This collection of essays, all by pre-eminent exponents of the history of political thought, explores the political ideologies of early modern Britain. Organised on a broadly chronological basis, the topics addressed by individual scholars reflect in general the themes initiated and inspired by the work of the distinguished intellectual historian, J. G. A. Pocock, for whom the collection is intended as a tribute. Each of the sixteen contributors has thought long and critically about Pocock's seminal contributions to the subject, and in each essay engages with the debates he has provoked. As a fitting conclusion to the volume, Professor Pocock has responded to the essays and provided his personal interpretation of the themes they invoke.

Contributors: J. H. Burns; Conal Condren; Mark Goldie; Istvan Hont; Lawrence E. Klein; William Klein; William Lamont; Michael Mendle; Nicholas Phillipson; J. G. A. Pocock; John Robertson; Gordon J. Schochet; Lois G. Schwoerer; Jonathan Scott; Quentin Skinner; Richard Tuck; James Tully.

IDEAS IN CONTEXT

POLITICAL DISCOURSE IN EARLY
MODERN BRITAIN

IDEAS IN CONTEXT

Edited by Quentin Skinner (General Editor), Lorraine Daston, Wolf Lepenies, Richard Rorty and J. B. Schneewind

The books in this series will discuss the emergence of intellectual traditions and of related new disciplines. The procedures, aims and vocabularies that were generated will be set in the context of the alternatives available within the contemporary frameworks of ideas and institutions. Through detailed studies of the evolution of such traditions, and their modification by different audiences, it is hoped that a new picture will form of the development of ideas in their concrete contexts. By this means, artificial distinctions between the history of philosophy, of the various sciences, of society and politics, and of literature may be seen to dissolve.

The series is published with the support of the Exxon Foundation.

A list of books in the series will be found at the end of the volume.

POLITICAL DISCOURSE IN EARLY MODERN BRITAIN

EDITED BY

NICHOLAS PHILLIPSON

Reader in History, University of Edinburgh

AND

QUENTIN SKINNER

Professor of Political Science, University of Cambridge

CAMBRIDGE UNIVERSITY PRESS

CAMBRIDGE UNIVERSITY PRESS
Cambridge, New York, Melbourne, Madrid, Cape Town,
Singapore, São Paulo, Delhi, Tokyo, Mexico City

Cambridge University Press
The Edinburgh Building, Cambridge CB2 8RU, UK

Published in the United States of America by Cambridge University Press, New York

www.cambridge.org
Information on this title: www.cambridge.org/9780521201933

© Cambridge University Press 1993

First published 1993
First paperback edition 2011

A catalogue record for this publication is available from the British Library

Library of Congress Cataloguing in Publication Data

Political discourage in early modern Britain/edited by Nicholas Phillipson and Quentin
Skinner.
p. cm. – (Ideas in contex)
Includes bibliographical references and index.
ISBN 0 521 39242 X
1. Great Britain – Politics and government – Historiography.
2. Political science – Great Britain – History. I. Phillipson,
Nicholas. II. Skinner, Quentin. III. Series.
DA300.P62 1993
320.941–dc20   92-9049   CIP

ISBN 978-0-521-39242-6 Hardback
ISBN 978-0-521-20193-3 Paperback

Contents

Contributors

J. H. BURNS is Professor Emeritus of the History of Political Thought at University College London. He edited both *The Cambridge History of Medieval Political Thought* (1988) and *The Cambridge History of Political Thought, 1450–1700* (1991).

CONAL CONDREN is Professor of Political Science in the University of New South Wales. His principal publications include *The Status and Appraisal of Classic Texts* (1985) and *George Lawson's Politica and the English Revolution* (1989). His edition of Lawson's *Politica Sacra et Civilis* was published in 1992 in Cambridge Texts in the History of Political Thought.

MARK GOLDIE is Fellow and Director of Studies in History, Churchill College, Cambridge. He is co-editor (with J. H. Burns) of *The Cambridge History of Political Thought, 1450–1700* and (with Robert Wokler) of *The Cambridge History of Eighteenth-Century Political Thought.*

ISTVAN HONT is University Assistant Lecturer in History and Fellow of King's College, Cambridge. He is the editor (with Michael Ignatieff) of *Wealth and Virtue: The Shaping of Political Economy in the Scottish Enlightenment* (1983).

LAWRENCE KLEIN teaches in the Department of History, University of Nevada. A pupil of J. G. A. Pocock, his forthcoming study of Shaftesbury will be published by the Cambridge University Press.

WILLIAM KLEIN, University of Madison, Wisconsin, studied with J. G. A. Pocock and is currently writing history text books for American high school students. He was a main contributor to *World Explorers and Discoverers* (1992).

WILLIAM LAMONT is Professor of History at the University of Sussex. His recent publications include *Puritanism and the English Revolution* (1991). He is currently preparing an edition of Richard

Baxter: *A Holy Commonwealth* for Cambridge Texts in the History of Political Thought.

MICHAEL MENDLE teaches in the Department of History at the University of Alabama. He is the author, among other works on the English Revolution, of *Dangerous Positions* (1985).

NICHOLAS PHILLIPSON is Reader in History at the University of Edinburgh. He is the author of *Hume* (1989) and *The Scottish Whigs and the Reform of the Court of Session* (1991). He is co-editor (with R. M. Mitchison) of *Scotland in the Age of Improvement* (1971) and editor of *Universities, Society and the Future*.

J. G. A. POCOCK is Harry C. Black Professor of History at The Johns Hopkins University. He was previously Professor of History and Political Science at Washington University in St Louis, Professor of Political Science at the University of Canterbury, Research Fellow of St John's College, Cambridge, and Lecturer in History at the University of Otago. *A full list of his publications appears at the end of this volume.*

JOHN ROBERTSON is a Fellow of St Hugh's College, Oxford, and Tutor and Lecturer in Modern History. He is the author of *The Scottish Enlightenment and the Militia Issue* (1985). He is currently preparing a new edition of *The Political Works of Andrew Fletcher* for Cambridge Texts in the History of Political Thought.

GORDON J. SCHOCHET is Professor of Political Science at Rutgers University. The author of *Patriarchalism in Political Thought* (1975; 2nd edition, 1988), co-author of *Moral Development and Politics*, and numerous articles, he is completing a book provisionally titled *John Locke and the Politics of Religious Tolerations* and preparing an edition of Locke's unpublished writings on toleration. With John Pocock, he is a member of the Steering Committee of the Folger Institute Center for the History of British Political Thought and the editor of the Center's six volumes of *Proceedings*.

LOIS G. SCHWOERER is the Elmer Louis Kayser Professor of History at the George Washington University. Her publications include *The Declaration of Rights, 1689* (1981) and, as editor, *The Revolution of 1688–1689: Changing Perspectives* (1992).

JONATHAN SCOTT is Fellow and Director of Studies in History, Downing College, Cambridge. His publications include *Algernon Sidney and the English Republic 1623–1677* (1988) and *Algernon Sidney and the Restoration Crisis 1677–1683* (1991) and he is currently working on *England's Troubles 1603–1702*, a study of English political and intellectual history in its European context.

QUENTIN SKINNER is Professor of Political Science in the University of Cambridge. His publications include *The Foundation of Modern Political Thought* (2 vols. 1978).

RICHARD TUCK is Lecturer in History and Fellow of Jesus College, Cambridge. His publications include *Natural Rights Theories* (1979), and he has recently completed an edition of *Hobbes: Leviathan* for Cambridge Texts in the History of Political Thought.

JAMES TULLY is Professor of Philosophy and Political Science at McGill University. His recent books include *An Approach to Political Philosophy: Locke in Contexts* (1992) and an edition for Cambridge Texts in the History of Political Thought of *Pufendorf: On the Duty of Man and Citizen* (1991).

Preface

When John Pocock published *Politics, Language and Time* in 1971, he opened his Introduction by remarking that 'during the last ten years scholars interested in the study of systems of political thought have had the experience of living through radical changes, which may amount to a transformation, in their discipline'. If it now seems clear that the 1960s did indeed witness the beginning of a revolution in our ways of thinking about the history of political theory, it is even clearer that John Pocock himself was one of the most active and important of the revolutionaries. We who have written the following collection of essays in his honour are all happy to acknowledge his inspiration and influence. We have profited from his insistence that the history of political theory should be written as a history of discourse, and we have sought at the same time to address ourselves to some of the specific questions he has raised about the evolution of early modern British political thought. We hope that the resulting volume will be read in the spirit in which we conceived it, as an affectionate and wholehearted tribute to a generous historian whose wide erudition, magisterial prose and insatiable curiosity about the mental world of Anglo-Saxon politics continue to generate a remarkable corpus of historical writing, one still capable of releasing those *frissons historiques* which we expect only from the finest of historians.

Some of John Pocock's most striking historical insights have arisen in the course of polemical engagements with other scholars and, perhaps most fruitfully of all, with his own earlier work. It is characteristic that his response to the essays in this volume should take the form of a series of suggestions for further research, together with a fascinating new synthesis of the entire early modern period of British political thought. As so often, John Pocock reminds us that the historian's quest is both a never-ending and a genuinely co-operative one.

John Pocock's first and epoch-making book, *The Ancient Constitution and the Feudal Law*, was published by the Cambridge University Press; so was his most recent set of studies, *Virtue, Commerce and History*. We are delighted that this volume in his honour should also have been accepted for publication by Cambridge, and are grateful to the officers of the Press for the many kindnesses they have shown us in the course of producing it. We owe particular thanks to the Press's Editorial Director, Jeremy Mynott, who gave us important advice at the outset about questions of scope and coverage, and to the editorial board of *Ideas in Context*, who welcomed our book into their series. We are also much indebted to Richard Fisher and Nancy-Jane Thompson, who acted with exemplary helpfulness at every stage, and to our sub-editor, Jean Field, who brought together, checked and corrected our disparate contributions with exceptional patience and meticulousness. We should also like to extend our thanks to all our contributors, who met their deadlines and revised their drafts with unruffled efficiency and goodwill. Finally, we owe a special debt to Felicity Pocock and to Gordon Schochet, both of whom gave us indispensable help and counsel when we were first planning our book. Our thanks to them all; and also, above all, to John Pocock himself for his friendship as well as his example.

NICHOLAS PHILLIPSON
QUENTIN SKINNER

PART I

CHAPTER I

George Buchanan and the anti-monarchomachs

J. H. Burns

In the opening chapter of *The Machiavellian Moment* John Pocock explores the themes of 'Experience, Usage and Prudence'. The analysis is characteristically wide-ranging; but it may fairly be said to find its focus in Sir John Fortescue's account of English law and the implications of that account for the exercise of prudence in positive legislation. At a much later stage in the book 'percipient North Britons' are recognised as significant contributors to the 'Atlantic republican tradition' which developed in an 'Anglophone civilisation'. In particular, Andrew Fletcher of Saltoun is presented as one of those Scots 'who understood the language of English controversy better, in some respects, than the English themselves'.[1] But Fletcher and those who followed his lead were formed also, it can be argued, by a specifically Scottish tradition of discourse which reflected a political experience differing from that of England and a vein of controversy in which, for one thing, the jurisprudence of the civil law had an especially important part. A major episode in the development of that tradition – and, more generally, in the early modern European debate on political authority – was the controversy precipitated by George Buchanan's dialogue *De jure regni apud Scotos*.

The political ideas Buchanan brought to bear in his defence of the deposition of Mary Queen of Scots were those of a humanist influenced above all by Ciceronian Stoicism. The vigorous polemi-

This is an abridged and modified version of a paper originally presented, in October 1990, as part of a seminar programme, directed by Dr Roger Mason at the Folger Institute Center for the History of British Political Thought, on the theme 'Scots and Britons: Scottish Political Thought and the Union of 1603'.
[1] J. G. A. Pocock, *The Machiavellian Moment: Florentine Political Thought and the Atlantic Republican Tradition* (Princeton, 1977), pp. 9–12, 17–22 (on Fortescue); 426–32 (on Fletcher); pp. 506 ff. (on 'Anglophone civilisation' and civic humanism).

cal interchanges provoked by that defence belong of course to the
argument over post-Reformation 'resistance theory'; but the debate
was not conducted primarily in the theological and scriptural terms
characteristic of so much of that controversy. The *De jure regni* was
first published, it is true, in the same year as the *Vindiciae contra
tyrannos*: the circumstances in which it appeared in print were those
created by the St Bartholomew massacres and the rise of the
Catholic League. It had been written, however, a dozen years
earlier;[2] and its purpose had never been merely sectarian or
confessional. Buchanan was, by the 1560s, a Latinist of European
renown, and he wrote, after political events that had created a
European scandal, to justify what his party had done in the eyes of
a public hardly to be satisfied by purely Protestant arguments.
Writing in that classical Latin of which he was an acknowledged
master, he turned to the humanist concepts which had shaped the
tradition of political thought to which he adhered.[3]

Thus the pivot on which Buchanan's political theory turns is the
Ciceronian hypothesis as to the origins of human society and the
basis of governmental authority within that society. It is both true
and important that Buchanan could, and doubtless did, draw here
on sources other than those of humanist learning. Contemptuous
though he was of the scholasticism of his early education, he built
his argument on foundations he and his fellow-humanists shared
with, among others, John Mair (whose pupil Buchanan had
been).[4] That the edifice he built was such as Mair for one would
surely have refused to enter is true; but the point need not be
pursued here. Similarly, there is no need in the present context to
explore certain ambiguities in the relationship between Buchanan's
thinking and the Ciceronian tradition to which it certainly

[2] On the date of composition see W. S. McKechnie in *George Buchanan: Glasgow Quatercentenary Studies 1906* (Glasgow, 1907), pp. 226–9; and cf. H. R. Trevor-Roper, 'George Buchanan and the Ancient Scottish Constitution', *English Historical Review*, Supplement 3, 1966. There is ample evidence, in Buchanan's correspondence and elsewhere, for the circulation of the dialogue in manuscript before the first printing in 1579.

[3] There is no attempt here to offer a full summary or analysis of the *De jure regni*. For recent accounts of it see Q. Skinner, *The Foundation of Modern Political Thought* (Cambridge, 1978), vol. II, pp. 339–48; R. A. Mason, '*Rex Stoicus*: George Buchanan, James VI and the Scottish Polity', in J. Dwyer, R. A. Mason and A. Murdoch (eds.), *New Perspectives on the Politics and Culture of Early Modern Scotland* (Edinburgh, 1982) pp. 9–33. An earlier brief analysis of my own is in 'The Political Ideas of George Buchanan', *Scottish Historical Review*, 30 (1951), 60–8.

[4] See on this Skinner, *Foundations*, vol. II, pp. 340 ff.

belongs.[5] It is more important to call attention to the fact that, in developing his argument and relating it more directly to the immediate issue with which he was concerned, Buchanan turned in another, but still a characteristically humanist direction – to history. Specifically, he turned to what has been called, appropriately enough, 'the ancient Scottish constitution'.[6] He argued (in a vein which was to be more elaborately developed in his *Rerum Scoticarum historia*) that the realm of Scotland exemplified in its laws and usages the general principles of society and government expressed by Cicero; and he justified the action taken in 1567 by an appeal to alleged precedent as well as to asserted principle. As we shall see, this historical argument was the cue for much of the debate that was to follow.

The debate was to be a protracted affair, prolonged in some sense to the threshold of the nineteenth century and even beyond; nor was it at any stage a purely Scottish debate.[7] It was inaugurated, nevertheless, by three Scots: Ninian Winzet, Adam Blackwood and William Barclay. All three had in one way or another moved from Scotland into European settings. It was Barclay who coined the term 'monarchomach', but Winzet and Blackwood were as aware as he was of the point the term was meant to make: that Buchanan's political principles threatened monarchical government as such, and specifically the hereditary monarchy which prevailed in most of the Europe they knew.

The senior figure in this anti-monarchomach triumvirate, Ninian Winzet, belonged, unlike the others, to Buchanan's own generation, sharing with him at least some adult experience of pre-Reformation Scotland and pre-Tridentine Catholicism. Moreover, Winzet had already engaged in controversy; and if his vernacular pamphlets of the early 1560s, directed against John Knox and the other Protestant leaders of the day, belong admittedly to a world somewhat different from that which is our concern here, yet there were important continuities. By the time Winzet responded to

---

[5] McKechnie (*Glasgow Quatercentenary Studies*, p. 258) may not have been too wide of the mark in suggesting that Buchanan's 'treatment of such topics . . . reflects merely the hazy state of contemporary opinion'. See also p. 18 below for the point made by William Barclay in regard to nature and 'utility' in Buchanan's theory.

[6] See Trevor-Roper, 'George Buchanan'.

[7] Thus, for example, German translations of the *De jure regni* were published in 1796 and 1821: cf. *Glasgow Quatercentenary Studies*, p. 455, where these are described in the splendid catalogue by David Murray of the Buchanan exhibitions in St Andrews and Glasgow.

Buchanan's dialogue in 1582, he had acquired, in Paris and Douai, the university training he had lacked twenty years before. Yet, writing now as abbot of the *Schottenkloster* at Ratisbon, his concerns were still very much the same as when he had debated with Knox. His old adversary was still vividly in Winzet's mind when he wrote the *Flagellum sectariorum* to which his *Velitatio in Georgium Buchananum* was an appendage.[8] From the outset in the 1560s Winzet had been preoccupied by the question of authority, albeit that concern had then been with ecclesiastical rather that with civil government. Now, facing the challenge of the *De jure regni*, he saw above all a problem in political theology. When he read the dialogue for the first time, he had just been arguing in the *Flagellum* that Knox and his like were 'ministers of sedition';[9] and he plainly saw Buchanan in precisely the same light.

For Winzet, then, authority in Christian society was a continuum extending across the entire structure, whether in its spiritual or in its temporal aspect. When this seamless garment was rent asunder by heresy and rebellion, it did not matter whether the first tear was made, so to speak, at the edge pertaining to kingship or at that which represented the traditional authority of the Catholic church. It was throughout a divinely constituted order that was being violated; and in this sense Winzet's political argument is a defence of the divine right of kingship against an onslaught which is as sacrilegious as it is seditious. To compare the *Velitatio* with the dialogue it attacked is to be struck by this difference especially: that whereas for Buchanan the argument from, or about, Scripture is subordinate and sometimes seems almost perfunctory, Winzet develops that argument elaborately and at an early stage in his campaign. A very substantial part of the *Velitatio* is devoted to scriptural exegesis and to theological exposition based largely on patristic sources. Winzet's professional preoccupation with such matters takes him, indeed, some considerable distance from anything that was strictly relevant to Buchanan's case. A good deal of space is given over to such matters as the problematic character of

[8] The two works were published together, with continuous pagination, at Ingolstadt in 1582. The fullest account of Winzet (but one needing considerable revision, which is not yet systematically available) is still that by J. K. Hewison in his Scottish Text Society edition of Winzet's *Certain Tractates*, etc., 2 vols. (Edinburgh, 1888, 1890).

[9] See especially *Flagellum*, pp. 20–1.

sola scriptura theology in general and the nature of the Eucharist in particular.[10]

The political theme is not lost sight of, however. Much of the discussion is concerned with the evidence afforded by the Bible, and especially by the Old Testament, as to the nature of kingship. On that evidence, of course, God had expressly authorised and established royal rule over his chosen people. By so doing, according to a powerful tradition of Christian thinking to which Winzet firmly attaches himself, God has consecrated kings and kingship in such a way as to secure them against the kind of attack Buchanan had launched. That attack culminated in the justification and indeed the advocacy of tyrannicide. In Buchanan's argument misgovernment, or even misconduct by a ruler in what might be regarded as matters of private, personal morality, constituted tyranny and made the delinquent king – or queen – a public enemy. For an individual citizen to kill such a self-declared criminal was legitimate and indeed praiseworthy. This is passionately rejected by Winzet. 'O tyrannical tyrannicide!' he exclaims: no one, amid all 'the pride, barbarity, and cruelty of the Calvinian spirit' had displayed its essential 'tyranny' more clearly than Buchanan.[11] In rebutting the attempt to justify the killing of a king even if his unjust rule does indeed amount to tyranny, Winzet relies in particular upon a scriptural instance to which he had already had recourse in his earlier vernacular writings. This was the treatment of Saul by David, his refusal to 'touch the Lord's anointed'.[12] The rite of anointing is crucial for Winzet as for other defenders of kingship in this period; and it confirms the impression that we are indeed dealing here with a 'divine-right' response to 'monarchomach' radicalism.

This being the case, and especially in view of the theological orientation of Winzet's thought, it is not surprising to find in the *Velitatio* an insistence on the parallelism between royal and priestly power. Kings, Winzet argues, are in political matters what priests are in matters divine – a kind of 'earthly gods' (*dii quidam terrestres*):

[10] Winzet's priorities are indicated in the dedication of the *Velitatio*: ' . . . ego pro meo munere et loco . . . ea maxime quae ex Dei verbo, verisque illis veteribus Dei verbi interpretibus . . . aut a iure nostri regni . . . agitare statui'.
[11] *Velitatio*, p. 171.
[12] See *Certain Tractates*, ed. Hewison, vol. I, p. 95; and cf. *Velitatio*, p. 177 (among several references).

they, like priests, are established by God as judges of his faithful people, and as such are answerable only to God.[13] That this sacred character should be combined with moral excellence is of course desirable; but such excellence – the essence of kingship as Buchanan portrays it – is neither a necessary nor a sufficient condition of royal power, which is, essentially, an effective power to *rule*. Winzet offers a list of the prerogatives this comprises. The detailed items need not detain us here. The most essential points are that the king alone disposes of the right to appoint magistrates, to enact laws (though this will require further consideration in a moment), to give judgement on doubtful cases, and to decide on issues of war and peace.[14] All this is summed up in the declaration that 'all power in matters political flows from the king as from its source'.[15]

So far, it seems, we have a straightforward statement of the kind of 'absolutism' that had been characteristic of one strand in European thinking about monarchy since at least the early fifteenth century, to say nothing of its earlier origins. The metaphor in which political power in all its subordinate forms 'flows' from the king is strongly reminiscent of the Neoplatonic element in such thinking to which Antony Black among others has directed attention.[16] Yet the same metaphor occurs elsewhere in Winzet's text with what might well seem to be a diametrically opposite sense and effect; for he also envisages circumstances in which the king's power itself 'returns to the people, from whom it originally flowed'.[17] The contradiction here, if contradiction there be, takes us an important step further in understanding the position Winzet takes up. Certainly, for him, all power comes from God. Certainly God has endowed royal power with a special sanctity. Certainly hereditary monarchy as it prevails in Scotland is the best form of government.[18] Yet is is also the case that all this can and should be mediated through the community for whose benefit God has ordained it. Almost at the outset of the *Velitatio* Winzet had acknowledged that 'in all

---

[13] *Velitatio*, p. 181.

[14] Ibid., pp. 265–6.

[15] Ibid., p. 266: 'tu nescire non potes, in regno solum esse Regem, a quo tanquam a fonte omnis in politicis rebus potestas dimanat'.

[16] A. J. Black, *Monarchy and Community: Political Ideas in the Later Conciliar Controversy 1430–1450* (Cambridge, 1970), pp. 57–67.

[17] *Velitatio*, p. 269: 'totum ius regni siue principatus . . . ad populum, unde profluxit, redire'.

[18] Winzet takes this point largely for granted, but his preference for hereditary kingship is evident throughout.

well-ordered kingdoms the royal authority is in the first instance conferred by the people'.[19] It is true and important that, here and throughout, Winzet makes, whether implicitly or explicitly, a sharp distinction between the *populus* and the mere *promiscua plebs*, having in mind always an organised body acting through some such mechanism as the Three Estates. The fact remains that the kingship he defends against what he calls Buchanan's *regnum populare* is a system in which king and people alike have an essential part to play. For example, fundamental changes in the law – changes in what Winzet calls the *leges politicae* – cannot be instituted by either party without the consent of the other.[20] And Winzet allows what Adam Blackwood had strenuously denied: namely, that there is a genuine sharing of power between king and community, each being (in a striking phrase) 'bound to the realm itself' (*ipsi regno . . . astrictus*).[21]

These mutual relationships constitute for Winzet the true *ius regni*. Plainly they imply limitations upon the king's power additional to those of divine and natural law which he shares of course with his subjects. Yet they leave intact, as Winzet understands the matter, that *liberum imperium* which the king must have if the realm is to be effectively ruled. The prerogatives of royal government are *not* shared with the community; nor does the community have any authority over its ruler corresponding (as Buchanan would have it) to his authority over each and all of his subjects. Though Winzet believes that what we would call constitutional restraints on royal power are effective, their efficacy does not depend upon any popular right to resist or depose a king guilty of misrule. Such a ruler – who becomes a tyrant only by stubborn persistence in misgovernment, not by isolated or occasional misdeeds – deprives himself by his tyranny of the authority which then reverts to the community. It would then indeed be legitimate, and even necessary, to take corporate action against one who was no longer, properly speaking, a king: yet the sanctity conferred by his anointing must still shield him from the violence Buchanan justifies and advocates.[22]

---

[19] *Velitatio*, p.154.
[20] Ibid., sig. xx 3 v; and cf. pp. 259–60.
[21] Ibid., p. 283: 'ius regni, ad quod tuendum communi iurisiurandi vinculo atque foedere & populus regi & rex populo & uterque ipsi regno est astrictus'.
[22] Ibid., pp. 273–5; and cf. p. 269.

Such being Winzet's concept of kingship, brief consideration may be given to two aspects of its application to the Scottish case he and his adversary had in view. The first of these is an episode that could be regarded – and had been regarded by John Mair in particular – as exemplifying the 'communitarian' basis of Scottish kingship: the disputed succession following the death of Alexander III, and the eventual accession of Robert Bruce. Here Winzet follows, not Mair's account, but one strand in the confused story told by Hector Boece. The succession, he insists, was strictly hereditary: John Baliol's leaving the throne was a voluntary act of abdication, following indeed his ignoble betrayal of his responsibilities as king, but involving no assertion of authority by the community either in deposing Baliol or 'electing' Bruce.[23]

The most interesting historical element in Winzet's *Velitatio*, however, is unquestionably his discussion of the reign of James III (1460-88). That reign and its dramatic ending were critically important for Buchanan, since the events of the 1480s could be presented as a clear (and recent) instance of the deposition of a Scottish king for tyranny. Much of the case has been shown by recent scholarship to turn upon what has become known as the 'legend' of James III – a legend developed for political purposes and elaborated by sixteenth-century historians.[24] Even Winzet's patron Bishop Lesley can be regarded as the prisoner, in this connection, of an ideological myth ill-attuned to his polemical purposes.[25] What is striking in Winzet's discussion is that, despite his close association with Lesley and his inevitable reliance on essentially the same sources, he emphatically rejects the received interpretation of the story. In the first place, while accepting the substance of the charges against James – and accepting in particular the fact of his ill-judged reliance on counsellors other than the nobility, with their vested right to give such counsel – he denies that these charges amount to an indictment for tyranny. Second, however, and perhaps more importantly, Winzet insists that there was no vestige of 'due process', of any kind of judicial constitutional procedure in James III's fate: he was, quite simply, killed by 'a few

[23] Ibid., pp. 254-6.
[24] See N. Macdougall, *James III: A Political Study* (Edinburgh, 1982), ch. 12, esp. pp. 282 ff.
[25] Macdougall, ibid., pp. 282-4. Winzet was closely associated with Lesley in the period between the Scots and Latin versions of the bishop's history (1570, 1578).

conspirators'.[26] The case, in other words, served Buchanan's argument no better than the more remote instances of deposition and tyrannicide he claimed to find in the Scottish annals.[27]

What Ninian Winzet sought to vindicate against Buchanan's radicalism, then, was a view of kingship exemplified (he claimed) both in the Bible and in the concrete historical reality of the Scottish realm. It is not a view that can be fitted neatly into our conventional categories of 'absolute' and 'constitutional' or 'limited' monarchy. Yet the more closely it is examined against the background of political thinking in the later Middle Ages, the more deeply its roots will be seen to run into that cultural soil. In a sense what might be termed the amateurism of Winzet's political thinking – and even as a theologian he cannot be regarded as a professional of high calibre – tends to enhance rather than to diminish its significance. His conservative response to the monarchomach challenge was grounded in the reflection of an intelligent observer upon the principles he believed to be embodied in the political system he had experienced. What we must now consider is whether and how the picture changes when we look at what the professionals – here, above all, the jurists – had to say in response to Buchanan's dialogue. The first such response was made by Adam Blackwood.

Blackwood's familiarity with legal scholarship may well have dated from his earliest years. Left fatherless at the age of eight after the battle of Pinkie (1547), he was educated by his uncle Robert Reid, Bishop of Orkney – 'undoubtedly the most learned of the prelates' in Scotland just before the Reformation.[28] Reid had a special concern for jurisprudence as an element in the improvement of Scottish education; and his nephew (nineteen when the bishop died in 1558) no doubt absorbed this nascent 'humanistic legal culture'[29] before his uncle sent him to Paris. There he imbibed humanism from less peripheral sources, with Adrien Turnèbe and Jean Dorat among his teachers. Reid's death briefly interrupted Blackwood's studies; but when he returned to Paris it was with the still more powerful patronage of the queen of Scots (and, briefly, of

---

[26] *Velitatio*, pp. 238–41, 254.

[27] Ibid., pp. 242–3.

[28] J. K. Cameron in J. MacQueen (ed.), *Humanism in Renaissance Scotland* (Edinbugh, 1990), p. 166.

[29] J. W. Cairns, ibid., p. 49.

France) herself. Legal preferment may well have been his goal throughout: his Paris arts degree was followed by law studies in Toulouse. It was, however, only after a substantial spell of arts teaching in Paris that Blackwood received the appointment as counsellor in the *parlement* of Poitiers which he held until his death in 1613.[30]

The recommendation to the queen (by Archbishop James Beaton, her ambassador in France) leading to this appointment was Blackwood's reward for his first polemical work, the *De conjunctione religionis et imperii libri duo* (Paris, 1575). When this was followed, six years later, by his reply to Buchanan's *De jure regni*,[31] it was (as with Winzet's *Velitatio*) a case of building a specific argument upon previously laid general foundations. The *De conjunctione* was published before the rise of the Catholic League had begun to call in question the royalist alliance between religious orthodoxy and loyalty to the crown. The book reflected the situation following the St Bartholomew's Day massacres; and for Blackwood it was the Calvinist heresy that threatened the bond between *imperium* and *religio*. Even when Buchanan's dialogue came to his notice, the politics and polemic of the League (which Blackwood was to attack in the third book he added to his *De conjunctione* in 1612, after the assassination of Henri IV) had not entered the radical phase which began in the mid 1580s. It was still possible for Blackwood to assert a Catholic royalism without having to look over his shoulder, as it were, at the alarming spectacle of a Catholic monarchomach.[32]

The core of that royalism was, it seems fair to say, essentially juristic. The formidable marginalia of the *Apologia* are drawn overwhelmingly from the civil and canon laws and their interpreters. The range of sources is impressively wide, extending as it

---

[30] On Blackwood see *DNB* v, 149–50; and cf. among the older authorities especially the *Elogium* in Blackwood's *Opera Omnia* (Paris, 1644) by Gabriel Naudé, whose association with the edition is a point of some interest.

[31] *Adversus Georgii Buchanani dialogum, de iure regni apud Scotos pro regibus apologia* (Poitiers, 1581; 2nd edn. Paris, 1588).

[32] J. H. M. Salmon (in J. H. Burns and M. Goldie (eds.), *The Cambridge History of Political Thought 1450–1700*, Cambridge, 1991, p. 234) argues that some elements in Blackwood's position – notably his deference to papal authority – were somewhat ill adapted to the *'politique* royalism' which was directed against Leaguer monarchomach ideology. It is, however, interesting to note that, despite this, the *Apologia* was reprinted with no significant changes in 1588, when the propaganda campaign against Henri III was developing in, for instance, the writings of Louis Dorléans, even if the extremism of Jean Boucher was still to come. Evidently Blackwood's royalism still retained its relevance.

does from the leading civilians and canonists of the later medieval centuries down to the juristic scholars of his own century and generation. This juristic learning is exhibited in the framework of the wider humanistic culture to be expected in one who had sat at the feet of Turnèbe and Dorat. Blackwood also pays due attention to the fact that he is arguing in a specifically Scottish context. Yet, though there are points of interest to be noted later in connection with his comments on Scottish history, the most important point here is a general one, and it alerts us to the fact that what we are being invited to consider is indeed a general theory of kingship.

The point Blackwood makes at the very outset is that Buchanan's dialogue is misleadingly titled. It is *not* in any substantial sense a discussion of the *jus regni* 'among the Scots': it is a general – and utterly misconceived – account of the nature of royal government as such. In the first place, the system Buchanan describes is one in which supreme authority lies not with the ruler, but with the people.[33] In addition, when he seeks to illustrate his argument by instances and institutions taken from, for example, Denmark or Venice, he is, on the one hand, digressing from his avowed concern with the situation in Scotland, and, on the other, drawing a false analogy, since those systems do not exemplify true kingship such as prevails among the Scots. The most important and striking case here is that of the Roman empire. This, after all, was the source of most of the language and conceptual equipment used by jurists in Blackwood's own civil-law tradition to describe and analyse political authority, and specifically to elucidate the power enjoyed by kings. For Blackwood, however, Roman imperial authority was essentially different from and inferior to truly royal power. One particularly remarkable passage is worth quoting:

The Senate and People of Rome had a certain authority over [the emperor]: the Senate and People of Scotland have no authority over [their kings]. The emperors had a limited power over the people: our kings have free and full power. The sovereignty (*imperium*) of the latter has always been pure and absolute (*merum . . . ac solutum*): that of the former depended on the will of others (*ex alieno nutu*). The first kind of lordship (*dominatio*) is called kingship (*regnum*), the second principate (*principatus*).[34]

[33] *Apologia*, 1581, p. 27: 'tu ademptam regi, populo maiestatem attribuis'.
[34] Ibid., p. 51.

The theme thus boldly enunciated pervades Blackwood's entire argument. Kingship – the ostensible subject of Buchanan's dialogue – is something quite different from the exemplary and dependent magistracy there envisaged. A king in the true sense of the term is a divinely constituted ruler, consecrated by the ceremony of anointing. That rite, Blackwood says, is *divinitatis symbolum ac veluti sacramentum*.[35] The point was one he had developed earlier, in the *De conjunctione*, where he had referred to 'the hidden and almost divine power' of the oil used in the Old Testament, by virtue of which 'those who were anointed with it became either Kings or priests' and their persons thenceforward sacrosanct.[36] Kingship, however, unlike priesthood in the Christian dispensation, is strictly hereditary: the heir becomes king immediately upon the death of his predecessor.[37] With this we have evidently passed from political theology to public law, and here Blackwood the jurist naturally comes into his own. We know already from the comparison with the Roman principate that a king's power is *merum ac solutum*. This means that the king is bound by no human law or ordinance: his authority is unconditional.[38] The king has complete command (*summam . . . imperii*); and in particular this means that he has full power over the laws.[39] Interestingly, Blackwood recognises that a power of this kind is essential in any political society, and he does not suggest that all such societies are governed by kings. Yet he clearly associates 'sovereignty' (for that is what is at issue here) with kingship: the term he uses to denote it is *regia potestas*.[40]

To the statement that a king conceived in Blackwood's terms is subject to no human law there is in a sense one exception. His authority being by definition strictly hereditary, the rules governing succession to the throne are beyond his power to change. Kings, Blackwood claims, *non regum sed regni sunt haredes*: they are heirs to the realm, not to the kings who have preceded them.[41] Now here, as

---

[35] This phrase is from an opening chapter seemingly added between the 1588 edition and the reprint in Blackwood's *Opera Omnia* (1644, p. 9). The theme, however, is a consistent one in his theory.

[36] *Opera Omnia*, 1644, pp. 232, 234.

[37] See *Apologia*, 1581, pp. 71–3, for a general discussion of the hereditary principle, including references to Baldus and Johannes Andreae.

[38] Ibid., p. 55.

[39] Ibid., p. 59.

[40] Ibid., pp. 197–8.

[41] Ibid., p. 113.

in Winzet, we have a concept of the *regnum* as an entity in some sense independent of *rex* and *populus* alike. Whereas, however, Winzet saw that entity as one to which king and people might equally be regarded as bound, with the implication that there were consequential limits upon royal power, Blackwood's use of the idea is quite different. The conclusion he draws immediately is that since kings succeed to the realm and not to their predecessors they cannot be bound by any agreements entered into by those predecessors. To this he adds that the king can make no law which he may not subsequently abrogate or repeal.[42] With these points in mind (though much could be added), there is no difficulty in recognising the vigour of Blackwood's absolutism; nor will it come as a surprise to find that his theory of government is grounded in a view of human society in which force is the essential basis of authority.[43]

To turn from Blackwood's own position to the critique of Buchanan he builds on that foundation is to find what is, effectively, a dual strategy. There is, first, what we may regard as an essentially theoretical argument intended to establish the inconsistent and even contradictory character of the opposing view. This turns very largely upon a logical analysis of Buchanan's concept of authority, indicating that it implies an untenable division of the essentially unitary sovereignty which is crucial for ordered government.[44] Whatever may be thought of the analysis – and it merits a close scrutiny which cannot be undertaken here – one point is clear and at least one comment seems permissible. The point to be made is that it is in this passage above all that we encounter the Blackwood who had studied and taught philosophy in Paris as well as reading law in Toulouse. The comment is that the dialectical skill Blackwood displays here is enough to cast doubt on A. J. Carlyle's remark that Blackwood's *Apologia* is 'somewhat crude'.[45]

The second element in Blackwood's anti-monarchomach strategy is historical rather than theoretical. We have noted already his insistence on the distinctively royal character of the Scottish monarchy. In his more specific discussion of the Scottish case

[42] Ibid., p. 114.
[43] Ibid., pp. 61–3.
[44] Ibid., ch. 33, pp. 293–307.
[45] *A History of Mediaeval Political Theory in the West*, vol. VI (Edinburgh and London, 1936), p. 437.

Blackwood argues, accordingly, that there was no question of any kind of popular election as a continuing element in the *lex regia*. Scottish kings ruled on the basis, simply, of the oath of allegiance sworn by the Scots not only to Fergus as their first king but to his posterity in perpetuity.[46] Consequently Blackwood's interpretation of events at the end of John Baliol's reign is essentially the same as Winzet's: Baliol abdicated; Bruce succeeded, not *populi suffragiis*, but by force of arms in vindication of his undoubted hereditary right.[47] The community has no say in the succession to the crown: *a fortiori* it has no right to depose a king who has come to the throne by legitimate hereditary succession. Accordingly Blackwood refuses to entertain the suggestion that the fate of James III exemplified the punishment of a tyrant.[48] For the most part, however, it is not so much Blackwood's dialectical skill or his juristic learning as his rhetorical powers that are at work in his discussion of the Scottish theme. Celebrating the antiquity and the continuity of the Scottish polity, he condemns Buchanan above all for his vain attempt to subvert this ancient, hereditary, absolute kingship – an undertaking as impious as it was futile.[49]

In the historiography of political ideas Blackwood may be said to occupy a middle point in a spectrum that runs from the virtually unknown Winzet to the comparatively celebrated William Barclay. To have been cited by John Locke in the *Second Treatise of Government* might in any case have assured Barclay of some notoriety.[50] There is, however, a good deal more to his reputation than that adventitious reference. If Locke saw Barclay as in some sense the advocate *par excellence* of absolute monarchy, that in itself reflects both the scale and the fame of the achievements of the man who coined the term 'monarchomach' itself. The *De regno* which Barclay published in 1600 had been begun twenty years or so before as a specific response to Buchanan; and Buchanan's ideas are never very far from the forefront of Barclay's mind throughout the prolix length of his book. However, having delayed his public entry into the controversy, he was able to take a broader view of the opposition.

---

[46] *Apologia*, 1581, pp. 159–62.
[47] Ibid., p. 188.
[48] Ibid., pp. 188–9.
[49] Ibid., p. 306.
[50] *Two Treatises of Government*, ed. P. Laslett (Cambridge Texts in the History of Political Thought: Cambridge, 1988), pp. 419–35.

Not only did he turn from Buchanan's dialogue to the *Vindiciae contra tyrannos*. Even more significantly, Barclay was able – and indeed obliged – to take account of the use of 'monarchomach' principles by Catholic as well as by Protestant writers. His third main antagonist in *De regno* was Jean Boucher. It was with the League and the Society of Jesus that Barclay had to contend, as well as with the Calvinists.[51]

Barclay's own career, as it happened, had brought him into a more direct and personal confrontation with the Jesuits. After graduating in arts at Aberdeen and spending some time at court, he had gone abroad to study law, first at Paris, then at Bourges. Ironically, it was to a Jesuit – his uncle Edmund Hay – that he owed his first major advancement: appointment to the chair of law in the new university of Pont-à-Mousson in Lorraine. The struggle against Jesuit influence in that university permanently embittered Barclay's attitude to the Society; but he carried the conflict to the level of political and ecclesiological principle both in the *De regno* and in the posthumously published *De potestate Papae* (1609). This ensured Barclay's place not only in the sixteenth-century debate about 'resistance theory' but in the conflict between Ultramontanes and Gallicans in the seventeenth century and beyond.

Like Blackwood, and to an even more formidable extent, Barclay in *De regno* mobilised the learning of the law against Buchanan and the other monarchomachs. He was, after all, a writer who devoted nearly four decades of his life to the study and teaching of the civil law. He wrote, to be sure, in full awareness of the theological aspect of the controversy in which he was engaged; but in that connection he relied to a considerable extent upon expert guidance. When he embarked on his reply to Buchanan, he seems to have turned for such guidance to the now all-but-forgotten Dutch Catholic author Cuner Peeters.[52] Once he had acquired Winzet's 1582 publication, however, it was above all to his fellow-Scot that Barclay looked for support in such things as scriptural exegesis: copious quotations

---

[51] On Barclay see *DNB*, III, 173–4; D. B. Smith in *Scottish Historical Review*, II (1914), 136–63; and, for his professional work, C. Collot, *L'Ecole doctrinale de droit public à Pont-à-Mousson* (Paris, 1965).

[52] *De Christiani principis officio* (Cologne, 1580; 2nd edn, Mons, 1581). Peeters (1532–80), usually known as Cunerus, bishop of Leeuwarden in Friesland, was mistakenly described by Carlyle (*Mediaeval Political Theory*, vol. VI, p. 434) as 'a Scotsman . . . who was Bishop of Louvain'.

from the *Velitatio* are a prominent feature of his text. Yet in the end
it is Barclay the jurist who commands attention. His work, diffuse
and often tedious though it is, displays an impressive range of
learning and reveals a sharp awareness not only of the reserves of
scholarship to be drawn from the past but also of the then current
vigour of legal commentary and exposition.[53] It has been argued
that Barclay, in seeking to combine the older traditions of legal
scholarship with the newer modes of juristic humanism, made
particular use of 'the historical method'; and certainly there are
significant signs of such a method in his handling of Buchanan's
ideas.[54]

It is to the fundamental positions adopted in the *De jure regni* that
Barclay turns at the outset of his *De regno*. Buchanan, he says, had
rejected the view that expediency or utility was the basis of social
organisation, looking instead to nature or the law of nature. This
distinction has no force in Barclay's eyes: *utilitas* is for him clearly
the foundation on which human society is built, while at the same
time there will never be any conflict between the dictates of utility
and those of nature.[55] More important perhaps is Barclay's
criticism of the assumption that natural law provides a ready-made
standard by which positive law can be evaluated and judged. In
fact, he points out – and it is here that 'historical method' manifests
itself – that positive laws vary widely in accordance with the
different conditions in which human societies find themselves and
the divergent traditions developed in those societies.[56] The essential consequences of this, in Barclay's argument, is the critical
importance of legislative sovereignty vested in a king. Human
affairs in all their diversity need firm government, and the most
effective way of providing that government is royal power. That
power is the source of positive law: it cannot therefore be subject to
any law of that kind.[57] A wise king will of course always take
counsel; but he cannot be obliged to follow it. Such bodies as
assemblies of estates exist by the king's concession and leave; and

---

[53] There are, e.g., references to Bodin, Hotman, Cujas and Rebuffi. Barclay also refers to his
later adversary Bellarmine, citing him more than once against Gerson.

[54] See Collot, *L'Ecole doctrinale*, p. 105.

[55] *De regno et regali potestate adversus Buchananum, Brutum, Boucherium & reliquos Monarchomachos,
Libri Sex* (Paris, 1600), vol. I, p. 11.

[56] Ibid., pp. 12–14.

[57] Ibid., pp. 124–5, 207–8.

similarly none of the magistracies requisite for the administration of the realm can claim any power beyond that which is conferred by royal appointment.[58]

This royal absolutism (to use a convenient term unknown of course, to Barclay and his readers) is grounded, it need hardly be said, in the ordinance of God. Yet it is scarcely the case that Barclay's conception of 'divine-right' kingship is wholly straightforward and unequivocal. His book was, as we have seen, written over a period of two decades; and there is some reason to think that he hesitated or wavered during those years between different ways in which his basic doctrine might be expressed. Thus is was possible to hold that royal power was always and everywhere – as it had certainly been in some cases, notably among the people of Israel – the result of direct divine intervention. On the other hand, it was possible for Barclay to accept that the people had a part to play in the establishment of kings. The king thus established would still be endowed by God with the absolute power Barclay regarded as essential to the task of ruling. Yet, on this view, there could have been some kind of instrumental act by the community, albeit that such an act must necessarily involve a total and final grant of power to the ruler.[59] Both in *De regno* and in *De potestate Papae* Barclay can agree (with Bellarmine, for instance) that succession to the crown is a matter for human law and that popular consent may in some sense be a necessary preliminary to a king's accession. The fact remains that a king once enthroned is entitled to his subjects' submission and obedience with all due honour and reverence; and all this by nothing less than divine precept.[60]

To rebel against a king, then, was to rebel against God. There can, on such an argument as Barclay's, be no place (it seems) in any circumstances for the kind of action against a ruler Buchanan sought to justify in the *De jure regni*. Yet, once again, matters prove to be rather less clear-cut than this. John Locke, it will be recalled, was both to point out and to exploit what he took to be Barclay's ambiguities on the subject of resistance to rulers.[61] It is highly significant in the present context that the two chapters of *De regno*

---

[58] Ibid., pp. 40–2.
[59] Ibid., pp. 110–14.
[60] See, e.g., *De potestate Papae an et quatenus in reges et principes seculares jus et imperium habeat* (Pont-à-Mousson, 1609), ch. 22, pp. 182–3.
[61] See n. 50 above.

from which Locke quotes are among those in which Barclay had drawn heavily upon Ninian Winzet's *Velitatio*. At the same time, Barclay was evidently (and inevitably) influenced by a powerful element in his own professional civil-law tradition. According to that view of the matter, human beings had an ineradicable right, rooted in natural law, to self-defence. This right, Barclay accepts, must pertain to a people suffering intolerable oppression by a tyrannical ruler: such a ruler may therefore be resisted. Yet Barclay is not here conceding the points made by Buchanan. He still maintains the sanctity of the king's person and specifically denies that there can be any question here of *punishment*: the right of self-defence confers upon inferiors no right to punish their super-iors. Even more important is the point that, if there is to be legitimate resistance, it must be by way of a collective or corporate act. There is no such right as that claimed by Buchanan for the individual subject to take upon himself the task of resisting the tyrant.[62]

When one looks at the crucial second passage from *De regno* cited by Locke, one finds, perhaps, a somewhat different perspective on the problem. Here Barclay will not allow that a king, as such, may be resisted – far less punished – even if the action is taken by the whole community and purports to be for their defence against oppression. Suppose, however, that the man who had been king were no longer so: suppose that he has, by certain extremities of misconduct, stripped himself of that royal dignity and sanctity which subjects are bound to respect. Then indeed, Barclay says (closely following Winzet at this point), the ex-king may suffer all the sanctions against which the king he once was had been hedged. Then, it seems, the people may of their own power and authority proceed against their oppressor – by force of arms if need be.[63] There is indeed a difficulty in this for Barclay, and one that lies so near the heart of the whole problematic area in early modern political thought with which this essay has been concerned that it may appropriately serve, in a moment, by way of conclusion. First, however, having regard to the specifically Scottish context of the discussion, it is necessary to take a brief look at Barclay's treatment of that context.

---

[62] *De regno*, 1600, p. 159.
[63] Ibid., pp. 212–14. This follows a passage in which Barclay opposes the view that a king can be brought before the ordinary courts of law.

Barclay had left Scotland (never, so far as we know, to return) when he was in his mid twenties. Yet his Scottish background and memories evidently remained vivid enough during the long years in Lorraine when, among other things, he wrote his *De regno*. This comes out in a number of varied incidental references as well as in the immediate context of conflicting interpretations of the Scottish past. Thus, when dealing with that crucial element in absolutist theory which refers to the king as acting 'of his certain knowledge' (*de certa scientia*), Barclay draws an analogy with a phrase used in the Scottish courts in regard to the basis of judicial decisions – 'the lordis motives'.[64] As for Barclay's general view of Scottish history and its significance for the debate in which he was engaged, it need hardly be said that he has harsh words for Buchanan as an historian.[65] It is perhaps fair to say – though the point needs fuller consideration than is possible here – that we find in Barclay even more than in Blackwood a 'celebratory' view of the historical record. He is concerned to record the warlike valour of the Scots, their impatience of alien rule, their stubborn loyalty to the royal house which had reigned over them for nearly 2,000 years.[66] William Wallace was a second Gideon; Baliol's submission to Edward I was a solitary (and ignominious) exception to an otherwise consistent rejection of foreign domination.[67] Though he refers more than once to the issue between Baliol and Bruce, Barclay seems not to have seen any need to refute at length those interpretations of the episode which might seem to undermine his own theory of kingship and its application to his native country.[68] Yet, as has already been said, the theory did have its problems; and to that problematic area we may now, finally, return.

To elucidate Barclay's difficulty it is helpful to go back to Ninian Winzet's *Velitatio in Georgium Buchananum*. Whatever may be thought of the positions advanced in that text, it is at least clear that Winzet adheres to a tradition in which the community of the

[64] Ibid., p. 102: 'Plurima eos [*sc.* Principes] mouere possunt, aliis ignota . . . in regno Scotiae eiusmodi causae vocantur simpliciter *the lordis motiues.*'
[65] Ibid., pp. 106–7. Barclay, unlike Winzet and Blackwood, had seen Buchanan's *Rerum Scoticarum Historia* (1582): he refers in particular to its last four books.
[66] See, e.g., ibid., p. 297.
[67] Ibid., p. 213. Barclay remarks here that Bodin (*Les six Livres de la République*, 1.ix) misinterprets the homage and fealty done by Scottish kings in respect of lands they held *in England*.
[68] Ibid., pp. 121, 213.

realm has institutional means of expressing, and, in certain circumstances, of executing its corporate will. To this extent Barclay and Winzet are in agreement. An organised political society – specifically, the realm of Scotland – has, especially though not exclusively in the Three Estates, an articulate collective life and being. For most of the time, no doubt, Winzet would agree that this life is latent rather than overt: it is a potentiality to be actualised only if and when misgovernment or extreme emergency produces a crisis with which the ordinary processes of royal government cannot deal. Now Barclay, in the phase of his argument which is so heavily indebted to precisely those elements in Winzet's thinking, plainly recognises a similar need for an institutional vehicle to activate the corporate life of the community. The trouble is that his general theory has already denied and precluded the existence of such institutions except insofar as they are allowed by royal concession and brought into being by royal summons; and even when they are in being they are subject always to the king's overriding authority. That there was a genuine dilemma here for the theory of monarchy in the late sixteenth century is, I suggest, quite clear. What was to become even clearer, and especially so to James VI and I, was that the dilemma would travel southwards from Edinburgh to London; and its horns would lose none of their sharpness when a king reacting vehemently against the teaching of George Buchanan encountered a parliament with – dare I say it? – rather more vigorous life in it than the parliament of Scotland.

CHAPTER 2

The ancient constitution revisited

William Klein

If human history is the story of painful journeys through violent upheavals, revolutions and conquests, it must equally be the story of growth, development and stability that are achieved as well as hoped for. The historian who reveals the violence rooted in the past of his civilised audience must therefore be a disturber of the peace; while a civilisation that blinds itself to the insight of the historian must rest its peace of mind on false foundations. It is this paradox that lies at the heart of Professor Pocock's first scholarly book, *The Ancient Constitution and the Feudal Law*, and that makes it still a book of general interest thirty-five years after its first appearance. What emerges from Pocock's examination of seventeenth-century English historical thought is a picture of the false consciousness of the ruling elites, which left them unprepared for the turbulence of their own century yet nevertheless became the basis for the disingenuous evasions of the ruling Whig ideology of the late seventeenth and eighteenth centuries.

At the heart of this ideology was the common-law view of the past, a view expressed with paradigmatic force by Sir Edward Coke at the beginning of the century. What interested Pocock about the Cokean core of Whig thought[1] was the degree to which Coke's view of the 'ancient constitution'[2] depended on a false (but not consciously falsified) view of history. Completely absent from Coke's

---

I would like to thank Ron Witt, Julie Solomon, Jane Tylus and Quentin Skinner for providing crucial criticisms of earlier drafts of this essay.

[1] In this Pocock was following his mentor Sir Herbert Butterfield, whose *The Englishman and his History* (Cambridge, 1945) is still a good introduction to the subject.

[2] As Charles Howard McIlwain pointed out in *Constitutionalism Ancient and Modern* (Ithaca, 1966; reprint of 1947 edn), pp. 23–7, the word 'constitution' was rarely used in our period to denote the whole complex of law and jurisdiction or, alternatively, the idea of regime or *politeia*, but both concepts were present. The question is, at what point did they combine? The older meaning was equivalent to 'statute'.

writings was any recognition that significant change ever confronted the common law. More specifically, for reasons that seem to
be of fundamental importance for the understanding of the ruling
ideology, Coke was insistent in denying that William the Conqueror imposed the Norman laws on the English in 1066 (and
consequently incapable of recognising the feudal character of
English law). The denial of sovereign activity of this magnitude in
the English past, linked to the insistence that everything fundamental to the common law had both developed through custom and
(paradoxically) existed from time immemorial, must, according to
Pocock, account in large measure for the way in which the lawyers
and politicians actually perceived and engaged with current constitutional questions. Hence the peculiar character of Whig thought,
which had to carry out constitutional change under the false
banner of stability.

Against this backdrop of Whig thought Pocock chronicled the
appearance of much more promising forms of consciousness, one
scholarly and ultimately Tory, the other republican. While James
Harrington's awareness of some of the more advanced scholarship
on feudalism aided him in arriving at a view of history as a
changing structure of social relationships based in law, it was his
republican sense of the dynamic and unstable *politeia* that gave his
history a real sense of movement. This form of thought was
therefore cut short by the restoration of the monarchy in 1660. The
pioneering work of the antiquary Sir Henry Spelman, on the other
hand, was paradigmatic for the Tory thought of Dr Robert Brady
because it developed, through a painstaking programme of comparative philological research, an ideologically useful critique of the
Cokean customary school of history. Like the continental legal
humanists who had developed dynamic, periodic visions of history,
Spelman saw the customary denial of the Conquest as relying on an
anachronistic use of documents. When philologically analysed, the
records of the common law showed that in fact William the
Conqueror had imposed a radically new system of feudal law on
England in 1066. This enlightened idea had wonderful royalist
potential, and Dr Brady accordingly seized on it in his elaboration
of a devastating *thèse royale* during the Exclusionist Controversy.
But though this mode of thought might have brought greater
sophistication to the constitutional thought of both Whigs and
Tories, it was effectively buried by the Glorious Revolution of 1688.

The *Ancient Constitution* became itself Whiggish, however, when it began to probe the period before the Restoration for the origins of the *thèse royale* and a pre-Whig reaction. Since the old chronicle tradition, which Pocock correctly saw was embodied in the work of Polydore Vergil, explicitly claimed that the Conqueror *had* changed the laws, it became something of a mystery, in Pocock's scheme, why the crown did not develop a Tory-like argument from history earlier than it did.[3] Pocock resolved this paradox by arguing that Coke's customary way of reasoning, along with his emphatic denial of the Conquest, was the product of a benighted 'mentality' common to crown and parliament alike. Before the Exclusionist controversy, the crown had essentially Tory views and the common lawyers had essentially Whig views, but neither had developed historiographically enlightened ways of putting them.[4] To this one could respond either that there *was* a Tory argument from conquest before the Restoration[5] or, alternatively, that there was *not* a Whig argument. It will be the aim of this essay to pursue the line of inquiry suggested by the latter response; that is, to attempt an understanding of the relevant thought of the first half of the century without imposing a prefiguration of the Whig/Tory dichotomy.

The problem with viewing Coke as an early Whig can be readily apprehended. Let us take for granted that the Whig Exclusionist William Petyt believed, as Pocock stated, that there 'must on no account have been a conquest by the Normans, for if all the laws of England had for one moment hung upon a conqueror's unrestricted will, they lived for ever afterwards by his permission and England was an absolute monarch to this day'.[6] This is a peculiar way of

---

[3] Pocock surmised that King James I's own argument from the Conquest was neither crucial to his case nor taken as a serious threat. See *The Ancient Constitution and the Feudal Law . . . A Reissue with a Retrospect* (Cambridge, 1987), pp. 42–3, 54.

[4] Pocock seems to have derived his model of enlightened despotism from Rosario Romeo, *Il Risorgimento in Sicilia* (Bari, 1950).

[5] In 'History and Ideology in the English Revolution', *The Historical Journal*, 8 (1965), 151–78, Skinner demonstrated that the *de facto* theorists developed absolutist arguments that relied on the Norman Conquest for illustration, and thus prepared the way for the *thèse royale* of the Exclusionist Controversy (he points out that Hobbes's *Dialogue on the Common Law* was published as an anti-Exclusionist tract, p. 170). Sommerville, in *Politics and Ideology in England, 1603–1640* (London, 1986), pp. 68–9, has pushed this type of argument back into the early Stuart period by arguing that some civilians traced the king's absolute power back to the Conquest. But it is not clear that the civilians believed they were arguing a controverted point against a proto-Whiggish party doctrine.

[6] 'Robert Brady, 1627–1700. A Cambridge Historian of the Restoration', *Cambridge Historical Journal*, 10 (1951), 189–90. This view is repeated in *The Ancient Constitution*, p. 53.

thinking, and not likely to occur to anyone who was not anticipating a *thèse royale* that did indeed hinge in such a way on an event
that took place 600 years earlier. The problem with constructing an
explanation as to why Coke thought in this way is that, as J. P.
Sommerville has already shown,[7] he simply did not think in this
way. Coke accepted the fact that William had conquered the land
and could well have changed the laws. Like other conquerors of
England, William recognised the excellence of English customs and
left them alone. In other words, he does not seem to have
anticipated a Tory argument from conquest.

But if we admit that Coke the Jacobean judge and author of the
Reports did not argue very much like a Whig polemicist, this does
not mean that there was no 'mentality' underlying his thought or
that his attitude towards the distant past was essentially irrelevant
to his general way of thinking (as Sommerville argues it was). In
this regard, Pocock's characterisation of Coke's thought (if not his
structural explanation) still remains the starting-point. Coke did
deny the effects of the Conquest, if not the fact of it, and he did so in
a manner which was every bit as paradigmatic as Pocock claimed.

In addition to the beginnings of a non-Whiggish reading of
Coke's mentality, *The Ancient Constitution* also contains an outline,
albeit somewhat buried, of a non-Whiggish chronology. It was
when 'the feudal interpretation entered the sphere of practical
politics' that attention shifted from maintaining the 'antiquity of
the law in general' to the 'antiquity of parliament'. Spelman as
usual is taken to have had the superior insight to recognise this
moment before it occurred when he applied the feudal interpretation to the history of parliament.[8] But the real moment came, as
Pocock recognised, during the Interregnum, when constitutional
innovation began to break up the vision of a unified body of law
and institutions so crucial to the common-law interpretation of
history. In *The Ancient Constitution* Pocock saw this occurring when
William Prynne responded to the army's attacks on the constitution, which led to Pride's Purge and the abolition of the House of
Lords.[9] Prynne was forced by circumstance to search in a Cokean

---

[7] 'History and Theory: The Norman Conquest in Early Stuart Political Thought', *Political Studies*, 34 (1986), 252–3.
[8] *The Ancient Constitution*, p. 120.
[9] In *The Machiavellian Moment* and in the Restrospect to *The Ancient Constitution*, the 1642 'Answer to the Nineteen Propositions' is taken to be the crucial moment.

manner for historical sanction for one element of the constitution – the House of Lords – above another, so that the result was entirely un-Cokean.[10] As Harrington was later to do, but in a much less dramatic fashion, Prynne made a crucial step in the direction of recognising historical change without the benefit of Spelman's comparative work in historical philology. He was able to see the ancient consitution as having been subject to historical forces in the past because the current constitution had been so subjected, not because sophisticated scholarly techniques had been applied to the study of documents.

With this trajectory from Coke to Prynne in mind we may return to examine Coke's world more carefully, sifting out aspects of Pocock's analysis and supplementing them with additional material. If, as Pocock suggested, it was Coke's place to assert 'the antiquity of the law in general' as opposed to one element of the constitution over another, we are led to wonder how 'the struggle of king and parliament'[11] could have been operative. Was not the king as much a part of the constitution as any other element? Indeed, it would appear that on this point Coke was as good a royalist as Brady. If it was part of the Tory thesis that 'the king enjoyed the advantage that every proprietor of land owed him the special and personal allegiance of the vassal' and that society was 'a pyramid of dependence upon a sovereign king',[12] Coke had arrived at this position by simply practising in the king's courts. While Coke denied that William the Conqueror instituted the common law, he did not deny that the king was the source of tenures, nor that he was the source of justice. Regarding tenures, Coke pointed out that 'all the lands within this realme were originally derived from the crowne, and therefore the king is sovereign lord, or lord paramount, either mediate or immediate, of all and every parcel of land within the realme'. Therefore the king is owed both liege homage as chief lord and a more general 'faith' as 'sovereign lord over all'.[13] It would not give the king greater authority to say that his ancestor the Conqueror divided the land among his followers, merely a more recent (and therefore less worthy) founding act than an act lost in

---

[10] *The Ancient Constitution*, pp. 156 ff.
[11] *The Ancient Constitution*, p. 42.
[12] *The Ancient Constitution*, p. 215.
[13] *1 Institutes*, L.2̍, c.1, sec.85.

the mists of time. Coke could admit the Conquest as a political act because the Conquest gave the king no more *legal* authority than the common law did. Far from being a comment on *ius conquestus*, or the political powers of the crown which might operate outside of the common law, Coke's work simply failed to consider the problem of a king as an outlaw.[14] But if Coke's denial of cataclysmic change at the Conquest was not a proto-Whig move against the royal prerogative, what was it?

To answer in terms of common-law mentality, but not to frame the answer in opposition to enlightenment, is to move from *The Ancient Constitution* to *The Machiavellian Moment*. Rather than view the common-law mind solely from the point of view of its incapacities in relation to enlightened historiographic discourse, and rather than develop an elaborate device to explain this incapacity as a function of uniquely English legal structures (which may not have been so unusual after all), we will instead simply ask, what was the common-law vision of the constitution existing in time? Since Coke borrowed his doctrine on the ancient constitution and its invulnerability to conquest from Fortescue, and since Pocock discussed Fortescue in the first chapter of *The Machiavellian Moment*, we may already seem to have Coke in the proper context. But some further points need to be made.

Pocock's discussion of Fortescue's *De laudibus legum Anglie* in *The Machiavellian Moment* is concerned to establish a contrast, following McIlwain, between the *jurisdictio* of the judges and the *gubernaculum* of the prince. Jurisdiction was the only realm Fortescue discussed seriously, and it is part of Pocock's point that Fortescue's understanding of law as the realm of experience, where prudence must fill in the gaps left by custom, was unable to encompass the mystery of statecraft and governance. This is clearly a key to Coke's view of the Conquest, but Fortescue's temporal consciousness is equally fundamental. Living in the deeply Christian world of late-medieval corporate monarchy, Fortescue imagined that the divine status of the *corpus mysticum* lifted the king's earthly institutions out of the realm of sublunary corruption and into the stable company of

---

[14] As McIlwain showed, the doctrine that the king can do no wrong could be used to void individual royal acts in court, where they violated the common law; but this did not provide a truly constitutional language for the political realm. See *Constitutionalism*, chapters 5 and 6.

angels and all other sempiternal creations.[15] His world of judges and jurors was accordingly a peaceful, slow-moving world with ample time for the making of laws in the customary way – over generations – and occasionally in the 'political' way – with the deliberation of the people. It was a world not of active citizens but of monarchical subjects, and in its pastoral insularity (chapter 29) it was undisturbed by the threats of fortune that charged the pages of, for instance, Leonardo Bruni's great work of republican civism, *Laudatio florentinae urbis*.[16] Indeed, according to Fortescue, the justices seem 'more contemplative than active. They thus lead quiet lives, free of all worry and worldly care.'[17]

To Fortescue, the English body politic, with king as head, people as heart and law as sinews, extended unchanged in essence (though subject to growth under the laws of Aristotelian physics) from its founding moment under Brut, when its principles were instituted (chapter 13). The problem of mutability and threat was so far from his mind (though he was living with the exiled Lancastrian prince) that he presented the several conquests of the passive body politic as a kind of Christian triumph. The Romans, Saxons, Danes and Normans all lay down their arms before the altar of the law, which stood undefended yet invulnerable in its sempiternal excellence (chapter 17). While it is true, as Pocock argues, that Fortescue was concerned to justify the peculiarities of English law as customary usages which could be apprehended only through experience, it was equally Fortescue's concern to show that the basic framework of the ancient constitution, the *institucionis regni politici formam*,[18] was

---

[15] A sempiternal body (neither eternal nor temporary), such as the law or the king's mystical corporation, occupied the same temporal space as the angels for the medievals, but this left them with a substantialistic view of historical entities very much like that of Livy, who, like Fortescue, traced all institutions back to the founding of the regime. See Ernst H. Kantorowicz, *The King's Two Bodies: A Study in Medieval Political Theology* (Princeton, 1957), pp. 273–7, 281, R. G. Collingwood, *The Idea of History* (New York, 1956: first edn, 1946), Part I.

[16] Here I am only expanding on the contrast implicit in Pocock's discussion. See Benjamin G. Kohl's translation and R. G. Witt's commentary in their edition, *The Earthly Republic: Italian Humanists on Government and Society* (University of Pennsylvania Press, 1978), pp. 121–75. I would like to thank Professor Witt for directing me to this text and discussing the contrasts with Fortescue.

[17] S. B. Chrimes (ed.), *De laudibus legum Anglie* (Cambridge, 1942), pp. 129–31. Fortescue cites Bruni's *Isagogicum de Philosophia Morali*, so it is tempting, even though there is no evidence for it, to think Fortescue composed his praise of the English laws in response to Bruni's praise of the city of Florence.

[18] *De laudibus*, p. 32.

original to the founding and unalterable by either a conquering prince or fortune. Fortescue imagined the polity as a natural organism bearing fruit in its maturity (chapter 36), and his comparative programme could extend no further than to contrast the lush growth of England's *dominium politicum et regale* with the withered bush of France's merely regal realm.[19] This was a vision of stable *jurisdictio* made oblivious to the devious operations of *gubernaculum*.

Fortescue's teaching provided an ideal setting for the post-Reformation 'Anglican' (contemporaneous with the Gallican)[20] school of law which grew up first alongside (but not necessarily in opposition to) the increasingly refined school of Tudor statecraft[21] and then the divine-right school of the early Stuarts. In John Selden's notes to Fortescue one can see the degree to which the new scholarly techniques left undisturbed the essentially monarchic vision. Selden was unwilling to accept the legendary founding by Brut, and he insisted that the various conquests of England did introduce new customs, which 'mixed' with the old. He refused to sanction Fortescue's notion that English laws were superior to French because of longer duration. But to Selden, no less than to Fortescue, the essential nature of a state is established at its founding. At that point the natural laws are limited to suit the 'conveniences' of that state. Though change will occur over time, the substance remains the same, like a ship repaired plank by plank.[22] Eventually the original matter of the law will have vanished, 'yet (by the civil law) [it] is to be accounted the same still'. But though he recognised that different states will have different laws, Selden was even less able than Fortescue to engage in comparative constitutional analysis: 'Neither are laws thus to be

[19] This crude, forensic comparative scheme is derived not from the *Politics* but from the *Rhetoric*, as Cary J. Nederman shows in 'Aristotle as Authority: Alternative Aristotelian Sources of Late Medieval Political Theory', *History of European Ideas*, 8 (1987), 37–41.

[20] See Donald Kelley on the Gallican legal scholars, who were perhaps, for all their erudition, less historicist and closer to the English lawyers than Kelley admits, *Foundations of Modern Historical Scholarship: Language, Law and History in the French Renaissance* (New York, 1970), esp. pp. 278–93, on Pierre Pithou.

[21] As an expression of this, with its fine comparative technique, full awareness of Aristotle's *Republic* and admiration for the Venetian constitution, see the magnificent diplomatic guide by Edmund Tyllney, *The Discriptione Regimentte and Pollicie as well Generall as particularly of Italy, France . . .*, Folger Library MS. V.b.182.

[22] Kantorowicz, in *The King's Two Bodies*, p. 295, showed that this notion of 'identity despite change' in the law, illustrated by the metaphor of a ship, originated in the Roman law (*Digest* 41,3,36), and was revived by Accursius.

compar'd. Those which best fit the state wherein they are, clearly deserve the name of the best laws.'[23] But these differences are inessential, so there is really nothing of importance to be learned from history.

Whatever the reasons for this theoretical retreat from history to natural law, it is clear that one outcome was that the common law was rendered immune to historicist attack. Selden did not explicitly respond to the various continental humanists who had turned the tables on Fortescue's chauvinistic argument by plausibly claiming that the English laws had actually been imposed by the Normans,[24] but we can see that his attitude towards history renders the whole question of conquest irrelevant. He could admit that the English received laws from the Normans without implying that the laws were thereby substantially changed. Regarding the *form* of government that the Conqueror may have imposed by the sword, Selden's scheme simply gave no guidance.

There appears to be a disjunction here between Selden's vast programme of research, which he had recently commenced, and his theory, which seems to make such research irrelevant. It was not until the preface to the 1631 edition of *Titles of Honour* that Selden seems to have formulated a theory equal to his research, but it does not appear that he ever produced an historical work in which the theory worked in tandem with the research. In this preface we learn that he had moved towards an appreciation of Aristotle's *Politics* and in fact developed the seeds of a legal relativism that would go beyond Aristotle. The notion that different states have different laws had now been linked to an awareness that constitutional change affects not simply the dispositions of laws but the 'nature of the Being' of practices such as the granting of titles of honour, and even the nature of justice itself: 'for that which may be most Convenient or just in one State, may be as Injust and Inconvenient in another'. He went on to regret the loss of Aristotle's pupil Theophrastus's comparative studies of constitutions and to complain, following Roger Bacon, that there had been no serious study

---

[23] Chrimes (ed.), *De laudibus legum Anglie*, notes, pp. 18–20. It may be misleading for Richard Tuck to take this Accursian position as representative of the humanism of Alciato, in *Natural Rights Theories: Their Origin and Development* (Cambridge, 1979), p. 83.

[24] Selden argued that the Conquest had introduced new customs in *Jani Anglorum facies altera* (1610). As Pocock has pointed out in his Retrospect to *The Ancient Constitution*, Selden would soon switch to denying that the Conquest had a significant effect.

of comparative constitutions in the universities leading to 'a true understanding *philosophicé*, . . . in such sort as that by comparing the manifold variety of several States and times (as we find them since those Grecians wrote) just precepts or directions might be doctrinally delivered concerning them'.[25]

If Selden was moving from one kind of intellectual world to another, and experiencing some confusion in the process, his lesser contemporaries in the 'Anglican' school of law seem on the whole to have been less worried about the shortcomings of the Fortescuean tradition. Their goal under most circumstances seems rather to have been to provide as sophisticated a version of that tradition as possible. Consequently, one could probably go further than Pocock in presenting a logically coherent version of the tradition. But my concern here is to show how two components of the system, custom and precedent (often conflated by Pocock), were able to operate within the general Fortescuean framework whenever that framework itself remained viable.

Without entering into the arcana of the philosophy of custom, which receives a full treatment in *The Ancient Constitution*,[26] we can perhaps move straight to the crucial use Coke made of custom in his constitutional thought. This is nowhere better illustrated, as Pocock astutely pointed out, than in the preface to the *Third Reports*, where he took a document from the Assize of 26 Edward III and used it to demonstrate the pre-Conquest existence of sheriffs, trials by oaths of twelve men, the king's courts, Chancery, and 'the entire science and practice of the common law'.[27] By a procedure that looks ridiculous from a historicist point of view, Coke read this document as an artifact of a stable system which was identical to his own. But since there were no records to the contrary (at least that anyone had coherently presented), it was fairly rational to presume that the system had subsisted under the guise of unwritten

[25] *Titles of Honor*, 3rd edn (London, 1672), 'Preface'. See Lord Ellesmere's condemnation of the study of 'the severall constitutions and frames of states and Common-wealths' and 'what Plato or Aristotle have written of this argument', in his argument in the *post-nati* case (1608), in Louis A. Knafla, *Law and Politics in Jacobean England: The Tracts of Lord Chancellor Ellesmere* (Cambridge, 1977), p. 247.

[26] But as McIlwain has shown in *Constitutionalism*, pp. 64–5, this notion of custom as the immemorial usage of the people also derives from Roman law and should not be thought of as peculiarly English.

[27] *The Ancient Constitution*, pp. 38–9.

custom rather than written (historically determinable) authority. The point to underline here, however, is that Coke used custom to argue for the sempiternity of the constitution as a whole, not the slow development of some aspect of it.[28]

The argument from custom was fundamentally different from the argument from precedent. A precedent was also 'unwritten' in that it was not statute and had to be received by the common law in order to have authority, and this required additional argumentation, but the evidence for a precedent was a written document. The search for a precedent thus became a form of historical research, and it was this sort of activity that the parliamentary lawyers and antiquaries excelled at. But it appears to be incorrect to suggest, as Pocock sometimes did, that pre-Whig members of parliament were ever engaged in searching for this kind of authority against the king as such.[29] If the king's policy asserted independent authority in some controverted area, parliament might then search for precedents of parliamentary involvement, and failing that, resort to custom. While this could lead to sophisticated criticism of documents, the purely partisan nature of the enterprise (like that of the Gallican school), carried out within the Fortescuean framework, ensured that the results were very far from being historical in any sense we would praise today.

When, on the contrary, the early Stuart antiquaries gathered to discuss historical questions in their cloistered settings, the result could be of historiographic value (though never, as far as I am aware, achieving the new type of understanding Selden was reaching towards). Often arriving at an impressive range of opinions about the origin of various institutions (British, Saxon, Danish, Norman or later), the method was sometimes genuinely philological, even if more genealogic than periodic. But this disinterested behaviour of necessity did not translate well from the private gathering to the various institutional settings, and the

---

[28] Pocock often sees the legal doctrine of custom as a precursor of the Burkean view of history, but in this case the key to Coke's thought is not development but stability; *The Ancient Constitution*, p. 19.

[29] *The Ancient Constitution*, pp. 16–17. Precedential competition among the various courts, especially between lay and ecclesiastical, was, however, common. How often this led to a dynamic view of the constitution *within* the law is a separate issue, and is no doubt worth pursuing.

discourses were not published until the eighteenth century (and then only a sampling).[30]

A good example of an antiquary who developed a sophisticated opinion about the genealogy of the common law itself (it was, like Norman law, essentially 'Danish', and therefore the Conqueror did not need to change it much) was a lawyer from Lincoln's Inn, William Hakewill (1575-1655).[31] His little discourse on the history of the common law does not seem to suggest any of the preconceptions about substantial duration we have encountered so far and it was fruitfully comparative. There is nothing to indicate his use of evidence (as is the case with some of the other discourses), nor what he thought about the development of the law once it had been established. Nor does he speculate on the form of the constitution of any of the racial groups discussed. But he does indicate a flexible historical consciousness on the limited question of the origin of 'the laws' taken as a whole, and his criticism of Fortescue and 'some late writers' on this score is refreshing.[32]

It is not surprising then to find that Hakewill was a master of the argument from precedent. His famous parliamentary speech of 1610 challenging the crown's right to impose new customs duties contains such a compelling critique of the judges' own precedents in Bate's Case, with such a sophisticated periodic theory of English kingship, that one is apt to miss the fact that it ultimately rests on a purely Cokean argument from custom, however cleverly put. Having established to his satisfaction that all the precedents of impositions were either illegitimate or in fact cases assented to in a parliament, he then confronted the fact that the earliest record of the parliamentary imposition of a 'new custom' or duty under Edward I left open the question of how the earlier ones were approved. The silence of the records had allowed the judges to argue 'that it began by the kings absolute power, and infer that the same power remains still'. But Hakewill claimed that the silence of

---

[30] Thomas Hearne (ed.), *A Collection of Curious Discourses* (Oxford, 1720). One uses these discourses with some trepidation. Hearne himself may have been a critical editor, but his successor for the 1771 edition certainly included a set of spurious discourses on the history of parliament.

[31] His brother George wrote an impressive treatise refuting the idea that the world was 'growing old', which Hans Baron discusses in relation to other humanist work on the same theme in *In Search of Florentine Humanism: Essays in the Transition from Medieval to Modern Thought* (Princeton, 1988), vol. II, pp. 70 ff.

[32] *Curious Discourses*, pp. 1-11.

the records was due to a fire in the Exchequer under Henry II. Since, as the Elizabethan antiquary Lambard showed, there were parliaments going back as far as King Ina, and since indeed the whole science of the common law was immemorial, one could not argue from silence that the king did anything by his absolute power. This was not to deny that the king *had* absolute power nor that he had used it on occasion, but rather to assert that most things in the law had begun 'by a tacit consent of king and people', and had continued 'by the long approbation of time beyond the memory of man'. Indeed, though the king might have originated some practices, 'yet no man can directly affirm but that most of them might begin by act of parliament, though now there bee no records extant of such antient parliaments'.[33]

Being concerned with the imperfect tense rather than the perfect, the legal antiquaries generally felt little need to explore the distant world of history proper. But there were occasions when space was left in multi-tiered parliamentary arguments for history. In their arguments regarding the legal status of the *post-nati*, the categories were: comparative history, civil law, reason and the law of nature, and the common law.[34] Ellesmere wearily rejected the first as irrelevant chatter, but the Commons had absorbed enough of the culture of the late Renaissance to be unable to resist appearing erudite in this venerable field of discourse. The man they chose to tell 'the stories of other countries' on this and other occasions, Sir Roger Owen (1573-1617), was indeed a man of remarkable erudition. But the question we must ask of Owen's erudition – as of Selden's – is how his erudition and capacity to engage in critical research informed his approach to questions of public doctrine.

Owen's contribution to the *post-nati* case is of some interest in this regard. He treated specific instances of Roman, Spanish and French history as precedents, and showed that, like Hakewill, he

---

[33] T. B. Howell (ed.), *A Complete Collection of State Trials* (London, 1816), vol. II, cols. 468–70. Not all ideological histories of parliament in this period were Cokean. Sir Robert Cotton's excellent tract demonstrating 'That the Kings of England have been pleased, usually, to consult with their Peers in the Great Council, and Commons in Parliament, of Marriage, Peace, and War' of 1621 had an aristocratic audience and so was able to repeat Arthur Hall's heresy that the Commons was not originally part of parliament. See Kevin Sharpe, *Sir Robert Cotton, 1586-1631: History and Politics in Early Modern England* (Oxford, 1979), p. 170, for the political context in 1621. On Arthur Hall's impeccable Elizabethan history of parliaments, see G. R. Elton, *Studies in Tudor and Stuart Politics and Government* (Cambridge, 1983), vol. III, pp. 268–71.

[34] *State Trials*, vol. II, pp. 563–4.

could be skilful at contextualising a precedent in such a manner
that it either appeared to agree with the Commons' case or
appeared illegitimate.[35] This required a certain degree of historical
consciousness and erudition, but in this case, since the precedents
were not English, they were irrelevant from the point of view of the
law. They might provide guidance for prudential action where no
English law or custom or example existed (and may suggest that in
this case the Commons saw themselves as partaking of statecraft)
but as Ellesmere pointed out, there was plenty of evidence from the
English crown's own complex territorial history. Prudence was
indeed required to solve this 'new case', but it was the sort of
prudence habitually used by judges in both the common and the
civil law to adjust the law to new circumstances. Judicial, not
political, activism was required; and the time-frame was not that of
the unstable republic battling with fortune, but of the durable body
of the law adjusting its precepts to the inconveniences brought by
the exposure of the *aevum* to *tempus*.[36]

If in this instance it appears that Owen's comparative history
had difficulty penetrating the law, there is a massive piece of
evidence indicating that he himself could conceive of no other
result. This is his voluminous treatise 'Of the Antiquitie Amplenes
and Excellence of the Common Lawes of England' (written from
1615 to 1616), which was never published but which seems to have
been intended for a judicial and even royal audience.[37] If it could
be said of Coke 'that he knew all there was to know about feudal
law in England except that it was feudal',[38] it could be said of
Owen that he knew both the former and the latter, and yet still
remained insular, patriotic and Cokean in his approach to the legal
past. The title of his treatise alone indicates this much, but the
outline of its programme of research is almost astoundingly
Cokean:

I shall perticularly instance, That the High Court of Parliament, the
Chauncery, the kings bench, the Common Place; the Exchequer, the
Sheriffe and his County Courts, the Bayliffe and their hundred Courts, the

---

[35] *State Trials*, vol. II, pp. 563–5.

[36] Knafla, *Law and Politics*, pp. 216–27.

[37] For an attempt to put the facts of Owen's life and writings in context, see my dissertation, 'Ruling Thoughts: The World of Sir Roger Owen of Condover', The Johns Hopkins University, 1987.

[38] *The Ancient Constitution*, p. 66.

Lords of Mannors and the Courte Barrons and Leetes, That the quallitie of the English Estates Tenure by knight service and Soccage; wardshipp, Reliefe, Herriotts, Escuage, That the same quantitie of Estates, Tenants for yeares, for life, in Taile in Fee Simple were afore the Conquest.[39]

And so it went, encompassing nearly every aspect of the English constitution, including in good 'Anglican' fashion the king's 'prerogatives over the Clergie'.

What is impressive about this effort to freeze time is that it was conducted with incredible erudition. Owen did not disappoint the reader when he promised that he would 'speake comparatively of the Lawes of other Nations'. After reading a section of the treatise mistakenly published in an edition of Raleigh's works, Sir Maurice Powicke drew these conclusions about the 'intellectual atmosphere' of the antiquaries:

The range of their reading is well-nigh incredible to us, who have been trained in a narrower discipline. An hour or so spent with a work like [Owen's treatise] ... is enough to show how exhilarating, and how dangerous, this reading was. It offered invitations to the comparative study of institutions and languages, but it held no thread of guidance in that vast labyrinth, and deluded men into the belief that they had mastered knowledge.[40]

Despite his comparative programme, despite his apparent mastery of the entire range of Sir Robert Cotton's library,[41] despite his impressive capacity to criticise source material (from chronicles to cartularies to Domesday Book), Owen had in the end to rely on Cokean arguments to arrive at the results he wanted. Indeed, to Owen Coke was 'the great God Pan of the Legal Oracles', and when in his sixteenth chapter he desired to prove the pre-conquest antiquity of King's Bench, Common Pleas and Exchequer, he reproduced and amplified Coke's argument from 28 Assize with infinite care and patience, refuting Lambard and other Elizabethans who had denied the antiquity of the full range of the

---

[39] British Library MS. Harley 1572, fos. 249 a-b. No holograph of the treatise exists, but I have attempted, in the first chapter of 'Ruling Thoughts', to demonstrate that all of the known fragments belong to the same treatise. The section cited is from chapter 8, the previous material having been preparatory to the main body of the treatise.
[40] F. M. Powicke, 'Sir Henry Spelman and the "Concilia"', *Proceedings of the British Academy*, 16 (1930), 350.
[41] On the library, see Kevin Sharpe, *Sir Robert Cotton, 1586–1631: History and Politics in Early Modern England* (Oxford, 1979), chapter 3.

constitution in this regard.[42] Unable to find documents to prove his case, Owen used the argument from silence (i.e., custom) to assert it.

But even when he developed an interesting argument about the shape of history, it is clear that he arrived at the theory by digesting some historical argument by a continental writer, and then framing an English parallel which would ensure that the structure of the common law retained an 'excellent' and 'ample' pedigree. This seems to be the procedure behind identifying the feudal structure of the English laws as essentially Germanic. There was a broad movement at this time within northern European nations to trace their roots to the Germanic barbarians, as a response both to the Reformation and to the rise of post-medieval nationalism. Hotman, John Thurnmaier, Albert Krantz, Joannes Goropius Becanus – these were some of the scholars engaged in Germanic genealogy.[43] Owen even borrowed the language of constitutionalism from the school of Hotman when he asserted that 'in theis Countreys where our Tenures hath bin in use, they have bin most free and least subject unto bondages'.[44] But the point was not developed in constitutional terms and was mainly used to defend the dignity of the feud against the humanists and other critics who had slandered wardship as a badge of servitude.[45]

Another tract, written by one Robert Hills during the debate on whether to abolish wardship in 1610, shows how a quick study of a continental author such as Guarrini Piso could result in a version of the 'de origine feudorum' topos and speculation about how the English case might fit into this civilian framework. But it was not so

[42] British Library MS. Harley 6605, fos. 64 ff.
[43] See chapter 7, on 'The Ancient Language', in Richard Foster Jones, *The Triumph of the English Language* (Stanford, 1953), and for the English movement, see Samuel L. Kliger, *The Goths in England* (Cambridge, MA, 1952). For Pocock's valuable point that truly Germanic thought is distinct from common law thought, see *The Ancient Constitution*, pp. 56–7.
[44] Inner Temple MS. 538.10, fo. 107a. This MS. was Petyt's copy of chapter 18.
[45] See the attack of Roderick Mors, in J. Meadows Cowper, *Henry Brinklow's Complaynt of Roderyk Mors* (Early English Text Society, 1874), chapter 5. Owen did end up admitting that the military aspect of the feud had gone into disuse and that therefore 'the life of the tenure is gone, being warfaringe by tenure, but the stinge of the Tenure, wardshipp, remaines, and that altered from the first foundation'. But I think it could be argued that my own complicated explication in 'Ruling Thoughts' of Owen's attitudes to the feud and to the advisability of abolishing wardship demonstrates that Owen did not have a clear way of dealing with constitutional change of this order, though my point was more or less the opposite. See 'Ruling Thoughts', chapter 2.

easy to locate the English evidence, to sort out what Domesday
Book may have to do with it all, and to escape the argument from
custom. In response to 'some forraigners' who had 'Injuriously
slandered our Lawes of this kinde', Hill argued, citing Coke's *Third
Report*, that English 'Tenures by knights service and the Prerogative
Royall of Warshipp are by Prescription and consequently farr more
antient then the Conquest or any memory of man, or other proofe
or Record.'[46] Owen cited dozens more of the feudists and worked
harder at interpreting the English material, but arrived at the same
result.

Aside from showing the degree to which the common-law mind
could become impervious to history, Owen shows why it had
become a matter of some urgency to cut short the less-dogmatic
approach of the Elizabethan antiquaries and to develop a more
defensive version of 'Anglicanism'.[47] Unlike Coke, Owen 'named
the names' of those continental and English heretics who denied
the antiquity of the common law,[48] and explicitly engaged in
rebuttal. There were fourteen foreigners who claimed that the
Norman laws were imposed on England by the Conqueror, including Bodin, Hotman, Charles Loiseau, Paulus Jovius, Paulus Aemi-
lius, Josiah Berault and René Choppin. Of these perhaps Berault is
the most interesting since his edition and commentary on the
customs of Normandy would seem to have provided a document
with which to engage in comparative analysis of English and
Norman feudal laws. But the question for Berault, no less than for
Owen and later Matthew Hale, was whether the Normans imposed
these customs on the English or the English on the Normans.[49]

Of the English authors who were not common lawyers, Owen
listed twenty. Though the monks Matthew Paris and Roger
Wendover were identified as the originators of the slander against
the common law, and Polydore Vergil as the progenitor of lies in

[46] Robert Hill, *Of Tenures in Knights Service, of Wardshipp Marriadge and Relief* . . ., Folger
Library MS., fos. 19b, 36b, where Piso is cited. Hill also cites seven other feudists. On
Piso, see Donald R. Kelley, 'De Origine Feudorum: The Beginnings of an Historical
Problem', *Speculum*, 39 (1964), 214.
[47] This is a question of chronology identified by Pocock but left unanswered.
[48] The naming takes place in chapter 8, British Library MS. Harley 1572, fos. 251a ff.;
rebuttal takes place in chapters 9 and 10.
[49] Josiah Berault, *La Coustume reformeé du pays et duché de Normandie* . . . (Rouen, 1612), p. 229;
Matthew Hale, *The History of the Common Law of England*, ed. Charles Gray (Chicago,
1971), chapter 6, 'Concerning the parity of similitude of the laws of England and
Normandy, and the reasons thereof'.

the modern period, it was the civilians John Cowell and Thomas Ridley who attracted Owen's most concentrated efforts at rebuttal. Again and again throughout the treatise Owen returned to them, making much of the threat that they and their profession posed to the common law.[50] Whether or not this threat of a Roman law 'reception' was taken seriously, the point is that the debate was carried out even more exclusively in terms of *jurisdictio* than it was in Fortescue. While Fortescue was worried about the political implications of a Roman law which gave the prince's pleasure the force of law, Owen was concerned simply to defend the common law as a set of jurisdictions against encroachment from a conflicting professional body. There was no concern with nor argument developed against a conflicting style of *gubernaculum*, and such a threat played no part in his denial of a conquest. He did state the erroneous argument that since all the kings are numbered since the Conquest 'this may somewhat intimate the Conquerour as a founder began a new manner of government of this Countrey more beneficiall for the succeeding kings by which they raigned and challenged their Prerogative Royall,'[51] but his research was aimed not at showing that the Saxons formed a different or less regal sort of government, but only that the common law was founded before the Conquest and not disturbed by it.

In fact, Owen had no sense that the present constitution was in any real danger of being subverted from above. The 'Clock of the Civill government' was 'well set and all the wheeles thereof movinge in order'. It was the civilians who were guilty of questioning 'the politique frame of the kingdome' with their (in fact rather minor) claims to a larger jurisdiction.[52] And it was in the context of Ridley's civilian version of history – which claimed, among other things, that the Lombard *Libri Feudorum* provided a model for the English feud, and that therefore it was legitimate for civilians to interpret the great Littleton – that Owen developed his static, Germanic view of history.

Conceptually, Owen's history was a thoroughly medieval treat-

[50] This threat was the subject of Maitland's lecture, *The English Law and the Renaissance* (Cambridge, 1901), but he did not mention Ridley and Owen's response.
[51] British Library MS. Harley 1572, fo. 263a.
[52] British Library MS. Harley 3627, fo. 59a. See Ridley's *A View of the Civile and Ecclesiastical Law* (1607).

ment of the law as a body whose 'substance' he was investigating.[53] The result was entirely consistent with the Accursian model of change, and indeed he cited the *locus classicus* in the *Digest* to characterise the continuum he was investigating:

If Plutarch and Alphanus in the Digest may hold it to be the same people of Rome at this day which was many hundred years aunciect, And it is the same Shipp of auncient Theseus which had only the forme of it and made of new boards clapt on at severall times, At this day in Syvill the Spaniards have the Shipp Victoria which first Sayled rounde the worlde, because by them if the same species of the thing continue it is the same thing. By better reason the Common Law may be said to be the same which was in the Saxons Kings times, because not only the species but the individua almost of each part of the Saxon or English Lawes as appeareth by the former division continue at this day in force. Consequently although God cannot be demonstrated to be a priore, yet precedency of the Common Law to the Norman Conquest may.[54]

This vision of the formal continuity and unity of the body of the law was very far from being historicist but it was obviously seen by its author as a viable ground for a defence against historicist criticism, and it is not a vision that is in any obvious way unsophisticated or inconsistent. The law so envisaged had even less of a constitutional aspect than it had for Fortescue, however, and it was certainly not seen as a response to a *thèse royale*. As a purely jurisdictional vision, it not only provided no suggestion of a check to the king's will, but placed the king squarely at the source of the law: 'Anciently likewise in the generation of the English Monarchy or any other such pollitique body All your writts or precepts of Justice issued from the handes or mouth of the king And in person where he dwelt he decided all causes.'[55]

It would appear, then, that the Cokeans were theoretically at least committed to occupying an un-Whiggish kind of 'fools eternity'.[56] If a modern historian wishes to find aspects of his own methods in the Cokeans, he can point to their ability to notice various changes in the law, to read documents, etc. But what was important to the development of their jurisprudence was rather a

---

[53] British Library MS. Harley 1572, fo. 122b.
[54] British Library MS. Harley 1572, fo. 250b.
[55] British Library MS. Harley 1572, fo. 214b (chapter 7).
[56] This is the phrase of Charles M. Gray, who denies its applicability to the Cokeans; Hale's *History of the Common Law*, p. xxiii.

confidence that their system of law was 'ample' enough to contain
solutions to problems that any case might present, 'ancient' enough
to have proved (in the manner indicated by Fortescue) its suitabi-
lity to the people it regulated, and 'excellent' enough to ward off
any competing claims of superior wisdom from rival systems. As a
body of law it had to be self-referring, self-sufficient and autochthonous if its practitioners were to claim the special competence
conferred on them by their clients. To admit that a conqueror had
imposed a foreign system of law in a foreign language, as the
civilians and humanists had asserted along with the chroniclers,
would be to deny those qualities – unless one were to take a
Seldenian view of natural law and history.

But as the basis of a claim to jurisdiction, the patriotic 'Anglicanism' of the Cokeans was not, in its origins, a doctrine touching
gubernaculum. Even when Cokean arguments were employed against
a royal policy in parliament, it would seem prudent to avoid
characterising them as proto-Whig either in constitutional or in
historical terms.[57] A view that was closer to being constitutional
was the cyclical view of the constitution which Owen tried to
suppress – the idea, which he found naively stated in Lambard,
that the Conqueror had buried the laws of Edward the Confessor,
but that successive confirmations of the Confessor's laws had
restored them whenever they had been allowed to lapse. This is the
view which came again to the fore in order to prepare the ground
for the Petition of Right, and which was at the core of the Leveller
view of the Norman Yoke.[58] It was the sort of view that could work
well in a providential time-scheme, and can accordingly be found
in Foxe.[59] But in this form it was no more palatable to Owen than
Lambard's view, though Owen treated both views as innocent
errors rather than intentional heresies.[60] It took the Interregnum,

---

[57] Once again, McIlwain's treatment seems fundamental. In *Constitutionalism*, p. 130, he
treats Coke's steps towards a constitutionalist view in 1621 as being taken 'unwittingly',
and he argues for a history of the period which is neither Whig nor Tory.
[58] See Christopher Hill, 'The Myth of the Norman Yoke', *Puritanism and Revolution* (London,
1965; first edn 1958); and more recently, R. B. Seaberg, 'The Norman Conquest and the
Common Law: The Levellers and the Argument from Continuity', *The Historial Journal*, 24
(1981), 791–806.
[59] *Acts and Monuments* (London, 1853), vol. I, p. 313; vol. II, pp. 105–7.
[60] British Library MS. Harley 1572, fo. 253b. In this sense, Lambard might be taken as a
'naive' chronicler in Skinner's terms, though Foxe's providential development of the
Conquest must be classed along with the Levellers' views as ideological.

which was to some extent prepared for by the debates of the 1620s, to provide the conditions in which constitutional arguments could flourish, with all that that implied about the consciousness of time; and it was not until Whig met Tory that the conditions for Whig historical thought were present.

Even with these new developments, however, the old juristic mode of discourse was not forgotten, since the lawyers still needed the notion that they had a stable body of law to work from, and since some of them found it difficult to think in any other way. Owen's history itself can even be seen entering the constitutional debates with the Levellers.[61] But even within purely juristic discourse one can already see in Hale a movement away from the static medieval view of Coke towards the evolutionary model of Blackstone.[62] When Hale used the metaphor of the ship in his *History of the Common Law of England* to illustrate continuity in the law, he admitted that in its 'long Voyage it had successive Amendments', and he saw the body politic as suffering 'accidental Diseases' in the 'right order of government'.[63] This sense of progress in the law and mutability in the constitution was clearly beyond the horizon of Coke and Owen, if still essentially juristic. But even more significant is the fact that Hale's attempt to show that William the Conqueror did not impose the Norman laws on England was motivated not only by the jurisdictional worries of the Cokeans, but by a new sense of threat issuing from the Tory *thèse royale*. His careful consideration of several forms of *jus conquestus* from the law of nations, followed by his denial of the Norman Conquest, was therefore much closer to being constitutionalist and Whig than anything to be found in Coke or Owen.[64] Though more

---

[61] Bulstrode Whitelocke quoted him at length, *Memorials of the English Affairs* (Oxford, 1853), vol. III, pp. 260–73, using his own copy, which is now in Longleat House, Longleat MSS. 209–11. I would like to thank the Marquess of Bath for permission to consult the MSS. Whitelocke also used Owen in his MS. treatise, 'Of the antiquitie and continuance of the Constitution of our Parliaments', British Library MS. Add. 15622.

[62] But one should not overrate the capacity of the moderns to think historically on issues that matter to them. Blackstone himself was committed to a substantialist doctrine, despite his historicist capacities. See Stephen Toulmin, *The Discovery of Time* (New York, 1965), pp. 118–19; and *The Return to Cosmology* (University of California, 1982), pp. 165–75, for the resistance in the human sciences to historicist approaches.

[63] *History of the Common Law*, pp. 30, 40.

[64] *History of the Common Law*, chapter 5. McIlwain points out in *Constitutionalism*, pp. 132–3, that Hale seems to have been the first to develop, in two other works, the crucial constitutional idea that the king's ministers can be punished for illegal governmental acts.

subtle and complex, Hale's version of history belongs with Petyt's bald Whiggism.

Both Petyt and Hale had a view of time, however, which was still Cokean, albeit reformed, in its insistence on the continuity of the *corpus juris*. In this sense, they were more in the world of the late-medieval corporate monarchy than in that of the post-revolutionary Restoration. Algernon Sidney, on the other hand, brought the Machiavellian model to the ancient constitution and explicitly rejected the old idea of continuance.[65] Insisting that 'the authority of a magistracy proceeds not from the number of years that it continued' (though hedging his bets by making an argument 'by prescription' anyway),[66] Sidney concluded that what was needed in the present 'circumstances' was not simply the upholding of the ancient constitution, since that had been radically corrupted, but 'new constitutions to repair the breaches made upon the old.'[67] This was a republican version of the myth of the confirmations which was essentially antithetical to the Cokean vision of history, and which Owen had tried to suppress. Sidney's synthesis of the old traditions with republicanism provided a much stronger form of Whiggism than that of Petyt, and it had a great future ahead of it.

It is not possible here, of course, to provide an adequate account of the transformation of the idea of the ancient constitution, but it should now be clear that such a chronicle would need to be organised around the moments that significantly affected the late-medieval, Fortescuean outlook and called for new formulations. This would include the jurisdictional crises of the Jacobean period (which provided the context for the early Cokeans), the crisis leading to the Petition of Right in the 1620s, the series of crises making up the Machiavellian moment, and finally (for our purposes) the Exclusionist Controversy. This would mean abandoning the structuralist determinism of the *Ancient Constitution*, along with its insistence on the immunity of certain kinds of discourse from the shaping influence of polemics, and moving instead towards the sort of analysis of discursive moments Pocock has elsewhere championed.

[65] See his sophisticated reading of Aristotle's *Politics* in section 10 of his *Discourses Concerning Government*, ed. Thomas G. West (Indianapolis, 1990).
[66] *Discourses*, pp. 178–9.
[67] *Discourses*, p. 527. See also his critique of corporate ideology in section 39.

CHAPTER 3

Arminianism: the controversy that never was

William Lamont

The relationship of Arminianism to the coming of the English Civil War satisfies two reasonable requirements of any controversy. It sparked off debate at the time; it continues to divide historians today.[1] In what sense then can it be called a non-existent controversy? Only in one sense, but an important one, namely that the theological issues raised by Arminians in the Netherlands at the end of the sixteenth century got a proper airing in England, neither just before the Civil War, nor even during it, but after it. The rival schools of historians explain this phenomenon differently; one ascribes it to censorship, and to the ability of a clerical elite to throttle debate – at least until the 1650s, while the other sees it as proof of the consuming lack of interest in such matters, until taken up by the politicians for their own self-serving ends. But at least they agree that the golden age of theological debate on Arminianism was in the England of the 1650s, not of the 1630s or 1640s.

That debate could be said to begin with Richard Baxter's _Aphorismes of Justification_ in 1649. His was a Puritan attack upon anti-Arminianism, just as it had been in New England between 1636 and 1638 when the ministers there attacked Anne Hutchinson (a parallel drawn on by Baxter and his supporters).[2] That attack was to drive a doctrinal wedge between Presbyterianism and Congregationalism, culminating in the Pinners–Hall schism at the

---

[1] Among the many important articles and books: N. Tyacke, _The Anti-Calvinists: the Rise of English Arminianism_ (Oxford, 1987); N. Tyacke, 'Puritanism, Arminianism and Counter Revolution', in C. S. R. Russell (ed.), _Origins of the English Civil War_ (London, 1983), pp. 119–43; P. White, 'The Rise of Arminianism Reconsidered', _Past and Present_, 101 (November 1983), 34–84; W. Lamont, 'Comment: The Rise of Arminianism Reconsidered', _Past and Present_, 107 (May 1985) 227–31; P. Lake, 'Calvinism and the English Church', _Past and Present_, 114 (February 1987), 32–76.

[2] D. Hall, _The Antinomian Controversy 1636–1638_ (Connecticut, 1968).

end of the century.[3] So the *real* debate about Arminianism had momentous consequences for the history of English nonconformity in the seventeenth century. That is not, however, the subject of this essay. I am concerned with the *false* debate about Arminianism, which tied it to a plot to take the Church of England to Rome. Those were the terms in which Baxter had himself entered the debate on the eve of the Civil War; he had joined the parrot cry against Arminianism, without knowing what the term meant (as he later disarmingly confessed). When he did know what the term meant, he gave up believing in a doctrinal conspiracy hatched by a group of Anglican divines. He did not, however, give up believing that a conspiracy had been hatched by a group of Anglican divines, but the villain of the piece was now no longer Arminius, but another Dutchman.

A Puritan exchanged one form of paranoia for another; one could end the matter there, and what follows would be a very short essay indeed. Such summary treatment would chime with the mood of the times. Professor Collinson recalls attending a routine undergraduate lecture at Oxford in the summer of 1981 and hearing Dr Christopher Haigh confess that he was heartily sick of the godly. His words, Collinson ruefully noted, 'seemed to strike an answering chord'.[4] Dr George Bernard has recently produced a magisterial survey of the Church of England from 1529 to 1649 which might be seen as the answer to Dr Haigh's (ungodly?) prayers.[5] In this handsome apologia for the Church of England, the godly are written out of the story. He is severe on Dr Tyacke, who had thought that the Laudian clergy, in pushing their Arminian theology, were ratting on the Calvinist traditions of the Church of England. Tyacke's account is flawed, says Bernard, because his 'tradition' starts in the 1590s – 'does he not start too much *in media res*?'[6] Bernard begins *his* story in 1529, and demonstrates that the Church of England for the next 120 years was both less Calvinist, and more accommodating, than its Puritan critics had alleged. He then poses his own question: why then 'did "Arminianism" become so universally unpopular by 1640?'[7] His answer is that it didn't.

[3] P. Toon, *Puritans and Calvinism* (Pennsylvania, 1973), pp. 85–101.
[4] P. Collinson, *Godly People* (London, 1983) p. xiii.
[5] G. W. Bernard, 'The Church of England c. 1529- c. 1642', *History*, 75, 224 (June 1990), 183–206.
[6] Ibid., p. 184.
[7] Ibid., p. 198.

But then how to explain a Civil War in which the 'Arminian' tendencies of leading clerics were made so much of in contemporary propaganda? Bernard finds that explanation elsewhere: 'It is, then, the obviously disastrous Scottish policy of Charles I and in particular the military defeats that he suffered at Scottish hands in 1639 to 1640 that offer the best explanation of criticisms made of royal religious policies in 1640–2.'[8] When it comes to explanations for Civil War, Bernard's time-scale is actually shorter, therefore, than Tyacke's: two years against fifty. In looking outside England for answers, Bernard is swimming with a strong historical tide. One thinks recently of the way in which a new understanding of James I's Scottish achievements has altered our views of his English record, or of Conrad Russell's elegant exposition of the English Revolution as a British problem, or of Hugh Kearney's imaginative retelling of the story of the British Isles as 'a history of four nations'.[9] But Bernard's is not any such attempt to integrate Scotland into his story, but rather to snatch at it as an escape route when his thoroughgoing revisionism was leading him into a *cul de sac*. We do know that the godly related Charles I's Scottish policy in 1639 and 1640 to what they perceived as his equally obviously disastrous English policy earlier, and therein lay its offence to them. But since Bernard only dealt with godly perceptions to demonstrate their falsity, Scotland can only be pressed into his argument as a *diabolus ex machina*.

If we shift our perspective from the Civil War to the Restoration we encounter a more solidly based revisionist exercise on behalf of the Church of England. R. S. Bosher had argued in 1957 that the Restoration Church Settlement had been captured, not by Arminians (now a dead letter), but by 'Laudians'.[10] There was some grumbling about that term, but the thesis itself commanded general assent until Dr Ian Green's pioneering work of 1978.[11] He showed how even those whom Bosher identified as 'Laudians' did *not* capture the key posts in the Restoration episcopate, and that the desire for persecution of nonconformity did not come principally

[8] Ibid., p. 204.
[9] Jenny Wormald, 'James VI and I: Two Kings or One?', *History*, 68, 223, (1983), 187–209; Conrad Russell, 'The British Problem and the English Civil War', *History*, 72, 236, (October 1987), 395–415; Hugh Kearney, *The British Isles: A History of Four Nations* (Cambridge, 1989).
[10] R. S. Bosher, *The Making of the Restoration Settlement* (London, 1957).
[11] I. M. Green, *The Re-Establishment of the Church of England 1660–1663* (Oxford, 1978).

from the episcopal benches. These are enduring historiographical gains and, since his was a study of conformism, it would be unfair to criticise him for giving the godly short shrift in the process. But Green is very good at entering the minds – not just of his clerics, but even of their supporters. Clarendon is notoriously difficult to read, but Green very sensitively relates his actions at the time of the Restoration, and his writing up of those actions in exile later, to his fundamental desire 'to obscure the king's true religious sympathies'.[12] Clarendon was in a better position than most to know what these were, but they were not exactly a closed book either to his (and the king's) opponents in 1660. Green himself records this revealing clash in October 1660 between Charles II and Baxter, the leading nonconformist:

Charles, through Clarendon, suggested a clause which would have granted freedom of worship to those who were not members of the state church; Baxter asserted that such freedom might be permitted 'tolerable Pasters', such as the sectaries; but not 'intollerable ones' such as Papists and socinians; Charles intervened to say that there were already 'Laws enough against the Papists'.[13]

That Baxter's rejection of the offer of a bishopric could have been related to the same worries as Clarendon's, about 'the king's true religious sympathies', is not given equal weight by Green. And so Baxter's refusal to throw in his lot with a church – acquitted now of being in thrall to a 'Laudian' conspiracy – seems, at kindest, hard to comprehend, at worst, the mark of a boor. Bosher gave attention in his study to the apologetic writings of a number of Anglicans in the 1650s (Cosin, Bramhall, Basire, Morley and Pierce among them).[14] They are ignored by Green, since what are they but the theoretical underpinning of a conspiracy now proved not to have taken place? They are not ignored by Baxter and other godly critics in 1660, however, although it is not the spectre of 'Laudianism' which is invoked by him then (it would be so in 1668, for reasons which will emerge later).

There are two key events then – the Civil War and the Restoration Settlement – in both of which the godly are cast in an

[12] Ibid., p. 206.
[13] Ibid., p. 30.
[14] Bosher, *The Making of the Restoration Settlement*, pp. 63–5.

almost incomprehensible role, clutching at the 'Arminian' alibi[15] to excuse their non-cooperation in one case, and at the 'Laudian' scapegoat in the other. But I am suggesting that they only seem almost incomprehensible because a serious attempt has not been made to engage with their point of view. And a figure that has recurred so far in the discussion is Baxter, because he himself was the first major Puritan to engage sympathetically with Arminianism in 1649, and then to decline a bishopric in 1660.

The historian is not hard up for material on Baxter. His archive, however, has been strangely under-used. I myself used it, particularly his prison notes in 1686, as the basis for a revaluation of his millenarian ideas.[16] I want now to do what Bernard and Green did not do, and that is to use his papers to bring a godly perspective to bear on the issues which they discussed. I have already argued that 'Arminianism' was, for Baxter, at least by 1647 (when he was writing the manuscript of his *Saints Everlasting Rest*), a side-issue; certainly so by 1649, when he published his first work, *Aphorismes of Justification*. 'Laudianism' was not a bogey for him either, in 1660. The idea of a conspiracy, associated with both these terms, persisted strongly with him, however, and his actions from fighting the Civil War to opposing the Restoration Settlement are unintelligible unless seen in that context. I have suggested that it was a Dutchman, other than Arminius, whom Baxter identified as his main antagonist. That man was Hugo Grotius. Bernard had acknowledged 'the inspiration of Hugh Trevor-Roper' behind his article on the Church of England,[17] yet oddly Grotius does not feature once in it. Oddly, since elsewhere Trevor-Roper has argued that 'as far as England was concerned, the most influential of the Dutch Arminians was not Arminius himself, but one of his admirers and supporters, the greatest of all the Dutchmen of that age, Hugo Grotius'.[18] Why did Grotius value Arminianism? Because it offered a more congenial view of the Creator than from the hard Calvinist perspective? Certainly, but he valued it for something else. And when Baxter came, during the period from

[15] Peter White actually uses the term 'Puritan alibi' for 'the rise of Arminianism' (see *Past and Present* 101 (November 1983), p. 54): itself revealing of the extent to which he is not prepared to read even *mistaken* perceptions as anything but *insincere*.

[16] W. Lamont, *Richard Baxter and the Millennium* (London, 1979).

[17] Bernard, 'The Church of England *c*. 1529- *c*. 1642, p. 183.

[18] Hugh Trevor-Roper, *Catholics, Anglicans and Puritans* (London, 1987), p. 52.

1647 to 1649, to a view of Arminianism not so very far from Grotius's, it was the 'something else' that chilled him to the marrow.

Grotius saw Arminianism as the way of ending the schism in the Catholic church. Here was the basis for union between liberal Calvinists in the Netherlands, Gallicans in France and Anglicans in England. Trevor-Roper has underlined the importance in this context of Archbishop Laud's presentation in 1639 to the university library, and to his own college library, at Oxford, of the Dupuy brothers' two-volume compilation of the liberties of the Gallican church. He has pointed out the Dupuy connection with de Thou, 'the closest Parisian friend of Grotius, now Swedish ambassador in Paris', and emphasised Richelieu's hand in the publication.[19]

It is this French connection which invests Grotius's plans with sinister implications for the godly. Until the reign of James II, Baxter had never felt that any of the Stuart kings had been wholly papist. This was small comfort, as we saw in the exchange in October 1660 between himself and Charles II, if a king was even 'half' papist, in the light of Grotius's schemes for reunion. Charles I may only have been a 'half' papist, but he was married to a 'full' French papist, Henrietta Maria. Charles II may have only been a 'half' papist, but he let a 'full' French papist, Louis XIV, run his foreign policy for him. Roman Catholicism was not monolithic, but this made the task of the vigilant Protestant more, not less, difficult. Protestants had only to turn their eyes to the Continent to see, in the Thirty Years War, France (first covertly, then overtly) fighting their Spanish and Austrian co-religionists. These divisions could be turned to Protestant advantage: witness the wooing of Henrietta Maria by Puritan parliamentarians before the Civil War,[20] or the rationalisation offered by Oliver Cromwell in the 1650s for throwing in his lot with Catholic France against Catholic Spain.[21] But they could also work to Protestant disadvantage. 'French' Catholicism had a bogus appeal lacking in its 'Italian' variant. What was Gallicanism but a revamped English imperialism? 'Italian' Catholics made no bones about the fact that they put pope above crown. 'French' Catholics, stressing the power of councils, did not seem to

---

[19] Ibid., pp. 100–1.

[20] R. M. Smuts, 'The Puritan Followers of Henrietta Maria in the 1630s', *English Historical Review*, 93, 366 (1978), 26–46.

[21] Oliver Cromwell, *Letters and Speeches*, ed. T. Carlyle (London, 1897), vol. III, p. 274.

threaten the power of kings in the way that their 'Italian' colleagues did. Anglican divines, who stressed the conciliar authority, could therefore pride themselves on being monarchists, indeed on being anti-Catholic, when they were really only being anti-'Italian'-Catholic.

There is no public document which voices the fears of Baxter and his fellow nonconformists on these matters with any accuracy. Much of his pamphleteering after 1660 was taken up with explaining away his earlier Cromwellian sympathies. It did him little good either, when his *Holy Commonwealth* joined Hobbes's *Leviathan* in the great book-burning of the 1683 Oxford Convocation. His memoirs were written as much to conceal as to expose; when he *had* seemed inadvertently to let secrets out of the bag there was the editor of his posthumously published *Reliquiae Baxterianae*, Matthew Sylvester, to apply sticking plaster to the text. It is to the private archive we need to turn to find out what made the great English nonconformist tick.

Nothing ever written by Baxter was more totally revealing than a short, undated, unfinished fragment which – from internal evidence – was written at the end of his life. He called it 'the true state of the present English divisions'. He began with a view of Charles II which he never committed to print, but which acquired credibility from the recent knowledge of his brother's reign: 'King Charles 2nd was a Papist if his brother and his bedfellow that gave him the Sacrament at his death may be believed.' Every nonconformist had to contend with this fact: there was nothing in the reigns of Charles I, Charles II or James II to suggest the model of an Emperor-Constantine-revived. But this same fact made credible dreams of a reunion between Rome and the Church of England. Baxter knew who was the architect of such schemes: 'Hugo Grotius (a man of incomparable worth for Learning and more for Judgement) was the great deviser of the terms and way.' Arminianism, as a doctrinal controversy, entered the English bloodstream as part of that greater design: 'And being deeply engaged in the Arminian cause, in Holland, that controversie must come in as one halfe of difference'. English theologians – that is, until Bishop Davenant got to work with his thesis of 'hypothetical universalism', which so profoundly influenced Baxter's subsequent compromise – did not then grasp 'how much of the disputes were frivolous (upon works not understood or things unsearchable)'.

Doctrine was always a side-issue: 'the maine work was a neerer approach to Rome, in order to the designed Concord'. This did not mean crudely that the Church of England had to turn papist, because on Grotius's terms, a papist 'is one that taketh all for right that popes should say or do, or that is for his uncontrollable power and will'. With such men there could be no compromise, but with men ready to whittle away the pope's powers, 'we should open our doors wide enough for them to come in to us'.[22]

This was Grotius's crucial error. He assumed that the issue was one of constitutional limitations, when it was one of territorial jurisdiction. In *The True History of Councils* (1682) Baxter rejected the proposition that the Italians were papists because they believed in the pope's absolute rule over councils, but the French were not papists because they 'would have the Pope rule only by the Canons or Church Parliament, and to be *singulis Maior, at universis Minor*'.[23] Baxter here brought together his mature thoughts on the Civil War with his attack on Grotius's reunion schemes. For that same Latin tag had been invoked (erroneously) by Richard Hooker's followers to justify parliamentary resistance in 1642. Not that parliament had been wrong to resist then, but to do so only on grounds of self-preservation (to avoid subjection to a foreign jurisdiction). The teachers to listen to here were not Hooker, but Bilson, Barclay and, paradoxically, Grotius himself. Grotius might be desperately unsound on church union, but he knew when subjects should not allow their throats to be cut. The constitutional arguments of the 1640s and the ecclesiastical controversies of the 1680s were thus symmetrically linked: French papists were to be resisted as firmly as Italian papists because 'their Designs . . . would bring us under a Foreign Jurisdiction, by the act of over-magnifying General Councils'.

What was the source of Baxter's fears? By 1668 he was in a position to identify it: ' you may see in Dr Heylyn what were the terms of that treaty for coalition . . . It was a Generall Council that our new Bishops (Laud and his party) would have ascribed this sovereignty to while they were in being'.[24] Baxter had known throughout the 1650s who 'our new Bishops were', and he named them and their apologists: men like Montague, Cosin, Pierce and

[22] (Dr Williams's Library) *Baxter Treatises*, 1, f. 261v, 264.
[23] Baxter, *The True History of Councils* (1682), preface.
[24] (Dr Williams's Library) *Baxter Treatises*, 1, f. 264.

Heylyn. He had even coined the epithet for them: 'Grotian'. There was a significant exchange between Baxter and Heylyn on this point in October 1658. Baxter had called Heylyn a 'Grotian'; Heylyn denied that he was (in the same way that Montague had claimed never to have read Arminius). Baxter professed to Heylyn satisfaction with this statement and hoped that others of 'the Prelaticall Divines' would also 'disdaine the Grotian Religion'.[25] His real feelings, however, came out in a letter a month later to a friend in which he says of Heylyn and Pierce that their design was that 'all the Protestant Churches must be unchurched'.[26]

Nevertheless it was not until 1668 – and the posthumous publication of the biography of Laud by Heylyn, *Cyprianus Anglicus* – that Baxter would use the term 'Laudian' as synonymous with 'Grotian'. Until that date he had not shown particular interest in the archbishop, even though the men he attacked were of his circle. But Heylyn's book was the eye-opener; the 'Grotians' were of his circle, because they were part of his design. It is a moot point whether the design was more in the biographer's mind than the subject's;[27] what counted was this particular reader's perception. After 1668 Baxter never refers to the episcopal fifth column without linking it to Heylyn's biography of Laud. The coalition-minded enemies who followed Laud down this dangerous path were, besides Heylyn, Bramhall, Gunning, Sparrow, Samuel Parker, Thorndike, Saywell and Beveridge. If he understood the French church right, Baxter argued in this manuscript fragment, it gives the pope no more than the Church of England does, and the Church of England gives no less to councils than the French do: 'And so we should close with the french in the essential part of their popery. But the whole kingdome clergie and Laity is sworne against all foreine Jurisdiction civil or ecclesiasticall'. Baxter's conformist heroes who, realising this, 'kept up the dislike of a Coalition with the Papists' were men like Usher, Downame, Abbott, Morton, Hall, Davenant, Brownig, Westfield and Isaac Barrow: they were the men whom nonconformists could do business with.[28]

[25] (Dr Williams's Library) *Baxter Correspondence*, II, f. 267–8.
[26] (Dr Williams's Library) *Baxter Correspondence*, II, f. 45.
[27] Royce MacGillivray, *Restoration Historians and the English Civil War* (The Hague, 1974), pp. 31–2.
[28] (Dr Williams's Library) *Baxter Treatises*, I, f. 264v, 265.

But the 'conformist' – 'nonconformist' distinction is itself illusory. Those who had bravely resisted the 'Grotian' designs before the Civil War had themselves been conformists. Here he cited Prynne, Bastwick and Burton. It is true that all three said they were defending Protestant imperialism against divine-right bishops; Prynne certainly meant it, even Bastwick may have done so initially, but Baxter's case is strained indeed when he presses Burton into a conformist straitjacket.[29]

The fragment breaks off at the crucial point of interconnection between this Grotian design and the Irish Rebellion of October 1641, which precipitated the English Civil War. Of the Irish rebels he says:

They boasted that they had the King's commission, its like falsely; Though some Scots writers say that he [Charles I] was in Scotland, and had there the possession of the Broad Seale of that Kingdome, and therewith signed a warrant for them to rise for his preservation, which they used to the destruction of the English: God only knoweth all the truth.[30]

This is the dramatic point at which the manuscript fragment breaks off. Even at the end of his life he thus suspends judgement on whether the Irish rebels had been granted a commission by the king to massacre Protestants;[31] the possibility that they had was, however, itself a justification for the self-preservative action taken by parliament. If Charles I, through his friend, the Earl of Antrim, had issued such a warrant it would be proof of how far the sovereign had gone in pursuit of 'Grotian' designs; even if he had not, the fact that suspicions could legitimately be entertained of such malpractice showed the damage that these coalition plans had already created to public confidence in the sovereign.

Baxter rehearsed two explanations for the Civil War for the whole of his life. The first – trotted out often in public – was to

---

[29] On Prynne, see W. Lamont, *Marginal Prynne* (London, 1963), *passim*; on Bastwick, see Frances Condick, 'The Life and Works of Dr John Bastwick, 1595–1654', unpublished University of London Ph. D. thesis, 1983; on Burton, see W. Lamont, 'Pamphleteering, the Protestant Consensus, and the English Revolution', in R. C. Richardson and G. M. Ridden (eds.), *Freedom and the English Revolution* (Manchester, 1986), especially pp. 78–9.

[30] (Dr Williams's Library) *Baxter Treatises*, 1, f. 266.

[31] Conrad Russell, 'The British Background to the Irish Rebellion of 1641', *Historical Research*, 61, 145 (June 1988), 177–9, examines the historical evidence for the widespread belief and is not impressed.

receive classic expression in the *Reliquiae Baxterianae* (especially when its editor had made discreet adjustments to the text). That was that the Civil War – the product of long-term constitutional grievances – had been stumbled into by men of goodwill on both sides (only the dividers on either side were villains). In retrospect, the best line to have taken would have been neutrality. Richard Hooker's populism had been one factor which had got in the way of that perception at the time. The second, more private version, is one that recurs in his manuscript papers, surfaces once publicly and dangerously in his *Holy Commonwealth* of 1659,[32] and which in substance is that offered in this manuscript fragment.

Three particular passages in the Baxter archive bear on these secret convictions of his about the origins of the Civil War. One is a letter to his admired confidant, John Durie, that tireless campaigner for church unity, on 20 November 1652. Baxter was then in the process of launching his own 'Ministerial Association', with Durie's ecumenical spirit as one of its inspirations. What he and Durie had to make sure was that their way was not Grotius's. Baxter knew the right way to do it: 'call an Assembly to consult, and charge the Duty on them (as Constantine did) and hold them to it and hold them in it'.[33] Constantine was the obvious model for Protestant imperialists, as he had been for John Foxe in his most influential of all sixteenth-century histories. Not for Durie or Baxter the sectarian revisionist perspective of Milton, or of John Owen (Cromwell's chaplain), in which Antichrist comes in with the first Christian Emperor. But the assumption of this 1652 letter, that Constantine knew how to deal with the clergy, is one that did not survive the chastened mood of the 1670s. Baxter and Marvell then would continue to have no truck with sectarian vilifications of Constantine, but going back into the history of church councils – to which the 'Grotian' Anglicans had propelled them – they could no longer rest with a simplistic Foxeian obeisance to Constantine.[34] Constantine, a good man, had not been tough enough with the ambitious prelates who, through their exaltation of councils, had

---

[32] I shall be producing a modern edition of Baxter's *Holy Commonwealth* for the Cambridge University Press series, *Cambridge Texts in the History of Political Thought*.

[33] (Dr Williams's Library) *Baxter Correspondence*, VI, f. 88v.

[34] See my essay, 'The Religion of Andrew Marvell: Locating the "Bloody Horse"', *The Political Identity of Andrew Marvell*, ed. C. Condren and A.D. Cousins (Scolar Press, 1990), pp. 135–56.

undermined his royal prerogative in a more insidious way than his opponents who had been straightforwardly exalting the papacy. The seventeenth-century parallels were, for Baxter and Marvell, irresistible. In 1652, however, Baxter was willing to give Charles I the benefit of the doubt; he had intended to give an imperial lead to church unity without realising that the way of going about it ensured its frustration: 'I beleeve that was the Late King's Designe (for I strongly conjecture he was much of Grotius's mind).' Unity was possible only by going back to those imperial traditions – robustly represented in the writings of Bishop Bilson – and this would mean a coming together of 'Episcopalians, Presbyterians, Erastians, Anabaptists, Separatists, Arminians, Lutherans, Calvinist Millenarians and some halfe-Antinomians' in 'Brotherly Associations'.[35] What is left out of the shopping list is as significant as what is put into it; no place in his church unity for full Antinomians (in 1652 he was in the thick of his Arminian controversies) or for Catholics, whether they were 'Italian' or 'French'.

Another insight into the nonconformist *mentalité* is conveyed by a letter he wrote some twenty years later, on 26 April 1673, to a royalist sympathiser, Edmund Hough. Hough was a young man on the make, who wanted to write a definitive history of the origins of the Civil War. We don't have his original letter, although he seems to have made some confident pronouncements about men's motives which irritated Baxter and fellow correspondents. Baxter thought that Hough suffered from two major defects. The first was that he leaned exclusively on Scripture for an explanation of politics. He needed a grounding in political theory; he must understand 'the principles of Grotius'. The second was that he hadn't been there: 'it is an unspeakable disadvantage that you were not a witness of the matters of fact, and know them but by papers and reports'.[36] Baxter had both these advantages, but one disadvantage. 1673 was not a good year for speaking out. 'Mens zeale of Royalty' had produced this dilemma for the nonconformist would-be historian of recent events: 'errors must not be cured, because the doubts must not be opened.' Censorship extended to letters: 'there is no debating such cases by letters, at a cheaper rate; especially at such distances'. Then comes this confession: 'I have many things to say

[35] (Dr Williams's Library) *Baxter Correspondence*, vi, f. 89–89v.
[36] (Dr Williams's Library) *Baxter Correspondence*, i, f. 70.

which your letters enable me not to do.' But at least he can steer Hough in the right direction: 'I cannot tell why you answer not what is said for the other cause (in the maine) in such papers as the political Aphorismes which I revoked.' The 'political Aphorismes' were an alternative title for his *Holy Commonwealth*, which by 1673 he had formally revoked, but was now pressing Hough to include in his bibliography. In case his meaning had not been spelled out clearly enough, Baxter went on in the letter: to deal briskly with Cavalier arguments based on paternity, primogeniture or conquest; to give the lie to royal absolutist claims by reference to parliament's own recent rejection of Charles II's Declaration of Indulgence; to show that no contract eliminated subjects' rights: 'consenting to government is not quitting the right but choosing the means to secure it'; to assert that *bonum publicum* is *finis regiminis*. Baxter, above all, affirms natural law: 'if you say that Kings hath power to send the footboies to kill all the Parliament or barre the city, and none may visit them, that you speake against the Law of Nature which is fundamentall to all human Laws'. He harps on the significance of private men's commissions in this context: 'for no man can be sure whether the Keeper of the Seale or some other hath not counterfeited it'. He refers to a Colonel Turner, hanged in London in 1660, for seizing a citizen's goods by a counterfeit commission under the King's Seal. He points to the power to manipulate royal commissions in the hands of the great offices, such as Keeper of the Seals or Lord Chancellor (a good debating point is made by reference to the recently disgraced Clarendon). He calls upon 'Barclay, Grotius etc.' as men who defended monarchy but not to the point of absurdity, where their own lives could be subject to a madman's whim. The letter ends, none too convincingly, with the claim that he won't tell Hough what others have said of his royalist apologia 'lest you should think that I speak but my own sense, while I am but telling you how you must satisfie others'.[37]

There is a third moment of revelation in the Baxter archive. Six years on from the rebuke to Hough we are plunged into the Popish Plot crisis. Baxter summarises in manuscript in 1679 a century or more of Catholic intrigue. The Great Fire fitted into this pattern: 'it was part of the Execution of the Papists Plot done by their

[37] Ibid., f. 71.

malicious Contrivance . . . now witnessed to our Rulers upon oath'. A solemn commemoration had been appointed from 23 October 1641 for the outbreak of the Irish Rebellion. This seemed to Baxter in 1679 – with such an embarrassment of riches before him – the supreme papist perfidy: 'I must profess that of all my Acquaintances I remember few that went into the Parliament Army, but such as by their fears upon the Irish Massacre, did seem and be moved to it, as thinking that there was no other way of Safety; And it is no wonder if Terror doe disturb Mens wits.' The murder of Berry Godfrey, even the Marian martyrdoms, paled into insignificance beside the terrible events of October 1641: 'how smal a matter was this in Comparison of the Irish Cruelties to murder of 200,000'. And so the connection was made with the English Civil War: 'by their Remonstrances [Parliament's] and the Irish Massacres we were frightened into the Apprehension of present dangers, and Mr. Hookers Doctrine of the Bodys Legislative Power, with Bishop Bilsons and Barclays and Grotius's Emuneration of Cases in which even Kings might be by Arms resisted'.

But Baxter would also make a connection, in his 1679 manuscript, between the historical pattern he was tracing in the seventeenth century and the breakdown of 'reconciling' moves between Anglicans and nonconformists at the time of the Restoration. Baxter could not then accept a bishopric in a church which had not broken with 'Grotian' coalition delusions: 'After all this Bishop Gunning desired Conference with me, and I was put by him to plead against a foreigne jurisdiction under foreign councils and Parliament, and gave him the sense of my reason in these Letters, thinking that the kingdome is sworne against a foreigne jurisdiction, tho I owned as extensive a concord as could be procured'.[38]

There is one strange, discordant note sounded in the archive. It comes at perhaps the lowest part in his life. In 1686 he was in prison and thought that he was dying. There was nothing novel about that. Baxter was always thinking he was dying. His first work in 1649 was published as his 'dying thoughts'. In 1686, however, objectively the claim seemed more impressive. James II was on the throne; there was no prospect of an immediate release; he was then aged seventy-one. At this blackest of moments he composed in prison a secret personal analysis. He did not spare himself. He now

[38] (Dr Williams's Library) *Baxter Treatises*, IV, f. 284, 287v, 288, 289v, 321v.

– according to his own analysis – recognised that he had made too much of the Roman Catholic attachment to the power of church councils:

And because the argument is of desperate consequences to princes lives, I adde that supposing Grotius and others say right, that *Regere et perdere* are inconsistent, and that Nations have a right of selfedefence, yet it is knowne that some Papist Kings do renounce the beliefe of the Lateran Council, and such others and of these King-destroying and deposing principles . . . so doth the King of France in particular, and its like other Princes, if we may judge by interest.

Hitherto Baxter, we have seen, had borrowed the bits of Grotius he liked – particularly, the recognition of self-preservation as the ultimate criterion – and turned them against the bits of Grotius he didn't like (the conciliar union, itself contravening Protestant imperial self-interest). Now he invoked Grotius for resistance still, but wondered whether princes (particularly the French variety) were really so blind to their self-interest? And thus, at a stroke, he rehabilitated the crucial Grotian distinction between 'French' and 'Italian' popery.

His penitence took more dramatic forms still. He had made too much of Heylyn's book on Laud as the Grotian source book: 'I too much censured publicly, as the destructive enemies of godliness [those who] were for the reconcilation with Rome, which Dr. Peter Heylyn describeth in the life of Archbishop Laud.' His other recantations are not so compelling. He had been too keen a critic of Arminianism before the Civil War (but he had never concealed his embarrassment on that point, from his first doctrinal publication in 1649 onwards):

I did ignorantly think that Arminianisme (which Dr. Heylyn maketh the chief matter of the strife) had bin a more intollerable pernicious evill to the Church than since I found it; and I proved in my Catholike Theologie (to this day unanswered) that it is of lesse consequence than I then imagined. And this conceit made me think the Bishops more injurious and former Parliaments accusations of Arminianisme more necessary than they were.

Finally he regretted, 'being young of undigested studys' (an Edmund Hough forty years back?), swallowing whole Richard Hooker, and his populist justifications for fighting the Civil War.[39]

---

[39] (Dr Williams's Library) *Baxter Treatises*, I, f. 193, 204v.

There was nothing sensational about Baxter's recognition, on
mature reflection, that he had underrated Arminius and overrated
Hooker; one cannot say the same about a recognition that he had
overplayed the Grotian card, and had read too much into Heylyn's
Life of Laud. What weight should we give it? First, these passages
are written at a time of morbid introspection. Second, all these
passages have been crossed out afterwards, and there is a marginal
annotation: 'All this is Apologeticall, because the Author is judged
seditious for his Paraphrase, and so as a prisoner dying wrote
this.'[40] Third, the passages may be revealing of his mood at the
time, but that mood did not last. The Glorious Revolution brought
Protestantism back on the throne, and revived his dreams of a
'National Church'.[41] Back then to his *Holy Commonwealth* of 1659:
no need for bogus retractions in 1689. Like father, like son: Papist
rebels, armed with (genuine or false) royal commissions to advance
the French interest, are to be resisted. And in one respect there is
an overlap between self-abnegation in 1686 and triumphalism in
1689: even in his depth of despair at the earlier date, and when he is
rounding on his younger self for having been attracted to Hooker,
he makes no apologies for having followed Bilson, Barclay and
Grotius in their advocacy of a 'natural right of self-defence for
whole Kingdoms'.[42] And in 1690 the other side of the coin is that he
won't allow this enthusiasm for Grotius's limited justification of
self-defence to extend to his justification for a conqueror (William
III?) filling a vacuum in the case when a government has been
dissolved.[43]

What the Baxter papers reveal as a whole is his fascination with
Grotius, but it is at the same time a discriminating fascination.
Nobody – except Bilson and Barclay – had got it better than
Grotius had on resistance theory; his stress on Reason influenced
profoundly Baxter's own great Arminian contribution, *Catholic
Theology*; his desire for Church unity would be echoed in Baxter's
own correspondence with men like Durie, Eliot, Poole and Mat-
her.[44] This dazzling Renaissance figure had one flaw (he equated
'popery' with the sovereignty of the pope) but that flaw was fatal: it

[40] Ibid., f. 200.
[41] (Dr Williams's Library) *Baxter Treatises*, VI, f. 287, 288, 291.
[42] (Dr Williams's Library) *Baxter Treatises*, I, f. 205.
[43] (Dr Williams's Library) *Baxter Treatises* VI, f. 294.
[44] (Dr Williams's Library) *Baxter Correspondence*, III, f. 44v.

vitiated all those high hopes of a 'third force' in Europe that wasn't Italian popery and wasn't Calvinism.

For a man with a mission – to expose the real nature of 'French' popery – Baxter himself had a handicap. He couldn't read French. This was where the improbable figure of Lauderdale comes into our picture. He it was, as a Cromwellian prisoner in the 1650s, who translated the relevant French works for Baxter, and fed him valuable tit-bits about the elusive Hugo Grotius. In September 1658 Lauderdale congratulates Baxter on his reply to Pierce, 'wherein you fully satisfy me of Grotius being a Papist'. He tells Baxter of meeting Grotius in Paris in 1637 when he was Swedish ambassador. Lauderdale was himself a young man then but 'I remember well he was then esteemed such a Papist as you call Cassandrian.' He refers to another who was 'a great admirer of Grotius, an Eminent enemy to Jesuites, and a moderate French papist'. A month later Lauderdale was sending him translations of works of Blondel and of Peter du Moulin the Elder.[45] (The two younger du Moulins – Peter and Louis – were to correspond with Baxter, for the rest of his life, on Grotius and Popish Plots[46]). He also obtained from Holland the works of Amyraut – along with Cameron and Davenant, the profoundest influence on Baxter's anti-Calvinist theology.

We began this essay with a big question – was Arminianism a pseudo-controversy? – and ended with a small answer. Combing through the papers of one nonconformist, we unravelled a consistent theme (if we overlook the section of the prison notes of 1686 which were subsequently crossed out). That theme was that nonconformists, however committed to the idea of a national church, could trust neither sovereign, nor significant sectors of the Church of England, while either thought that Grotius's principles were not popery. And Arminianism – which had once seemed integral to that question – had been written off by this particular nonconformist as a side-issue, as early as the late 1640s.

What weight are we to give to this finding? The cynic might suggest: not much. One foreigner had been substituted for another in the nonconformist's demonology. One shouldn't altogether discount chauvinism in the backlash against Arminianism. Prynne

[45] (Dr Williams's Library) *Baxter Correspondence*, III, f. 50.
[46] (Dr Williams's Library) *Baxter Correspondence*, III, f. 120; VI, f. 69v.

sniffed out its alien pedigree: one seminal figure, Thompson, was a 'dissolute, ebrious, prophane, lascivious English-Dutchman' whilst 'the exotique Frenchman', Baro, 'being at the very best a Foraigner, doth only marre, not help their cause'.[47] But this charge will not stick with Baxter. It was answered most effectively by an unknown correspondent in an undated letter in the archive. This writer was a supporter of the drive for church unity in the apologetics of Grotius, Cassander and Erasmus. He thought that Catholic controversialists had been foolish to attack Baxter, simply because he had written against Grotius on one particular point: 'tis true that he has written much against Popery and to prove Grotius a Papist because he is for the Council of Trent and the Popes Universall Primacy in Government by the Canons'. But, the writer went on, moderate Catholics would agree with much of that; no man had done more than Baxter, in his doctrinal controversies, to reconcile Protestantism with Rome by his early recognition of Arminianism as the controversy that never was. He had even courageously refused to identify pope with Antichrist. The correspondent then chided Baxter's detractors: 'If you would have men goe as farre as Cassander and Grotius, and he will but draw them as farre to one half or three quarters of the way, and that more effectively than any other man, is it your interest to destroy or shame him because he can goe no further?[48] This was the point. Baxter was not a papist-under-the-bed bigot. He was, instead, a three-quarters Grotian whose refusal to run that final quarter's-worth-of-distance is what, in the final analysis, determined where he stood on the issues that tested the godly conscience in the second half of the seventeenth century.

What do we gain by such a discovery? We know – not least from the offer of a bishopric – how vital was Baxter's role in the Restoration Settlement. We know – from public and private sources – how many of the godly hoped for a coming together of Owen and Baxter, of Independent and Presbyterian, after the Restoration. Baxter disappointed therefore the hopes of two different sorts of animal in these separate negotiations. He might be written off by historians (as he was by many of his contemporaries) as a wrecker by nature. A different conclusion suggests itself from

[47] William Prynne, *Anti-Arminianism* . . . (1630), pp. 268–70.
[48] (Dr Williams's Library) *Baxter Correspondence*, vi, f. 186.

this glimpse in the archive: that he could have done business with one set of divines if he had given up worrying about Grotianism when he stopped worrying about Arminianism; conversely, he could have done business with the other set if he had continued to fear Arminianism as much as he went on fearing Grotianism.

To take such scruples seriously seems to be running against the most powerful historiographical tide of the moment. When Christopher Haigh shows the unreality of the godly case against the pre-Reformation church, when Ian Green demonstrates that there was no Laudian takeover of the Caroline episcopate, when John Morrill shifts historical attention in the Interregnum away from Puritan agitation to Anglican survivalism, considerable gains in our historical understanding are achieved.[49] A necessary historical balance, we feel, has been struck. The temptation to go beyond this is understandable, from treating the godly remonstrances with a pinch of salt to discounting them altogether. What may be overlooked, in such a process, is that a revisionist check upon excessive godly claims can come as much from within as from without. C. H. George deflated Michael Walzer's claims for puritanism as a closed brotherhood of 'revolutionary saints', not by turning to what their opponents said, but to what they said themselves. Kenneth Fincham holds in a sensitive balance what those outside said about Jacobean bishops as well as what they themselves said and did; the result is as convincing a rebuttal of conventional criticism of the earlier episcopate as Green's is for the later, but with an evenhandedness lacking in the Restoration study. I challenged William Haller's picture of Prynne as a revolutionary nihilist by analysing Prynne's own writings.[50] If an older generation of historians were too credulous about the claims made by the godly, one form of redress is obviously to tap other sources, but another is to go back to those same sources with a more critical eye.

As Baxter reminded Hough, he had the priceless advantage of

---

[49] Christopher Haigh, 'Anticlericalism and the English Reformation', *History*, 68, 224 (October 1983), pp. 391–407; John Morrill, 'The Church in England, 1642–9', *Reactions to the English Civil War 1642–1649*, ed. John Morrill (London, 1982), pp. 89–115.

[50] Michael Walzer, *The Revolution of the Saints* (London, 1966) and his 'Puritanism as a revolutionary ideology', *History and Theory*, 3 (1963–4), 59–90; C. H. and K. George, *The Protestant Mind of the English Reformation 1570–1640* (Princeton, 1961); K. Fincham, *Prelate as Pastor: The Episcopate of James I* (Oxford, 1990); C. H. George, 'Puritanism as History and Historiography', *Past and Present*, 41 (December 1968), 77–104; for Haller's view of Prynne, see W. Haller, *The Rise of Puritanism* (New York, 1938), p. 219.

being there, whether in 1641 waiting in bed for his throat to be cut by Irishmen, or in 1659 negotiating with Peter Gunning and finding to his chagrin unreconstructed Grotianism, or in 1688 welcoming the new Constantine-deliverer. The historian has the priceless advantage, too, of access to Baxter's personal papers, not just his printed statements, even if admittedly they are in an untidy and semi-legible form. For all those reasons it is not cocking a snook at revisionism to argue that his views should be taken seriously. Can we go further than this, and argue that he was right?

Baxter thought that the Church of England had never rid itself of Grotius's delusion, that union with Rome was possible on Rome's modified terms. He was influential enough to impose this perspective on a significant number of fellow nonconformists. This is a matter of historical importance, even if it can be shown to be false. Whether true or false, it was sincerely held; this essay has shown that the gap between Baxter's public and private positions on this matter (not on others) is non-existent (apart from the prison aberration which we discussed), and that words like 'alibi' are way off the mark. However, suppose he was *right*? That a significant number of Anglican clergymen went on believing in Grotius's dream? Before we write this off as godly paranoia, we will need to absorb the important findings of Anthony Milton's doctoral research when they are published. His investigation (which is outside the scope of the present essay) is into the historical basis for the belief in the Laudian conspiracy to reconcile the Church of England with Rome. Montague, Grotius and Heylyn will be found to be as pivotal in Milton's argument as they are in Baxter's polemics.[51]

To attempt to recreate the thought-processes of one of the godly is not, in any case, to subscribe to them. Fifty years before Christopher Haigh wanted us to look behind the conventional gibes at the unreformed English church, Lucien Febvre was asking the same of the French. If both were unimpressed by contemporary laments about decay for their respective institutions, Febvre took the argument further. The question, he famously said, had been badly put. Why did the reformers themselves think in the way they did? This needed a new kind of history, to engage with the

---

[51] Anthony Milton, 'The Laudians and the Church of Rome *c.* 1625–1640', unpublished University of Cambridge Ph.D. thesis, 1989.

reformers' dreams, prophecies and sensibilities. One by-product of such a quest would be that witchcraft would seem not nonsense, but a mental revolution.[52]

Such an ambitious programme was tied to the sources. Exceptionally, as we have seen, this is not a problem with Richard Baxter: I was able to exploit this lucky documentary windfall to show the 'rational' Baxter as a creature of millenarian drives which would never, incidentally, have surprised Febvre. In this essay I have gone back to the same sources to show how Baxter was haunted by the compelling figure of Grotius – half admiring, half fearing him. And another objection consequently may be levelled at this approach, from the opposite side of the historiographical divide.

Revisionist historians can regret the waste of effort in teasing out the thought-processes of the irrelevant godly. But there are other historians (not all of them denominational) who can lament, not that Baxter is taken too seriously, but that he is not taken seriously enough. To them what matters is his piety, his ecumenism, his charity.[53] Coleridge thought so too. For him Baxter was 'the good man'. It was a pity he was, on the other hand, so credulous about 'Irish stories of ghosts, apparitions and witches'.[54] And now, following Febvre, it is precisely those 'Irish stories' which the twentieth-century historians seize upon! Isn't the whole process reductive?

The answer is simply that it is not. Recognise the force of anti-Catholicism, and Baxter's refusal to go along with the 'Pope Joan' fiction becomes heroic.[55] Note the centrality of the Protestant identification of Rome with Antichrist, and Baxter's refusal to make it becomes audacious.[56] Note how universal (Muggleton and a few other eccentrics excepted) was the acceptance of witchcraft beliefs – and there was no more powerful theoretical contributor incidentally to that debate than Baxter – and his scrupulous handling of practical investigations in his own parish becomes

[52] Lucien Febvre, *A New Kind of History*, ed. Peter Burke (London, 1973), pp. 44–108.
[53] Hugh Martin, *Puritanism and Richard Baxter* (London, 1954), p. 8; G.F. Nuttall, *Richard Baxter* (London, 1965), pp. 114–32; F. J. Powicke, *The Reverend Richard Baxter Under the Cross* (London, 1927), p. 266.
[54] S. T. Coleridge, *Notes on English Divines*, ed. D. Coleridge (London, 1853), I, p. 250.
[55] (Dr Williams's Library) *Baxter Treatises*, VII, f. 45.
[56] Baxter, *A Paraphrase on the New Testament* (1684).

impressive.[57] And finally recognising, as this essay makes clear, that for Baxter one-quarter of Grotius meant the ruin of Protestantism, there is something awesome about his refusal to let it blind him to the virtues of the remaining three-quarters.

We can understand why historians have become heartily sick of the godly, but there is a price, we may suggest, to be paid for not listening to their voice.[58] That price may be thought too high when a leading historian can argue, in a survey stretching over a century, that what was wrong with the Church of England can be compressed into an analysis of its last two years, and that only Scotland can explain the English Revolution.

[57] Baxter, *A Key for Catholicks* (1659), pp. 184–5. Cf. Baxter, *The Certainty of the Worlds of Spirits* (London, 1691) with Muggleton's scepticism: W. Lamont, 'Lodowick Muggleton and "Immediate Notice"', C. Hill, B. Reay and W. Lamont, *The World of the Muggletonians* (London, 1983), p. 120.

[58] Christopher Haigh has restated the revisionist thesis which this essay has criticised in a review article, 'The English Reformation: A Premature Birth, a Difficult Labour and a Sickly Child', *The Historical Journal*, 33, 2 (1990), 449–59.

CHAPTER 4

'Scientia Civilis' in classical rhetoric and in the early Hobbes

Quentin Skinner

I

One of John Pocock's most characteristic and fruitful procedures as an historian has been to fix his attention on what he likes to call the 'language' of public debate.[1] His main concern has been to uncover the wide variety of discriminable idioms and modes of speech in which the societies of early modern Europe conducted their political arguments.[2] But he has also shown that a sensitivity to the range of these idioms can engender new insights into the character of even the most closely analysed texts. Not without a touch of justified pride, he has recently reminded us of two important cases in which his studies of political language have yielded such results. As he has expressed it, one consequence of becoming attuned to nuances of vocabulary is that the historian 'is constantly surprised

I am deeply grateful to Susan James, Noel Malcolm, James Tully and my co-editor for many helpful comments on earlier drafts of this chapter, and to Colin Burrow for helping me to clarify its theme.

[1] See especially J. G. A. Pocock, 'Languages and their Implications: The Transformation of the Study of Political Thought', in *Politics, Language and Time* (New York, 1971), pp. 3–41 and 'Introduction: the State of the Art', in *Virtue, Commerce and History* (Cambridge, 1985), pp. 1–34, esp. pp. 2–7. As Pocock makes clear in both essays, he is not in general referring to languages in the ethnic sense, but merely to different styles of speech within a given vernacular. But it is important to recall (as Pocock does in *Virtue, Commerce and History*, p. 7) that many early modern political writers worked in two natural languages – Latin and their native tongue – with a skill amounting to bilinguality. As a consequence, it is often necessary to 'hear' the Latin words, and *a fortiori* the Roman sources, lying behind their vernacular pronouncements if the meaning and resonances of the latter are to be understood. As I shall try to show in what follows, this emphatically applies in the case of Hobbes.

[2] His two classic studies in this mode have been on the language of law and history in early modern England, and of Florentine republicanism in the development of the Atlantic republican tradition. See, respectively, J. G. A. Pocock, *The Ancient Constitution and the Feudal Law: A Reissue with a Retrospect* (Cambridge, 1987) and J. G. A. Pocock, *The Machiavellian Moment* (Princeton, 1975).

and delighted to discover familiar languages in texts equally
familiar, where they have not been noticed before – the language of
prophetic exegesis in *Leviathan*, the idiom of denouncing paper
credit in *Reflections on the Revolution of France* – though making these
discoveries does not always enhance his respect for previous
scholarship'.[3]

My aim in what follows will be to pay homage to this aspect of
John Pocock's theory and practice in two connected ways.[4] I
propose in the first place to return to Hobbes, concentrating
specifically on the earliest formulations of his political philosophy. I
wish in particular to focus on the views he expresses about the
nature of civil science in *The Elements of Law*, first circulated in 1640,
and in *De cive*, first published in 1642.[5] My object, moreover, will be
to point to the presence in these texts of a particular idiom, a
distinctive vocabulary, whose importance for Hobbes's intellectual
development has not I think been fully appreciated. The vocabulary I have in mind is the one characteristic of the classical and
especially the Roman art of eloquence,[6] the principles of which
were initially popularised by Cicero in his *De inventione*[7] and *De
oratore*,[8] later elaborated by Quintilian in his *Institutio oratoria*[9] and
subsequently taken up by their countless humanist admirers in the
course of the Renaissance.[10] I hope to indicate the pervasive extent

---

[3] Pocock, *Virtue, Commerce and History*, p. 11. Pocock is here referring respectively to his
essays, 'Time, History and Eschatology in the Thought of Thomas Hobbes', *Politics,
Language and Time*, pp. 148–201 and 'The Political Economy of Burke's Analysis of the
French Revolution', *Virtue, Commerce and History*, pp. 193–212.

[4] I do not mean to imply that this approach has guided the whole of Pocock's practice. As
he himself stresses in *Virtue, Commerce and History*, esp. pp. 6, 8, 12, he has been at least as
much preoccupied with the effects of *parole* upon *langue*, and thus with the consequences of
speech.

[5] For these dates see Hugh Macdonald and Mary Hargreaves, *Thomas Hobbes: A Bibliography* (London, 1952), pp. 9–10, 16.

[6] This brings out a point about 'context' which Pocock himself has always been at pains to
emphasise: that the intellectual context we need to invoke to understand a given text may
at once be very remote chronologically and yet very close from an interpretative point of
view. I have discussed this issue further in *Meaning and Context*, ed. James Tully
(Princeton, 1988), pp. 274–5.

[7] Cicero, *De inventione*, trans. and ed. M. M. Hubbell (London, 1949). Subsequent page
references will be to this edition, but translations will be my own.

[8] Cicero, *De oratore* trans. and ed. E. W. Sutton and H. Rackham, 2 vols. (London, 1942).
Again, subsequent page references will be to this edition, but translations will be my own.

[9] Quintilian, *Institutio oratoria*, trans. and ed. H. E. Butler, 4 vols. (London, 1920–2). Once
again, subsequent page references will be to this edition, but translations will be my own.

[10] For guides to the rhetorical literature produced in early modern England see T. W.
Baldwin, *William Shakespeare's Small Latine & Lesse Greeke*, 2 vols. (Urbana, 1944) and W.
S. Howell, *Logic and Rhetoric in England, 1500–1700* (Princeton, 1956).

to which this tradition of thinking about the idea of *scientia civilis* sets the terms for Hobbes's own consideration of the same theme.

II

As the opening of Cicero's *De inventione* makes clear, his special concern as a theorist of *eloquentia* is with the character of *civilis ratio*, and in particular with the place of the *ars rhetorica* within a *scientia civilis*.[11] Quintilian later announces the same general theme – while invoking Cicero's analysis – in the course of discussing the definition of rhetoric in Book II of the *Institutio oratoria*. Although Quintilian refuses to equate the science of politics with the study of eloquence, he agrees that rhetoric is at once a *scientia* in its own right and at the same time an indispensable part of the *scientia* which is concerned with the *officia* of public life.[12]

Cicero begins the *De inventione* by suggesting that the form of knowledge or *scientia* needed for the proper conduct of civic affairs is, above all, a knowledge of how to establish a *civitas* and subsequently maintain it in a state of friendship and peace. The distinctive claim he goes on to advance is that 'a large and crucial part' of this *scientia civilis* is occupied by eloquence, and specifically by 'that form of artistic eloquence which is generally known as rhetoric, the function of which is that of speaking in a manner calculated to persuade, and the goal of which is that of persuading by speech'.[13]

Cicero's argument in favour of this central conclusion takes as its starting-point the question of how cities were originally founded. He assumes that men, the *materia* of cities, must come together in a union of a mutually beneficial and honourable kind if they are ever to succeed in realising their highest opportunities.[14] He further assumes that, at some determinate point, some mighty individual must have recognised this fact and taken it upon himself to mould

11 Cicero, *De inventione*, I.I.I. to I.VI.8, pp. 2–18.
12 Quintilian, *Institutio*, II.XV.33–8, vol. I, pp. 314–18.
13 Cicero, *De inventione*, I.V.6, pp. 12–14: 'Eius [sc., civilis ratio] magna et ampla pars est artificiosa eloquentia quam rhetoricam vocant . . . Officium autem eius facultatis videtur esse dicere apposite ad persuasionem; finis persuadere dictione.'
14 See Cicero, *De inventione*, I.II.2, pp. 4–6 on the need for men as the *materia* of cities to congregate *in unum locum* and act together in a manner at once *utilis* and *honestus* if they are to realise their highest *opportunitas*.

the available human material into just such a unified shape.[15]
Cicero is thus led to consider what qualities must have been
possessed by such founding fathers or artificers of cities. He stresses
that they must of course have been men of *ratio* and hence of
sapientia.[16] But he insists that they must also have been men of
eloquentia. Given that 'wisdom is in itself silent and powerless to
speak',[17] it follows that 'wisdom without eloquence cannot do the
least good for cities'.[18] We can thus be sure that 'cities were
originally established not merely by the *ratio* of the mind, but also,
and more readily, by means of *eloquentia*'.[19]

The same assumptions are later reiterated by Quintilian in an
important passage from Book II of the *Institutio oratoria* which is
closely modelled on the opening of the *De inventione*. 'It does not
seem to me possible that the founders of cities could ever have
succeeded in bringing wandering multitudes together to form
peoples without moving them by a trained voice' and hence
'without the addition of the highest powers of oratory'.[20] Reason,
and hence *scientia*, possess in themselves no inherent powers to
persuade us of the truths they enunciate; the emotional force of
eloquentia is always needed if *ratio* is to be empowered and given
effect.[21]

Cicero and Quintilian are both careful to add that a true orator
will never rely exclusively on such emotional appeals to win over an
audience. Rather they see themselves as answering and overcoming
precisely this misunderstanding of the rhetorical arts, a misunderstanding which they in turn associate with Greek philosophy. They
trace the prejudice in part to Aristotle, whose *Art of Rhetoric* begins –
in the words of Hobbes's translation – by marking a contrast
between the logical method of instruction by means of '*Scientificall
proofes*' and the method of instructing 'by the *Rhetoricall*, and shorter

---

[15] See Cicero, *De inventione* I.II.2, pp. 4–6 on how some *magnus vir* must have *compulit* this *materia*.
[16] See Cicero, *De inventione*, I.I.I, p. 2 on the *ratio* of the *magnus vir*, and I.II.2, p. 4 on his also being *sapiens*.
[17] See Cicero, *De inventione*, I.II.3, p. 6 on *sapientia* as *tacita* and *inops dicendi*.
[18] Cicero, *De inventione*, I.I.I, p. 2: 'sapientiam sine eloquentia parum prodesse civitatibus'.
[19] Cicero, *De inventione*, I.I.I, p. 2: 'urbes constitutas . . . cum animi ratione tum facilius eloquentia'.
[20] Quintilian, *Institutio*, II.XVI.9–10, vol. I, pp. 320–2: 'Equidem nec urbium conditores reor aliter effecturos fuisse ut vaga illa multitudo coiret in populos, nisi docta voce commota; nec . . . sine summa vi orandi.' (To go with *populos*, I have read *multitudo* as equivalent to *multitudines*.)
[21] See Quintilian, *Institutio*, II.XVI, 14–17, vol. I, pp. 322–4.

way'.[22] But they mainly associate the animus against rhetoric with Socrates's attack on Gorgias.[23] As Quintilian observes, 'Socrates was only willing to concede to Gorgias the power of persuading, not of instructing.'[24] Socrates's radically sceptical criticism was that, since rhetoricians always aim to persuade, it follows that they cannot be said to teach.

The Roman writers concede that, as Cicero puts it at the beginning of *De oratore*, to think of an orator as someone who moves an audience by persuasion alone would indeed be to reduce the art of rhetoric to nothing more than 'an inane and laughable form of garrulity'.[25] The true orator 'must always be possessed in addition of sufficient *scientia* to understand very many matters' if his powers of *oratio* are to have compelling force.[26] The point to which they continually return, however, is that *ratio* without the addition of *eloquentia* can never hope to persuade. The image Cicero invokes is that of a battle, a war of words, in which the orator is forced to struggle with his audience to make them see the truth, or to act aright, often against their will.[27] Quintilian later picks up the same imagery, arguing that 'since our hearers will be changeable, and truth will always be opposed by so many evils, we must be ready to use our art to fight for it'.[28] The orator thus comes to be viewed as an heroic figure battling for the truth by speaking in the most 'winning' way.[29] As Quintilian declares towards the end of his treatise, 'we as orators stand armed in battle formation, contending for matters of the highest importance and exerting ourselves to gain the victory'.[30] It follows that we not only need to be armed, but that

[22] Thomas Hobbes, *A Briefe of the Art of Rhetorique* in *The Rhetorics of Thomas Hobbes and Bernard Lamy*, ed. John T. Harwood (Carbondale, 1986), pp. 39–40.

[23] For a discussion of Plato's attack on the rhetoricians in the *Gorgias*, see for example Cicero, *De oratore*, I.x.46–8, vol. I, pp. 34–5. For Cicero's defence of rhetoric against Socrates see *De oratore*, III.xvi.60–1, vol. II, p. 48.

[24] Quintilian, *Institutio* II.xv.18, vol. I, p. 308: 'cui [sc. Gorgias] Socrates persuadendi, non docendi, concedit facultatem'.

[25] Cicero, *De oratore*, I.v.17, vol. I, p. 14: 'verborum volubilitas inanis atque irridenda est'.

[26] Cicero, *De oratore*, I.v.17, vol. I, p. 12: 'Est enim et scientia comprehendenda rerum plurimarum.' Cf. also I.xii.51, vol. I, p. 38.

[27] On the orator's need to fight, and thus to wield the appropriate weapons, see Cicero, *De oratore*, I.viii.32, vol. I, p. 24; III.xxxiv.139, vol. II, pp. 108–10; III.lii.200, vol. II, p. 158.

[28] Quintilian, II.xvii.29, vol. I, pp. 336–8: 'Sin et audientium mobiles animi et tot malis obnoxia veritas, arte pugnandum est.'

[29] Quintilian repeatedly invokes the metaphor of speaking 'winningly' and thereby achieving *victoria*, especially when he discusses forensic oratory in Book v. See Quintilian, *Institutio*, v.viii.1, vol. II, p. 190; v.xii.22, vol. II, p. 308; vi.iv.4, vol. II, p. 502; etc.

[30] Quintilian, *Institutio*, x.i.29, vol. IV, p. 18: 'nos vero armatos stare in acie et summis de rebus decernere et ad victoriam niti'. Cf. also XII.ix.21, vol. IV, p. 448.

'our weapons must shine with a splendour that will terrify our opponents, just as steel strikes the mind and eye all at once'.[31]

The true orator is thus defined, *pace* Socrates, as a man who possesses the capacity to teach and persuade at the same time. This power or *vis* is due, Cicero and Quintilian repeatedly assert, to the fact that he combines *ratio* with *oratio*, and hence *sapientia* with *eloquentia*. The consequence, as Quintilian puts it in a phrase that echoes throughout the *Institutio oratoria*, is that he is simultaneously able *docere, movere et delectare*, to teach, to move and to delight.[32] 'The duty of such an orator', he adds, 'is always to teach, even though the power of eloquence is certainly at its greatest in its capacity to move.'[33]

This brings the Roman theorists to the main practical question they address. How can an orator hope to speak and write in such a way as to attain his threefold goal? They begin by arguing that he needs to make it his aim not merely to state or affirm what he takes to be the truth, but by some means to put it forward or hold it out (*ostendere*) in such a way as to win attention for it.[34] As Hobbes was later to put it with elegant ambiguity in *Leviathan*, the task of the rhetorician is to speak in such a way that the truth is 'preferred'.[35] To achieve this goal, what the orator needs to understand above all is how to augment (*augere*) what he wants his audience to believe, and how to extenuate (*extenuare*) any objections that might be urged against his case. According to Cicero in *De oratore*, this ability to stretch the truth comprises the essence of the orator's art. 'The highest achievement of eloquence consists in knowing how to amplify the matter of our speech in this way.'[36] We need to know 'not only how to augment something and raise it to a higher level, but also how to extenuate and if necessary disparage it as well'.[37] Quintilian later reiterates the same commitment, going so far as to

---

[31] Quintilian, *Institutio*, x.i.30, vol. iv, p. 18: 'arma . . . fulgorem inesse qui terreat, qualis est ferri, quo mens simul visusque praestringitur'.

[32] For this triad see for example Quintilian *Institutio*, iii.iv.2, vol. i, p. 396; viii. pr. 7, vol. iii, p. 180; xii.ii.11, vol. iv, p. 388.

[33] Quintilian, *Institutio*, iv.v.6, vol. ii, pp. 138–40; 'Non enim solum oratoris est docere, sed plus eloquentia circa movendum valet.'

[34] See for example the discussion in Quintilian, *Institutio*, iv.ii.64, vol. ii, p. 84.

[35] Thomas Hobbes, *Leviathan*, ed. Richard Tuck (Cambridge, 1991), p. 484.

[36] Cicero, *De oratore*, iii.xxvi.104, vol. ii, p. 82: 'Summa autem laus eloquentiae est amplificare rem.'

[37] Cicero, *De oratore* iii.xxvi.104, vol. ii, p. 82, 'non solum ad augendum aliquid et tollendum altius dicendo sed etiam ad extenuandum atque abiciendum'.

declare that 'the whole power of oratory consists in knowing how to augment our speech or diminish it'.[38]

It is at this point, the Roman theorists agree, that the specific techniques associated with the *ars rhetorica* need to be brought into play. They single out two in particular, assigning them such paramount importance that, among a number of their Renaissance disciples, the techniques in question were eventually equated with the whole art of rhetoric.[39] One is said to be *pronunciatio* or delivery, the ability to accompany one's utterances with the most persuasive gestures and tones of voice. The other is *elocutio* or excellence of style, the relevance of which to written as well as spoken eloquence caused it to be regarded as the most important accomplishment of all.

Cicero and Quintilian both treat *elocutio* as the heart of rhetoric, and both of them divide their analysis of the concept into two parts. The first feature of a truly persuasive style is said to be the capacity to speak with *decorum* and above all with *perspicuitas*.[40] But the other and even more important characteristic of 'winning' speech is said to be *ornatus*, the ability to add appropriate and memorable *ornamenta* or *exornationes* to the statement of one's case.[41] It is easy to overlook the significance of this latter claim, especially if the term *ornatus* is translated (as it generally is) merely as 'decoration' or 'embellishment'.[42] This misses the metaphorical force of the argu-

[38] Quintilian, *Institutio*, VIII.III.89, vol. III, p. 260: 'Sed vis oratoris omnis in augendo minuendoque consistit.' Cf. also the important discussion at VIII.IV.1–3, vol. III, pp. 262–4.

[39] This view was developed in particular by Ramus and Talon as part of their attempt to reform the Paris arts curriculum in the middle of the sixteenth century. See especially Omar Talon, *Rhetorica* (1548) (Cambridge, 1631), chapter I, p. 2: 'Partes Rhetoricae duae sunt: Elocutio & Pronunciatio.' On the origins and implications of this claim see Walter Ong, 'Ramist Rhetoric', in *The Province of Rhetoric*, ed. Joseph Schwartz and John A. Rycenga (New York, 1965), pp. 226–55. Among English rhetoricians of the later sixteenth century who adopted this perspective the most important were Dudley Fenner, Abraham Fraunce and Charles Butler.

[40] On *perspicuitas* see esp. Quintilian, *Institutio*, I.VI.41, vol. I, p. 130; II.III.8, vol. I, p. 220; VIII.II.1–2, vol. III, pp. 196–8; VIII.II.22, vol. III, p. 208.

[41] On *ornatus* see esp. Cicero, *De oratore*, Book III, *passim*, esp. III.V.19, vol. II, p. 16; III.V.25, vol. II, p. 20; III.XIV.53, vol. II, p. 42; III.XX.76, vol. II, p. 62, etc. See also Quintilian, Book VIII, *passim*, esp. VIII.III.1–14, vol. III, pp. 210–18; VIII.III.40, vol. III, p. 232; VIII.III.61, vol. III, p. 244, etc.

[42] This has given rise to the misleading impression that those concerned with *ornatus* were merely interested in 'superficial elocutionary devices' and 'gratuitous verbal ornament'. For these claims see William J. Kennedy, *Rhetorical Norms in Renaissance Literature* (New Haven, 1978), pp. 1, 4. See also Barbara J. Shapiro, *Probability and Certainty in Seventeenth-Century England* (Princeton, 1983), pp. 228–9.

ment, which depends on the fact that, in classical Latin, the term *ornatus* is at the same time the word ordinarily used to describe the accoutrements of war.[43] What the rhetorical theorists are claiming is that the 'ornaments' of language, and above all the figures and tropes of speech, ought *not* to be viewed as mere decorations; they ought instead to be regarded as weapons that the orator must learn to wield if he is to have any prospect of winning the war of words. As Quintilian explains in Book VIII, it is by means of *ornatus* and the apt use of *ornamenta* that we are able to speak in such a way that the facts 'are thrust forward and displayed to the mind's eye'.[44] It is therefore by means of *ornatus* that we are able 'to augment or diminish anything in whatever direction we desire'.[45] The skilful use of *ornatus* is accordingly seen as the key to everything: the orator who fights with these flashing weapons will always have the best prospect of vanquishing his opponents and gaining victory for his side of the argument.[46]

The man who masters the power of words is seen in consequence as a figure of almost superhuman strength. His art is habitually described as magical in character, and as having the effect of turning the orator into a force of nature. One pervasive (and enduring) set of metaphors speaks of his ability to seize and hold people's attention, to captivate and enrapture them.[47] A further and equally familiar range of images speaks of his power to sway people in such a way that they are transported or carried away.[48] To these metaphors the *De oratore* adds an allusion to the idea that oratory, like music, is a bewitching art, one with the power of a *carmen* to charm, of a *cantus* to enchant.[49] Quintilian similarly speaks of the orator as having almost godlike powers, and on two occasions

---

[43] The significance of this point is well brought out in Walter J. Ong, *Ramus, Method and the Decay of Dialogue* (Cambridge, Mass., 1958), p. 227 and in Brian Vickers, *In Defence of Rhetoric* (Oxford, 1988), pp. 314–15.

[44] See Quintilian, *Institutio*, VIII.III.62, vol. III, p. 244: 'exprimi et oculis mentis ostendi'.

[45] Quintilian, VIII.III.40, vol. III, p. 232: 'augere quid velimus an minuere'.

[46] Quintilian, VIII.III.5, vol. III, p. 213.

[47] The verbs are *capere, rapere, tenere*. See for example Cicero, *De oratore*, I.VIII.30, vol. I, p. 22; III.XXV.97, vol. II, p. 76; Quintilian, *Institutio*, VI.II.3, vol. II, p. 418; VIII.III.4–5, vol. III, p. 212; X.I.111, vol. IV, p. 62; XII.X.61, vol. IV, p. 484.

[48] The verbs are *impellere, auferre, ducere*. See for example Cicero, *De oratore*, I.VIII.30, vol. I, p. 22; II.XLIV.185, vol. I, p. 330; Quintilian, *Institutio*, VIII.III.5, vol. III, p. 212; IX.IV.129, vol. III, p. 578; XII.X.50, vol. IV, p. 478.

[49] Cicero, *De oratore*, II.VIII.34, vol. I, p. 222: 'Qui enim cantus moderata oratione dulcior inveniri potest? Quod carmen artificiosa verborum conclusione aptius?'

mentions Aristophanes's remark that, when Pericles spoke, the impact of his eloquence was like a thunderstorm.[50] Cicero and Quintilian are thus led to defend an extraordinarily elevated view of the *ars rhetorica* and its place in public life. It is true that they allow themselves an occasional doubt as to whether the techniques they describe amount to a genuine *scientia*.[51] They concede that an orator can never hope to demonstrate the truths he propounds, and thus that, strictly speaking, his goal is *verisimilitudo* rather than truth.[52] They similarly admit that, since it is always possible to argue on both sides of any question, the most that can be said for the orator's skills is that they enable him *disserere*, to put forward plausible contentions for discussion and debate.[53] Nevertheless, they think of the orator's art as being *utilis* or socially valuable in the highest degree,[54] and as representing a major *beneficium* or benefit both to its practitioners and to society at large.[55] Above all, they think of the figure of the orator not merely as an ideal citizen, but as nothing less than a perfect exemplar of humanity.

To see how they arrive at this last and loftiest conclusion, we need to consider what Cicero and Quintilian conceive to be the different styles and tasks of eloquence. They both take from Aristotle the claim that there are three different *genera* of oratory: the demonstrative, concerned with praise and vituperation; the forensic, concerned with accusation and defence; and the deliberative, concerned with offering advice about the most expedient way to act.[56] They tend, however, to set the first of these aside,[57] and to concentrate almost exclusively on the arts of pleading and tendering advice. They thus arrive at a view of the orator as a man who either devotes himself to arguing for justice in the courts, or else to counselling his fellow-citizens on the best lines of public policy to pursue.[58]

---

[50] See Quintilian, *Institutio*, II.XVI.19, vol. I, p. 324 and XII.X.65, vol. IV, p. 486.
[51] See for example Cicero, *De oratore*, I.XXIII.108–9, vol. I, p. 76 and II.VII.30, vol. I, p. 218.
[52] See for example Quintilian, *Institutio*, II.XVII.39, vol. I, p. 342.
[53] See for example Cicero, *De oratore*, III.XXI.80, vol. II, p. 64 and III.XXVII.107, vol. II, p. 84.
[54] See for example Quintilian, *Institutio*, II.XVI.1–19, vol. I, pp. 318–24.
[55] See for example Quintilian, *Institutio*, XII.VII.7–8 and 12, vol. IV, pp. 422, 426.
[56] See for example Quintilian, *Institutio* III.III.14, vol. I, p. 390 (noting the threefold division) and III.IV.1, vol. I, p. 390 (attributing it to Aristotle).
[57] See for example Cicero, *De oratore* II.LXXXIV.341, vol. I, p. 456, explicitly noting that he will leave out panegyric altogether.
[58] For explicit statements to this effect see Cicero, *De oratore*, III.XXXI.122, vol. II, pp. 94–6 and Quintilian, *Institutio*, XII.II.6–7, vol. IV, p. 384.

As they both emphasise, however, these activities constitute at the same time the most important duties of the *bonus civis* or true *vir civilis*. As Cicero puts it towards the end of *De oratore*, the kind of knowledge or *scientia civilis* required of a good citizen centres above all 'on justice, on civic duty, and on how cities should be established and ruled'.[59] Quintilian underlines the same point in the Preface to his *Institutio oratoria*, arguing that 'the man with the capacity to play a full civic role' is the man 'who is able to guide cities with his advice, to establish them firmly by means of laws, and to correct their behaviour by means of his legal judgements'.[60]

It follows that in writing *de oratore*, about the ideal orator, they see themselves as writing at the same time *de cive*, about the ideal citizen. Quintilian makes the point most explicitly in the closing section of his treatise, the section in which he sketches the portrait of a perfect orator. 'Having employed his powers as a speaker in the giving of legal judgements and in the offering of advice, both in public assemblies and in the meetings of the senate' the orator may be said to have discharged 'every duty of a good citizen'.[61] To suggest that such a figure might be other than the best of men amounts, for Quintilian, to nothing better than a contradiction in terms.

We are even justified in concluding, both Cicero and Quintilian suggest, that the *bonus orator* is not merely a *vir bonus* and a *bonus civis*, but is possibly the most humane of men, the man in whom the distinctive attributes of humanity attain their highest peak. To see why this is so, we need only reflect that the quality which makes us distinctively human is not so much our faculty of *ratio* or reasoning; what separates us from brute creation is rather our power of *oratio*, our unique capacity for speech. 'But if it is true', Quintilian goes on, 'that we receive from the gods nothing finer than the power of speech, what can possibly be more worthy of cultivating with effort and labour, or in what regard can we more desire to exceed our fellow-men, than in the exercise of that very power by which men

---

[59] Cicero, *De oratore*, III.XXXI.122, vol. I, p. 96: 'de iustitia, de officio, de civitatibus instituendis et regendis'.

[60] Quintilian, *Institutio*, I.pr.10, vol. I, p. 10: 'vir ille vere civilis [est vir] qui regere consiliis urbes, fundare legibus, emendare iudiciis possit'.

[61] Quintilian, *Institutio*, XII.XI.1, vol. IV, p. 494: 'His dicendi virtutibus usus orator in iudiciis, consiliis, contionibus, in omni denique officio boni civis.'

exceed the animals?'[62] Quintilian's analysis thus culminates in the claim that, as Cicero had already expressed it at the start of *De inventione*, the greatness of the orator derives from the fact that 'he is the man who is pre-eminent over all other men in the very quality that makes men pre-eminent over the beasts'.[63]

III

When Hobbes turned away from his optical and other scientific investigations at the end of the 1630s in order to compose *The Elements of Law*, he saw himself as turning, in the words of his own Epistle Dedicatory, to consider the principles of another type of science, a science 'of justice and policy in general'.[64] Speaking at the end of *The Elements* about the dissolution of government, Hobbes again describes the knowledge needed to prevent the decline and fall of commonwealths as a form of science. We need an understanding of 'that science in particular from which proceed the true and evident conclusions of what is right and wrong, and what is good and hurtful to the being and well being of mankind'.[65]

In presenting his enterprise in these terms, Hobbes is clearly alluding to the classical conception of a *scientia civilis* which the humanist rhetoricians of the Renaissance had revived. What then is the nature of the relationship between the classical and humanist understanding of civil science on the one hand, and Hobbes's attempts to restate the principles of such a science on the other?

Among those who have explored Hobbes's development as a philosopher, the consensus has been that, by the time he completed the initial statements of his political theory – *The Elements* in 1640 and *De cive* in 1642 – he had largely abandoned his earlier interests in the rhetorical culture of classical and Renaissance humanism. Leo Strauss's monograph, *The Political Philosophy of Hobbes*, presents the most influential argument along these lines. Strauss rightly speaks of Hobbes's 'humanist' period, in the course of which he

---

[62] Quintilian, *Institutio*, II.xvi.17, vol. I, p. 324: 'Quare si nihil a dis oratione melius accepimus, quid tam dignum cultu ac labore ducamus, aut in quo malimus praestare hominibus, quam quo ipsi homines ceteris animalibus praestant.'

[63] Cicero, *De inventione*, I.iv.5, p. 12: 'is qui qua re homines bestiis praestent ea in re hominibus ipsis antecellat'.

[64] Thomas Hobbes, *The Elements of Law Natural and Political*, ed. Ferdinand Tönnies, 2nd edn, introd. M. M. Goldsmith (London, 1969), p. xv.

[65] Hobbes, *Elements*, p. 176.

made a serious study of the classical authors, including such rhetorical theorists as Cicero and Quintilian.[66] According to Strauss, however, Hobbes devoted himself to these writers only during the 1620s, after which we may speak of his humanist period as coming to an end.[67] He returned to his youthful philosophical studies, made his epoch-making (if confusing) 'discovery' of geometrical method, and turned to the preoccupations characteristic of his 'mature period' as a political scientist.[68]

Recently, however, David Johnson has challenged this view of Hobbes's intellectual development.[69] Johnson stresses that, even though it may be true that Hobbes severed himself after the 1620s from his humanist background, he later reverted to a number of key humanist beliefs. Above all, Johnson observes, *Leviathan* discloses a new and characteristically humanist scepticism about the powers of reason and science to persuade us of their truths, together with a new and corresponding awareness of the value of eloquence.[70] Hobbes had come to see, as he was to put it himself in chapter x of *Leviathan*, that 'the Sciences are small Power; because not eminent', and that 'Eloquence is power; because it is seeming Prudence'.[71]

Johnson could have carried his argument much further. When Hobbes asks in the Review and Conclusion of *Leviathan* how men can ever be 'sufficiently disposed to all sorts of Civill duty',[72] he not only addresses the question in exactly the language already used by

---

[66] Leo Strauss, *The Political Philosophy of Hobbes: Its Basis and Its Genesis*, trans. Elsa M. Sinclair, Phoenix edn (Chicago, 1963), pp. 30–3, 82.

[67] Strauss, *Hobbes*, pp. 32–3, 44, 64.

[68] Ibid., pp. 42, 95–6, 112, 138–9.

[69] See David Johnson, *The Rhetoric of Leviathan* (Princeton, 1986). Two other challenges to Strauss's interpretation should be mentioned. J. W. N. Watkins, *Hobbes's System of Ideas* (London, 1965) endorses Strauss's conception of a humanist phase, but follows Tönnies in accepting Hobbes's authorship of the *Short Tract* and in dating the *Tract* to c.1630, arguing in consequence that even the earliest versions of Hobbes's political theory are grounded in his 'scientific' thought. See Watkins, *Hobbes's System*, esp. pp. 27–46. A different challenge is presented by Gigliola Rossini in 'The Criticism of Rhetorical Historiography and the Ideal of Scientific Method: History, Nature and Science in the Political Language of Thomas Hobbes', *The Languages of Political Theory in Early-modern Europe*, ed. Anthony Pagden (Cambridge, 1987), pp. 303–24, who sees Hobbes as concerned at all times with applying to politics an ideal of scientific method. Both accounts rest on the questionable presupposition that Hobbes applies a single conception of science to the moral and physical sciences alike. On this point see the important article by Noel Malcolm cited in note 85, *infra*. For a valuable survey of the literature of Hobbes's so-called rhetorical strategies see Conal Condren, 'On the Rhetorical Foundations of *Leviathan*', *History of Political Thought*, 11 (1990), 703–20.

[70] Johnson, *Rhetoric*, pp. 98, 131–2.

[71] Hobbes, *Leviathan*, ed. Tuck, p. 63.

[72] Ibid., p. 483.

the classical theorists of eloquence; he deploys it in such a way as to uphold exactly their sceptical point of view. He begins by noting that questions of civil duty arise in connection with both the forms of oratory they had particularly singled out – that is, 'in all Deliberations, and in all Pleadings'.[73] He then stresses, just as they had done, that *ratio* is of course indispensable if the right decisions or judgements are to be reached. 'The faculty of solid Reasoning, is necessary: for without it, the Resolutions of men are rash, and their Sentences unjust.'[74] But he then declares, just as they had done, that *ratio* in the absence of *eloquentia* can never hope to prevail. For 'if there be not powerfull Eloquence, which procureth attention and Consent, the effect of Reason will be little'.[75] The solution he goes on to suggest, moreover, is exactly the one they had already proposed. As we have seen, they had argued that we must be ready to deploy the techniques of *ornatus* in such a way that, by adding *eloquentia* to *ratio*, we can hope to thrust forward or 'prefer' the truth. Hobbes follows them to the letter. The answer, he agrees, lies in recognising that 'Reason and Eloquence' may 'stand very well together'. This is because, 'wheresoever there is place for adorning and preferring of Errour, there is much more place for adorning and preferring of Truth, if they have it to adorn'.[76]

Although Johnson's view of Hobbes's intellectual development strikes me as more accurate than that of Strauss, one aspect of his argument is I think open to doubt. Although he has rightly pointed to the humanist and especially the rhetorical dimensions of *Leviathan*,[77] he remains content to endorse Strauss's contention that, at

[73] Ibid., p. 483.
[74] Ibid., p. 483.
[75] Ibid., p. 483.
[76] Ibid., pp. 483–4.
[77] In speaking of the 'rhetoric' of *Leviathan*, however, Johnson is not in general referring to Hobbes's use of the *Ars rhetorica*; he is using the term in a modern and wider sense to refer simply to Hobbes's literary strategies. The same is true of two helpful articles by Tom Sorell, 'Hobbes's Persuasive Civil Science', *The Philosophical Quarterly*, 40 (1990), 342–51 and 'Hobbes's UnAristotelian Political Rhetoric', *Philosophy and Rhetoric*, 23 (1990), 96–108. Although Hobbes makes systematic use of the classical and humanist devices of *eloquentia artificiosa* in *Leviathan*, this is not an aspect of his civil philosophy which has yet been studied in a non-anachronistic way, as M. M. Goldsmith notes at the end of his recent review-article, 'The Hobbes Industry', *Political Studies*, 39 (1991), 135–47. I am currently attempting to complete such a study myself, and have already tried to sketch the context for Hobbes's use of the *Ars rhetorica* in 'Thomas Hobbes: Rhetoric and the Construction of Morality', *Proceedings of the British Academy*, 76 (1990) 1–61. Among existing studies, I have found useful Jeffrey Barnouw, 'Persuasion in Hobbes's *Leviathan*', *Hobbes Studies*, 1 (1988), 3–25 and especially Frederick G. Whelan, 'Language and its Abuses in Hobbes' Political Philosophy', *The American Political Science Review*, 75 (1981), 59–75.

the time when Hobbes first began to formulate his civil science, he had broken away from his youthful humanist interests. This means, according to Johnson, that if we compare *Leviathan* with *De cive*, and even more with *The Elements of Law*, we find that the earlier texts contain a far more purely 'scientific' version of Hobbes's political theory, a version largely independent of humanist assumptions and unaffected by them.[78]

It is this conclusion which seems to me questionable. It is certainly true that Hobbes's conception of a civil science in *The Elements* and *De cive* stands in sharp contrast with classical and humanist beliefs. But it is misleading to suggest that Hobbes had set his concern with the rhetorical tradition 'to one side' by the time he came to write these works, and still more misleading to add that he became 'less and less interested' in 'the formal study of rhetoric'.[79] My aim in what follows will be to show that, on the contrary, Hobbes's original presentation of his civil science was worked out in close relationship with – and often in the form of a direct commentary on – the understanding of *scientia civilis* orig- inally articulated by the classical theorists of eloquence.

IV

When Hobbes republished his *De cive* in 1647, he inserted a new Preface addressed 'To his readers' in which he included a survey of his philosophical method and a summary of what he took himself to have achieved.[80] He begins by reiterating that his concern is with the idea of a *scientia civilis*,[81] and he singles out the name of Cicero among 'the philosophers of Greece and Rome' who prided them-

---

[78] Johnson, *Rhetoric*, pp. xviii–xix, 11–13, 22–5, 26–9.
[79] Ibid., pp. 23n., 24.
[80] See Howard Warrender, 'Editor's Introduction', in Thomas Hobbes, *De cive: The Latin Version* (Oxford, 1983), p. 9. The Preface itself, headed 'Praefatio ad Lectores' is at pp. 77–84.
[81] Note that, when quoting from *De cive*, I have made my own translations from Hobbes's Latin text. It is true that Howard Warrender, 'Editor's Introduction', in Thomas Hobbes, *De cive: The English Version* (Oxford, 1983), pp. 4–8, claims that the English translation of *De cive* published in March 1651 was the work of Hobbes himself. As many scholars have pointed out, however, this cannot possibly be the case. For references to the literature see Quentin Skinner, 'Thomas Hobbes on the Proper Significance of Liberty', *Transactions of the Royal Historical Society*, 5th series 40 (1990), 121–51, at p. 122n. It is because the 1651 translation has no standing that I have preferred to work from Warrender's edition of the Latin text.

selves on the contributions they made to 'what is unquestionably the worthiest of all the sciences'.[82] He follows their account of its subject-matter, arguing that civil science chiefly centres on 'the doctrine of civic duty', and can thus be described (in Cicero's own words) as a *scientia iustitiae*, a science of justice.[83] He also endorses the classical view that such a science must be purposive in character. This aspect of Hobbes's argument has largely been overlooked by recent commentators, who have generally assumed that for Hobbes all sciences must take the same anti-teleological form.[84] As Noel Malcolm has recently pointed out, however, Hobbes marks a sharp distinction between natural and civil science, although he allows that both are capable of amounting to genuine sciences.[85] The aim of the natural sciences is to understand the behaviour of physical bodies; and in this case, Hobbes agrees, we must always adopt a purely mechanistic approach. But the aim of civil science is to understand the behaviour of one particular type of artificial body, the body of the *civitas*. The peculiarity of such bodies stems from the fact that men are at once their artificers and their *materia*; and this means, according to Hobbes, that we cannot avoid asking about the purposes for which they are brought into existence.[86] When Hobbes turns to consider these purposes, moreover, he again voices general agreement with the classical point of view. Cities are founded primarily 'in order to preserve life', and more specifically in order to show us 'the royal road to peace'.[87] This is why we are justified in speaking of the exceptional *utilitas* of civil science. 'For nothing could be more useful than to find out how this can be done.'[88] Finally, Hobbes reiterates the classical belief that what a student of civil science needs above all to comprehend is the nature and range of the qualities that enable men, the material of cities, to mould themselves successfully into

---

[82] Hobbes, *De cive*, p. 77 on 'Cicero, caeterique Philosophi Graeci, Latini', and p. 78 on 'scientia civilis' and on this form of *scientia* as 'dignissima certe scientiarum'.

[83] See Hobbes, *De cive*, pp. 77–8 on *scientia civilis* as a *doctrina officiorum* and a *scientia justitiae*.

[84] The misleading character of this assumption is well brought out in Tom Sorell, 'The Science in Hobbes's Politics', in *Perspectives on Thomas Hobbes*, ed. G. A. J. Rogers and Alan Ryan (Oxford, 1988), pp. 67–80.

[85] Noel Malcolm, 'Hobbes's Science of Politics and his Theory of Science', in *Hobbes oggi*, ed. Andrea Napoli in collaboration with Guido Canziani (Milan, 1990), pp. 145–57.

[86] See Hobbes, *De cive*, pp. 79–80 and cf. Malcolm, 'Science of Politics', pp. 147, 149, 151–2.

[87] See Hobbes, *De cive*, pp. 78–9 on *civitates* being founded *vivendi causa* and in order to show us *via regia pacis*.

[88] Hobbes, *De cive*, p. 79: 'qua re utilius nihil excogitari potest'.

those particular shapes.[89] We need 'rightly to understand the character of human nature, what makes men either fit or unfit to bind themselves together into a *civitas*, and how far men need to agree among themselves if they wish to form such a unity'.[90]

There is a sense in which Hobbes still retains his classical allegiances as he turns to enquire into the nature of the qualities required. For he fully agrees that, as Cicero had put it at the start of the *De inventione*, the attributes we must indispensably possess if we are to succeed in bringing men together in the form of a *civitas* are *ratio* and, in consequence, *sapientia*.[91] It is at this point, however, that Hobbes suddenly parts company with, and turns against, the familiar classical account. As we have seen, the Roman theorists had argued that, in the absence of *eloquentia*, the qualities of *ratio* and *sapientia* can never hope to have the least effect. By contrast, it is crucial to Hobbes's project both in *The Elements* and in *De cive* to repudiate exactly this contention, and to insist on the contrary that the force of *ratio* is capable in itself of persuading us to accept the truth.

Hobbes first throws down this challenge in the superbly confident Epistle Dedicatory to *The Elements*.[92] His chief ambition, he declares, is to construct a science of justice and policy on the basis of right reason alone; to 'reduce this doctrine to the rules and infallibility of reason'.[93] The possibility of creating such a science arises from the fact that there are 'two principal parts of our nature'.[94] One is of course passion; but the other is reason, 'which', as he later adds in discussing the laws of nature, 'is no less of the nature of man than passion, and is the same in all men', since 'God almighty hath given reason to man to be a light unto him.'[95] This being so, there need be no barrier in principle to our employing our reason to lay the foundations for a science of civil life which, 'passion not mistrusting, may not seek to displace'.[96] But if this can

---

[89] On the *materia* and *forma* of *civitates*, see Hobbes, *De cive*, p. 79.

[90] Hobbes, *De cive*, pp. 79–80: 'qualis sit natura humana, quibus rebus ad civitatem compaginandam apta vel inepta sit, & quomodo homines inter se componi debeant, qui coalescere volunt, recte intelligatur'.

[91] See Hobbes, *De cive*, p. 81 on the indispensability of following the dictates of *ratio*.

[92] For an excellent analysis which concentrates on this aspect of the *Elements*, see Johnson, *Rhetoric*, ch. 2, pp. 26–65.

[93] Hobbes, *Elements*, p. 1.

[94] Ibid., p. 1.

[95] Ibid., pp. 75, 99.

[96] Ibid., p. 1.

be done, the resulting foundations, being principles of reason, will be 'inexpugnable'. We shall have no inclination to dispute them; rather we shall find ourselves ineluctably persuaded of their truth. As a result, we can hope to inculcate them in such a way as to produce a form of learning, in matters of justice and policy, that will finally be 'free from controversy and dispute'.[97]

The *De cive* is pervaded by a no less confident belief in the power of *ratio* to convince. Hobbes begins by remarking in the Dedication – in a direct allusion to the classical art of eloquence – that he expects to persuade 'by the firmness of *rationes* and not by any outward diplay of *oratio*'.[98] When he discusses the laws of nature in chapter 2, he goes on to speak of the infallibility of *recta ratio*, describing it not merely as an undoubted law but as 'no less a part of human nature than any other faculty or passion of the mind'.[99] And when he considers the duties of sovereigns in chapter 12, he assumes that 'the opinions they need to insert into the minds of men'[100] can and ought to be inserted 'not by commanding but by teaching, not by the fear of penalties but by the perspicuity of reasons'.[101]

If *ratio* is sufficient to insert doctrines into the mind, there would seem to be no place for the various techniques of persuasion on which the classical theorists of rhetoric had laid so much emphasis. This is indeed the inference Hobbes proceeds to draw, thereby repudiating as explicitly as possible the classical and humanist belief that any effective civil science must be founded on a union of reason and eloquence.

The point is cunningly made at the start of *The Elements* in the form of an apparent concession to humanist pieties. Hobbes remarks in his Epistle Dedicatory that he needs to apologise for his *elocutio*. 'The style', as he puts it, 'is therefore the worse, because I was forced to consult when I was writing, more with logic than with rhetoric.'[102] What this trope of modesty succeeds in conveying, however, is the subversive suggestion that, contrary to common

---

[97] Ibid., pp. 1–2.
[98] Hobbes, *De cive*, p. 76: 'neque specie orationis, sed firmitudine rationum'.
[99] See Hobbes, *De cive*, p. 99 on *recta ratio* as a *lex* and as 'non minus pars naturae humanae, quam quaelibet alia facultas vel affectus animi'.
[100] Hobbes, *De cive*, p. 198: 'opiniones . . . animis hominum inseruntur'.
[101] Hobbes, *De cive*, p. 198: 'non imperando, sed docendo, non terrore poenarum, sed perspicuitate rationum'.
[102] Hobbes, *Elements*, p. xvi.

belief, the task of laying the foundations of a civil science is one in which the art of rhetoric has no necessary place.

Hobbes turns the tables even more adroitly in *De cive*. He now professes to endorse the classical belief that *eloquentia*, and hence a capacity to speak with *elegantia* and *perspicuitas*, are indispensable to civil science. But he insists that, when we speak with *eloquentia*, and in consequence manage to offer 'an explication of our beliefs and conceptions which is at once *perspicua* and *elegans*',[103] the art we are deploying is the *ars logica*, not the *ars rhetorica* at all. It follows that, when we say that eloquence is indispensable to civil science, this is only to say that we must reason logically; it is not in the least to say that we need to call upon the artificial aids associated with 'that form of powerful eloquence which is separated from a genuine knowledge of things'.[104]

As the *De cive* particularly emphasises, Hobbes believes that he has in fact succeeded in founding a civil science on such infallible principles of *recta ratio*. Staking out this claim in his Preface, he presents it in the form of a scathing series of allusions to the rival view of *scientia civilis* made familiar by the classical and humanist writers on eloquence. The classical theorists had argued that *eloquentia* is indispensable in the first place if we are to win the *attentus* of an audience. Hobbes retorts that the interest of his topic is quite sufficient in itself to hold the attention of his readership.[105] The classical theorists had gone on to argue that civil science can never hope *demonstrare*, to demonstrate its findings, but only *disserere*, to discuss and debate them. Hobbes responds with the lie direct: *non enim dissero sed computo*.[106] The classical theorists had added that, because civil science cannot hope *demonstrare*, we must always seek *suadere*, to employ the 'probable' techniques of rhetoric in such a way as to persuade. Hobbes replies that in *De cive* there is only one argument – his preference for monarchy – which attempts *suadere*, and which is *non demonstrandum sed probabiliter*.[107] For the

103 See Hobbes, *De cive*, pp. 192–3, claiming that the *ars* which yields true *eloquentia*, and thus serves as the 'sententiae & conceptionum animi perspicua & elegans explicatrix' is the *ars logica*.
104 See Hobbes, *De cive*, p. 193: on '*eloquentia potens*, separata rerum scientia'.
105 Hobbes, *De cive*, p. 77.
106 Ibid., p. 82.
107 Ibid., p. 83.

rest, he insists, everything is 'so evidently demonstrated'[108] that, as he was later to boast in *De corpore*, *De cive* is not only an exercise in civil science, but the only such exercise in the entire history of philosophy with a genuinely scientific character.[109]

V

As Hobbes sets about the construction of a civil science on the basis of right reason alone, he is led to develop a theory which appears to have little or no connection with classical and humanist thought. Nevertheless, we cannot hope to understand the distinctive shape and character of his resulting argument without making reference to the rival conception of *scientia civilis* articulated by Cicero, Quintilian and their followers. The reason is that, at a number of crucial points, Hobbes works out his own views about the nature of language and politics in the form of a critical reaction to – and even a satirical commentary on – the classical and humanist ortho-doxies.

There are two moments in particular at which Hobbes's own argument is couched in the form of just such a critical response. The first is when he lays out his theory of language in the opening chapters of *The Elements*, and especially when he presents his views in chapter 5 about the value of signs and names; the second is when he moves on to his connected discussion in chapter 13 about the use of these signs to teach and affect others.

As we have seen, when the classical theorists discussed the value of speech they permitted themselves a remarkably elevated tone, declaring that it is due to *oratio* even more than *ratio* that men 'exceed' the beasts. When Hobbes addresses the same issue in chapter 5 of *The Elements*, he frames his argument in the form of a satirical deflation of exactly this point of view. It is true, he observes, that 'the invention of names hath been necessary for the drawing of men out of ignorance', and that it is due to 'the benefit of words and ratiocination' that men 'exceed brute beasts in knowledge'.[110] However, he adds, it is likewise due to the invention

---

[108] See Hobbes, *De cive* p. 82 for the claim (referring to his conclusions drawn from Scripture) that *evidentissime demonstro & concludo.*

[109] Thomas Hobbes, 'Elements of Philosophy. The First Section. Concerning Body', in *The English Works*, ed. W. Molesworth (11 vols., 1839–45), vol. I, p. ix.

[110] Hobbes, *Elements*, p. 22.

of names and our capacity to communicate them in speech that we acquire the connected ability 'to multiply one untruth by another'. So while it is true in a sense that men exceed the beasts as a result of having the benefit of speech, it is no less true that 'by the incommodities that accompany the same they exceed them also in errors'.[111]

When Hobbes turns in chapter 13 to consider 'the use and effect' of this power of speech in teaching,[112] he again presents his argument in the form of a critical commentary on the assumptions and vocabulary of classical humanism. He begins by affirming that what it means to teach is always to demonstrate something beyond dispute. 'The infallible sign of teaching exactly, and without error, is this: that no man hath ever taught the contrary.'[113] This is because, in genuine teaching, we always begin with 'something from experience' and proceed 'from the imposition of names' to infer unquestionable truths and thereby convey knowledge.[114] It follows that to persuade cannot be to teach. As Hobbes goes on, it is when 'there be not such evidence' that 'such teaching is called PERSUASION, and begetteth no more in the hearer, than what is in the speaker' – that is, 'bare opinion' as opposed to genuine knowledge.[115] But as Hobbes later observes, it is precisely this alternative and spurious method of teaching that rhetoricians practise and recommend. They are not interested in 'demonstration and teaching of truth'; they are only interested in 'the power of winning belief of what we say'.[116] They may thus be said – and here Hobbes alludes to his own translation of Aristotle's *Rhetoric* – to 'take another way'.[117] They 'not only derive what they would have to be believed, from somewhat believed already, but also by aggravations and extenuations make good and bad, right and wrong, appear great or less, as it shall serve their turns'.[118]

In *De cive* Hobbes goes on to denounce the classical and humanist belief that such methods are indispensable if there is to be

---

[111] Ibid., p. 22.
[112] Ibid., p. 64.
[113] Ibid., p. 65.
[114] Ibid., pp. 64, 66.
[115] Ibid., pp. 64–5.
[116] Ibid., p. 177.
[117] Ibid., p. 177. Cf. note 22 above for the passage to which Hobbes alludes.
[118] Hobbes, *Elements*, p. 177. Here again Hobbes is alluding to his own translation of Aristotle's *Rhetoric*. See Hobbes, *Briefe*, ed. Harwood, p. 40, where rhetoric is defined as 'that Faculty, by which wee understand what will serve our turne'.

any prospect of winning the war of words. 'It is the vice of *eloquentia*', Hobbes retorts, 'that it takes as its goal, as all the masters of rhetoric teach, not truth – except *per accidens* – but victory.'[119] Hobbes's reply is of course doubly unfair. Some of the acknowledged masters of rhetoric – for example, Aristotle – had made no use of such militaristic metaphors in describing the art. And although others – such as Cicero and Quintilian – had undoubtedly made use of them, they had always insisted that the rhetorician's true goal must be to employ the techniques of persuasion to gain victory for the truth. But Hobbes refuses to recognise that a rhetorician might have any such scruples. When he published his translation of Aristotle's *Art of Rhetorique* in 1637, he ruthlessly inserted the claim – giving the impression that Aristotle had made it – that 'the end of *Rhetorique* is victory; which consists in having gotten *beleefe*'.[120] And when he discussed the nature of rhetoric in chapter 12 of *De cive* he again insisted that 'whereas the goal of Logic is truth, that of Rhetoric is Victory'.[121]

The implication, duly drawn in *De cive*, is that rhetoricians can never be said to teach. The whole of Hobbes's argument, in other words, amounts to nothing more than a restatement of the anti-sophistic stance which the Roman theorists of eloquence had associated with Greek philosophy. As we have seen, they had taken it to be Socrates's view that, since the goal of rhetoric is *suadere*, the rhetorician can never be said *docere*. While they believed themselves to have overcome the criticism, Hobbes simply reverts to it. As *De cive* declares, the *munus* or gift of rhetoric is *non docere, sed suadere*.[122] Reason and rhetoric are once again treated as polar opposites.

It is evident that Hobbes later found his own forthright scepticism something of an embarrassment. As we have seen, by the time he came to publish *Leviathan* he had reached the conclusion that, without the aid of eloquence, truth and reason can never hope to prevail. It therefore comes as no surprise to find that none of the passages from *The Elements* and *De cive* in which the art of eloquence is assailed for preferring victory to truth recur in *Leviathan* at all. If

[119] Hobbes, *De cive*, p. 178: 'Eloquentiae vitium, cuius finis (ut magistri Rhetoricae omnes docent) non veritas est (nisi per accidens) sed victoria.'
[120] Hobbes, *Briefe*, ed. Harwood, p. 41. Harwood duly notes (p. 41n) that Hobbes's remark is an interpolation.
[121] Hobbes, *De cive*, p. 193: 'Illius [sc. logica] finis veritas est; huius [sc. rhetorica] victoria.'
[122] Ibid., p. 178.

we turn back to these earlier texts, however, the contrast could hardly be more striking: both in *The Elements* and in *De cive*, Hobbes takes up the precise vocabulary of the classical rhetoricians in order to repudiate their basic assumptions point by point. Above all, he repudiates their image of the ideal orator as someone who moves men's minds by combining wisdom with eloquence in such a way as to amplify and extenuate the truth. Hobbes retorts that to speak of someone who 'by moving men's minds is able to amplify hope and extenuate dangers' is not to speak of adding eloquence to wisdom at all.[123] It is to speak of 'a powerful eloquence separated from wisdom and from a genuine knowledge of things',[124] an eloquence which is not joined with wisdom 'but is almost always disjoined from it'.[125] It is not to speak of *ratio atque eloquentia*; it is to speak of an eloquence *praeter rationem*, beyond reason and apart from it.[126]

VI

The other and even more important point at which Hobbes presents his argument in *The Elements* and *De cive* in the form of a critical commentary on the classical theory of eloquence is in discussing the nature and duties of citizenship. As we have seen, the Roman rhetorical theorists had insisted that, in writing *de oratore*, about the perfect orator, they were also writing *de cive*, about the ideal of citizenship. The climax of Quintilian's treatise comes with the claim that a good orator cannot but be a good citizen and a good man. Nothing is more indicative of Hobbes's continuing preoccupation with this particular tradition of thought than the fact that, in publishing the first version of his own civil science, he used his title to signal the fact that he too took himself to be writing *de cive*, about the ideal of citizenship. In doing so, moreover, he reiterated the precise reasons given by the classical theorists for supposing that good orators make especially valuable citizens. His chapter comparing different forms of government notes that the classical theorists chiefly had in mind the government of 'popular states'.[127] And in these commonwealths, he observes, it is usual for

[123] Ibid., p. 193: 'spem amplificare, pericula extenuare . . . commovendo animos'.
[124] Ibid., p. 193: '*eloquentia potens*, separata a rerum scientia, hoc est, a sapientia'.
[125] Ibid., p. 193: 'a *sapientia* . . . disiungitur haec [sc. rhetorica] vero fere semper'.
[126] Ibid., p. 193.
[127] Ibid., ch. x, p. 176.

'everyone to take part in public business, and to display and thrust forward (*ostendere*) their *prudentia, scientia* and *eloquentia* in deliberating about matters of the greatest difficulty and public significance'.[128] This in turn means, he agrees, that it becomes 'indispensable not merely to deliver long and sustained orations, but also, in order to win goodwill, to present them to one's auditors with an eloquence characterised as much as possible by *ornatus* and elegance'.[129]

It is precisely this ideal which Hobbes then sets himself to challenge and destroy. He expresses deep misgivings in the first place about the classical picture of the *bonus civis* as a man continually engaged in counselling, debating and tendering advice in all matters relating to the running of the commonwealth. For Hobbes it is vital that citizens should recognise themselves as subjects, men who are subject to law rather than appropriately employed in acting as legislators.[130] He accordingly thinks of the main duties of citizenship as lying in the private rather than in the public sphere, and in consequence treats the classical image of the active citizen as little better than a portrait of a conceited meddler. The point is pressed with great vehemence in the chapter on forms of government in *De cive*. 'The only reason why anyone devotes himself to public rather than to family affairs is because the former seem to provide him with an opportunity of displaying his eloquence, by means of which he can hope to acquire the reputation of being a clever and prudent man.'[131] But this, Hobbes goes on, is inherently dangerous:

The gift of eloquence consists of being able to make good and evil, profitable and unprofitable, honest and dishonest seem greater or lesser than they are in fact, and injustice to appear as justice, solely in such a

[128] Ibid., p. 176: 'ubi [sc. in a *status popularis*] scilicet negotia publica omnes tractant, prudentiam, scientiam, eloquentiamque suam in deliberationibus circa res maximae difficultatis & momenti publice ostentandi'.
[129] Ibid., p. 176: 'necesse habet perpetua & longa uti oratione; eamque existimationis causa, audientibus quantum potest ornatam gratamque eloquentia reddere'.
[130] Hobbes almost always translates *civis* not as 'citizen' but as 'subject'. See, most revealingly, *Leviathan*, ch. xxi. The chapter-heading in the Latin edition appears as 'De libertate civium', but in English as 'Of the Liberty of Subjects'. See Thomas Hobbes, 'Leviathan' in *Opera Philosophica* (Amsterdam, 1668), p. 104 and compare Hobbes, *Leviathan*, ed. Tuck, p. 145.
[131] Hobbes, *De cive*, p. 179: 'Nihil enim est propter quod non malit quisquam *rei familiari* potius, quam *publicae* vacare, praeterquam quod locum esse videt facundiae suae, qua possit ingenii & prudentiae existimationem acquirere.'

way as appears to conduce to the speaker's own ends. For this is what it means to persuade. Nor do such people attempt to relate what they say to the nature of things, but merely to the passions of their minds. From which it follows that they deliver their judgments not by *recta ratio* at all, but merely by a passionate impetus of the mind.[132]

Hobbes's main and most savage criticism, however, is that it is only necessary to find a man who possesses these talents and is at the same time a person of little wisdom in order to arrive at the very definition of a treasonous citizen. With this contention Hobbes impugns the classical ideal of eloquence in a way that must have struck his original readers, schooled in the ways of humanism, as shockingly paradoxical. Far from regarding the figure of the orator as being, in Ciceronian phrase, of the greatest benefit to cities and the key to preserving them, Hobbes professes to find an intrinsic connection between the practice of eloquence and the destruction of civil life.

He begins his defence of this claim in *The Elements* by conceding that it will doubtless appear 'a contradiction, to place small judgment and great eloquence, or, as they call it, powerful speaking, in the same man'.[133] The concession is likely to strike a modern reader as puzzling, since there is obviously nothing *contradictory* about the claim that someone might at once be a powerful speaker and a person of weak judgment. The puzzle can easily be resolved, however, if we treat Hobbes's way of putting the point as further evidence that he is chiefly thinking about the classical theorists of eloquence. With their doctrine that good orators necessarily make good citizens, they had certainly implied that it must be contradictory to suppose that someone might be eloquent without at the same time being wise.

Hobbes declares in response that, if we reflect on those who breed in others a disposition to sedition, we find that they invariably possess three qualities. They are 'discontented themselves'; they are 'men of mean judgment and capacity'; and they are 'eloquent men or good orators'.[134] Hobbes takes as an example

[132] Hobbes, *De cive*, pp. 177–8: 'Eloquentiae autem munus est, *Bonum* & *Malum, utile* & *inutile, Honestum* & *inhonestum*, facere apparere maiora vel minora quam revera sunt, & *Iustum* videri, quod *iniustum* est, prout ad finem dicentis videbitur conducere. Hoc enim est persuadere ... neque orationem suam naturae rerum, sed affectibus animorum convenientem esse student. Unde accidit non recta ratione, sed impetu animi sententias ferri.'
[133] Hobbes, *Elements*, p. 175.
[134] Ibid., p. 175.

the case of Catiline, quoting Sallust's epigram to the effect that 'he was a man of considerable eloquence but small wisdom'.[135] To this Hobbes adds in his own most epigrammatic style that 'perhaps this was said of Catiline, as he was Catiline: but it was true of him as an author of sedition. For the conjunction of these two qualities made him not Catiline, but seditious.'[136]

To justify this profoundly anti-humanist conclusion, Hobbes begins by recalling what the classical theorists of eloquence had said on behalf of their art, citing their own characterisations almost word for word. Rhetoricians are basically interested in 'the power of winning belief'. So they seek to arouse 'the passions of the hearers' by means of 'aggravations and extenuations' of the truth. But this means that 'many times a man is made to believe thereby, that he sensibly feeleth smart and damage, when he feeleth none'. And this, Hobbes adds, is sufficient to make his point:

This considered, together with the business that he hath to do, who is the author of rebellion, (viz.) to make men believe that their rebellion is just, their discontents grounded upon great injuries, and their hopes great; there needeth no more to prove, there can be no author of rebellion, that is not an eloquent and powerful speaker, and withal (as hath been said before) a man of little wisdom.[137]

The *De cive* launches a similar attack on the *ars verborum* 'by means of which good can be represented to the mind as being better, and bad as being worse, than is really the case'.[138] Again Hobbes denounces the seditious implications of the art, and again he treats the case of Catiline as the best exemplification of his case. To this he adds a further caustic allusion to the classical writers when he mentions the leadership of Pericles, 'of whom it has been remarked that with his orations he thundered and flashed lightning'.[139] As we have seen, the remark was in fact Quintilian's; he had offered it in illustration of his central conviction that good orators make the best citizens. When Hobbes repeats it, however, he does so in order to make the opposite point. The outcome of Pericles's thunderings, he observes, was that 'the whole of Greece was brought to a state of

---

[135] Ibid., p. 175: 'Eloquentia satis, sapientia parum.'
[136] Ibid., p. 175.
[137] All quotations in this paragraph come from Hobbes, *Elements*, p. 177.
[138] Hobbes, *De cive*, p. 133 on the *ars verborum* 'qua Bonum, Melius, Malum Peius repraesentatur animo quam revera est'.
[139] Ibid., p. 133: 'diciturque *Pericles* suis quondam orationibus, tonuisse, fulgurasse'.

collapse'.[140] Far from reminding us of the supposed connection between powerful eloquence and wise government, what the case of Pericles illustrates is the fact that 'the tongue of man is nothing other than a trumpet of sedition and war'.[141]

Before bringing his discussion in *The Elements* to a close, Hobbes has one further satirical allusion to make to the classical theorists of eloquence. As we have seen, both Cicero and Quintilian had maintained that the great benefit or *beneficium* of rhetoric stems from the power of those who practise it to proffer counsel and advice in such a way that those who hear it are bewitched and carried away. Hobbes enthusiastically seizes on the suggestion that deliberative oratory constitutes an almost magical art. He recounts the story of the daughters of Pelias, who wished 'to restore their old decrepit father to the vigour of his youth'.[142] They sought the counsel of Medea, who advised them to chop him in pieces 'and set him boiling with I know not what herbs in a cauldron'.[143] The effect of Medea's deliberative oratory proved fatal; as Hobbes remarks with studied understatement, Pelias's foolish daughters 'could not make him revive again'.[144] But the reason for their folly, as *De cive* makes especially clear in repeating the anecdote, was that they were *ductae* – transported or carried away – by the spellbinding force of Medea's speech.[145] The moral is that we are indeed justified in saying that the power of rhetoric 'is as the witchcraft of Medea'.[146] But the consequences are by no means as benign as the theorists of eloquence like to presume. Far from invigorating the body politic, the force of oratory tends to have a deadly and irrational effect. When Hobbes retells the story in *De cive*, he ends by bringing out the play on words underlying his argument in such a way as to deliver his strongest rebuke to the classical theorists of *scientia civilis*. The effect of eloquence upon commonwealths, he declares, is not beneficial but poisonous: a form of *veneficium*, not *beneficium*.[147]

---

[140] Ibid., p. 133: 'tonuisse, fulgurasse, & confudisse [sic; sed recte *confundisse*] totam Graeciam'.
[141] Ibid., p. 133: 'hominis autem lingua tuba quaedam belli est & seditionis'.
[142] Hobbes, *Elements*, p. 178.
[143] Ibid., p. 178.
[144] Ibid., p. 178.
[145] Hobbes, *De cive*, p. 194.
[146] Hobbes, *Elements*, p. 178.
[147] Hobbes, *De cive*, p. 194.

VII

By the time Hobbes came to write *Leviathan*, his sense of the adversaries against whom he needed to pit himself had undergone a considerable change. His denunciations of Aristotle and the scholastics are more violent than ever,[148] but his earlier fulminations against the humanist art of eloquence are largely withdrawn. We find no reference in *Leviathan* to Sallust's portrait of Catiline, no criticism of Quintilian's equation between the figure of the good orator and the good citizen and above all no suggestion that eloquence may be a treasonous art. And although the tale of Pelias is recounted once more, Hobbes now uses the story to convey a different moral, one unconnected with the value of rhetoric.[149] By this time, in short, his views about *scientia civilis* had completely changed. Whereas the point of his original discussion in *The Elements* had been to establish 'how want of wisdom and store of eloquence may stand together',[150] the suggestion he now wished to leave with his readers was that 'reason and eloquence' may 'stand very well together'.[151]

With this allusion to his own previous position, Hobbes explicitly recants his earlier scepticism about the value of the rhetorical arts. We are left confronting the sharpest volte face to be found at any point in the evolution of his civil philosophy.[152] *Leviathan* endorses the familiar call for a union of reason and eloquence, and hence of rhetoric and philosophy. By contrast, as I have sought to show, the earlier versions of Hobbes's civil science owe much of their shape and character to the repudiation of precisely these humanist beliefs.

---

[148] One example, as David P. Gauthier, *The Logic of Leviathan* (Oxford, 1969), pp. 143–4, rightly stresses, is that, by comparison with *The Elements* and *De cive*, Hobbes's criticisms in *Leviathan* of Aristotle's views on liberty and citizenship are far more vehemently expressed.

[149] Hobbes, *Leviathan*, ed. Tuck, p. 234. Hobbes now uses the anecdote to illustrate the dangers inherent in any desire for political change.

[150] Hobbes, *Elements*, pp. 175–6.

[151] Hobbes, *Leviathan*, ed. Tuck, pp. 483–4.

[152] This obviously raises the question of why Hobbes should have changed his mind. It would take at least another essay to offer anything like a satisfactory answer. Suffice it to say for the moment that Hobbes himself appears to provide the clue when, in *Behemoth*, he describes the English Civil Wars of the 1640s essentially as a triumph of rhetoric over rationality. The inference – drawn most clearly in *Leviathan* – is that the art of rhetoric, even if reprehensible, cannot after all be safely ignored. See Thomas Hobbes, *Behemoth*, ed. Ferdinand Tönnies, 2nd edn, introd. M. M. Goldsmith (London, 1969), esp. pp. 3, 24, 39–41, 68–9, 109, 144, 158–60.

Part II

CHAPTER 5

Parliamentary sovereignty:
a very English absolutism

Michael Mendle

In 1642, the houses of Parliament articulated England's first clear, widely understood theory of parliamentary sovereignty. The development had its consequences. The assertion of sovereignty brought the country to the constitutional impasse that, joined with religious and political strains, brought on the Civil War. Then and later, it also encouraged a constitutionalist backlash against the parliamentary regime, leading to the development of a new liberal sensibility and other kinds of parliamentary sovereignty.

Yet that first assertion of parliamentary sovereignty has been belittled or denied. Taken part by part, it was far from revolutionary – even banal, so much so that some scholars detect no significant difference on the eve of civil war between the political theory of parliament and the theory of the king.[1] Nevertheless, as a whole the theory was quite remarkable, as much in the rejection of possible positions as in the selection of its components. For all its seeming moderation, it was a theory that Charles would not accept, and no conceivable king – no king, that is, in the Tudor or Stuart mould – could have accepted, without forfeiting the most essential and traditional rights of the English monarchy.

In two important respects, the theory of parliamentary sovereignty of 1642 was absolutist. In the first place, 'sovereignty' and 'absolutism' were overlapping terms. Bodin himself defined sovereignty as the 'most high, absolute, and perpetual power'. Recollecting Bodin in the debates on the Petition of Right, Edward Alford argued that '"sovereign" power [was] free from any condition'. Pym would not allow the word 'sovereign' to be attached to the

---

[1] For a recent rebuttal of the no-significant-difference thesis, Johann Sommerville, 'Ideology, Property and the Constitution', in *Conflict in Early Stuart England* (London, 1990), pp. 47–71. For a recent restatement, Conrad Russell, *The Causes of the English Civil War* (Oxford, 1990), ch. 6.

king's 'power', and Coke rejected 'sovereign power' as 'no parliamentary word'.[2] In the second place, the theory of parliamentary
sovereignty worked out in 1641 and 1642 drew upon the linguistic
and conceptual resources of one of the main varieties of royal
absolutism in the preceding Stuart decades. Parliamentary sovereignty was claimed in the way that Charles's lawyers and lay
theoreticians had made a case for Charles's absolute power – in
respect of the necessary superiority in extreme situations of the
executive over the legislative function.

   In this regard, it must be emphasised that the theory of
parliamentary sovereignty was specifically an English absolutism,
developed in response to the claims of the common law and the
ancient constitution. Like the royal absolutism upon which it drew
(some would say, perversely), parliamentary sovereignty usually
paid deference to law and the constitution. Alternatively, as with
Henry Parker, parliamentary absolutists openly cast off the
shackles of constitutional legality. In both cases, the ancient
constitution and the common law were never far from the thoughts
of royal or parliamentary absolutists.

                                I

'Sovereignty' meant more than one thing in early Stuart England.
Sometimes it was closely tied to the medieval notion of *plenitudo
potestatis*, which had arisen in the contests of imperial and papal
power. At other times it drew mostly upon the concept of sovereignty associated with Jean Bodin. Both of these senses partook
fully of the common stock of European ideas about sovereignty and
absolutism. The distinguishing feature, however, of England's
parliamentary sovereignty is that it drew most of all from a third
approach to sovereignty that unlike the others was rooted in a
formula expressive, of all things, of England's limited monarchy.
While the sources of the different senses were tangled beyond
separation, and the contemporary meanings overlapped and exer-

---

[2] Jean Bodin, *The Six Bookes of a Commonweale*, ed. by Kenneth Douglas McRae (Cambridge,
   Mass., 1962), p. 84; cf. the French text ('la souveraineté est la puissance absolue &
   perpetuelle'), cited Appendix B, p. A75. *Proceedings in Parliament 1628*, 5 vols., ed. Mary
   Frear Keeler, Maija Jansson Cole and William B. Bidwell (New Haven, 1977–83), vol. III,
   pp. 495–6; cf. Robert Mason, vol. III, pp. 527, 530. For a good treatment of these passages,
   J. P. Sommerville, *Politics and Ideology in England 1603–1640* (London, 1986), pp. 168–9.

ted sympathetic influence upon each other, the fact that the three different kinds or aspects of sovereignty could produce antipathetic reactions in a single individual militates against dismissing their independent pressure.

In an adaptation of the medieval *plenitudo potestatis*, sovereignty had been an important component of the political theory of England's withdrawal from Rome.[3] As an autonomous political unit of the highest order – an empire – England owed subjection to no earthly power, and its king possessed supremacy in both church and state. This sense of sovereignty had been strongly shaped by a foreign–domestic polarity. The bishop of Rome was a foreign power and his English clerical supporters foreign agents. The medieval statutes of praemunire reflected this fusion of anticlericalism and xenophobia, which had been an element of royal–clerical conflict at least since the days of Henry II, whose Constitutions of Clarendon had outlawed clerical appeals to foreign powers. The old statutes and chronicles continued to resonate into the sixteenth and seventeenth centuries. From the Act in Restraint of Appeals (1533) to Stephen Gardiner's Henrician *De vera obedientia* and the Elizabethan Protestant state supremacists such as Richard Hooker and Thomas Bilson, royal supremacy was a highly palatable forcemeat of patriotism and the species of political theology usually called the divine right of kings.[4] Henry Parker, the foremost early champion of parliamentary sovereignty and a great debunker of unlimited kingship in other situations, was also capable, in this context, of stating his 'beliefe ... that the Prince is the Head, the Fountaine, the Soule of all power whatsoever, Spirituall, or Temporall'. Princes possessed 'divine graces' higher than 'the sense of Laick or Secular will beare'.[5] For William Prynne, a godly – an imperialist, anti-papal – prince unobjectionably wielded all manner of power;

---

[3] For medieval theories, Michael Wilks, *The Problem of Sovereignty in the Later Middle Ages* (Cambridge, 1963).

[4] Walter Ullmann, 'This Realm of England is an Empire', *Journal of Ecclesiastical History*, 30 (1979), 175–203. G. R. Elton (ed.), *The Tudor Constitution*, 2nd edn (Cambridge, 1982), pp. 341n, 353, and G. R. Elton, *Reform and Reformation* (Cambridge, Mass., 1977), pp. 133–8. Stephen Gardiner, *De vera obedientia* (Roane, 1553; repr. Leeds, 1966); for Gardiner's changing calculus, Rex Pogson, 'Stephen Gardiner and the Problem of Loyalty', in Claire Cross, David Loades and J. J. Scarisbrick (eds.), *Law and Government under the Tudors* (Cambridge, 1988) pp. 67–89. Claire Cross, *The Royal Supremacy in the Elizabethan Church* (London, 1969). Bilson's and Hooker's support for the royal supremacy was firm, but not utterly unconditional.

[5] *A Discourse Concerning Puritans* (1641), pp. 17–18, 35.

but when Prynne's prince lost his imperialist credentials by becoming part of the popish plot rather than its target and antagonist, Prynne turned against royal absolutism.[6] Clericalists were sometimes troubled by the claims of sovereignty; infuriating (though also useful) ambiguity attended the parliamentary or non-parliamentary status of the royal supremacy. These issues notwithstanding, if sovereignty had stopped at the level of asserting the full independence of the English king–church–state, it would never have reached the status of being unparliamentary.

However, Bodin was to make this prospect impossible.[7] Although Bodin's *Six Bookes of a Commonweale* were translated only in 1606, his ideas were current earlier in their French and Latin versions. Bodin's ideas travelled well, being amenable to reduction into easily portable slogans (e.g., that sovereignty cannot be divided). Moreover, the natural-law tradition, an important component of Bodin's own outlook, could readily assimilate many Bodinian notions on its own. While Bodin was not the only source of English absolutism (as Johann Sommerville stresses), the absolutism found in late Elizabethan and early Jacobean clerical circles was comfortable with Bodinian sovereignty.[8]

To Bodin, the 'licentious anarchy' of France's civil wars was 'worse than the harshest tyranny', whose scourge he had not felt.[9] Insofar as civil collapse was the principal terror, sovereignty was power of the kinds and extent necessary to prevent it. While this power could be analysed into its components – legislation (Bodin's central political act), taxation, war and peace, appointment of magistrates, and final legal jurisdiction – no part of sovereignty could be alienated from the rest without destruction of the whole. A sovereign had no 'companion', and the components (or 'marks') of sovereignty could not be divided or shared.[10] Bodinian sovereignty

---

[6] William M. Lamont, *Marginal Prynne 1600–1669* (London, 1963), pp. 108–17. See also William M. Lamont, *Godly Rule* (London, 1969).

[7] J. H. M. Salmon, *The French Religious Wars in English Political Thought* (Oxford, 1959) and 'Bodin and the Monarchomachs', *Renaissance and Revolt* (Cambridge, 1987), pp. 119–36; Julian H. Franklin, *Jean Bodin and the Rise of Absolutist Theory* (Cambridge, 1973) and *John Locke and the Theory of Sovereignty* (New York, 1978). For a strong treatment of these views and others, Quentin Skinner, *The Foundations of Modern Political Thought*, 2 vols. (Cambridge, 1978), vol. II, pp. 284–301.

[8] Sommerville, *Politics and Ideology*, pp. 38, 46.

[9] Bodin, *Six Bookes*, p. A70. Salmon, 'Bodin and the Monarchomachs', p. 135, argues that 'the concept of sovereignty was a *thèse de circonstance*'.

[10] The marks of sovereignty are discussed in Book I, chapter 10; Bodin, *Six Bookes*, p. 155.

looked inward, pointing its accusing finger at would-be sharers of the royal power. It is easy to see how Bodinian sovereignty could be construed as unparliamentary.

A third and distinctively (if not entirely) English source of sovereignty was, paradoxically, a part of England's anti-absolutist tradition. To see how this result came about, it is useful to examine the several counters to assertions of Bodinian-clerical royal sovereignty. One response can be briefly dismissed. Full-blown monarchomach ideas played only an incidental role in Protestant England after the accession of Elizabeth. The trappings of monarchomach thought were often useful, but monarchomachism's decisive contribution of a theory of resistance to tyranny is lacking in the development of English opposition to royal absolutism, or, later, to the first form of the theory of parliamentary sovereignty. This should not be surprising: the question before 1642 was the nature of the law; in 1642 it was who controlled the state, not how to resist it.

Potentially more promising was the claim that England possessed a mixed government on classical lines. Tudor and early Stuart England had been acclimated to the classical ideal of the balanced or mixed state consisting of monarchical, aristocratic, and democratic elements. Loosely construed, mixed government was consonant with the common English assumption that effective governance required the co-operation and, in legislation and taxation, the consent of landed society. However, the details of English governance made classical theory harder to apply the more closely one examined English institutions. Amongst other obstacles were the irreducible place of the clergy in the polity (their standing as an 'estate'), the poor correspondence of the lower house of parliament's members to the classical image of 'democracy', and the apparent disrespect to the king in considering him on a par with his houses of parliament. These technical limitations were not fatal, but there was little motive to overcome them after English mixed government became tainted (perhaps unfairly) with Presbyterian extremism and traces of monarchomach sensibility.[11] Ironically, once freed of its earlier associations, mixed government became

---

[11] Michael Mendle, *Dangerous Positions* (University, Ala., 1985), pp. 38–97. For a different view, Corinne Comstock Weston, *English Constitutional Theory and the House of Lords 1556–1832* (London, 1965), pp. 9–43.

serviceable as a constitutionalist critique of parliamentary absolutism.

Finally, Bodinian sovereignty confronted a related but distinct sense that English monarchy was limited by human law, a doctrine rooted in Bracton and in England's medieval past, and in full flower in the seventeenth century.[12] Bridging the eras was Sir John Fortescue's enormously influential formulation: England was a *dominium politicum et regale*, a monarchy whose power ran in two channels.[13] While the formula had strong links to continental juristic and scholastic thought, Fortescue used the phrase in an assertively nativist way, to distinguish England's system from France's, and the common from the civil law.[14] France was a *dominium tantum regale*, a 'merely regal' – hence, an absolute – monarchy. The king alone could make law and tax his subjects, in accordance with the Roman-law view that *quod principi placuit legis habet vigorem*.[15] In England these powers, which the king exercised in parliament, and the activity of the king's 'ordinary' (viz., professional, common law) judges were 'political', subject to the law.

Equally, the king also ruled 'regally' or 'royally', free of external control. The eponymous mission of *De laudibus legum Anglie* dictated that Fortescue extol the 'political' (i.e., legal) controls on the king more than he indicate their limits; Fortescue left the regal category more or less to define itself as the residuum after the political side was subtracted. However, he recognised that the king had to protect the realm from invasion and domestic rapine or 'be

[12] Bracton's judgement (Bracton, *On the Laws and Customs of England*, translated and ed. Samuel E. Thorne (Cambridge, Mass., 1968), 2 vols., vol. II, pp. 33) that the king had no peer among men but was 'under the law, because the law makes the king', became a seventeenth-century commonplace. For Bracton's seventeenth-century reputation, D. E. C. Yale, '"Of No Mean Authority": Some Later Uses of Bracton', in Morris S. Arnold (ed.), *On the Laws and Customs of England: Essays in Honor of Samuel E. Thorne* (Chapel Hill, 1981), pp. 383–96. From Bracton's day forward, the approach described here as distinctively English drew in various ways upon Roman law and scholastic theory, but it did so with a high degree of selectivity, and often with a sense of national distinctiveness.
[13] One of J. G. A. Pocock's most important retrospective emphases in the reissue of *The Ancient Constitution and the Feudal Law* (Cambridge, 1987) is the centrality now afforded to the Fortescuean perspective; see Part II, chs. 1 and 2.
[14] See Felix Gilbert, 'Fortescue's "Dominium Regale et Politicum",' *Medievalia et Humanistica*, fasc. 2 (1944), pp. 88–97, and Francis Oakley, 'Jacobean Political Theology: The Absolute and Ordinary Powers of the King', *Journal of the History of Ideas*, 29 (1968), 323–46.
[15] *De laudibus legum Anglie*, ed. and translated by S. B. Chrimes (Cambridge, 1939), pp. 25, 79, 81–9.

adjudged impotent'.[16] Others filled the gap, perhaps bringing to the regal category more than Fortescue had intended.[17] By the usual later reckoning, amongst other things a king could 'regally' issue proclamations, make war and peace, appoint officers, coin money and regulate trade. While in principle such powers could be denominated with some precision, many thought the king possessed an inalienable responsibility to preserve the kingdom; with the magnitude of the responsibility went, necessarily, an equivalence of means.[18] To preserve the independence of the *dominium regale* the 'statesmen' of 1628 tried to leave an explicit role for the king's 'sovereign' power, which the law supremacist Alford rejected precisely because it allowed for 'a regal as well as a legal power'.[19]

In the assertively nationalistic legal and political culture of the early seventeenth century, Fortescue's *dominium politicum et regale* (or what it had come to mean) had great appeal. It saved the phenomena: the kingdom's institutional practice and working assumptions had bowed neither to Bodinian analytical scorn nor to common-law chauvinism. It also admirably served prejudice, brokering a place for the 'good' sovereignty that fought enemies abroad and conspirators at home and provided for the kingdom's occasions as they emerged, without the 'bad' sovereignty of the *rex asinorum*. However happy the result, this put the entire weight of Fortescue's formula upon the *et*. Where did proclamation (more generally, conciliar competence) end, and legislation begin? While it was generally accepted that regulation of trade, particularly foreign trade, was within the *dominium regale*, when did its revenue-producing potential become covert, illegal taxation? Did national security, or the mere alleging of national security, override otherwise controlling legal principles within the *dominium politicum*? On the other side, could the *dominium regale* function if hamstrung by legal prigs and self-interested manipulators of a notoriously malleable legal system? At a higher level of abstraction, the question was the relation of the law to the two kinds of rule. Law was the peculiar responsibility of the *dominium politicum*; but did law stop there? Were there simply two zones, one legal and the other extralegal? Or did

---

[16] *De laudibus*, p. 89.
[17] Cf. Oakley, 'Jacobean Political Theology', p. 345.
[18] Cf. Corinne Comstock Weston and Janelle Renfrow Greenberg, *Subjects and Sovereigns: The Grand Controversy over Legal Sovereignty in Stuart England* (Cambridge, 1981), pp. 8–34.
[19] *Proceedings in Parliament 1628*, vol. III, p. 494.

the law overarch the whole structure, delineating zones of its own
activity and inactivity, much as the divine will could either act or
not act, and in the latter case exercise a permissive rather than a
direct providence? If so, was that omnicompetent law the common
law or something else, presumably greater?

The conundrums of the Fortescuean *et* gave rise to a distinctive
political theology. Fortescuean binary kingship, when linked to the
notion of a law embracing both kinds of kingship, resembled
notions developed in orthodox trinitarian theology and ecclesiology.[20] The third person of the Trinity had been thought not only
to have inspired the written testaments, but also to have guided the
church through time, including its apprehension of the sacred
mysteries, thus becoming a continuing source of truth. In the
political parallel – Fortescue himself described the body politic as a
'corpus misticum' – the law (particularly a high-blown notion of
the common law) served the same role, revealing the unity of
otherwise potentially competitive claims of the two 'persons' of
kingship.[21] Like the Holy Spirit's authoritative tradition, the
common law was a wisdom both aboriginal and accumulative,
existing from time out of mind but constantly restated or revealed
in time. Like the 'artificial reason' of the common law, the *lex non
scripta* of the Holy Spirit went beyond any single figure (e.g., a
church father), although individuals, like common-law judges,
contributed to its declaration.[22] The church's standard for inspired
tradition was doctrine accepted *semper, ubique* and *ab omnibus*;[23] Sir
John Davies thought the common law a *jus non scriptum* written 'only
in the heart of man' but also 'connatural to the nation'. Continuous
use was probation of its 'reason and convenience'.[24]

Like some expositions of the great mystery of Christian faith,

[20] Oakley, 'Jacobean Political Theology', p. 332, suggested that the distinction between the
absolute and ordinary powers of the king is rooted in a similar distinction canonists made
of the powers of God.

[21] *De laudibus*, p. 30.

[22] Considering the corporate nature of the king's judgements (no king gives judgements 'by
his own lips, yet all the judgements of the realm are his, though given by others'),
Fortescue was prompted to consider them the 'judgements of God'. *De laudibus*, pp. 23, 25.

[23] Jaroslav Pelikan, *The Emergence of the Catholic Tradition (100–600)*, vol. 1 of *The Christian
Tradition* (Chicago, 1971), pp. 333–9.

[24] Sir John Davies, *Primer Report*, in David Wootton (ed.), *Divine Right and Democracy*
(Harmondsworth, 1986), pp. 131–3. Thomas Hedley developed the notion of time as the
trier of custom; Elizabeth Read Foster, *Proceedings in Parliament 1610*, 2 vols. (New Haven,
1966), vol. II, p. 175.

Fortescuean kingship sometimes seemed to be a cat chasing its own tail. Though written by a civilian, Sir Thomas Smith's enormously popular *De republica Anglorum* is a case in point. As Smith had it, the king-in-parliament and the king alone were both absolute, and the task of the law was somehow to sort all this out. Yet the law gave the king (in his single capacity) a dispensing power – that is, a power temporarily to void its own effect.[25] Thomas Hedley, in 1610, arrived at what Professor Pocock has dubbed a 'doctrine of consubstantiality', in which parliament, which was supreme by the common law, could not annihilate the source of its own supremacy.[26]

For these delicacies Bodinian theory had no use. Like his religion, Bodin's political theology was unitarian.[27] The phenomena-saving subtleties of Fortescuean thought were gibberish, and mixed government (a mixture of sovereign powers) was treason. While Bodin sternly admonished kings to adhere to law, he steadfastly rejected notions of enforceable human limitation upon the sovereign; the prince would answer for his failings, but in no earthly tribunal. In politics (though of course not in theology), Bodin's unitarian views generally matched those of the absolutist university and court clerics. Unlike Bodin, who regarded legislation as the central act of sovereignty, English clerical absolutists may have emphasised (or so their opponents thought) the king's unfettered right to tax his subjects, an English absolutist preoccupation for which Bodin had considerable distaste.[28] Yet both agreed on the unity of royal power and the divine right of sovereigns, a right that ultimately came, as Bodin, James I and court clerics variously put it, from the earthly sovereign being God's 'liuing & breathing image'.[29]

[25] For this view of Smith, see my *Dangerous Positions*, pp. 51–6.
[26] *The Ancient Constitution and the Feudal Law*, p. 271; in Pocock's usage law and parliament are, respectively, Father and Son. Hedley in *Proceedings in Parliament 1610*, vol. II, pp. 173–4.
[27] For Bodin's religious views, Paul Lawrence Rose, *Bodin and the Great God of Nature* (Geneva, 1980), and J. Samuel Preus, *Explaining Religion* (New Haven, 1987), pp. 3–20.
[28] For Bodin, the property rights of subjects were so serious that they led Bodin very nearly to contradiction. For Bodin's complex and difficult attitudes toward taxation, Franklin, *Jean Bodin*, pp. 86–92; see Bodin, *Six Bookes*, pp. A71, 108–11. While in no exact sense can the apologists of Stuart absolutism be described as Socinian in theology, the attempt was made to tar them with that brush: see Francis Cheynell, *The Rise, Growth, and Danger of Socinianisme* (London, 1643).
[29] Bodin, *Six Bookes*, p. 109. Cf. *The Political Works of James I*, ed. Charles Howard McIlwain (Cambridge, Mass., 1918), p. 307 (Speech of 21 March 1610); cf. pp. 4 (Sonnet to *Basilikon Doron*), 53–5 (*Trew Law*).

A gulf of conception and an ocean of temperament separate the Fortescuean outlook from Bodinian-clerical absolutism. Had it been the only alternative to limited monarchy, Bodinian absolutism would not have posed a serious threat to the way the English viewed their institutions. However, in early Stuart England a different species of absolutism, working within the Fortescuean tradition, posed a much more formidable challenge. Fortescuean absolutism took the binary character of the English monarchy as given, showed a proper respect for the municipal law of the kingdom, and conducted its argument in terms of the claims of both sides of the Fortescuean *et*. England could take great pride in its government of laws. But there were times, so it was argued, when the *dominium politicum* had to yield to the *dominium regale* – instances of general emergency and 'reason of state', and of the precedence of the general welfare over private right. When these cases 'emerged' – this was a casuistical sort of absolutism of the greater good, or lesser evil – the relevant action fell under the unimpeded 'royal' or 'absolute' side rather than the political, 'legal' or 'ordinary' side. When conflicts between the two sides arose, the absolutists argued that the king alone (or the *dominium regale*) had ultimate control; the point of having a king was to have an actor for these situations. Of course, invocation of *arcana imperii* and reason of state was in no sense peculiarly English, and the complex of ideas about the supremacy of the common good was deeply graven in the European natural-law and humanist traditions.[30] However, not only the idiom but the institutional and functional context of Fortescuean absolutism had strongly English resonances. If the political side had to do with judgement, legislation and taxation, with corresponding institutional loci in the courts and parliament, the regal side dealt with 'government' (*gubernaculum*), policy and equity, belonging in theory to the king alone, and in practice and common assumption to the king in conjunction with his personally selected advisers.

Fortescuean absolutism offered lawyers and counsellors an opportunity to pay homage to the law while finding reason to make an exception to it. In Bate's Case in 1606, Chief Baron Fleming happily conceded that interference with the subject's private right was matter for the king's 'ordinary power', expressed through

---

[30] Skinner, *Foundations*, vol. I, pp. 58–65, 248–54; vol. II. pp. 171–3.

courts of common law and through parliament; direct taxes upon individuals or their goods could only proceed 'by parliament'. However, Fleming insisted, the imposition upon currants fell upon the entry of currants into the kingdom, not upon Bate or his goods. That pertained to the king's 'absolute' power or 'government', which was intended for the common good. When the king invoked that power, the dispute was effectively settled.[31]

The same approach shaped both the Five Knights' Case and the parliamentary argument it engendered in 1628. Paul Christianson has shown Fortescue's *dominium politicum et regale* was a leitmotif in the case, and the prosecution's modish use of reason of state was an 'updated' version of the powers of the king under the *dominium regale*.[32] The King's Bench's response to the prisoners' writs of habeas corpus was lukewarm and deliberately not precedential, keeping the prisoners in custody but giving their attorneys room for further manoeuvre. Later, the Attorney-General, Sir Robert Heath, attempted to twist the court's half-hearted action into a far-reaching precedent. In the parliament of 1628, when Heath's machination was exposed, both houses of parliament reacted with alarm. The issue became whether the king possessed on his regal side a right in any circumstance to imprison without following the due course of the common law.[33] Like the imprisonment of the Five Knights, the levying of ship money involved a pretence of national security; the original writs spoke of danger, and Charles canvassed the judges on their view of an extraparliamentary charge levied when the 'whole kingdom is in danger'. Like Bate's Case, the ship-money levy was manifestly a revenue-raiser. However, propo-

---

[31] *State Trials*, vol II, cols. 388–91. The Exchequer court, Fleming (col. 389) insisted, was merely 'guided' rather than 'direct[ed]' by common law, and followed its own precedents and even 'pollitick reasons' in preference to common law, when matters so dictated; his colleague Clark concurred, even calling into question the value of statutes as directing precedents (col. 382). This suggests a view of the overarching law broader than the common law alone, an issue that returned with some vengeance in 1628 and 1642. For the circumstances of the case, and the obvious deviation of the legal logic and the practical situation, Pauline Croft, 'Fresh Light on Bate's Case', *Historical Journal*, 30 (1987), 523–39.

[32] Paul Christianson, 'John Selden, the Five Knights' Case, and Discretionary Imprisonment in Early Stuart England', *Criminal Justice History*, 6 (1985), 66, 72.

[33] See John Guy's superb treatment, 'The Origins of the Petition of Right Reconsidered', *Historical Journal*, 25(1982), 289–312. For treatment of the debates of 1628, see ibid., pp. 298–311; Christianson, 'John Selden, the Five Knights' Case, and Discretionary Imprisonment in Early Stuart England', pp. 72–82; and Pocock, *Ancient Constitution*, pp. 289–305 *passim*.

nents argued that ship money was not a tax (which was parliamentary), but a response by the *dominium regale* to a public emergency, akin to creating a firebreak by pulling down structures adjacent to the one on fire. While one of the king's attorneys, Sir John Bankes (who bluntly located all sovereignty within the *dominium regale*) and one of the judges, Crawley (who believed that kings could legislate without parliament), pushed for a loosely Bodinian notion of royal sovereignty, the preponderance of royalist opinion was that the king could levy ship money under the aegis of the *dominium regale* though not under the *dominium politicum*. Necessity, the *arcana imperii* and the general welfare legitimated what would otherwise have been illegal.[34]

II

Before the Long Parliament found its sea legs in the storms of 1640 to 1642, objectors to this subtle, English absolutism could make several replies. The most direct route was that taken in 1610 by James Whitelocke, who denied that the *dominium regale* included absolute power. That, including the 'power of erection of arbitrary government', belonged only to the king-in-parliament.[35] As it turned out, the most direct route was the one least travelled. For partisans of the law, like Hedley, Whitelock's parliamentary solution was cold comfort; for Bodinians, Whitelock's appropriation of their terminology was the usual divided-sovereignty nonsense; for devotees of the facts, it was simply wrong.

Opponents could also point to the abuse of the common good or national security to advance the king's private interest, or to avoid dealing with the *dominium politicum*. In the courts, this argument was a non-starter, since the judges would not consider it. In the political arena, it had great value, since it stated the facts, on the one hand, thought at great prejudice to the king or his ministers, on the other. A third, predictable approach was to take cover under a contrary absolutism of the law; like the ancient trinitarian heterodoxies, one imbalance tended to generate a compensatory opposite. Thus in the matter of impositions, opponents denied a right to impose 'by

---

[34] For a fuller treatment of argument in the case, Michael Mendle, 'The Ship Money Case, *The Case of Shipmony*, and the Development of Henry Parker's Parliamentary Absolutism', *Historical Journal*, 32 (1989), 516–20.

[35] *State Trials*, vol. II, cols. 482–3.

any absolute authority of the King's Majesty without assent of parliament'. The right of property was 'original', they contended, and not taxable except by the parliament's consent.[36] These claims continued, and in a parallel development in 1628 opponents of discretionary imprisonment by king and council wished it to be declared illegal, without exception or reservation. The Commons so voted on 3 April, and so they steadfastly held through repeated attempts by the king's partisans or more circumspect lords to allow for a saving clause in the Petition of Right for the king's sovereignty. *Lex terrae*, specifically defined as the 'due process of law' and the common law, controlled every possible case of imprisonment or detention.[37] The insistence of Coke, Selden and others that they stood for both liberty and prerogative sounds like the prompting of a disturbed Fortescuean conscience. More accurate, perhaps, was the arch-villain Heath's view that the Commons made 'their proposition so unlimited and so large' that it was incompatible with monarchy in the Fortescuean mode.[38]

The anger and urgency of 1628 were not indefinitely sustainable. In the ship-money case, even Hampden's partisans paid obeisance to the need in emergencies to go beyond the common law's normal processes. Instead, opponents of ship money denied that an emergency on the scale necessary to suspend positive law existed. This may testify to the drift of opinion during Charles's personal rule; however, in the new world of 1640, the old hostility to the assertion of *dominium regale* over the *dominium politicum* resurfaced. Oliver St John, notably, adjusted his position. As Hampden's counsel, he made grudging room for necessity; in parliament he was much more hostile.[39]

However, as a staple of *parliamentary* thought this approach had more of a past than a future. Tentatively in the summer of 1641,

---

[36] The first phrase is from the unsuccessful bill against impositions of 1610; the second from the petition of temporal grievances of 7 July 1610. See *Proceedings in Parliament 1610*, vol. II, pp. 266–7, 411. The point is repeatedly made in several key speeches: vol. II, pp. 152 (Fuller); 185 (Hedley); 223, 237 (Whitelocke).

[37] Heath was correct (*Proceedings in Parliament 1628*, vol. V, p. 292) that 'How this *lex terrae* [in Magna Charta, c. 29] is to be expounded, is the main apple of contention.' He insisted that the *lex terrae* was broader than the common law; Sergeant Ashley spoke (to his peril) of a 'law of state' separate from the common law and superior to it in respect of 'natural equity'. By contrast, Littleton specifically argued that the common law was the law of the land. *Proceedings in Parliament 1628*, vol. V, pp. 281, 282, 287, 292, 293.

[38] *Proceedings in Parliament 1628*, vol. V, p. 281.

[39] Michael Mendle, 'The Ship Money Case', pp. 518–21.

and more openly in early 1642, the houses of parliament embarked on a different approach to the meaning of the Fortescuean *et*: parliamentary absolutism. Parliament had been viewed as the embodiment of the *dominium politicum* both as legislature and court. Now the houses claimed as well to be on the other side of the conjunction, as the ultimate custodian of the powers traditionally inherent in the *dominium regale*. In the full, final version, in the name of the powers historically associated with the *dominium regale*, parliament had the capacity to do what partisans of the *dominium politicum* had denied to the *dominium regale* – bypass the law of the land. This, of course, could be viewed as an assertion of unitary absolutism in the natural-law tradition. Some elements of Henry Parker's thought, for example, can certainly be seen in this light, and are reminiscent of Johannes Althusius's populist reversal of Bodinian absolutism.[40] But that is not how the problem was generally conceived, as frustrated seekers of Bodinian sovereignty in the parliamentary position have repeatedly noted. The idiom of the debate lies elsewhere, in an adaptation of the royal version of Fortescuean absolutism.

Parliamentary absolutism, like its Fortescuean royal predecessor, was a species of casuistry; to understand it is necessarily to be submerged into the complexes of events – the cases – of its emergence. Nevertheless, what emerged in 1642 as parliamentary absolutism is to be found in a larval state in the claim, advanced particularly in the House of Commons, that parliament was the king's 'great council'.[41] While the mere words meant little (and were commended by their seeming banality) the claim to be the great council was closely linked to the persistent Tudor and Stuart skirmishing over liberty of speech in parliament. Speech in the Lower House fell foul of the monarch when it moved without royal authorisation into the *dominium regale* – matters, for example, of war and peace, and of the domestic affairs or marital arrangements of the royal family. When threatened, members jealous of their privilege invoked their status as members of the great council (rather than the 'high court of parliament', useful for judicial

---

[40] Otto von Gierke, *The Development of Political Theory*, trans. by Bernard Freyd (New York, 1939; reprinted New York, 1966).

[41] This section draws upon my article, 'The Great Council of Parliament and the First Ordinances: The Constitutional Theory of the Civil War', *Journal of British Studies*, 31 (1992), 133–62.

matters, or the 'representative body of the kingdom', for matters of
supply and legislation). A hostile royalist attacked this presumption of men to be 'counsellors in all things', and in 1621 James
thought the Commons sought to use freedom of speech to control
the *dominium regale*.[42] The Commons' stock reply to these charges
was to distinguish between an appropriate role (sanctioned by the
writs of summons) of offering advice on matters within the *dominium
regale*, and an inappropriate direct assumption of executive power,
or, as it was termed, 'determination'.[43] James and Charles never
entirely conceded the distinction. Nevertheless, the 'great council'
became an established figure in political rhetoric, and some
ground was conceded with respect to unrestricted parliamentary
discussion.

In 1641 the situation changed decisively. By the summer of 1641,
the houses of parliament began to act openly as, indeed, they had
been acting (if not covertly then unassertively) since November
1640: separately and conjointly the houses began to function much
as had the privy council and other executive organs of the king,
including the recently abolished Star Chamber and High Commission. Meanwhile the council, hobbled by management difficulties
and further crippled by bridge appointments and fear of action,
began to wither away.[44] At this time the houses of parliament
began first to exercise independently of the king the executive role
hitherto assumed to be the duty of king and council – not only to
advise but also, in some very specific circumstances, to determine.

The immediate crisis was provoked by the king's imminent
departure for Scotland in the summer of 1641. Fears of a new
military coup (possibly involving the Covenanting army still sitting
in the north of England) generated a sense of genuine emergency.
Emergency was also opportunity, in particular to press the
executive-grabbing elements of a programme Pym had recently
outlined in the Ten Propositions. The new and volatile element in
the mixture was the king's expected journey. Who was to assume

[42] 'A True presentation of fore-past parliaments to the view of present times and of
posteritie', Folger Shakespeare Library MS. v. b. 189, p. 14. J. R. Tanner (ed.),
Constitutional Documents of the Reign of James I A.D. 1603–1625 (Cambridge, 1960), pp. 282–5.
See also Conrad Russell, *Parliaments and English Politics 1621–1629* (Oxford, 1979), pp.
92–3, 138–42.
[43] See, e.g., Tanner, *Constitutional Documents*, pp. 284, 289.
[44] For the council's earlier difficulties, Conrad Russell, *The Causes of the English Civil War*
(Oxford, 1990), pp. 189–90, 194–5.

the functions of the king in his absence? The royal assent to legislation could be given by a *custos regni*. However, the debates over the custos reveal that an authority was sought for action more suitable than legislation for 'emergent Occasions for the Safety of the Kingdom'.[45] Shortly afterwards the king made his way to Edinburgh, and the two houses, acting as the supreme council of the king, adopted in his absence the first 'ordinances' of the Long Parliament.

From the start parliamentary ordinances received two different interpretations. One view, now conventional but in its time neither the *maior* or *sanior* opinion, held that an ordinance was an action of the two houses alone rather than the king and the houses. This opinion probably took colour from one of Coke's false steps, his belief that an act of parliament differed from an 'ordinance of parliament' by having the assent of king, Lords, and Commons, rather than 'one or two of them'.[46] The problem here, noticed in our time by Professor Foster and in the seventeenth century by Sir Matthew Hale, was that Coke's ordinance in parliament was fanciful.[47] Had Coke's view been prevalent, even widespread, the king would never have passed by the first ordinances in silence. The other view was that an ordinance was an exercise of power by the *dominium regale*, and that, as the great council, the two houses were part of it. One could take the antiquarian route and seek antecedents of the 1641 ordinances in the medieval past, as did D'Ewes, who was probably taken in by Coke's misapprehension. However, the operative model was close to hand. Ordinances were still being made throughout the sixteenth and seventeenth centuries – made, that is, by the king in council. What had changed was the name: the royal ordinance in its most common form was the proclamation.[48] In summer 1641, the houses, acting as the great

[45] BL MS. Harl. 479, ff. 140b, 141a (9 August); *Lords Journal*, 4.356 (10 August) (hereafter *LJ*).
[46] *The Fourth Part of the Institutes* (London, 1804), pp. 24–5.
[47] Elizabeth Read Foster, 'The House of Lords and Ordinances, 1641–49', *American Journal of Legal History*, 21 (1977), 158; D. E. C. Yale (ed.), *Sir Matthew Hale's The Prerogatives of the King* (London, 1976), p. 175.
[48] On this crucial point, see James F. Larkin (ed.), *Stuart Royal Proclamations*, (vol. II: *Royal Proclamations of King Charles I 1625–1646* (Oxford, 1983), p.v; W. S. Holdsworth, *A History of English Law* (Boston, 1934), vol. II, p. 99, n.7; F. W. Maitland, *The Constitutional History of England* (Cambridge, 1920), p. 256, where proclamations, though considered legislation, are also a manifestation of a 'certain ordaining power'. My argument on this point has been anticipated by Sheila Lambert, 'The Opening of the Long Parliament,' *Historical Journal*, 27 (1984), 283.

council, assumed the governing (not legislative) role of the privy council in the absence of the king.[49]

According to prevailing theory, the king's absence from the country created a temporary 'defect' in the king's capacity, similar to the defects of illness or infancy, and in this case (an emergency by definition) the king's councils were to function as if the king had been in their midst.[50] Without special authorisation, the privy council met and transacted minor business during the king's absence; the great council of parliament did the like for more important matters. The first ordinance (perhaps reflecting a prior phase of planning for a more extensive 'commission' to treat directly with the Scots in Edinburgh) arranged for sending 'committees' of the houses to the king then in Scotland.[51] Another established a day of thanksgiving for the peace lately concluded between the kingdoms of England and France; its printed version, by the king's printer, closely mimicked a royal proclamation in appearance and substance, and was distributed to the sheriffs by messengers who normally performed that service for royal proclamations.[52] A third made an administrative adjustment to a tax-payment procedure.[53] Of the two most aggressive of the 1641 ordinances, one sought to disarm recusants and their families, the other attempted to prevent English soldiers from leaving the kingdom (and entering into Spanish pay). Both touched matters customarily regulated by proclamation.[54]

Only two ordinances received internal critique in parliament. The first raised the term 'ordinance' out of the dust, but did little to clarify it. The ambiguities were more usefully explored in the debates concerning the ordinance to disarm recusants. Proponents claimed that the ordinance merely executed existing law – the stock role of a proclamation. But Selden and D'Ewes thought the broad seizure provisions of the ordinance strayed into questions of life and property, matters for the *dominium politicum* either in the courts of

---

[49] It is significant that all four proclamations issued from June to August 1641 were by the advice of parliament (Larkin nos. 319–22).

[50] For the notion of defects, *Sir Matthew Hale's The Prerogatives of the King*, pp. 93, 106–32.

[51] *LJ* 4:372. The development of the ordinance can be traced in BL MS. Harl. 164, ff. 16b, 32b, 47a,b; Harl. 479, ff. 138a, 140b, 141a, 158b, 159, 160, 161a.

[52] *LJ* 4:383. BL 669 f. 3 (12); cf. 669 f. 3. (8). BL Harl. Ms. 164, f. 81b. Larkin (ed.), *Stuart Royal Proclamations Volume II*, nos. 39, 47, 89, 107, 329, 448, 509.

[53] *LJ* 4:375.

[54] *LJ* 4:385, 394. Larkin (ed.), *Stuart Royal Proclamations, Volume II*, nos. 62, 182.

common law or in the threefold assent of an act of parliament.[55] No one, however, argued that the great council had no business with executive matters, or that it could not act in the absence of the king; even the king, who was informed by Nicholas of the houses' activities, did not lift an eyebrow.[56]

Thus the houses moved from advice to determination, and from a secondary to a primary role as the king's council. If it is astonishing that so much was assumed on the one side and conceded on the other, to an equal extent it is unsurprising that in the next confrontation the king's apologists tried to recover lost ground. The occasion was provided by the manoeuvres from January to March 1642 that resulted in the militia ordinance, which from the first was promoted as an executive response to an emergency. Significantly, bicamerality was not a feature of the first versions of the ordinance; the early texts call for the king's assent.[57] It is true that some radicals had already come to bicameral conclusions, and that the king's denial of the threefold ordinance and an earlier 'petition' to the same effect usefully laid a paper trail for the leap into a bicameral ordinance.[58] The point remains, however, that the militia ordinance was seen not as a legislative act but as an executive action to save the kingdom. To a Bodinian, the houses' failure to take forthright legislative action marks their timidity or conservatism. From a Fortescuean vantage point, by overriding but not changing the law of the land the houses claimed precisely the sort of right that had historically been identified with the king alone, and with the practical absolutism of the early Stuarts.

That is how the king's spokesmen saw the houses' appeal that the king join with them in the emergency reordering of the militia. Already cloaking his cause in the 'rule of law'[59] in a message of 28 February, Charles refused his assent to the militia ordinance,

[55] BL Harl. 164, f. 70a.
[56] John Evelyn, *Diary and Correspondence*, ed. William Bray, 4 vols. (London, 1872), vol. IV, pp. 60, 64.
[57] *Commons Journal* 2:406 (hereafter *CJ*); *The Private Journals of the Long Parliament, 3 January to 5 March 1642* (hereafter *Private Journals I*), ed. Willson H. Coates, Anne Steele Young, and Vernon F. Snow, pp. 551–2.
[58] In the August 1641 debates on ordinances, Henry Marten argued that an ordinance had 'force and power' equal to an act of parliament, perhaps with bicamerality in mind; BL MS. Harl. 164, ff. 70a, 78b–79a. For 1642, *Private Journals I*, pp. 229, 237, 287, 298, 302, 309–15, 318–22.
[59] See Russell, *The Causes of the English Civil War*, ch. 6.

distinguishing the 'arbitrary' method of executive action (even if he were party to it) from an 'Act of Parliament'.[60] The refusal provoked the unveiling of the bicameral ordinance. The houses reasserted the emergency to 'the State' posed by its 'Enemies', the evil counsellors who wrote in the king's name, and by the king's departure into 'remote Parts' far from parliament. On 5 March the houses at last adopted the bicameral version of the ordinance.

III

These salvoes began the war of words: the printed onslaughts of charge and countercharge, attack and indignation, and, unmistakably, statements of two rival theories of the constitution. Parliament's own justifications came embarrassingly out of the old royalist book. The king's refusal to accept the militia ordinance created an even more 'urgent and inevitable Necessity' than that existing before. Such necessity called for obedience by a law more 'fundamental' than the recognised law of the land.[61] Later, as the houses discovered they were not bound by judicial precedents, they also discovered that they conjointly constituted the supreme judicature.[62] This completed the circle; taken together the two propositions amounted to a parliamentary claim to be its own inspiration. It was true that without the king the houses could not legislate. It was also true that they did not have to. They had mastered the art of absolutism through the *dominium regale*, including the ability to determine when the common law and due process obtained and when they did not. That was why the houses stood by their insistence that the militia ordinance was in no proper sense a law, but an action of the 'highest Councell' (and approved by the self-same body as 'the supream court') in the face of the king's 'dangerous absenting' himself from it.[63] And that is also why the houses offered the same logic for the violation of individual property rights as had the promoters and justifiers of ship money:

[60] *CJ* 2:459–60; Edward Husbands (comp.), *An Exact Collection*, (London, 1643) p. 91. This point closely mimicked debates within the house and probably reflected Hyde's judgment of the most effective form of resistance.

[61] The fundamental law claim was resisted by fainter hearts. *CJ* 2:479, *LJ* 4:646; *The Private Journals of the Long Parliament, 7 March to 1 June 1642*, ed. Vernon F. Snow and Anne Steele Young (hereafter *Private Journals II*) (New Haven, 1987), pp. 41–4.

[62] *CJ* 2:481, 486–7; *LJ* 4:650; *Private Journals II*, pp. 48, 55–6, 60; *An Exact Collection*, p. 114.

[63] *An Exact Collection*, pp. 171, 196–7, 207, 265.

to save the kingdom from 'hazard or danger' parliament could 'dispose of any thing' of king or subject.[64] The law of self-preservation had become the highest law, even the ancient constitution (the 'most ancient Law of this Kingdome').[65]

Royalists knew how to respond, although Falkland and Hyde were silently embarrassed by their share in the making of the August and September ordinances. Now, though, as the parliamentary leviathan rose from the deep, their pens stabbed at the absolutist monster they had earlier helped fashion. The houses' claim to supreme judicature amounted to a bicameral suspending power. With other elements of executive supremacy, it led to 'an Arbitrary way of Government' and the abandonment of Magna Charta.[66] The houses had also destroyed the appropriate relation of king to parliament, a relation that was seen in surprisingly reactionary terms. Fond remembrance of days before the non-dissolution act of 1641 remodelled the constitution mingled with born-again assertions of the old distinction between legitimate advice and unwarranted 'absolute determination'.[67] In this respect the famed, flawed *Answer to the XIX Propositions* joined other royal declarations in claiming the ancient constitution as the royalists' sworn cause. Fusing the ancient constitution and the language of classical mixed government, the *Answer* argued that the ancient balance of one, few and many had been destroyed by the recent high-handedness of the third 'estate'. Although each 'estate' had a share in legislation, the *Answer* emphasised that each 'estate' also had functions specific to it and no other. To the king belonged the 'government' (in the old medieval sense of *gubernaculum*) and the power of appointment of officers for law, state and war. Conversely, the Commons, in no uncertain terms, had no 'share in the government, or the choosing of them that should govern'.[68]

Shortly after the *Answer* appeared, the war of words spread from the defined battleground of official statements to the street warfare of often-anonymous pamphlets. A critical step came with the emergence of the Observator, Henry Parker, whose official role as

[64] Ibid., p. 267.

[65] Ibid., p. 197, cf. p. 207.

[66] Ibid., pp. 126, 250–1.

[67] Ibid., pp. 110, 146; *LJ* 4:640–1. One royalist declaration even attempted to justify Queen Elizabeth's muzzling of Peter Wentworth (*An Exact Collection*, p. 287).

[68] *His Majesties Answer to the XIX Propositions of both Houses of Parliament* (1642), pp. 18–20. For a detailed discussion of the *Answer*, see Mendle, *Dangerous Positions*, pp. 5–20.

secretary to the Committee of Safety was not linked publicly to his authorship of *Observations upon Some of His Majesties Late Answers and Expresses*. Trying to limit the damage caused by recent royalist attacks, especially the king's reply to the declaration of both houses of 26 May, Parker responded head on, proudly pleading guilty to most of the major charges. The king had charged that the houses claimed an 'absolute' power of 'declaring law'. Parker replied that the power had to reside somewhere, and 'no where . . . more safely then in Parliament'. To the charge that the houses were not bound to precedents, Parker replied that there was no greater 'obligation' than a parliament's 'Justice and Honour', *mutatis mutandis* a formula infuriatingly familiar to common-law critics of royal absolutism. When confronted by the houses' claim to be judges of necessity without the king and thereby to 'dispose' of all things, Parker replied that this power devolved upon the houses when the king 'deserted' the 'whole body of the State'. To the king's charge that houses claimed 'Soveraign power' unfettered by the king's negative voice, Parker responded that the 'power is not claimed as ordinary; nor to any purpose, but to save the kingdom from Ruine'.[69]

Parker was himself a 'counsellor', who had once relished the 'primacy of order' accorded to the first person in the Trinity, identifying the Father with power, and the Son and Spirit with wisdom and goodness. Perhaps personal proclivity led him to exalt the executive role of parliament, to see parliament's role as great council as the 'maine question', and the king's obligation to recognise that parliament supplied the remedy to 'all defects' inherent in monarchy as the principal corollary.[70] Whatever their motives, others took similar roads. In an early example of the dilemma of divided allegiance, the earl of Warwick explained that he obeyed parliament rather than the king because 'they are the

---

[69] *An Exact Collection*, pp. 297–8; *Observations upon Some of His Majesties Late Answers and Expresses* (1642), pp. 45–6. *Observations* is reprinted in William Haller (ed.), *Tracts on Liberty in the Puritan Revolution, 1637–42*, 3 vols. (New York, 1934), vol. II, pp. 167–213. For Parker's earlier respectful treatment of absolutist language, Mendle, 'The Ship Money Case', pp. 521–6.

[70] *Observations*, pp. 5, 25; cf. pp. 6–13. Parker's work as a counsellor and its bearing on his thought is discussed in my 'Henry Parker: The Public's Privado'. in *Religion, Resistance, and Civil War*, Proceedings of the Folger Institute Center for the History of British Political Thought, vol. III (Washington, 1990), pp. 151–78. The trinitarian figure is in *The True Grounds of Ecclesiasticall Regiment* (1641), pp. 19, 85. See also the revealing *The Contra-Replicant* (1643), pp. 18–19.

great Councell'.[71] William Prynne's serial tract known as *The Soveraigne Power of Parliaments and Kingdomes* was little more than an attempt to buttress the official parliamentary position with the weight of the kingdom's records, as Parker had tried to support it with the spring steel of his political science.[72]

Parker himself also began the process of returning to a unitary theory of sovereignty, founded in the consent of the people to all government over them. That was how Parker squared his own circle, finding a way to exalt the power of the king against the clergy but not fashion from it a yoke for his people. Parker's populism quickly found its limits: the conciliar standing of the houses of parliament in the summer of 1642 was not enhanced by intimate contact with popularity.[73] But popular sovereignty possessed its own sources of energy. In a later, theoretical essay, *Jus populi*, even Parker drifted momentarily to the centre of gravity of monarchomach thought, a theory of resistence.[74] Others, whether parliamentarian or royalist, pursued parallel paths, encouraged by the loose language of the *Answer to the XIX Propositions*.

For a while, the two theories of sovereignty uneasily co-existed. In the longer run, unitary theories of sovereignty came to command the field.[75] The emergency became permanent, and particularly as the houses taxed their way to military victory, the executive nature

[71] Pocock, *Ancient Constitution*, pp. 313–14, addresses this issue in the period under consideration. Warwick's letter, addressed to Pym and presented to both houses, received official endorsement and was printed in several versions. See *CJ* 2:654, 655 (4 July 1642); *LJ* 5:185; House of Lords Main Papers (4 July 1642); BL E.154(9) and E.154(13).

[72] Prynne's *Soveraign Power* is discussed thoughtfully in Lamont, *Marginal Prynne*, pp. 85–119. Lamont's puzzlement over Prynne's failure to embrace full Bodinian sovereignty is lessened by recognition that Prynne was simply following the official line. Prynne's tract was issued in four parts, each with a different title. Thomason bound them together in BL E.248(1–4).

[73] *The True Grounds of Ecclesiasticall Regiment*, pp. 89–93 *Observations*, pp. 1, 5, 13–16. It is appropriate to state here that Parker's populism has obvious links to earlier consensualist thought, including that associated with the monarchomachs. In this respect it is the more interesting that Parker binds these universalising notions so tightly to executive, absolute power.

[74] *Jus populi* (London, 1644), pp. 55–69. The anonymous *A Question Answered*, which I believe Parker to have written (*Dangerous Positions*, pp. 187–8), does entertain the question the limitation of obedience (rather than resistance); *Observations* considered the same notions (pp. 4, 21, 44), but in general used populist notions more to explain adherence to parliament than resistance to kings.

[75] Though I remain puzzled by several features of the treatment of C. C. Weston and J. R. Greenberg, *Subjects and Sovereigns: The Grand Controversy over Legal Sovereignty in Stuart England* (Cambridge, 1981), it is indubitable that legislation and 'co-ordination' were very much part of the post-1642 debate.

of an ordinance was increasingly inapt. Never a fig leaf but no longer a goal, the constitutional theory that is the subject of this essay became more remote and subject to ridicule. Nevertheless, the questions posed by the parliamentary absolutism of 1642, as by the Fortescuean royal absolutism of earlier decades, remained painfully alive. By the end of 1643, as the original war of words was dying down, it was beginning to be replaced by a constitutionalist critique of the parliamentary regime coming from old royalists, common-law sticklers, and new radicals. Slightly changed, the old questions endured. If an old priest lurked within the new presbyter, was the old king to be found in the new parliament? Was it an improvement to have found that what a king could not do, a perpetual bicameral parliament could? *Quis custodiet custodes?*

CHAPTER 6

The civil religion of Thomas Hobbes

Richard Tuck

Twenty-one years ago, John Pocock observed with characteristic trenchancy that:

The two books [of *Leviathan*] in which Hobbes expounds Christian faith and its sacred history are almost exactly equal in length to Books I and II; yet the attitude of far too many scholars towards them has traditionally been, first, that they aren't really there, second, that Hobbes didn't really mean them.[1]

It comes as a shock to realise that the first version of this essay dates back to 1968.[2] Pocock had already seen the way in which a new understanding of Hobbes might be approached, at a time when most scholars were pre-occupied with the so-called 'Taylor–Warrender' debate, and it has taken the intervening twenty years for the rest of us to catch up. He urged that we should take the theology of Books III and IV of *Leviathan* utterly seriously, and recognise that though Hobbes's civil sovereign was empowered to interpret Scripture as he thought fit for the needs of civil peace, there was still an independent place for the word of God in Hobbes's thought.

The authority by which the sovereign interprets the prophetic word is clearly distinct from the authority by which the word is uttered; and since the word, its content, its transmission and its authors constitute a history, the secular ruler finds himself inhabiting a history which he did not make – it does not owe its being to the natural reason which produced him – and which indeed looks forward to a time when his authority will be exercised by the risen Christ. The word and the history it connotes are given him,

---

[1] 'Time, History and Eschatology in the Thought of Thomas Hobbes', in *The Diversity of History: Essays in Honour of Sir Herbert Butterfield*, ed. J.H. Elliott and H.G. Koenisberger (London, 1970), pp. 149–98, at p. 160, reprinted in J.G.A. Pocock, *Politics, Language and Time* (London, 1972), pp. 148–201, to which my citations refer.
[2] See ibid., p. 151, n.10.

and his authority as interpreter begins only from acceptance of it as *datum*. Hobbes therefore, as a private man, a subject and (so he tells us) a Christian, inhabiting the same history, finds it desirable to pursue an accurate interpretation of the same data, and does not wait in mindless quiet for the sovereign to interpret it to him.[3]

Pocock went on to depict Hobbes's interpretation of this data as essentially the acceptance of a particular eschatological vision: that Christ will return to earth in a corporeal form, and will rule over the resurrected saints. In the meantime, death means extinction, the soul has no existence after death, nor does a spiritual realm intrude on the present physical world. Christianity means simply the acceptance of the truth of this prophetic history, and the posture of waiting submissively for the return of Christ.

There is no doubt that this eschatological vision is present in Books III and IV of *Leviathan*, and equally no doubt that though compatible with Hobbes's general philosophical materialism (in ways convincingly documented by Pocock) it is clearly not *entailed* by it – most materialists have, after all, not been eschatological Christians. Something more is needed before we can explain why Hobbes put this theology forward. Pocock's own explanation was that by putting forward this particular eschatology, Hobbes was able to refute the assertions of those who claimed spiritual authority prior to the return of the risen Christ:

The tactical thrust of Hobbes's argument is now clear. It is directed against new presbyter as well as old priest, and against new saint as well as old scholastic – against anyone, that is, who may claim that the process of salvation authorizes his civil actions or power in the present.[4]

But as we shall see, and as I have already shown elsewhere,[5] the clear desire to refute *all* claims to spiritual authority only appears in Hobbes's work at the same time as the eschatology itself – that is, in *Leviathan*. Hobbes's earlier works in which he discusses religious matters at some length, the *Elements of Law* of 1640, *De cive* of 1641-2, and the *Critique of Thomas White* of 1643, all accord a much greater role to a separate ecclesiastical authority than does *Leviathan*, and all were correspondingly much more acceptable to the orthodox clergymen amongst whom (it must be remembered)

---

[3] Ibid., p. 168.
[4] Ibid., p. 187.
[5] First in 'Warrender's *De cive*', *Political Studies* 33 (1985), 308–15.

Hobbes seems to have felt most at home in the England of the 1630s. Not until *Leviathan* appeared did they express disquiet about Hobbes's ideas – a disquiet voiced most vividly by his old friend Henry Hammond, the former archdeacon of Chichester, who wrote to Matthew Wren the former bishop of Ely on 14 October 1651, asking 'have you seen Mr Hobbes' Leviathan, a farrago of Christian Atheism?' A week later he wrote again, saying that Hobbes,

having in France been angered by some Divines, and having now a mind to return hither, hath chosen to make his way by this book, which some tell me takes infinitely among the looser sons of the Church, and the king's party, being indeed a farrago of all the maddest divinity that ever was read, and having destroyed Trinity, Heaven, Hell, may be allowed to compare ecclesiastical authority to the kingdom of fairies.[6]

So we need to provide two separate, though linked explanations: one of why Hobbes chose to attack ecclesiastical authority in the late 1640s, and the other of why he chose to join his attack to the kind of theology that was so bewilderingly expounded in the second half of *Leviathan*. Pocock drew our attention to the tremendous importance of these issues for a proper understanding of *Leviathan*; what I want to do in this essay is suggest a slightly different way of looking at them from the way which he proposed.

The best place to begin a study of Hobbes's religion as he expounded it before 1651 is the *Critique of Thomas White*. This was a long manuscript criticism of White's *De Mundo* which Hobbes composed in Paris in 1643, and which was not published until 1973. Because the work is still not well known, even among professional Hobbes scholars, I will quote from it more extensively than would be necessary in the case of the other works. In the course of the *Critique*, Hobbes was obliged to clarify his views on a number of theological issues, and his remarks are often extremely illuminating. For example, he explained very clearly what he meant when he said (as he did in all his works) that nothing could truthfully be said of God other than that he exists – and in the process furnished a most original dissolution of the problem of evil.

Personally, while I hold the nature of God is unfathomable, and that propositions are a kind of language by which we express our concepts of the natures of things, I incline to the view that no proposition about the

[6] (Anon), 'Illustrations of the State of the Church during the Great Rebellion', *The Theologian and Ecclesiastic*, 9 (1850), 294–5.

nature of God can be true save this one: God exists, and that no title correctly describes the nature of God other than the word 'being' [*ens*]. Everything else, I say, pertains not to the explanation of philosophical truth, but to proclaiming the states of mind that govern our wish to praise, magnify and honour God. Hence those words 'God sees, understands, wishes, acts, brings to pass' and other similar propositions which have only one meaning for us – 'motion' – display, not the Divine Nature, but our own piety, who desire to ascribe to Him the names most worthy of honour among us. Therefore [the words cited] are rather oblations than propositions, and the names [listed], if we were to apply them to God as we understand them, would be called blasphemies and sins against God's ordinance (which forbids us to take His name in vain) rather than true propositions. Neither propositions nor notions about His nature are to be argued over, but are a part of our worship and are evidences of a mind that honours God. Propositions that confer honour are correctly enunciated about God, but the opposite ones irreligiously; we may reverently and as Christians say of God that He is the author of every act, because it is honourable to do so, but to say 'God is the author of sin' is sacrilegious and profane. There is no *contradiction* in this matter, however, for, as I said, the words under discussion are not the propositions of people philosophising but the actions of those who pay homage. A contradiction is found in propositions alone.[7]

For Hobbes, therefore, all theology was essentially a question of the authoritative character of the language in which we 'did homage' to God: whatever seemed to us to do him honour, was a description that could fairly be applied to him.

From the beginning of his developed philosophy, Hobbes recognised that the control of public meanings was the essence of the civil sovereign's role; as he said in the most striking passage of the *Elements of Law*, 'the civil laws are to all subjects the measures of their actions, whereby to determine, whether they be right or wrong, profitable or unprofitable, virtuous or vicious; and by them the use and definition of all names not agreed upon, and tending to controversy, shall be established'.[8] So in the 'kingdom of God by nature' described most fully in *De cive* chapter xv, all religious utterances intended to honour God are given their meanings by the civil sovereign (xv.17). There is even a certain nostalgia in these early works for the ancient world's attitude to religion – thus in the *Elements of Law* Hobbes observed that the conflict between God's

[7] *Critique du* De mundo *de Thomas White*, ed. Jean Jacquot and H.W. Jones (Paris, 1973), ff. 396–396v, trans. H.W. Jones (Bradford, 1976) p. 434, slightly emended.
[8] *Elements of Law*, ed. F. Tönnies, second ed, M.M. Goldsmith (London, 1969), pp. 188–9.

commands and those of the sovereign was not 'a controversy that was ever taken notice of amongst the Grecians, Romans, or other Gentiles; for amongst these their several civil laws were the rules whereby not only righteousness and virtue, but also religion and the external worship of God, was ordered and approved'.[9]

But at the same time Hobbes argued in these works that this capacity of the civil laws to determine meaning stopped at the frontiers of Christian faith and theology, where a *future life* was concerned. It was true that in a Christian *civitas* the term 'church' meant the same as *civitas* – there could be no universal church without a universal state; and it was accordingly true that the sovereign was the ultimate interpreter of Christian doctrine in his capacity as head of the church. But in his works of 1640 to 1643, Hobbes denied that the sovereign should use his own natual reason to interpret doctrine (as he could have done if solely a natural religion had been involved). In a passage in *De cive* to which I have elsewhere drawn attention on a number of occasions, Hobbes wrote that

For the deciding of questions of Faith, that is to say, *concerning God*, which transcend humane capacity, we stand in need of a divine blessing (that we may not be deceiv'd at least in necessary points) to be derived from CHRIST himselfe by the imposition of hands. For, seeing to the end we may attaine to aeternal Salvation, we are oblig'd to a supernatural Doctrine, & which therefore it is impossible for us to understand; to be left so destitute, as that we can be deciv'd in necessary points, is repugnant to aequity. This infallibility our Saviour *Christ* promis'd (in those things which are necessary to Salvation) to his *Apostles* untill the day of judgement; that is to say, *to the Apostles, and Pastors* succeeding the *Apostles* who were to be consecrated *by the imposition of hands*. He therefore who hath the Soveraigne power in the City, is oblig'd as a Christian, where there is any question concerning *the Mysteries of Faith*, to interpret the Holy Scriptures by *Clergy-men* lawfully ordain'd.[10]

So what Hobbes favoured at this stage was substantially what we might anachronistically call 'Anglicanism' of a rather Laudian type: an autonomous national church headed by the civil sovereign, but with the sovereign under a duty to use apostolically ordained clergymen in deciding doctrine. Though in one sense Hobbes took

9 Ibid., p. 145.
10 *De Cive: The English Version*, ed. Howard Warrender (Oxford, 1983) XVII.28, p. 249. For my earlier discussions of this passage, see my 'Warrender's *De Cive*', p. 313; *Hobbes* (Oxford, 1989) p. 85.

away ecclesiastical autonomy, in another sense he reinforced it, for the determination of *Christian* meanings had to lie in practice with the men who stood in the apostolic succession to Christ (which need not include the sovereign himself, though of course it might do so – see *Elements of Law*, II.7.11). His attacks on autonomous ecclesiastical power were attacks on the notion of a church which did not have to issue its rules to the citizens without going through the legislative channels of the sovereign; but they were not attacks on the doctrinal hegemony of a clergy.

Indeed, Hobbes was willing at this time to accord an overwhelming importance to an apostolic church. Again, this is put most clearly and surprisingly in the *Critique of White*, and in particular in chapter 39, where Hobbes discussed Thomas White's explanation of why most men do not attain 'happiness' (*felicitas*). Hobbes distinguished here between 'worldly happiness', consisting in 'riches, titles and physical pleasure' – where the explanation for a man's failure to attain them was the usual Hobbesian story of contingency and inadequate prudence – and 'true happiness, namely that which has been laid up for the faithful in a future age'. In the case of this 'true' happiness,

the sole cause of enmities [the MS here is corrupt, and the editors conjectured 'inimicorum'] is lack of faith. All men without exception fall into three categories: (*i*) the main one, consisting of those who themselves know what it is best to do; (*ii*) those who, knowing nothing themselves, admit that they must be ruled by those more wise; and (*iii*) those who neither know [anything] themselves nor will trust others. In the first category are those who know the path to happiness, namely those to whom the Holy Ghost has pointed the way through supernatural revelation; such were the Apostles, and such now alone is, and ever will be, a Church, formed into one person. In the second category are those who, having no supernatural revelation accorded them, admit that they must be ruled by one who *has* [had this revelation], i.e., a Church. In the third are those who themselves neither know what the path to a future life is, nor believe in a Church, nor perform what a Church teaches as being necessary to the winning of felicity. So the main reason why men fall out of that everlasting happiness is a lack of belief in a Church, i.e. simply a lack of Christian faith.[11]

---

[11] *Critique du De mundo*, ff. 444–6, trans. pp. 481–3. I have emended the translation: in particular, I have replaced Jones's translation of *Ecclesia* as 'the Church' by 'a Church'; as I have just remarked, Hobbes at this time did not believe in a universal church as a single 'person'.

Elsewhere in the *Critique* he argued that a Christian church would have no reason to deceive in doctrinal matters such as the nature of God: 'she has received without controversy these dogmas from the Apostles that handed them down, and there is no reason why the Apostles should have wished to deceive a Church of days later than their own'.[12] Accordingly, in the *Elements of Law* he had freely admitted that 'we who are Christians *acknowledge* that there be angels good and evil; and that they are spirits, and that the soul of man is a spirit; and that these spirits are immortal', and that while 'to know it, that is to say, to have natural evidence of the same: it is impossible', it is 'the holy men of God's church succeeding one another' whom we should trust in matters of faith.[13]

An important and surprising feature of Hobbes's argument at this time is that one of the things he was trying to do was to protect theology from philosophy – more or less the opposite of what is conventionally supposed to have been his ambition. Because there are no meanings other than those established by some authority, there can be no philosophical argument against theological dogmas, since the meaning of the terms involved is given purely by the *fiat* of the church. In chapter 26 of the *Critique*, Hobbes attacked White's whole project of giving philosophical foundations to theology as fundamentally unsound and politically dangerous – 'it must not be thought that the articles of faith are [philosophical] problems; they are laws, and it is inequitable for a private individual to interpret them otherwise than as they are formulated'.[14] Looming over any discussion of this kind in the 1640s was the figure of Galileo, and Hobbes in the *Critique* met this difficulty head on, and with far less perseverance for Galileo's cause than might have been expected:

Perhaps someone will ask: 'What then, will the philosopher not be allowed to investigate the cause of motion?' Or, if this is not the case, 'What is it, then, that we shall assign to philosophy as her proper function?' First, I reply that nothing may be fixed as true or false by natural reason, except on supposition, because terms and names are acceptable only inasfar as we understand them . . . If, therefore, either the meaning is changed, or the thing which has been named cannot be grasped by the mind, every power to syllogise falls to the ground at once . . .

---

[12] Ibid., f. 337v, trans. p. 364.
[13] *Elements of Law*, pp. 55,58.
[14] *Critique du* De mundo, f. 288v, trans. p. 307.

Second, I say that the philosopher is indeed free to enquire into the nature and cause of motion, but that as the investigation proceeds he will stumble upon a proposition that is now held by the Christian faith and that seems to contradict a conclusion he has established earlier. He can infer (if he has previously reasoned correctly): 'I do not understand under what meaning of terms that proposition is true'. So, for instance, he says: 'I do not see, or it is beyond my grasp, how that which is not moved moves something else, or how that which exists is not spatially located, or how something incorporeal sees, hears, understands, wills, loves, hates, etc.' This is the attitude both of a balanced mind and, as I have said, of one that reasons correctly. But he cannot conclude that it is false; for how can anyone know whether a proposition is true or false that he does not understand? Whoever, then, has followed this way of proceeding will not impinge upon the Church's authority, which he acknowledges and conforms to, nor will he therefore philosophise the less freely, being one who has been allowed to advance as far as correct reasoning leads him.[15]

In chapter 39, he repeated that White's fundamental error was to seek to subordinate theology to philosophy, and that if anything the opposite was the case:

To settle whether the world is infinite, whether unique, whether existing from all time, whether eternal; likewise whether the human soul is immortal, whether free-will exists, and whether or not there are incorporeal substances lacking quantity; likewise what titles we must set upon God, and whether He could have founded a better world; likewise concerning the blessedness and unhappiness of a future age – all these questions, which are discussed in [White's] *Dialogues* as philosophical matters, the theologians claim to determine . . . Either, then, these are not philosophical matters; or philosophy, even the true, must be subject to theology. However, when I say 'theology' I am saying 'the leaders of the Church', whose task it is to regulate all dogmas; for these will be seen to be able either to strengthen or to overthrow the fixed tenets of faith.[16]

So Hobbes's theological position in the early 1640s was very far removed from the kind of arguments set out in *Leviathan*. He deliberately avoided committing himself to a definite, let alone an heretical, view on all the issues which later led to his condemnation by former friends of a more orthodox cast of mind. What those issues were, incidentally, can be seen most plainly from the terms of the bill introduced into parliament in 1666 to 1667 and specifically aimed at *Leviathan*: it would have made punishable by imprison-

[15] Ibid., ff. 289–289v, trans. pp. 307–8. See also ff. 132v–133, trans. pp. 162–3.
[16] Ibid., f. 452v, trans. p. 490.

ment or banishment the denial of 'the essence, powers or attributes of God the Father, Son or Holy Ghost, given to them in Scripture, or the omnipotency, wisdom, justice, mercy, goodness or providence of God in the Creation, Redemption or Governance of the world'; the denial of 'the divine authority of any of the canonical books contained in the Old and New Testaments, received in the Church of England'; and the denial of 'the immortality of men's souls, the resurrection of the body, and the eternal rewards in Heaven or eternal torments in Hell'.[17] These were precisely the kinds of issue which Hobbes had been careful to leave unchallenged in his early works; even his well-known later 'mortalism' (i.e. his belief that the soul had no existence after the death of the body) is (as David Johnston has recently pointed out[18]) not to be found in these works, where he repeatedly says that the immortality of the soul is a matter of Christian faith decidable by the authority of the church.

The change in Hobbes's views from this cautious position to that represented by Parts III and IV of *Leviathan* is relatively simple to describe. The special position of the Christian Church *vis-à-vis* the civil sovereign was abrogated, and the sovereign made the interpreter of Scriptural meanings with the same autonomy as he possessed in the interpretation of all other meanings. The apostolic succession was denuded of all significance; indeed, Hobbes asserted that even the Apostles themselves did not possess a monopoly of interpretative power: 'when a difficulty arose, the Apostles and Elders of the Church assembled themselves together, and determined what should be preached, and taught, and how they should Interpret the Scriptures to the People; but took not from the People the liberty to read, and Interpret them to themselves'.[19] However, at the same time Hobbes suggested a new, and highly idiosyncratic, version of some of the salient doctrines of Christianity, and in particular of its eschatology. The core of this new theology is in chapter 38, 'Of the Signification in Scripture of ETERNAL LIFE, HELL, SALVATION, THE WORLD TO COME, and REDEMPTION'. Hobbes explained the status of his theological conjectures at this point in

[17] *Historical Manuscripts Commission*, 8th Report I, pp. 111–12. See my 'Hobbes and Locke on Toleration', in *Thomas Hobbes and Political Theory*, ed. Mary G. Dietz (Lawrence, Kans. 1990), pp. 153–71.
[18] David Johnston, 'Hobbe's Mortalism', *History of Political Thought*, 10 (1989), 647–63.
[19] My edition of *Leviathan* (Cambridge, 1991), pp. 355–6.

the following words (which, as I have observed elsewhere, also illustrate that Hobbes at this point in *Leviathan* did not believe that the royal cause was finally lost):[20]

> because this doctrine (though proved out of places of Scripture not few, nor obscure) will appear to most men a novelty; I doe but propound it; maintaining nothing in this, or any other paradox of Religion; but attending the end of that dispute of the sword, concerning the Authority, (not yet amongst my Countrey-men decided,) by which all sorts of doctrine are to bee approved, or rejected.[21]

But since Hobbes intended *Leviathan* to be taken seriously by the future sovereign,[22] we may suppose that he also wished the sovereign to take seriously this theology, and to make it the public doctrine of England. Even in the last few pages of *Leviathan*, where he accepted that the new regime in England was well established, he still hoped that his theology might be established as the new religion of the country.

> In that part which treateth of a Christian Common-wealth, there are some new Doctrines, which, it may be, in a State where the contrary were already fully determined, were a fault for a Subject without leave to divulge, as being an usurpation of the place of a Teacher. But in this time, that men call not onely for Peace, but also for Truth, to offer such Doctrine as I think True, and that manifestly tend[s] to Peace and Loyalty, to the consideration of those that are yet in deliberation, is no more, but to offer New Wine, to bee put into New Cask, that both may be preserved together. And I suppose, that then, when Novelty can breed no trouble, nor disorder in a State, men are not generally so much inclined to the reverence of Antiquity, as to preferre Ancient Errors, before New and well proved Truth.[23]

The most striking feature of Hobbes's new theology is indeed the sharp division he now drew between Christianity and the religions of antiquity. As we saw above, there was a certain nostalgia in the *Elements of Law* for the religious arrangements of the ancient world, a nostalgia which closely paralleled the attitudes of (say) Grotius to the similarities of ancient and modern religion – Grotius frequently used ancient examples to illuminate general truths about religion, holding that 'the true Religion, which has been common to all

---

[20] See ibid., p. x.
[21] Ibid., p. 311
[22] Ibid., p. xxxv.
[23] Ibid., pp. 489–90.

Ages', was built upon the four fundamental principles of mono-
theism, the immateriality of God, his care for the world and his
creation of it.[24] This attitude was to be the source of late
seventeenth- and early eighteenth-century English Deism, and one
can easily imagine Hobbes having developed into a kind of English
Grotian. But *Leviathan* aborted this development: chapter 12 contains an impassioned denunciation of the religion of the gentiles for
fostering *fear* in the hearts of men. Natural man, Hobbes argued,
has constant fear about the uncertain outcome of his actions, and
'this perpetuall feare, alwayes accompanying mankind in the
ignorance of causes, as it were in the Dark, must needs have for
object something . . . In which sense perhaps it was, that some of
the old Poets said, that the Gods were first created by humane
Feare: which spoken of the Gods, (that is to say, of the many Gods
of the Gentiles) is very true.' Philosophical contemplation, on the
other hand, arrives at the idea of a God without fear: the deduction
of a First Cause is made by philosophers 'without thought of their
fortune; the solicitude whereof, both enclines to fear, and hinders
them from the search of the causes of other things.'[25]

The great idea Hobbes seems to have had in Paris in the late
1640s is that there could be a version of Christianity wholly
detached from the religion of the gentiles, if the traditional
doctrines both of the immateriality of the soul and of *hell* were
overthrown. It was commonplace among modern, Grotian theorists that Christ came not to issue commands but to deliver counsel
– counsel being advice, not law, and therefore, without any threat
of sanction hanging over the recipient.[26] Hobbes however perceived
that any doctrine of an immaterial soul and eternal torment must
add a whole new set of fears to those which men possess by nature.

The idea of an immaterial soul led straightforwardly (as he
repeatedly said) to a fear of ghosts and occult forces in this life (and
the rhetorical use of the term 'ghost' is very striking throughout
Leviathan). The theology of Hell, moreover, gave men a wholly new
set of things to fear. Uninstructed about a future life, we would fear
death as the greatest of terrors; but the idea of Hell has persuaded
us that there are many other things to fear *as well* – Hell has not
removed our natural fear of dying, but it has added to it a fear of

[24] *Of the Rights of War and Peace* (1738), II.45.1, p. 442.
[25] *Leviathan*, pp. 76–7.
[26] See e.g. *Of the Rights of War and Peace*, I.2.9, pp. 47–8.

eternal pain. In chapter 38 Hobbes duly set out his new interpretation of (extremely slender) Scriptural evidence about the afterlife: the Scriptures teach that those whom God has decided to save – those who have kept his laws – will be resurrected and will live on earth for ever, while sinners will be judged and suffer a second, definitive death. The 'eternal' torments for the wicked, of which Scripture speaks fairly clearly (particularly in Matthew 25), Hobbes ingeniously explained away by postulating that even after the Day of Judgement the wicked might continue to breed as normal, and that their descendants might sin and therefore suffer torment before dying themselves – and that this process might continue for ever. Christianity, interpreted in this way, was the only religion which did not add to the natural burden of fear which men carry, and indeed offered them an entirely new hope – the hope of *eternal* life.

It may be significant that Hobbes's views about hell were very close to those of the Socinians, who also believed in eternal death for the damned and eternal life for the saved.[27] It is certainly striking that Hobbes looks rather like a Socinian in the other two principal areas of Socinian theology, scepticism about the Athanasian doctrine of the Trinity and unhappiness about the conventional idea of the atonement.[28] Humanist scholars of the Bible were constantly liable to find themselves teetering on the edge of Socinianism,[29] and there may be nothing more to be said about this resemblance; but Hobbes must have been fully aware of the parallels contemporaries would draw between his theology and that of the Socinians.[30]

It is sometimes said that Hobbes's object was to make men more fearful of the sanctions which could be brought to bear on them, and thereby to discipline them into obedience; and both Pocock and David Johnston have suggested that it was the desire to give the sovereign a monopoly on sanctions which led Hobbes to eliminate Hell. But the theology of *Leviathan* points in a very different direction, and one which (I think) is more in keeping with Hobbes's general intentions. Hobbes wished to *relieve* men of their

[27] See e.g. D.P. Walker, *The Decline of Hell* (London, 1964), pp. 73 ff.
[28] For this last, see my *Leviathan*, pp. 319–20.
[29] Compare the claims made about such scholars in H.J. McLachlan, *Socianism in Seventeenth-Century England* (Oxford, 1951).
[30] For such a parallel, see William Lucy, *Observations, Censures and Confutations of Notorious Errours in Mr. Hobbes his Leviathan . . .* (1663), pp. 291–391.

fears: in a state of nature, the constant exercise of our own judgement about what is dangerous is a nerve-wracking and wearying business, which leaves (as he constantly emphasised) little time for anything else. The basic fear of death cannot be eliminated; but by transferring our judgement to the sovereign, we are relieved of the responsibility of thinking about it. The psychological character of Hobbes's theory is very similar to that of the late Renaissance sceptics who believed that the path to 'wisdom' lay in the renunciation of both belief and emotion, and that the wise man would not be led into upsetting and dangerous courses of action by any cognitive commitments. Pierre Charron, one of these sceptics whose works clearly influenced Hobbes, devoted *Les trois Veritez* (1595) to an argument that the wise man will choose his religion according to these criteria – to have a religion is far more psychologically reassuring than to go without one, to be a Christian is better than being a non-Christian, and to be a Catholic is better than being a Protestant. The argument of *Leviathan* is that a religion without future punishment is far better than a religion with it, and that such a religion is in fact on offer in the form of a deviant interpretation of Christianity itself.

The central puzzle about Parts III and IV of *Leviathan*, to which Pocock originally drew our attention, can be described as one about their emotional intensity. Why should Hobbes have felt so deeply about the theology described in Part III? The political point could have been made independently of the theology – to say that the sovereign is the sole authoritative interpreter of Scripture is a sufficiently striking and alarming claim, without the added complication of a new eschatology. But if I am right in putting the liberation of men from fear as the point of the eschatology, then we can begin to see why Hobbes felt deeply about it: the psychological work of the sovereign would not be done unless fear of an after-life could be eliminated. The point of the sovereign, on Hobbes's account, was after all to reduce the burden on men and to relieve them of the obligation to act on principles which were not clearly conducive to their self-preservation. Moreover, it was only if the sovereign was recognised as sole interpreter, that the new eschatology stood a chance: clearly, the traditional apostolic churches were not going to accept a theology of this kind, and in Part IV Hobbes gave a witty but passionate account of the history of the church and its progressive corruption by the religion and philosophy of the gentiles in order to explain why this was so (again, this was a much stronger dissociation of true Christianity from antiquity than was to be found in his earlier works). It may therefore be that an explanation of the theology in terms of the ecclesiology has got the matter the wrong way round: Hobbes broke with the Anglican tradition because the Church of England was not sufficiently purged of the religion of the gentiles. If this is right, he gave up on the apostolic tradition *before* he turned to the civil sovereign as sole interpreter of Scripture.

But there remains a harder question, as to why this happened to him at Paris between 1647 (when the second edition of *De cive* was published) and 1650 (when he refused to allow an English translation of it).[31] The explanation hinted at by the exiles seems to have been his connection with the court of Queen Henrietta Maria.[32] This was clearly true as far as the purely political side of Hobbes's argument went, since it was an important part of the queen's policy to persuade first her husband and then her son to abandon the Church of England, if doing so would win them back their throne. But there was no political reason for Hobbes to adopt the eschatology of *Leviathan* in order to argue the queen's case – and indeed, his doing so made the case seem even less plausible to opponents such as Clarendon. However, there was another feature of the queen's court which may have been relevant, and that was its Catholicism. Pocock linked Hobbes's theology to the radical Protestantism of the Interregnum in England; but during the 1640s Hobbes actually spent far more time with Catholics than with radical Protestants, and some of the theological issues he addressed in *Leviathan* seem to be responses to the debates among French and English Catholic writers.

For example, at the end of 1643 Denis Petau ('Petavius'), professor of theology at the Sorbonne and a prominent Jesuit, began to publish an encyclopaedia of patristic theology, the *Theologicorum Dogmata*. The book made an instant impression on the learned public: Petau had long been admired by people like Grotius, Mersenne and Gassendi, and they were delighted with his first volume.[33] Petau carefully documented the often profound

---

[31] My 'Warrender's *De Cive*', p. 311.

[32] See my *Leviathan*, pp. xxiv–xxv.

[33] Marin Mersenne, *Correspondance*, ed. P. Tannery, C. de Waard and R. Pintard (Paris, 1932–   ) vol. xiii, p. 121, xiv, pp. 618–19, xiv, p. 487, n.3, xv, p. 491; R. Pintard, *La Mothe le Vayer, Gassendi, Guy Patin* (Paris, 1943), pp. 60,85.

disagreements over Christian theology among the early fathers, with (it seems) two principal and related objectives in mind. One was to attack the theology of the Jansenists, and in particular their explicit reliance upon the teachings of Augustine: as Mersenne observed (with approval), Petau had been led to criticise Augustine himself as part of his critique of Jansenism because 'it is difficult to refute the one without the other'.[34] The best way of diminishing Augustine's authority was to show the prevalence among respected early theologians of quite different views. But Petau's other objective was to demonstrate that there could be no adequate interpretation of Scripture other than that given formally by the church itself – no private views, even those of the most authoritative theologians, could in the end carry any weight with a Christian, though they might enjoy some provisional status. Good citizens (he remarked) must initially be bound by the letter of the law in their disputes and cannot 'wrest the right of interpreting it and fitting it to their case', but the praetor is entitled to modify it as he sees fit. The church was in the same position: the commonly accepted meanings of Scripture must be followed by *privati*, but the church can always exercise its authority and reinterpret Scripture.[35]

Petau's volumes thus depicted a very different early church from that presented in the Anglican tradition. To some extent despite himself, he showed that the early Christians had not believed in a stable body of doctrine which had become corrupted after Nicaea (the usual Anglican view), but had indulged instead in a wide range of deviant theologies. Petau also documented the constant intrusion of Greek philosophy into these theologies: one of his main claims was that the philosophies of Plato and Aristotle had corrupted Christianity and given rise to heresy (see e.g. the *Prolegomena*, Chapter III). His fair-mindedness in setting out these theologies led him to be accused of Socinianism, an accusation he easily refuted; but he had provided an extensive new set of insights for anyone who wished to put forward an account of Christianity purged of philosophical error, and he had done so in a context which Hobbes would have found (in principle) very appealing – namely the idea that the sovereign of the church must be wholly free to interpret Scripture.

---

[34] *Correspondance*, vol. XI, p. 359.
[35] *Theologicorum Dogmata* (Paris 1644–   ) I *Prolegomena* I.9.

To find Hobbes taking up some of the ideas of the anti-Jansenists may be surprising: surely his account of liberty and the freedom of the will put him far more in the Jansenist camp? It was after all frequently said by contemporaries that Hobbes should be bracketed with the Calvinists (and therefore by extension the Jansenists) as a believer in a strong theory of predestination.[36] The issues were however more complicated than this simple categorisation would suggest. The Jansenists argued that naturally men (since the Fall) will always wish to perform sinful actions, since it is these which seem psychologically appealing to their fallen nature. To prevent this, God directly and supernaturally (through his grace) wrests the wills of the elect and turns them towards righteous actions. Against this, the Jesuits asserted that men could naturally will what is right, in the sense that they could freely co-operate with God's grace or resist it. Neither of these two positions is of course very similar to Hobbes; but it is striking that there was a Catholic theory, albeit one which verged on heresy, which was extremely close to Hobbes.

This was the theory put forward by Thomas White and his followers such as Henry Holden and John Sargeant, according to which God can not 'infuse' anything into the will – the will always chooses what the mind judges to be the best course of action according to the natural desires of the agent. To secure righteous actions, therefore, God has either to arrange the prior material conditions appropriately, so that the natural process of ratiocination leads the agent to do the right thing, or has directly to intervene in the mental life of the agent, the 'phantasms and spirits' over which men have little or no voluntary control.[37] Since it was God who does this, it could correctly be described as a 'supernatural' act; but he operates through a process of natural causation. In his edition of Rushworth's *Dialogues* (which he may in fact have composed himself) White spoke sardonically of the conventional idea of grace – 'to supply the weaknesse they imagine in the motives, they bring in the helping hand of omnipotency under the

---

[36] See e.g. Thomas Pierce, Αυτοκατακριοις *or, Self-condemnation* . . . (1658), *passim*.
[37] See particularly White, *Institutionum Sacrarum Peripateticis Inaedificiendis* (n.p., 1652), pp. 111–13.

name of *Grace*.[38] This was of course precisely Hobbes's view of God's grace,[39] and one of White's critics accused him and his followers of putting forward ideas 'not very far from *Hobbes's doctrine*'.[40] White's theology thus cut across the arguments of Jansenists and anti-Jansenists – Holden wrote against Arnault, but White and Sargeant were attacked (ironically, as Pelagians) by Jesuits.[41]

Hobbes's discussion of hell may also owe something to these English Catholics. Beginning with the work of another of his friends, Kenelm Digby, in the early 1640s, they developed a distinctive eschatology. They accepted the arguments which Hobbes put forward in all his philosophical works, that only material objects can exhibit change; but whereas Hobbes concluded that the human mind, whose sense-impressions alter, must therefore be material, they concluded that the immaterial human soul (which Digby at least identified with the Cartesian ego) must therefore be incapable of change. At death, argued both Digby and White (who each referred in flattering terms to the other's work), the soul survives completely unchanged and unchangeable, and Hell is the continued experience by the unrighteous of an unsatisfiable longing for material goods. White marshalled an impressive set of Scriptural and moral arguments against the conventional notions of eternal fire and the other physical punishments.[42]

Hobbes's dismissal of hell then makes some sense as a rejection of this theory – *any* mental life, on his account, must involve change; as he said in *De corpore*, static 'perceptions' could not really be perceptions. If a man

---

[38] *Rushworth's Dialogues . . . corrected and enlarged by Thomas White* (Paris, 1654), sig. **8v. For some scepticism about Rushworth's hand in the composition, see George H. Tavard, *The Seventeenth-Century Tradition. A Study in Recusant Thought* (Leiden, 1978), pp. 158–60; for White's circle in general, see John Henry, 'Atomism and Eschatology: Catholicism and Natural Philosophy in the Interregnum', *British Journal for the History of Science*, 15 (1982), 211–39.

[39] See e.g. *Leviathan*, pp. 406–7.

[40] [Peter Talbot], *Blakloanae Haeresis* (Ghent, 1675), p. 250.

[41] For Holden's attacks on Arnault, see his *DNB* entry; White and Sargeant were accused of Pelagianism by the Jesuit Archbishop of Dublin, Peter Talbot, in his *Blakloanae Haeresis* of 1675.

[42] Kenelm Digby, *Two Treatises . . .* (Paris, 1644), pp. 443–5; White, *The Middle State of Souls* (n.p., 1659) pp. 97ff. (a translation of a work which appeared in 1653, and which drew on other theological work of White during the 1640s); Henry, 'Atomism and Eschatology', pp. 223ff.

should look only upon one thing, which is always of the same color and figure, without the least appearance of variety, he would seem to me, whatsoever others may say, to see, no more than I seem to myself to feel the bones of my own limbs by my organs of feeling; . . . it being almost all one for a man to be always sensible of one and the same thing, and not to be sensible at all of any thing.[43]

It would follow that a hell of the Digby–White kind was impossible, and if White's arguments against the conventional idea were accepted, then only the Socinian theory remained as a plausible interpretation of Scripture.

Other similarities between Hobbes and these writers are often striking. For example, White and Holden agreed with the argument put forward in *Leviathan* that there should be a *rapprochement* with the Independents in England – Holden was allegedly a leading advocate at Queen Henrietta Maria's court of a deal with the Independents,[44] while White published a notorious book to that effect, *The Grounds of Obedience and Government* (London, 1654). Even after the Restoration there were links: the two people singled out by name in the proceeding on the Atheism Bill of 1666 were Hobbes and White, while Sergeant was apparently forced to flee into exile at the same time under pressure from attacks by Tillotson.[45] It would not be surprising if it was the experience of prolonged and intellectually satisfying debates with these Catholics, of which the *Critique of White* is the most vivid testament, which led Hobbes to his own theological position – in which, in a sense, the national church under its civil sovereign simply takes over the absolute interpretative power accorded to the universal church in the Catholic tradition, and a material body is given once again to the ghost of the Roman empire.

But though we might gain a fuller understanding of Hobbes's theology by considering it against this background, we cannot really capture its spirit this way. Hobbes by 1651 was fundamentally unlike all these writers because, as Pocock noticed, he was a kind of utopian. *Leviathan* is not simply (and maybe not at all) an analysis of how political societies are founded and conduct themselves. It is also a vision of how a commonwealth can make us freer

---

[43] *English Works*, vol. 1, ed. W. Molesworth (London, 1839) p. 394.
[44] *The Nicholas Papers*, vol. 1, ed. G.F. Warner (Camden Society, 1886) p. 226.
[45] Tavard, *The Seventeenth-Century Tradition*, p. 233.

and more prosperous than ever before in human history, for there has never yet been a time (according to Hobbes) when the errors of the philosophers were fully purged from society, and men could live a life without false belief. Revolutionary moments tend to breed utopianism, and perhaps we have always overlooked the greatest of the English revolutionary utopias.

CHAPTER 7

The rapture of motion:
James Harrington's republicanism

Jonathan Scott

When a thing is in motion, it will eternally be in motion, unless somewhat els stay it.

Thomas Hobbes, *Leviathan* (1651)[1]

When he beheld . . . the rapture of motion . . . into which his spheres were cast, without any manner of obstruction or interfering . . . [he] abdicated the magistracy of Archon.

James Harrington, *Oceana* (1656)[2]

I have opposed the politics of Mr Hobbes, to show him what he taught me.

James Harrington, *The Prerogative of Popular Government* (1658)[3]

I

English republicanism has proved a rich intellectual terrain. This may be some compensation for its abject practical failure. For contemporaries the English republic was the Rump Parliament, the disreputable fag-end of an august political institution. It fell victim to the turbulence of the times, not once but twice. All the bodies upon whose truncation or abolition it was founded preside prosperously over its failure to this day. Yet through the window of this brief break with political custom there shone an intense ideological light. English republican thought was remarkable, both for the depth of its reach back into the past, and for its internal variety. The republican experience became a prism, receiving the broadest rays of antiquity and the Renaissance and refracting them for the use of modern Europe and America. Among their number the

---

[1] Thomas Hobbes, *Leviathan*, ed. C.B. MacPherson (London, 1984), p. 87.
[2] James Harrington, *Oceana* in *The Political Works of James Harrington*, ed. J.G.A. Pocock, (Cambridge, 1977), p. 342. The words 'were cast' have been moved in this quotation to make the sense clearer.
[3] Ibid., p. 423.

republican writers included some of the most innovative and influential of a century exceptionally endowed with both.[4] This was an extraordinary achievement.

Our understanding of English republican thought rests upon two foundations. One, the older, is the study of its most distinguished author, James Harrington. The other is that of English republicanism in general, which has particularly blossomed since the Second World War. John Pocock has done most to bring the two together, by precisely locating Harrington's *Oceana* within its wider republican ideological context.[5] For Pocock, Harrington was 'a classical republican, and England's premier civic humanist and Machiavellian'.[6]

What Pocock has taught us above all is that there was such a relationship: between republican thought in general, and Harrington's in particular. This was by no means obvious even to the best of earlier Harrington scholars. When Felix Raab, for instance, detected the presence of fourteen different Harringtons in the scholarly literature, he called for a synthesis 'rigidly disciplined by direct reference to the text'.[7] This left unanswered however the question of the context within which this text would be read. It was precisely the variety of such contexts which accounted for this Harringtonian proliferation. To this failure to relate *Oceana* to the ideological tradition from which it emerged was linked a tendency to conflate the two. It was Perez Zagorin who declared that with Harrington 'republican thought may be properly said to begin', thus mistaking for a beginning what was in some sense the beginning of the end.[8] Even where the existence of such an independent ideological tradition was recognised, Harrington's stature has always overshadowed, and sometimes been allowed to define it. This is no sounder than taking Machiavelli to be the definer of orthodox Florentine humanism, or Hobbes of mainstream natural-law theory. Zera Fink clothed all the English classical republicans in Harrington's outrageous Venetian attire;

[4] I count Harrington here under 'innovative'; Sidney under 'influential'.
[5] Pocock built here, as he has stressed, on the work of Zera Fink (see note 9). J.G.A. Pocock, 'James Harrington and The Good Old Cause: A Study of the Ideological Context of his Writings', *Journal of British Studies*, 10, 1 (1970); *The Machiavellian Moment* (Princeton, 1975), esp. pp. 350–400; *The Political Works of James Harrington*, Introduction, pp. 6–42.
[6] Pocock (ed.), *Political Works*, p. 15.
[7] F. Raab, *The English Face of Machiavelli* (London, 1964), ch. 6, p. 187.
[8] P. Zagorin, *A History of Political Thought in the English Revolution* (London, 1954), ch. 11.

no small matter since here (as elsewhere) Harrington was wilfully disobeying Machiavelli.[9] Even Pocock himself christened some later republicans 'neo-Harringtonian' for repeating an early republican view of history from which Harrington himself had borrowed. This cart may need reintroduction to the horse: these republicans were not neo-Harrington; Harrington was, as we shall see, neo-republican.

It is true then, that Harrington's *Oceana* cannot be understood outside the context of the republican ideological tradition from which it emerged, and to which it was in turn a conscious contribution.[10] At the heart of this context sits classical republicanism. This essay begins from this conclusion; its purpose is, however, to offer a reassessment of Harrington's relationship to that tradition. This will oppose the history of J.G.A. Pocock, to show him what he taught me. For we are dealing here not only with the most idiosyncratic member of the republican intellectual flock. The more we look at Harrington the more we detect, under that loose sheepskin cover, a full set of whiskers and a low growl. It is true that from a certain perspective Harrington's politics look classical, his economics Aristotelian.[11] In some sense they were. But from the perspective which counts, that of classical republicanism itself, and of the whole republican experience from 1649 to 1683, there is reason to look again.

We must begin by sketching this wider context: that of the English republican experience as a whole. We may then see where Harrington stands within it. Although we will find everyone involved reading the same map of this terrain, Harrington's compass appears to have been issuing bearings of a distinctly independent character. We consequently find him occupying

---

[9] Z. Fink, *The Classical Republicans* (Urbana, 1945). J. Scott, *Algernon Sidney and the English Republic 1623–1677* (Cambridge, 1988), ch. 2, and pp. 15, 32, 111.

[10] The summary of the tradition which follows draws upon Scott, *English Republic*; and *Algernon Sidney and the Restoration Crisis 1677–1683* (Cambridge, 1991). The best expression of this self-consciousness remains Sidney's to a friend in Paris in 1677: 'The design of the English [republicans] had been, to make a Republic on the model of that of the Hebrews, before they had their Kings, and of Sparta, of Rome, and of Venice, taking from each what was best, to make a perfect composition.' Paris, Bibliothèque Nationale, Fr. MS.23254, fols. 99–101.

[11] John Pocock's pre-*Machiavellian Moment* trajectory towards this subject is most helpfully laid out in *The Ancient Constitution and the Feudal Law* (Cambridge, 1957), ch. 6; *Politics, Language and Time* (London, 1972), chs. 3–4, see esp. p. 112.

exceedingly exotic territory.[12] Our final task will be to examine that compass, and understand how he got there. One side-effect of this process may be the recognition that the study of political language, while it is essential for, can also be a distraction from our perception of political substance. If classical republicanism was a language, why do we find its foremost English practitioner speaking in a North Derbyshire accent which Machiavelli would have found incomprehensible?

II

The English republican paradox, of practical failure and ideological success, was not coincidental. Political instability and intellectual fertility have long walked hand in hand (for Plato, as for Machiavelli, and for Hobbes). And throughout its history the practical and intellectual aspects of the English republican experience remained closely linked. This experience spanned thirty-five years (1649-83); that is, a single generation. For it was the product of a single group, bound by a common political experience. For all its variety, all the branches of English republican ideology issued from this one trunk, rooted in the practical experience of republicanism. We may divide its development into five stages.

It was the centrality of political practice that made the first stage (1649-53) the most important. Notoriously the fact of English republicanism arrived slightly in advance of the theory.[13] The consequent depth of a despised government's need for political legitimation bred its own rich ideological harvest. For European and domestic audiences respectively, John Milton and Marchamont Nedham both showed in their different ways that it would be necessary to reach back behind the whole medieval experience of monarchy to a time free from the 'superstitious reverence for kings'.[14]

---

[12] See for instance Milton's complaints about Harrington's republic in 1659, a year of more general republican attack upon his thought. J. Milton, *Readie and Easie Way* in *Complete Prose Works*, vol. VII (New Haven, 1980), pp. 441, 445–6.

[13] By this I mean positive, as opposed to the negative theory which dominated the engagement controversy. Nedham distinguished himself on both fronts, making the transition in Part 2, Chapter 5 of his *The Case of Commonwealth of England Stated* (1650), ed. P.A. Knachel (Virginia, 1969), pp. 111–28.

[14] J. Milton, *Second Defence of the English People* (1654), Introduction; Scott, *English Republic*, pp. 23–4.

In its second stage, in opposition to the Protectorate, and centred upon the year 1656, republicanism extended its range. This now spanned the considerable intellectual distance from Harrington to Vane. And this marriage of political adversity with intellectual diversity remained characteristic. It was evident in 1659, as republicanism stared its own failure in the face. It persisted as the restored monarchy was assailed from continental exile in 1665 to 1666. And we see it in the last phase of English republican activity, both practical and intellectual, in London in 1680 to 1683. One last time the capital became a republican bastion: even a sheriff, Slingsby Bethel, published something. It took a further wave of exiles and executions to bring this singular chapter of English history to a close.

This was not the end, of course, for the republican ideology. This displayed a prodigious capacity for posthumous (and international) reinvention.[15] But it was the end for the practical experience by which it had been sustained. In all its phases it was the product of men linked with that experience, at first or second hand. Milton and Nedham had been employed by the republican Council of State. Their achievement was built upon by a series of members of that council. In stages two to three (1656, 1659) there was the republican leader Henry Vane. In four to five, there was Vane's close friend and protegé Algernon Sidney. Joining Sidney in the latter was another council member and his own second cousin Henry Neville. All of these senior republican politicians were patrons of other writers (Vane of Sidney and Stubbe; Sidney of Bethel; Neville of Harrington) as well as authors in their own right.

As the product, then, of a common experience and linked authorship, it is not surprising that this ideology shared some characteristics and an identifiable core. English republicanism, it has been said, 'was a language, not a programme'.[16] Indeed it was at least four languages, and usually some combination of them. All drew, logically enough, and with more or less adaptive flair, on the republic's own pre-1649 intellectual heritage. Natural-law theory was the language of civil-war independency (and its other political

[15] C. Robbins, *The Eighteenth Century Commonwealthsman* (Cambridge, Mass., 1959); Pocock, *Machiavellian Moment*; Scott, *English Republic*, ch. 1.
[16] Pocock (ed.) *Political Works*, p. 15. For the remainder of this paragraph see Scott, *English Republic*, ch. 2.

offshoots, including the Levellers).[17] Interest theory had, by 1648, become the political language of the new model army.[18] Classical republicanism involved a considerable realignment of early Stuart Renaissance culture. Republicanism also employed an historical adaptation of the ancient constitutionalism of the same period. Milton used this, along with classical republicanism and natural-law theory. Nedham used classical republicanism and interest theory. Vane used interest and natural-law languages. Sidney used all four: interest theory to connect with the Dutch republicans in 1665 and 1666; classical republicanism, natural-law theory and ancient constitutionalism to respond to Robert Filmer's (early Stuart) attack upon them in *Patriarcha*. All of these languages are important, but it is upon classical republicanism that we must focus for the context of Harrington's *Oceana*.[19]

The character and much of the range of English classical republicanism was established by its pioneers. Milton emphasised its antique basis; Nedham its Renaissance revival. Milton's key sources were Aristotle, Cicero and Livy. Nedham's *Mercurius Politicus* developed the Livian republicanism of Machiavelli. Both writers used many other sources, classical, medieval and early modern: among the most important were Plato, Polybius, Tacitus, Guicciardini and Grotius. Between them, and particularly around this core of Aristotle, Livy and Machiavelli, they laid the basis for everything to come.

Thirty years later, at the other end of the republican chronology, Sidney and Neville remained secure within this tradition. This is true of Sidney in particular, whose political thought reads like Milton and Nedham in a fit of mutual congratulation (no mean feat). At its core sit the same Aristotelian natural-law theory, the same Ciceronian rhetoric of liberty, and the same Livian and Machiavellian militarism that lay at the heart of the Rump's own ideology. Both men borrowed the Anglo-Saxon ancient constitu-

---

[17] Ibid., pp. 16–17 and note 8.
[18] Ibid., chs. 12–13; *The Humble Remonstrance of his Excellency the Lord Fairfax* (November 1648); M. Kishlansky, 'Ideology and Politics in the Parliamentary Armies 1645–9', in J.S. Morrill (ed.) *Reactions to the English Civil War* (London, 1982).
[19] See especially Fink, *The Classical Republicans*; the works of Pocock in notes 5 and 11 above; and Blair Worden, 'Classical Republicanism and the Puritan Revolution', in Pearl Lloyd-Jones and Blair Worden (eds.), *History and Imagination: Essays in Honour of Hugh Trevor-Roper* (London, 1981). This author has made the point (*English Republic*, ch. 2) that even classical republicanism can only be seen as 'a' language in the loosest of senses.

tionalism ('the Gothic polity') adapted by Milton from Tacitus (*Germania; Agricola*) and Hotman (*Francogallia*). Neville became the translator of Machiavelli's works.[20] None of this is surprising, since both men had, as we have seen, been members of the republic's Council of State. Yet the durability and grip of this early ideology also reflects both the high profile of the propaganda organs through which it had been disseminated, and some salient characteristics of the republic's own political life.

Milton wrote, theatrically, for a European audience. Nedham's *Mercurius*, the Rump's official journal, 'flew every week to all parts of the nation for more than ten years'; 'tis incredible what influence [it] had'. When we find Nedham's writing referred to by a contemporary as 'like a weaver's beam' – around which subsequent ideology spun itself – we have reason to pay attention.[21] Of these practical political characteristics, two in particular generated and typified English republican ideology. The first was an emphasis on arms: the equation of political liberty with military strength. English republicanism was deeply militaristic because these elements of Livy (Milton) and Machiavelli (Nedham) spoke to the republic's own extraordinary military achievements. The conquest of England, Ireland and Scotland, and the humbling of the mightiest naval power in Europe, all within four years, left an indelible mark upon everybody involved. The second characteristic was an equally pervasive awareness of contingency, for the republic's life, though militarily glorious, was turbulent and short. Nedham took to the republican stage pointing at Fortune's wheel: there is 'a perpetual rotation of all things'.[22] Milton exited from it bewailing the same movement, 'making vain . . . the blood of so many thousand valiant Englishmen, who left us in this libertie, bought with their lives'.[23] Sidney improved upon the Machiavel-

[20] A. Sidney, *Discourses Concerning Government* (1698); H. Neville, *Plato Redivivus* (1680), *The Works of the Famous Nicholas Machiavel* (1675); J.H. Salmon, *The French Religious Wars in English Political Thought* (Oxford, 1959), p. 160. See Nathaniel Bacon, *A Historical and Political Discourse of the Laws and Government of England* (1648); J. Milton, *A Defense of the People of England* (1651), in *Complete Prose Works*, vol. IV, ed. D.M. Wolfe (New Haven, 1966), pp. 479–83; Scott, *English Republic*, p. 107.

[21] These quotes are from Wood, cited in the introduction to Milton's *Complete Prose Works*, vol. IV, pp. 53–6.

[22] Nedham, *Case of the Commonwealth*, p. 7.

[23] J. Milton, *Readie and Easie Way* (1659), *Prose Works*, vol. VII (New Haven, 1980), pp. 358–9.

lian insight that political change was unavoidable, insisting that it was essential.[24]

There was indeed then, a Machiavellian moment in England. As a whole English republicanism both faced, and embraced, its instability in time. As a body of thought it was distinguished by an openness, a flexibility, and a scepticism entirely characteristic of the humanistic context from which Machiavelli's own had emerged.[25] In Nedham and Sidney in particular it had two supreme Machiavellians, who understood and supported every hard decision taken before them by the master. The most important of these was the choice of vigour, of armed force and of the 'tumults' they would bring, at the expense of longevity and stability. Faced with the choice, for them as for Machiavelli, the longevity of Venice could not compare with the *grandezza* of Rome. That Harrington was a participant in this tradition is, however, much less clear.

III

Harrington's relationship to the republican experience, both practical and intellectual, was most unusual. On the one hand he did indeed draw heavily upon this classical republican heritage. Almost every major feature of *Oceana* was prefigured in some way between 1649 and 1656. One the other hand, everything so borrowed was fundamentally transformed. The intention and result was to produce a body of thought completely different in kind. *Oceana* is, in fact, a deliberate subversion of classical republicanism with its roots in a post-humanist rebellion linked to that of Hobbes. We will need to consider each of these relationships – of dependency and transformation – in turn.

One of *Oceana*'s fundamental laws, rotation of office, has long been recognised as a hobby-horse of Nedham's *Mercurius Politicus*. It was also a feature of the republican Council of State's own political practice.[26] But the other, the agrarian, or at least the concerns behind it, had also been adumbrated in this period. Milton had used Cicero's *De lege agraria* in his *Defence of the English People*

---

[24] Scott, *English Republic*, pp. 30–5; *Restoration Crisis*, chs. 10–11.
[25] This is no less true of figures like Vane and Stubbe than of those whose ideas have been discussed here: see Scott, *English Republic*, pp. 105–12.
[26] Ibid., pp. 36, 100.

(1651).[27] Nedham, in one three-issue run of *Mercurius* (no. 5, 101-3, 6-27 May 1652) had insisted upon three essentials of republican policy that lie at the heart of *Oceana*. They were that a free state must 'limit . . . the wealth' of its citizens, and particularly its senators, 'that none of them grow over rich'; that it must limit their term of office 'that the affairs of the commonwealth [not] be made subservient . . . to a few persons'; and 'that the people be conti-nually trained up in the exercise of arms'.[28] In these three policies, drawn from Aristotle, Cicero, Livy and Machiavelli, Nedham anticipated both of *Oceana*'s basic laws, and its armed citizenship. Moreover Nedham illustrated the first principle, as Harrington was to do, by reference to the 'policy of Harry the 8, who when he disposed of the Revenues of the Abbies' followed the example of Brutus in distributing 'the Royal Revenues among the people'.[29] When the pamphlet *A Copy of a Letter from an Officer in Ireland* used this same historical account in early 1656 its author was accused of stealing from the still-unpublished *Oceana*. The reality may have been more complicated.[30] Harrington himself noted the anticipa-tion of his concept of the balance by Aristotle ('You have Aristotle full of it in divers places, especially where he says that immoderate wealth . . . [is] where one man or a few have greater possessions than the . . . frame of the commonwealth will bear').[31]

These borrowings form part of what was a wholesale adoption by Harrington of the sources and the range (classical, medieval and Renaissance) of the early republican tradition. These included aspects of interest and natural-law theory, and the history of the Gothic polity. What is more important however is the use to which these borrowings were put. For the distance between the type of thought upon which Harrington drew, and the type to whose construction he now set himself, was extreme. It was a transition from general principles to specificity; from the sceptical humanism of the Renaissance to the pursuit of perfection, fixity and perma-nence. Harrington set his sights upon this extraordinary objective: political immortality. To this would be sacrificed all the fundamen-

---

[27] Milton, *Complete Prose Works*, vol. IV, pp. 485–6.
[28] *Mercurius Politicus*, pp. 1,586–7, p. 1,594.
[29] Ibid., pp. 1,586–7.
[30] See below; and Pocock, *Political Works*, pp. 10–12; Scott, *English Republic*, pp. 115–16.
[31] Harrington, *Political Works*, p. 166; see also M. Downs, *James Harrington* (Boston, 1977), pp. 24–6.

tals of the classical republican tradition. And behind this intellectual chasm lay divergent assumptions about nature itself.
According to Harrington: 'A man is sinful yet the world is perfect,
so may the citizens be sinful, and yet the commonwealth be
perfect.'[32] According to Algernon Sidney: 'Nothing can or ought to
be permanent but that which is perfect. And perfection is in God
only, not in the things he has created.'[33]

The peculiarity of Harrington's relationship to the republican
experience begins with its practical dimension. Alone of the major
republican writers Harrington was not himself actively involved in
the cause. He was not, that is, an exponent of the *vita activa*, in
practice any more than in theory. This is important not only
because the sceptical qualities of English republican thought are
closely related to the political practice of its authors (as was true of
Machiavelli). We will shortly have reason to question the quality of
political participation in *Oceana* itself. It is also important because
Harrington himself placed great emphasis upon it:

Some have [said] that I, being a private man, had been ... mad ... to
meddle with politics; what had a private man to do with government? My
Lord, there is not any public person, not any magistrate, that has written
in politics worth a button. All they that have been excellent in this way
have been private men.[34]

Hardly less importantly, Harrington's personal involvement in
England's troubles in the middle of the century had been on the
other (royalist) side. As an intimate of the captured Charles I he
'passionately loved his Majestie', and contracted 'so great a griefe'
at his death that 'never any thing did goe so neer to him'.[35] Among
the subsequent features of *Oceana* remarkable within the republican
canon were a denial of the right of political resistance (shared with
Hobbes),[36] and an insistence upon the right of defeated royalists to
full citizenship which embroiled him in controversy with other
republicans including Nedham, Stubbe and Vane.[37] At the same

[32] Harrington, *Political Works*, p. 320.
[33] Sidney, *Discourses Concerning Government* in *Sydney on Government: The Works of Algernon Sydney* (1772), p. 406.
[34] *The Examination of James Harrington*, in *Political Works*, p. 858. See also p. 395.
[35] J. Aubrey, *Brief Lives*, ed. O.L. Dick, (London, 1958), p. 124.
[36] Zagorin, *Political Thought*, p. 140.
[37] See particularly Stubbe's *An Essay in Defence of the Good Old Cause* (1659) written under Vane's patronage. J.C. Davis, 'Pocock's Harrington: Grace, Nature and Art in the Classical Republicanism of James Harrington', *Historical Journal*, 24, 3 (1981) discusses this feature of *Oceana*.

time he was attacked by royalists for dabbling in republican theory
and betraying an impeccably loyal background.[38]

Harrington's one personal link with the republican experience
was through his friend Henry Neville. It was Neville who persuaded him to stop writing bad poetry and turn to political
thought. Subsequently Hobbes claimed of *Oceana* that Neville 'had
a finger in that pye' and (as Aubrey remarked) ''tis like enough'.
Neville was also rumoured to be the author of *A Copy of a Letter*
(1656) already mentioned.[39] Certainly when Neville's own *Plato
Redivivus* was published twenty-four years later its editor remarked
that it was no fairer to accuse Neville of borrowing Harrington's
ideas than to accuse Harrington of borrowing those of *A Copy of a
Letter*.[40] When *Oceana* was published, Samuel Hartlib noted in his
'Ephemerides': 'Oceana a Polit[ical] Book about all Govern-
m[en]ts written by Mr Harrington. Mr Nevil the witt commends it
as one of the best books written in that kind.'[41]

In *Oceana* Harrington used classical republicanism as that other
ex-royalist Hobbes had used (and similarly subverted) natural-law
theory: to research the tragedy of the civil wars, and to find a way
out of them. Both *Leviathan* and *Oceana* have the same object:
stability and peace. As Harrington restated Hobbes: 'The ways of
nature require peace. The ways of peace require obedience unto
laws. Laws in England . . . must [now] be popular laws; and the
sum of popular laws must amount unto a commonwealth.'[42]

What is most immediately unusual about *Oceana* (within the
republican tradition) is its utopian form and the extreme particularity of its orders. These features are related to the object of
permanence. It is through a constitutional order that will be eternal
that Harrington seeks his exit from civil war. One can only imagine
the bafflement of Machiavelli (for whom internal 'tumults' were
essential to republican greatness) faced with Harrington's

[38] J. Lesley, *A Slap on the Snout of the Republican Swine*, quoted in Downs, *Harrington*, pp. 40–1.
[39] J. Aubrey, *Brief Lives*, pp. 124–5. See footnote 33. A copy of the *Letter* in Cambridge
University Library features a contemporary attribution to Neville.
[40] Neville, *Plato Redivivus* in C. Robbins (ed.), *Two Republican Tracts* (Cambridge, 1969), p.
68.
[41] Samuel Hartlib 'Ephemerides' (1656), transcript p. 65, Hartlib Papers, Sheffield
University. I am indebted for this reference to Dr Jan Kumpera, visitor to the Hartlib
Papers Project from Pilsen, Czechoslovakia, and the translator of Harrington's *Oceana*
into Czech (1986).
[42] Harrington, *The Art of Lawgiving, Works*, p. 660.

fifth order: requiring that upon the first Monday next ensuing the last of December the bigger bell in every parish throughout the nation be rung at eight of the clock in the morning, and continue ringing for the space of one hour.[43]

Set out in 'The Model of the Commonwealth'; bounded by 'The Preliminaries' on one side and 'The Corollary' on the other, Harrington's 'orders' account for the bulk of *Oceana*'s length. They are the most important (though the least read) part of the work. And they may have had an interregnum model of their own of sorts. This was the reigning constitution, the Instrument of Government (enacted December 1653).[44] *Oceana* shares the Instrument's concerns with property qualification, with the composition of the governing bodies, with tenure and rotation of office, with political participation more generally and with the size and distribution of Horse and Foot. Since Harrington said he began writing in 1654, and since what he was offering Cromwell in *Oceana* was an elaborate alternative to the Instrument, it makes sense to read it in this way.

Our major concern in the work of 'England's premier civic humanist' must be with the quality of civic participation these orders allow. Civic humanism, Pocock reminds us, was 'a style of thought . . . in which . . . the development of the individual towards self-fulfillment is possible only when [he] . . . acts as a citizen . . . [in] a conscious and autonomous decision-taking political community'. This 'polis, or republic . . . had to be conceived of as finite and localised in time, and therefore as presenting all the problems of particularity'.[45] Yet what is striking about *Oceana* is precisely the absence of these characteristics. *Oceana* is not to be finite in time (nor, incidentally, localised in space). Its triumph over particularity, over time itself, is exactly the purpose of the construction: 'it hath no principle of mortality'.[46] And this purpose is achieved by an equivalent conquest of the participatory capacities of its citizens.[47] Nobody is autonomous in *Oceana*, for everyone

---

[43] *Political Works*, p. 214.

[44] J.P. Kenyon (ed.), *The Stuart Constitution 1603–1688* (Cambridge, 1966), pp. 333–6.

[45] Hans Baron, *The Crisis of the Early Italian Renaissance*, discussed in Pocock, *Politics, Language and Time*, p. 85.

[46] *Political Works*, p. 321.

[47] Colin Davis has pointed out that 'in *Oceana* no citizen does anything in a fully moral sense, and what he does do he doesn't do for very long'. J.C. Davis, *Utopia and the Ideal Society* (Cambridge, 1981), p. 209; 'Pocock's Harrington', ibid. This article is indebted to Davis's work.

is enslaved to the state. The 'people' have no moral political personality; they are 'materials' (Harrington's word) in the greater construction of the Commonwealth. Thus Oceanic political participation is actually restricted to the tedious repetition of prescribed rituals which cannot be changed. Moral behaviour has been abolished with its precondition, choice. Members of the popular assembly work in silence upon pain of death. Even 'self-consciousness' is unnecessary since 'it is not possible for the people, if they can but draw the balls, though they understand nothing at all of the ballot, to be out'. It is upon the grounds of this rigid control of civic participation that Harrington defended his part-royalist citizenship against republican criticism. Sedition was impossible because the quality of civic behaviour could not affect the quality of the state. Most noticeable throughout *Oceana* is the strength of the language Harrington uses to describe this control of the exercise of power. 'Receive the sovereign power . . . hold her fast, embrace her forever . . . The virtue of the lodestone is not impaired or limited, but receiveth strength, by being bound in iron.'[48]

Since the quality of his citizenship counted for nothing ('a man may be sinful, yet the world be perfect') Harrington boasted that he had rendered redundant the moral basis of political science. Thus he criticised Machiavelli:

'If a commonwealth' saith he [Machiavelli] 'were so happy as to be provided often with men that, when she is swerving from her principles, should reduce her unto her institution, she would be immortal.' But a commonwealth . . . swerveth not from her principles, but by and through her institution . . . a commonwealth that is rightly instituted can never swerve . . . wherefore it is apparent . . . Machiavel understood not a commonwealth as to the whole piece.[49]

The truth is that we see in Harrington's *Oceana*, no less than in Hobbes's *Leviathan*, the abolition of the participatory basis of classical citizenship. In both cases the reason is the same: that this is what it takes to achieve peace. Unlike Hobbes, however, while abolishing the *substance* of participation Harrington does, throughout *Oceana*, preserve and ritualise the external appearance of it. This civic 'motion' plays, as we will see, a vital function within the work. The result, however, is a classical republican Trojan horse.

---

[48] *Political Works*, pp. 222,230.
[49] Ibid., pp. 321–2.

Within an empty shell there has been pushed into the world a fundamentally different type of politics. Even the linguistic 'shell' is full of peculiarities which should alert us to the fact that something is wrong.

While removing choice, the precondition of Aristotelian virtue, Harrington has also abolished 'liberty', the foundation of the classical republican tradition.[50] In its place he has substituted another foundation, not moral but material: the balance of property. Equally absent is *fortuna*, the precondition of Machiavellian *virtu*.[51] For *fortuna* is precisely that element of contingency which Harrington's system has eradicated. Gone, too, is Milton and Sidney's free 'Gothic polity'. In *Oceana* this has become the unstable and (therefore) imperfect 'Gothic balance'. This use of 'balance' is in turn a transformation of Polybius, for whom it had meant a stabilising balance within the three-part classical constitution (the one, the few, and the many). In Harrington this stability is provided by the 'balance of dominion', the material foundation upon which the whole constitutional superstructure will rest. That constitution in turn has an internal balancing principle which is not tripartite but bi-polar. It is the superstructural twin of the balance of property: the second of Harrington's great 'discoveries'. 'That which great philosophers are disputing upon in vain is brought into light by two silly girls: even the whole mystery of a commonwealth, which lies only in dividing and choosing.'[52]

---

[50] Classical liberty was active and collective: the self-government of cities, rather than individuals. *Oceana* is not free in these terms: its 'citizens' do not rule themselves; its empire of laws is not of its own making. Following Aristotle this liberty also presupposed individual choice: civic virtue, the moral quality upon which the free city depended, involved the voluntary placing by the citizen of private means and talents at the service of the public (Sidney and Milton particularly emphasised this). That there is little such choice in *Oceana* should not surprise us since it is (as we will see) a material rather than a moral political construct. Hobbes had rejected the Aristotelian concept of liberty (Q. Skinner 'Thomas Hobbes on the Proper Signification of Liberty', *Transactions of the Royal Historical Society*, 5th series, 40 (1990), 140–1). Harrington stated: '[Hobbes's] treatises of liberty and necessity . . . are the greatest new lights, and those which I have follow'd, and shall follow'; 'as is admirably observed by Mr Hobbs . . . [the human] will is caus'd, and being caus'd is necessitated'. It should not surprise us then that Harrington viewed the Commonwealth as a constitutional 'frame' which 'causeth everyone to perform his certain function . . . necessarily'; see below p. 160 (and note 80). James Cotton, 'James Harrington and Thomas Hobbes', *Journal of the History of Ideas*, 42 (1981), 416–17.

[51] In its place we get a single phrase: the definition of 'empire' (political power) as 'the goods of fortune': *Political Works*, p. 163. Needless to say the word here has a different meaning, and performs a different function.

[52] *Political Works*, p. 172.

What so delighted Harrington about this discovery, its simplicity, is precisely what is apt to strike the humanistic observer as so
ludicrous about it. It is vintage Harrington: all the problems of
politics throughout the ages have been solved by one material
object (the cake: the superstructural image here of dominion) and
one mechanism for disposing of it (dividing and choosing). That
political behaviour might amount to anything more serious or
complicated than the division of material spoils seems not to have
occurred to him. That this metaphor for the relationship between
two assemblies is irrelevant to the great majority of transactions in
which they would engage has equally been ignored. Exactly the
same syndrome is visible in *Oceana*'s treatment of the key republican term 'interest'. Another moral fundamental, the relationship
between private and public interest had exercised all classical
thinkers from the Greek (Plato, Aristotle) to the English (Milton,
Vane, Sidney). Harrington, however, had little difficulty with it.
'Whereas the people, taken apart, are but so many private
interests ... if you take them together they are the public
interest.'[53] Again, that the transition from one to the other might
hinge on anything more than the collection of citizens ('the being of
a commonwealth consisteth in the methodical collection of the
people');[54] that it might hinge on the quality rather than quantity
of participation, seems not to have occurred to him. The appropriate response to all this came from Mathew Wren who, increasingly exasperated by *Oceana*'s meaningless use of words like 'virtue',
'interest' and 'soul', demanded of Harrington the moral philosophy
within which their meaning could be located. Harrington's reply
shows that he had no answer, and may not have understood the
question.[55]

Oceana, then, both abandons and mutilates a good deal of
classical language. Even where the words are retained the meanings have changed. We must turn away from the apparently clever
things in *Oceana* to see what is really clever about it. Historical
attention has focussed upon its main building blocks, which come
in three pairs. There are the two 'discoveries': the balance of
dominion (in the foundation), and dividing and choosing (in the

---

[53] Ibid., p. 280.
[54] Ibid., p. 214.
[55] M. Wren, *Considerations upon Mr Harrington's Oceana* (1657) p. 20; Harrington, *The Prerogative of Popular Government* (1658); *Political Works*, p. 415, and Book I, ch.5 in general.

superstructure). There are the basic laws which follow from them: the agrarian, and rotation. And there are the historical (The Second Part of the Preliminaries) and constitutional (The Model) frameworks through which each principle is elaborated. Modern admiration, perhaps credulity, has particularly attached to the former in the wake of Karl Marx. It remains to be seen whether the decline of Marx will prefigure the decline of Harrington. Altogether more important however is the nature and intention of the whole construct.

IV

Wren understood *Oceana* immediately because he was a participant in the same intellectual world: that of 'natural philosophy'.[56] Natural philosophers in the middle of the century varied considerably in their methods and objectives. These ranged from the deeply religious to the almost secular, and from the empirically to the metaphysically grounded. They also squabbled incessantly, and Harrington and Wren, when they were not arguing with one another, were arguing with Hobbes, and quoting Hobbes against one another. All however were indebted to Bacon's search for 'the pure knowledge of nature', the handiwork of God. For Bacon 'the true end' of such knowledge was a 'restitution . . . (in great part) of man to the Sovereignty and power . . . which he had in the First state of creation'. Through the understanding of nature 'natural philosophy proposes to itself, as its noblest work of all, nothing less than the renovation of things corruptible'.[57]

Harrington's debt to Bacon is widely understood. Less so, however, is his much greater debt to a more immediate influence. Once again Wren saw it instantly:

---

[56] On this context see Craig Diamond, 'Natural Philosophy in Harrington's Political Thought', *Journal of the History of Philosophy* 16, 4 (1978) 387–98. Diamond emphasises Harrington's attraction both to Neoplatonism and to the 'new mechanical philosophy', both features of his thought noted here.

[57] Bacon, *Works*, vol. III, pp. 264–5, 286; vol. IV, p. 721, quoted in Davis, *Utopia*, pp. 124–5. The Hartlib Circle formed one wing of this enterprise, which may partly explain *Oceana's* appearance in Hartlib's 'Ephemerides', and a utopian form to Harrington's work more like Hartlib's *Macaria* and Bacon's *New Atlantis* than like other republican works. See Charles Webster, *Samuel Hartlib and the Advancement of Learning* (Cambridge, 1971) and *The Great Instauration* (London, 1975). *Oceana* includes, as Pocock noted, an 'academy of provosts' which looks like Hartlib's 'Office of Addresses': *Political Works*, pp. 251–2.

though Mr Harrington professes a great Enmity to Mr Hobs in his politiques, underhand notwithstanding he . . . does silently swallow down such Notions as Mr Hobs hath chewed for him.

To this Harrington replied, candidly: 'It is true that I have opposed the politics of Mr Hobbes, *to show him what he taught me* [my emphasis] . . . I firmly believe that Mr Hobbes . . . will in future ages be accounted, the best writer at this day in the world.'[58]

Although it has often been quoted, this statement by Harrington has not been taken literally by historians. The similarity of Hobbes's and Harrington's ecclesiology has been noted,[59] but no equally close relationship between their political thought has been discerned. This is, not least, because the first part of *Oceana*'s Preliminaries is a point-by-point refutation of *Leviathan*; and because the connection has not been obvious between 'the theorist of absolute sovereignty and the theorist of the commonwealth of participatory virtue'.[60] But how does *Oceana* look if we accept literally the claim of its author that he wrote it, opposing *Leviathan* in the process, to show Hobbes what he had taught him?

Like Harrington, Hobbes believed that it was only upon the principles of nature that a science of government could be erected. Political art was an imitation of nature, the art of God. 'Nature is by the Art of Man . . . so imitated, that it can make an Artificial Animal . . . For by Art is created the great Leviathan called Commonwealth . . . which is but an artificial man.'[61] Hobbes was also a sceptic, who had become alienated from both classical history and Baconian empiricism as roads to knowledge. For according to Hobbes 'experience concludeth nothing universally'. Both history and experimentation produced information about human perception, not about the world, unless they were grounded in a theory of perception 'set in the context of a general metaphysical theory'.[62] It was Hobbes's metaphysical assumptions which formed the basis of *Leviathan* (and, as we will see, of *Oceana*).

For Hobbes the world, or nature, consisted of material in motion.

---

[58] Wren, *Considerations*, p. 41; Harrington, *Prerogative*, in *Political Works*, p. 423.
[59] Pocock, *Political Works*, Introduction, ch. 5; M. Goldie, 'The Civil Religion of James Harrington, in A. Pagden (ed.), *The Languages of Political Theory in Early Modern Europe* (Cambridge, 1988).
[60] Pocock, *Machiavellian Moment*, p. 397.
[61] *Leviathan*, p. 81.
[62] Hobbes, *Elements of Law*, I.4.10, and Richard Tuck, *Hobbes* (Oxford, 1989), p. 49.

Leviathan was subtitled 'the Matter, [and] Form . . . of a Common-wealth', the purpose of the 'form' being to give direction to this motion. Natural motion was perpetual unless arrested or diverted by pressure (motion) from a different direction: 'when a thing is in motion, it will eternally be in motion, unless somewhat els stay it'.[63] Hobbes's famous picture of a state of nature as a 'war of all against all' expressed this ballistic vision. Nature was an unregulated billiard table full of perpetually moving and colliding balls. Yet man's greatest fear was of the permanent cessation of motion (death). Hobbes built upon this fear a series of universal 'laws of nature' the object of which was peace.[64] In a commonwealth this object would be secured by the public sword. The members of this commonwealth accepted some collective restraint on their motion (peace) in exchange for protection from the prospect of its end (death). They accepted Leviathan's restraining hand upon the billiard table.

In his growth towards this position Hobbes had passed many Harringtonian landmarks. He had been an accomplished humanist scholar and poet. He had been deeply impressed by Venice, and by Bacon.[65] It is significant however that his major humanist achievement was a translation of Thucydides' *History of the Peloponnesian War* (1628), the magisterial account of a brutal and catastrophic conflict which had all but destroyed the golden age of Greece. This can only have reinforced Hobbes's interest in peace, and his scepticism about the popular political participation which had turned to *hubris* and then disaster in ancient Athens.

The first chapter of Harrington's reply to Wren, *The Prerogative of Popular Government* (1658), turns upon a lengthy argument over Hobbes's *Thucydides*. Later in the *Prerogative* Harrington remarked that his 'opinion that riches are power is as ancient as the first book of Thucydides . . . and not omitted by Mr Hobbes or any other politican'.[66] The cause of the argument was Wren's taunting of Harrington's division of history into 'ancient' and 'modern prudence'. For Harrington's abandonment of classical usage included the exchange of 'history' for this Hobbesian term. According to

---

[63] *Leviathan*, p. 87.
[64] Ibid., part 1, chs. 14 and 15.
[65] Tuck, *Hobbes*, ch. 1.
[66] Harrington, *Political Works*, pp. 397–400, 412.

Hobbes, prudence was a derivation from experience: it was 'a Presumption of the Future, contracted from the Experience of time Past'.[67]

Both Zagorin and Raab discerned in *Oceana* a Hobbesian search for universal laws of nature, tethered however by a Machiavellian historical empiricism governing their recovery. This did not, then, interfere with their perception of Harrington as a Machiavellian and a humanist. For Harrington (said Zagorin) the principles of politics must 'come from history, and history alone'.[68] Yet this is not actually what Harrington said. According to Harrington: 'Policy is an art. Art is the observation or imitation of nature . . . by observation of the face of nature a politician limns his Commonwealth.' Therefore 'No man can be a politician except he be first a Historian *or a Traveller*' (my italics). Except he be, that is, an observer of nature, either in 'what has bin' or 'what is'.[69] Lycurgus became a supreme politician in Sparta without any knowledge of history: 'Lycurgus, by being [only] a Traveller, became a legislator; but in times when prudence was another thing.'[70] In the ancient world prudence (the political observation of nature) was recorded in what is, not only (as in the Gothic world) in what has been.

For Harrington, then, history was indeed Hobbesian prudence. 'Experience of time past' was one kind of experience of the world. Although it 'concludeth nothing universally' it could be used to recover, and demonstrate, principles which were otherwise derived (from nature). *Oceana* used the terms ancient and modern prudence in just this way.[71] Nor, similarly, could unaided experimental (as opposed to historical) empiricism give true knowledge. But like prudence experimental demonstration could reveal to the world the

---

[67] Hobbes, *Leviathan*, p. 98.
[68] Raab, *Machiavelli*, ch. 6; Zagorin, *Political Thought*, ch. 11.
[69] Harrington, *Political Works*, p. 417; Raab, *Machiavelli*, pp. 193, 249.
[70] Harrington, *Political Works*, p. 310.
[71] Harrington makes this relationship between history and nature, discovery and demonstration clearest in *A Note Upon the Foregoing Eclogues*, *Political Works*, pp. 580–1. Having said elsewhere that 'the doctrine of the balance is as old in nature as herself, and new in art as my writing', he continues: 'The doctrine of the balance, not being sufficiently discovered or heeded by ancient historians and politicians, is the cause why their writings are more dark . . . in the principles of government than otherwise they would have been; nevertheless he who . . . shall rightly answer these quaeres out of story, must strike the inevitable light of this truth out of nature; which once mastered, the whole mystery of government . . . becometh as obvious and facile . . . as the meanest of the vulgar arts.'

universal principles inherent in nature itself. In this connection both Harrington and Hobbes admired the anatomist Harvey. His demonstration, from the dissection of particular bodies, of the universal principle of the perpetual circulation of the blood, accorded perfectly with the metaphysical assumptions of both men.[72] For *Oceana*, like *Leviathan*, and following it, assumes a world of material in perpetual motion.

The First Part of *Oceana*'s Preliminaries is structured as an argument between 'The Leviathan' and Machiavelli. On the face of it Harrington abhors the one, and adores the other. Upon Machiavelli he heaps praise as the 'onely retriever of ancient prudence'; and it is precisely 'that which Machiavel . . . hath gone about to retrieve . . . that *Leviathan* . . . goes about to destory'.[73] Even in the first Preliminary however, this relationship is not what it seems: there is even something dishonest about it, for in both cases Harrington protesteth too much.

Machiavelli, having been slapped on the back as an old friend, is then systematically reprimanded. Every important decision made by him within the Florentine humanist tradition is up-ended. He had sensationally rejected Venice for Rome: Harrington disagrees, accusing him of 'Saddling the wrong horse.'[74] He had disparaged the political role of the gentry: Harrington corrects him, and insists that they are indispensable.[75] He had concluded as a fundamental principle that a state cannot have preservation and expansion, it must choose; Harrington observes that this is incorrect, they are compatible. All of this culminates in the statement that 'Machiavel understood not' republican politics 'as to the whole'. In particular the fundamental of the balance 'hath [been] missed . . . narrowly and more dangerously by him . . . [yet] the balance . . . though unseen by Machiavel, is that which interpreteth him'.[76] This is the language of the used-car salesman. Machiavelli's civic humanist world having been dismantled, a material principle foreign to it now poses as the key by which to unlock its true meaning.

No more is *Oceana*'s relationship to Hobbes what Harrington initially makes it appear. For the argument of the First Preliminary

---

[72] Tuck, *Hobbes*, pp. 48, 53; for Harrington's use of Harvey see below (and also 77).
[73] Harrington, *Oceana*, in *Political Works*, p. 161.
[74] Ibid., p. 277.
[75] Ibid., pp. 166–7, 173.
[76] Ibid., p. 166.

is actually the squabbling of siblings: it derives from a deeper intellectual cousinage (and rivalry). When it is complete Harrington proceeds (as we will see) to erect the 'Model of the Commonwealth' upon Hobbesian foundations. Harrington's initial argument with Hobbes has one basis: this relates to means, rather than assumptions or ends. Hobbes's scepticism has led him to reject ancient prudence: one kind of 'experience of the world'. Even so he grasps (unlike Machiavelli) the material basis of government. 'But Leviathan, though he seems to skew at antiquity, following his furious master Carneades, hath caught hold of the public sword, unto which he reduceth all manner and matter of government.'[77] Harrington's point is that to reject the prudence (experience) of the ancients, as *Leviathan* did, on the grounds that 'the Greeks and Romans . . . derived . . . [politics] not from the principles of nature but . . . the [particular] practice of their own commonwealths' is 'as if a man should tell famous Harvey that he transcribed the circulation of the blood not out of the principles of nature, but out of the anatomy of this or that body'.[78] In other words Harrington thought the ancients had perceived the principles of nature, Hobbes did not.

Harrington wrote *Oceana* to demonstrate, on the contrary, that ancient prudence was perfectly conformable with Hobbes's metaphysics. More importantly, and to his intense excitement, Harrington succeeded by this route in constructing a *better* political form for a world of material in perpetual motion. As Wren disgustedly observed of *Oceana*'s orders: 'this libration is of the same nature with a perpetual motion in the mechanics'.[79] By its own metaphysical criteria *Leviathan* was crude. It could only produce peace from a ballistic world by restraining motion. Harrington believed he had transcended this need. Leviathan's hand could come off the billiard table, to be replaced by an intricate frame or cage. This allowed the balls to move perpetually, though along preconceived paths. All danger of collision was thereby removed. Thus Harrington explained in *A Discourse upon this Saying* (1659):

at Rome I saw [a cage] which represented a kitchen . . . the cooks were all cats and kitlings, set in such frames, so tied and so ordered, that the poor creatures could make no motion to get loose, but the same caused one to

[77] Ibid., pp. 165, 174
[78] Ibid., pp. 162, 178.
[79] Wren, *Considerations*, p. 67, quoted by Harrington in *Political Works*, p. 430.

turn the spit, another to bake the meat, a third to skim the pot and a fourth to make green sauce. If the frame of your commonwealth be not such as causeth everyone to perform his certain function as necessarily as this . . . it is not right.[80]

How much is left in *Oceana* of classical liberty (self-government, collective and individual) is clear enough from this passage. The truth is of course that Harrington's peace was achieved by restraint on motion of a different, subtler, but no less pervasive kind.

All this Harrington accomplished by erecting, following Hobbes, an artificial copy of the natural art of God. Nature was a universe whose planets and stars (Harrington's 'orbs' and 'galaxies') moved in perpetual circular motion. By so copying nature's perfection Harrington believed he had harnessed for politics its very immortality. *Oceana* is full of the wild excitement produced by this extraordinary ambition. This culminates (in 'the Corollary') in an exultant paraphrase of *Leviathan's* own famous opening paragraph. Passionately admiring his own creation, Harrington's lawgiver

conceived such a delight within him, as God is described by Plato to have done, when he finished the creation of the world, and saw his orbs move below him. For in the art of man, being the imitation of nature which is the art of God, there is nothing so like the first call of beautiful order out of chaos and confusion as the architecture of a well ordered commonwealth. Wherefore Lycurgus, seeing . . . that his orders were good, fell into deep contemplation how he might render them . . . unalterable and immortal.[81]

Both the scale of this enterprise, and the emotions and language attending it, make Harrington's later descent into madness less of a distant journey than it has hitherto appeared.[82]

Thus in the main body of the work, 'the Model', *Oceana's* concerns are *Leviathan's*. They are material and motion; 'the matter and forme of a Commonwealth'.[83] *Oceana* has a material foundation (the balance) fixed by the agrarian law. The superstructure emerging from it has its own internal mechanism for motion (rotation). 'In the institution or building of a commonwealth, the

---

[80] *Political Works*, p. 744 (also quoted by Davis, 'Pocock's Harrington').

[81] Harrington, *Political Works*, p. 341.

[82] Aubrey, *Brief Lives*, p. 126. As Aubrey says, Harrington was 'a Gentleman of a high spirit and a hot head'. Prolonged exposure to *Oceana's* wheeling 'orbs' and 'galaxies' make the later picture of the philosopher sitting in the sun surrounded by swooping bees and flies seem more of a reduction in scale than a change in kind.

[83] Harrington left a summary of his politics in these terms in *A System of Politics*, *Political Works*, pp. 834–54.

first work is no other than fitting and distributing the materials. The materials of the commonwealth are the people.'[84] The 'form of the commonwealth is motion'. 'In motion consisteth life . . . [and] the motion of a Commonwealth will never be current, unless it be circular.'[85] It is in imitation of the heavens that 'the motions of *Oceana* are spherical'. Order by order, the 'materials' of *Oceana* are pitched into perpetual circulation, 'the parishes annually pour themselves into hundreds, the hundreds into tribes, the tribes into galaxies'.[86] Like *Leviathan's* 'Artificial Man' this is also a giant imitation of Harvey's human body.

so the parliament is the heart which, consisting of two ventricles, the one greater and replenished with a grosser store, the other less and full of a purer, sucketh in and gusheth forth the life blood of *Oceana* by a perpetual circulation.[87]

Perfectly constructed, it followed from the teaching of Hobbes that such a commonwealth:

should be immortal, seeing the people, being the materials, never dies, and the form, which is motion, must without opposition be endless. The bowl which is thrown from your hand, if there be no rub, no impediment, shall never cease; for which cause the glorious luminaries that are the bowls of God were once thrown forever.[88]

Thus when Olphaus Megelator, having 'cast the great orbs of this commonwealth into . . . perpetual revolution . . . observed the rapture of [their] motion . . . without any manner of obstruction or interfering, but as it had been naturally', he saw that his work was done. He 'abdicated the magistracy of Archon'.[89]

Harrington did indeed then write *Oceana*, opposing *Leviathan* in the process, to 'show Hobbes what he taught me'. This was not only that ancient prudence could be the ally, rather than the enemy, of their common enterprise. It could furnish the way to the first perfect fit between their metaphysical assumptions (material in motion) and their political objective (peace). For Hobbes, classical republicanism was a recipe for perpetual civil war. This was demonstrated by the violence of the classical Greek, republican

[84] Ibid., p. 212.
[85] Ibid., p. 248.
[86] Ibid., p. 245.
[87] Ibid., p. 287.
[88] Ibid., p. 229.
[89] Ibid., p. 342.

Roman, and Renaissance Italian political worlds. Machiavelli had recognised this, and turned the 'tumults' of Rome from its greatest liability into its chief political asset. But Harrington turned to an entirely different construction: a world of perpetual motion, locked into permanent peace.[90]

The problem for Harrington was that Hobbes had been right. As he wrote *Leviathan* Aristotle, Cicero, Livy and the rest were being welded by the real classical republicans into a genuinely Machiavellian ideology of vigour, instability and war. This process began with Milton and Nedham, and culminated with Sidney.[91] Despite opposing one aspect of Hobbes's post-humanist rebellion Harrington of course shared its assumptions and its objective. He consequently echoed its substance. Upon the altar of peace he sacrificed the moral and the participatory bases of the classical republican tradition. *Oceana* is a dead landscape: a political Frankenstein's monster raised from the anatomists' slab. It is not art's imitation of, but its triumph over nature. It is a world without liberty, and without meaningful political activity. But it is clever, and it establishes its author as the greatest English disciple, not of Machiavelli, but of Hobbes.

It would be a mistake to ignore the humanist context from which the thought of both Harrington and Hobbes emerged. Both remained humanists of a kind. Their classicism was not, however, civic humanism: that of *quattrocento* Florence, of Machiavelli, or of his genuine English followers. It was that of the generation who had witnessed the Spartan humiliation of Athens. Its ruling spirits were not Aristotle, Cicero, Machiavelli; but Plato, Lycurgus, Thucydides.[92] It was aristocratic and circumspect; it spoke of the

---

[90] Harrington allowed for foreign war (having carefully separated foreign and domestic government). Here too, however, the ultimate object was peace, gifted to a war-ravaged Europe by the establishment of a universal empire. 'A commonwealth . . . is a minister of God upon earth . . . for which cause . . . the orders last rehearsed are buds of empire, such as . . . may spread the arms of your commonwealth like an holy asylum unto the distressed world, and give the earth her Sabbath of years or rest from her labours, under the shadow of your wings.' *Political Works*, p. 323.

[91] See Scott, *Algernon Sidney and the Restoration Crisis*, chs. 11–13.

[92] The links with Thucydides have been mentioned. The one classical philosopher for whom Hobbes retained frank admiration was Plato (J.W.N. Watkins, *Hobbes' System of Ideas* (London, 1965), p. 80). The influence of Plato throughout *Oceana* is pervasive. Lycurgus was not, of course, a member of this generation but a symbol for it; his strong presence in the writing of both Plato and Harrington reflects this. Machiavelli had explicitly dissociated himself from the Spartan example: *Discourses*, Book 1, ch. 6 (ed. Crick), pp. 121–4.

dangers of uncontrolled political participation; the importance of harmony and peace; the ultimate evil of war. After England's own shattering conflict we hear in the great writings of the Interregnum these far echoes from the Peloponnesian War.

CHAPTER 8

Casuistry to Newcastle:
'The Prince' in the world of the book

Conal Condren

Margaret, 'Mad Meg', Cavendish was apt to exclaim that she read nothing: and Hobbes, that had he read more he would have known less. William Cavendish prided himself on remaining largely unpoisoned by the printed page, despite the dangers of a university education;[1] and thus qualified was appointed a governor to Charles, Prince of Wales. Straight away he warned his charge against books.[2]

Although such affectations of pre-print recidivism should be taken with a pinch of salt, they are important in helping to disguise and rationalise the resources through which the political inheritance of early modern Britain was being transformed. Increasingly in the seventeenth century, printed texts were becoming principal reservoirs of values, idioms of discourse, and the vocabulary through which the present was patterned and with the aid of which the future was plausibly projected. This essay concerns one such text, Machiavelli's *Prince*, and the way in which its style of discourse was creatively adapted in a long *Advice* by William Cavendish, husband to Meg, friend to Thomas, mentor to Charles; and, *inter alia* playwright, courtier, horseman, translator, soldier, free-form speller and, above all, Machiavellian.

When considering *The Prince*, I take the term Machiavellian to

An initial version of this paper was given in June 1990 to the Early Modern British History seminar at Selwyn College, Cambridge, convened by Mark Goldie and John Morrill; I would like to thank them and all who participated, especially Jeremy Maule, Jonathan Scott and Quentin Skinner.
[1] Margaret Cavendish, *Life of the Thrice Noble, High and Puissant Prince, William Cavendish, Duke Marquess, and Earl of Newcastle* (1667), ed. C.H. Firth (1986), p. xxx, xxxiv, xxxvii, liii–iv; John Aubrey, 'Hobbes' in *Brief Lives*, ed. Oliver Lawson Dick, (Harmondsworth, 1962), p. 234.
[2] *Clarendon State Papers* (1773), vol. II, pp. 7–8, (19 March, 1637). The letter followed shortly, Harleian MS 6988, art.62.

refer to a sub-species of deliberative rhetoric, organised, as such rhetoric had been since antiquity, around the appropriation of *honestas* and *utilitas*; but couched in a personal rather than a public register.[3] This refinement of classical rhetoric remained predicated on the contingency of human affairs and thus employed not syllogistic reasoning but enthymemic generalisations about character and circumstance, reinforced with the shared resources of history. Further, I take this princely idiom to constitute neither a 'language' (which would involve a multidimensionality it lacks); nor any fixed or elaborate doctrinal matrix. Rather, it provided a fairly coherent semantic organisation within political language and was used to suggest a powerful reductionist economy of priorities to which we metonymously attach Machiavelli's name as providing the supreme encapsulation of a discernible, if fluid tradition.

Cavendish probably presented his *Advice* to Charles in 1659. It survives as the 'Fair' copy, there being a rougher version from which it was polished.[4] Many of the views the *Advice* contains were adjusted for public consumption in Margaret's *Life* of William; but otherwise it has been a largely lost text of the Restoration.[5] The little attention it has received has concerned whether it illuminates

---

[3] For a valuable study of Machiavelli within the *genera* of classical rhetoric, see J.F. Tinkler, 'Praise and Advice: Rhetorical Approaches in More's *Utopia* and Machiavelli's *The Prince*', *The Sixteenth Century Journal*, 19 (1988), 187ff. Many of the specific doctrines used and adapted by Machiavelli have of course a similarly classical, especially Ciceronian derivation through which were also mediated such writers as Aristotle on tyranny.

[4] The original 'Welbeck' MS. is now probably amongst the Portland Papers held in the University of Nottingham Archives and was transcribed by Arthur Strong, *A Catalogue of the Letters and Other Historical Documents Exhibited in the Library at Welbeck* (London, 1903), Appendix, pp. 173–236. On the Portland deposits generally see R.J. Olney 'The Portland Papers', *Archives* 19, 82 (1989), 78–87. The 'Fair' copy, given to Charles, is in the Bodleian, Clarendon MS. 109. This has been transcribed with an introduction by Thomas P. Slaughter, *Ideology and Politics on the Eve of the Restoration: Newcastle's Advice to Charles II*, American Philosophical Society (Philadelphia, 1984). See also Gloria Anzilotti, *An English Prince: Newcastle's Machiavellian Guide to Charles II*, (Pisa, 1988). This is a modernised collation of the 'Welbeck' and 'Fair' copies. Anzilotti catalogues (with increasing exasperation) Slaughter's deviations from the MS., although, as she is modernising, she does not additionally list his numerous spelling errors. Anzilotti also disputes Slaughter's dating *c.*1658, claiming that the *Advice* was written between 1652 and early 1653. There are no good grounds for this and internal evidence, which she mistranscribes, makes it impossible (see below note 31).

[5] Margaret Cavendish, *Life*, 1667 edn., part 4. About thirty of the eighty-five sayings seem to come from the *Advice*.

Charles's policies;[6] and whether Cavendish's views were derived from *Leviathan*.[7] The exception is Gloria Anzilotti who has valuably pointed to a connection between the *Advice* and *The Prince*. Unfortunately, her enthusiasm for the 'exquisitely' Machiavellian Cavendish and her rather libertarian notion of inference, has created a procrustean bed of coincidences into which neither writer quite fits.[8] Cavendish's familiarity with Machiavelli's *Prince*, in some form, cannot be doubted; appropriately for my theme, it is a text that surfaces in the rough copy of the *Advice* only to be displaced in the copy given to Charles.[9] The point of comparison, however, is not to suggest any exclusive, let alone slavish dependence on Machiavelli, but to locate the *Advice* firmly within the tradition to which Machiavelli is central. Consequently, some similarities between the *Advice* and *The Prince* are of no more significance than those between the *Advice* and other works.

Qualifications aside, *The Prince* does seem to act as a pretext for the *Advice*, circumscribing its themes and vocabulary. Like *The Prince* the *Advice* emphasises *utilitas* more than *honestas*; it stresses the importance of necessity and occasion; political power is understood as a reified thing to be held in one's hands. Further, Cavendish operates in terms of characteristically Machiavellian disjunctions, between appearance and reality; ideal and real; friend (*qua* ally or dependant) and foe; and like Machiavelli, he urges that for safety's sake the princely reader should see politics as an extension of war, and thus cast himself in the role of indefatigable soldier.

Before turning to the *Advice*, however, I want first to examine an earlier letter, which not only establishes Cavendish's long and easy

---

[6] See Slaughter, *Ideology and Politics*, p. xi, for discussion and Strong, *A Catalogue*, p. vii. The consensus seems to have been that Charles never read it; but he might not have needed to inasmuch as the idioms and doctrines were probably quite familiar to him. Clarendon, to whom the *Advice* was attributed may have read it; his jibe that Cavendish was as well suited to be a general as a bishop, seems to be a conceit on Cavendish's claim that one who is fit to be the Archbishop of Canterbury is not fit to be a general, 'Fair' copy, p. 67.

[7] Slaughter, *Ideology and Politics*, at length.

[8] Anzilotti, *An English Prince*, e.g. p. 64. The justifications for this harsh judgement on an otherwise useful book, are in the footnotes below (see 11, 15, 17, 31, 33, 52, 67).

[9] Cavendish remarks that people having read *The Prince* think they know all about policy; Strong, *A Catalogue*, p. 190. Anzilotti plausibly hypothesises that in making the 'Fair' copy, Cavendish's eye jumped between mentions of Caesar in consecutive lines. The Latin translation of *Il Principe* was sold in an auction from the estate of the Dukes of Newcastle *c.*1718; *Biblioteca nobilissimi Principiis Johannis Ducis Novo-Castro*, 1718–19, p. 62. There is much else by Machiavelli in the catalogue; but in any case availability would not have been an issue by the time of Interregnum, either in Italian, other languages, or by cribs, digests and critiques.

familiarity with Machiavellian discourse, but provides something against which to indicate change and continuity in his employment of it.

Cavendish issued his early warning against books to Charles in the context of a substantial letter about the nature and purpose of princely education.[10] The letter began by evoking a theory–practice topos which is also central to *The Prince*, chapter 15. Cavendish urges the study of matter and things rather than words and language (p. 326); for 'too much contemplation spoils action and virtue consists in that'.[11] Concentrate on useful arts, 'especially those that are most proper for War'. One 'cannot be a good contemplative man and a good Commonwealth's man therefore take heed of too much book' (p. 327).

The Cavendish preference for ignorance, then, is situated in the context of some widespread Renaissance, even bookish distinctions between theory and practice, and between the active and the contemplative.[12] As with writers like Machiavelli, it is to the active life of *negotium* that virtue is co-opted and for which *utilitas* acts as a principal criterion of judgement. Central to action is war. For Cavendish the only exception to the caveat upon reading is history, its usefulness being insured by the constancy of human nature. Since history writing was overwhelmingly about politics and war, his advice is little different from that standard advice Machiavelli also gives on reading matter fit for a prince.[13] According to Cavendish, history books will allow the young prince to wade in times past most beneficially if he concentrates on judgement and unchanging nature.

Beware, he continues, of too much devotion, 'for one may be a good man but a bad king';[14] history shows how many in seeming to

---

[10] Harleian MS. 6988, 62. Page numbers to the letter are to C.H. Firth (ed.), *Life*, Appendix, pp. 326–30.

[11] Anzilotti seizes on the word virtue to infer an exclusive Machiavellian derivation: *An English Prince*, p. 63, where Machiavelli is said to use the word in the same way, which he did, sometimes. Slaughter, however, notes how widespread it was to extol action over words, citing Winstanley and Hobbes, p. xvii. To these one might add Shakespeare (*Hamlet*), and Cicero.

[12] The most extreme statement is perhaps to be found in Lorenzo Valla, *De Professione religiosorum*, but in the interim the *vita contemplativa* has changed from monastic life to book learning. See also William Scott, *An Essay on Drapery* (1635), a text which adapts, though with less vigour than the *Advice*, Machiavellian nostrums to the citizen *qua* merchant.

[13] *The Prince*, ch. 14.

[14] Ibid., chs. 15, 18.

gain a heavenly throne have lost one on earth. Devotion should be
genuine but kept to the point. Yet, he demurs, such matters are
beyond his sphere and Charles has a good and discreetly learned
tutor in Dr Duppa, Bishop of Chichester. The advice nevertheless
continues; if a prince does not show reverence for God he cannot
expect reverence from his subjects (p. 327): 'no Obedience no
Subjects, no Subjects – then ye Power is off that side and whether it
be in one or more then that's King, & thus they will turn tables
with you' (p. 328). Watch also for the 'Bible Madd', 'one way you
may have a Civil War ye other a private Treason & he that cares
not for his own life is a master of anotherman's' (p. 328).[15]

Cavendish, descanting upon fear as an interest that stabilises
political relationships, uses the contemplative associations of devotion, love, to treat religion as a *religio*, a binding force maintaining
the prince's position.[16] A prince's display of devotion to a higher
power sets an example for the subjects to follow; the 'Bible Madd'
are dangerous because no display of love or capacity to generate
fear is a sufficient bond. The image is that of the cloaked assassin, a
haunting Renaissance theme. The defeat of those who would
render unto Caesar on the battlefield, by those who would render
only unto God, seems, despite the European wars of religion,
beyond Cavendish's vision; he will have re-focussed by the time of
the *Advice*.

Returning to the irrelevancy of books ('ye greatest Captains were
not ye greatest schollars') he proceeds to paraphrase and partially
quote *The Prince*: divinity and moral philosophy teach 'what we
should be, not what we are . . . and many Philosophicall Worlds &
Utopia's Schollars hath made and fansied to themselves such
worlds as never was, is or shall be, and then I dare say if they
govern themselves by those Rules what men should be not what
they are they will miss ye Cushion very much' (p. 328).

The dichotomy between ideal and real, recalling that between
theoretical and effective truth which Machiavelli had woven into
the chapter Cavendish quotes, brings the letter back to its begin-

---

[15] Anzilotti misreads this, taking Cavendish to be warning Charles about becoming 'Bible Madd' himself. Perhaps she has been misled by the belief that Machiavelli was totally irreligious, and so Cavendish as an English clone had to be also; *An English Prince*, p. 63.

[16] Cf. Machiavelli, *Discourses*, vol. 1.1–9, pp. 9–13 (Milan, 1973 edn), Something of Cavendish's pragmatic attitude to religion is to be gleaned from his *Declaration*, 1642, in defence of having Catholics in his army; see also Clarendon, *History of the Great Rebellion* (1702), vol. II, bk. 8, pp. 391–2.

ning; and the assimilation of divinity and moral philosophy implicitly sweeps these and the tutor responsible for their inculcation to the margins of relevancy.

The marginalising of Dr Duppa is neither discourteous nor overt, for courtesy is vital. 'Making a leg' (p. 328) costs little and pays dividends. A prince's dislike kills his subjects, therefore he should speak well of people and 'seeme' greatly to dislike hearing bad of others. Those who speak ill of others are usually traitors underneath; those who hear the prince's kind words will give their hearts, '& more you cannot have' (p. 329). Yet, do not confuse civility with familiarity. All that separates a king from a subject is ceremony, even the wisest 'shake for fear of it' (p. 329). Know then, when to play the king and never leave the kingly persona aside, but remember it is only a persona: kings are ultimately ordinary mortals. Charles can, he concludes, make his name immortal only by brave acts abroad and by justice at home (p. 330).

The final section of the letter is a series of succinct variations on the Machiavellian topos of appearance and reality, predicated on a belief in the fragility of political relationships. Courtesy is a necessary appearance epitomised in 'making a leg', in *seeming* to dislike ill-words which are themselves cloaks for an underlying reality of disloyalty. Ceremony is a contrived hierarchy masking a reality of equality which, in fooling even the wise, 'maskers the Commonwealth' (p. 329). For all the initial martial emphasis, role play is the essence of kingship, ceremony the central prop in the theatre of power. The letter has not been seen principally as a political statement;[17] yet, once placed in the context of Machiavellian discourse, its character becomes apparent. As author and audience are cast in the appropriate roles, it comes within the 'advice to the princes' genre; and moreover, shares major topoi with *The Prince*, works within the same loaded disjunctions of appearance and reality, the ideal and the real, and paraphrases portions of a central chapter.

Cavendish's letter and his *Advice* frame a tumultuous period which was also the apogee of Machiavellian theory in England.[18] What helps us identify the period as one of such crisis was that it so strained the resources of inherited rhetoric. No form of discourse

[17] Despite her emphasis on Machiavellian *virtù*, this is Anzilotti's perplexing conclusion, p. 77.
[18] See especially J.G.A. Pocock, *The Machiavellian Moment* (Princeton, 1975).

nor locus of textual wisdom could explain the Civil War and its aftermath with sufficient authority.[19] Yet it was precisely the violent instability of a world at the nexus of war and politics that made Machiavellian princely idioms of discourse as relevant as they remained disquieting. Their public use was apt to be supplementary and circumspect.

As Cromwell could be seen as a new prince, so he could be understood through Machiavellian categories; and with his armed ascendancy went the ceremonial theatre that dispatched the old, all appearance and 'helpless right' as Marvell had it.[20] In the Engagement controversy that followed, there is a clear sense in which the Machiavellian casuistry of necessity and interest (vulgarised through stage personae such as Cavendish's Monsieur Device in *The Country Captain*)[21] could be further adapted to ease the conscience of the subject. Some Engagers advised accepting the new regime partly on grounds of necessity and self-interest; appealing to fear and a notion of reality as opposed to traditional love, and the ideal, they stressed the contingent nature of keeping faith.[22] For men such as Ascham and Nedham, to stand upon traditional oaths as if the world were ideal was very much to 'miss ye cushion'. Equally those hostile to the Engagers saw them as casuistic subverters of morality; co-opting the appeal to *utilitas*, it was argued that to ease the bonds of oath-taking was foolish, only heightening the instability everyone wished to avoid. Such accusations had been levelled at *The Prince* earlier in the century; their republication at the end of the Engagement controversy may not have been coincidental.[23]

[19] The point is made succinctly by J.G.A. Pocock, 'Political Thought in the Cromwellian Interregnum', in *W.P. Morrell, A Tribute*, ed. G.A. Wood and P.S. O'Connor, (Dunedin, 1973), esp. p. 22.

[20] Marvell's casting Cromwell as a new prince was first discussed by A.J. Mazzeo, in *Reason and Imagination* (New York, 1962).

[21] *The County Captain*, 1649, an ill-timed comedy at the expense of the parliamentary army.

[22] For the institutional background to the Engagement and the perceptive discussions of it in parliament see Blair Worden, *The Rump Parliament*, (Cambridge, 1977), pp. 225–32; for valuable discussions of the controversy, on which I am largely drawing here, see Pocock, 'Political Thought in the Cromwellian Interregnum'; John Wallace, 'The Engagement Controversy: An Annotated Check List', *Bulletin of the New York Public Library*, 68 (1964), 384–405; Quentin Skinner, 'Conquest and Consent', in G.E. Aylmer, *The Interregnum: A Quest for a Settlement* (London, 1972); and Glenn Burgess, 'Usurpation, Obligation and Obedience in The Thought of the Engagement Controversy', *The Historical Journal*, 29, 3 (1986) 515f.

[23] Thomas Fitzherbert, *An sit utilitas in scelere* (Rome, 1610), esp. chs. 6–7; *The First Part of a Treatise of Politicks* (Douai, 1608; Second Part, 1610; republished 1652), see esp. ch. 34.

More broadly, it was the dogma so powerfully expressed by Machiavelli that history is a series of variations on themes dictated by unchanging human nature, that encouraged the desperate imposition of the past upon the present. So people, Sisyphus-like, pushed a barrow of ever-bigger books up a hill of controversy. In this way the events of '41' or '49' (suggesting a sort of history by numbers) were made to have a resonance at the Restoration which was fashioned to avoid their return.[24] The very term 'Restoration' evoked Civil War memory by displacement to the extent of forming an almost retrospective view of the future. It is little wonder, then, that Cavendish should develop the themes of his early letter, playing his own Monsieur Device to an out-of-country captain. Perceiving recent history through his neo-Florentine spectacles he may have thought reiteration was wisdom. Perhaps it was; for in re-casting himself in the role of prince's adviser, he cast Charles as new prince more fittingly than he had when Charles had been a young unchallenged heir to a well-established throne.

I am bold humbley to presente this booke . . . writt perticulerly for your Majestie [there is] no oratory in it, or any thing stollen out of Bookes, for I seldome or Ever reade any, but these Discourses are out of my long Experience to presente your Majestie with truths, which greate Monarkes seldome heares . . . ye honesteste . . . wisest, that a Dutyfull servante can offer to so Gracious A Master. (pp. xiii;5)[25]

The king's appreciation will cause him great joy, yet should Charles disapprove then 'through it into the fier so it may become a flameing Sacrefice of my Duty to your Majestie' (pp. xiv;5). Cavendish was never averse to burning a good book. Dedications may be formulaic, but as Anzilotti notes, this is distinctly like Machiavelli's to Lorenzo.[26] Each author writes as personal adviser, each emphasises personal experience, integrity, the importance of

---

[24] The perceived repetition of history is not only found in explicit fears and warnings; George Lawson, *Politica sacra et civilis* (1660), rehearses arguments he probably put forward in his lost engagement tract c.1650. In 1681 Edward Cooke (himself repeating Edward Hyde) urged more reading of Machiavelli, a writer 'much studied of late', in order to avoid the repeated ruin of civil war; for he claims, it is Machiavelli who shows that by attending to the past we can avoid its repetition. *Memorabilia*, cited in Jonathan Scott, *Algernon Sidney and the Restoration Crisis, 1677–83* (Cambridge, 1991), p. 82.
[25] The parenthesised numbers in the text are to the *Advice*: those before the semi-colon to the 'Fair' copy (Clarendon 109), those after to Slaughter's version of it in *Ideology and Politics* because of its availability.
[26] Anzilotti, *An English Prince*, p. 66.

rare truths simply told. Almost all that is absent from the *Advice* is Machiavelli's thinly veiled request for work and his claim to have studied history – as Cavendish had urged Charles to do before and as he is now about to use it.

The text so stamped, we are ushered into the world of *The Prince*, noticeably more than that of *The Discourses*. The common authorial bifurcation between the noble historian of one work and the spawner of the other, enabled some writers to explore an ever-changing range of contaminants to republican virtue.[27] Such a nicety of distinction allows Cavendish to take up a rigorously precise agenda of debate to one side of the issues of virtue and corruption in the public realm. Under fifteen headings he pursues one question. How can Charles maintain his power over a commonwealth he does not yet possess? Under the auspices of this quintessentially Machiavellian question are the following sub-themes which I shall discuss in turn: the foundations of power; the species of power; the danger to Charles's power; trust and the delegation of power; and the loss of power. Throughout, the imagery of power is as tactile as Machiavelli's; it is a thing to hold 'in your owne hands' (a favourite phrase) and so, as in *The Prince*, the verbs central to the semantics of policy are: to lose, to gain and to maintain.[28]

Repeatedly, Cavendish insists that the 'foundation' (pp. 39;35) of power is in arms and in money;[29] 'without an Army in your owne hands, you are but a king upon ye Curtesey of others, and Cannot bee Lasting' (pp. 1;5). Again, all ammunition must be in the king's own hands (pp. 1;6); being a supreme judge means little without 'ye power to Determyne, which is Armyes, for otherwise ye factious & vaine Disputes of Sophesterall Devines, & Lawyers, & other Philosophicall Booke men will Raise Rebellions' (pp. 1;5). Even without such book men 'ye prentices of a shrove tuesday would teare ye Bishopps Moste Reverent Lawne sleeves . . . & cutt his throte to Boote' (pp. 39;34–5). In a rare appeal to *honestas* he writes

---

[27] Pocock, *The Machiavellian Moment*, at length, for the range of dangers to virtue and stability from standing armies to paper money and luxury.

[28] For an examination of their centrality see especially, J.H. Hexter, *The Vision of Politics on the Eve of the Reformation* (London, 1973), pt. 3.

[29] According to Margaret Cavendish, *Life*, p. 69, William had been urging Charles to get his armies into his own hands since 1650 and he was, of course, to be one of those princes who acquired power through the arms of others (*The Prince*, ch. 7), which is exactly what Cavendish fears.

'Armes . . . is your Juste power . . . Sr' (pp. 39;34–5), 'your power
is nothing butt Armes'; and, evoking a broader *utilitas* because
of them, every subject 'may sitt safe under his owne vine'
(pp. 40;35).[30]

England's 'Brasson walls' (pp. 6;9), the navy, is as vital as the
army. Through their navy, 'these Rebells' have become a scourge
of Europe (pp. 6;9); so too for Charles, an annually augmented
navy will be a defence at home and a terror abroad (pp. 6;9).[31]
Indeed, once properly settled, Charles should embark upon a war
with France or Spain, there being nothing like a 'forren warr, for
your Majesties Safety' (pp. 88;75). Holland and Ireland too are
seen as supports to the foundation in arms, even their description
being invaded by martial imagery. The one is seen as an 'outworke'
(pp. 85;73), the other as part farm and part armed camp from
whence an army might always be transported on 'Any occasion
that is necessary' (pp. 77;67).[32] Charles then must be a Renaissance ruler-commander of his own standing armies, ever ready to
seize the occasion in the name of necessity, be the act one of
suppression or glorious expansion. But ever sensible of the objections of some self-styled Machiavellians, amongst others, to the
innovation of standing armies, Cavendish urges that the reality of
force should have a minimal appearance – 'people loves not ye
cudgell' (pp. 3;7).

The necessity of direct control has come to mean, as it did not for
Machiavelli, command of the purse; money replaces Machiavelli's
law as a foundation of power.[33] Indeed, Cavendish explicitly
affirms what Machiavelli had denied in *The Discourses*; money is 'ye
sinews of warr' (pp. 54;46). Hence, he urges, 'pay the soldere
alwayes your selfe by your owne officers, that they may wholy

---

[30] Ibid., pt. 4, p. vi, princes are half armed if their subjects are unarmed.

[31] Anzilotti mistranscribes as 'those Rebells', which makes Cavendish seem to be referring
to Queen Elizabeth and her sailors. It is this misread passage which makes Anzilotti's
date for the original *Advice* impossible. Slaughter's guess of around 1658 to 1659 seems
much nearer the mark, but if anything a shade early.

[32] Such a martial image of Holland was not new; see Jonathan Scott, *Algernon Sidney and the
English Republic* (Cambridge, 1989), p. 128. Cf. also Margaret Cavendish, *Life*, pt. 4,
where the urgings to war are more general and cautious.

[33] Because Anzilotti treats Cavendish as a fairly slavish follower of *The Prince*, she foists the
same foundations on Cavendish, which is bluntly to contradict his argument. The only
difference she allows is that Cavendish leans more heavily than Machiavelli on the role of
commerce (p. 72); by a similar angle of inclination Marx leaned more heavily towards
communism than Prince Metternich.

Depend upon your Majestie' (pp. 6;9). In a world without the unlikely prop of Roman virtue every soldier seems close to being a mercenary; a soldier would always 'follow ye money' (pp. 49;42). In sum, 'they that have The Armes, have ye purse, & they that have ye purse, hath obedience, so that Armes is all' (p. 3).[34]

The immediate corollary is that trade becomes an aspect of security. Only the merchant brings 'Honye to ye Hive' (pp. 41;35) and any good statesman must understand commerce (pp. 44;38). So, Cavendish outlines policies which also reinforce his advisory credentials. Charles must destroy monopolies, promote exports, tie merchants to his interests, exploit the excise; force even 'sturddy vagarant Roggs to work' (pp. 49;42) and learn from the industrious Dutch in the Fens. Conversely, he should not debase the coinage; ultimately it is counter-productive. Finally, he must understand the underlying and variable relationships between money supply and value. 'Plenty of money, makes Every thinge Deere, & scaresety of Money of nesesety muste make Every thing cheepe' (pp. 41;36). The point of this monetarist excursion is not to develop a capitalist economy for its own sake, or even (a subordinate aim) to create a wealthy industrious commonwealth; rather, it is to bring sufficient honey to the king bee, that he may sweeten the workers in the battlefield. *The Prince*, then, may more easily than *The Discourses* be accommodated to a commercial world.

Hitherto, ex-commander Cavendish has sounded like an early modern Maoist, peering for power down the barrel of a gun; but he also greatly elaborates his understanding of ceremony from his early letter. This now becomes a theory of symbolic power; and Charles is portrayed as being as dependent on this species of power as he is upon force. 'Seremony though itt is nothing in itt Selfe, yett it doth Every thing, – for what is a king, more then a subiecte, Butt for seremony, & order, when that fayles him, hees Ruiend' (pp. 52;44).[35] And this is true of every social distinction (pp. 52;44:20;20). Superficially Cavendish might be thought to be re-writing Shakespeare's *Henry V* (something else he no doubt seldom if ever read) or blimpishly trying to suggest some semiotics of primordial hierarchy.[36] There was a time, he recalls, when only a

---

[34] Cf. Margaret Cavendish, *Life*, pt. 4, p. vii.
[35] Ibid., p. xxv.
[36] *Henry V*, Act 4, scene 1. See also Scott, *An Essay*, for a similar emphasis with respect to trade, p. 27.

baroness could have a bedside carpet or two; 'now every Turkey merchants wife, will have all her floore over with Carpetts'. Making 'no Difference between great Ladys & Citizens wifes in aparell is abominable' (pp. 53–4;46).

The whiff of nostalgia here overlays a more significant scent. Such ritualised conventions affirm and display predictable hierarchical relationships precisely where force cannot.[37] An army may give power over the naked but cannot itself be held together by force; money may be its blood but discipline provides the will to make it seek its quarry as required. This is a discipline which seems to be less the Stoic virtue of Machiavelli than a habit of accepting authority through the signs of status. Even money, as Cavendish's comments on prices show, works only through convention. The essence of ceremony then, lies not in a natural quota of turkey carpets but in a habitual acceptance of status which is affirmed even in ritualistic display. Without ceremony in this socially cementing sense there is only force, which seems to suggest some violent state of nature. This is close to Hobbes, perhaps, but closer to Hume for whom habit was the true *religio*.[38] The point is elaborated by a digression into the nature of convention. Most of what we accept is socially inducted convention:

Education is a mighty matter, – they call itt a Second nature, but I beleeve it is converted into nature, & is nature itt Selfe, for Iff wee Consider nature, no more then weeping Laughing, hungrey, Thurstey, Eateing, drinking, urenising & ye Sege &c, but very These, are altered perpetually by Custome, butt all ye reste is very Custome. (pp. 80;69)[39]

Unimproved, natural wit leaves man little better than 'a well Educated Dogg' (pp. 81;69–70). Yet Cavendish affirms that 'custome is ye great Tirante of man kinde' (pp. 81;70).[40] What makes our world seem stable and natural strikes the foreigner as bizarre (pp. 81;70). With respect to language, Cavendish considers pre-

[37] Pepys remarks on the notorious Cavendish extravagance and singularity, *Diary*, 26 April and 2 May 1667. Here is the serious rationale for it which is at one with the aristocratic view that money maketh man.

[38] See e.g. *Human Understanding*, V, pt. 1, pp. 36–8; and 'Of the Origin of Government' and 'Of the Original Contract', in *Political Essays*, ed. Charles W. Hendel (New York, 1953).

[39] Virtually a quotation from and commentary upon Cicero *De finibus*, 5.25.sec.74: 'consuetudini quasi alteram quandam naturam effici'.

[40] *Othello*, Act 1, scene 3; Bacon, *Essays*, 1625 (Oxford, 1962): 'Of Custom and Education', 'We See also the Raine or Tyrannie of Custome, What it is', and it is the 'Principall Magistrate of Man's Life', p. 164. His text is Machiavelli on conspiracy.

cisely what seems its least conventionalised aspect, figuration. Custom determines our ways of 'simulising'; thus where we might associate 'white' with 'snow', a piously educated man will see a 'sirplis', and that upon a preacher in a pulpit and 'presently hee . . .is at his prayers, with holly Eiaculations' (pp. 82;71).

The general point is as old as Herodotus, as polemical as Nash, and as fresh as the discovery of the Americas;[41] but taken perhaps from a Montaignesque into a Machiavellian idiom of advice, it defines the very limits of security. Nothing is immutable, may not be shaken or changed; hence the 'mighty matter' of education must figure on the prince's agenda. As the Tuscans had seen liberty as a flower of vigilance and industry, so princely security is the blossom of these suspicious virtues in an artificial world.[42]

Certainly all must have occasional holidays, horse racing and tilting for the nobility; morris dancing and shrovetide hen thrashing for the plebs, but all constrained by convention and designed to 'free your Majestie from faction and Rebellion' (pp. 75;64). As everything is a function of ceremony and convention there is no absolute security in lineage and tradition. By implication there is a sense in which every prince is new and may grow old staying so. Similarly, where ceremony is most preserved society is most secure; and presumably as Charles becomes more settled, ceremonial power will dominate at home, force abroad.[43]

Charles, it seems must maintain his power much like a Machiavellian prince, but the Reformation and Civil War have required significant adjustments, more of which are apparent when Cavendish turns to consider the principal dangers to Charles's power; they are less nobles, people or foreign princes than lawyers, priests and London.

Unruly, rich and armed, the city is virtually a free state within the commonwealth. It needs a new charter and the interests of its merchants must be fostered; above all it must be disarmed and hemmed in by the King's own garrisons. Only then will Charles be 'Mestroe Dell Campoe' (pp. 1;5). London's wealth 'was ye bane

---

[41] Montesquieu, *The Persian Letters*, helped to keep the theme fresh in the eighteenth century at least until Oliver Goldsmith's *A Citizen of the World* (1762).

[42] Quentin Skinner, *Ambrogio Lorenzetti: The Artist as Philosopher*, Proceedings of the British Academy, 72 (1986), 7–8, 31ff., it being partially from this ground that Machiavelli's *Prince* flowered.

[43] Cf. *The Prince*, ch. 2, where one is left with the strong impression that hereditary rulers are usually so safe as not to need much advice.

and loss of your Royall Father . . .Looke to your greatest mischeefe to keepe this Citie from Hurtinge you' (pp. 2;6–7). The threat of London clouds the whole *Advice*, it seems to provide a microcosm for Charles's relationship with the commonwealth as a whole, 'Every corporation, is a petty free state, Againest monarkey' (pp. 47;41). Effectively, his state is of a kind Machiavelli had considered so difficult to maintain, one used to its own laws and liberties. With respect to Scotland, Cavendish urges tender handling for just this reason (pp. 75;65).[44] As Machiavelli remarked, such states could always be incited to rebellion in the name of liberty and the public propagation of that word was a sustained worry for Cavendish; the point is reinforced by turning to the other principal dangers to Charles's power.

If Charles is to be a king, the church must be in his hands. The problem is that priests are more like wasps than bees bringing honey to the hive (pp. 13;15), for they are bookish and disputatious. Specifically, Charles must fear papacy and presbytery, tied like Samsons's foxes in their hostility to his power: one would replace him with an alien monarch, the other would destroy monarchy (pp. 11;12–13).[45] 'Iff [the civil and ecclesiastical states] . . .Bee not governed in Cheefe by one & ye same person. They cannot be sayd to bee parts of ye same Monarcky' (pp. 10;1). In this succinct summation of Elizabethan and Jacobean Erastianism, Cavendish seems to be following a dominant reading of Hooker's '*Ecclesiastical Polesy*'. The Church of England is to be preferred not only because of its apostolic legitimacy (passingly mentioned) but above all because it teaches passive obedience and is dependent for its own survival upon the monarchy (pp. 14;16). No bishop does indeed mean no king. Therefore, episcopal appointments must be made principally on political criteria (pp. 14;16). Bishops must control priests and education – both of which have slipped through the hands of the monarch. Schools must be limited, for an illiterate population is easier to control (pp. 19;20); and university students must be vetted for sound views. There must be

---

[44] *The Prince*, ch. 5.
[45] *Judges* 1:4. This clearly reflects the continuing fear that the monarchy did need keeping to the straight and narrow of a *via media* of its own church. Charles was to prove little more reliable than his father, James intolerably less so. See Mark Goldie, 'Danby, The Bishops and the Whigs', in *The Politics of Religion in Restoration England*, ed. T. Harris, Paul Seaward and M. Goldie (Oxford, 1990), pp. 75ff.

no lecturing clergy; the Word should be preached only through officially printed and sanctioned sermons (pp. 19;20); controversies must be restricted to Latin (pp. 21;21). The bishops themselves must be kept within their domain lest they generate envy and disaffection amongst the gentry (pp. 17;17–18). All this done, a great danger can become a true *religio*, but only if it 'bee in your owne Hands, which Is the Drum & the Trumpett, for Disputts will never have and Ende & make new And Great Disorders, butt force quietts all things this amongst the rest' (pp. 24;23).

Lawyers too constitute an institutionalised danger with their own group interest. After the Reformation this class 'crepte upp' and 'Swelde to bee to bigg for ye kingdom' (pp. 25;24). It helped foment and continue the rebellion (pp. 25;24). It has impoverished the king's subjects and so Chancery should be abolished, but 'Start chamber' kept (pp. 26;24).[46] Again, have fewer schools 'for if you Cutt of much reading, & writing, ther muste bee fewer Lawyers' (pp. 25;24). Like bishops, judges must be chosen with care; but on occasion, the king must exercise judgement himself; in doing so Cavendish suggests 'put ye Displeaseing parte still uppon your Servants, And keepe ye pleaseing & mercifull part still, for your Majestie to Doe' (pp. 34;31).[47] This echo of the peremptory justice of Cesare Borgia in the Romagna, is followed by another, fainter one.[48] It is necessary, he writes, sometimes to be cruel to be kind, in the long term the more merciful judge may prove the more harsh (pp. 32–3;30).[49] Just as within the church the Word should be printed to be controlled, so the introduction of a public register of deeds, would diminish suits and superannuate surplus lawyers (pp. 35–6;32).

For Cavendish the vital similarity between priests and lawyers is that each constitutes a caste of book-men whose own power, derived from education, lies in an accepted right to mediate public meanings. Controlling them means commanding education and the volatile contingency of public discourse, made urgent as disquieting numbers of men and women can read. The priest will

---

[46] Margaret Cavendish, *Life*, pt. 4, p. xxvii, which more blandly and generally attributes to Cavendish the belief that professions which get too large are bad for the kingdom.

[47] Ibid., p. 1iii. Princes should judge ordinary people's cases because thereby they can identify extortions and corruption in the magistrates, and this pleases the people.

[48] Cf. *The Prince*, ch. 7.

[49] Ibid., ch. 17. The paradox of being cruel to be kind was a widely established commonplace.

expound God's will in his own interest, thus he becomes a king: 'The Lawyeres sayes The kinge is to bee obayd, butt not againste ye Lawe – & ye Lawyeres will Expound ye Lawe to their best advantage to Rule' (pp. 38;34). Again, 'there are three hundreth Several opinions, on this smale texte, This is my Body, so that in their Severall Kingdomes, men judge itt & wee muste obay their Judgementes, whether itt be right or wrong, Because it standes for righte, as Long as that Authorety Hath power to judge itt' (pp. 80;69). Here certainly, the voice is more Hobbesian than Machiavellian, and the hostility to books, reiterated from before the Civil War, has an additional and contradictory rationale. In the *Advice* books remain symbols of the contemplative life, irrelevant to action, virtue and the effective truth of things (not books, but practice does everything in the world) (pp. 21;22). Yet, books are now also dangerous; they represent uncontrollable opinion and the open debate of what had been accepted.[50] As language itself was conventionalised and politically significant, so the burgeoning print culture, especially through its arbitrating professions, was a political force helping, as it were, to keep every prince new. Controversy, Cavendish writes, is a civil war with the pen, which pulls out the sword soon after (pp. 20;21). Mastery of the book might just keep Charles a prince; these are the axioms of L'Estrange. They might have been abstracted from writers as different as Hobbes, Milton or Chillingworth, all of whom exhibit a general awareness of the importance of print.[51]

The insistence upon personal control presupposes problematic loyalties; the delegation of power is thus seen as a necessary evil in Charles's political relationships. Delegation is more necessary and more evil, as it were, as one moves from the small-scale Renaissance principality or the direct world of courtly politics, to the sprawling indirect government of the compound commonwealth of Britain. The Machiavellian problem of control couched in the

---

[50] The crucial text here is Montaigne's *Essays*, a major theme of which concerns the book as an elusive and uncontrollable problem. His tone is ironic and ruminative. The pamphlet wars which accompanied civil wars gave an urgency to such reflections. Cf. Margaret Cavendish, *Life*, pt. 4, p. xxxi – even equivocations in law and religion should be discouraged, as they can lead to trouble.

[51] See Hobbes, *Leviathan*, ed. Richard Tuck (Cambridge, 1990), ch. 18, pp. 124–5, to whom Cavendish is verbally close; but Milton's *Areopagitica* is predicated on a similar appreciation; see also William Chillingworth, *Charity Maintained*, in *Works* (Oxford, 1838), vol. I, ch. 2, Answer, p. 157.

G

vocabulary of love, fear, and interest, is intensified as Cavendish's problem of delegation. The metaphoricity of *mantenere* is extended. All agents, Cavendish argues, must be tied to the king by self-interest, otherwise they cannot be relied upon to do his business. What is true of judges, priests and merchants is true of freeholders, who having great dependence upon the king are greatly at his command (pp. 35;31). The nobility, also dependent upon the monarchy for its position, is always for monarchy, if not always for the monarch. Thus taking from the nobility and giving to the commons was a great error (pp. 54;46), for there is a weaker community of interest between king and people. Machiavelli's advice as to wherein the prince should put his trust, nobility or people, is reversed on a relentless argument from *utilitas*.[52] As it occurs in the context of discussing ceremony, it is clear that Cavendish considers the conventions of rank and patronage to constitute the bond which ties the monarch and his friends together like another pair of Samson's foxes against the real possibility of a republic.

Reading men, therefore is more important than reading books, knowing the bait on which 'to hooke Them withall, Gaynes . . . business' (pp. 80;69).[53] It is in this context that Cavendish invokes one of the most familiar of all Machiavellian topoi, under the heading of government in general.[54] It is a draconian reduction of a huge topic, but a reasonable if collapsed translation of two passages from *The Prince*, chapter 17.

There hath been a greate question for kinges, whether they Should Governe, by Love or feare . . . if ye people Love him, there is nothing that Hee can desire, that ye Subiecte will not grante [Cavendish's ostensible position in 1638] but those that are for governing by feare, Say shrodly, they say, that Love Depends of them & not of The King, & that thier Love is . . . Alterable, – upon Every, & no occasion, – but with feare Say they Dependes uppon ye king. (79;68)

He concludes that both should be used, 'as occasion serves' using

---

52 Cf. *The Prince*, ch. 9, where the argument is also based on an appeal to *honestas* (the people are more honourable than the nobles). Anzilotti, *An English Prince*, p. 70, seems to imply a similar bias in Cavendish.

53 Cf. Margaret Cavendish, pt. 4, p. xlii: 'those which have Politick Designs, are for the most part dishonest, by reason their Designs tend more to Interest, then Justice'.

54 Machiavelli was commenting upon Cicero, *De officiis*, II, 7, 23–4. See Quentin Skinner and Russell Price (eds.), *The Prince* (Cambridge, 1988), p. xvii.

force only 'uppon Nesesety'.[55] A few years later, Margaret would reiterate the topos in Cavendish's name with the conclusion that one should always rule justly; her's was a Prince and a thrice-noble lord, modified for public consumption.[56]

Cavendish's understanding of justice itself suffers a similar reduction when translated into the vocabulary of a princely idiom. Justice, instructs Cavendish, is of two sorts, commutative and distributive. The former is a relation between individuals, the latter is in the king's own hands, a reward for service (pp. 35;31–2). Thus a major philosophical distinction dwindles into a form of self-interested patronage.

Central to the *Advice* is the ever-present past of the Civil War. It was the most crucial tense in the grammar of seventeenth-century political argument. For one untempted by the improving possibility of republican government (in order to keep the reformation on its feet), it underlined the inadequacy of Machiavellian answers to still detectably Machiavellian questions. The final sub-theme of the *Advice*, the loss of political power, effectively casts Charles I in the role of failed prince.

In 1638 Cavendish had urged that Charles read history with an eye to human nature and failures of judgement; he now follows his own advice by listing eleven 'errors of state' (several of them 'the Greateste'). All are forms or causes of loss of direct control. The first was want of money, the results of which were inflammatory taxes and a dependence upon parliament. Only financial independence keeps parliament within bounds (pp. 57;49–50). Second, the peerage was devalued by the selling of titles (pp. 56;48). This upset ceremonial expectations and created an enlarged upper House more factious than the lower (pp. 58;50). Make a man a lord and he will think himself capable of any office.[57] Therefore the fewer the

---

55 Cavendish is clearly closer here to Machiavelli than to Cicero. He never even considers the possibility that rule through fear is ultimately counter-productive, as Cicero believed; and although not dealing as Machiavelli did with the difficult choice of ruling through love or fear, he concludes precisely as Machiavelli did that 'a wise ruler should rely on what is under his own control'. *The Prince*, ed. Skinner and Price, p. 61. The continual insistence upon having everything of importance, especially arms 'in youre own hands', suggests that Cavendish did not discuss choosing *in extremis* between love and fear, because the answer was obvious. Or he may have thought it a silly question. The distinction between symbolic power and force suggests that there could never be a government without both.

56 Margaret Cavendish, *Life*, p. 4, p. li the 'best way of government always has been just rewards and punishments': Cicero, for public consumption.

57 Cf. *The Prince*, ch. 9.

lords, the less the faction and *ergo* the more direct the control (pp. 58;50). Third, court factions were unsuppressed and parliament became a court for their intrigues (pp. 58–9;51). Fourth, allowing judicial power to pass into the hands of parliament and tolerating its destruction of great men, was misguided 'Raginoe del Stato' (pp. 59;51). The remedy: 'keepe ye Power of punishmente only In your Selfe' (pp. 60;52). The fifth error was to reward enemies not friends. This mistaken state maxim weakened the king's allies and encouraged the belief that opposition aided advancement, thus the activities of 'Henery Martin that Holly Soule' (pp. 61;53).[58]

The sixth error was to allow the prerogative to be disputed, especially by lawyers and divines, who at least should have known that all governments are above the law (pp. 62;54).[59] Seven, too many privy councillors were created, again resulting in faction and loss of control. Eight, parliaments were allowed to sit too long, institutionalise themselves and debate at leisure, independently of the king; and ninth, the news of debates and much else went unchecked. With 'weekely Corants' (pp. 65;54) every man became a statesman. Charles must clamp the press so that 'all our Discourse will bee of Hunting & Hawkeing, Boling, Cocking, & such things' (pp. 65;56).[60]

The corollary of an uncontrolled press is an augmented need for intelligence in which (the tenth failing) Charles I had not been well served: 'nothing Should bee spared for Intelegence' (pp. 66;57). The final error lay in choosing the wrong men for the wrong jobs because they were either ill suited or ill stationed. Ill stationed men upset social expectations, and flouting social conventions will, it seems, lose a king control over those whose social identities depend upon the fit between station and responsibility.

---

[58] It was to be a source of discontent that Charles did reward enemies more than friends (a thinly disguised irritant for Margaret Cavendish). But Machiavellian criteria could justify such a policy. With limited resources potential enemies at least needed tying to one's interest. Judging how far this could be done at the expense of nervous and expectant friends was a continuous test of prudence for Charles and for James. Cavendish would have predicted the outcome.

[59] This is as close as Cavendish gets to a theory of sovereignty of the sort that a post-Bodinian world would lead us to expect would interest him. A king and all governmental forms are above the law. Whether a government is in one or more, it is still the transcendent power (pp. 62;54).

[60] Margaret Cavendish, *Life*, pt. 4, p. xlvi: not everything should be put into gazettes, as they encourage public debate.

There are positive lessons to be learned from the 'Rebells', concerning command structure; and certainly from the greatest politician of the age 'D'e Richlew' (pp. 66;57), especially concerning his use of arms and money; but principally a mythologised model of Elizabeth's reign stands in counterpoint to the failings of the last two. As Slaughter correctly remarks, if Cavendish wanted to re-establish an *ancien regime* it was not that of Charles's father.[61]

Slaughter also suggests that the *Advice* is important because it represents a resurgent attachment to tradition;[62] but in some form public deference to tradition was so widespread, that Cavendish's respect for it has little significance. Indeed, the reverse is nearer the truth. In a world of tradition-centred public rhetoric, the new prince's problem is that *per se* he is an innovator.[63] Cavendish, like Machiavelli, seems to recognise this; a number of his recommendations are explicitly innovatory; there is implicit complaint in calling custom a tyrant and a clear note of frustration in saying that country people object to anything new (pp. 50;43). One might say, then, that as the logic of Machiavelli's position involves innovation, Cavendish, in extending the coverage of *The Prince* to Charles, takes a Trojan horse into a tradition-centred world. What is interesting in the *Advice* is the interplay of tradition and innovation at the interstice of public and private discourse; a point reinforced by Margaret's public modifications of the *Advice* (sometimes to the point of disingenuousness), in which a respect for tradition and traditional values are altogether less qualified.[64]

Slaughter's major contention, however, is that the *Advice* is 'clearly' and 'largely Hobbesian'.[65] But again, the claim is inferentially indiscriminate and something significant is largely overlooked. Slaughter catalogues a range of doctrinal similarities between the two men (a shared Erastianism seems to excite him)[66] but these are all too widespread to justify inferring any specific relationship at all. Yet he barely touches on the clear coincidence of

---

[61] Slaughter, *Ideology and Politics*, p. xii.
[62] Ibid.
[63] Pocock, *The Machiavellian Moment*, ch. 6.
[64] See footnotes 46, 47, 52, 55 above; this conclusion further qualifies my argument in 'Radicals, Conservatives and Moderates in Early Modern Political Thought: A Case of Sandwich Islands Syndrome?', *History of Political Thought*, 10, 3 (1989), 538-9.
[65] Slaughter, *Ideology and Politics*, p. xiii.
[66] Ibid., p. xv where Cavendish is said to be reflecting the anticlerical views of the Hobbes circle.

views concerning the book and the politics of interpretation. In any case, as Slaughter accepts, the theoretical scope of *Leviathan* and the *Advice* are hardly comparable; and as I have shown, the Machiavellian style of discourse which circumscribes the *Advice* is also characteristic of the letter, which handsomely predates *Leviathan*. If Hobbes did have any specific impact on the *Advice* it is more likely to have been with respect to the dangers of the public word.

It would of course, be just as wayward to claim that Hobbes too was essentially Machiavellian.[67] Machiavelli's princely idiom does not exist in a self-contained tradition, neither does it consist of fixed policies and nor amount to a proper 'language'. Consequently, there is bound to be an elusive slippage between what we might and might not call 'Machiavellian'. But the language metaphor at least suggests, in the technical senses, Machiavelli's princely discourse as a pidgin or a creole. *If* it had ever been only a pidgin in Renaissance courts, a limited vocabulary shared by groups of political calculators meeting in the world of *negotium*, it was by Cavendish's day certainly a courtly creole; as such there was nothing to stop its employment in the diversified economy of *Leviathan*.[68] So, the vocabulary of *lo stato*, in terms of which Cavendish operates, could be appropriated to that of the sovereign state. In a small way this is to see *Leviathan* marking a Machiavellian moment. It is also to encapsulate a broader problem; that of determining the point at which *lo stato* as passive estate and area of control becomes a concept of political community. If there is ambivalence in Machiavelli, it is carried over into Cavendish for whom 'state' denotes a community, indeed a commonwealth; but its connotations are still overwhelmingly of an object to be possessed.

As I have suggested, the semantic resource we attach to Machiavelli's name was one of the more flexible in the attempts to make sense of British political experience in the seventeenth century. Cavendish's creative mastery of this resource provides a

---

[67] To Anzilotti it is too obvious to need evidence: 'Hobbes has his own words and work to vouch for the source of his thought'; *An English Prince*, p. 63, also p. 67.

[68] Edward D'Acres prefaced his translation of *The Prince* (1640) with an apology for taking the work out of elite circles and thereby running the risk of putting it into inexperienced hands ('Epistle To The Reader'). He justified himself in Baconian terms claiming that the revelation of evil is medicinal (A3). As D'Acres seems to understand, the force of *The Prince* depends considerably on whether it is seen as a private manuscript or as a public book.

dimension which complements, albeit with some tension, the public Machiavelli we have come to associate with that bleak and other-worldly *romanitas* of those on the edges of the political stage.[69]

In their private inscriptions the aristocrats of the court like Cavendish stand between those who publicly denigrated *The Prince* and those who preached from the *Discourses*; they were at home with its criteria of judgement.[70] What is instructive about the Advice in particular is that we can see something of how a semantic resource both informs and is transformed. The transformation was sufficient and facile enough for Arthur Strong to have concluded that the *Advice* is nothing but robust English common sense; and Slaughter that in its conservatism (*sic*) one sees the authentic origins of the Tory party.[71] The most significant aspect of the change in use is not the obvious departure from specifically Machiavellian conclusions, for there traces of the tradition, even the seminal text, must remain clear. It lies in the preoccupation with public language and the book (Machiavelli seems not to have thought much about either). Cavendish wrote with a similar innocence in 1638, but, adhering to his dismissive attitude to books, he came also to fear their power. Once conceived in terms of power, discourse *has* to be in the hands of the prince; it is an extreme extension of the metaphor of *mantenere* made plausible by the physicality of books and presses.

Finally, the *Advice* in all its glorious conversational verve, is an antidote to the now tawdry myth that the Restoration was a return to normality, or even a culmination of the 'revolution'.[72] For men such as Cavendish it could be no such thing, 'some Disputative Scoffers, will tell your Majestie this was a thing this rebellion that never Hapynd before, nor never will Hapen agen' (pp. 2;6). He should not believe them. Cavendish treats rebellion as an ever-present incubus symbolising and insuring the newness in even the

---

[69] As John Pocock has shown, Harrington is a central figure here, see *The Machiavellian Moment*, chs. 11–13.

[70] Jonathan Scott has pointed out to me that Sidney's *Court Maxims* bear a striking resemblance to much of Cavendish's *Advice*, so we are dealing with something that goes beyond commitment to monarchy, but is still characteristic of aristocratic courtly circles.

[71] Strong, *A Catalogue*, p. vii; Slaughter, *Ideology and Politics*, p. xii. One of these 'germs of the Tory party' is said to be a love of religious truth. Cavendish's love has eluded me as it did his contemporaries, see e.g. Clarendon, *History of the Great Rebellion*, bk. 8., pp. 391–2. The portrait is quite consistent with the *Advice*.

[72] Ronald Hutton, *The Restoration, A Political and Religious History of England and Wales, 1658–1667* (Oxford, 1985), p. 1, for the belief that no one doubts that the Restoration was a culmination of the Revolution.

most *ancien regime*. In this way, Machiavelli's preoccupation with
political uncertainty in time is extended to the imagined corners of
the commonwealth of Britain.[73] Twenty years later another would
warn in true Cavendish style, that some rebels now are more fox
than lion, more of the pen 'than glittering steel'.[74] When such *furbi*
had re-written the book of the Great Rebellion, the monarchy
would fall again.

---

[73] Pocock, *The Machiavellian Moment*, chs. 6–7, where this preoccupation is shown to pervade
all Machiavelli's political works.
[74] Anon, *The Character of a Rebellion* (1681), p. A2.

PART III

Between Lambeth and Leviathan: Samuel Parker on the Church of England and political order

Gordon J. Schochet

Samuel Parker was a remarkable and multi-faceted man. Well known in his day – although hardly well regarded – as a formidable and sharp-tongued polemicist and enemy of dissent, he has been all but forgotten. A handful of literary scholars interested in Andrew Marvell's *Rehearsal Transpros'd* – which was a response to several of Parker's tracts – knows at least one side of him,[1] and the critical consensus is that Parker was an unworthy opponent who was easily driven from the field of battle.[2] Parker's name appears from time to time in works on Restoration ecclesiology and religious thought – especially in reference to his attacks on nonconformity and toler-

The research out of which this essay has grown has enjoyed the generous support of both the Research Divison and the Fellowship Divison of the National Endowment for the Humanities, the Folger Institute of the Folger Shakespeare Library and its Center for the History of British Political Thought, the Center for the History of Freedom of Washington University and Rutgers University. Some of the ideas were presented to the 1991 meeting of the American Society for Eighteenth-Century Studies. On that occasion, Richard Kroll, Hugh Ormsby-Lennon, Joseph Levine and especially Patricia Brückmann made a number of helpful and encouraging suggestions, as did, at other times, Moti Feingold, J.G.A. Pocock, Patrick Moloney and the editors of this book. It is a pleasure to acknowledge my indebtedness to all these institutions and people. Lena Cowen Orlin and Louise Haberman deserve separate and particular thanks.

[1] In order of publication, John M. Wallace, *Destiny His Choice: The Loyalism of Andrew Marvell* (Cambridge, 1968), pp. 184–207, *passim*; Andrew Marvell, *The Rehearsal Transpros'd* and *The Rehearsal Transpros'd, The Second Part* (1672 and 1673), ed. D.I.B. Smith (Oxford, 1971), Editor's Introduction, *passim*; Annabel M. Patterson, *Marvell and the Civic Crown* (Madison, 1978), pp. 175–210, *passim*; and Warren L. Chernaick, *The Poet's Time: Politics and Religion in the Work of Andrew Marvell* (Cambridge, 1983), pp. 120–50, *passim*.

[2] The *DNB* entry, rather more judiciously (and correctly), reports that 'Parker held his own'. It is the case, however, that Parker, somewhat out of character, did not reply to Marvell's second attack in 1673.

ation[3] – and here too the received opinion is that he was a relatively minor figure.[4]

Intelligent, well read, prolific, and possessed of diverse interests, he was an advocate of the new science, an astute critic of the Restoration Platonists and what he saw as their misuses of language,[5] a more than merely competent natural-law theorist, and a high church apologist for the Anglican establishment. But he was intemperate and mean spirited in his attacks on dissenters, ruthlessly absolutist in his political theory and – at the end of his life – an ally (and possibly a pawn as well) of James II's in the king's attempt to further the interests of Roman Catholics. (James, ignoring Archbishop Sancroft's recommendation of Robert South, had appointed Parker bishop of Oxford in 1686.[6]) Because he consistently cast his lot with what was ultimately the losing side in Restoration politics, history has buried Parker in either defamation or obscurity, yet another instance of Whiggery triumphant that would have pleased many of his contemporaries.

While this essay is not directly concerned with resuscitating Parker – that would require a far more extensive treatment than is attempted here – it necessarily possesses something of the character

---

[3] See, for instance, Tim Harris, Paul Seaward and Mark Goldie (eds.), *The Politics of Religion in Restoration England* (Oxford, 1990), pp. 20–1 and 199–200; Norman Sykes, *From Sheldon to Secker: Aspects of English Church History, 1660–1768* (Cambridge, 1959), p. 81; G.R. Cragg, *Puritanism in the Period of the Great Persecution, 1660–1688* (Cambridge, 1957) p. 230; and C.E. Whiting, *Studies in English Puritanism from the Restoration to the Revolution, 1660–1688* (London, 1931), pp. 497–506. Among older works, see H.F. Russell Smith, *The Theory of Religious Liberty in the Reigns of Charles II and James II* (Cambridge, 1911), pp. 47, 49, and 80; William H. Hutton, *The English Church from the Accession of Charles I to the Death of Queen Anne (1625–1714)* (London, 1903), p. 205; and John Hunt, *Religious Thoughts in England from the Reformation to the End of the Last Century*, 3 vols. (London, 1870–3), vol. I, pp. 405–7 and vol. II, pp. 10–13. The most extensive discussion is in A.A. Seaton, *The Theory of Toleration under the Later Stuarts* (Cambridge, 1911), pp. 154–70.

[4] For an important if somewhat overstated exception to this characterisation, see Richard Ashcraft, *Revolutionary Politics and Locke's Two Treatises* (Princeton, 1986), esp. pp. 41–54.

[5] For some discussion, see Hugh Ormsby-Lennon, 'Rosicrucian Linguistics: Twilight of a Renaissance Tradition', in *Hermeticism and the Renaissance: Intellectual History and the Occult in Early Modern Europe*, ed. Ingrid Merkel and Allen G. Debus (Washington, DC, 1988), esp. pp. 333–4 and nn.

[6] Hutton, *English Church*, p. 222, and Sykes, *Sheldon to Secker*, p. 31, citing George D'Oyly, *The Life of William Sancroft, Archbishop of Canterbury*, 2 vols. (Oxford, 1821), vol. I, pp. 235–6.
   At the same time, Thomas Cartwright was appointed Bishop of Chester, and Gilbert Burnet described them as 'the two worst men that could be found out', calling them 'the fittest instruments that could be found among all the clergy, to betray and ruin the church'. *History of his Own Time*, vol. IV, 695 and 696 (reprint edn (Oxford, 1823), vol. III, pp. 134 and 136). Cf. Hutton, *English Church*, pp. 300–1.

of a 'revisionist' work. There is no general scholarship on Parker, and prevailing judgements about his worth seem overly simplistic and incorrect. Parker can stand as a representative of the political and religious establishment against which the nonconformists and their liberal, Anglican allies and 'radical' political reformers contended. He steadfastly resisted all attempts to alter English society and was a most formidable opponent, for – like Rousseau one hundred years later – Parker understood enough of the 'modern' world that was coming into being around him to be deeply troubled by it and to resist its growth.

He regarded social diversity and religious sectarianism as the harbingers of chaos and anarchy; they were the uncontrollable forces that would be unleashed by toleration and permissive comprehension. In many respects, he was what would today be termed a 'reactionary'. But he was not merely a devotee of the 'ancient wisdom' who took his stand against the 'moderns', for he was also enough of a Baconian nominalist – and therefore himself something of a 'modern' – to believe that there was a dangerous deception inherent in the essentialist conception of language to which the Platonists of his day subscribed. This much, along with a commitment to sovereign absolutism, he shared with Hobbes, from whom he departed on virtually every other issue.

J.G.A. Pocock is one of the few scholars who has recognised the complexity of Parker's relationship with Hobbes. Moreover, he has seen in the works of this uncelebrated Restoration divine something more than a cantankerous defence of the High Church establishment against its latitudinarian and nonconformist critics.[7]

Pocock explores Parker's early attribution to Hobbes of doctrines akin to those of the Platonists and enthusiasts. Such a view of Hobbes seems radically incorrect – in terms of both seventeenth-century and modern perspectives – for it is at odds with the more familiar understanding of Hobbes as a hard-headed materialist (and atheist as well, in all probability) who himself launched profound attacks on the mysterious and ethereal doctrines of his Platonist contemporaries. But Pocock ingeniously argues that there is an important Restoration sense of atomism in terms of which 'even Hobbes's brand of atheism could be termed as enthusiasm'.[8]

---

[7] J.G.A. Pocock, 'Thomas Hobbes, Atheist or Enthusiast? His Place in Restoration Debate', *History of Political Thought*, XI: 4 (winter, 1990: Hobbes issue), 737–49.

[8] Ibid, p. 747.

Thus, at least this aspect of Parker's interpretation of Hobbes can be vindicated. And Parker himself is certainly a fitting subject for a volume of essays inspired by Pocock's scholarship.

I

Relatively little is known of Parker's biography aside from his life as a cleric and author, and what facts there are seem not to be in dispute.[9] Born in 1640, he was matriculated at Wadham College, Oxford, in 1656 (BA 1659), where he was known as a dedicated Presbyterian; he became an equally zealous Anglican after the Restoration. He remained at Oxford and was ordained in 1664 and subsequently attracted the attention of Gilbert Sheldon, archbishop of Canterbury, who made Parker his chaplain in 1667. In 1670 he became archdeacon of Canterbury and later that year was installed prebendary there. By 1673 he held the rectory of Ickham in Kent and was also master of Edenbridge Hospital. After that, the progress of his clerical career came to a halt. Perhaps because of the death of his patron, Archbishop Sheldon, in 1675, he did not receive further advancement to a bishopric that, according to Gilbert Burnet, he expected,[10] until 1686. And even then, William Sancroft, Sheldon's successor, did not favour Parker's elevation and agreed to consecrate him only because he feared a praemunire suit.[11]

Parker's appointment to the bishopric was politically motivated,

[9] The following biographical remarks are based largely on the account in the *DNB*, q.v., which draws on all the available sources, including occasional autobiographical references in Parker's writings, scattered comments on Burnet's *History* and comments by Parker's critics.
Other than a Latin *History of His Own Time*, Parker apparently left no manuscripts. The *History* was published in Latin in 1726 (*Reverendi amodum in Christo Patri, S. Parker . . . de rebus sui temporis commentariorum libri quatuor* (not seen; title from British Library *Catalogue*)) and twice translated, in 1727 and 1728, with minor textual differences. The 1728 edition contains 'An Impartial Account of Parker's Life, and of his Conversation with Presbyterianism to Popery' and says of Parker himself, 'The boasted Lyon a meer Mouse appears'. (*Bishop Parkers History of His Own Time* (1728), title page. I have used the 1727 edition but have provided page references to the later one as well.) The work stops in 1680 and does not say much about Parker himself. It does reveal Parker's animus toward dissenters, and provides some insight into the activities of the Archbishop of Canterbury Gilbert Sheldon – Parker was his chaplain from 1667. It is used to advantage in Victor D. Sutch, *Gilbert Sheldon, Architect of Anglican Survival, 1640–1675* (The Hague, 1975), which has little to say about Parker.
[10] Burnet, *History*, vol. IV, 696 (edn 1823, vol. III, 137).
[11] Ibid., vol. IV, p. 696 (edn 1823, vol. III, p. 138).

and by the next year he was promoting the cause of the king's co-religionists at Oxford. He published an attack on the Test Act, attempted to persuade his diocesan clergy to declare their gratitude and loyalty to the king, and when it was reported that James intended to make appointments at the universities that would be in the interests of Roman Catholics, Parker encouraged his own nomination to the vacant presidency of Magdalen College. The refusal of the fellows to accept Parker was overcome only by the forcible seizure of the president's lodgings in late October 1687, two months after his appointment and eight months after the death of the last president. The entire affair caused much bitterness, and many members of the college did not recognise Parker's legitimacy. He spent the next four months – the last of his life – admitting Roman Catholics to College fellowships, resisting only when the king called for the admission of nine more.

There was no doubt about his sympathies for the Roman Catholic cause, and it was widely believed that he had actually converted before his death. However, he received the sacraments according to the Anglican practice and declared his adherence to the Church of England to the fellows of the College. He died on 21 March 1688, and was buried three days later. Exactly fourteen months later, as the culmination of a series of events that the ever-contentious Parker would have found disastrous, King William III accepted as law what has since been known as the Act of Toleration. Parker lost on all fronts, for the Act granted a limited religious freedom to many of the despised nonconformists and provided nothing at all for Roman Catholics.

Parker's literary career had been no less stormy than his brief term as bishop. A productive, intelligent and witty writer who had a great command and understanding of the language, he published more than twenty books and pamphlets, many 300 or more pages long and repetitious (but not dreary) and all controversial and polemical. Somewhat surprisingly for a clergyman, he published no sermons, and there seem to be no references to any that he delivered. His verbal skills apparently did not lend themselves to oratory.

His writings parallel his clerical life. They are united by persistent concerns with order, morality and political stability, issues that seem to have been the driving intellectual forces of Parker's life and the vehicles through which he pursued his apparent ambitions for status within the church. As Burnet observed, 'He was a covetous and ambitious man; and seemed to have had no other sense of religion but as a political interest, and a subject of party and faction.'[12] It is not surprising, then, that – with the exception of his first published work,[13] a criticism of the doctrine of the pre-existence of souls (which was part of his attack on Platonic mysticism and essentialism),[14] and contentious discussions of transubstantiation and the invocation of saints in his last work – there is no theology *per se* or direct discussion of the substantive meaning of theological principles in Parker's writings.

Much of his writing was also marked by attacks on the philosophy of Hobbes, distrust of the 'common people' and the insistence upon strong public power – absolute sovereignty, which Parker said was divinely ordained – as the only viable response to an otherwise unavoidable disorder. There is a coherence and loose if stubborn consistency that tends to unite Parker's writings as well. Until 1686, he does not appear to have changed his opinions at all.

Two of his earliest works, published in 1666 and 1667, were criticisms of the Platonism of his day – and its role in furthering the doctrines of nonconformity – and defences of the new science; they followed his election to the Royal Society (in which he was never active).[15] Shortly after the start of his association with Archbishop Sheldon, he began his direct and overt attack on dissenters. That period, which opened with his best-known work, the *Discourse of*

[12] Ibid., vol. iv, p. 696 (edn 1823, vol. iii, p. 138).
[13] *Tentamina Physico-Theologica de Deo* (1665).
[14] Samuel Parker, *An Account of the Nature and Extent of the Divine Dominion and Goodnesse* (Oxford, 1667), pp. 171–89. This work was published as part of the second edition of Parker's *A Free and Impartial Censure of the Platonick Philosophy* (Oxford, 1667). Each work has a separate title page but the pagination is continuous. The attack on the pre-existence of souls was presumably aimed at [Joseph Glanvill], *Lux Orientalis; or, An Enquiry into the Opinions of the Eastern Sages concerning the Praeexistence of Souls* (Cambridge, 1662).
[15] *Free and Impartial Censure* and *An Account of the Nature*. Both works identified Parker on their title pages as a 'Fellow of the Royal Society'. Parker was elected FRS on 13 June 1666, having been proposed by John Wilkins. He was never an active fellow, paying only his admission and no further subscriptions. His name does not appear in membership lists after 1684, and he was apparently expelled in 1685 for non-payment (Michael Hunter, *The Royal Society and Its Fellows, 1660–1700*, British Society for the History of Science Monographs, 4 (Chalfont St Giles, 1982), pp. 198–99, 99, and 153 n. 10). Parker's *Free and Impartial Censure* was commended by Henry Oldenburg in a letter to Robert Boyle of 8 June 1666 (*The Correspondence of Henry Oldenburg*, ed. A. Rupert Hall and Marie Boas Hall, vol. iii (Madison, 1966), p. 155), but otherwise there appears to be no mention of him in the context of the Royal Society.

Ecclesiastical Polity,[16] lasted until 1673 and the conclusion of his exchange with Marvell.[17]

Parker's *Ecclesiastical Polity* grew out of failed attempts to pass comprehension and toleration bills in late 1667 and early 1668;[18] reactions to the moderately permissive comprehension advocated by Simon Patrick in his 1669 *Friendly Debate between a Conformist and a Non-Conformist*[19] (one of the most widely cited books on the subject during this period); debates over the renewal of the Conventicle Act in 1670; and the possibility that same year that King Charles would issue a Declaration of Indulgence[20] – which he did in 1672 (and which parliament forced him to withdraw the next year) –

---

[16] [Samuel Parker], *A Discourse of Ecclesiastical Polity* (1670). All references are to the 3rd edition (1671), which was a page-for-page reprint of the first. The first edition must have been in print in 1669 despite its 1670 date, for John Owen's reply (see below) carried a 1669 imprint.

[17] *Ecclesiastical Polity* attracted a number of responses, most notably [John Owen], *Truth and Innocence Vindicated: In a Survey of Discuss concerning Ecclesiastical Polity* (n.p., 1669), to which Parker replied in his voluminous (750 pages) *A Defence and Continuation of the Ecclesiatical Polity* (1671). His next publication was his anonymous 'A Preface Shewing What Grounds There Are of Fears and Jealousies of Popery', prefixed to John Bramhall, *Bishop Bramhall's Vindication of Himself and the Episcopal Clergy from the Presbyterian Charge of Popery* (1672). (The 'Preface' was republished as a separate work in 1673 – still anonymous – as *A Discourse in Vindication of Bp. Bramhall and Clergy of the Church of England, from the Fanatick Charge of Popery* (1673); I have used the original edition, cited as [Parker], 'Preface to Bramhall'. The 'Preface' is the work that ultimately provoked Marvell into writing *The Rehearsal Transpros'd*. Parker answered Marvell with [anon.], *A Reproof to the Rehearsal Transprosed, in a Discourse to Its Author* (1673). Marvell's rejoinder, *The Rehearsal Transpros'd, The Second Part*, ended the controversy.

[18] The earlier part of this attempt is little known, for the proposed bills were never introduced in parliament and are therefore not included in the official history. There are two contemporary accounts. One – which I am editing for publication – is a lengthy manuscript that Thomas Barlow (later Bishop of Oxford) wrote and bound as a preface to a collection of comprehension and toleration tracts from 1667 to 1668 (Bodleian Library Printed Book B.14.15.Linc.); the other is in *Reliquiae Baxterianae: or Mr. Richard Baxters Narrative of the Most Memorable Passages of His Life and Times*, ed. Matthew Sylvester (1696), Bk. III, pp. 9–17, 23–25, and 32–49. Excerpts from the Barlow manuscript were printed as an editorial preface to Herbert Thorndike, *The True Principle of Comprehension: or, A Petition against the Presbyterian Request for a Comprehensive Act*, in Thorndike, *Theological Works* (Oxford, 1854), vol. v, pp. 301–8. There are discussions based on these sources in Sykes, *Sheldon to Secker*, pp. 72–4; Roger Thomas, 'Comprehension and Indulgence', in *From Uniformity to Unity, 1662–1962*, ed. Geoffrey F. Nuttall and Owen Chadwick (London, 1962), pp. 200–3; Walter G. Simon, 'Comprehension in the Age of Charles II', *Church History*, 31 (1962), 440–8; and the same author's *The Restoration Episcopate* (New York, 1965), ch. xi.

[19] See [Parker], *Ecclesiastical Polity*, Preface, p. iii.

[20] Ibid., pp. 165–6.

despite Parliament's recent stand against dissenters.²¹ Archbishop Sheldon opposed toleration and comprehension,²² and his biographer has said that the views of *Ecclesiastical Polity* were those of Sheldon 'expressed through the vitriolic pen of his chaplain'.²³

After five years of silence, Parker returned to literary activity. He ignored current political issues but was preoccupied instead with the Church of England and religiosity in general. Between 1678 and 1685 – during the period of the Popish Plot, the Exclusion Controversy, the Rye-House Plot, and Monmouth's Rebellion – Parker published, *inter alia*, essays on divine providence and on the law of nature and its basis in divinity and a number of apologies for and defences of the Anglican establishment, its historical legitimacy and its roots in primitive Christianity.²⁴ While still argumentative, the tone of Parker's writings was more subdued – almost gentle by comparison – than it had previously been, and there is little to direct the reader to the tumultuous politics of the day.

As bishop of Oxford and near the end of his life, he returned to his more accustomed polemical manner, serving his new patron, King James, with a literary attack on the Test Act and a covert defence of the entitlements of Roman Catholics,²⁵ just as he was serving him in deed at Magdalen College. The politics surrounding Parker's tract are intriguing and reveal Parker at his most opportunistic. On 4 April 1687, James had issued a Declaration of

---

21 In 1670 – perhaps as early as 1669 – the Earl of Shaftesbury presented to Charles a 'Memorial . . . on Indulgence to Dissenters, Naturalization of Foreigners, and Registration of Titles to Land' in which he urged the King to issue a declaration granting dissenters relief from the Penal Laws. See W.D. Christie, *A Life of Anthony Ashley Cooper, First Earl of Shaftesbury, 1667–1683*, 2 vols. (London, 1871), vol. II, Appendix 1 (pp. v–ix); the title seems to have been Christie's invention. Archbishop Sheldon and, through him, Parker could certainly have known that the King was considering indulgence that early.
On the indulgence declaration, see Frank Bate, *The Declaration of Indulgence, 1672: A Study in the Rise of Organized Dissent* (London, 1908), a work that is seriously out of date. More recent discussions are Douglas R. Lacey, *Dissent and Parliamentary Politics in England, 1661–1689* (New Brunswick, N.J., 1969), pp. 63–70, and Thomas, 'Comprehension and Indulgence', pp. 206–12.
22 See Parker, *History*, pp. 22–3 (edn 1728, pp. 32–3).
23 Sutch, *Gilbert Sheldon*, p. 109.
24 Samuel Parker, *Disputationes de Deo, et Providentia Divina* (1678); Samuel Parker, *A Demonstration of the Divine Authority of the Law of Nature and of the Christian Religion* (1681); S[amuel] Parker, *The Case of the Church of England, Briefly and Truly Stated* (1681); Samuel Parker, *Religion and Loyalty: Or, a Demonstration of the Power of the Christian Church with It Self* (London, 1684); and Samuel Parker, *Religion and Loyalty, The Second Part* (1685).
25 Samuel Parker (signed the last page), *Reasons for Abrogating the Test, Imposed on all Members of Parliament* (1688).

Indulgence in which he declared that 'the execution of all and all manner of penal laws in matters ecclesiastical ... [are] immediately suspended'.²⁶ At the same time, James was preparing to summon a parliament. In an attempt to control the elections and to ensure that the Commons was sympathetic to the policies of the Declaration, he ordered a survey of magistrates, justices of the peace, and other local officials throughout England. They were asked if they would, as prospective members of parliament, support repeal of the penal laws and the Test Act, if they would use their influence to elect persons so pledged and, finally, whether they would 'support the King's Declaration for Liberty of Conscience, by living friendly with those of all perswasions, as subjects of the same Prince, and good Christians ought to doe'.²⁷

The Declaration aroused fears in moderate and high churchmen alike, both because of the encouragement it gave to Roman Catholics and because of the possibility that the king might acquire the support of the dissenters. The next year, in a manoeuvre designed to force the hand of the church, the king reissued the Declaration²⁸ and ordered that it be read in all the parishes in the country, thus provoking the famous Trial of the Seven Bishops. Parker was dead by time the second Declaration was issued, but his attack on the Test Acts had been licensed on 10 December 1687; it made him one of the few high-ranking officials of the church who had supported James in one of the last series of acts before his expulsion.

²⁶ James II, 'His Majesty's Gracious Declaration to All His Loving Subjects for Liberty of Conscience' (1687), reprinted in Andrew Browning (ed.), *English Historical Documents, 1660–1714* (Oxford, 1953), doc. 146, pp. 395–6.

²⁷ George Duckett (ed.), *Penal Laws and Test Acts: Questions Touching Their Repeal Propounded in 1687–8 by James II . . . from the Original Returns in the Bodleian Library* (London, 1883), Introduction, p. ix. The returns from this survey were never made public, but they were finally published by Duckett. See also John Carswell, *The Descent on England: A Study of the English Revolution of 1688 and Its European Background* (New York, 1969), pp. 105 ff.

²⁸ The reissue – dated 24 April 1688 – contained a new preamble and postscript. In the latter, James announced his intention 'to call a Parliament that shall meet in November next at the furthest' and expressed his hope that his subjects would 'lay aside all private animosities and jealousies' and would 'choose such members of Parliament as may do their parts to finish what we have begun.' James II, 'The King's Declaration for Liberty of Conscience', reprinted in Browning, *Documents*, doc. 149, p. 400. The events of the next few months, of course, rendered James's plans moot, and there is no little irony in the fact that his alleged intentions to heal the divisions of the kingdom solidified and unified the opposition to his government. For a detailed discussion, see Richard E. Boyer, *English Declarations of Indulgence, 1687 and 1688* (The Hague, 1968).

II

The principal issue at stake for Parker was always the survival of the English state and its established church, which he regarded as inseparably bound together. Setting aside for the moment the possible contradictions introduced by his willingness after 1686 to permit relative religious freedom to some Catholics, Parker never wavered from his belief that religious diversity would destroy England. Despite his self-interested motives and apparent indifference to the finer points of theological disputation, he seems to have been altogether sincere in his dedication to the Church of England and in his continuing belief in its divine and historical legitimacy.

His fears for its destruction at the hands of the Presbyterians and their nonconformist allies were certainly genuine, and suggest that he shared more than a title with the author of the original *Ecclesiastical Polity*.[29] Richard Hooker, fearing the influence of the Puritans whom he urged to sit quietly in the Church of England without compromising their consciences, had written his *Ecclesiastical Polity*, he declared in 1593 in the opening sentence of his Preface, '*Though for no other cause, yet for this; that posteritie may know we have not loosely through silence permitted things to passe away as in a dreame, there shall be for mens information extant thus much concerning the present state of the Church of God established amongst us, and their carefull endeavour which woulde have upheld the same.*'[30]

Parker, of course, was not nearly so gentle, and there is no danger of his ever being called 'judicious'. His *Ecclesiastical Polity* was aimed at the '*Wild and Fanatique Rabble*' who, through '*Folly and Ignorance*' would destroy the '*publick Peace and Settlement of [the] Nation*'.

> ... *these Brain-sick People, if not prevented by some speedy and effectual Remedy, may in a little time grow to the Power and Confidence, as to be able* ... to restrain the Highest Powers of Church and State ... to turn the still People of a State or Nation into War and Blood: *or* ... *to tye the Hands of Authority, to*

---

[29] In his only reference to Hooker, Parker said that the *Laws of Ecclesiastical Polity* was 'as full and demonstrative a Confutation' of the nonconformists' cause as could be made and that ''tis Unanswerable': *Ecclesiastical Polity*, p. 200.

[30] Richard Hooker, *Of the Laws of Ecclesiasticall Politie* (1593, *et seq.*), Preface, text from the Folger Edition of *The Works of Richard Hooker*, ed. W. Speed Hill, 5 vols. (Cambridge, Mass., 1977–90), vol. I, p. 1.

instigate the People of God to Rebellion, and once more involve the Kingdom in Blood and Confusion.[31]

Such was the legacy of toleration.

The aim of the work, as its title-page asserted, was to demonstrate 'The Authority of the Civil Magistrate over the Consciences of Subjects in Matters of External Religion' and to show 'The Mischiefs and Inconveniences of Toleration'.

Parker opposed toleration because it would have legitimated the freeing of large numbers of people from the discipline of the Church of England. If the common people are 'suffered to run without restraint', he wrote in 1666, 'they will break down all the banks of Law and Government'.[32] The only thing to be done with (and to) them was to punish and persecute them in accordance with the Clarendon Code, and to drive them back into the established church. For the masses were waiting *'to fall into the snare of an abused and vicious Conscience'* prepared for them by the dissenting ministers.

There is no Observation in the world establish'd upon a more certain and universal Experience, than that the generality of mankind are not so obnoxious to any sort of Follies and Vices, as to wild and unreasonable conceits of Religion; and that, when their heads are possess'd with them, there are no principles so pregnant with mischief and disturbance than they. And if Princes would but consider, how liable mankind are to abuse themselves with serious and conscientious Villanies, they would quickly see it to be absolutely necessary to the Peace and Happiness of their Kingdoms, that there be set up a severe Government over mens Consciences and Religious perswasions, than over their Vices and Immoralities.[33]

It followed, then, that *'Indulgence and Toleration is the most absolute sort of Anarchy'*.[34]

Parker objected to a permissive or negotiated comprehension in which the Presbyterians would have been granted concessions on church practices they found offensive as a condition of ecclesiastical reunion. He insisted on the contrary that they should be forced to conform, which would not injure their 'tender consciences' and was necessary for the social good. He side-stepped the issues involved in

---

[31] [Parker], *Ecclesiastical Polity*, Preface, pp. ii–iii.
[32] Samuel Parker, *An Account of the Nature and Extent of the Divine Dominion and Goodness* (1666), 2nd edn (Oxford, 1667), p. 219.
[33] [Parker], *Ecclesiastical Polity*, Preface, pp. xlii–xliii.
[34] Ibid., Preface, p. lxv.

the disputes over indifferency. The problem was not the resolving
of personal consciences that was so important to the dissenters but
finding the 'most prudent and expedient way of settling' the
conflicts that would inevitably arise because mankind is not
infallible. Everything pointed to 'an absolute necessity of a
Supreme Power in all Publick Affairs', giving Parker the opportunity to make his most absolutist pronouncements.

Even granting that this 'Supreme Civil Power' itself was 'imperfect and liable to Errors and Mistakes', he continued,

yet 'tis the least so, and is a much better way to attain Publick Peace and
Tranquility, than if they were entirely left to the ignorance and folly of
every private man, which must of necessity be pregnant with all manner of
Mischiefs and Confusion . . . And if it so happen, that some private
persons suffer from this method of proceeding, yet *this private injury has an
ample Compensation from the Publick benefit that arises from it.*[35]

From this argument, Parker derived 'the necessity of subjection
and obedience to all Authority', for 'The miseries of Tyranny are
less, than those of Anarchy.'[36]

Parker was conspicuously silent about the Roman Catholic
recusants and the persistent charge that the Anglican church was
too sympathetic to popery in general even though it was widely
believed that Catholics were a threat to the security of England.
His 1672 'Preface' to Bishop John Bramhall's *Vindication of Himself*
attacked the '*Geneva Faction*' and the '*natural Tendency of fanatick and
enthusiastick Principles, to wild and seditious Practices*' and repeated
many of the arguments from *Ecclesiastical Polity* for more than fifty
pages before taking up its ostensible question. And then Parker
concluded that the 'Danger . . . of the Return of Popery into this
Nation' came exclusively from '*the Nonconformists [sic] boisterous and
unreasonable Opposition to the Church of* England', which was undermining '*the Power and Reputation*' of Anglicanism. Left alone, the
established church '*could easily beat back and baffle all the Attempts of
Rome and all its Adherents*'.[37] The real problem was the '*Disorders and
Disturbances in the State*' created by the nonconformists, who '*are
fermented with a Republican Leven*' and devoted to '*the Good Old Cause*'.
In short, they were nothing more than revolutionaries and regicides.[38]

35 Ibid., pp. 212–13.
36 Ibid., pp. 213 and 215.
37 [Parker], 'Preface to Bramhall', sigs. [A4ᵛ], [a5ᵛ], and c4ᵛ.
38 Ibid., sig. [c6].

About the allegations of popery in the Anglican church itself or the putative Catholic menace, Parker had nothing more to say until his attack on the Test Act in 1688.[39] And here, he took – however hypocritically – what for him was something of a theoretical high ground by appealing to principles and the 'rights' of parliament and of Englishmen, which he claimed were abridged by the Test.[40]

Until that point in his life, Parker's writings had looked to the preservation of the order, peace and stability of England as a homogeneous society with uniform religious practice. Even the new science of the Royal Society was essential to the achievement of this goal, for its experimental, Baconian perspective exposed and destroyed the allegorical mystifications and errors of Platonism.[41]

References to Hobbes – generally critical – are a further constant that runs through Parker's writings until his attack on the Test Act. But there is a certain tension in his relationship with Hobbes. For the most part, Parker felt that the threat posed to English society by Hobbes and his materialist philosophy was no less great than that of the nonconformists, and he argued that Hobbesian doctrines undergirded dissent. These criticisms grew stronger and more frequent over the years, starting with subtle rejections of the 'mechanical' philosophy and an insistence that there was God-given 'propriety' – at least in one's self – even in the Hobbesian state of nature.[42]

At the same time, however, there was a number of important similarities between them, evidenced not simply in Parker's insistence upon the absolutism of sovereign power but including his hard-headed linguistic nominalism and rejection of the 'dark and aenigmatical Representations' of Platonists and Rosicrucians – whom he also frequently called 'Enthusiasts' and 'Fanaticks' (which were barely disguised terms for nonconformists[43]) – as well as the 'empty words' of their 'Metaphors and Allegories'[44]. At one

---

[39] In his manuscript *History*, however, he defended the restoration of lands that had been seized from Roman Catholics during the Interregnum, saying that they were 'the patrimony of papists that had stood by the King, and who had not only approved themselves Gentlemen of firm fidelity to his Majesty, but were indeed the rightful Owners'. Parker, *History*, p. 48 (edn 1728, p. 72).

[40] Parker, *Reasons for Abrogating the Test*, esp. pp. 1, 6, and 65.

[41] Parker, *Free and Impartial Censure*, pp. 47 and 55.

[42] Parker, *Free and Impartial Censure*, p. 34, and *Account of the Nature*, pp. 130–2.

[43] On the practice of identifying the Rosicrucians with religious and political dissidents throughout the Restoration, see J.R. Jacob, *Robert Boyle and the English Revolution: A Study in Social and Intellectual Change* (New York, 1977), pp. 163–4.

[44] Parker, *Free and Impartial Censure*, pp. 73 and 78.

point in his *Ecclesiastical Polity*, Parker put both these contentions together, saying:

So that all the Magistrate's Power of instituting Significant Ceremonies amounts to no more than a Power of Determining what shall or shall not be *Visible Signs of Honour*, and this certainly can be no more Usurpation upon the Conscience of men, than if the Sovereign Authority should take upon it self (as some Princes have done) to define the signification of Words. For as Words do not naturally denote those things which they are used to represent, but have their Import Stampt upon them by consent and Institution, and may, if Men would agree to it among themselves, be made marks of things quite contrary to what they now signifie.[45]

It would be easy to conclude that Parker was following Hobbes in all this, but neither Parker's nor Hobbes's linguistic theories were at all unusual in the period. Also, Parker frequently cited Bacon in support of these apparently Hobbesian positions,[46] who might also have been Hobbes's source. A further, important difference between Hobbes and Parker was that the latter's arguments were embedded in and utterly dependent upon a commitment to theism and a profound belief in the goodness of God's will. And it was a theism that appears to have been altogether sincere; certainly none of Parker's critics accused him of atheism.

Of central importance to Parker was Hobbes's reduction of motivation to self-interest, which could only result in a denial of obligation and would render it impossible for people ever to escape from the 'supposed . . . natural state of War'.[47] This doctrine, Parker contended, was identical to the views of the nonconformists. '*With what a greedy confidence*', he asked, '*do they* [i.e., dissenting ministers] *swallow down the Principles of the* Malmsbury Philosophy, *without any chewing, or consideration?*'[48]

the result of all their Principles is, That every Wise Man will by any means consult his own Interest and Security, and that his Interest and Security consists chiefly in the preheminence of his Strength above Men, so that the more he oppress them, the more he acts up to the Laws of Nature, and Principles of Wisdom.[49]

Groundless as this state-of-nature theory is, it has become the

45 [Parker], *Ecclesiastical Polity*, p. 108.
46 Parker, *Free and Impartial Censure*, pp. 29, 61, possibly 90, and 93.
47 [Parker], *Ecclesiastical Polity*, p. 132.
48 Ibid., Preface, p. xxv.
49 [Parker], 'Preface to Bramhall', sig. [d8ᵛ]. See also *Ecclesiastical Polity*, Preface, p. xxvi.

'Standard of our *Modern Politics*'.[50] Similarly, the Hobbesian doctrine of liberty of conscience and its concomitant notion 'That
Mankind is free from all obligations antecedent to the Laws of the
Common-wealth' have become the bases of the nonconformists'
belief that they cannot be bound to obey any magisterial impositions in religious matters.[51]

Operationally, Parker's conception of the relations between the
church and state of England was Erastian – another point of
contact with Hobbes. However, this was a position he explicitly
rejected when he turned to Anglican apologetics in the 1680s:

> in a Christian state men are not Christians by vertue of the Law of the
> Common-wealth, but it is the Law of God that constitutes the Being and
> Formality of a Christian Church . . . the whole cause of *Erastianism* is run
> upon a palpable Contradiction. For if the Church be a Society founded
> upon Divine Right, it must have at least as much power of Government
> within it self as is necessary to its own Peace and Preservation; otherwise,
> it is no Society, much less of any Divine appointment.[52]

But the rejection was more apparent than real. Without explaining
precisely how he had moved from the divine institution and
consequent political independence of the ecclesiastical establishment, Parker said to those latitudinarians who regarded church
government as indifferent, 'unless the Christian Church be subject
to Government, it can be no more than Rabble and Riot . . . and
forever obnoxious to unavoidable disorders and confusions'.[53] For-
tunately, the Church of England 'is established by the Law of the
Land, and by the Law of Christ'.

> For unless we suppose that the Church was originally settled by our
> Saviour with divine Authority, we deny his Supremacy over his own
> Church: and unless we suppose that the supreme Government of King-
> dom has power to abett and ratifie our Saviours establishment by Civil
> Laws, we deny his Majesties Supremacy over his Christian Subjects.

---

[50] [Parker], *Ecclesiastical Polity*, p. 118.
[51] Ibid., p. 137.
[52] Parker, *Case of the Church*, p. 35. This work too has many negative references to Hobbes, to
whom the first fifty pages are devoted.
[53] Parker, *Case of the Church*, p. 251. Comprehension and indulgence were once again in the
air when Parker published this work. Both houses of the second Exclusion Parliament
considered such proposals, but the king adjourned the session before final action could be
taken. See Henry Horwitz, 'Protestant Reconciliation in the Exclusion Crisis', *Journal of
Ecclesiastical History*, 15 (1964), 201–17.

It was, at best, a weak and confused argument. It led Parker into the embarrassing position of having to deny the divine legitimacy of the goverment of any Protestant church that differed from that of the Church of England: 'If in anything any other Churches deviate from the Primitive Institution, they must stand and fall to their own Master'. But he would not be 'so uncharitable as to go about to un-church them, or renounce brotherly communion with them'.[54]

There was a more satisfactory solution available that went back to 1661. That year, in his *Irenicum*, Edward Stillingfleet argued that historical investigations revealed the ancient status of both episcopacy and synodical rule. The actual structure of church government was therefore a matter of indifference and legitimately subject to magisterial regulation. The history and needs of England justified Anglican episcopacy, which dissenters were obliged to accept and which they could do without violating either their consciences or their duties to God.[55] Parker could not endorse this contention both because it would have forced him to admit that in some significant sense church government was arbitrary – which was precisely the Hobbesian contention he had gone to such lengths to criticise – and because he had effectively denied the category of indifferency.

In his *Ecclesiastical Polity* he had contended that pronouncements by lawful authority transformed what might otherwise be indifferent into necessity. What liberty of action there was disappeared in the face of the sovereign's command, for the duty to obey the orders of superiors is part of the duty that is owed to God.[56] And he had further attacked the appeal to indifferency as a subterfuge – along with the claims of tender conscience – resorted to by dissembling nonconformists.[57] Any sinfulness was between the magistrate and God and did not involve the subject.[58] This assertion of non-resistance thus removed the last ground of appeal that had been left to dissenters; it rivals Hobbes's most extreme statement of the

[54] Parker, *Case of the Church*, pp. 264–5 and 268.
[55] Edward Stillingfleet, *Irenicum, A Weapon-Salve for the Churches Wounds* (1661), 2nd edn. (1662) Preface, sig. (a2)ʳ.
[56] [Parker], *Ecclesiastical Polity*, pp. 94 and 259–60.
[57] Ibid., pp. 175–6.
[58] Ibid., pp. 112–14.

absolute duty of obedience to the sovereign, and there is nothing in Parker's later writings to suggest that he had changed his mind.

Parker's contemporaries accused him of Hobbesism, and it is not difficult to understand why. John Humphrey said that while Parker was 'so stoutly confuting Mr *Hobbs*' he had 'become a young *Leviathan* himself'.[59] Henry Stubbe, using the same language, noted that Parker was 'in the *Pulpit* declaimed against as a *young Leviathan*',[60] and Marvell said that Parker's 'Principles confine upon the *Territories* of Malmsbury' and that his 'Arrogance . . . surpasses by far' the *Leviathan*.[61] Parker even admitted that his claim that 'as to the most important parts of Religion, there is a publick Conscience, to which Men are to attend, and not to their own . . . is somewhat a rank Dotrine, and favours not a little of the Leviathan', but insisted that his words were taken out of context.[62]

Obviously, these charges were meant to discredit Parker and his arguments by associating them with the disreputable Thomas Hobbes. As Parker himself well knew, the fact that he had attacked Hobbes was irrelevant to the rhetoric of criticism, for he had resorted to the same tactics in linking the nonconformist to Hobbes.

He was still doing it in 1681 when he complained that 'Atheism and Irreligion . . . [had] become as common as Vice and Debauchery.' Once again, the culprit was Hobbes, for:

The Plebians and Mechanicks have philosophised themselves into Principles of Impiety . . . And they are able to demonstrate out of the *Leviathan*, that there is no God nor Providence, but that all things come to pass by an eternal Chain of natural Causes: That there are no Principles of Good and Evil but only every Man's Self-interest, nor any Self-interest but onely of this present Life: That humane Nature is a meer Machine, and that all the contrivances of the minds of Men are nothing but mechanical Results of Matter and Motion.[63]

In response, Parker wrote a treatise on the law of nature that was based not on self-interest and materialism but on the benevolence

[59] [John Humphrey], *A Case of Conscience . . . Together with Animadversions on a New Book Entitled Ecclesiastical Polity* (1669), p. 12; see also p. 11.
[60] [Henry Stubbe], *Rosemary & Bayes: Or, Animadversions upon a Treatise Called The Rehearsal Trans-prosed* (1672), p. 18.
[61] Marvell, *Rehearsal Transpros'd*, ed. Smith, p. 47; see also *The Second Part*, p. 214.
[62] [Parker] *Defence and Continuation*, p. 279.
[63] Parker, *Law of Nature*, Preface, pp. ii and iii. In many respects, this work was written in response to Hobbes; the early portions contain numerous negative references to him. See, e.g., Preface, pp. viii, xii, xiv, xxiiii, and pp. 29 and 38 of the text.

of God and 'happiness' and 'pleasure' – including, of course, salvation – as the ends of human activity.

Parker's book was derived from Richard Cumberland's *De Legibus Naturae* of 1672. He commended Cumberland as one 'who has not only hit upon the right Notion of the Law of Nature, but has, in a method heretofore proper onely to mathematicks, demonstrated its obligation'.[64] Cumberland's massive treatise was conceived as a response to Hobbes, so it was appropriate to Parker's aims in several respects.

The natural law to Parker rested upon 'the supposition of an Author of Nature' and directed people to the 'one great end of Morality, and that is universal and mutual Love, Kindness and Benevolence between all rational Creatures'.[65] The 'total obligation' of the law of nature was resolved 'into the will of God', which had to be accepted as 'the first inducement of... Obedience'.[66] Its end, for Parker, was to enable people to achieve their proper happiness. 'And here unavoidably comes in the Happiness of a future state.'[67]

In *form*, Parker's natural-law theory is somewhat Thomist and resembles that of John Locke's *Two Treatises*. The book is the most temperate and restrained that Parker wrote. Even the attacks on Hobbes are relatively moderate; apart from the stinging comments in the Preface about 'Plebians and Mechanicks', there is little to suggest that the author had also written the polemical essays of the early 1670s. There is a strikingly 'modern' quality to Parker's argument as well, for the overwhelming tenor of the book is to make moral behaviour rather than grace the source of salvation, which is also the case in *Ecclesiastical Polity*.[68]

In his last work, the old Samuel Parker returned, at least in style if not in content. Conceived by Shaftesbury as 'the first *Sacrament*' of the Popish Plot, the Test Act of 1678, according to Parker, 'was the

---

[64] Parker, *Law of Nature*, Preface, p. ix. See Linda Kirk, *Richard Cumberland and Natural Law: Secularisation of Thought in Seventeenth-Century England* (Cambridge, 1987), pp. 83–6, for a discussion of the relationship of Parker's work to Cumberland.

[65] Parker, *Law of Nature*, Preface, pp. ix and xix. See also pp. 23–4 and 27–8.

[66] Ibid., pp. 72 and 73.

[67] Ibid., pp. 29, 47, 50, and 86.

[68] Parker was accused of precisely this reduction by Owen and Marvell. This aspect of the dispute is put into context in Dewey D. Wallace, Jr, *Puritans and Predestination: Grace in English Protestant Theology, 1525–1695* (Chapel Hill, 1982), pp. 166–70; Wallace does not discuss Parker's *Natural Law*.

very Master-piece of little *Achitophel's* Wickedness'.[69] By requiring that members of both houses of parliament disavow transubstanti- ation and declare that the Roman Catholic adoration of the Virgin Mary and other saints is 'superstitious and idolatrous',[70] the Act 'doth . . . utterly destroy the natural *Rights* of *Peerage* and [it] turns the *Birth-right* of the English *Nobility* into a *precarious* Title'.[71] More generally, Parker attacked the Test as 'a Law of an *Ecclesiastical* Nature, made without the Authority of the *Church*, contary to the Practice of the Christian World in all Ages'. It was a temporal encroachment 'upon this sacred *Prerogative* of the *Holy Catholick Church*' and a 'daring *Invasion* of our *Saviour's* own *Kingdom*'.[72] The argument about Erastianism was picked up, and this time Parker made the outrageous claim that the Independents had been in league with the Erastians during the Interregnum, 'leaving no standing Authority in the Christian Church over private Chris- tians, but leaving every Man to the arbitrary Choice of his own Communion'.[73]

Parker's final objection to the Act was that it obliged the nobility 'to swear to the Truth of such *abstruse* and *uncertain* Propositions, which they neither *do* nor *can*, nor indeed *ought* to understand'. These were matters 'chiefly handled by the *Schoolmen* and *Metaphys- icians* Skill, in whose writing is the least part of a Gentlemans education'.[74] The rest of the tract was devoted to defending the claim that the Chuch of England 'agrees with the Tradition of the *Catholick* Church both *Roman* and *Reformed*, in asserting the *Certainty* of the *real Presence*, and the *Uncertainty* of the *Manner* of it'[75] and attacking this particular notion of 'idolatry' as 'a Stabbing and

---

[69] Parker, *Reasons for Abrogating*, p. 10. The allusion, of course, was to John Dryden's *Absalom and Achitophel* (1681), in which Shaftesbury was depicted as 'the false *Achitophel* . . . A Name to all succeeding Ages Curst' (lines 150–1). Text from *The Works of John Dryden*, vol. II: *Poems, 1681–1684* ed. H.T. Swedenberg, Jr (Berkeley, 1972), p. 10.

[70] 'An Act for the More Effectual Preserving the King's Person and Government by disabling Papists from Sitting in Either House of Parliament', 30 Car. II, stat. 2, cap. 1 (Second Test Act, 1678), reprinted in Browning (ed.), *Documents*, doc. 144, p. 392.

[71] Parker, *Reasons for Abrogating the Test*, p. 1. The Act did not deny Peers their titles but only barred them from sitting in the House of Lords. Parker's complaint, presumably, was that membership in that House was a right of peerage. The Act also applied to members of the House of Commons, but Parker did not claim that the exclusion of Roman Catholics from that body violated anyone's 'rights'.

[72] Parker, *Reasons for Abrogating*, pp. 6–7 and 8.

[73] Ibid., pp. 64–5.

[74] Ibid., pp. 9 and 10.

[75] Ibid., p. 47.

Cut-throat Word' that was introduced into English religious discourse by the Puritan destroyers of the church and the monarchy in the 1640s.[76]

These arguments were apparently offered in support of James's projected plans to have the parliament repeal the 1678 Test Act. Not a word was said about the Declaration of Indulgence nor about whether the king was empowered to suspend laws that dealt with ecclesiastical matters. And Parker's old contentions about the need for religious uniformity as a prerequisite of political stability and the consequent entitlement of the sovereign to impose religious practices on his subjects were quietly forgotten. Roman Catholicism in 1687 was presumably less of a threat to the Anglican establishment than Presbyterianism had been in the 1670s. Such was the price Parker was willing to pay for the satisfaction of his ambitions.

[76] Ibid., p. 71.

CHAPTER 10

Priestcraft and the birth of Whiggism

Mark Goldie

Anticlericalism has long been integral to our idea of the Enlightenment. This used to encourage an heroic mythology of secularisation, in which reason did battle with religion, free-thought with
bigotry. Few historians today would endorse so Manichaean a
picture, for European thought in the eighteenth century is now seen
to have been characterised by an ameliorated Christianity rather
than by a militant crusade to overthrow it. Yet even so, the attack
on priestcraft, on clerical dogmatism and religious intolerance,
remains stubbornly central to the story of Europe's passage from
Reformation zeal to Enlightenment eirenicism. That even devout
Catholics thought it important to clip the wings of Jesuits is a
propensity distinctive of the age of Enlightenment.

The historical prominence of anticlericalism renders England's
position puzzling. For it is commonly supposed that, in the words
of a *Times* leader in 1984, England 'has had no intellectually
sanctioned tradition of anticlericalism since the Reformation' – and
a fortiori no Enlightenment. John Pocock, deploying one of his more
colourful metaphors, has written that 'to try to articulate the
phrase "the English Enlightenment" is to encounter inhibition; an
ox sits upon the tongue'. The English, by disposing of Laudian and
Calvinist fanaticism in the Civil War, and popery and tyranny in
the Glorious Revolution, were able to breathe easily the air of
intellectual liberty. Consequently there was 'simply no *infame* to be

---

For commenting on a draft of this essay I am indebted to the editors and to Justin Champion
and Sylvana Tomaselli. The themes of this essay are richly illuminated in Justin Champion's
Pillars of Priestcraft Shaken: The Church of England and its enemies, 1660–1730 (Cambridge, 1992),
based on 'The Ancient Constitution of the Christian Church: The Church of England and its
Enemies, 1660–1730' (Ph.D. thesis, University of Cambridge, 1989). See also P. Harrison,
'Religion' and the Religions in Enlightenment England (Cambridge, 1990).

crushed' and the voices of the intelligentsia lacked the antagonism which Continental clergies provoked.[1]

Despite this, there have recently been two kinds of attempt to give substance to the notion of an English Enlightenment. The first, expressed by Roy Porter, argues that because we have now come to see that it is mistaken to define the Enlightenment monolithically, as an atheistic or revolutionary assault on an *ancien régime*, it follows that England need not be bereft of an Enlightenment. The Enlightenment was not a crusade but a tone of voice, a sensibility. It preferred civility to enthusiasm, experience to metaphysics, the pursuit of happiness to the rule of the saints, the benevolent ethics of Jesus to the wrath of an unforgiving Father. And these goals 'throve in England *within* piety'. Pocock has similarly attempted to shift the ox. The English Enlightenment is not less substantive, if harder to perceive, for being 'conservative and in several ways clerical', the property of ruling elites rather than of clandestine rebels, an 'enlightenment *sans philosophes*'.[2]

Unquestionably the temper of English thought underwent a steady transformation in the decades after 1660, and the attempt to trace its modifications is one of the most demanding of current preoccupations. For who can satisfactorily define a society whose vaunted virtue was an ineffable 'politeness', and whose most beloved philosopher, the third earl of Shaftesbury, wrote only a rag-bag of coffee-house epistles and allusive essays?[3] Some of the most rewarding studies dwell literally on modulations of voice – the manner, for instance, in which the text of Colonel Ludlow's canting, Scripture-sodden memoir was spruced into Augustan sobriety by its editor John Toland.[4]

[1] J.G.A. Pocock, 'Post-Puritan England and the Problem of the Enlightenment', in *Culture and Politics: From Puritanism to the Enlightenment*, ed. P. Zagorin (Berkeley, 1980), pp. 91, 106; J G A Pocock, 'Clergy and Commerce: The Conservative Enlightenment in England', in R.J. Ajello (ed.), *L'Eta dei Lumi: Studi Storici sul Settecento Europe in onore di Franco Venturi* (Naples, 1985), pp. 525–8; J.G.A. Pocock, *Virtue, Commerce and History* (Cambridge, 1985), pt. III. See also Franco Venturi, *Utopia and Reform in the Enlightenment* (Cambridge, 1971).
[2] Roy Porter, 'The Enlightenment in England', in *The Enlightenment in National Context*, eds. Roy Porter and Mikulas Teich (Cambridge, 1981), p. 6; Pocock, 'Clergy and Commerce', p. 528. See also John Gascoigne, *Cambridge in the Age of the Enlightenment* (Cambridge, 1989).
[3] See Lawrence Klein, *Shaftesbury and the Culture of Politeness* (Cambridge, forthcoming), based on 'The Rise of Politeness in England, 1660–1770' (Ph.D. thesis, The Johns Hopkins University, 1983).
[4] Edmund Ludlow, *A Voyce from the Watch Tower*, ed. A.B. Worden (London, 1978).

The second type of attempt to give substance to the English Enlightenment has no truck with the insipidity of such Fabian approaches. It unabashedly restores to centre-stage the guerilla warfare waged by insurgent atheism against Christianity and gives pride of place to English writers. The most pronounced proponent of this view is David Berman. The procedure is gnostic: there is an esoteric atheistic doctrine to be unearthed, which fear of persecution precluded from public utterance. In other versions of this approach, conspiracy, arcana and secret societies are central to the story: hidden beneath the urbane moderate Enlightenment of official Newtonianism lay the clandestine freemasonry of the radical Enlightenment.[5]

Whilst historians of the first school decode inflections in the runes, those of the second dig up broadswords. The difficulty with the latter, the histories of atheism, is that they present a sharply disjunctive view of Christianity and infidelity, negating the pervasive intellectual and rhetorical debt to classical and Christian theology owed by the critics of the churches. The quest for the origins of irreligion overlooks how profoundly English radical writing remained religiously committed: to a Ciceronian idea of *religio*, cleansed of *superstitio*; to the search for the *prisca theologica*, a 'pure' and 'primitive' religion; and to the devising of a civil theology fit for a Whig commonwealth, a polity that knew how to distinguish the 'priest of God from the priest of Baal'.[6]

We can accept that there was a militant anticlericalism in English political discourse, but we must also recognise that it was grounded in an unfolding tradition of Christian reformism. Atheism, if it existed at all, was marginal. The broad stream of critical reflection on religion was hostile not to piety but to the vanity of dogmatizing, not to scripture but to theocracy. In the wake of England's wars of religion, it sought to transform the Established Church into a civil religion. Pocock takes the essence of this process to be the 'polemic against enthusiasm'. But we should

---

[5] David Berman, *A History of Atheism in Britain* (London, 1988); Margaret C. Jacob, *The Radical Enlightenment* (London, 1981). See also *Atheism from the Reformation to the Enlightenment*, ed. M. Hunter and D. Wootton (Oxford, forthcoming); John Redwood, *Reason, Ridicule and Religion: The Age of Enlightenment in England, 1660–1750* (London, 1976). For a parallel treatment see David Wootton, *Paulo Sarpi: Between Renaissance and Enlightenment* (Cambridge, 1983). For discussion see James E. Force, 'The Origins of Modern Atheism', *Journal of the History of Ideas*, 50 (1989), 153–62.

[6] The last phrase occurs in John Dennis, *Priestcraft Distinguished* (1715), sig. A.

add another facet, the polemic against priestcraft, for, fundamental
to the animus of early Whiggism, was, in Hobbes's phrase, the
'unpleasing' of priests.

The case made here is a prima facie one. It rests upon Whig
perceptions as exemplified in their pamphlets. To put the case fully
would require an institutional and intellectual history of the
Restoration church: the divines would have to be judged independently of Whig barratry. Suffice it to say, Whig anticlericalism was
not quixotic. Its target, Restoration Anglicanism, was more vigorous, more adamantine, than is generally allowed. Or, at least, it
became so by about 1675, when there came of age a confident and
aggressive style of Anglicanism for which the phrase 'High Church'
was quickly coined. When the Anglican phoenix rose from the
ashes of the Puritan revolution it had an urgent need to assert its
distinctive identity. The groundworks and bastions of the restored
church were manifold: from the revanchism of the anti-Puritan
gentry in the Cavalier Parliament, to the flourishing of patristic
theology in the purged universities; from the heresy-hunting that
Hobbes, Newton and Locke feared, to the censors' expurgation of
Puritan devotional and poetic writing; from the stubborn piety
visible in churchwardens' accounts, to the pert young divines'
raucous defence of the *jure divino* authority of kings and bishops.[7]
But undoubtedly the most tangible element was the repression of
nonconformity. The makers of the Act of Uniformity of 1662
embarked upon the last attempt in English history coercively to
create a church that was indefectibly the whole commonwealth at
prayer. If the attempt sometimes faltered, by the early 1680s the
'church party', gradually acquiring the new name of Tory, had
launched what was, with the possible exception of the 1580s, the
most ferocious religious persecution of England's Protestant era.[8]

In the 1690s the Whig financier and MP Thomas Papillon could
offer the following definitions of Whig and Tory: 'Under the name
of Whigs is comprehended most of the sober and religious persons
of the Church of England that . . . put no . . . stress on the forms

---

[7] There is not yet a sufficient account of the Restoration church. But see John Spurr, *The
Restoration Church of England* (Yale, 1991); Tim Harris, Paul Seaward and Mark Goldie
(eds.), *The Politics of Religion in Restoration England* (Oxford, 1990); Tim Harris, *London
Crowds in the Reign of Charles II* (Cambridge, 1987).

[8] See Mark Goldie, 'The Theory of Religious Intolerance in Restoration England', in *From
Persecution to Toleration*, eds. O.P. Grell, J.I. Israel and N. Tyacke (Oxford, 1991).

and ceremonies, but look on them as human institutions, and not as the essentials of religion, and are willing that there might be a reformation to take away offence.' The Tories, by contrast, are those 'that stickle for the forms and ceremonies, and rail against the endeavour to discountenance all those that are otherwise minded'.[9] At issue was not just that a minority of cussed Puritans were brutally treated. It was that, for many, the Restoration church had embarked on a tragically mistaken project and had exhausted religious energies in futile directions. It neglected holy living, preferring credal and ritual formalism to moral reformation. Locke's *Third Letter Concerning Toleration* (1692) railed against those who put coercive uniformity above pastoral care and moral discipline.

The collapse of the Restoration church in 1689 produced, amongst Whigs, a prolonged sigh of relief. The Toleration Act, the induction to the episcopal bench of the hitherto beleaguered Latitudinarians, and the end of press censorship, marked the defeat of Archbishop Sancroft's vision of a purified Anglican Zion. It was a sea-change that casts doubt on recent talk of 'the long eighteenth century' as an historical entity stretching uninterruptedly beyond 1660. In the defeat of those whom the diarist Roger Morrice called 'the hierarchists' a decisive shift in English culture occurred.[10]

This is not to say that the contest between church and state came to an end, nor that the need for vigorous Whig litanies on the evils of churchmen ceased to exist. The High Church cry of the 'Church in Danger' provoked Whigs to fulfil the warning. A series of polemics stretched into the Walpolean era: the Occasional Conformity controversy, which spilled into the furore over Matthew Tindal's *Rights of the Christian Church* (1706); the Bangorian Controversy (1717–20), which produced John Trenchard's and Thomas Gordon's relentlessly anticlerical newspaper *The Independent Whig* (1720–1);[11] the clash between Sir Robert Walpole and Bishop Gibson and the quarrels over the Quaker Tithe bill and Mortmain

---

[9] *Memoirs of Thomas Papillon, 1623–1702*, ed. A.F.W. Papillon (Reading, 1877), pp. 374–5.

[10] Dr Williams's Library, London: Morrice MS Q, *passim*.

[11] It was translated into French by Holbach. Trenchard also published *The Natural History of Superstition* (1709) and Gordon an edition of Barbeyrac's *The Spirit of Ecclesiastics in All Ages*. See Marie P. McMahon, *The Radical Whigs, John Trenchard and Thomas Gordon* (Lanham, Md, 1990).

Act in the 1730s.[12] Selections from these affrays were anthologised in Richard Barron's four-volume *Pillars of Priestcraft Shaken* (1768). His preface harmonised with the manifestos of the Continental *philosophes*. He offered 'everlasting reasons for opposing all priests, and an unanswerable argument against all their claims of power and authority'. The aim of his collection was 'to emancipate the minds of men, and to free them from those chains in which they have been long held to the great disgrace both of reason and Christianity'.[13]

The anticlerical animus allows us to see Whiggery in an unconventional light, less in terms of civil doctrines concerning constitutionalism and the right of revolution, and more in terms of ecclesiology: the struggle of temporal and spiritual, *regnum* and *sacerdotium*. No historian of medieval political thought would neglect ecclesiology; it behoves historians of the seventeenth century not to do so either.[14]

English Whiggism was born as much in anticlericalism as in constitutionalism, and church history was as natural a stamping ground for Whig polemicists as was parliamentary history. As John Pocock and William Lamont have shown, the Whigs steadily secularised an eschatological drama, inherited from the canonical works of early English Protestantism, and especially from John Foxe. It was a vision of history in which the temporal sphere, whether embodied in a Godly prince or a Godly people, gradually asserted its rights against the pretensions of a usurping clergy. The stuff of medieval history was not only parliament and barons, but also praemunire and provisors, legates and interdicts, mortmain and mulcts, prelacy and simony. A mind attuned to the struggle against *imperium in imperio* did not suspend this mode of explanation with the Henrician Reformation. Just as there was a centuries-long contest prior to the Reformation – Henry II's battle with Becket, the Constitutions of Clarendon, Wycliffe and the Lollards – so the

---

[12] See Stephen Taylor, 'Sir Robert Walpole, the Church of England, and the Quakers Tithe Bill of 1736', *Historical Journal*, 28 (1985), 51–77; and, generally, J.C.D. Clark, *English Society, 1688–1832* (Cambridge, 1985).

[13] Richard Barron, *Pillars of Priestcraft Shaken* (1768), vol. I, pp. iii, vi.

[14] For recent moves toward what might be called a 'neo-medievalism' in studying seventeenth-century political thought, see Brian Tierney, *Religion, Law, and the Growth of Constitutional Thought, 1150–1650* (Cambridge, 1982); Conal Condren, *George Lawson's 'Politica' and the English Revolution* (Cambridge, 1989); Francis Oakley, *Omnipotence, Covenant and Order: An Excursion in the History of Ideas from Abelard to Leibniz* (Ithaca, 1984).

struggle to perfect the work of the Tudor Reformation remained onerous and unyielding.[15]

The Whigs borrowed the Foxean vision of history, drained it of its 'enthusiasm', but retained its historical and juridical assumptions. The idea of sovereignty remained strongly conditioned by notions of the autonomy of the secular sphere, an outlook embedded in the Henrician Act in Restraint of Appeals to Rome: 'this realm of England is an empire'. *Imperium* was the rightful attribute of the state and all priestly seeking after political power was a praemunire, an *imperium in imperio*.[16] The Protestant tradition had oscillated between an Erastian reverence for the prince's role in protecting the pursuit of godliness and a populist tradition of not tarrying for the magistrate. In the same way, early Whiggery was as capable of deep respect for sound Protestant kingship, as of denigrating monarchs who failed in this role. Foxean rhetoric was pervasive in Restoration writing and, on the whole, early Whiggism remained profoundly reverential to monarchy. When Israel Tonge helped Titus Oates expose the Popish Plot, that seedbed of the Whig movement, his theme was the history of Romish conspiracies to destroy monarchy – loyalty to the crown was the badge of true Protestant Englishmen.[17] Even the plebeian Baptist John Bunyan clung, in the 1680s, to the doctrine that 'Antichrist shall not down but by the hand of kings'.[18]

The crux is the transformation of the Puritan into the Whig. Puritans believed that the English church was 'but halfly reformed' and that elements of popery remained insidiously intermixed. Their first answer to Laudian prelacy was Presbyterian power, a polity governed by a godly ministry schooled in Genevan discipline. But the Covenant, the hectoring Scots, and the heresiographers who damned all rival sects, did not endear themselves. The

---

[15] Pocock, 'Post-Puritan England'; William Lamont, *Godly Rule* (London, 1969); William Lamont, *Richard Baxter and the Millennium* (London, 1979). The Henrician roots are traced in G.D. Nicholson, 'The Nature and Function of Historical Argument in the Henrician Reformation' (Ph.D. thesis, University of Cambridge, 1977).

[16] For the persistence of the rhetoric of *imperium in imperio* see J.A.W. Gunn, *Beyond Liberty and Property* (Kingston and Montreal, 1983), ch. 2.

[17] Israel Tonge, *Jesuitical Aphorisms* (1679); Israel Tonge, *The Northern Star* (1680).

[18] See W.R. Owens, '"Antichrist must be pulled down": Bunyan and the Millennium', in *John Bunyan and his England, 1628–88*, ed. A. Laurence, W.R. Owens and S. Sim (London, 1990). For another unexpected version of a Whig and Dissenting ideal of kingship see Manuel Schonhorn, *Defoe's Politics: Parliament, Power, Kingship and Robinson Crusoe* (Cambridge, 1991).

recoil from them provoked Milton's famous judgement that 'new
presbyter is but old priest', and brought forth the pithy sacrileges of
John Selden's *Table Talk*. The religious polemics of the 1640s also
generated the voguish phrases by which the wits would bruise the
clerics in Restoration coffee-houses – 'black-coats', 'levites', 'canting tribe' and 'Baal's priests'. A substantial segment of Protestancy
came to believe that priestly usurpation took not one but three
forms: prelatical and presbyterial as well as popish. As Protestants
shed the rule of the saints, this triad came to haunt their search for
a civil religion, and in this awakening the Puritan became the
Whig.

   I take as the cynosure of Whig anticlericalism the birth of a new
word in the political lexicon, 'priestcraft'.[19] Anticlericalism was
anciently embedded in English writing; it is in Chaucer and
Tyndale. But the term 'priestcraft' appeared when the pervas-
iveness of clerical turpitude amongst rival, putatively Protestant,
churches began forcibly to demand explanation. It was not until
the end of the seventeenth century that the term became widely
used, and usually as a reflection upon the Restoration church. But
the word was coined in 1657.[20] It occurs in James Harrington's
Pian Piano, a defence of *Oceana* against Henry Ferne, doctor of
divinity, sequestered archdeacon of Leicester and royalist pamphleteer. Ferne thought it 'lamentable' that lay authors launched 'a
quarrel against the Church of England' and were 'so boldly
meddling in matters of religion, as if they had forgot or did not
understand their article of the Catholic Church'. By 'Catholic
Church' Ferne meant of course not the Roman church but Christ's
universal church, of which the Anglican was the authentic English
branch. He believed that it was for divines and not laymen to
determine what was 'the government of the Christian church, the
form and functions left by Christ and his apostles, according to
which the church acted three hundred years before the civil power
became Christian'. The Christian must ever remember that there
was a church for three centuries before the Emperor Constantine

---

[19] I have discussed elsewhere the role of 'priestcraft' in the evolution of the concept of
ideology: 'Ideology', in *Political Innovation and Conceptual Change*, ed. T. Ball, J. Farr and
R.L. Hanson (Cambridge, 1989).

[20] A search of Civil War writing might prove me wrong. *A Corrector of the Answerer* (1646) has
'clergy craft' (p. 7).

converted, before the civil arm began to shape the externals of the church.

Harrington argued, on the contrary, that in 'every well ordered commonwealth', the senate 'ever had the supreme authority, as well in matters of religion as state'. He thought Ferne's attitude typical of divines, whose habit it was to identify 'the church' with themselves alone. 'Now wherever the clergy have gained this point, namely that they are the Catholic Church', and wherever they have rendered it unlawful for the laity to discuss or make settlements in church government, then in such cases 'neither government nor religion have failed to degenerate into mere priestcraft'. In such societies, divinity becomes a monopoly trade and the religious freedom of the laity is curtailed. If the craft of divines is exemplified in the Roman church, it is by no means limited to it, and because Harrington detected this trait in all priests, he coined his new word. Priestcraft was popery universalised.[21]

Harrington's clerical critics accused him of following Hobbes's *Leviathan* in matters of religion. This association of the republican with the monarchical absolutist might seem odd. But it does not require much foreshortening of historical explanation to say of Hobbes that, ecclesiologically, he was a Whig; nor of theoretical explanation to say that the Erastian defence of the Christian laity transcended differences over civil constitutions. At the end of *Leviathan* Hobbes wrote of the 'three knots' of popedom, prelacy and Presbytery which tied up the freedom of the apostolic Christians during the Dark Ages. They were untied during the Reformation: the first under the Tudors, the latter two in quick succession in the 1640s. We are now, he concluded, 'reduced to the independency of the primitive Christians', which 'is perhaps the best'. After 1660 Hobbes dissembled this remarkable endorsement of the congregationalism of the Puritan revolution.[22] Both Harrington and Hobbes were mistakenly sanguine that the revolution had crushed priestcraft and that the grand cycle of the Reformation was complete. The Restoration church would disabuse them: the struggle continued. As Pocock has persuasively shown, Hobbes's

---

[21] *The Political Works of James Harrington*, ed. J.G.A. Pocock (Cambridge, 1977), pp. 371, 372, 383. See, more fully, Mark Goldie, 'The Civil Religion of James Harrington', in *The Languages of Political Theory in Early-Modern Europe*, ed. Anthony Pagden (Cambridge, 1987).

[22] In the Latin edition of *Leviathan* (1668) ch. 47 was revised and abridged.

Leviathan was Protestant eschatology refashioned and, as such, was seminal for Whig anticlericals and Erastians in the ensuing decades, as they grappled with resurgent Anglicanism.[23]

Hobbes, incidentally, does not seem to have used the word 'priestcraft', although his texts abound with synonyms. When, however, a translator turned his little-known *Ecclesiastica Historia* into English he did make use of the term, to encapsulate a theme that John Aubrey described as 'the history of the encroachment of the clergy (both Roman and Reformed) on the civil power'. Aubrey also wrote, when summarising Edmund Waller's elegy on Hobbes, that Hobbes had 'pulled down all the churches, dispelled the mists of ignorance, and laid open their priestcraft'.[24]

The word 'priestcraft' rarely occurred in print before the 1690s, but there was a flurry at the time of the Exclusion Crisis. The impetus came from the opening line of John Dryden's great anti-Whig poem *Absolom and Achitophel*: 'In pious times, e'r priest-craft did begin'. Since Dryden was referring to Charles II's promiscuity and to an age when sexual licence was not yet decreed a sin, we may take him to be alluding to the scoffing Whig's habit of treating the laws of marriage as amongst priestly inventions. The replies to *Absolom* adopted a more narrowly ecclesiastical construal of the term. Samuel Pordage offered a history of popery and its latter-day recurrences, beginning, 'In impious times, when priest-craft was at height'. His moral was that a righteous king was one who drove away Baal's priests. Another versifier turned the word against the regicide Calvinists of the 1640s: ' . . . the old priestcraft cant: / Who once did consecrated daggers chant'. A third poet was closer to Pordage's Whiggery. 'In gloomy times, when priestcraft bore the sway', then it was that 'the priest sate pilot even at empire's helm'. This poet looked forward to great Absolom's – the duke of Monmouth's – triumph, when the 'cowed sanhedrim shall prostrate lie'. For him, the essence of the Whig struggle was to prevent English churchmen building a Protestant popery, in which

---

[23] J.G.A. Pocock, 'Time, History and Eschatology in the Thought of Thomas Hobbes', in *Politics, Language and Time* (New York, 1971); James R. Jacob, *Henry Stubbe, Radical Protestantism and the Early Enlightenment* (Cambridge, 1983).

[24] John Aubrey, *Brief Lives*, ed. Andrew Clark, 2 vols. (Oxford, 1989), vol. I, pp. 358, 394; Hobbes, *Ecclesiastical History* (1722), pp. 77, 127. The translator freely inserted material. For Hobbes's anticlericalism see David Johnston, *The Rhetoric of Leviathan* (Princeton, 1986).

'the mitre . . . above the diadem soar'd'. The war was, in Edmund Hickeringill's words, against any kind of popery that 'exalts the mitre above the crown, and the crozier above the sceptre'.[25] The rhetoric of the crisis that gave birth to Whiggery had at its heart the mortal struggle between mitre and sceptre.

'Priestcraft' suddenly became commonplace in the 1690s. *The Folly of Priestcraft* (1690) and *Priestcraft Expos'd* (1691) were the first tracts to put the word in their titles.[26] In 1691 a Whig gentleman visiting Oxford wrote to a friend that he could no longer stand the university's 'air of nauseous priestcraft'.[27] In 1692 the Whig Samuel Johnson remarked that William of Orange's glorious advent was 'unblessed by bishops, and puzzled by a little priest-craft'.[28] In 1695 Locke's friend William Popple painted a word-picture of a great prelate: 'The church's finest pillar: double famed / For orthodoxy and for discipline. / (Terms, without which, all priestcraft would decline.) / In ceremonial forms he was so nice; / Discord in them he more abhor'd than vice.'[29] In 1697 John Toland was reported as holding that 'religion is a plain and easy thing, and that there is not so much in it, as priestcraft would persuade'. He opened the new century with a rousing epigram: 'Religion's safe, with priestcraft is the war, / All friends to priestcraft, foes of mankind are.'[30] In 1702, John Dennis offered a double definition. Priestcraft 'comprehends all that the arts of designing men cause to pass for religion with the unthinking part of the world'. 'All that the clergy do to advance their temporal greatness is priestcraft . . . and

---

[25] Samuel Pordage, *Azariah and Hushai* (1682), p. 1; anon., *A Panegyrick on the Author of Absolom* (1681); anon., *Absolom Senior* (1682), pp. 1, 2, 14, 27; Edmund Hickeringill, *Curse ye Meroz* (1680), p. 2. Cf. *Directions to Fame* (1682), p. 11. Another early usage is by the Whig propagandist Henry Care, who sneered at churchmen 'whose priestcraft is preferment merely': *A Weekly Pacquet of Advices* (1678–83), vol. IV, no. 16.

[26] The former of these is a play about Catholicism under James II. Two other early titles are John Dennis, *The Danger of Priestcraft* (1702); and Edmund Hickeringill, *The History of Priestcraft* (1705). Hickeringill had a long and troublesome career attacking the phenomenon.

[27] Somerset Record Office, MS. DD/SF 417 (H. Thomas to Edward Clarke, 7 November 1691). He offered greetings to Clarke's friends at the Grecian and Dick's coffee-houses, the homes of advanced Whig thought.

[28] Samuel Johnson, *Works* (1713), pp. 265, 306.

[29] British Library, Add. MS. 8888, fo. 96.

[30] British Library, Add. MS. 5853, fo. 385 (James Bonnell to John Strype); Toland, *Clito* (1700), p. 26. Toland's first use of the word was on the last page of *Christianity not Mysterious* (1696). There are two fine studies of Toland: Robert Sullivan, *John Toland and the Deist Controversy* (Harvard, 1982); Stephen H. Daniel, *John Toland: His Methods, Manners, and Mind* (Kingston and Montreal, 1984).

consequently such priestcraft is destructive to government.'[31] Gilbert Burnet, chronicling the 1690s, recorded that 'it became a
common topic of discourse to treat all mysteries in religion as the
contrivances of priests, to bring the world into a blind submission
to them: priestcraft grew to be another word in fashion'.[32]

We may take as an epitome of the early English Enlightenment
analysis of priestcraft Sir Robert Howard's *History of Religion*
(1694). Howard had been a courtier, a Whig MP, and fashionable
playwright since the 1660s; he was now a privy councillor in
William III's government. He announced the subject of his book to
be 'how religion has been corrupted, almost from the beginning, by
priestcraft'. Its chief characteristic was the pursuit of clerical power
by the forcible imposition of unnecessary creeds. The clergy by
'priestcraft contrived notions and opinions, to engage people to
submit implicitly to their directions'. This had been the practice of
pagan priests; it was 'followed to this day, in what is called the
Church of Rome'; and he wished that 'among the most reformed
Christians these methods of priestcraft were not so much, and
violently pursued'.

The true religion of the gospel was 'plain and easy', but the
gospel had been overlain and the laity gulled by the 'inventions of
priests', whose manufacture of extravagant doctrines 'neither
reason will justify' nor 'religion require'. The doctrine of purgatory
– here Howard offered the most familiar of Protestant instances –
was an invention 'wholly the subject matter of power and profit':
through masses for the dead the priests mulcted the living. Even
the conduct of philosophy had been cynically subjugated to serve
hieratic ambition, for the medieval universities had enforced a diet
of Aristotelian metaphysics, a system at the heart of university
curricula wherever priestly power was entrenched. But worst of all,
the 'most cruel contrivance of priestcraft . . . is persecution'. From
the moment that Christianity first received the support of the civil
power, under Constantine, creed-making, excommunication, and
the violent 'extirpation of heresy' had been the hallmark of priestly
Christianity. The civil power had too often been the church's

---

[31] Dennis, *Danger of Priestcraft*, pp. 6–7, 15. For other early examples see Matthew Tindal, *An
Essay Concerning the Power of the Magistrate* (1697), pp. 115, 185; Matthew Tindal, *A Letter to
a Member of Parliament* (1698), pp. 21–4; Charles Blount, *The Oracles of Reason* (1693), sig.
a3ʳ.
[32] Gilbert Burnet, *A History of his Own Times*, 2 vols. (London, 1838), vol. II, p. 649.

compliant arm in punishing schism and heresy, 'the magistrate their stirrup-dog'.[33]

Howard's themes were standard weapons in the Whig armoury. Hostility to Aristotelianism, to the philosophy of the 'schoolmen', and to the persecution of speculative opinions as heresies, were keynotes in the anticlerical refrain. Howard's attention to the church of the fourth century was also a common preoccupation; in his remarks lay the seed of that most magisterial of Enlightenment indictments of priestcraft, Gibbon's *Decline and Fall*. The interpretation of the reigns of Constantine and Theodosius, under whom the secular arm began to invest the church with temporal authority, became the historical fulcrum in the wars of clericalists and Erastians, for, as Gibbon later remarked, 'the ecclesiastical institutions of his [Constantine's] reign are still connected by an indissoluble chain, with the opinions, the passions, and the interests of the present generation'.[34]

Of special importance in Whiggish church history was the Council of Nicaea in AD 325, at which St Athanasius secured the credal definition that bears his name. To sneer at the Nicene Fathers, amongst whom the enforcement of speculative theologies began, became an invariable topic for the anticlericals. 'From this creed-making', wrote Howard, 'came persecutions, almost equal to those of the heathen emperors.' What struck him forcibly was that the theological quarrel had hung upon a tiny distinction between two Greek words which differently expressed the nature of Christ's oneness with God. In 1673 Hobbes's disciple Henry Stubbe called it a dispute 'about trifles'. In 1676 the Puritan poet Andrew Marvell styled it a quarrel over 'but one single letter of the alphabet . . . an iota'. In 1691 *Priestcraft Expos'd* talked of 'the destruction of millions . . . for the sake of an iota'. And a century later Gibbon contrived a famous phrase: 'the difference of a single diphthong . . . between the *Homoousians* and *Homoiousians*'.[35]

There is a further significance in Howard's attention to the fourth century. Constantine had long been a powerful motif in

---

[33] Sir Robert Howard, *The History of Religion* (1694), pp. iv, vii, 5, 22, 27, 43, 69, 74–80, 85–8, 103.

[34] Edward Gibbon, *The History of the Decline and Fall of the Roman Empire*, 12 vols. (London, 1827), vol. III, p. 237.

[35] Howard, *History*, p. 85; Jacob, *Stubbe*, p. 123; Marvell, *Mr Smirke* (1676), p. 62; anon, *Priestcraft Expos'd* (1691), p. 14; Gibbon, *Decline*, III, 339.

Protestant rhetoric as the archetype of the Godly Prince. Reformation propagandists had awarded Henry VIII the mantle of the modern Constantine. The secular prince and not the usurping bishop of Rome was the bearer of Christ's promises, the defender of the faith and head of the visible church. But the Constantine topos was ambivalent. He could be portrayed as a tower of Christian leadership; or as a prince too easily swayed by the prelates around him. Here the image became tarnished, for the prince succumbed to flattery and became the tame agent of ecclesiastical ambition. When Howard, Marvell and others, discussed the relationship between Constantine and his bishops, they were covertly expounding the relationship between Stuart monarchy and Anglican prelacy. The king should not become the feeble holder of the priest's stirrup, helping the church into the saddle of a pseudo-popish power. That had been Charles I's crime, and Milton, in *Of Reformation* (1641) had brilliantly brandished the image of Constantine against Charles. Similarly, it came to seem that Charles II and James II were victims of prelacy, or of popery itself.

The 1690s are rich in the history and sociology of priestcraft. *Priestcraft Expos'd* pronounced that the government of England 'would be immortal' if it could return to 'the conduct of primitive Christianity'. The Reformation had promised such a renovation, until the Stuart age threw up a priesthood 'panting after Protestant encroachment with no less ardour than their predecessors had done, after popish usurpation'. The tract offered a lengthy account of the struggles of medieval monarchs to resist ecclesiastical domineering. Its author had a Puritan voice, for he listed Archbishops Whitgift and Laud amongst the 'pontifical prelates . . . burdensome to the nation'. But he also had a civic humanist voice in citing Machiavelli and in contending that 'heathen legislators never admitted their priesthood to civil preferments'. He saw the Glorious Revolution as an opportunity for the final crushing of the 'levitical Orlando Furiosos'.[36]

The most influential epitome of these doctrines occurred in the preface to Robert Molesworth's *Account of Denmark* (1694), a bestseller, especially on the Continent, where Pierre Bayle commended it as full of the lustre of English liberty. Molesworth analysed the relationship between ecclesiasticism and liberty. A

---

[36] *Priestcraft Expos'd*, preface, and pp. 1, 15, 19, 26, 44, 57, 63 and *passim*.

simple model, he argued, might suggest that whilst Roman priests have a 'firm adherence to the most exquisite tyranny', Protestant priests 'have an entire dependence on their kings and princes'. But the simple model was defective, for Protestant societies have too often complacently imagined that their clergies were fully reformed. It was in the nature of any priestly class that it was improbable that 'the character of priest [will] give place to that of true patriot'. It would be wise to commit education 'to philosophers instead of priests', and prudent of statesmen to 'keep . . . ecclesiastics within their due bounds, and . . . curb those who if they had power would curb all the world'.[37]

John Locke's books were quickly construed within the same framework of thought. A clerical enemy of his *Reasonableness of Christianity* (1696) summarised his religion as containing the single Hobbesian truth that Jesus is the Messiah 'and that our stickling for the rest is only sect and party, and priestcraft, and narrowness of spirit'. Locke's tract was one of the 'fashionable papers' that devalued the clergy as 'a designing sort of men; nay, their very office [is] exposed as a trade'.[38] The Quaker Benjamin Furly applauded Locke, telling him that he was 'fully assured that priestcraft will fall, and cannot stand long against that light, that has so far opened men's eyes to see through the tiffany cover of their [the priests'] fulsome authority'. Another wrote of Locke's works that 'true and free reasonable religion' had been rescued from 'the great trade of priestcraft (in fashion in every church)'. His books, said William Molyneux, will 'abridge the empire of darkness'. Locke's friends wrote sneeringly of 'the Druids', the 'levites' and the 'cassocked tribe'. Even before his death his admirers were constructing a podium for him, the philosopher who vanquished the priestly darkness of mankind's infancy.[39]

Howard's and Locke's books were jointly congratulated in William Stephen's *Account of the Growth of Deism* (1696), as having done sterling service to 'a priest-ridden people'. They had 'distinguished betwixt religion and priestcraft' and cleansed Christianity

---

[37] Molesworth, *An Account of Denmark* (1694), sig. b2ʳ–b8ᵛ.
[38] R. Willis [?], *The Occasional Paper* (1697–8), No. 1, p. 21; cf. pp. 19–20, 40–1; No. 5, pp. 3–4.
[39] *The Correspondence of John Locke*, ed. E.S. De Beer, 9 vols. (Oxford, 1976–), vol. v, p. 3; vol. vi, p. 38; vol. vii, pp. 144, 225. cf. vol. v, pp. 64, 300, 339; vol. vii, pp. 431, 209, 772. Locke's religion is authoritatively explored in John Marshall, 'Locke in Context: Religion, Ethics, and Politics' (Ph.D. thesis, The Johns Hopkins University, 1990).

of those 'circumstantials and appendages' which were 'designed to uphold the power of the clergy over the people'.[40] Stephens was that rare thing, a Whig Anglican clergyman, and one of his sermons was to be reprinted in Barron's *Pillars of Priestcraft Shaken*.

The main task of the *Account of Deism* was to explain the rise of credal indifference. Stephens looked back to the 1640s and judged that the priests had only themselves to blame. He noted the habit of Protestant gentlemen of going on a Continental Grand Tour, during which they were encouraged to see how popery was less a religion than a collection of self-serving trickeries. When they returned to England, educated in a sceptical sense of priestly conniving, they witnessed the wrangling of Anglican and Presbyterian parties, and 'could not forbear to see that both these Protestant parties, under the pretence of religion, were only grasping at power'. Consequently, anyone who had lived in England since the Civil War had 'no need of going over the water to discover that the name of church signifieth only a self-interested party'.

Stephen went on to provide an unfamiliar retrospect on Restoration politics. We are accustomed to assume that Whigs identified the autocratic inclinations of the crown as the chief enemy of English liberties. But Stephens took the view that the primary enemy was not the crown, but the re-established episcopal church. The crown was only collusively guilty in so far as it feebly succumbed to the bishops' supremacy. He sarcastically commented that 'as certain as the cross is above the crown, so sure a thing is it, that the bishop will be above the king'. This proposition was sufficiently proven by looking 'back to King Charles's Restoration'. Charles II, who 'for two years after his return, reigned in the hearts of all his people, was by the Act of Uniformity reduced to be king of the Church party'. That Act betrayed the healing spirit of 1660. This contrast between 1660 and 1662 was a common Whig refrain: through it they avowed their loyalty to monarchy, but not to its subversion by the ambitions of narrow-spirited Anglicanism. The

---

[40] Stephens, *An Account of the Growth of Deism in England* (1695; Augustan Reprint Society, 1990), pp. 18, 19, 25. He also commended Sir Matthew Hale. Henry Hill wrote that Stephens had 'distinguished so nicely between religion and priestcraft that he has made all ambitious priests to stink, even from Aaron down to this day': *A Dialogue between Timotheus and Judas* (1696), p. 6; cf. p. 26. See also R. Willis, *Reflexions on a Late Pamphlet* (1696), pp. 27, 33, 39.

tragedy was that the king had succumbed to being the servant of the prelates. England had become little more than a theocracy, 'the secular arm directed by the spiritual power', in which the 'Protestant high priests do all of them rival the sovereign power'.

Two features of Stephens's analysis stand out. The first is a doctrine about the symbiosis of crown and clergy: the claim that the institutional power of the latter is predicated on their ideological services to the former. A 'posse of the clergy' preach up absolutism, but in requital the 'clergy require the king to do their persecuting journey-work', for 'if a king will submit to this drudgery, he shall have the *vox cleri* on his side'.[41] Thus *jure divino* doctrines were not only wrong-headed, but corruptly self-serving. The clergy's betrayal of their evangelical calling was the essence of their priestcraft, and consequently the defence of Whig civil theory must go hand in hand with exposing the *trahison des clercs*. This maxim of the crown's and clergy's corrupt mutuality was repeated countless times in Whig writing. Matthew Tindal wrote that the clergy taught absolute obedience since 'the only way to secure tyranny in the Church was to get it established in the state'. Popple's version was more brusque: 'Church and state . . . in league combined . . . Claw me and I'll claw thee.'[42]

The second feature of Stephen's argument was that he was not hostile to strong monarchy, but to its perversion. In succumbing to the clergy a patriot prince becomes a servant of a faction, and so by definition a tyrant, one who betrays the common good. The virtuous prince resists the clerical incubus. For Stephens, Restoration history is the story of attempts to counsel Stuart kings in their duty to enhance Christian liberty, and not to mire the commonwealth in the dregs of popery and prelacy. His was the Reformation ideal of the Godly Prince in Whig dress, a continuation of Foxe's story of the struggle of the secular sphere to put the clerical satan behind it. His tone was Erastian: the governance of religion lay with the secular arm, for the liberty of the Christian believer depended upon the strength of the Godly ruler in reminding the clergy that its role was ministerial and not priestly, edificatory and not coercive. None of this precluded Whig civil doctrines about

---

[41] Stephens, *Account*, pp. 5–6, 7, 9, 10, 23.
[42] Tindal, *Letter*, p. 21; Locke, 'Sacerdos' in Lord King, *The Life of John Locke*, 2 vols. (London, 1830), vol. II, pp. 89–90; British Library, Add. MS. 8888, fo. 114. Cf. Dennis, *Danger of Priestcraft*, pp. 16–17; Gibbon, *Decline*, vol. III, p. 280.

constraints on monarchical prerogative, but it did demand that properly constituted monarchs should exercise supremacy over the churchmen. Edmund Hickeringill likewise urged that history warned princes against 'trusting their supremacy . . . out of their own keeping' to popes, bishops and presbyters. Let not 'the silly bigot-magistrate' be 'the surrogate of the priest's revenge'.[43]

Stephens wrote about the Restoration era in hindsight, but he echoed a view that had been voiced twenty years previously. In 1675 there appeared a tract called *A Letter from a Person of Quality to his Friend in the Country*. It has good claims to be the manifesto of the Whig party. It was brief, pungent and deeply shocking to the church's sensibilities. It was condemned by the House of Lords to be burnt, and the publisher feared that 'the bishops would prosecute him'. It has often been attributed to Locke, and certainly came from the stable of his patron Shaftesbury. John Pocock has treated the *Letter* as the seminal text of neo-Harringtonian constitutionalism, for it endorsed the notion that an independent aristocracy was the essential balance in the constitution. But his account omits to note that the tract was overwhelmingly concerned with ecclesiastical power. It argued that the possibility of a Godly Prince and a Godly church had been destroyed because the true foundations of the Restoration had been fatally undermined. A 'distinct party' of 'the High episcopal man and the old Cavalier' have plotted to establish absolute monarchy so that they may enjoy 'all the power and office of the kingdom'. The vital steps were the penal statutes of the 1660s, and especially the Act of Uniformity, by which 'our church became triumphant'. The tide had been temporarily halted during the Cabal administration (when Shaftesbury was himself in office), but since then it had been inexorable. The projects after 1673 of the earl of Danby's 'church party' were 'the greatest attempt . . . against the king's supremacy since the Reformation'. The 'great churchmen' have now captured the king's government and they planned to perfect their tyranny. The king has become the church's lapdog, yet the church will be careful to shore up the crown by preaching the divine right of kings. In a rousing peroration the tract declared that the two modern idols are

43 Hickeringill, *Curse Ye Meroz*, pp. 17, 11–12; E. Hickeringill, *The Black Nonconformist* (1682), sig. b1ᵛ.

bishop and king who must 'be worshipped as divine in the same temple by us poor lay subjects'.[44]

The same refrains can be found in Andrew Marvell, a friend of Harrington and Milton, and associate of Shaftesbury's Whigs. One of his most vicious anticlerical satires is *Mr Smirke, or the Divine in Mode* (1676). It lampooned an up-and-coming clergyman, a man 'constantly treading in the footsteps of preferment', destined for a bishopric and anxious to get into the saddle of prelatical power. The object of Marvell's attentions was probably Francis Turner, later bishop of Ely, and, had it not been for the Glorious Revolution, likely heir to Archbishop Sancroft at Canterbury. Turner played a singular role in the evolution of the idea of priestcraft, for as well as being the target of Marvell's ire, he was, after his arrest in 1690 for Jacobite plotting, also the butt of *Priestcraft Expos'd*. Marvell's satire drew a general moral. 'If we of the laity would but study our self-preservation, and . . . be as true to our separate interest as those men [the clergy] are to theirs, we ought not to wish them any new power for the future.' The aim of the priests, and especially of the bishops, was 'the engaging men's minds under spiritual bondage, to lead them canonically into temporal slavery'.

Mr Smirke closed with 'a short historical essay, touching general councils, creeds, and impositions in religion'. It expressed, in historical parable, the point of view more overtly put in *The Letter from a Person of Quality*. Marvell examined the reign of Constantine, for 'from his reign the most sober historians date the new disease which was so generally propagated, that it hath given reason to inquire whether it . . . were not inherent to the very function' of priesthood. The disease disclosed itself 'first in ambition, then in contention, next in imposition, and after . . . in open persecution'. The 'pitiful' Council of Nicaea embroiled the gospel in obscure philosophic terminology: *homoousios, hypostasis, essentia, substantia*. So began the 'trade of creed-making' by which 'bishops . . . throw the opposite party out of the saddle'. With every creed came an oath or test, and so 'the dextrous bishops step by step hooked within their verge, all the business and power that could be catched, . . . first to a spiritual kind of dominion, and from that encroached upon and

---

[44] *A Letter from a Person of Quality* (1675), pp. 1–3, 8, 24–5, 34; J.G.A. Pocock, *The Machiavellian Moment* (Princeton, 1975), pp. 406, 415–16. See Mark Goldie, 'John Locke and Anglican Royalism', *Political Studies*, 31 (1983), 61–85 repr. in *John Locke: Critical Assessments*, ed. R. Ashcraft, 4 vols (London, 1991), vol. I, pp. 151–80.

into the civil jurisdiction'. Princes have been foolish and unmindful
of their duty enough to let them get away with it. The bishops
'crept . . . by court insinuations and flattery into the princes'
favour, until those generous creatures suffered themselves to be
backed and ridden by them'. But, 'in persecution the clergy . . .
wisely interposed the magistrate betwixt themselves and the
people, not caring . . . how odious they rendered him'. Marvell's
readers would be in no doubt as to the moral of his best-selling
tract: Charles II, like Constantine, had the opportunity to be 'the
universal apostle of Christianity', and yet, like Constantine, was
apt to render his regime odious by becoming the cat's-paw of
episcopal tyranny. Marvell did not wish to unking his prince: he
wished him to *be* one.[45]

I turn finally to exemplify these themes by examining one
moment in Restoration history in which the ecclesiological dimension of proto-Whiggism is especially manifest. The Cabal regime
(1667-73) was a cross-grained phase, its eponymous members
pulling in a Catholic as well as a Dissenting direction. But plainly it
involved attempts to escape the Anglican dominion of the Clarendon years and to lighten the yoke of uniformity. The king now
shunned the prelates and complained of 'the ambition, covetous-
ness and the scandal of the clergy'. In 1669 there was even strong
talk of expropriating episcopal lands.[46] The culmination was the
king's edict of toleration, the Declaration of Indulgence of 1672. It
was prefigured in the informal suspension of the penal laws during
1668 and 1669, which provoked the Cavalier Parliament to pass the
vicious Conventicle Act, which Marvell described as 'the quintes-
sence of arbitrary malice'. The Cavaliers repeated their response
when, in 1673, they forced the king to withdraw his Declaration
and sack his ministers. The scene was set for the king's capitulation
to Danby's church party, and for Shaftesbury's move into opposition.

It is commonly supposed that the Indulgence was fatally flawed
because it was a prerogative act contrary to statute and hence an
affront to the rule of law and parliament. The familiar grid is that of

---

[45] Marvell, *Mr Smirke*, pp. 10, 44, 50–1, 58-62, 67, 70; *Priestcraft Expos'd*, p. 12. Cf. Gibbon,
   Decline, vol. III, pp. 343–4. On Marvell's political poetry see the studies by Wallace (1968),
   Patterson (1978), and Cherniak (1983).
[46] Samuel Pepys, *Diary*, ed. R. Latham and W. Matthews (London, 1970–83), vol. IX, pp.
   36, 45, 72–3, 347, 360, 473, 485.

absolutism in contention with constitutionalism. But this is to focus narrowly upon constitutionality as modern Whigs conceive it.[47] Contemporaries also perceived the issue as an ecclesiological quarrel about religious liberty and the church's hegemony. Since parliament was the source of persecuting laws, it is hard to see why the friends of liberty should wish unequivocally to defend it. In fact, a constellation of Puritans and future Whigs backed the crown. William Penn did so; so did Henry Stubbe, the Hobbesian Independent; and so also Marvell, in his *Rehearsal Transpros'd.*[48] Locke did so in position papers for Lord Chancellor Shaftesbury, who impressed on the king that he was God's 'vice-regent' in spirituals. As late as 1675, the Shaftesburian *Letter from a Person of Quality* defended the Indulgence.[49]

Amongst the defences of the crown three strands of argument are discernible. The first was vilification of the church party. John Owen, once Cromwell's 'archbishop', rehearsed 'the severe and destructive penalties' by which 'the prelates' pressed conformity 'to the utmost punctilio'. The king had a 'noble' disposition towards indulgence, which ought not to be 'sacrificed to the interests of any one party'. John Humfrey wrote of 'episcopal bigots' who are 'blinded' by their 'God of . . . uniformity'; and Nicholas Lockyer, an old Cromwellian, of the 'bishops' cruel courts . . . backing the Common Prayer with armies'.[50]

The second element was the Erastian insistence that the royal supremacy, entrenched at the Reformation, entailed the crown's personal governance of the church. Humfrey, Stubbe, and Philip Nye, a redoubtable Puritan of the Westminster Assembly, drew upon Marsilian, Gallican and Grotian materials. Humfrey wrote, 'kings and emperors (says Grotius . . .) are equally to take care of sacred and secular things . . . the Nonconformists therefore deny not the authority of the king in matters ecclesiastical'. Stubbe's discussion of early Christian emperors invoked Henrician doctrines

[47] For example, C.C. Weston and J.R. Greenberg, *Subjects and Sovereigns: The Grand Controversy over Legal Sovereignty in Stuart England* (Cambridge, 1981), pp. 162–76.

[48] William Penn, *Works* (1726), vol. I, p. 168; Jacob, *Stubbe*, ch. 6; Marvell, *The Rehearsal Transpros'd* (1672), p. 162.

[49] *A Letter*, pp. 4–5; Marshall, 'Locke in Context', ch. 3. See also Richard Tuck, 'Hobbes and Locke on toleration', in *Thomas Hobbes and Political Theory*, ed. M.G. Dietz (Lawrence, Kans., 1990).

[50] John Owen, *Works*, (London, 1850–3), vol. XIII, pp. 519–22, 534; Nicholas Lockyer, *Some Seasonable and Serious Queries* (1670), p. 11; John Humfrey, *The Authority of the Magistrate about Religion* (1672), p. 10.

which invested quasi-sacerdotal powers in the crown. Charles, by his Indulgence, 'revives the primitive policy of Constantine, and acteth like a bishop'.[51]

The final element was the dramatic claim that since, by the laws of God and nature, civil coercion in religion was never permissible, the Indulgence, far from being the exercise of arbitrary state power, was instead a renunciation of such power. As Edmund Waller, the poet and future Whig, told the House of Commons, the king had promised to 'stick to his Declaration' and thereby '*not* invade our rights and liberties'. In its most paradoxical form, this argument appeared in the title page of Humfrey's tract, which aimed at a 'confutation of that misshapen tenet, of the magistrate's authority over the conscience in the matters of religion . . . for vindication of the grateful receivers of his Majesty's late Declaration'. The central point, Lockyer argued, was that statutes cannot prevail against Scripture: the Conventicle Act was against 'the express word of God, the positive law of the nation, the law and light of nature' and hence was 'null and void'. It had been passed by 'violent faction, by strength of vote, against all the force of unanswered reason'. The Quaker Penn agreed that statutory impositions cannot 'invade divine prerogative'. Humfrey succinctly concluded that 'the Act of Parliament is against the command of God: the king permits what God bids'.[52]

The same case was presented more sustainedly by John Owen. Liberty of conscience is a natural right. People take up the bonds of society because of the 'inconveniences' that would otherwise befall them. In so doing they abandon only those liberties necessary for the purchase of the 'advantage which public society does afford'. They do not forgo their religious liberties, which are inviolable. The mind's assent 'followeth the evidence which they have of the truth of any thing', and coercion can only alter 'outward actings', not the 'inward constitution' of the mind. True religion can never be obtained by force, and the magistrate can only be concerned with 'public peace and tranquility'. Why, therefore, should not the

[51] Humfrey, *Authority*, pp. 36–7; Stubbe, *A Further Justification of the Present War* (1673), p. 32; Philip Nye, *The King's Authority in Dispensing with Ecclesiastical Laws* (publ. 1687). Cf. Owen, *Works*, vol. XIII, p. 540; Matthew Henry, *The Life of the Rev. Philip Henry* (London, 1825), p. 129; anon., *Vindiciae Libertatis Evangelii* (1672). For Humfrey's Marsilianism see Condren, *Lawson's 'Politica'*, ch. 12.
[52] *The Parliamentary History of England* (London, 1808), vol. IV, p. 518; Lockyer, *Some Seasonable*, p. 13 and title-page; Humfrey, *Authority*, p. 28 and title-page.

magistrate, 'knowing their minds and persuasions to be out of his reach and exempted from his jurisdiction', indulge them? The argument is remarkably close to Locke's *Letter Concerning Toleration*, but it was here used by Cromwell's chaplain to defend Charles II's prerogative.[53]

The remarkable meld of Puritan divinity and Erastian tolerationism visible in these debates is best epitomised in a letter of 1669 which Lewis du Moulin, a minister who had defended the Cromwellian church and who had been ejected at the Restoration, wrote to Richard Baxter, doyen of the Presbyterians. With relish he declared that 'the toleration will be the downfall of the hierarchy'. He pronounced that 'all church power is popery' and condemned Catholics, Anglicans and Calvinists equally on that account. He praised Erastus for 'laying open the grand cheat of ecclesiastical jurisdiction', and marvelled at the fact that God 'hath permitted that men ill-principled as Grotius and Selden, yea Hobbes as bad as can be, should come nearer the truth than many good men'.[54] Du Moulin's grandfather had narrowly escaped the Massacre of St Bartholomew, that epitome of Catholic barbarism; a descendant would serve at the court of Frederick the Great, the Enlightened despot who gave religious toleration to Prussia. Du Moulin's letter of 1669 stands on the cusp between Reformation and Enlightenment, for when a Presbyterian found religious truth in Grotius, Selden and Hobbes, then indeed the Puritan had become the Whig. To be a Whig in later Stuart England was to be as the Prophet Elias slaying the priests of Baal.

---

[53] Owen, *Works*, vol. XIII, pp. 373, 389, 526–8, 530, 532.
[54] Dr Williams's Library, London: Baxter Letters 5, fo. 192 (*c.* November 1669). On Du Moulin see Mark Goldie, 'The Huguenot Experience and the Problem of Toleration in Restoration England', in *The Huguenots and Ireland*, ed. C.E.J. Caldicott, H. Gough and J-P. Pittion (Dublin, 1987), pp. 188–95; Lamont, *Baxter*, pp. 64, 133, 249, 264.

The right to resist: Whig resistance theory, 1688 to 1694

Lois G. Schwoerer

During and immediately after the Revolution of 1688–9, English-men faced an issue as important and troubling as any to be discussed in an early modern nation; did the people, however that word was understood, have the right to resist the king, and if so, on what grounds, to what degree, and through what agency? The circumstances of the Revolution and the need to legitimise it thereafter provoked intense debate among Whigs, Tories and Jacobites, who – their political thinking shaped by resistance theories that had been developed during the Reformation on the Continent and in Scotland, and in England during the Civil Wars, the Interregnum, and at the time of the Exclusion Crisis – argued questions concerning active resistance, passive resistance and non-resistance more comprehensively than ever before.[1] My focus in this essay is on Whig resistance theory only. Mark Goldie has studied Tory resistance theory, especially as it was articulated by Anglican divines, and Paul Monod has illuminated Jacobite theory as expressed from 1688 to 1788.[2] Whig resistance theory has also been studied by Richard Ashcraft, H.T. Dickinson and J.P. Kenyon, but not exhaustively for the years with which I am concerned.[3] I will argue that Whig resistance theory from 1688 to

[1] Mark Goldie, 'The Revolution of 1689 and the Structure of Political Argument. An Essay and Annotated Bibliography of Pamphlets on the Allegiance Controversy', *Bulletin of Research in the Humanities*, 83 (1980), 496–9, Table III for party designations.

[2] Mark Goldie, 'The Political Thought of the Anglican Revolution', *The Revolutions of 1688. The Andrew Browning Lectures 1988*, ed. Robert Beddard (Oxford, 1991), pp. 102–36. Paul Monod, *Jacobitism and the English People, 1688–1788* (Cambridge, 1989). See also J.C.D. Clark, *English Society 1688–1832. Ideology, Social Structure and Political Practice during the Ancien Regime* (Cambridge, 1985) and J.A.W. Gunn, *Beyond Liberty and Property* (Kingston and Montreal, 1983).

[3] Richard Ashcraft, *Revolutionary Politics and Locke's Two Treatises of Government* (Cambridge, 1986); Conal Condren, *George Lawson's 'Politica' and the English Revolution* (Cambridge, 1989); H.T. Dickinson, *Liberty and Property. Political Ideology in Eighteenth-Century Britain*

about 1694 was richer and more complex than has been understood, that intellectual and ideological tensions existed within it, occasioned in part by the pressure of circumstances, the challenge of Tory and Jacobite criticism, and Whig views on other political issues, and that the theory, its tensions unresolved, was transmitted to the eighteenth century where it influenced British radicals throughout the era and American colonists at the time of their revolution.

Whig resistance theory was developed in parliamentary debate and in approximately one hundred tracts and pamphlets published between the autumn of 1688 and 1694.[4] Many were anonymous, but some were written by known political figures and clergymen. The known authors included Gilbert Burnet (in 1688 and 1689 William of Orange's principal English propagandist), Peter Allix (a Huguenot scholar), Samuel Masters (an Anglican cleric), Samuel Johnson (an Anglican cleric better known as a Whig pamphleteer and former chaplain to the Whig martyr, William Lord Russell), John Humfrey and Robert Ferguson (Presbyterian ministers in 1688 and 1689, Ferguson later becoming a Jacobite), John Wildman (a former republican), Charles Blount (a deist) and Daniel Defoe. Locke, of course, also discussed resistance in his *Two Treatises of Government*. Some scholars have recently shown that his book did not enjoy contemporary popularity, but others insist that Lockean ideas found in lesser tracts were more important than sometimes recognised.[5]

Exchanges in the press and in debates were often bitter. The breakdown in press controls in the winter of 1688 and 1689

(New York, 1977); J. P. Kenyon, *Revolution Principles. The Politics of Party 1689–1720* (Cambridge, 1977); Julian H. Franklin, *John Locke and the Theory of Sovereignty: Mixed Monarchy and the Right of Resistance in the Political Thought of the English Revolution* (Cambridge, 1978).

[4] Goldie, 'The Revolution of 1689 and the Structure of Political Argument', pp. 476, 484, 485, 490. Goldie found 192 tracts in the Allegiance controversy printed between 6 February 1689 and the end of 1694; of these 89 were Whig, 50 Tory and 53 Jacobite. Approximately ten additional pamphlets on resistance appeared before 6 February during the autumn and winter of 1688–9.

[5] For example, Kenyon, *Revolution Principles*, and Martyn Thompson, 'The Reception of Locke's Two Treatises of Government 1690–1705', *Political Studies*, 24 (1976), 184–91. But see Richard Ashcraft and M.M. Goldsmith, 'Locke, Revolution Principles, and the Formation of Whig Ideology', *Historical Journal*, 16 (1983), 773–800, and Lois G. Schwoerer, 'Locke, Lockean Ideas, and the Glorious Revolution', *Journal of the History of Ideas*, 51 (Oct.–Dec. 1990), 531–48.

encouraged an unaccustomed and shortlived freedom of the press, and the faltering mechanisms of pre-publication censorship to 1695 (when those mechanisms were removed) assured a freer press than before. The number of printed tracts promoting a Whig position exceeded those advancing passive resistance or non-resistance from 1688 to 1694, and were supplemented by reprints of earlier English, Scottish and continental tracts arguing resistance theory from diverse points of view.[6] The need to develop a theory of resistance which would legitimise the Revolution and the Settlement and ease tender consciences was urgent, and ideas about resistance were central to the political discourse of these years in ways not heretofore acknowledged.

I

Whig theorists of resistance during and immediately after the Revolution had to respond to an abhorrence of resistance that was deeply embedded in Restoration culture – in its hierarchical social structure, deferential assumptions, and underlying respect for kingly authority and law. Since the return of the Stuarts, the government (king and parliament co-operating in legislation), the Anglican church (through sermons, homilies and above all the Homily on Obedience), and Tory writers and spokesmen had denounced and even tried to outlaw all theories of active resistance. The legal maxim, 'The King Can Do No Wrong', a powerful bulwark against resistance, was reinforced as early as 1660 by the presiding judge at the regicides' trial.[7] In 1661 the Act to Preserve the Person and Government of the King made it treason not only to restrain the monarch but also to write, preach, or speak against royal authority.[8] Also in 1661 a comprehensive 'Non-Resistance oath' was imposed on all office holders obliging them to swear that 'it is not lawful, upon any pretence whatsoever, to take arms

---

[6] Goldie, 'The Revolution of 1689 and the Structure of Political Argument', p. 484.

[7] Janelle Greenberg, 'Our Grand Maxim Of State, "The King Can Do No Wrong"', *History of Political Thought*, 12 (Summer 1991), 209–28, makes the point. The act attainting the regicides declared that neither peers, commons, or people 'collectively' or otherwise have 'any coercive power over' kings of the realm. *Statutes of the Realm*, ed. A. Luders, Sir T. Edlyn Tomlins, J. France, W.E. Taunton and J. Raithby, 11 vols. (London, 1810–28), vol. v, p. 288.

[8] J. R. Jones, *Country and Court England 1658–1714* (London, 1978), pp. 142–3. *Statutes of the Realm*, vol. v, p. 304.

against the king'.[9] In 1661 the oath was extended by the Militia Act to officers and soldiers in the militia, in 1662 by the Act of Uniformity to all schoolmasters, university professors and readers, and churchmen, and in 1663 by an act to regulate vestries, to all vestrymen.[10] In 1675 the court's effort to extend such an oath to members of parliament passed the House of Lords and failed in the Commons only because of a prorogation.[11]

The government had also attempted to censor ideas justifying resistance. In 1663 Roger L'Estrange, the first Surveyor of the Imprimery, had drawn up a list of seditious propositions and pamphlets which was approved by the king. Among the propositions was that the king's power was fiduciary and the subjects' allegiance conditional, that the king possessed two bodies (his person and his authority), and that the king's person might be resisted, but not his authority.[12] Twenty years later the banned books were burned in Oxford on 21 July 1683, the day that Lord Russell, the Whig party leader in the House of Commons during the Exclusion Crisis, was executed in London for his role in the Rye House Plot.[13] The banned ideas were part of Whig resistance theory, and many of the books were reprinted in 1689. Finally, the government punished persons (among them the Reverend Samuel Johnson) for publishing tracts favouring resistance. The government's policy was clear: the expression of certain ideas, including the right to resist, would not be tolerated.

Whigs were also faced with the challenge of Tory and Jacobite theories of passive resistance and non-resistance, which enjoyed greater popularity than is sometimes realised.[14] During the Restoration, Tories mirrored faithfully the policies in state and church that encouraged abhorrence of the idea of resistance. After the Revolution Tories and Jacobites reflected the concerns of those

[9] In the Corporation Act (1661); conveniently found in J.P. Kenyon, *The Stuart Constitution. Documents and Commentary* (2nd edn, Cambridge, 1978), pp. 351–2.

[10] Ibid., pp. 337, 355. *Statutes of the Realm*, vol. v, pp. 309, 364–70, 446–7.

[11] David Ogg, *England in the Reign of Charles II*, 2 vols. (2nd edn, Oxford, 1962), vol. II, pp. 532–3.

[12] Roger L'Estrange, *Considerations and Proposals In Order to the Regulation of the Press: Together With Diverse Instances of Treasonous, and Seditious Pamphlets, Proving the Necessity Thereof* (1663), pp. 11–24. The banned books are arranged under categories of ideas.

[13] University of Oxford. *The Judgment and Decree of the University of Oxford Past in their Convocation July 21, 1683, Against certain Pernicious Books and Damnable Doctrines* (Oxford, 1683).

[14] See titles in n. 2 above.

people troubled about their conscience, the moral legitimacy of the event, and the apparent violation of the principle of hereditary succession. Using the language of divine-right kingship and relying on Scripture, Tories and Jacobites insisted upon a theory hallowed by time: that England's king receives his authority directly from God, possesses an indefeasible hereditary right to the crown and is, therefore, not to be resisted by force. This was a theory of absolute, not arbitrary government. Following the early theories of Luther and Calvin, Tories and Jacobites held that a Christian has a religious duty to resist an evil prince in ways that might go beyond prayer and tears to civil disobedience.[15] While a king could do no wrong, his ministers could undoubtedly do so, and they had been a fair target for disaffected Tories between 1686 and 1688.[16] Both Roger North, a prominent Tory during the reign of Charles II, and the Reverend Charles Leslie, an obdurate Nonjuror in the early eighteenth century, insisted that a royal government was constrained by a king's coronation oath, promises to his people, laws of justice and honour, and self-interest.[17]

In all of this, Tories and Jacobites frequently used the same political language as Whigs. They, too, called upon an ancient constitution, Magna Charta, English law and history, and natural law. They, too, claimed England's common and positive law for themselves. But their major emphasis was on divine law and the obligation oaths imposed on conscience.[18] After the Revolution, in an effort to ease the consciences of Tories who had subscribed to the new oath of allegiance with its *de facto* clause, Tory thinkers invoked the comforting idea of Providence to explain the Revolution and justify obedience to the new monarchs. Finally, Tories and Jacobites underscored the actual and theoretical possibilities of anarchy and popular tyranny that (they said) were encouraged by Whig resistance theories. In Leslie's view, such ideas would return power to the people, 'setting 10000 tyrants over us instead of one'.[19] Overall, Tories and Jacobites attempted to demonstrate that all

---

[15] Goldie, 'The Political Thought of the Anglican Revolution', pp. 113, 114, 116.
[16] Monod, *Jacobitism and the English People*, p. 19; Goldie, 'The Political Thought of the Anglican Revolution', pp. 107–8.
[17] Monod, *Jacobitism and the English People*, p. 18. Goldie, 'The Political Thought of the Anglican Revolution', p. 116.
[18] Goldie, 'The Political Thought of the Anglican Revolution', pp. 118–21.
[19] Quoted in Monod, *Jacobitism and the English People*, p. 19; cf. p. 20

forms of Whiggism and all Whig theories of resistance were merely covers for rebellion, republicanism, and anarchy. The basic challenge to the Whigs was to articulate a theory of resistance that would allow them to avoid or deflect such charges.

II

Many of the Whig responses to the Tory and Jacobite critique drew in different ways upon approximately twenty-five reprints of earlier English, Scottish, and continental tracts dealing with resistance. In a few instances, they drew also upon previously unpublished manuscripts.[20] We know little about the circumstances of their publication, but it was in the interests of Whigs to multiply the number of tracts that supported resistance, and it seems likely that they were responsible for the reissues.[21] Johnson himself brought out some of his previous work.[22] Richard Baldwin, the printer of many reissues, was surely driven by ideological as well as economic reasons.

Earlier work was sometimes edited to apply its message to 1688–9. Algernon Sidney's ideas, as expressed at his trial and in his scaffold speech, were reprinted as *Sidney Redivivus: Or The Opinion Of the Late Honourable Collonel Sidney, As to Civil Government*. John Milton's *The Tenure of Kings and Magistrates*, first printed in 1650 to justify the trial and execution of Charles I and banned in 1663, was shortened, refocussed on 1689, and printed under the provocative title *Pro populo adversus tyrannos: Or The Sovereign Right And Power Of The People Over Tyrants*. George Lawson's *Politica sacra et civilis* was

---

[20] I count 25 reprints of resistance tracts out of approximately 85 reprints from a list I have been compiling for many years. Goldie listed 18 reprints in the Allegiance debate: 'The Revolution of 1689 and the Structure of Political Argument', pp. 522–3. Condren found 19 reprints: *George Lawson's 'Politica'*, p. 151.

[21] Some resistance tracts may have been republished by Tories and/or Jacobites to embarrass Whigs. *Killing no Murder Briefly Discoursed in Three Questions* (1657, 1659) is such a possibility. The tract could be read either to identify James II with Cromwell, or William of Orange with Cromwell. The latter equation was a theme in Jacobite satire and tracts, and at least one notable picture, a reissued Cromwellian print, substituted William for Oliver. See Lord Macaulay, *The History of England*, ed. C.H. Firth, 6 vols. (1913–15), vol. III, p. 1433.

[22] *Remarks upon Dr. Sherlock's Book, Intituled The Case of Resistance of the Supreme Powers Stated and Resolved* (1689), Preface, p. i: Johnson credited himself with printing this unpublished manuscript. A tract with this title appeared in 1690, but the text is different from the 1689 issue.

also reprinted in 1689, possibly by John Humfrey, with a significant marginal emendation.[23]

Many of the books banned in 1663 and burned in 1683 were reprinted in 1688 and 1689. Thus, George Buchanan's *De jure regni apud Scotos* (1579) made available his radical ideas about what has been termed popular sovereignty and the right of 'every individual citizen', even those from the lowest class, to depose a ruler.[24] Philip Hunton's *A Treatise of Monarchy* (1643, 1680) provided a text filled with ideas of the king's two bodies and of sovereignty residing in three co-ordinated powers, king, Lords and Commons, just as Charles I had said in his famous *Answer to the Nineteen Propositions*. Although Hunton argued for the right to resist an erring king, he did not justify deposing and punishing the king. *Vindiciae contra tyrannos* (1579), written probably by Phillipe du Plessis-Mornay, a sixteenth-century French reformer, located the right of resistance in magistrates and 'the assembly of Estates', and assigned magistrates a religious duty and moral right to resist a monarch with force if he ruled as a tyrant.[25] Also reprinted was Johnson's *Julian the Apostate* (1682), which identified the Emperor and his fall with the 'popish' Duke of York.[26] Another Johnson tract, *The Opinion is This: That Resistance may be Us'd*, printed first in 1683 to vindicate the memory of Lord Russell, was also reissued. The reprints, many of which offer exceedingly radical statements, were an important feature of the debate about resistance theory.

III

All Whig statements about resistance were derived from some form of a theory of contract (usefully distinguished as constitutional contract or philosophical contract)[27] and were articulated in several sometimes intersecting political languages: the ancient

---

[23] Condren, *George Lawson's 'Politica'*, p. 154.

[24] Quentin Skinner, *The Foundations of Modern Political Thought*, 2 vols. (Cambridge, 1978), vol. II, pp. 342–5; also R. A. Mason, 'Knox, Resistance and the Moral Imperative', *History of Political Thought*, 1 (Fall 1980), 411–36.

[25] Julian H. Franklin, translator and editor, *Constitutionalism and Resistance in the Sixteenth Century. Three Treatises by Hotman, Beza, & Mornay* (New York, 1969), pp. 39–44, 148–9, 152, 154, 161, 169, 189, 190–1, 196. Also Skinner, *The Foundations of Modern Political Thought*, vol. II, pp. 332–7.

[26] *Julian* was licensed on 22 December 1688 and had a fourth edition the next year.

[27] Härro Hopfel and Martyn P. Thompson, 'The History of Contract as a Motif in Political Thought', *American Historical Review*, 84 (1979), 940–3.

constitution,[28] law, history (of England and other nations), Reformation theories of revolution,[29] natural rights, and the Bible, often combined in the same tract. But while these statements shared common assumptions, they differed widely on key theoretical issues such as the origins of government, the meaning of the word 'people', whether a monarch's tyranny resulted in dissolution of the government and whether and under what circumstances limited or unlimited resistance was legitimate. These differences allowed Tories and Jacobites to ridicule Whig ideas of resistance as incoherent and obliged later generations of Whigs to search for resolution of their incoherence and ambiguity.

The concept of how government began divided Whigs. Theorists who promoted philosophical contractarianism, such as Ferguson, Humfrey and of course John Locke, offered a non-historical account. They explained that men in a state of nature created a community by their individual and free consents, and that the community, by a second or 'rectoral' compact, entrusted power to a government in a contractual relationship (according to Ferguson)[30] or a fiduciary one (according to Locke, whose concept of trust reinforced the sovereignty of the people).[31] The community reserved certain rights and liberties to itself in a constitution, while the Legislative made laws for society consonant with the law of nature so that men would have 'standing' rules to govern them, not the arbitrary will of a prince.[32] Government, whether seen as a trust or a contract, was divine only in the sense that God ordained that man should have government. As Humfrey put it, 'the powers that be are the government of every Country according to its own Constitution'.[33]

On the other hand, constitutional contractarians, such as

---

[28] J.G.A. Pocock, *The Ancient Constitution and the Feudal Law. A Study of English Historical Thought in the Seventeenth Century. A Reissue with a Retrospect* (1957; reprint edn, Cambridge, 1987).

[29] Skinner, *The Foundations of Modern Political Thought*, vol. ii, chs. 7–9.

[30] Robert Ferguson, *A Brief Justification of the Prince of Orange's Descent into England, and of the King's late Recourse to Arms* (1689), in *A Collection of State Tracts, Publish'd on Occasion of the Late Revolution in 1688. And during the reign of King William III*, 3 vols. (1705–6), vol. i, p. 136.

[31] Peter Laslett (ed.), *John Locke: Two Treatises of Government* (Student edition, Cambridge, 1991), *Second Treatise*, chs. i, ii, viii. (All references to Locke's *Treatises* are to this edition.) On trust see ibid., pp. 112–16; John Dunn, *The Political Thought of John Locke. An Historical Account of the Argument of the Two Treatises of Government* (Cambridge, 1969).

[32] Locke, *Second Treatise*, pp. 283–4, 411. Laslett (ed.), *Locke, Two Treatises*, pp. 112–13.

[33] John Humfrey, *The Free State of The People of England Maintained* (London, 1702), pp. 9–10.

Masters, Allix and Johnson, held that England's government originated in historical time. It was shaped by the common law, exemplified in an ancient constitution, the medieval mythical laws of King Edward the Confessor, Magna Charta, and by statutory law. The law bound subjects to obedience and kings to rule in accordance with it. England's government, wrote one author, is a 'Paction and Contract between the Supreme Authority and the People'.[34]

Whereas all Whigs used the words 'original contract' and 'original compact' they assigned different meanings to them. For Locke the 'original compact' was the agreement every man makes both to form a society – a 'Body Politick' – and to submit to the decisions of the majority of that society. The 'original compact' is the 'beginning' of lawful government whose purpose is to preserve 'property', that is, material things, as well as 'Lives, Liberties and Estates' and religion.[35] Admitting that no physical copy of the 'original compact' existed, Locke explained that government was established before records were kept, implied that common sense showed its existence, and, in a rare use of history, offered examples from such places as Rome, Venice and the American Indians.[36] In contrast, Whig constitutionalists identified the 'original contract' concretely with the oath English kings took at their coronation. Allix, invoking medieval authorities, such as the *Mirror of Justices*, Bracton and Fortescue, sarcastically remarked that if the coronation oath were not proof of a contract, then when a king takes the oath he should immediately explain that he did so only in 'mockery and masquerade'.[37] For Johnson the coronation oath was the 'fundamental contract' or 'downright bargain' by which the king

---

34 William King, *A Dialogue between Two Friends, a Jacobite and a Williamite, Occasion'd by the Late Revolution of Affairs, and the Oath of Allegiance* (n.p., n.d. [1689]), in *State Tracts*, vol. I, p. 293. Also, Samuel Masters, *The Case of Allegiance in our Present Circumstances consider'd* (licensed 21 March 1689), p. 10. Cf. Thomas Hodgin [?], *An Inquiry into the nature and Obligation of Legal Rights* (1693; 2nd edn, 1696), in *State Tracts*, vol. II, pp. 396, 397, 398, Samuel Johnson, *Reflections on the History of Passive Obedience* (1689), p. 11, and *A Brief Account of the Nullity of King James's Title* (licensed 27 July 1689), in *State Tracts*, vol. I, p. 282.
35 Laslett (ed.), *Locke, Two Treatises*, pp. 102–8; Locke, *Second Treatise*, pp. 268, 352, 353.
36 Locke, *Second Treatise*, pp. 332–6.
37 [Peter Allix], *An Examination of the Scruples of Those who Refuse to Take the Oath of Allegiance* (licensed 16 April 1689), pp. 4, 5, 6, 13, 22. See also Masters, *The Case of Allegiance in our Present Circumstances consider'd*, p. 9. Daniel Whitby, *An Historical Account of Some Things Relating to the English Government*, in *State Tracts*, vol. I, pp. 590, 592. *Animadversions on a Discourse entituled, God's Ways of Disposing of Kingdoms* (1691), p. 38.

binds himself to uphold the law.[38] If the king failed to do so, the people were released from their contractual relationship and had a legitimate right to resist him.

The identification of the coronation oath with the 'original contract' appeared also in the Convention. For example, when the Lords discussed a draft of the 'abdication and vacancy' resolution (which referred to James II having broken the 'original contract'), their legal advisor, William Petyt, appealed to history to show that the original contract was the king's coronation oath. Tory peers objected to the words 'original contract', some denying that any such thing existed, and there was talk of substituting the words 'coronation oath' for 'original contract'.[39] But the Convention dropped the words 'original contract' from the resolution and no more was heard of substituting the 'coronation oath'. After the Revolution, some Whigs, in an equation underscoring the specificity of the concept, identified the 'original contract' with the Bill of Rights, one MP declaring, 'The Foundation of the Government is the Bill of Rights . . . This is our original Contract.'[40]

Another matter of fundamental importance to Whig resistance theorists was the right of self-preservation, and again they conflated several political languages in discussing it. If the king failed to provide protection, a duty he assumed as part of the contract with his people, the 'natural Liberty of self-defence returns', wrote an anonymous pamphleteer.[41] Engraved in everyone's heart, the right of self-defence was so powerful that no human law could be valid against it. Defined as a 'natural right . . . superior to human laws, and of greater force', the right of self-preservation was both a law of God and the 'Magna Charta of all Constitutions'.[42] In collapsing

[38] Samuel Johnson, *Remarks upon Dr. Sherlock's Book*, pp. vi, x, xii. Cf. Samuel Johnson, *An Argument Proving, That the Abrogation of King James by the People of England from the Regal Throne, and the Promotion of the Prince of Orange, one of the Royal Family, to the Throne of the Kingdom in his stead, was according to the Constitution of the English Government, and Prescribed by it. In Opposition to all the false and treacherous Hypotheses, of Usurpation, Conquest, Desertion, and of taking the Powers that Are upon Content* (1692), p. 30.
[39] Lois G. Schwoerer, *The Declaration of Rights, 1689* (Baltimore and London, 1981), pp. 205–7.
[40] Anchitell Grey, *Debates of the House of Commons*, 10 vols. (1763), vol. x, p. 75.
[41] *An Inquiry . . . Legal Rights*, in *State Tracts*, vol. II, p. 403.
[42] Ibid.; Charles Blount, *The Proceedings Of The Present Parliament Justified By the Opinion of the most Judicious and Learned Hugo Grotius* (London, 1689), p. 16; *Political Aphorisms; or, The True Maxims of Government Displayed* (London, 1690) in *State Tracts*, vol. I, pp. 398–9; Timothy Wilson, *Conscience Satisfied: In a Cordial and Loyal Submitting to the Present Government of King William and Queen Mary* (1690), pp. 36, 38, 44; *A Dialogue between Two Friends*, in *State Tracts*, vol. I, pp. 288–9.

the right of resistance into the right of self-preservation, these anonymous Whig writers justified resistance as a *response* to acts of tyranny. Locke, however, extended the implications of the concept of self-preservation. Referring to the 'Native and Original Right' of society to preserve itself, Locke asserted that people had the right to prevent as well as resist tyranny. As he put it, 'Men can never be secure from Tyranny, if there be no means to escape it, till they are perfectly under it.'[43] This formulation shifted resistance from reaction to tyranny, to action that prevented tyranny, and, as Jacobites saw, opened the question of who is to judge when such action might be taken.

But who were the 'people' to whom the king was accountable? And in whom did the right of resistance inhere? Men who embraced a theory of natural law interpreted the word 'people' more expansively than other Whigs, but none defined precisely what he meant. It is debatable whether Locke had in mind males of the 'lowest social classes', as Ashcraft thinks,[44] but it is certain that he (and men such as Humfrey and the author of *Political Aphorisms* (Defoe?)[45]) did not equate the term with the representative body or the current political nation. Although Locke did not recommend suffrage reform or enlarging the Convention, the author of *A Letter to a Friend* (Wildman?) urged members of the Convention to do just that.[46] Among other Whigs, Johnson adhered to the broadest interpretation, one perhaps identical to Locke's.[47] Allix, however, referred to the 'people' only as men of 'rank and interest in the State'.[48] Generally, the word 'people' in Whig discourse meant the legislative body.

The majority of MPs in the Convention, whether Whig or Tory, held the latter view. When Sir Robert Howard declared that a dissolution of government had occurred and power now resided in

[43] Locke, *Second Treatise*, p. 411.

[44] Ashcraft, *Revolutionary Politics*, p. 311. Gordon J. Schochet, 'Radical Politics and Ashcraft's Treatise on Locke', *Journal of the History of Ideas*, 50 (1989), 501–4.

[45] The author plagiarised the work of Locke and others: Ashcraft and Goldsmith, 'Locke, Revolution Principles, and the Formation of Whig ideology', pp. 773–93.

[46] [Wildman], *A Letter to a Friend, Advising him, in this Extraordinary Juncture, How to free the Nation from Slavery Forever*, in Sir Walter Scott (ed.), *A Collection of Scarce and Valuable Tracts . . . Selected from . . . Public as well as Private Libraries, Particularly That of the Late Lord Somers*, 13 vols. (1809–15), vol. x, p. 196 (hereafter *Somers Tracts*).

[47] See Melinda Zook, 'Early Whig Ideology, Ancient Constitutionalism and the Reverend Samuel Johnson'. Forthcoming in the *Journal of British Studies*.

[48] Allix, *An Examination of Scruples*, p. 10, cf. p. 32.

the people collectively, outraged denial was voiced.[49] A Tory (Sir Robert Sawyer) asserted that if the theory were true, then the Convention was not representative of the people of England. A Whig rejoined that the Convention spoke for all who 'are fit to have a share in [the government]'.[50] In the Declaration of Rights the 'Lords Spiritual and Temporal' and the 'Commons' together were said to make 'a full and free representative of this nation'. The Commons was composed of men who 'were of right' to be elected, the document declared. With few exceptions, then, Whigs identified the 'people' with traditional political elite society, and in so doing clearly restricted the 'right' to resist.

This attitude towards the 'people' brought the status of the Convention into question. Again natural-law theorists and constitutional contractarians travelled different routes to reach the same end. The former regarded the Convention as the surrogate for the 'people' and as possessing the power to 'mend the great frame of government', which a regular parliament could not do.[51] In a tract handed directly to MPs, Humfrey described the Convention as having a 'higher capacity than a parliament'.[52] Anonymous writers reiterated the point.[53] But constitutional contractarians, such as Masters, simply felt that the Convention was the only body competent to judge the present issues, and that its decision was binding on people outside.[54]

Whigs also had to face the question brought into focus by the Revolution itself – whether and under what circumstances might the commands of a king be resisted? Only a very few would have agreed with *Pro popolo adversus tyrannos*, which admitted the right of people to rid themselves of any ruler whom they found simply incompatible. Biblical passages were cited to support the extraordi-

[49] Grey, *Debates*, vol. IX, pp. 19–20; Lois G. Schwoerer, 'A Jornall of the Convention at Westminster begun the 22 of January 1688/9', *Bulletin of the Institute of Historical Research*, 49 (1976), 250–1.
[50] Schwoerer, 'A Jornall', 252–3, 254–5, 256; Grey, *Debates*, vol. IX, pp. 13, 17–19, 22. Debate in the House of Lords contained similar points. See Danby's notes reprinted in Henry Horwitz, 'Parliament and the Glorious Revolution', *Bulletin of the Institute of Historical Research*, 47 (1974), 36–52; also Schwoerer, *The Declaration of Rights, 1689*, pp. 205–8, 214.
[51] E.S. de Beer (ed.) *The Correspondence of John Locke* (8 vols., Oxford, 1976–89), vol. III, p. 576.
[52] John Humfrey, *Good Advice Before It Be Too Late; or, A Breviate for the Convention* (1689), in *Somers Tracts*, vol. X, p. 200.
[53] *A Brief Collection of some Memorandums* (1689), p. 7. Also *Four Questions Debated* (1689), p. 9.
[54] Masters, *The Case of Allegiance*, pp. 20, 22.

nary assertion that the people may 'depose' a king, 'though no Tyrant', simply by their right as 'free-born Men, to be Govern'd as seem to them best'.[55] More circumspectly, the editor of *Sidney Redivivus* maintained that an erring king must 'expect . . . Revenge taken by those that he hath Betray'd'.[56] One anonymous pamphleteer hesitantly suggested that the Bible showed that subjects might correct a king while he reigned, admitting at the same time that Scripture usually commanded that such correction be left to God.[57] But all other pamphleteers maintained that resistance to a lawful monarch executing his duties according to law was forbidden. This is their key position.

For the most part, Whigs limited the conditions under which resistance to an erring king was allowed. To royal incompetence or inconsequential acts, people must respond with forbearing patience. That a private person may not resist the king to serve his private purposes is assumed, but Locke, although agreeing, does give private persons a *right* to resist when their cases might serve as precedents.[58] Also, as we have seen, Locke allowed people the right to resist to *prevent* tyranny. If a *minority* of the people are disaffected, they should emigrate.[59] If the king attempts to make amends for his actions, the people must accept these changes, for at law a defendant may purge his failure any time before final judgement.[60] When appeal to legal processes was possible, resistance to the king was impermissible.[61] People should depend first upon petitioning the king and opposing his ministers.[62] People must never disobey a legal command, even if this meant suffering 'manifest injustice, abuses and particular wrongs'.[63]

---

[55] *Pro popolo adversus tyrannos*, pp. 10–11.

[56] *Sidney Redivivus*, pp. 3–5. Cf. Thomas G. West (ed.), *Discourses Concerning Government* by Algernon Sidney (Indianapolis, 1990), pp. 519, 522–3.

[57] *A Dialogue between Two Friends*, in *State Tracts*, vol. 1, p. 296.

[58] For example, Locke, *Second Treatise*, p. 402; *The Scrupler's Case Considered* (London, 1683, repr. 1689), pp. 6–8.

[59] *A Political Conference Between Aulicus, a Courtier; Demas, a countryman; and Civicus, a Citizen: Clearing the Original of Civil Government, the Powers and Duties of Soveraigns and Subjects* (1689), pp. 17, 19.

[60] Ibid., p. 22.

[61] Locke, *Second Treatise*, pp. 403–4, a proposition which he explains in an elaborate analogy to a highway robbery.

[62] *The Works of the Right Honourable Henry Late L. Delamer, and Earl of Warrington* (London, 1694), pp. 364–5. Locke, *Second Treatise*, p. 403.

[63] John Wildman, *A Memorial from the English Protestants. To their Highnesses the Prince and Princess of Orange, Concerning their Grievances* (November 1688), in *State Tracts*, vol. 1, p. 33.

Only when the king's illegal acts afflicted – or threatened – the majority of people, only when there occurred a 'long train of Abuses ... all tending the same way' (as Locke put it) was resistance legitimate. A king ruling by his will becomes a tyrant; he is therefore no king and may be opposed.[64] Legitimate resistance then is not to a king, but to a tyrant. Therefore, it is not treason by the laws of England. But resistance to a legal king ruling by law is rebellion and treason at law.

What, then, were the rights of a people in respect to kings who violated the law and their oaths? Did this lead to the dissolution of government? Whig answers varied. For Locke, James's acts released people from their allegiance, returning them to the community (not to the state of nature), and thus dissolving the government. When this happened, the people were 'at liberty to provide for themselves by erecting a new Legislative, differing from the other, by the change of Persons, or Form or both'.[65] With the possible exception of Ferguson, who went beyond Locke in suggesting that James's acts had returned the people to a state of nature,[66] natural rights thinkers agreed that tyranny returns the people to the community. Burnet, in *An Enquiry Into the Measures of Submission To The Supreme Authority* (a tract printed 'By Authority' and betraying views he later disavowed), declared that James's miscarriages constituted a 'dissolution of the government', that is, a 'breaking of the whole constitution'.[67] In early 1689 *A Letter to a Friend* and Humfrey's *Good Advice* continued this line of thinking.[68] The result was to sanction resistance and the creation of a new government.

Constitutional contractarians arrived at the same conclusion, but with different implications. A king's violations of the law did *not* dissolve government, but rather unkinged him and released the people from their allegiance to him. An anonymous writer main-

---

[64] Locke, *Second Treatise*, pp. 398–401.

[65] Laslett (ed.), *Locke, Two Treatises*, pp. 407–11. Condren points out that Locke and Tyrrell drew these ideas from Lawson without acknowledgement: *George Lawson's 'Politica'*, p. 84.

[66] James's subversion of the 'fundamental laws of society' had absolved his subjects from their allegiance and restored them to their 'State and Condition of Primitive Freedom.' See *A Brief Justification*, in *State Tracts*, vol. I, pp. 136–7.

[67] Gilbert Burnet, *An Enquiry Into the Measures of Submission To The Supream Authority. And of the Grounds upon which it may be Lawful, or Necessary for Subjects, to Defend their Religion Lives and Liberties* (1689), pp. 6–7.

[68] *A Letter to a Friend*, in *Somers Tracts*, vol. x, pp. 195–6. Humfrey, *Good Advice*, in *Somers Tracts*, vol. x, p. 200.

tained that the result was only to 'empower the people to declare themselves free from subjection to him', not make for a 'new Constitution'.[69] Members of the Convention agreed. They rejected the idea of dissolution advanced by Howard in the speech mentioned earlier.[70] Sawyer and others underscored the consequences of *that* notion, among them the disastrous effect on property. 'If we were in the state of Nature', said one MP 'we should have little title to any of our estates'.[71] This was exactly what the Whigs wanted to avoid and a principal reason for disavowing dissolution theory. It was also what Tories and Jacobites accused them of supporting.

Critical to Whig theories of resistance, then, were James's specific violations of the law. For, as Locke put it, if James had *not* violated the law, 'our complaints were mutiny and our redemption rebellion'.[72] James's acts thus invalidated the charge of rebellion levelled against Whigs. In fact Locke's theoretical examples of acts that cause a dissolution of government – an Executive who rules by 'his own Arbitary Will', corrupts the election process by 'Sollicitations' of the representative, or turns over the government to a foreign power (the pope) – correlated with steps James had actually taken.[73] Timothy Wilson, calling upon the Biblical story of David and Saul to support his point that religion was a man's property, declared that James's threat to Protestantism legitimated resistance to him.[74] Wildman's *Memorial* also emphasised James's violation of English property rights through his use of the dispensing and suspending powers. Englishmen consequently had 'no legal Right to their Estates, their Wives and Children, or their Lives'.[75] The same connection between property and resistance theory appears in pamphlets written by constitutional contractarians. The most striking formulation was that of Johnson, who wrote that 'every Liege-Subject of England has a Legal Property in his Life, Liberty and Estate' and drew the conclusion that 'a Legal Possession may be Legally Defended'.[76]

---

[69] *A Political Conference*, p. 22.
[70] Grey, *Debates*, vol. IX, p. 20.
[71] Ibid., vol. IX, p. 18; Schwoerer, 'A Jornall', p. 258.
[72] James Farr and Clayton Roberts, 'John Locke on the Glorious Revolution: A Rediscovered Document', *Historical Journal*, 28 (1985), 396.
[73] Locke, *Second Treatise*, pp. 409, 410–11, 412.
[74] Wilson, *Conscience Satisfied*, p. 21.
[75] Ibid., p. 35.
[76] Johnson, *Remarks upon Dr. Sherlock's Book*, pp. 12, 15, 19.

The effect, then, of James's misgovernment was to legitimate everything the Prince of Orange and the people of England had done. Turning the charge of Tories and Jacobites on its head, Johnson declared that *James* was the 'Usurper and a Rebel', not William of Orange nor the people of England.[77] The people may oppose a usurper with good conscience.[78] One writer appealing to Hooker, Grotius and English history, declared that 'the Kingdom . . . [in 1688] was not taken from a Sovereign Prince against His Will; but himself, by his own Act, dissolved the Bond of Union between Prince and People'.[79] In the Convention Sir George Treby offered the same pretence, declaring, 'We have found the Crown vacant, we have not made it so.'[80] This reasoning meant that there was no resistance to a *king*, for there was no king to resist; the king had changed himself into a tyrant. One's conscience was clear, because the right to resist a tyrant *was* legitimate; it was justified by law, oaths, conscience, historical example, and Biblical precept.

James's miscarriages were debated in the Convention and itemised in the Declaration of Rights and in the Bill of Rights (a statute) as grievances of the nation. Looked at from the viewpoint of ideas about resistance, these documents taken on a theoretical significance beyond their recognised constitutional importance.

Whigs differed over what form resistance to a king-turned-tyrant could legitimately take. For Masters, no other resistance than a judicial procedure was allowed.[81] Some tract writers tacitly endorsed the use of force and the deposition of the prince.[82] A few explicitly sanctioned the use of force and deposition. Locke held that if a king rules illegally, he 'puts himself into a state of War' with his people, and 'in that state' people have the right to use force against him in an 'Appeal to Heaven'.[83] Blount, citing Grotius, argued that the people may 'justly . . . resist [the king] by force' if he offers violence either to them or their laws.[84] In the Convention, the hot-blooded Delamere, who had issued a call to his tenants to

---

[77] Johnson, *Reflections on the History of Passive Obedience*, p. 7.
[78] Johnson, *The Opinion is This*, p. 3.
[79] *Animadversions on a Discourse entituled, God's Ways of Disposing of Kingdoms* (London, August [?] 1691), p. 38. Cf. *Inquiry . . . Legal Rights*, in *State Tracts*, vol. 2, p. 409.
[80] Grey, *Debates*, 9: 13.
[81] Masters, *The Case of Allegiance*, p. 13.
[82] *A Brief Account of the Nullity of King James's Title*, in *State Tracts*, vol. 1, p. 284.
[83] Locke, *Second Treatise*, pp. 419–27.
[84] Blount, *Proceedings*, p. 10. Cf. *The Doctrine of Passive Obedience*, in *State Tracts*, vol. 1, p. 368.

join William of Orange, was notable for his announcement that if James returned he would 'fight against him' and, if necessary, 'die' with his 'sword in his hand'.[85] In his view, using prayers and tears against arbitrary power was like binding Sampson's arms with 'cords'.[86]

Assisting Whig resistance thought were two ideas that had been condemned at the Restoration. One was the gloss placed on the legal maxim, 'The King Can Do No Wrong'. In the Convention Howard was the first to explain that the maxim had been miscontrued of late and that 'lawyers of old' like Bracton and Fortescue interpreted it to mean that when the king violates the law, he ceases to be a king and may be resisted. Sir William Polteney dismissed the maxim entirely as disproved by James's miscarriages.[87] Whig tract writers argued along the same lines, William Atwood adding that the maxim applied only to private persons, not to parliament, which had the authority to punish erring kings.[88]

The second was the notion of the king's two bodies. Masters explained that the nation's allegiance to James was only to him as king, not as a person, and that when he violated the law, he lost the 'Right' to and 'Power' of his office.[89] In the Convention, Polteney bluntly denied that it was a traitorous position to distinguish a king's person and his power, whatever the Restoration law said.[90]

Many Whigs conceived of the right to resist as a civil right of the people. Some, however, regarded resistance as a moral duty and a religious responsibility. In terms similar to those used in Reformation resistance tracts, Masters argued that resistance was a 'necessary duty'.[91] Other pamphleteers insisted that for a man to stand idly by in the face of tyranny was for him to be guilty of tyranny by association.[92] Johnson invoked the Bible (1 Samuel 8:18) to argue

---

[85] For these and other fighting words, see Robert Beddard, 'The unexpected Whig Revolution of 1688', *The Revolutions of 1688*, ed. Beddard, pp. 81–2.

[86] Delamere, *Works*, pp. 366, 367.

[87] Schwoerer, 'A Jornall', pp. 250, 255.

[88] Greenberg, 'Our Grand Maxim Of State', p. 227. Cf. Daniel Defoe, *Reflections upon the Late Great Revolution* (1689), pp. 3–4.

[89] Masters, *The Case of Allegiance*, pp. 15–16. Cf. *A Political Conference*, p. 30; *Doctrine of Passive Obedience*, in *State Tracts*, vol. 1, p. 368.

[90] Schwoerer, 'A Jornall', p. 255.

[91] Masters, *The Case of Allegiance*, p. 14.

[92] *The Doctrine of Passive Obedience*, in *State Tracts*, vol. 1, p. 370.

that God would give no comfort to such persons. If men will not resist a usurper, they must suffer.[93]

To buttress further their resistance theory, Whigs undertook to answer specific accusations levelled against them by Tories and Jacobites. To take but one example, a major charge (described by Burnet as the 'true difficulty')[94] was that in supporting the Revolution people had violated their oaths of allegiance to James II, thereby destroying the integrity of their conscience. One response was to appeal to reason: Masters advised that conscience must not be blindly 'follow[ed]', but rather 'inform[ed]' by reason and common sense.[95] Another argument was jurisprudential: England's government was based on law and no subject was bound to adhere to an oath to a king bent on destroying the law. The intention of the framers of the non-resistance oath was to protect the king and the 'whole Society', and so the oath applied only when the interests of monarch and people were conjoined. One writer offered a rule-of-thumb judgement: if an oath were 'repugnant to Piety, Justice or Charity' it was invalid.[96] The effect was to neutralise oaths and deny that they were promises sanctioned by God.

Whigs also attempted to undermine Tory and Jacobite use of Scripture as a capping argument by insisting upon a rational approach to the Bible. Defoe remarked in the spring of 1689 that Biblical citations should be used for rhetorical purposes only, and Johnson, reiterating the thought three years later, disparagingly remarked that 'the Bible is a Miscellaneous book, where dishonest and time-serving men may ever, in their loose way, find a Text for their purposes'.[97] But the Bible provided powerful backing to any argument and Whigs were ready with their own interpretation of key passages. For example, they represented Romans 13:1, a favourite text of Tories and Jacobites, which commanded 'every soul [to] be subject unto the higher powers', as God's instructions to the Jews not to disobey *lawful* authority, and as referring *only* to

---

[93] Johnson, *Reflection on the History of Passive Obedience*, p. 12.
[94] Burnet, *Enquiry into the Measures of Submission*, p. 5.
[95] Masters, *The Case of Allegiance*, pp. 1–2, 14–15.
[96] *A Dialogue between Two Friends*, in *State Tracts*, vol. 1, pp. 297, 298, 300.
[97] Daniel Defoe, *Reflections upon the Late Great Revolution*, in *State Tracts*, vol. 1, p. 251; Johnson, *Argument Proving*, p. 41.

lawful authority.[98] Whigs maintained that a rational reading of the Bible showed that God did not require subjects to destroy themselves in obeying a prince or to sit idly by while a prince acted illegally and violently.[99]

IV

Whigs travelled different theoretical routes to reach the end of justifying resistance. Their failure to develop a single theory mirrored their broader political views at the time of the Revolution and their party development in the years immediately following. The variety in their resistance theory well exemplifies the 'varieties of Whiggism' that John Pocock has helped us to discern.[100] Using multiple political languages, Whigs developed resistance ideas that diverged principally over certain key theoretical questions which they were unable to resolve. But, whether articulated in the language of natural rights or ancient constitutionalism,[101] Whig resistance theory was a radical construct when compared to Tory and Jacobite ideas about passive resistance and non-resistance. All Whigs sanctioned the right of the people (variously defined) to resist established authority under certain circumstances. Claiming this right was a defiant rejection of the political and religious policies and societal assumptions of Restoration England and of the intellectual suppositions of Tories and Jacobites. Whig resistance theory is another reason for rejecting the thesis that the Revolution of 1688–89 was an entirely conservative affair. On the other hand, nearly all Whig resistance theory, whatever the charges of Tories and Jacobites, was conservative in the restrictions it imposed on the right to resist. The usual polarities of 'radical' versus 'conservative' categories do not illumine Whig resistance theories.

All Whig versions of resistance theory reflected tension between

---

[98] A Dialogue between Two Friends, in State Tracts, vol. 1, p. 294. Johnson, Reflections on the History of Passive Obedience, p. 7.

[99] The Doctrine of Passive Obedience, in State Tracts, vol. 1, p. 370. A Dialogue between Two Friends, in State Tracts, vol. 1, p. 294. Pro popolo adversus, p. 12.

[100] J.G.A. Pocock, 'The varieties of Whiggism from Exclusion to Reform', Virtue, Commerce and History Essays on Political Thought and History, Chiefly in the Eighteenth Century (Cambridge 1985), pp. 215–310.

[101] Janelle Greenberg, 'The Confessor's Laws and the Radical Face of the Ancient Constitution', English Historical Review, 104 (1989): 611–37, underscores the radical implications of ancient constitutionalism.

a desire to sanction resistance to an erring prince and to preserve law and property. Their underlying argument was that of the right of self-preservation which can never be stripped from a person. Jurisprudential arguments, linked to the protection of law and property, lie also at the heart of Whig resistance theory. The right to resist is encircled with conditions that limit it (with one or two exceptions) to a 'defensive' response to the illegal actions of established authority. 'Defensive' resistance may legitimately occur (there is a qualifying nuance in Locke's work) *only* when the whole society is threatened by the prince's illegal acts. Those acts are the critical element; they transform the king into a tyrant; they dissolve the government; there is no resistance to a king. Legally, there can only be resistance to a tyrant, who has no treason laws to protect him. Resistance to a tyrant is not rebellion, but a civil right and, for some, a religious and moral imperative.

Whig resistance theory assumes that the people identify with the law and that the law serves their interests. If a king rules by laws that do not protect the liberty and property of a minority people, that minority enjoys no right of active resistance and is invited to emigrate. If a disaffected minority actively resists a king who rules by laws harmful to them, their resistance is rebellion, an act of treason. By distinguishing resistance from rebellion, Whig thinkers constructed a thesis that in practice was inapplicable to minorities and so failed to serve minority interests.

Whig resistance theory as articulated during and immediately after the Revolution had a long reach. It was heard in the early eighteenth century when the battle of ideas and words was renewed with increased vituperation. In 1705, Dr Benjamin Hoadly, the Latitudinarian cleric supportive of Whig causes, reacting to Tory and Jacobite ridicule of and challenge to the Revolutionary settlement and its justification, indignantly criticised the continuing view of the Revolution as a 'usurpation'.[102] Through Hoadly's works and such tracts as *The Judgment of Whole Kingdoms and Nations* (printed in 1710 in response to the uproar occasioned by the Sacheverell Trial),[103] Whig resistance theories were transmitted to

---

[102] Benjamin Hoadly, *The Measures of Submission To The Civil Magistrate Consider'd* (1706), pp. 19–21.

[103] *The Judgment of Whole Kingdoms and Nations, Concerning the Rights, Power, and Prerogative of Kings, and the Rights, Privileges, and Properties of the People* (1710), p. 46. The author was possibly Defoe: see Ashcraft and Goldsmith, 'Locke, Revolution Principles, and the Formation of Whig Ideology', pp. 796–800.

the 'Real Whigs' and so on to late-eighteenth-century radicals in Great Britain and the American colonies.[104] The former put them in the service of reform, the latter invoked them to legitimate another Revolution whose leaders, like their intellectual forebears, were intent upon making their resistance to established authority seem as legal as possible.

[104] Caroline Robbins, *The Eighteenth-Century Commonwealthman* (Cambridge, Mass., 1959).

CHAPTER 12

Placing the 'Two Treatises'

James Tully

Since the Laslett 'revolution' in Locke scholarship John Pocock and others have cleared away the myth of the dominant place of the *Treatises* in early modern political thought. The myth consists in eight false but widely held assumptions: that the *Treatises* are (1) the mainstream Whig apology for the revolution of 1688; (2) the synthesis of Whig political thought in the early 1680s; (3) the paradigm of radical Whig and eighteenth-century 'commonwealth' demands and idioms; (4) the dominant form of political thought in eighteenth-century Britain; (5) the ideology of early capitalism; (6) the basic text of liberalism; (7) the exclusive ideology of the American revolution; and finally, (8) the inescapable political thought of the United States.[1]

---

[1] J.G.A. Pocock, *The Ancient Constitution and the Feudal Law* (Cambridge, 1987), pp. 235–8, 353–65; *The Machiavellian Moment: Florentine Political Thought and the Atlantic Republican Tradition* (Princeton, 1975), pp. 423–4, 435–7, 456–7, 507, 516; 'The Myth of John Locke and the Obsession with Liberalism', in J.G.A. Pocock and Richard Ashcraft, *John Locke* (Los Angeles, 1980), pp. 1–24; 'John Locke and the 1680s', unpublished paper presented to the 'John Locke and the Political Thought of the 1680s' symposium of the Conference for the study of political thought and the Folger Institute for Renaissance and Eighteenth-Century Studies, Washington D.C. (21–23 March 1980); 'Cambridge Paradigms and Scotch Philosophers: A Study of the Relations between the Civil Humanist and the Civil Jurisprudential Interpretation of Eighteenth-Century Social Thought', in I. Hont and M. Ignatieff (eds.), *Wealth and Virtue: The Shaping of Political Economy in the Scottish Enlightenment* (Cambridge, 1983), pp. 235–52, at 239–40, 243–4, 251; 'Recent Scholarship on John Locke and the Political Thought of the Late Seventeenth Century – A Review Article', *Theoretische Geschiedenis*, 11,3 (1984), 251–61; 'Virtue, Rights, and Manners: A Model for Historians of Political Thought', *Virtue, Commerce, and History* (Cambridge, 1985), pp. 37–51; 'Authority and Property: The Question of Liberal Origins', in *Virtue*, pp. 103–24; 'The Varieties of Whiggism from Exclusion to Reform: A History of Ideology and Discourse', in *Virtue*, pp. 215–310, 217–18, 223–42, 258; 'Between Gog and Magog: The Republican Thesis and Ideologia Americana', *Journal of the History of Ideas*, 48, 2 (1987), 325–46; 'Transformations in British Political Thought', *Political Science*, 40, 1 (July 1988) 160–78, 169–74; 'Introduction', *Edmund Burke, Reflections on the Revolution in France* (Indianapolis, 1987), pp. vii–lvi, xii–xiii, xxvii, xlvii; 'States, Republics, and Empires: The American Founding in Early Modern Perspective', in T. Ball and J.G.A. Pocock, *Conceptual Change and the Constitution* (Lawrence, Kans. 1988), pp. 55–78, 58–9.

Pocock discovered a complex, non-Lockean republic of letters that had been neglected as a result of the 'assumption that everything in intellectual life after the year 1688 could be explained by his [Locke's] presence in the context'.[2] The ancient constitution and Harringtonian republicanism; a multidimensional 'dialectic' between virtue and the corruptions of commercial society and parliamentary patronage; liberal languages of manners, polish, politeness, civility, sympathy and sociality; and a 'republican synthesis' in America – all these came into view as the Locke myth receded. While the roles of Locke's other publications appeared 'authoritative' and 'incalculable', the *Treatises* seemed at first sight to be different from these languages and relatively marginal to them. Unconventional in the 1680s, they came into play in the eighteenth century when a theory of popular resistance was needed – with Molyneux in Ireland, the English radicals after 1770 and the American revolutionaries – and among the Scottish jurists.

This pluralistic picture of the formation of modern political thought was always presented by Pocock as a provisional and non-comprehensive series of sketches. Digs for traces of the *Treatises* on the site were temporarily prohibited until a better picture of non-Lockean forms of thought emerged, and warnings went up not to make new myths out of his heuristic classifications of the linguistic evidence into languages of virtue, rights, manners and so on. Then he invited others to join in 'redefining' the places of a non-mythical Locke in this motley landscape.

Pocock acknowledges that two anomalies in his classifications of linguistic data need to be resolved. First, whereas he classifies the ancient constitution and republicanism as different in kind from natural law and natural rights respectively, they are in fact used interchangeably in the same contexts, and often by the same author, from Milton to Jefferson. Second, he classifies Harrington and Sidney as different in kind from Locke (republican versus jurist), whereas writers from Defoe to Jefferson interpret all three authors as the same kind of theorists. Pocock has briefly noted four similarities that cut across his classifications and thus explain both anomalies. He has marked them as 'suggestive' and worthy of study.[3] Without diminishing the dissimilarities he has unearthed, I

---

[2] 'John Locke', p. 1.
[3] 'Myth of Locke', p. 12; cf. 'Authority and property', p. 67.

would like to approach the same labyrinth from the perspective of these four similarities and use them to draw the non-mythical *Treatises* into the picture.

Four aspects of the *Treatises* that are similar to ancient constitutional and republican writing are: the forms of government and property in the state of nature; the social history of their development; their modern or 'civilised' forms; and the way modern government is limited. I will summarise these and then draw on them throughout the essay.

In the state of nature people exercise political power directly in forms of self-government. All have the right and civic duty to judge alleged violations of the laws of nature in *ad hoc* tribunals and execute their judgements with punishments appropriate to the violation and sufficient for reparation. They also have the right to exercise their labour power and appropriate the products of their labour without the consent of others. This gives rise to property rights within the laws of nature, which are enforced through the *ad hoc* system of government. The labour-based system of property initially develops on the base of a hunting and gathering economy, marked by fixed consumption, replacement production and low population growth. It persists with some changes through the transition to an agricultural economy in which vacant land is appropriated without the consent of others and rights are acquired in it by means of agricultural improvement.

Second, a history of social, economic, demographic and psychological changes explains the transition to modern systems of institutionalised government and property. Hunting and gathering are supplemented by domestication of animals, agriculture and applied arts; population increases, trade widens, money is introduced, and self-love and the elastic desire for more than one needs come to structure human motivation and so disrupt the pre-monetary stage of limited desire and fixed needs. People seek to enlarge their possessions, either by an ethic of industriousness and agricultural improvement, in which they sell their surplus on the emerging market for money, or by misusing political power to expropriate the property of others. Available land becomes scarce, disputes break out over land title and appropriation without consent. People reform their system of government and property, introducing temporary kings or chiefs for war-fighting and councils for internal affairs of kin-groups and small nations, but the system itself is inadequate to cope with the property disputes and insecurities that arise.

Third, people then make the transition to modern forms of government and property. They form 'political societies' out of the temporary monarchies and councils, first on familial affection and trust, then by consenting to form communities and conditionally entrusting their political powers to institutionalised monarchies and representative legislatures, so that they have 'a common established law and judicature to appeal to, with authority to decide controversies between them and punish offenders'.[4] Similarly, they give up their right to appropriate without consent so that the complexities of appropriation, ownership, and trade can be regulated by a legal system which establishes territorially defined sovereignty, fixed and registered property in land and a common dispute procedure. The legal system is designed to preserve property and regulate it in accordance with the public good.

Fourth, the new system of states and property law solves the disputes that undermined the earlier system but it has its own problem. Everyone is affected by self-love and the desire for more than is needed; flattery, luxury and ambition corrupt governments and lead to abuses of power. The history of political societies is marked by the rise of corrupt monarchies and representative bodies and by attempts to check, limit and balance them. In addition to these internal mechanisms, the people place a limit on their governors derived from part of the old system of self-government which continues as the foundation of the new. The people entrust their power to government subject to three conditions: that it is exercised lawfully, subject to their representatives' consent, and bound by natural law. The people impose these constitutional limits on government by the duty and right of judging whether they have been violated, and, if they have, by punishing the violators with removal, just as they would judge and punish a violator in the state of nature.

I

If these four aspects are placed in the Exclusion debate one can see why natural law and ancient constitutional arguments are used

---

[4] John Locke, *Two Treatises of Government*, ed. Peter Laslett (Cambridge, 1962), 2.87 (spelling modernised).

interchangeably by writers such as James Tyrrell and Algernon Sidney, and why a number of writers throughout the early modern period say that natural law and the ancient constitution are the same.[5] First, the system of *ad hoc* government is similar to pre-Norman and Saxon liberties and English birth-rights in ancient-constitutional and republican writings such as the *Mirrour of Justice* (which identifies the two and is recommended by Locke), Nathaniel Bacon's history of Saxon liberties, Harrington's armed proprietors, and Henry Neville's *communitas militum*. In both types of account, political power and property derive from the people, not the king. Second, the type of history in which the development of government and property is related to underlying social changes is employed by ancient constitutional republicans and natural-law Whigs alike: Tyrrell, William Temple, William Atwood, Sidney, Neville and John Wildman among others. Notwithstanding the enormous differences, there is no reason why Locke's type of history should not be interpreted as 'Harringtonian' in this regard. Third, similar accounts of modern systems of government and property by Locke and these authors serve a similar purpose: to ground the independence of property from the king and to subject the exercise of power to consent and limitations.

Locke himself shows how natural law and ancient constitutional analyses complement each other. According to the ancient constitution, institutions such as country courts, the Commons, conjoint sovereignty, and freehold property in Common law are seen as emanations of Saxon liberties. The Norman Conquest superimposed over these an illegitimate double yoke: absolute monarchy and a system of property that emanates from William's feudal right of conquest. This feudal system of kingship and property is defended by Robert Brady and Robert Filmer. Locke reasserts the popular origins of property in response to Filmer's criticism and attacks Filmer's feudal theory that property derives from royal sovereignty. In 'Of Conquest' he takes up the Norman Conquest. Many people base the English monarchy on the Conquest and conclude that it is absolute, but, Locke states, the historical argument is against it, thereby endorsing the ancient constitutional

---

[5] See Richard Ashcraft, *Revolutionary Politics and Locke's Two Treatises of Government* (Princeton, 1986), pp. 181–227, especially pp. 189–90, 210–12, 217, 222; and Pocock's discussion, *Ancient Constitution*, pp. 357–62, 'Recent Scholarship', p. 256. I am indebted to both authors in this section.

thesis of his close Whig associates, Atwood, Tyrrell and William Petyt. Then he shows that a natural-law argument can make the identical point. If William had 'a right to make war on this island', as the absolutists claim, conquest would have entitled him to despotical (non-consensual) power only over the lives of Saxons and Britons who fought against him; not over Normans who came with him nor over non-combatants and future generations of Saxons and Britons. Neither would William have had any sovereignty over the prevailing system of property, even of those who fought against him, nor any right to dispossess future generations. Locke employs the 'continuity theory' of conquest of British imperial constitutional law – which holds that the legal and political institutions of the conquered survive a conquest – to overthrow the Norman yoke.[6] Hence, although Pocock is right to observe that Locke 'displays little or no interest in the antiquity of the Commons, not much more in the problem of the Norman Conquest, and none to speak of in the history of feudal tenure', it is just enough in the context to make it clear that his natural-law arguments, like those of other exclusionists, are addressed to these very issues.[7]

The fourth aspect – the scheme of consent, limit and resistance – is central to 'radical' Whig and republican writers of the early 1680s and 1689 as well. Pocock has shown that much of the debate from 1642 to 1689 was organised around the question of whether sovereignty was held conjointly by king, Lords and Commons or absolutely by the king. Conjoint sovereignty could be proven historically by showing the antiquity of the Commons.[8] Notwithstanding, Locke points out, there is no remedy within the English conjoint constitution of king-in-parliament if the king overrides the powers of parliament and, *eo ipso*, dissolves the constitution, as Charles did in March 1681 by dissolving parliament and ruling without it, and James did in 1687 and 1688. To acquiesce is just to concede royal sovereignty, to call on parliament to act is to grant it sovereignty, and no constitutional court of appeal exists. The way to preserve or restore the constitution of conjoint sovereignty is to have an outside body judge and redress the dispute: namely, the

[6] Locke, *Treatises* 2.177–80. Contrast Pocock, *Ancient Constitution*, p. 237.
[7] Pocock, *Ancient Constitution*, p. 354.
[8] Pocock, 'Recent Scholarship', pp. 253–6; 'Authority and Property', p. 66; 'Varieties of Whiggism', pp. 218–23, *Ancient Constitution*, pp. 308–12, 348–9.

people.[9] It is not surprising, then, to find Locke, who upholds the conjoint sovereignty of king-in-parliament, and the majority of Whigs and republicans employing the language of consent, limit and resistance to restore the constitution.[10]

The move, Locke recalls, was forced on them by the Tories' publication of Filmer's defence of absolute monarchy in which he eliminated all elements of popular consent and limitation.[11] Filmer argued that the leading defence of conjoint sovereignty was one based on a theory of consent, limit and resistance. He then cited the major exponents of such a view, including Grotius and many mainstream writers, and criticised them. This structured the debate around two possible answers and the Whigs simply turned to the broad tradition of respectable authorities Filmer had unwittingly created for them by casting his critical net so widely. Locke rested his 'radical' right to resist on the authority of the royalist William Barclay.

The *Treatises* were read as a theory of consent, limit and resistance partly because it was associated with one interpretation of the 1688 revolution. When it was rewritten and published in 1689 it formed part of the 'radical' Whig interpretation. The official interpretation, put out in 1689 after considerable arm-twisting in the Convention and embraced by the mainstream Whig oligarchy, was that no dissolution of government occurred and the Convention was simply a parliament. The more radical interpretation was that James's absolutism dissolved the government, the Convention was therefore a constituent assembly, and William, in assenting to the Bill of Rights, recognised the consensual or contractual limits of his power.[12]

Pocock finds the *Treatises* atypical of radical Whig and commonwealth political thought for three reasons. First, he suggests that the dissolution of government entails the dissolution of the constitu-

---

[9] Locke, *Treatises*, 2.149–52. See Julian Franklin, *John Locke and the Theory of Sovereignty* (Cambridge, 1978) and Pocock, 'Recent Scholarship', pp. 252–3, 'John Locke', p. 4, 'Varieties of Whiggism', pp. 223, 225.

[10] 'Consent, limit, and resistance' is the majority language in the Whig literature of Exclusion and 1689 according to Ashcraft, *Revolutionary*, p. 190n, and Mark Goldie, 'The Revolution of 1689 and the Structure of Political Argument', *Bulletin of Research in the Humanities*, 83 (Winter 1980) 473-564, 489; and Pocock, 'Varieties of Whiggism', p. 224.

[11] Locke, *Treatises*, 1.126.

[12] Mark Goldie, 'The Revolution' and 'The Roots of True Whiggism 1688–94', *History of Political Thought*, 1, 2 (June, 1980), 195–236.

tion in Locke's theory, and, accordingly, that it is incompatible with an (indissoluble) ancient constitution.[13] It is true that a prominent Whig, Atwood, repudiated the *Treatises* on this ground, but such a Hobbesian interpretation is a commonplace of the official attacks on dissolution theories in general. Furthermore, the thrust of the theory runs in the other direction. A monarch who rules without limits threatens to dissolve the constitution, whereas the people, in resisting this, preserve it. Such a ruler dissolves the trust between himself and the people, placing himself in a state of nature with respect to them, like a criminal, yet the constitutional and legal structure of society continues in force. Therefore, Locke's 'moderate' theory of dissolution of government can be compatible with the ancient constitution, which itself continues through various changes in persons and forms of government.

Second, Locke leaves the powers to reform representation and to call and dissolve parliament with the executive, which also has the discretion to act against the law for the sake of the public good. The only check on these prerogatives is the right of the people to judge and resist if they are used against the public good. A demand of radical constitutionalism, on the other hand, is constitutionally entrenched annual parliaments.[14] Notwithstanding this difference, although Locke says he will not address the question of 'whether periods of the legislative should be left to prerogative or set constitutionally', he actually favours the conventional English system for two reasons: the contingencies of events and need to assemble are too variable for a set period, and the prerogative system has worked well in the past in the long run. The reason the people and not the legislature must check the abuse of prerogative in the last instance is that Locke takes for granted the customary English 'self-checking' constitution of king-in-parliament, in which the legislature cannot act as superior to the king without dissolving the constitution.[15] These are classic historical and constitutional arguments, perhaps written to show his republican associates that

---

[13] Pocock, 'Myth of Locke', pp. 4–6; 'Recent Scholarship', pp. 251–3, 256–8; 'Authority', p. 65; 'Varieties of Whiggism', pp. 217–18, 223–32, 258; 'Transformations', pp. 170–2.

[14] Pocock, 'Varieties of Whiggism', pp. 227–8; *Ancient Constitution*, p. 361.

[15] Locke, *Treatises*, 2.160–7. In Locke's (and Britain's) system of king-in-parliament the king checks factional politics in parliament, the basic flaw in republics and democracies, and the parliament checks the separate interests of the king, the basic flaw in absolute monarchies. Only if this internal mechanism fails do the people act.

their ahistorical and abstract demand is out of line with the conventions of ancient constitutionalism.

Third, Locke does not focus on executive corruption. This type of corruption is presented in an idiom which prefigures eighteenth-century debates, according to Pocock, in *A Letter from a Person of Quality* (1675). This is a somewhat unsettling element in the non-Lockean interpretation of classical republicanism because the author has always been assumed, but not proven, to be Locke. Pocock's interpretation, I believe, is that the analysis of executive corruption may not have been written by Locke and, more importantly, that the same sort of analysis is absent from the *Treatises*.[16] Yet the argument of the *Letter* is that the best means to check the temptation to executive corruption is the threat of resistance and this is repeated in the *Treatises*. Moreover, the terms and history Locke presents of how ambition, luxury and flattery 'taught princes to have distinct and separate interests from their people' and how the people found 'out ways to restrain the exorbitances' are similar to those in later varieties of Whiggism.[17]

Under the prevailing mythical interpretation of the text as an ahistorical theory of liberal individualism these similarities were difficult to see, partly because rights were interpreted as liberties or trumps, shielding the individual against interference. This interpretation makes it appear that rights are in opposition to civic duties of republicanism.[18] However, as I have tried to show, the primary *use* of rights by Locke and republican–Whig writers is to constrain or limit the king or parliament to act within a known and recognised constitutional structure of lawfulness: to subject their governors to the rule of law by exercising their rights.[19] From the perspective of this 'constitution-enforcing' conception of rights, the central distinction is not between republicanism and rights – for the problem of the people subjecting rulers to the rule of law is at the

---

[16] Pocock, *Machiavellian Moment*, pp. 406–16; 'Varieties of Whiggism', p. 226.
[17] Locke, *Treatises*, 2.106, 107, 110–12, 162.
[18] This is precisely Pocock's point in 'Myth of Locke', 'Authority and Property', 'Mobility of Property', 'Beyond Gog', 'Virtue, Rights, and Manners', and 'Cambridge Paradigms'.
[19] This constitution-enforcing conception of rights emerged during the trial of John Hampden in 1637 and the demands of participation, liberty and popular defence were made in its terms in the Civil War and Bill of Rights. Richard P. Claude, 'The Classical Model of Human Rights Development', *Comparative Human Rights* (Baltimore, 1976), pp. 6–50, especially pp. 12–20.

heart of the republican tradition as well – but between a system in which the people are passive subjects ('slaves'), as in the theories of Filmer and other absolutists, and one based on consent in which the people engage in governing their governors, as in the theories of Milton, Harrington, Sidney and Locke.[20]

II

Once Pocock had laid out his sketches of eighteenth-century political debates and removed mythical assumptions (4), (5) and (6), he correctly conjectured that Locke's other writings had an incalculable influence. Scholars have since confirmed that most of the themes of the commercial society literature were formulated with multiple references to Locke's writings on psychology and motivation, history, ethics, epistemology, natural law, political economy, religion, education, explanation of behaviour, labour and sociology of manners.[21] It is also possible to see that the *Treatises* played significant roles in the debates in addition to the ones first noted by Pocock.

Although the *Treatises* are not 'republican' in the senses Pocock has delineated, they are linked with Sidney's republican *Discourses* throughout the century.[22] Whigs associated both with the unofficial interpretation of 1688 and read them as theories of how executive and parliamentary corruption could be held in check by the bridle of popular consent, limit and resistance. This reading was disseminated by Daniel Defoe. Pocock underscores the importance of Defoe as 'the ideologist of the Whig order' while highlighting the non-Lockean aspects of his writings. [23] Yet, from the complementary perspective of consent, limit, and resistance, Defoe is, as Goldie discerns, 'Locke's later populariser'.[24]

[20] The same connection between Locke and the republican tradition is drawn by Quentin Skinner in 'The State', in T. Ball, J. Farr and R.L. Hanson (eds.), *Political Innovation and Conceptual Change* (Cambridge, 1989), pp. 90–131, 114–16.
[21] Such as Stephen Buckle, John Dunn, Knud Haakonssen, Istvan Hont, Michael Ignatieff, John Marshall, Ronald Meek, James Moore, Michael Silverthorne, David Norton, Barbara Shapiro and Charles Taylor.
[22] Caroline A. Robbins, *The Eighteenth-Century Commonwealthman* (Cambridge, Mass., 1959); discussed by Pocock, 'Varieties of Whiggism', especially p. 260 where he warns against 'a naive and crude antithesis between republican and Lockean forms of radicalism'.
[23] Pocock, 'Myth of Locke', p. 15.
[24] Goldie, 'The Revolution of 1689', p. 509. Cf. Ashcraft, *Revolutionary*, pp. 565–6, and R. Ashcraft and M.M. Goldsmith, 'Locke, Revolution Principles and the Formation of Whig Ideology', *Historical Journal*, 26, 4 (1983), 773–800. Pocock notes the complementarity at 'Varieties of Whiggism', p. 228 n.45 and 'Transformations', p. 172.

When Hume criticised an extreme version of consent theory, he modestly called it a 'complete refutation of the political systems of Sidney, Locke, and the Whigs, which all the half philosophers of the nation have implicitly embraced for nearly a century'.[25] In addition to substantiating the popularity of Locke and Sidney, Hume set out the extreme 'Atwoodian' version of consent theory that was used as a strawperson by later critics and as a stalking-horse by later radicals. Among the 'half philosophers' were the respectable republican Whigs of Scotland who praised Locke and Sidney and defended the moderate version of their common theory of consent, limit and resistance as they found it presented by Jean Barbeyrac in his authoritative notes to Pufendorf's *On the Law of Nature and Nations*.[26] The *Treatises* were republished in this republic–Whig milieu in 1764.[27] In 1781, Josiah Tucker praised the moderate version of Locke's theory that government rests on consent and trust and the right to resist flagrant abuses of power. He went on to criticise the extreme version – that individual consent is universally required – and associated this interpretation with Molyneaux, the London radicals and the American revolutionaries, linking them to republicans like Andrew Fletcher. He was never quite sure if the extreme or the moderate version was Locke's own view.[28] Thomas Elrington published an annotated edition of the *Treatises* in 1798 to defend the moderate interpretation and save Locke from his critics and self-proclaimed radical followers alike – to distinguish 'between the system of Locke and the theories of modern democrats'.[29]

Pocock correctly concluded that Locke's analysis of property did

[25] Letter to Lord Elibank in 1748 on 'Of the Original Contract', E.G. Mossner, 'New Hume Letters of Lord Elibank', *Texas Studies in Language and Literature*, 4, 3 (1962), cited in James Moore, 'John Locke and the Scottish Jurists', unpublished paper presented to the 'John Locke and the Political Thought of the 1680s' symposium (1980), p. 20. I am indebted to this important article in this section. It is noted by Pocock, 'Cambridge Paradigms', p. 251.
[26] Jean Barbeyrac (ed.), *Samuel Pufendorf, On the law of nature and nation*, trans. of the 1706 edition (1726), 7.8.6. (p. 720) n.1. Moore, 'Locke', p. 22.
[27] John Locke, *Two Treatises of Government*, ed. Thomas Hollis (London, 1764). See Moore, 'Locke', pp. 30–1.
[28] Josiah Tucker, *A Treatise concerning Civil Government in Three Parts* (1781), (London, 1967); discussed by Pocock, 'Josiah Tucker' and 'Varieties of Whiggism', p. 263. Tucker mentions the followers of the moderate interpretation at p. i, praises it at pp. 3–5, and raises his doubts at pp. ii–iv.
[29] John Locke, *An Essay concerning the True Original Extent and End of Civil Government*, annotated and ed. by Thomas Elrington (Dublin, 1798).

not play a role in the conceptualisation of credit, speculation and mobile property in the debates over virtue and commercial society. Recently, however, scholars have shown that Locke's history of property and government plays significant roles. Gershom Carmichael, Francis Hutcheson and Adam Smith worked out the shared picture of the development of commercial society with reference to Barbeyrac's editions of Pufendorf. In his notes Barbeyrac argued that Locke presents a superior account of the history of property and the *Treatises* entered the debate by this route.[30]

The first trope Locke vouchsafes is his premise that 'in the beginning all the world was America'.[31] This grounds the convention that all societies in the world are the same at the beginning and can be ranked on one scale of world-historical development. Amerindian societies are by definition primitive and can be studied to see what politics and property were like at the beginning of European society. On top are European societies, 'civilised' by virtue of their property and state formations.[32] This Eurocentric convention enframes the eighteenth-century debate and theories of development to this day.

The second convention is that Amerindian societies are based on hunting and gathering. The aboriginal peoples have rights only in what they catch, gather and cultivate, and anyone has the right to appropriate uncultivated land without consent. Therefore, Locke concludes, Europeans have the right to settle, cultivate and acquire rights in land in the 'vacant place of America' without the consent of the native peoples, who have no 'reason to complain or think themselves injured by this man's incroachment'. If the native people resist, they violate natural law and 'may be destroyed as a lion or tiger, one of those wild savage beasts'.[33] The argument, which is spliced into the chapter on conquest, serves to justify English colonisation in America: to dispossess aboriginal peoples of their land, on the ground that they have no rights to it because they do not cultivate, and no sovereignty because they lack institution-

---

[30] Barbeyrac, *On the Law*, 4.4.4. (p. 365), n.4. Moore, 'Locke'; and Istvan Hont, 'Needs and Justice in the *Wealth of Nations*', in I. Hont and M. Ignatieff (eds.), *Wealth and Virtue*, pp. 26–43.

[31] Locke, *Treatises*, 2.49. (This premise is not original to Locke.) For its role in the eighteenth century see Ronald Meek, *Social science and the Ignoble Savage* (Cambridge, 1976); discussed by Pocock, 'Mobility of Property', p. 116, and 'Cambridge Paradigms', p. 242.

[32] Locke, *Treatises*, 2.30.

[33] Locke, *Treatises*, 2.36–7, 11. Cf. 1.130–1.

alised 'political societies', and to 'destroy' them by war if they resist, because resistance proves them to be 'savages'. This is one of the most contentious issues of the era and, as Locke repeats throughout the chapter, his theory of appropriation without consent solves it. The form of justification Locke advances is called the agriculturalist argument. It was employed by English colonists and propagandists from the 1620s on. Locke and Emeric de Vattel (in 1758) are recognised as its two most influential proponents.[34]

The right to appropriate without consent in America is the feature of Locke's theory that the Scottish theorists single out as superior to Pufendorf's argument that consent is required. As Smith typically comments, 'in North America . . . where the age of hunters subsists, theft is not much regarded. As there is almost no property amongst them, the only injury that can be done is the depriving them of their game.'[35] Whether or not they were aware of the use to which it was standardly put, they wove this Lockean thread into the fabric of their Eurocentric theories of modernisation.

The third convention Locke transmits is the superiority of European commercial agriculture to Amerindian hunting and gathering. He advances many of the arguments used throughout the debate by both agricultural republicans and commercialists: commercial agriculture uses the land more efficiently (versus Amerindian 'waste'), supports a larger population, engenders the division of labour and trade and, the most influential standard of modern times, produces more commodities. When Locke tries to explain why anyone would engage in commercial agriculture rather than hunting, gathering and replacement agriculture, he answers that only 'the hopes of commerce with other parts of the world, to draw money to him by the sale of the product' can explain it. Smith's explanation is: the 'opportunity of commerce, and consequently, . . . [the] opportunity of increasing their wealth by

34 Emeric de Vattel, *The Law of Nations or the Principles of Natural Law*, trans. C.G. Fenwick (Washington, 1902), 1.8.81, 1.18.207–10. I have discussed Locke's arguments and their roles in the justification of dispossession of the American Indian in 'Rediscovering America: John Locke and Aboriginal Title', unpublished paper presented to the tercentennial symposium on John Locke, Christ Church, Oxford, 4–7 September 1990 (to be edited by John Rogers and published by Oxford University Press).
35 Adam Smith, *Lectures on Jurisprudence*, ed. R.L. Meek, D.D. Raphael, and L.G. Stein (Indianapolis, 1982) 1.33 (p. 16). See Moore, 'Locke', for more examples.

industry'.[36] Locke's description of commercial agriculture as a superior ethic of the 'industrious' and 'rational' 'improvement' of 'waste-land' provides some of the stock images of the later debate in Britain and America.

Finally, one criterion Pocock used to differentiate the mythical Locke from the debates over commercial society is his 'indifference to virtue'.[37] Yet non-mythical Locke, like many of his contemporaries, treats civic virtue similarly to later apologists of commercial society who argued that it belongs to an earlier age. In his educational writings he attacks the Renaissance cult of virtue, glorification of war, cruelty and reputation, saying it is immoral and inappropriate to the instrumental use of war and the politics of 'preservation' of modern times. In the *Treatises* he locates love of virtue in the early age of direct government and uses its presence to explain how the system, which depends on participation and dedication to the public good, works. With money, population, and the desire for more than one needs, self-love undermines the system and gives rise to political corruption and the need for institutions, checks and enforced public duties to replace the decay of virtue.[38]

III

In challenging myths (7) and (8), Pocock has never denied the importance of the *Treatises* to the American patriots in justifying their revolt. He accepts the view that it is a major language of the revolution and of its authoritative justification, Jefferson's *Declaration of Independence*.[39] Like Bailyn, he seeks to show that non-Lockean languages of republicanism also played a significant role in America throughout the eighteenth century and did not disappear in the nineteenth.[40] I would like to point out some roles of the

---

[36] Locke, *Treatises*, 2.48–9; and Smith, *Lectures*, iv.61 (p. 223).

[37] Pocock, 'Myth of Locke', 18, 'Virtue, Rights, and Manners', p. 48, 'Cambridge Paradigms', p. 248.

[38] Locke, *Treatises*, reading 2.110–11 along with 2.12–13 and 124–6.

[39] Pocock, *Machiavellian Moment*, p. 516; 'Myth of Locke', p. 8; 'Between Gog', p. 339; 'Varieties of Whiggism', p. 267; 'Transformations', p. 175; 'States, Republics', pp. 58–9; (especially) 'Introduction', p. xiv, n. 24.

[40] Bernard Bailyn, *The Ideological Origins of the American Revolution* (Cambridge, Mass., 1967); Pocock, *Machiavellian Moment*, pp. 506–52; 'Between Gog', p. 41.

Treatises in this more complex picture, drawing attention again to areas of overlap.

To appreciate these roles it is necessary to understand the controversies over title to land in America that Locke thought he had solved. The dispossession of native Americans of their land rested on four distinct and conflicting titles.[41] The first was the Lockean claim that Europeans were entitled to the land they cultivated without native consent. It was normally supplemented by a deed of purchase with resident natives, which could then be registered under colonial law. The purchase (superfluous on Lockean grounds) was explained as necessary to mollify the otherwise contentious Indians. Colonial governments supported this title by giving preference to actual settlement and cultivation, whether legal or not, where it did not conflict with their own grants.

A land grant from a colonial government is the second form of title. The authority of the colonial government could be based on a grant from the crown in the case of proprietary colonies. This created a class of proprietors in conflict with the settlers who preferred to work their own land and claimed title under the agriculturist argument. One remarkable conflict of this type was the 1719 rebellion in Carolina. Settlers overthrew the system of property controlled by the proprietary government, which was set up by Shaftesbury and Locke in 1668, and placed the colony under crown rule. John Norris based his justification of the revolt against Locke's constitution on the *Treatises*.[42] The rebellion against large land grants in New Jersey in 1747 is another instance in which the *Treatises* are cited to justify revolt.[43]

The independent authority of a colonial assembly to grant land was often based on a stretch of the *Treatises*: the right of people to migrate, conquer and form independent political societies was used to underwrite the 'compact' theory of colonial independence. Coupled with the denial of native land rights, the assembly had full title.[44] These grants created a class of landowners often in conflict

---

[41] See Tully, 'Rediscovering America' for background and further references to this section.
[42] John Norris, *The Liberty and Property of British Subjects Asserted in a Letter from an Assemblyman in Carolina to his Friend in London* (London, 1726).
[43] *New Jersey Archives*, first series, 5.7 (1746–51) 42, cited in Stanley Dowertz, *The Unvarnished Doctrine: Locke, Liberalism and the American Revolution* (Durham, N.C., 1990), p. 211, n. 35.
[44] James Otis, *Rights of the British Colonies Asserted and Proved* (Boston, 1764), pp. 25–31; and Thomas Jefferson, below.

with the poorer settlers and with rival elites bearing title from an adjacent colony claiming jurisdiction over the same land.[45]

On the third title, an individual or a company of speculators would purchase tracts of land from a native sachem on the assumption that the first nations possessed aboriginal title to their territory and thus could alienate lots of it. Roger William's use of this deed title was contested by agriculturist arguments in the most celebrated non-native land struggle of the seventeenth century.[46] Conflicting 'deed games' became common as land speculators poured into the western lands in the 1740s. Samuel Wharton, whose notorious land speculation companies involved large tracts of land claimed by Virginia, argued the strongest case in *Plain Facts* (1781).[47] After citing Grotius, Pufendorf and colonial history, he argues (against the standard interpretation) that Locke's natural right to the means of preservation gives the Indians a natural (alienable) right to their hunting territories, and thus that the taking of their land must be based on agreements. Disputes broke out among farmers bearing the agriculturist title, land speculators bearing deeds from Indians or colonial assemblies, and the first nations claiming sovereignty.

Standing above these conflicting claims is the crown's exclusive title to land in British North America based on the theory of discovery and continuity in imperial constitutional law.[48] On crown title, native American societies are recognised as independent, sovereign nations. In virtue of discovery the crown has the sole right, exclusive of all other European nations, to trade with the first nations and acquire Indian lands. Since native sovereignty survives or 'continues' through discovery, native land is acquired by the crown through treaties. To be valid the treaties must be between the crown representatives and native sachems, in public, and not negotiated under duress. Valid cession extinguishes native

[45] See Georgina C. Nammack, *Fraud, Politics, and the Dispossession of the Indians* (Norman, Okla., 1968); and below.

[46] Francis Jennings, *The Invasion of America: Indians, Colonialism and the Cant of Conquest* (New York, 1975), pp. 128–45.

[47] Samuel Wharton, *Plain Facts: Being an Examination into the Rights of the Indian Nations of America to their Respective Countries, and a Vindication of the Grant from the Six United Nations* . . . (Philadelphia, 1781), pp. 7, 15. See Robert A. Williams, *The American Indian in Western Legal Thought: The Discourse of Conquest* (Oxford, 1990), pp. 257–64, 277–9, 288–9, 298–300.

[48] See Bruce Clark, *Native Liberty, Crown Sovereignty: The Existing Aboriginal Right of Self-Government in Canada* (Montreal, 1990); R.L. Barsh and J.Y. Henderson, *The Road: Indian Tribes and Political Liberty* (Berkeley, 1980), pp. 31–61.

title, activates crown title, and the crown then grants land to non-natives. Unceded land remains under native jurisdiction. All non-native land in America derives from the crown, as in feudal law, but as the result of treaties, not conquest. By 1776 hundreds of treaties had been signed in the colonies, while western lands and several areas within the colonies remained unceded and reserved as Indian lands. The crown did not recognise the right of colonial assemblies to grant land and the continual friction between royal governors and colonial legislators, and their respective landholding elites, was a major cause of the revolution.

The security of the British empire in America depended upon the assistance of the native nations, especially the Iroquois confederacy, for survival, military support against the French and commercial partnership in trade from Florida to Hudson's Bay. This delicate balance of native, French and British power was continuously threatened by settlers, speculators and colonial assemblies encroaching on Indian lands and causing the natives to defend their property by force of arms and to support the French. The purpose of centralising property allotment under crown title was thus to protect the first nations from the unbridled land-hunger of the colonists in order to secure the stability of the imperial system as a whole. The effect was to alienate the colonials whose land titles did not derive from the crown.[49]

In a precedent-setting case from the 1690s to 1740s (currently in court again) the Mohegan nation appealed to the Privy Council to recognise their sovereignty and prohibit the taking of their land by the colony of Connecticut. Two Royal Commissions (1705, 1743) found in favour of Mohegan sovereignty.[50] The strongest case against native sovereignty was written by John Bulkley in 1724.[51] After introducing the famous Mr Locke he denies sovereignty to native Americans on the ground that they lack political societies and justifies the right of Europeans to settle and cultivate without consent. He explains that once settlers introduced money the Indians developed a desire for more than they needed and claimed

---

[49] Jack M. Sosin, *Whitehall and the Wilderness: The Middle West in British Colonial Policy, 1760–1775* (Lincoln, 1961).

[50] J.H. Smith, *Appeals to the Privy Council from the American Plantations* (New York, 1950), pp. 417–42.

[51] John Bulkley, 'An Inquiry into the Right of the Aboriginal Natives to Land in America' (1724), in Roger Wolcott, *Poetical Meditations* (New London, Conn., 1725).

prior title to the land the industrious settlers cultivated, thus causing the quarrels and contentions. The entire case is based on detailed quotation and paraphrase of the relevant sections of the *Treatises* (aspects 1–3 above). In 1743 William Samuel Johnson repeated the Lockean argument that the Mohegan lack sovereignty because they lack institutionalised political societies and added that they are 'savages' resembling 'Lyons, Wolves or Beasts' with whom the English may thus use force.[52]

As the Iroquois and British defeated the French in the Seven Years War more settlers and land speculators transgressed Indian lands on the frontier and colonies advanced conflicting claims. The nations of the Northwest united under the leadership of the Ottawa chief Pontiac and rose in defence of their property. To protect natives and interlopers alike, the crown, in the Royal Proclamation of October 1763, drew a boundary down the backs of the colonies from Canada to East Florida and proclaimed territories to the west to be under native sovereignty. All settlement was to proceed under the crown title treaty system, settlers west of the boundary were ordered to move back, land speculation (involving many of the revolutionary leaders) was nullified and Virginia's charter claim to western land truncated.[53] When settlers and speculators transgressed the boundary and caused further hostilities, the crown responded with the Quebec Act of 1774. Based on the conquest and continuity theory, it recognised the right of French Canada to its religion (Catholicism) and legal system (the civil law). Further, because the French Canadians were traders, not settlers, and adopted native ways, and so were trusted by the Indians, they were put in charge of the military and trading forts that ran down the 1763 boundary, and the western lands were annexed to Canada.[54] Henceforth, the imperial constitution became a federation of native, French Canadian and British layered sovereignty (the constitutional basis of Canada). Finally, parliament enacted legislation to finance the debt from the Seven Years War and the costs

---

[52] Smith, *Appeals*, pp. 434–5, n.109.

[53] Jack Stagg, *Anglo-Indian Relations in North America to 1763 and an Analysis of the Royal Proclamation of 7 October 1763* (Ottawa, 1980). For the reaction of land speculators, including Benjamin Franklin and George Washington, see Francis Jennings, *Empire of Fortune: Crowns, Colonies and Tribes in the Seven Years War in America* (New York, 1988); Sosin, *Whitehall*, pp. 79–127, 181–210, 239–58, and Williams, *The American Indian*, pp. 233–325.

[54] *The Quebec Act*, Geo. III cap.83, Adam Shortt and A.G. Doughty (eds.), *Documents Relating to the Constitutional History of Canada* (Ottawa, 1907) 2 vols., vol. I, pp. 406–9.

of securing the system from both the Spanish in the south and the defiant rebels within. From the perspective of the patriots, the whole attempt to consolidate the four conflicting land titles under crown title and recognise native and French Canadian forms of government and religion was seen as 'a posture of hostility', and rebellion followed.[55]

Turning to the ways in which the *Treatises* were used to address these issues in the revolutionary literature, I should like to start with Thomas Jefferson. The first feature of his writing is the reassertion of the convention of using both ancient-constitutional and natural-law genres in *A Summary View of the Rights of British America* (1774).[56] This convention is also upheld by another Locke–Sidney patriot, James Otis, who (to circumvent the crown charter origins of the colonies) appeals to 'natural rights', which, he immediately adds, were 'better understood, and more fully enjoyed by our ancestors, before the coming in of the first Norman tyrants than ever after, 'till it was found necessary, for the salvation of the kingdom, to combat the arbitrary and wicked proceedings of the Stuarts'.[57] In this quotation Otis, like Jefferson, adds the unofficial interpretation of 1688 to the ancient constitution–natural rights tradition. The most influential identification of Saxon liberties, 1688, and natural rights is the anonymous *Historical Essay on the English Constitution* (1771).[58]

Second, Jefferson combines the Lockean natural-law theories of conquest, the formation of political societies and appropriation with an ancient-constitution and Norman-yoke history of England to prove the independence of colonial legislatures and undermine the crown's title to grant land. According to Jefferson, his Saxon ancestors left northern Europe, settled in thinly populated Britain and established a system of common laws which is 'the glory and protection of that country'. Their former country did not claim sovereignty over them and they held land in 'absolute dominion' or 'allodial' property, an independent form of property that persists in common law. Feudal property was imposed after the Norman

[55] See Jack P. Greene, '"A Posture of Hostility": A Reconsideration of Some Aspects of the Origins of the American Revolution', *Proceedings of the American Antiquarian Society*, 87 (1977), 27–68.

[56] Thomas Jefferson, *A Summary View of the Rights of British America*, ed. T.P. Abernethy (New York, 1943).

[57] Otis, *The Rights*, p. 31.

[58] Anon., *Historical Essay on the English Constitution* (London, 1771).

conquest and feudal lawyers put out the fiction that all property derives from the crown.

Like their Saxon ancestors, Britons conquered and settled in America under the natural right to leave their country and set up independent societies by compact. They established common-law freehold property by two titles: allotments from their own assemblies and, otherwise, 'each individual . . . may appropriate to himself such lands as he finds vacant, and occupancy will give him title'. For, defying crown title, 'his Majesty . . . has no right to grant lands of himself. All the lands within the limits which any particular society has circumscribed around itself are assumed by that society and subject to their allotment only.' Although the colonial charters were compacts between independent colonial assemblies and the crown, stipulating consent and limits, later kings claimed sovereignty and the right to grant land on the fictitious feudal interpretation of the charters and introduced the Norman yoke into America, which the settlers may resist with 'a vigorous exertion of their own force'. This historical summary, he concludes, is the view of 'a free people claiming their rights, as derived from the law of nature, and not a gift of their chief magistrate'.[59]

The justification of revolt in the Declaration of Independence is based on an application of Locke's theory of consent, limit and resistance to the steps taken by the crown to secure the crown title system.[60] The 'injuries and usurpations' that led to 'the establishment of absolute Tyranny over these States' include the following. The 1763 Royal Proclamation is condemned for 'raising the conditions of new Appropriations of Lands'. The constitutional pluralism of the Quebec Act is characterised as 'abolishing the free system of English Laws in a neighbouring Province, establishing therein an arbitrary government, and enlarging its boundaries so as to render it at once an example and fit instrument for introducing the same absolute rule into these colonies'. The crown's protection of native peoples and property from further usurpation is described, in war-justifying terms, as having 'endeavoured to bring

[59] Jefferson, A Summary View, pp. 4–22.
[60] For the Lockean aspects of the Declaration, see Ronald Hamowy, 'Declaration of Independence', Jack P. Greene (ed.), Encyclopedia of American Political History (New York, 1984), vol. I, pp. 455–65; endorsed by Pocock, 'Introduction', p. li, n.24.

on the inhabitants of our frontiers, the merciless Indian Savages whose known rule of warfare is an undistinguished destruction of all ages, sexes and conditions'.[61]

The main Lockean argument in the Declaration and the rebel literature as a whole is that revolt was justified because property was taken without consent. The premise is that the Royal Statutes and parliamentary legislation to consolidate and enforce crown title were enacted without the consent of the colonists and the Declaratory Act asserted the right of parliament to so act 'in all cases whatsoever'. The Lockean patriots appealed to chapter 11 (sections 138–40) to redescribe this as taking their property without consent, thereby destroying property altogether, transgressing natural-law limits, introducing slavery and arbitrary government, and so furnishing grounds for resistance.[62] The *Treatises* also seemed apposite for three specific reasons: the patriots claimed to be defending the Lockean interpretation of 1688 against court Whigs; the use of paternalistic terms in some imperial literature; and the fact that Molyneux had set a crucial precedent by successfully employing the same sections of the *Treatises* for British Protestant parliamentary independence.[63]

The use of the *Treatises* by the patriots was challenged by the Lockean loyalists defending crown title. They had the advantage of being in agreement with Locke, who governed Carolina by the authority of crown grant, regulated the colonies from the Board of Trade, and placed them under imperial authority in the *Treatises*. In sum, loyalists interpreted the *Treatises* in their 'moderate' version – government by king-in-parliament rests on consent and trust and is subject to limits enforced in the last instance by resistance. The revolutionaries in England and the colonies, they responded, in propounding the extreme version, misinterpreted the theory to fit

[61] James Brown Scott (ed.), *The Declaration of Independence* (New York, 1917), pp. 4, 5, 6. For the similar reaction of other patriots to the Quebec Act see Charles H. Metzger, S.J., *The Quebec Act: A Primary Cause of the American Revolution* (New York, 1936). For the background to Jefferson's language of savagism see Bernard Sheehan, *Savagism and Civility: Indians and Englishmen in Colonial Virginia* (Cambridge, 1980).

[62] See Stanley Dowertz, *The Unvarnished Doctrine*, pp. 65–97. He takes his demonstration of the role of the *Treatises* in justifying the revolution to be a challenge to Pocock's thesis, but, as far as I can see, Pocock has never denied Locke's role.

[63] Barsh and Henderson, *The Road*, pp. 3–19; Bailyn, *The Ideological*, pp. 311–18.

their interests and, as Tucker elaborated, created a mythical theory unworkable in practice.[64]

The actions the crown took to consolidate the system were done for the 'public good' of the colonial system as a whole and thus were not an abuse of prerogative. Turning the republican ideology around, they remarked on the ingratitude and civic irresponsibility of the patriots in not assisting British troops in the Seven Years War and not shouldering the duties of the system which preserved them.[65] There is nothing illegitimate in claiming the supremacy of king-in-parliament 'in all cases whatsoever', Joseph Galloway explained, for this is precisely Locke's doctrine of legislative supremacy. In sections 138 to 140 Locke does not say that the consent of every individual is required, but the consent of their representatives, and this was given in parliament. Therefore, there was no violation of established or natural law.[66] They also underlined Locke's point that the use and enjoyment of property evinces consent and entails obedience, and then presented proposals for reform.[67]

The patriots replied that the consent of colonial assemblies was required, on the presumption that colonial charters were Lockean compacts. Loyalists cited the terms of the charters and British history in reply; challenged the extreme role the revolutionary writers gave to individual consent in the formation of polities; and emphasised the moderating role of familial affection and trust.[68] Furthermore, the loyalists were commercialists, and accused the republican patriots of not understanding a modern commercial

---

[64] For the Lockean loyalists see Peter J. Smith, 'The Origins of Commercial Whiggism, Loyalism and the Federal Idea (Ottawa University of Carleton Ph.D. thesis, 1983), ch. 4; and Janice Potter, *The Liberty We Seek: Loyalist Ideology in Colonial New York and Massachusetts* (Cambridge, Mass., 1983).

[65] See William Knox, *The Controversy between Great Britain and Her Colonies Reviewed* (1769), and *The Justice and Policy of the Late Act of Parliament [The Quebec Act] . . .* (1774). After extensively quoting Locke's theory of king-in-parliament in *The Controversy* he concludes, '[t]his is the British constitution', p. 69.

[66] Joseph Galloway, *A Candid Examination of the Mutual Claims of Great Britain and the Colonies . . .* (New York, 1775), p. 4; Knox, *The Controversy*, pp. 67–8, 71–2.

[67] Galloway, *A Candid Examination*, pp. 15, 18 (*Treatises* 2.120); Knox, *The Controversy*, p. 69.

[68] Galloway, *A Candid Examination*, pp. 10, 35–7 (appealing to the ancient constitution, Saxon liberties and 1688); Allan Ramsay, *Thoughts on the Origin and Nature of Government* (1769); and Tucker, *A Treatise*, pp. 122–201.

political system.[69] In book 4 of the most famous of all loyalist tracts, Adam Smith presented the classic loyalist defence of the British system of parliamentary and commercial union and refuted the rebels' main arguments, especially their republican charge that the executive 'corrupted' the colonial assemblies.[70]

It was the native leaders who were in the best position to see the basic injustice in the patriots' arguments. In hundreds of diplomatic protests to Sir William and Guy Johnson, chiefs like the Mohawk Thayendanega (Joseph Brant) submitted that it was their property that had been taken by the colonists without consent, and thus they who had the right to resist and protect their property by fighting with the British for security under crown title.[71] The majority of native or first nations fought as loyalists; many moved north to Canada after the war, defeated the American invasion of 1812 and maintained protection under the Royal Proclamation. The patriots had one last reply. They tarred and feathered loyalists, burnt their houses, smashed their presses, expropriated their property, declared native peoples savages and declared war on both.[72]

IV

The war expelled the loyalists, removed the yoke of crown title and opened the west to conquest, removal and imperial expansion against native and British defence.[73] But the question of which title would serve as 'license for empire' remained unanswered.[74] In the

---

[69] The Locke–Smith language of the loyalists is highlighted in Smith, 'The Origins', chapter 4, and 'The Dream of Political Union: Loyalism, Toryism and the Federal Idea in Pre-Confederation Canada', in Ged Martin (ed.), *The Causes of Canadian Confederation* (Fredericton, 1990) pp. 148–71. Pocock notes the Smithian elements in Tucker: 'Josiah Tucker', pp. 161–2, 188–9.

[70] Adam Smith, *An Inquiry into the Nature and Causes of the Wealth of Nations*, ed. R.H. Campbell and A.S. Skinner (Oxford, 1976) 4.7.b. (p. 585), 4.7.c (pp. 619–23). See Smith, 'The Dream', pp. 163–4.

[71] See Charles Thomson, *Causes of the Alienation of the Delaware and Shawanese Indians from the British Interest . . .* (1759). The diplomatic speeches of the chiefs are collected in Francis Jennings, William N. Fenton, Mary A. Druke and David R. Miller (eds.), *Iroquois Indians: A Documentary History of the Diplomacy of the Six Nations and their League* (Woodbridge, Conn., 1985), and discussed in Jennings, *Empire of Fortune*; and Dorothy V. Jones, *License for Empire: Colonialism by Treaty in Early America* (Chicago, 1982).

[72] Walter Stewart, *True Blue: The Loyalist Legend* (Toronto, 1985).

[73] Colin G. Calloway, *Crown and Calumet: British–Indian relations, 1783–1815* (Norman, Okla. and London, 1987).

[74] Jones, *License for Empire*, pp. 157–86; and Barsh and Henderson, *The Road*, pp. 37–61.

K

Declaration Jefferson carefully wrote that power devolves to 'independent states', not the state of nature, so Virginia would gain jurisdiction over its western land in the Ohio valley.[75] Virginia proclaimed jurisdiction in 1779. Thomas Paine, another defender of the universal rights of man and speculator in the Indiana Company, replied in the *Public Good* that Virginia had no jurisdiction, not because native Americans had any rights, but because the feudal power of the crown devolved intact to the Continental Congress.[76] In addition, the agriculturist argument was used as a general rationale for the taking of Indian lands by figures as diverse as H.H. Brackenridge (1782), John Adams (1818) and President Jackson (1829). Jefferson instructed the chiefs of 20,000-year-old hunting and gathering societies on the Lockean virtues of conversion to agriculture and private property.[77]

Pocock mentions two republican themes in this period: the necessity of an imperial republic to conquer and expand, associated with Jackson's Machiavellian virtue and ruthlessness in the wars against the Creek and Seminole nations, and the Harringtonian ideal of a virtuous republic founded on an all-white 'fee-simple' empire, associated with Jackson and Noah Webster.[78] Overlapping Lockean themes can be brought into this picture by examining how the chaos over title to land was settled.

The conflicts were finally resolved and the system of property of the United States established by John Marshall, Chief Justice of the Supreme Court, in three landmark decisions (1810, 1823, 1832).[79] In *Johnson v. M'Intosh* (1823) the plaintiffs claimed land in the state of Illinois which they said they purchased from Illinois and Piankeshaw Indians in 1773 and 1775, when the land was

[75] Noted by Pocock, 'States, Republics', p. 59.
[76] Thomas Paine, *Public Good, Being an Examination into the Claims of Virginia to the Vacant Western Territory* . . . (1780), in Philip S. Foner (ed.), *The Complete Writings of Thomas Paine* (New York, 1945), pp. 303–33.
[77] John Adams, 'Letter to William Tudor', 23 September 1818, in Charles F. Adams (ed.), *The Works of John Adams Second President of the United States* (Boston, 1856), 10 vols., vol. x, pp. 359–62; H.H. Brackenridge, *Atrocities: Narratives of the Perils and Sufferings of Dr. Knight and John Slover among the Indians* (1782) (Cincinnatti, 1867), in Virgil J. Vogel (ed.), *This Country was Ours: A Documentary History of the American Indian* (New York, 1972), pp. 104–6; President Andrew Jackson, first annual message 1829, in Vogel, *This Country*, pp. 107–10; Thomas Jefferson, 'Speeches to the Indians', in Saul K. Padover (ed.), *The Complete Jefferson* (New York, 1943), pp. 449–514.
[78] Pocock, *Machiavellian Moment*, pp. 531–42, with a gesture towards Locke's role at p. 542.
[79] *Fletcher v. Peck* (1810) 10 US (6 Cranch) 87; *Johnson and Graham's Lessee v. M'Intosh* (1823) 8 Wheaton 543 (USSC); *Worcester v. State of Georgia* (1832) 6 Peters 5150 (USSC).

within the boundaries of Virginia. The same Indian nations later ceded the land to the American government, which granted it to the defendant. The plaintiffs appealed to Grotius and Pufendorf for the validity of their agreement.

The defendants responded that the agreement was invalid because 'the whole theory of their [European nations'] title to land in America rests on the hypothesis that the Indians had no right of soil, as sovereign, independent nations'. The natives are in the state of nature (citing *Treatises*, 2.87–9, 143, 123–30), with property limited to their wants and actual uses (citing 2.25, 34–40). It is a violation of the natural rights of Europeans for the Indians to claim rights in the land and to try to exclude them from cultivating land they merely roamed over (citing 2.36–48):

the Indians had no individual rights to land; nor had they any collectively, or in their national capacity; for the lands occupied by each tribe were not used by them in such a manner as to prevent their being appropriated by a people of cultivators. All proprietary rights of civilized nations on this continent are founded on this principle.

Combining this with conquest theory (as in *Treatises*, book 2, p. 184), all land titles in America rest on the fundamental title of the crown by discovery and conquest, which 'overlooks all proprietary rights in the natives' and is now held by the American government.[80] Accordingly, one of the most celebrated cases associated with a western fee-simple agrarian empire, from which the native people were removed or killed if they resisted, could be pleaded in Lockean terms without reference to Harrington or virtue.

In his decision Marshall set aside the Lockean argument and explained that, in theory, crown title in America rested on discovery and continuity, laying it out in accordance with the Royal Proclamation (as above). Nonetheless, he continued, overlooking hundreds of treaties, theory was not followed. America was acquired by conquest and discontinuity of native sovereignty: the feudal-law theory of Norman conquest. The conqueror is usually expected to respect the property of the conquered, to extend citizenship to them and to govern them either by assimilation or as a distinct people. But, these conventions were 'incapable of application' because 'the tribes of Indians inhabiting this country were fierce savages, whose occupation was war, and whose subsistence

---

[80] 8 Wheaton 543 (USSC) at 567–71. 'A people of cultivators' is a phrase from Vattel.

was drawn chiefly from the forest'. They could not be left in possession of their country because this would leave it a 'wilderness', and they could not be governed conventionally because they were 'brave', 'high-spirited', and 'fierce'; 'ready to repel by arms every attempt on their independence'. Europeans had no choice but to enforce their claims by the sword or abandon the continent. Bloody wars ensued. Settlers advanced, Indians receded, the land was 'no longer occupied by its ancient inhabitants', and the Indian title of occupancy, which holds only in peacetime, no longer applied to the now-vacant land. The crown then exercised its exclusive title and all land in the colonies 'was parcelled out according to the will of the sovereign power'.

Marshall repudiates Jefferson's thesis that the colonies were independent bodies with the authority to grant title. Arguing that the crown always had the exclusive right to grant land in Virginia, he reasserts the very feudal-law title that, according to Jefferson, the rebellion had been fought to overthrow. Crown title now belongs to the American government and holds over western lands as well, subject only to the Indian title based on occupancy. He concedes that title by conquest and discontinuity is unjust – 'opposed to natural right, and to the usages of civilized nations' – but he concludes that he will uphold it on the ground of necessity of state, as 'indispensable to that system under which the country has been settled' and which 'certainly cannot be rejected by the courts of justice'.[81]

According to Marshall in *Johnson v. M'Intosh*, therefore, the property system of the original United States is derived neither from Harrington nor Locke but from the Norman yoke; its patron philosopher is the Virginia landowner Sir Robert Filmer. Nine years later, in *Worcester v. the State of Georgia*, concerning the Cherokee nation, he took a different view. Explicitly following the Royal Proclamation of 1763, he decided that the federal government, like the crown before it, recognises and protects the Indians as distinct, self-governing nations with exclusive jurisdiction over their territories.

---

[81] 8 Wheaton 543 (USSC) at 572–5, 585–6, 587–92, 585–6. For the conflict between Marshall and Jackson, mentioned by Pocock, *Machiavellian Moment*, pp. 536–7, see J.C. Burke, 'The Cherokee Cases: A Study in Law, Politics and Morality', *Stanford Law Review*, 21 (1968–9), 500–31.

V

Pocock has shown how the specialisation, dependency and 'effeminacy' of commerce and parliamentary patronage were sources of the male anxiety over virtue in early modern Britain and America. This essay suggests an additional source. Britons in North America were surrounded by a civilisation based on an ethic of virtue and honour. Women did the agricultural work that men deemed too undignified for them. Native men ridiculed the 'unmanly' life of the male settlers: their constraining clothes, immobility, private property and especially their long days behind a ploughhorse, ankle-deep in manure with a yoke on their necks. By contrast, the natives engaged in hunting, political discussion and diplomacy, and fighting in defence of their nations and independence. Great men were accorded honour and respect, especially for valour in war, by their own citizens and many Europeans. Their political organisations were freer and more egalitarian than anything the newcomers knew. They reminded many settlers and Europeans of the freedom and independence of the state of nature, Saxon liberties and classical republics. Native eloquence in diplomacy reminded many of Cicero and their valour in war of the noble deeds of classical heroes.[82]

Yet the settlers coveted the land of the indigenous peoples and took it, destroying native cultures and reducing a population estimated at as high as 10,000,000 to 250,000.[83] The question of virtue that this experience raised was put forcefully by Joseph-François Lafitau: was a civilisation based on the virtue of the Hebrews, Greeks and Romans being destroyed by a European civilisation based on corruption and self-love?[84] He, like Samuel Johnson and others, answered yes. The reason why the settlers enlarged their possessions of land in America, Locke acknowledged, was the hope of drawing money to themselves by sale of the

---

[82] The most famous British presentation of Amerindians as classical republicans is Cadwallader Colden, *The History of the Five Indian Nations of Canada* . . . (London, 1747), pp. 2–19. See James Axtell, *The Invasion Within: the Contest of Cultures in Colonial North America* (Oxford, 1981); and William Brandon, *New Worlds for Old: Reports from the New World and their Effect on the Development of Social Thought in Europe 1500–1800* (Athens, Ohio, 1986).

[83] H.F. Dobyns, *Their Numbers Become Thinned: Native American Population Dynamics in Eastern North America* (Knoxville, 1983).

[84] Joseph-François Lafitau, *Moeurs des sauvages Ameriquans comparées aux moeurs des premiers temps* (Paris, 1724).

products, based on a corrupt desire for more than one needs that was unknown to Amerindians.[85]

To overcome the resulting anxiety and reassure themselves of the virtue of their corruption they frequently made use of various myths of their superiority. One of the most important was to inscribe native civilisations into a worldview in which they were seen as a primitive stage in a fictitious world-historical scheme of development with European practices on top. Once Locke's premise that 'in the beginning all the world was America' was in place, British superiority was reassured. The British could go on, as Pocock has demonstrated, to debate among themselves the relative merits of Locke's rights-bearing and industrious agriculturist, Harrington's virtuous republican and Smith's polished and civilised commercialist, for all three were defined and used in contrast to, and in supersession of, the Amerindian they displaced in practice – the propertyless and wasteful hunter–gatherer, the fierce and vicious savage, the rude and primitive Indian. Even accounts of the distinctiveness and value of native practices can be contemplated with equanimity within this worldview, for they appear as unthreatening romantic nostalgia for forms of life that must convert or perish in the face of progress.[86]

This mythical worldview has been so successful that many later political theorists read the early modern texts and adopt the terms of the debates without even noticing the civilisation whose displacement they were used to justify.[87] The uncritical continuation of modern political thought in the Eurocentric terms of the Lockean, republican and commercial languages serves to hold the myth in place and so hide the real history from view. This feature of the *Treatises* is on a margin of early modern political thought, but a margin that is a horizon in which modern political thought takes place.

---

[85] Locke, *Treatises*, II.48–9, 108, and Tully, 'Rediscovering America'.

[86] See Robert F. Berkhofer, Jr., *The White Man's Indian: Images of the American Indian from Columbus to the President* (New York, 1978); Roy H. Pearce, *The Savages of America: A Study of the Indian and the Idea of Civilization* (Baltimore, 1965); and Alden T. Vaughan, 'From White Man to Red Skin: Changing Anglo-American Perceptions of the American Indian', *American Historical Review*, 87 (1982), 917–52.

[87] Pocock is an exception to the usual acceptance of the myth. He has lamented the rise of progressive and universalising forms of history in *Ancient Constitution*, pp. 228–54; written of the 'contemplated genocide' of the aboriginal peoples in *Machiavellian Moment*, p. 511; and written from a post-imperial, anti-mythical, and contingent historical perspective, which he associates with the Maori and non-native sensibility of his home country of Aotearoa in 'Between Gog', pp. 332–5.

PART IV

CHAPTER 13

Shaftesbury, politeness and the politics of religion

Lawrence E. Klein

In the early eighteenth century, the language of 'politeness' concerned sociability and gentlemanliness and cannot as such be said to have been a peculiarly political language.[1] However, it was a language that was easily politicised and, indeed, has come to appear central to understanding early-eighteenth-century political culture, especially Whiggism.[2] Nonetheless, there has been little detailed analysis of how 'politeness' operated as a political idiom, even in the writings of Joseph Addison, Richard Steele and the third earl of Shaftesbury, who crystallised the notion.[3] Indeed, there has been almost no writing at all on Shaftesbury (1671–1713), although his Characteristicks of Men, Manners, Opinions, Times, first published in 1711, deployed 'politeness' for political purposes in an elaborate and highly sophisticated manner.[4] This essay takes Shaftesbury seriously as a Whig writer of the first importance. In

[1] On the contours of the language of 'politeness', see Lawrence Klein, 'The Third Earl of Shaftesbury and the Progress of Politeness', Eighteenth-Century Studies, 18 (1984–5), 186–214.

[2] This point has been made by J.G.A. Pocock in 'The Varieties of Whiggism from Exclusion to Reform', in Virtue, Commerce and History (Cambridge, 1985), pp. 234–39; J.W. Burrow, Whigs and Liberals: Continuity and Change in English Political Thought (Oxford, 1988), p. x; and Nicholas Phillipson, Hume (London, 1989), pp. 23–30, and other writings of Phillipson cited there. I have explored some aspects of the politics of 'politeness' in 'Liberty, Manners and Politeness in Early Eighteenth-Century England', Historical Journal, 32 (1989), 583–605.

[3] The most helpful observations on Addison are in Nicholas Phillipson's articles (see previous note). For an account of Addison as a middle-class Lockean, see Edward A. Bloom and Lillian D. Bloom, Joseph Addison's Sociable Animal (Providence, 1971), pp. 11–12, 20–1, 87–8, 114–17.

[4] Some basic sources on Shaftesbury are Robert Voitle's biography, The Third Earl of Shaftesbury, 1671–1713 (Baton Rouge, 1984); Stanley Grean's philosophical account, Shaftesbury's Philosophy of Religion and Ethics: A Study in Enthusiasm (Athens, 1967); and A.O. Aldridge's 'Shaftesbury and the Deist Manifesto', Transactions of the American Philosophical Society (Philadelphia), N.S. 41 (1951). Shaftesbury has never been given adequate treatment as a political writer, nor has Characteristicks been adequately interpreted as an ideological document.

283

turn, taking Shaftesbury seriously illuminates the ways in which 'politeness' could operate as a medium of political discourse.

One remarkable feature of Shaftesbury's writing is the degree to which his discussion of religious and ecclesiastical matters was penetrated by the idioms of sociability and 'politeness'. He contended that *Characteristicks* was, among other things, a 'Plea for *Complacency, Sociableness*, and GOOD HUMOUR *in Religion*'.[5] One direction in which this claim points is Shaftesbury's 'deism', a contemplative worship of divine order arising out of natural affective sociability.[6] Shaftesbury eschewed virtually all the distinctive attributes of Christianity and indicted certain Christian doctrines for their hostility to true sociability, though he was also capable of maintaining that Christianity was 'in the main, A *witty* and *good-humour'd Religion*'.[7]

However, polite religion implied more than certain doctrinal preferences, for it endorsed a specific social configuration of religion, a religion operating within society according to principles of sociability and politeness. The pressure to construct a sociable model of religion arose from the fact of religious conflict and the political problems of ordering the ensuing commotion. The central issue in this essay is the way that Shaftesbury used sociability and 'politeness' to grasp the nettle of religious politics.

Shaftesbury responded to politicised religious conflict by urging the necessity of free, tolerant, sociable discussion of religion, according to the standards of polite gentlemanly conversation. He juxtaposed such public discourse to more constrained arrangements. Writing that 'a proper way to render the most sacred Truth suspected' was by 'supporting it with *Threats*, and pretending to *terrify* People into the Belief of it',[8] he opened perspectives on both the psychology and sociology of religion. He could then avail himself of some traditional tools of religious polemic, namely,

---

[5] 'Miscellaneous Reflections' (II, iii), III, 111 (Robertson, II, 224). References to the components of Shaftesbury's *Characteristicks* are to the title of the component, followed by the part and section (in parentheses) and the citation of the volume and page of the 1714 edition of *Characteristicks*. The 1714 edition, the second, was published after the third earl's death but included his corrections and revisions of the first edition of 1711. References are also given in parentheses to the modern edition of *Characteristicks* by John Robertson (London, 1900).

[6] See, among other places, 'The Moralists' (I, iii), II, 210–17 (Robertson, II, 20–3), and 'Miscellaneous Reflections' (II, iii), III, 114–15 (Robertson, II, 226–27).

[7] 'Miscellaneous Reflections' (II, iii), III, 98–9 (Robertson, II, 217).

[8] 'Miscellaneous Reflections' (II, iii), III, 107 (Robertson, II, 222).

arguments against 'enthusiasm' and 'priestcraft', which he incorporated into his campaign for politeness in the context of a thoroughly Whiggish politics. Attacking the High-Church party as an enemy of public discourse, he could pursue the polemical agenda of the Whigs while he also defined the limits of religion in the modern polity.

Taking Shaftesbury seriously as a political writer involves some adjustments in the usual approach to him. Commentators on both his philosophy and his politics usually focus on the later 1690s, when Shaftesbury wrote *An Inquiry Concerning Virtue* and joined the Country opposition in association with Robert Molesworth, Walter Moyle, John Toland and other 'commonwealthmen'.[9] However, his master achievement, *Characteristicks*, was produced more than a decade later.[10] It is there that we find the mature philosophy as well as the mature politics, the work for which Shaftesbury was known in the eighteenth century.

Opening the first volume of *Characteristicks*, the reader comes upon 'A Letter Concerning Enthusiasm', addressed to an anonymous lord (in fact, John, Baron Somers). The address is gentlemanly, and the style is that 'familiar' albeit crafted 'way of *Chat*' that many readers of Shaftesbury, in the eighteenth century and since, have found odiously affected.[11] Shaftesbury remarks that, since the modern world is disenchanted, a modern writer cannot imitate the ancients, who, seeking inspiration from the muses, began their works with apostrophes to them. Instead, staying within the perimeter of the social, Shaftesbury looks to the noble lord for

[9] Philosophical commentators from Henry Sidgwick to D.D. Raphael confine themselves to *An Inquiry* as do, for the most part, anthologies of the 'British moralists'. Typical characterisations of Shaftesbury as an oppositionalist Whig are A.B. Worden, introduction to Edmund Ludlow, *A Voyce from the Watch Tower, Part Five: 1660–1662* (Camden Fourth Series, vol. XXI, London, 1978), 39–46; Caroline Robbins, *The Eighteenth Century Commonwealthman* (Cambridge, 1959), pp. 56, 88–95, 128–33; and David Hayton, 'The "Country" Interest and the Party System', in Clyve Jones (ed.), *Party and Management in Parliament* (New York, 1984), pp. 44, 52.

[10] *Characteristicks*, first published in 1711, included revised versions of five previously published pieces (*An Inquiry concerning Virtue*, 1699; *A Letter concerning Enthusiasm*, 1708; *Sensus Communis: An Essay on the Freedom of Wit and Humour*, 1709; *The Moralists, A Philosophical Rhapsody*, 1709; *Soliloquy: Or Advice to an Author*, 1710), to which the extensive 'Miscellaneous Reflections' was added.

[11] 'Miscellaneous Reflections' (II, iii), III, 97 (Robertson, II, 216). A guide to the polite (or 'courtly') register is Carey McIntosh, *Common and Courtly Language: The Stylistics of Social Class in Eighteenth-Century English Literature* (Philadelphia, 1986).

inspiration. Indeed, before proceeding with the argument, Shaftesbury envisages the lord with whom he can then imagine himself in
face-to-face discussion. Thus, 'A Letter' – as, indeed, the entirety of
Characteristicks – is intended as a literary representation of gentlemanly conversation.[12]

This fact is of more than literary importance, since the literary
representation of gentlemanly conversation points to the ideological crux of this text, which Shaftesbury lays bare in what follows.
Having been invited to imagine what he is reading as a dialogue
between gentlemen, the reader of 'A Letter' is then treated to a
defence of open-ended public discussion, in which Shaftesbury
endorses '*Freedom of Censure*' and the 'impartial and *free Censure* of
Manners'. Such freedom becomes a major theme in 'A Letter' and
the other essays comprising *Characteristicks*. For instance, in 'Sensus
Communis', which follows 'A Letter', Shaftesbury endorses 'a
Liberty in decent Language to question every thing, and an
Allowance of unravelling or refuting any Argument, without
offence to the Arguer'.[13] The decency and inoffensiveness referred
to here indicate the constraints which, according to Shaftesbury,
should control public discourse: one benefit of the gentlemanly
mode is the social discipline it imposes on participants. However,
notwithstanding such limitations, public discourse conducted on
the model of gentlemanly conversation has its own cognitive value,
since Shaftesbury associates conversability with rationality: 'there
can be no rational Belief but where *Comparison* is allow'd, *Examination* permitted, and a sincere *Toleration* establish'd'.[14] Thus, the
Shaftesburian public is a self-sustaining discursive realm in which a
diversity of manners and opinions, having been displayed and
expressed, can be assessed, approved, corrected or dismissed.
Shaftesbury intends his writing to display procedures of gentlemanly conversation which the text explicitly endorses.

Moreover, the first pages of 'A Letter' establish the political
valence of Shaftesbury's endorsement of a free public discourse

---

[12] 'A Letter concerning Enthusiasm' (i), I, 3–9 (Robertson, I, 5–9). On Shaftesbury's
conversational literary practice: Klein, 'Shaftesbury and the Progress of Politeness', pp.
205–11; Robert Markley, 'Style as Philosophical Structure: The Contexts of Shaftesbury's
Characteristicks', in Robert Ginsberg (ed.), *The Philosopher as Writer: The Eighteenth Century*
(Selinsgrove, 1987), pp. 140–54; Jack Prostko, '"Natural Conversation Set in View"
Shaftesbury and Moral Speech', *Eighteenth-Century Studies*, 23 (1989–90), 42–61.

[13] 'Sensus Communis' (II, iv), I, 69 (Robertson, I, 49).

[14] 'Miscellaneous Reflections' (II, iii), III, 104 (Robertson, II, 220).

among gentlemen: "'Tis only in a free Nation, such as ours, that Imposture has no Privilege; and that neither the Credit of a Court, the Power of a Nobility, nor the Awefulness of a Church can give her Protection or hinder her from being arraign'd in every Shape and Appearance'.[15] Here Shaftesbury specifies the institutional co-ordinates of English liberty, associating it with an order of gentlemanly discourse that has liberated itself from the discursive trammels of state and church.

This was clearly a Whiggish project in the civic mode. Shaftesbury drew inspiration from the ideal of a self-ruling community based on principles of equality, reciprocity and the commitment to public virtue.[16] The institutional threats to liberty of discourse – 'Court', 'Nobility', 'Church' – corresponded neatly to the elements of the English constitution that James Harrington had thought outmoded by historical development. Like Harrington, Shaftesbury was an optimist about the direction of history and the condition of liberty.[17] It is true that Harrington's continuators in the Restoration reassembled his analysis to produce a view of modernity as inimical to liberty and virtue, a view to which Shaftesbury was much drawn in the 1690s. However, by the time he was writing the components of *Characteristicks* in the middle years of Anne's reign, he was concerned to assert the compatibility, rather than any hostility, between post–1688 Whiggism and liberty. For Shaftesbury, the Revolution Settlement was a Whiggish triumph, and the Whig accession to power merely reflected the new political prominence of English gentlemen at large.[18] Post-

---

[15] 'A Letter concerning Enthusiasm' (ii), I, 9–10 (Robertson, I, 9).

[16] Hannah Arendt, *The Human Condition* (Chicago, 1958), Part II; J.G.A. Pocock, 'Civic Humanism and Its Role in Anglo-American Thought', *Politics, Language and Time* (New York, 1973), pp. 85–96; *The Machiavellian Moment* (Princeton, 1975), pp. 49–80. For a broad definition of the civic tradition that includes but is not confined to the civic idioms explored in the works of J.G.A. Pocock, see John Robertson, 'The Scottish Enlightenment at the Limits of the Civic Tradition', in Istvan Hont and Michael Ignatieff (eds.), *Wealth and Virtue: The Shaping of Political Economy in the Scottish Enlightenment* (Cambridge, 1983), pp. 137–41.

[17] See, for instance, 'Miscellaneous Reflections' (III, i), III, 150–1 (Robertson, II, 249), where Shaftesbury anticipates the modernist attitudes of Baron Hervey in *Ancient and Modern Liberty Stated and Compared*. For Harrington, J.G.A. Pocock, introduction, *The Political Works of James Harrington* (Cambridge, 1977), especially 50ff. and 77–99.

[18] Some Shaftesburian endorsements of the Revolutionary settlement and its consequences can be found in: 'Sensus Communis' (III, i), I, 108 (Robertson, I, 73); 'Soliloquy' (II, i), I, 215–16 (Robertson, I, 141); 'Miscellaneous Reflections' (III, i), III, 150–1 (Robertson, II, 249).

1688 England was not a Harringtonian republic, but it was a polity in which both monarchical and ecclesiastical power were conceived by Shaftesbury to have been crucially abrogated.

There was, of course, a big distance between Harrington and Shaftesbury in other respects. Though Shaftesbury argued against standing armies in quite neo-Harringtonian ways in 1697 and 1698, his mature writing lacked the military dimension that has loomed so large in J.G.A. Pocock's account of the civic tradition.[19] In thinking civically, Shaftesbury turned the republic of freeholders into a republic of polite gentlemen and reconstituted the community of armed citizens as a community of discourse or what we can call a public. For Shaftesbury, post-1688 England was potentially and ideally a republic of gentlemen defined by their autonomy, virtue and philosophical enlightenment.

In effect, Shaftesbury abandoned the civic emphasis on institutions in favour of a concentration on manners.[20] At best, according to Shaftesbury, the social and political arrangements secured by 1688 offered a framework for moral, social and cultural refinements still to come. His concern with manners was mediated, specifically, by standards of gentlemanly conversation. When he referred to the 'imposture' likely to be perpetrated by state and church, he raised the image of an enemy of gentlemanly conversation, for the impostor was pretentious, prone to make false or untested claims and impose them on others, by the vigour or unctuousness of his presentation. This instance illustrates Shaftesbury's reliance on early modern traditions of civil conversation and interpersonal politeness in producing a normative vision of the modern public.[21]

Over the centuries, the tradition of civil conversation had generated standards for interchange among gentle people that conduced to refined sociability. Civil conversation assumed equality among participants and insisted on a reciprocity in which participants were sometimes talkers and sometimes listeners. It was described as a zone of freedom, ease and naturalness (though these terms assumed highly qualified meanings in so obviously

[19] Among many places, 'Machiavelli, Harrington and English Political Ideologies', in *Politics, Language and Time*, pp. 112–28; *Machiavellian Moment*, pp. 196ff., 406–22. For Shaftesbury's connections with the oppositional movement in the later 1690s, see note 9 above.
[20] See J.G.A. Pocock, 'Virtues, Rights and Manners: A Model for Historians of Political Thought', in *Virtue, Commerce and History*, pp. 37–50, especially 48–50.
[21] Klein, 'Shaftesbury and the Progress of Politeness', pp. 188–91, 198–200.

artificial an activity). In this tradition, conversation was an opportunity for self-display at the same time as its norms disciplined self-expression for the sake of domestic peace.

Writers about the principles of conversation were generous with their recommendations and proscriptions. Those engaged in conversation were warned against taciturnity, stiffness, self-effacement and withdrawal, which starved conversation. However, they were also warned against excesses of assertiveness and sociability, which smothered conversation. It was wrong to dominate a discussion, push one's opinions too relentlessly, or strive for effect. Self-righteousness, self-solemnity and gravity were odious. To terminate a conversation with dispatch, one needed only to be pedantic or magisterial!

Politeness as gentlemanly conversation was crucial to Shaftesbury's construction of the public. Public discussion on the model of conversation emerged as a realm in which submission to the disciplines of equality, liberty and reciprocity created an arena for rational persuasion. At the outset of *Characteristicks*, he defended the public sphere with reference to politeness: 'Justness of Thought and Stile, Refinement in Manners, good Breeding, and Politeness of every kind, can come only from the Trial and Experience of what is best. Let but the Search go freely on, and the right Measure of every thing will soon be found.'[22] And he reiterated in many ways this interaction of discursive freedom and politeness throughout *Characteristicks*.

Thus, Shaftesburian politeness described a politics of manners and opinions that focussed on the status of discourse in society. Discourse was politicised because its status was entwined with questions of power and institutions. In advocating politeness, Shaftesbury projected a culture of, for and by gentlemen. This was a deeply political proposition since it involved a transfer of authority from state and church to the arena of public gentlemanly discourse.

Shaftesbury's new vision of British society and culture, based on the hegemony of gentlemen in conversation, has to be seen in relation to two other contexts. On the one hand, the project arose out of a concern for religion, opinions and manners that had

---

[22] 'A Letter concerning Enthusiasm' (ii), I, 10 (Robertson, I, 10).

entered political discussion during the preceding decades. In fact, Restoration political discussion provided specific materials that Shaftesbury would deploy in his writings. However, the project was also shaped by the immediate needs of Whig polemic, of which Shaftesbury was very aware. *Characteristicks* spoke to the partisan controversies of the first decade of the eighteenth century.

In the middle of the seventeenth century, diversity of opinion together with passionate conviction in the absence of authority had proved a volatile combination of ingredients. One quandary posed by the civil breakdown was that religion, which was supposed to be a social cement, had instead precipitated civil disruption. What had gone wrong with religion was a pressing question, and diagnoses often found answers in analyses of religious passions, interests and opinions. More particularly, since the Civil War had made people wonder how Christians could act so indecently, it exposed rather embarrassingly the tension between religious profession and behaviour and necessitated discussion of manners, which, as Hobbes pointed out, were a function of passions and opinions.[23]

Those who wrote about these issues during and after the Civil War period sought to rehabilitate the civil character of religion through a series of disciplines. These disciplines were social, psychological, epistemological and forthrightly political.

An important tactic in the disciplining of religion (ordinarily found in Anglican polemic against Dissent) was to disparage enthusiasm.[24] While 'enthusiasm' often referred simply to bad behaviour in the name of religion, it also had a richer potential for addressing the problem of manners. As used by Henry More and John Glanvill, 'enthusiasm' pathologised wayward religion, linking it to disturbances of the mind and body: it was a disorder of 'temper', associated with errant humours, passions and imaginations. Thus, attacking enthusiasm redirected religious discussion from issues of doctrine to estimations of social personality.

While attacks on enthusiasm aimed to bring religious experience and expression under psychological and social control, they were

[23] Thomas Hobbes, *Leviathan*, ed. Michael Oakeshott (Oxford, 1947), p. 63 (chapter 11).
[24] See particularly Susie I. Tucker, *Enthusiasm: A Study of Semantic Change* (Cambridge, 1972); Michael Heyd, 'The Reaction to Enthusiasm in the Seventeenth Century', *Journal of Modern History*, 53 (1981), 258–80; Frank Manuel, *The Changing of the Gods* (for Brown University, by University Press of New England, 1983), pp. 34–51.

also used to bring religious insight under epistemological control. In hindsight, such efforts might appear 'secularist', but they were intended to save religion from itself, providing more secure foundations for faith. Since enthusiasm involved the unfounded conviction of certitude, it was a foil in the search for a firmer understanding of God and nature. Restoration epistemology dealt in reassessments of reason, certainty and probability, language and so forth. However, it also offered new constructions of the social spaces of inquiry and the procedures, habituated in such spaces, for validating knowledge claims. Such constructions often assigned an important place to conversation and mutual exchange, an emphasis that Shaftesbury's own discursive interests would renew.[25]

Such critiques of enthusiasm were accompanied by a constructive activity, a reassertion of the civilising qualities of religion. Occupying the high ground, an assortment of Anglicans, from Samuel Parker to Benjamin Whichcote, represented true religion as sociable. Their emphasis on sociability, good manners, decency, civility and charity was designed to reassure people that true religion fostered rather than destroyed the polity. This emphasis provided a practical standard against which professions of religious belief could be judged and the distortions of enthusiasm assessed. As his endorsements of Whichcote and Restoration divines indicate, Shaftesbury's sociability was partly rooted in this Anglican language (though it is a mistake simply to elide the categories 'Latitudinarian' and 'deist').[26]

An important polemical advantage followed from this Anglican emphasis on religious sociability. If the enhancement of human social life was to be a significant feature of Christian practice, then clerics would have to devote careful attention to spiritual and eleemosynary duties and eschew political engagements in favour of

[25]Barbara Shapiro, *Probability and Certainty in Seventeenth-Century England* (Princeton, 1983), pp. 74–118; Henry G. van Leeuwen, *The Problem of Certainty in English Thought 1630–1690* (The Hague, 1963); Richard Ashcraft, 'Faith and Knowledge in Locke's Philosophy', in John W. Yolton (ed.), *John Locke: Problems and Perspectives* (Cambridge, 1969), pp. 194–223; Steven Shapin and Simon Schaffer, *Leviathan and the Air-Pump: Hobbes, Boyle and the Experimental Life* (Princeton, 1985), chapters 7 and 8.
[26] Shaftesbury's first publication was a preface to an edition of sermons by Whichcote, whom Shaftesbury labelled 'the Preacher of Good-nature': Benjamin Whichcote, *Select Sermons of Dr. Whichcot. In Two Parts*, ed. Anthony Ashley Cooper (1698). See Roger L. Emerson, 'Latitudinarianism and the English Deists', in J.A. Leo Lemay (ed.), *Deism, Masonry and the Enlightenment* (Newark, Delaware: University of Delaware Press, 1987), pp. 19–48.

pastoral ones. Thus, the rejection of enthusiasm and the vogue of sociability were congruent with an Erastian stance towards ecclesiastical politics, civil controls on the church complementing the new epistemological, psychological and social standards for religion. When a demand for civil control of the church was infused with the anti-clerical spirit, the demand could be reinforced with the language of 'priestcraft'.[27]

By the middle of the seventeenth century, it had become clear that Protestant churches were as liable to unfortunate extensions of clerical power as 'popery' was. The introduction into discussion of the term 'priestcraft' (by James Harrington) provided a means to generalise about exaggerated clerical claims, whether Catholic or episcopal or Presbyterian. According to the critique of priestcraft, a church must be dependent on the state for its authority and wealth since, on its own, the clerical estate aimed to aggrandise itself. Clerics were said to confect beliefs that they imposed on believers in order to secure clerical power more firmly. Moreover, a powerful clergy tended to substitute its own interest for the public's and could easily mount itself as a rival to the state.

As we shall see, Shaftesbury set into play the idioms of both anti-enthusiasm and anti-priestcraft. However, the use he made of them depended on the difference in circumstances between the Restoration moment when they arose and the post-1688 moment when he deployed them. Among other things, Shaftesbury wrote with the needs of Whig polemic in the reign of Queen Anne in mind.

It is often noted that, in the aftermath of the 1688 Revolution, the Whigs had to transform themselves from a Country to a Court party. It is less noted that the Whigs also had to reposition themselves in relation to the church. When parties first appeared in the 1670s, the labels 'church' and 'Presbyterian' were as frequently used as the labels 'Tory' and 'Whig'. This was true notwithstand-

---

[27] See Mark Goldie's essay in this volume, pp. 209–31, and his other essays cited there. In addition J.G.A. Pocock, introduction, *The Political Works of James Harrington* (Cambridge, 1977), pp. 77–99; Richard Tuck, *Hobbes* (Oxford, 1989), pp. 30, 65, 73–6, 78–9; Richard Tuck, 'Hobbes and Locke on Toleration', in Mary G. Dietz (ed.), *Thomas Hobbes and Political Theory* (Lawrence, Kans., 1990), pp. 153–71; John Marshall, 'The Ecclesiology of the Latitude-men 1660–1689: Stillingfleet, Tillotson and "Hobbism"', *Journal of Ecclesiastical History*, 36 (1985), 407–27; Justin Champion, 'The Ancient Constitution of the Christian Church: The Church of England and Its Enemies 1660–1730', University of Cambridge doctoral dissertation 1989.

ing the large number of Whigs, including the first earl of Shaftesbury, who were conforming members of the Church of England. The core of Whiggism was not Dissent but hostility to the ecclesiastical establishment, a posture shared by both conformists and nonconformists.[28]

The 1688 Revolution placed the Whigs in a new relation to the church since the defence of the Settlement necessitated a defence not only of the Toleration Act but also of the Established Church (albeit a church firmly dominated by the state).[29] In the same way that an Old Whig might ask himself whether he could make peace with a court, he might find himself asking whether he could make peace with a church.

Such questions became urgent once a self-consciously High-Church group of clerics and laymen began to make moves in the second half of the 1690s that threatened the Whig understanding of the Settlement. Asserting the rights of Convocation and the ignominy of occasional conformity, this group challenged the Whig commitments to state supremacy and toleration. During the Restoration period, divisions *within* the Church of England did not become themes of political dissension; but, in Anne's reign, the divisions within the church were politicised on partisan lines. The debate that emerged between High Church and Low Church, mapped on the partisan distinction between Tory and Whig, was something new, spawning a succession of paper battles, setting Atterbury versus Wake and Kennett, Atterbury versus Hoadly, Sacheverell versus Dennis, Drake versus Toland.[30]

Shaftesbury wrote as a Whig in an environment in which party differences entailed differences of religious perspective. Moreover, he was implicated in the new responsibility of the Whigs for the defence of the Established Church against its internal enemies. Therefore, no matter how natural his innermost religion and how anti-clerical his innermost ecclesiology, his writing constituted an endorsement of the current order in church and state. He was well

---

[28] Mark Goldie, 'Danby, the Bishops and the Whigs', in Tim Harris, Paul Seaward and Mark Goldie (eds.), *The Politics of Religion in Restoration England* (Oxford, 1990), p. 80.

[29] We need a treatment of the Whig theory of the church in the eighteenth century. Some brief remarks appear in: H.T. Dickinson, 'Whiggism in the Eighteenth Century', in John Cannon (ed.), *The Whig Ascendancy* (New York, 1981), pp. 41, 46–7.

[30] Norman Sykes, *From Sheldon to Secker* (Cambridge, 1959), pp. 85–101; G.V. Bennett, *The Tory Crisis in Church and State, 1688–1730* (Oxford, 1975), pp. 44–118; John Spurr, '"Latitudinarianism" and the Restoration Church', *Historical Journal*, 31 (1988), 61–82.

aware not only of the Country roots of Whiggism but also of its Presbyterian ones and of the ease with which Anglican Tories had traditionally smeared the Whigs as unmannerly enthusiasts.[31] Therefore, Shaftesbury urged a sociable Anglicanism firmly under the sovereign's power. The Erastian goal was amply served by the traditional arguments against priestcraft, but a sociable Anglicanism required asserting the sociability of the Low Church against the enthusiasm of the High-Church party.

The more specific elements of Shaftesbury's religious politics are adumbrated in a letter he wrote to a young protégé on the eve of his ordination.[32]

Attacking 'the Conceit & Pride wch is allmost naturally inherent to the Function & Calling you are about to undertake', Shaftesbury exhorted: ' . . . since we think fitt to call it Priesthood, & have brought *Preists* into Christianity (a thing wch in my Reading & Capacity I cou'd never discover or apprehend) see, that this Preisthood be of a kind not to make Thee say or think of Thyself in the presence of another *that thou art holyer than he*'. Of course, the parenthetical remark revealed a profound anticlericalism and points us towards the ultimately un-Christian character of Shaftesbury's religion. However, the rest of the passage points towards Shaftesbury's religious politics, since it emphasised the irregularities to which the priest's social relations were prone. The standing liability of the clerical profession was conceit, the unwarranted and unsociable assumption of authority. Accordingly, in Shaftesbury's portrayal, the standard tool of the cleric was intimidation. Such spiritual authoritarianism was the psychological outcome of the inherently unequal and unreciprocal relationship between priest and believer. Since civil conversation demanded equal and reciprocal relations, the cleric naturally gravitated to the margins of sociability and politeness.

---

[31] He said that the Tories were used to seeing 'the Poor Rivall Presbitereans as unpolite, unform'd, without Literature, or Manners' and that *Characteristicks* aimed to identify the Tories 'not as Corrupters merely of Morals & Publick Principles; but as the very Reverse or Antipodes of Good Breeding, Schollership, Behaviour, Sense & Manners' – in a letter to John Somers, 30 March 1711, P.R.O. 30/24/22/4, ff. 153–6.

[32] P.R.O. 30/24/20/143, Shaftesbury to Michael Ainsworth, Reigate, 30 December 1709. An edition version of this letter appears in *Several Letters Written by a Noble Lord to a Young Man at the University* (London, 1716), pp. 42–4.

However, in the same letter, Shaftesbury associated religious psychology with religious politics:

He thou ownst to be thy Master & Legislator made no Laws relating to civil power or interfering with it. So that all the Pre-eminence, Wealth or Pension wch thou receiv'st or expects't to receive by help of this assum'd Character, is from the Publick, from whence both the Authority & Profit is deriv'd, & on wch it legally depends: all other Pretensions of *Preists* being Jewish & Heathenish, & in our State Seditious, disloyal & Factiouse, such as is that Spirit wch now reigns in our Universitys, & where the high Church (as they are call'd) are prevalent.

The propensity of clerics to psychological domination was matched by the appetite of churches for wealth and power. Despite their popularity in High-Church enclaves, such pretensions were to be dismissed since the church, as described by Jesus and established in English law, had a specifically secular foundation.

Shaftesbury elaborated the themes of this letter throughout *Characteristicks*. There, the psychosocial and institutional dimensions of the church were analysed in terms of the corruptive force of enthusiasm and priestcraft, which Shaftesbury assimilated to the idioms of sociability and 'politeness'.

Shaftesbury extended and also transformed the theme of enthusiasm. 'Enthusiasm' was used in an entirely negative sense during the Restoration decades, but, by the 1690s, this was changing, as more positive usages by Dryden and John Dennis witnessed.[33] In appropriating 'enthusiasm' to help explain the standards of politeness, Shaftesbury both transvaluated the term and found new objects for its aspersive use.

Shaftesbury's rehabilitation of the affections as foundations of moral agency sanctioned a re-estimation of such a passionate phenomenon as enthusiasm. Shaftesbury embraced it as an important expression of natural affection, saying of himself: 'So far is he from degrading *Enthusiasm*, or disclaiming it in himself; that he looks on this Passion, simply consider'd, as the most *natural*, and its Object as the *justest* in the *World*.'[34] Enthusiasm was natural and universal.

---

[33] For Dryden, see *OED*, s.v. 'enthusiasm'. For Dennis, see Edward Niles Hooker (ed.), *The Critical Works of John Dennis* (Baltimore, 1939), vol. I, pp. 6, 201, 215–16, 227–8. His *Advancement and Reformation of Modern Poetry* (1701) is the major reference, though he was using the term as early as 1693.

[34] 'Miscellaneous Reflections' (II, i), III, 33 (Robertson, II, 176).

This was to rebel against a major tendency of fifty years of Anglican polemic. However, it also allowed an important shift in the term's polemical uses. 'A Letter' was provocative because Shaftesbury used the appearance in London in 1706 and 1707 of French millenarians not just to ridicule this band of 'enthusiasts', but also, and more significantly, to offer a broad critique of public discourse.[35] Since enthusiasm was rooted in human nature, it could be found in all forms of secular and religious life and could all too easily be perverted by zealots. Indeed, zealots could be found inside the Established Church as well as at its borders. Thus, Shaftesbury took a stock element of Anglican polemic and turned it against the high-church wing of the Anglican church, which Shaftesbury labelled 'enthusiastic', 'zealous' and 'fanatic'.

In keeping with the traditional discourse of 'enthusiasm', Shaftesbury defined religious enthusiasm as uncontrolled passion, a condition in which basically sound affections grew to extremity, liberating themselves from any control by mind and eventuating in irrationality and loss of autonomy.[36] What matters here, however, is that Shaftesbury's caricature of the zealot emphasised his unsociability and so played into his politics of discourse. All enthusiasm, according to Shaftesbury, was built on a temperamental substratum of melancholy, which expressed itself in solemnity and gravity. Gravity refused to be questioned and sought rather to impose on others. In fact, '*Gravity* is of the very Essence of Imposture'. The impostor's unwarranted claim to authority opposed the principles of gentlemanly discourse, which deflated pretension through 'a sober kind of Chearfulness, and by a more easy and pleasant way of Thought'.[37]

Thus, in 'The Moralists', the 'serene, soft, and harmonious' enthusiasm of Theocles, the good guru, was contrasted with 'the fierce unsociable way of modern *Zealots*; those starch'd, gruff Gentlemen, who guard Religion as Bullys do a Mistress, and give us the while a very indifferent Opinion of their Lady's Merit, and their own Wit, by adoring what they neither allow to be inspected

---

[35] On the entire incident of the French 'prophets', Hillel Schwartz, *The French Prophets: The History of a Millenarian Group in Eighteenth-Century England* (Berkeley, 1980) and *Knaves, Fools, Madmen, and That Subtile Effluvium: A Study of the Opposition to the French Prophets in England, 1706–1710* (Gainesville, 1978).

[36] 'Miscellaneous Reflections' (II, i; v, iii), III, 40–1, 305 (Robertson, II, 180, 345).

[37] 'A Letter' (ii), I, 11–13 (Robertson, I, 10–12).

by others, nor care themselves to examine in a fair light'.[38] Here, enthusiasm verged on the barbarous. Marked by rigidity and coarseness, its aggressiveness implied a claim to unquestioned authority and a horror of openness, freedom and inquiry. Thus, the High Churchman cum enthusiast with his love of dominion failed to meet sociable standards. He was the opposite of the person who, in social interaction, brought out others, helped them fulfil themselves and fostered their sense of autonomy.

As High-Church enthusiasm was hostile to public discourse, so public discourse was the enemy of enthusiasm. Though the spiritual temperature had fallen since the Middle Ages, religious enthusiasm still survived because people were afraid to question it: 'if something of this militant Religion, something of this Soul-rescuing Spirit, and Saint-Errantry prevails still, we need not wonder, when we consider in how solemn a manner we treat this Distemper, and how preposterously we go about to cure Enthusiasm'.[39] It was in the cause of curing enthusiasm that Shaftesbury mounted his defence of raillery as a key ingredient of public discourse.

Thus, the conceit inherent in the clerical estate was exaggerated by enthusiasm so that the enthusiastic cleric became a moral and spiritual terrorist. However, Shaftesbury was anxious to relate the psychology of religious domination to the history of religious institutions. Turning to the idea of priestcraft, he worked out the implications of ecclesiastical worldliness for the history of politeness and public discourse. In the 'Miscellaneous Reflections' that comprise *Characteristicks'* third volume, he narrated a history of regimes in which the mantle of clerical tyranny had been translated from east to west. Egypt served as the *locus classicus* of a priest-ridden polity, the first and best case of the hierocratic state. Not surprisingly, Shaftesbury says it was there 'where first Religion grew unsociable'.[40]

The main feature of Shaftesbury's account of Egypt was the mutually supporting relationship between priesthood and superstition. The number of priests tended to increase because the priesthood was a hereditary caste with no limits to its numbers or

---

[38] 'The Moralists' (i, iii), ii, 218 (Robertson, ii, 24–5).
[39] 'A Letter' (ii, iv), i, 20, 32 (Robertson, i, 16, 24).
[40] 'The Moralists' (iii, i), ii, 387 (Robertson, ii, 122).

wealth and, as their number grew, so did the number of religious beliefs. Shaftesbury gave several reasons for this, though a particularly interesting one, in light of the question of sociability, was the Egyptians' 'solitary idle Life, whilst shut up in their Houses by the regular Inundations of the NILE'. However, the underlying explanation was economic. In ancient Egypt, Shaftesbury said, the priests maintained themselves with whatever contributions they received from believers, gifts of land and other items that remained the property of the clergy in perpetuity. It was, therefore, in the interest of an ever-increasing number of priests to offer an ever-increasing body of doctrine, until the entire culture was enveloped in a fog of superstition.

The economic dimension of this account allowed Shaftesbury to give it a Harringtonian twist. The growth of the priesthood ultimately subverted the state. Once the Egyptian state had acquiesced in the hereditary priesthood and failed to set limits on clerical wealth and influence, it was no surprise 'that we shou'd find the *Property* and Power of the *Egyptian* Priesthood, in antient days, arriv'd to such a height, as in a manner to have swallow'd up the State and Monarchy'. Deploying a Harringtonian maxim ('That *Dominion* must naturally follow *Property*'), Shaftesbury said that no state could withstand the encroachments of a powerful clergy indefinitely.[41]

All of this meant that ancient Egyptian religion was unsociable. The relation of priests to believers was unequal, manipulative and authoritative, denying the autonomy of the believer. However, Egyptian religion was unsociable in a more basic sense too. As the Egyptian pattern of religion spread, so did beliefs and rites, religions and ceremonies. 'Thus Provinces and Nations were divided by the most *contrary* Rites and Customs which cou'd be devis'd, in order to create the strongest *Aversion* possible between Creatures of a like Species . . . From hence the Opposition rose of Temple against Temple, Proselyte against Proselyte.' Thus, the fruit of zealotry, cultivated by a priesthood, was religious warfare, the ultimate expression of religious unsociability.[42]

Egypt was more than a cautionary example since its influence spread throughout the ancient world, particularly among the Hebrews, whose dependence on the Egyptians for institutions and

[41] 'Miscellaneous Reflections' (II, i), III, 45–50 (Robertson, II, 184–7).
[42] 'Miscellaneous Reflections' (II, i), III, 60–2 (Robertson, II, 194–5).

ideas Shaftesbury spent considerable effort trying to establish.[43] More immediately relevant was Shaftesbury's treatment of later Roman paganism, which he saw as replicating the key features of ancient Egyptian religion: an ever wealthier and more numerous priesthood, a weakening state, and a multiplication of fantastic beliefs that required more gifts to support the priesthood. The conversion of the emperor made Christianity the heir of the material and psychological equipment of the later Roman heathen religion. Christianity solidified on the structural and spiritual perversities of Roman religion. Thus, the situation of medieval Europe was very similar to that of the ancient Egyptian hierocracy.

However, according to Shaftesbury, medieval Europe had reached a new plateau in the history of religious unsociability. The medieval church replaced the unified public culture of antiquity with multiple enthusiasms.[44] A world of spiritual bullying supplanted the classical antique culture of inquiry, scepticism and toleration.

The consummation of these developments was the rise of the medieval Catholic church, an elaborate mechanism for the nurturing of a hierarchy. The achievement was founded on psychological observation of 'the various *Superstitions* and *Enthusiasms* of Mankind; and . . . the different Kinds and Force of each': 'All these seeming Contrarietys of human Passion they knew how to comprehend in their political Model and subservient System of Divinity.' Thus, the Roman church began with the very insights that underlay Shaftesbury's own *Inquiry concerning Virtue*: the foundational importance of the affections, their multiplicity and dynamism, the malleability of the consciousness founded on them. However, where *An Inquiry* used the psychology of affection and consciousness to foster moral responsibility, the church used it to establish a system for manipulating believers. Dismissing the good sort of enthusiasm ('*that* ENTHUSIASM which ran upon *Spirituals*, according to the simpler Views of the divine Existence'), the Catholic church dedicated itself to the alternative enthusiasm, 'which ran upon external Proportions, Magnificance of Structures, Ceremonys, Processions, Quires, and those other Harmonys which captivate *the Eye* and *Ear*. On this account they even added to this *latter* kind, and display'd *Religion* in yet more gorgeous Habit of Temples, Statues,

---

[43] 'Miscellaneous Reflections' (II, i), III, 50–8 (Robertson, II, 187–93).
[44] 'Miscellaneous Reflections' (II, ii), III, 77–82 (Robertson, II, 204–07).

Paintings, Vestments, Copes, Miters, Purple, and the Cathedral Pomp.'[45] In short, the Roman church cultivated a visual and ritual 'Awefulness' which allowed it to conquer Europe and erect an 'almost Universal Monarchy'. Catholic magnificence had offered shelter to imposture for centuries because it subdued those acts of intelligence that might have exposed the preposterousness of Catholic belief and practice.

Shaftesbury made explicit the relevance of his observations on Catholicism to the role and mission of the Church of England. He suggested that some English Protestants, impressed by the grandeur of the Roman church, wanted to imitate it. He then wondered whether the spiritual domination of the Roman church 'seems less intolerable' on account of its age and duration than 'under the petty Tyrannys and mimical Politys of some new Pretenders'.

The former may even *persecute* with a tolerable Grace: The latter, who wou'd willingly derive their Authority from the former, and graft on their *successive Right*, must necessarily make a very aukard Figure. And whilst they strive to give themselves the same Air of Independency on the Civil Magistrate; whilst they affect the same Authority in Government, the same Grandure, Magnificence, and Pomp in Worship, they raise the highest Ridicule, in the Eyes of those who have real Discernment, and can distinguish *Originals* from *Copys*.[46]

The object of ridicule here was the Anglican High Church, which sought independent authority for the church from the civil authority, made much of apostolic succession, and elaborated the mystery of ritual. In the long run, the High-Church zealots were heirs of not only the Catholics but also the Egyptians.

J.P. Kenyon has asserted that the challenge faced by post-1688 Whigs 'was not whether they could establish a new, abstract model of the constitution, but whether they could offset the entrenched theories of Toryism, and at the same time live down their damaging association with political radicalism under Charles II'.[47] This observation has a double significance for this essay.

For one thing, Shaftesbury wrote under the conditions described by Kenyon. Though he had a streak of the Old Whig in him, *Characteristicks* was post-Revolution Whig apology, dedicated to

[45] 'Miscellaneous Reflections' (II, ii), III, 90–1 (Robertson, II, 212–13).
[46] 'Miscellaneous Reflections' (II, ii), III, 93–4 (Robertson, II, 215).
[47] J.P. Kenyon, *Revolution Principles: The Politics of Party, 1689–1720* (Cambridge, 1977), p. 2.

seizing higher ground from Tories. Of course, Shaftesbury was not just writing pamphlets. Rather, he sought a critical altitude from which he could trace a new map of society, politics and culture. He operated at that level described by John Burrow as 'the reflective articulation of the educated classes' political culture'.[48]

The meridian on Shaftesbury's map was the gentleman. Assuming that post-1688 politics ought to be those of a gentlemanly oligarchy, he proceeded to propose an appropriate culture to support it. The social, political, religious, philosophical and aesthetic aspects of this culture were set within a gentlemanly framework, articulated by Shaftesbury in the language of 'politeness'. In this essay, we have seen how Shaftesbury submitted religious and ecclesiastical matters to the discipline of politeness. This involved a relocation of political and cultural authority, transferring it from the church to the social world of polite philosophical gentlemen who were linked by the ties of conversation. Shaftesbury's vision did not appeal to High-Church Tories. However, Shaftesbury's account of politeness gave a religious and political dimension to the culture about which he philosophised and thus made political and religious claims on those who practised it. Moreover, in representing English culture in the image of the polite gentleman, Shaftesbury's account had significant purchase among those who found themselves inscribed so conspicuously and so favourably in *Characteristicks*.

Kenyon's remark also reminds us that political discourse is usually generated in charged rhetorical situations. The satisfaction of theoretical impulses and the conquest of technical problems motivate some writers and therefore shape some texts. Indeed, there are places in Shaftesbury's writing (frequently examined sections of 'An Inquiry concerning Virtue' and 'The Moralists') where he sought to provide a theoretical grounding for the polite public. However, Shaftesbury was only fitfully a theoretical writer, and, as this essay shows, much of his discussion relied on forms of persuasion other than formal argument. What is most interesting about Shaftesbury is not that he offered the authority of a public as an alternative to ecclesiastical and magisterial authority, but the way in which he did it – by refashioning the scenes of English politics and culture according to the requirements of politeness.

---

[48] Burrow, *Whigs and Liberals*, p. 6.

CHAPTER 14

Propriety, property and prudence: David Hume and the defence of the Revolution

Nicholas Phillipson

The publication of the *History of England* finally established Hume's reputation as a Tory. The Whiggery of George III's reign could probably have survived the effects of his attack on reason, which had destroyed the epistemological foundations on which its theories of natural rights and contract depended. But, in what Hume called 'the historical age', it was much less easy to ignore an assault on Whig historiography which was not only intellectually devastating but was set out in a work which was becoming a bestseller at home and abroad.[1] The *History of England* had destroyed the credibility of traditional claims that England was a country which possessed an ancient constitution whose principles had been periodically reaffirmed and perfected in the course of a long and continuous history. So far as the history of the modern age was concerned, Hume had drawn on Harrington and Clarendon to develop a strikingly subtle account of the catastrophes of the Civil War. It had taken place, he argued, in a country which had entered its post-feudal age but had not yet entered the age of commerce. It was the story of a court and parliament engulfed by Arminian superstition and Puritan enthusiasm and a country dominated by a gentry which had been freed from the bondage of feudal tenures but lacked the political understanding needed to secure their property and avoid the quicksands of religious zealotry. So far from being a Whiggish story about a struggle to preserve English liberty from Stuart despotism, Hume's account of the Civil War was a story about the failure of modern prudence and the fall of a king whose virtues and sufferings commanded the sort of sympathy Whigs only expected from Tories. But most important of all, the *History of England* had ended with a nuanced and dismayingly problematic account of the

[1] D. Hume–W. Strahan [August 1770], *Letters of David Hume*, ed. J.Y.T. Grieg, 2 vols. (Oxford, 1932), vol. i, p. 230.

Revolution, the Convention Parliament and the accession of William III. As Hume told it, James II's astonishing and unexpected flight, the opportunism of men who were doubtless animated by public spirit, and the prudence of a cautious and forceful prince accounted for a peaceful transfer of power and for preventing the rapid declension of politics into ideological turmoil and popular tumult. Was the Revolution to be seen as an act of providence, fortune or usurpation; as a revolution which had returned power to the people or a *ricorso* which had returned the constituion to its first principles? Hume's was an account which carefully kept alive the unwelcome question, whether the Revolution was, as the Whigs insisted, a Whig revolution whose future would only be safe in their hands. And if not, it raised the further question, how could it be defended.[2]

There can be no doubt of Hume's interest in this most fundamental of questions. He had already raised it at the end of Book III of the *Treatise* – significantly the only such departure into a question of contemporary politics in that metaphysical work. He had dealt with the question again in 1747 in two of the last of his *Essays Moral and Political*, 'Of the Original Contract' and 'Of Passive Obedience' in classic assaults on the theories of rights, divine and natural, on which party polemic was founded. Duncan Forbes has described Hume as a 'philosophical' or 'sceptical' Whig at war with the narrowly provincial political culture of modern England, turning to the natural jurisprudence of Grotius and Pufendorf for new intellectual resources with which to rebuild it.[3] But natural jurisprudence has its own place in the history of political polemic in post-Revolution Britain, as a source of theories of limited resistance which were free of radical, exclusionist associations and were available to Whigs and Tories who sought a more 'moderate' defence of the Revolution and the Revolution Settlement.[4] This

---

[2] This modifies Duncan Forbes's account in *Hume's Philosophical Politics* (Cambridge, 1975), pp. 91–101, 320. Forbes complains that, here and elsewhere, Hume was 'a precise thinker, but a notoriously careless writer', *The History of Great Britain: The Reigns of James I and Charles I*, ed. D. Forbes (Harmondsworth, 1970), p. 27. Here and elsewhere I argue that this apparent imprecision was part of a carefully conceived plan to reconstruct contemporary culture. See my *Hume* (London, 1989), *passim*.

[3] D. Forbes, *Hume's Philosophical Politics* (Cambridge, 1975).

[4] M.A. Goldie, 'Tory Political Thought, 1689–1714', Unpublished Ph.D. thesis, University of Cambridge, 1977, esp. pp. 21–2, 79–88 and ch.5, demonstrates how Grotius could be exploited by both Whig and Tory apologists. The debts of that arch-Whig apologist Benjamin Hoadley to Grotius and Pufendorf as well as to Locke would repay study.

essay deals with Hume's defence of the Revolution and the Hanoverian Succession and his search for an intelligible and polemically convincing account of the principles of limited resistance. It deals with a non-Christian sceptic's interest in the language of manners that developed in Anne's reign, during the so-called 'range of party' and the paper war that broke out in Grub Street in a periodical press which was then in its infancy. And it suggests that there is light to be shed on the development of Hume's conception of the Science of Man as well as his political thought, by regarding him as a philosopher who looked back to the reign of Anne and saw it as an age in which the agenda of modern political discourse had been set.

The discourse that interested Hume had developed in the latter years of William III's reign and reached a climax during the Sacheverell Trial and the General Election campaign of 1710. These were years in which party conflict was sharpened by fears of oligarchy, Whig or Jacobite, by bitter disputes about the relationship between the Anglican church and dissent and by the conduct of a war which was turning Britain into an imperial polity. These apprehensions were brought into polemical focus by the language of the Exclusion Crisis and an astonishingly virulent revival of the classic debate about election and divine right, resistance and passive obedience which was orchestrated by Grub Street and the resources of a newly established and rapidly expanding periodical press. Henceforth the history of political discourse would be inextricably entwined with the history of an institution which offered political writers new and powerful opportunities for manipulating opinion. Hume's philosophical interest in opinion, his political desire to create a casuistical bridge to link philosophy and practical morality, can be traced to this extraordinary moment in the history of British political culture.

So far as the history of the periodical press is concerned, the responsiblity for reviving the exclusionist debate lay with the country Whig John Tutchin, whose thrice-weekly *Observator* first appeared in 1702.[5] His was a garrulous and eclectic attempt to reconstruct a Whiggery which was threatened by the Junto as well as the High-Church party. But it was the High-Church party

---

[5] Tutchin has understandably been neglected. But see J.P. Kenyon, *Revolution Principles: The Politics of Party, 1689–1720* (Cambridge, 1977), pp. 105–6.

which provided the debate with its cutting edge in a brilliant and iconoclastic assault on all forms of Whiggery by Charles Leslie's *Rehearsals*.[6] This attack on Whiggery was directed against its most formidable theorist, 'the Great Lock', 'the oracle of the party'.[7] During the Exclusion Crisis Locke had devoted the First Treatise of Government to a classic attack on Filmer's patriarchalism in order to clear the gound for his own defence of resistance. Leslie now proposed a tit for tat. A successful attack on the Second Treatise would discredit the authority of the First and clear the ground for a restatement of Filmerian principles in such a way as to demonstrate the necessity of an apostolic Anglican church for maintaining the principles of monarchy. Leslie's assault on Locke took the form of a sceptical attack on theories of natural rights which was set in an Augustinian framework. Such theories were shown to be no more than *opinions* which had roots in the imagination and pride of a fallen species, which bred distrust of political authority and laid the foundations of 'the kingdom of ME', a quasi-Hobbesian realm regulated by the vagaries of opinion and political craft.[8] In this view, there was no such thing as an intelligible theory of limited resistance based on rights that were vested collectively in a people or their representatives; indeed Defoe's claim that the rights of resistance were vested in the 40/- Freeholders was met with the withering retort, 'Is none a Free born Englishman but a Freeholder? Have we exchanged absolute Kings for absolute Freeholders?'[9] Theories of limited resistance were simply subtle cloaks for the sort of oligarchic rule that had been responsible for the Revolution Settlement, the Act of Settlement and the abominable Toleration Act which threatened the apostolic claims of the church. As such, they did nothing to shake the old High Church view that the Revolution had been an act of necessity, a providential

---

[6] Leslie on the other hand, deserves attention, J. Dunn deals perceptively but in passing with his critique of Locke; *The Political Thought of John Locke* (Cambridge, 1969). See also M.A. Goldie, 'Tory Political Thought', esp. chs. 10–11. Leslie's political thought was developed at length in *The Rehearsal of Observator* which was later republished as *A View of the Times, their Principles and Practices. By Philalethes* (1708–9). It was usefully summarised in *The New Association of those called Moderate Church-Man with the Modern-Whigs and Fanaticks, to Undermine and Blow-up the Present Church and Government*, Part III (1702–3). See also *The Finishing Stroke* (1711).

[7] *Rehearsals*, 14–21 April 1705; 15–22 December 1705. The critique of Locke was begun on 11–18 August and continued until 13–20 October 1705.

[8] *Rehearsals*, 28 October–4 November 1704.

[9] *Rehearsals*, 16 March 1708. Cf. 6–13 January 1704/5 and 3 August 1706.

intervention to preserve the church and the constitution from popery and despotism. And it had established a regime which would last only until it was divinely ordained that the succession should return to its rightful heritors.

Whigs and Revolution Tories ('false brethren' in the high Anglican argot[10]) responded by using wit and satire to ridicule the absurdities of divine-right theory, by attempting to shore up appeals to natural rights by appeals to the Common Law and the public interest and by calling for a reformation of manners to restore the trust on which the preservation of the Revolution depended. This attempt to invoke conventional as well as natural rights provoked two influential responses which were to be of particular importance in shaping Hume's understanding of the inadequacies of contemporary political thought. Daniel Defoe, and Richard Steele and Joseph Addison addressed the problem of creating a language of interest which would reinforce the increasingly shaky authority of the language of rights on which the legitimacy of the Revolution depended and rescue it from the charge that the Revolution Settlement was simply a Whig usurpation. Here Defoe was to be the most adept and interesting of Leslie's opponents. In his long philosophical poem *Jure Divino: A Satyr in Twelve Books. By the Author of The True Born Englishman* (1706) he ridiculed a political theory which made more sense of the experience of the nomadic world of the patriarchs of the Old Testament than that of a free commercial polity and could only offend the 'reason' and 'common sense' of the modern citizen. Its cutting edge was a defence of limited resistance which was based on an unashamedly eclectic appeal to Grotius, Pufendorf and Locke to the common law, to Harrington and to the progress of society since the rise of commerce.[11] This appeal to the public interest as well as

---

[10] Thus the title of Sacheverell's classic pamphlet, *The Perils of False Brethren, both in Church and State* ... (1709).

[11] Defoe is generally seen as playing an important part in the transmission of Locke's second treatise into Augustan/Whig political culture. See, for example, Martyn Thomson, 'Daniel Defoe and the Formation of Early Eighteenth Century Whig Ideology', unpublished paper delivered at the Folger Institute Center for the History of British Political Thought, October 1986, Paula Backsheider, *Daniel Defoe: his Life* (Baltimore and London, 1989), pp. 169–72, and in this volume James Tully, 'Placing the *Two Treatises*', p. 262. In my view these claims overlook the damage inflicted by Leslie on Locke's reputation as a 'moderate' Whig and the highly eclectic context in which Defoe found it necessary to call on his authority. Indeed, it can be argued that Defoe was attempting to appropriate Locke for a non-exclusionist defence of the Revolution by placing him in the context of natural jurisprudence.

natural rights was sharpened here and in *The Review* by a proto-Humean regret that the English had failed to develop an adequate understanding of their constitution and of the public interest at a time when their country was being transformed by war, commerce and empire. As he put it, 'It is an *English* disease and too peculiar to this Nation, not to see their own Interest, and to interrupt their real happiness by Feuds, Discontents, and private Murmurings for Trifles, needless Diversions, and unreasonable heats.'[12]

But new conceptions of interest required a reformation of manners to propagate and sustain them. Defoe saw this as a matter of curbing the superstition and enthusiasm of an ungrateful people and the pride, ignorance and xenophobia on which it fed, by encouraging moderation in the use of political language. He had a clear sense of the potential of the press in shaping the tavern and coffee-house conversation of citizens engaged in the ordinary business of life in London and the provinces. As he showed in the most famous of his satires, 'The True-born Englishman' and 'A Short Way with Dissenters', part of the job could be done by exploiting the resources of raillery and satire in an Erasmian and Shaftesburian spirit, encouraging the friendly conversation that would prevent the spirit of raillery from turning into cynicism.[13] But it was also a matter of combating ignorance with the sort of instruction he offered in *The Review*, in essays on politics, diplomacy, war and trade which were designed to explain the changing interests of Britain to the city. Intellectually, the enterprise was broadly Ciceronian, an exercise in exploiting the resources of the press and the city to encourage conversation which would generate new ideas of prudence, curb faction, restore trust and secure the constitution.

This enterprise hinged on the cultivation of *moderation* in the use of political and religious language; but that, Leslie remarked caustically, was simply to encourage hypocrisy:

It is a Catholicon, and Cures all Diseases! Take but a Dose of this and thou mays't Drink Poison, and Break all the Ten Commandments without any Offence! It Reconciles Churches, or No Churches, Christ and Belial, Light and Darkness! It can Transform a Rebel into a Saint, and Satan to

---

[12] *Jure Divino* (1706), pp. xi, 12n.
[13] Defoe marshalled his most potent exercises in satire in two volumes *A True Collection of the Writings of the Author of the True Born Englishman. Corrected by Himself* (1703–4).

an Angel of Light! It can make a Schismatick, a true Friend of the Church; and a Whore an Honest Woman!'[14]

This was to expose, in a peculiarly Anglican setting, the classic tensions between prudence, honesty and Christian virtue which were inherent in neo-Ciceronian ethics. Defoe seems to have addressed the problem by appealing to the *candour* beloved of English dissenters who recognised honesty in argument as a sign of Grace. But it was Richard Steele and Joseph Addison, both devout members of the Church of England, who addressed the problem most directly by developing an elaborate language of manners which showed how propriety, reinforced by the cultivation of taste and natural theology – what contemporaries called politeness – could encourage Christian virtue. This enterprise was explicitly Ciceronian and designed to explore the resources of conversation as an instrument for generating a reformation of manners.[15] The numerous and astonishingly popular essays on manners, morals, taste and religion that were written for the *Tatler, Spectator* and *Guardian* between 1709 and 1714 provide a closely textured and fascinating analysis of the cultural fabric of the modern British city.[16] But it was an analysis which was designed to show how cultivating the arts of conversation could reform the morals as well as the manners of citizens whose behaviour was shaped by the imagination, the passions and, above all, pride 'the most ordinary Spring of Action among Men.'[17] Indeed the *Spectator* was presented as 'remedium efficax et universum' for pride, party and spleen.[18] It was designed to show how ill-suited the pursuit of Christian virtue on Augustinian lines was to cultivating the prudential virtues needed in the daily life of a free commercial polity and to advocate the pursuit of 'virtue and decency' on Ciceronian terms as the path which would lead to a true understanding of virtue.[19] In this idiom,

[14] *Rehearsals.* 13–20 January 1704–5. Cf. 3–10 February 1704–5.
[15] In what follows, I refine the discussion of politeness I offer in *Hume*, ch. 2. There I make no distinction between languages of propriety and politeness. Here, I present the latter as a variant of the former. Were I to reformulate my earlier discussion, Defoe would appear as employing the language of propriety rather than the language of politeness.
[16] Between 1709 and 1711 the *Tatler* published, thrice weekly, 271 essays; between 1711 and 1714, the *Spectator* published 635 daily essays; in 1713, the *Guardian* published 175 daily essays. And that is not to mention the many essays which appeared in short-lived and ephemeral reviews like the *Old Whig* and the *Freeholder* of 1715 to 1716.
[17] *Spectator*, no. 394.
[18] *Spectator*, no. 547.
[19] *Spectator*, no. 104.

perfecting the art of conversation meant paying attention to the principles which regulated it. Doing so would teach the citizen that conversation was a regular form of human activity, controlled by the constraints of friendship and social approval and the decorum on which it depended. He would learn to value moderation in the use of language, to respect the judgement of his friends and understand the advantages that flowed from the careful use of language.

But an essential element in the appeal of Spectatorial propriety lay in its demonstration of the manner in which politeness could bridge the gap between prudence, honesty and virtue. Steele, and more especially, Addison, were particularly attentive to the processes by which manners and language were internalised, became 'easy' and could be regarded as conforming to 'reason' or 'common sense' (here, as in Defoe, the terms were virtually interchangeable). Indeed Steele's much-loved honest country gentleman, Sir Roger de Coverley, declared that unless these conditions were met, morality would be out of step with nature and the public good and a man's conduct would always be 'hopping'.[20] But the history of the Civil War and the commotions of the previous century had demonstrated in ways which Hume would elaborate with the most brilliant insight, how behaviour which was apparently 'honest' could sustain the most disastrously disruptive forms of superstition and enthusiasm.[21] Here it was a matter of cultivating discretion, 'an accomplishment' as well as a virtue, which had the power to curb 'narrow Views of Self-interest' and encourage the development of more 'extensive' views of interest and morality.[22] As such it had the potential to act as 'the Perfection of Reason, and a Guide to us in all the Duties of Life.'[23] Politeness was the skill which would perfect discretion and ensure that propriety became a vehicle of

---

[20] *Spectator*, no. 6.
[21] Thus the portrait of Archbishop Laud, subtly derived from Clarendon, showed how Arminian superstition could divert virtue and learning from service to the public to service to the church and could erode the prudence on which the court and country would have to draw if the constitution was to be preserved. D. Hume, *The History of England. From the Invasion of Julius Caesar to The Revolution in 1688.* 6 vols., ed. W.B. Todd (Indianapolis, 1983), vol. v, pp. 222–9. Thus, Lord Russell, executed for his part in the Rye House plot, is presented as a man whose party zeal, nourished by 'a social temper and cloathing itself under the appearance of principle, it is almost impossible for a virtuous man, who has acted in public life, ever thoroughly to eradicate', ibid. vol. vi, p.435.
[22] *Spectator*, no. 224.
[23] *Spectator*, no. 225.

virtue. It was first and foremost, a matter of cultivating the arts and
sciences and of generating a general conception of the world which
had its roots in 'reason' and 'common sense' and could be perfected
by cultivating a love of beauty. As such, it was an accomplishment
that relied on awakening the 'poetic imagination' by means of
imaginary conversations with the authors of works of art and
literature and their heroes and heroines.[24] These imaginary conversations provided an escape from the prudential world to one in
which understanding was ruled by general and more elevated
principles which allowed the citizen to receive the truths of
aethestics and natural theology and to prepare himself for the
friendly, conversational relationship with the Deity which Anglicans since Hooker's day had long been accustomed to enjoy. In the
last resort, then, it was natural theology which underwrote Spectatorial ethics and the language of propriety on which the moderate
defence of the Revolution was seen to depend.

It was, of course, inevitable that propriety and politeness would
be associated with Whiggery. Its dependence on natural theology
pointed quite explicitly towards the latitudinarian world of the
Toleration Act and Occasional Conformity and equally explicitly
rejected the Augustinian foundations on which the apostolic claims
of High-Church Toryism rested. But equally, its moral theology
was far from proof against critics like Swift and Mandeville who
rightly refused to find in them any adequate answer to the different
languages of self-love on which Augustinian and Hobbesian ethics
depended. Thus, for Mandeville, Steele's' 'artful Encomiums' to
encourage the improvement of manners were nothing but a series of
tricks like those made use of 'by the Women that would teach
Children to be mannerly' which pleased their parents and gratified
their pride.[25] As for the benevolence which Shaftesbury and Addison
had invoked to persuade their readers that virtue could be cultivated
without self-denial, that simply constituted 'a Vast Inlet to Hypocrisy, which being once made habitual, we must not only deceive
others, but likewise become altogether unknown to our selves.'[26]

[24] See especially the essays on 'The Pleasures of the Imagination', *Spectator*, nos. 411–21. The
same theme is reiterated, often with greater terseness and acuity throughout the *Guardian*.
[25] *The Fable of the Bees. Or Private Vices. Publick Benefits*. By Bernard Mandeville. Ed. F.B.
Kaye (Indianapolis, 1988), pp. 52–3. On Mandeville as a critic of politeness see D.
Castiglione, 'Mandeville moralized', *Annali della Fondazione Luigi Einaudi*, vol. XVII, 1983,
pp. 239–90.
[26] *Fable of the Bees*, p. 331.

For all Defoe's and the *Spectator*'s efforts, it still seemed hard to defend the Revolution other than on narrowly prudential or providential grounds.

Hume's defence of the Revolution and the Hanoverian Succession rested on a highly distinctive theory of limited resistance which was integral to his Science of Man. Its roots lay in a classic sceptical assault on reason which undermined the epistemological founda- tions on which all known languages of rights, divine and natural, depended and led Hume to conclude 'Tis not . . . reason, which is the guide of Life, but custom.'[27] This assault on traditional claims about the authority of reason in regulating human conduct was, of course, comprehensive in scope and intellectually decisive, but it is interesting to notice that Hume, like Defoe, Addison and Steele before him chose to mount his assault by attacking 'strict' Christian claims about rationality in general and those of Malebranche, the most sophisticated and influential of modern Augustinians, in particular. In his attack on reason he was willing to concede – with reservations – to the Augustinian proposition that the ordinary behaviour of human beings was shaped by imagination, pride and custom. What interested him particularly was the role of custom and habit in shaping the imagination and socialising the pride of sympathetic beings who possessed the power of language. It was this critique of 'strict' Christian metaphysics, then, that formed the basis of his celebrated analysis of the process of convention-making out of which human beings fashion the societies they inhabit. The natural theology of the polite press did not offer Hume a system of theology which was capable of directing him to his new, historicist, science of man.

Thus armed, Hume used his theory of convention to develop a pagan critique of the language of propriety.[28] Language itself was a product of 'company and conversation' and of the search for social approval and the exercise of restraint.[29] But these principles

---

[27] D. Hume, *A Treatise of Human Nature*, ed. L.A. Selby-Bigge. Second edition ed. P.H. Nidditch (Oxford, 1978), p. 652 (henceforth cited as *Treatise*).

[28] I am particularly indebted to Donald W. Livingston's discussion of conventions in *Hume's Philosophy of Common Life* (Chicago and London, 1984), esp. ch. 3. The following discussion of convention-making as a venture in developing the resources of the language of propriety develops my discussion in *Hume*, ch. 2–3.

[29] *Enquiries Concerning the Human Understanding and Concerning the Principles of Morals* by David Hume, ed. L.A. Selby-Bigge (2nd edn, Oxford, 1966), p.209. Henceforth cited as *Enquiries*.

themselves were a function of that fundamental principle of
sociability, sympathy, of which, Hume wrote,

no quality of human nature is more remarkable both in itself and in its
consequences, than that propensity we have to sympathize with others,
and to receive by communication their inclinations and sentiments,
however different from or even contrary to our own.[30]

Hume's critique of reason had offered a classic demonstration of
the power of language to deliver those general propositions about
the world which were absolutely necessary for the conduct of
ordinary life; herein, he concluded, lay the necessity of submission
to its authority. Hume proposed a new definition of necessity which
was neither Christian – in the sense of constituting a denial of free
will – nor, as some modern commentators have suggested, biologi-
cal. It was a form of obligation which derived from considerations
of interest and force of habit. If considerations of interest explained
the necessity which obliged human beings to enter into linguistic
conventions, it was habit which ensured that those conventions
became, as Addison and Steele, though not Hume, put it, 'easy'.
Thus, if our initial interest in convention-making derived from a
general sense of its interest to those who had entered into it,
linguistic conventions reinforced by interest and habit rather than
reason were the source of those general ideas on which knowledge,
or rather, understanding, depended. Ciceronian claims about the
authority of language in shaping the civic personality and neo-
Ciceronian perceptions about the role of conversation in making
the resources of language available to sociable beings were pressed
to new and radical metaphysical depths.

   The full – not to say, revolutionary – power of this convention-
based language of custom as a tool for analysing human behaviour
was by no means apparent in the *Treatise*. That power would only
be fully apparent once Hume was in a position to demonstrate how
considerations of interest and force of habit interacted and shaped
the behaviour of particular individuals, sects and societies in
particular historical circumstances. Something of this was to be
evident in his long essay 'The Natural History of Religion' in which
he traced the origins of religious belief and the progress of
civilisation from its polytheistic to its monotheistic state in what

---

[30] *Treatise*, p. 316.

Pocock has recently shown to be an uncharacteristically eccentric piece of historical scholarship.[31] But the full force of this model would not be apparent until Hume had abandoned metaphysics for that neglected masterpiece, the *History of England,* in which he offered a series of extraordinary demonstrations of the manner in which new and perhaps fantastical conceptions of interest could undermine even the most fundamental and apparently stable cognitive habits.[32] But Hume had no particular reason to be interested in habit in the *Treatise.* For that work was, first and foremost, a study of metaphysics which was concerned with the *origins* of ideas and with the interest-considerations on which our initial adherence to linguistic conventions depends.[33] And it was, above all, concerned with the origins of those *general* ideas which shape our social behaviour and the precise nature of the interests on which they are founded. In the first two books of the *Treatise* Hume had offered an analysis of convention which drew on the experience of that most exceptional of beings, the non-Christian Pyrrhonian philosopher. In the third book 'Of Morals', published a year later, he made the first of his formal appeals to the candour of 'ordinary readers',[34] to the experience of the 'vulgar' rather than the 'learned' and to the intelligence of the 'honest gentlemen' who 'have carried their thoughts very little beyond those objects, which are every day expos'd to their senses',[35] invoking the only cognitive experience he could assume had forced them to reflect on the nature and necessity of general rules in the conduct of ordinary life. This was their recognition of the need for rules of justice and for political authority to secure their property. This formative experience was the outcome of the tension between any individual's natural desire to increase his own possessions and those of his family and friends at the expense of others; and the countervailing,

---

[31] J.G.A. Pocock, 'Cudworth, Brucker and Hume: The Paradox of the Natural History of Religion', Unpublished paper delivered at the Folger Institute Center for the History of British Political Thought, September 1986.

[32] On which see my *Hume,* esp. chs. 5–6.

[33] It is worth reflecting that Hume's science of man deals with human beings who have acquired the capacity for language and are in a position to exploit its resources. It does not, therefore apply to infants who are short of verbal language skills and who, in acquiring the rudiments of language, can be expected to be interest-orientated rather than habit-orientated. I am grateful to Kurtis Kitigawa for fascinating conversation on this point.

[34] *Treatise,* Book III, 'Advertisement'.

[35] *Treatise,* p. 272.

defensive recognition of the need to restrain his natural acquisitiveness in the interest of preserving the right to exclusive enjoyment of what he already possessed. Interest taught the necessity for
restraint and the need for rules of justice. Interest obliged him to
enter into conventions which articulated the laws of nature, defined
the general interests of society and provided him with an understanding of the need for political authority and a sense of the
'common', 'general' or 'public' interest. For the ordinary reader,
reflecting on the nature of property and justice was shown to be the
key to understanding the nature of convention-making and the
origins of those general ideas on which civil society depended.
Understanding property was to be the key to understanding
propriety.

As Hume's classic discussion of the origins of justice shows, it
was in 'Of Morals' that Hume's account of conventions and
convention-making and the interest-calculations on which it rested,
was at its most developed and it was here, therefore that he
confronted directly the problem of bringing the language of propriety into alignment with the language of natural jurisprudence.[36]
But what was equally important was his sceptical insistence on the
potentially bewildering variety and diversity of interests which
regulated ordinary human intercourse in a commercial world and
the necessity of adhering to linguistic conventions in order to
acquire general ideas of our interests. Indeed, in a remarkable
analysis which is worth quoting at length, Hume went so far as to
insist on the importance of *forgetfulness* in shaping our moral
conduct. *Ataraxia* would enable the modern sceptic to bypass the
Augustinian and Mandevillian dilemmas which threatened to
unsettle the language of propriety:

Being thus acquainted with the nature of man, we expect not any
impossibilities from him; but confine our view to that narrow circle in
which any person moves, in order to form a judgement of his moral
character. When the natural tendency of his passions leads him to be

---

[36] On Hume's theory of justice as a contribution to the development of the natural
jurisprudence tradition established by Grotius and Pufendorf, see especially D. Forbes,
Hume's Philosophical Politics and K. Haakonssen, *The Science of a Legislator: The Natural
Jurisprudence of David Hume and Adam Smith* (Cambridge, 1981). What is argued in the
present essay, however, is that whatever contribution Hume may be said to have made to
such a 'tradition', his account of the principles of justice is written in a language whose
linguistic foundations and whose agenda were significantly different from those of that
tradition's founders.

serviceable and useful within his sphere, we approve of his character, and love his person, by a sympathy with the sentiments of those, who have a more particular connexion with him. We are quickly oblig'd *to forget our own interest* in our judgements of this kind, by reason of the perpetual contradictions we meet with in society and conversation, from persons that are not plac'd in the same situation, and have not the same interest with ourselves. The only point of view, in which our sentiments concur with those of others, is when we consider the tendency of any passion to the advantage or harm of those who have any immediate connexion or intercourse with the person possess'd of it. And tho' this advantage or harm be often very remote from ourselves, yet sometimes 'tis very near us, and interests us strongly by sympathy.'[37] [my italics]

This intricate reasoning allowed Hume to conclude, famously, that such social intercourse 'makes us form some general inalterable standard by which we may approve or disapprove of characters and manners'. As such it constituted a prudential language which 'tho' the *heart* does not always take part with those general notions, or regulate its love and hatred by them, yet are they sufficient for discourse, and serve all our purposes in company, in the pulpit, on the theatre, and in the schools'.[38]

But what matters here is the manner in which Hume applied this analysis to the Revolution and the Hanoverian Succession and to the problem of formulating a theory of limited resistance. At one level, his theory pointed to a theory of resistance that was universal and unlimited. As the only foundation on which the conventions on which political obligation rested was interest, the so-called right of resistance was by its nature universal and unlimited. 'Since 'tis impossible, even in the most despotic governments to deprive [the people] of it.'[39] On the other hand, since the primary motive for submitting to government was a recognition of the necessity of political authority to secure the rules of justice, it followed that the roots of political obligation were to be found in a 'natural' disposition to submit to established political authority. Thus 'there is nothing but a great present advantage, that can lead us to rebellion, by making us overlook the remotest interest which we have in preserving peace and order in society.'[40] Thus our 'right' to rebel, or rather, our interest in rebelling, was limited simply by

[37] *Treatise*, pp. 602–3.
[38] *Treatise*, p. 603.
[39] *Treatise*, pp. 563–4.
[40] *Treatise*, p. 545.

considerations of prudence which might be reinforced by 'a separate sentiment of morality' which would encourage subjects to assign peculiar 'rights' to those in power and to assume peculiar obligations not to resist them.[41] As Hume concluded,

Time and custom give authority to all forms of government, and all successions of princes; and that power, which at first was founded only on injustice and violence, becomes in time legal and obligatory. Nor does the mind rest there; but returning back upon its footsteps, transfers to their predecessors and ancestors that right, which it naturally ascribes to the posterity, as being related together, and united in the imagination. The present *king* of *France* makes *Hugh Capet* a more lawful prince than *Cromwell*; as the establish'd liberty of the *Dutch* is no inconsiderable apology for their obstinate resistance to *Philip* the second.[42]

Hume's theory of limited resistance was a theory about the prudential limitations that restrained an exercise of power that no members of a polity would indulge except in the face of the most extreme forms of despotism, or, as the *History of England* was to show, unless they were deluded by the most violent forms of superstition and enthusiasm. As such, Hume concluded, the Revolution and the Hanoverian Succession only could and only ought to be defended on prudential grounds provided always that prudence was discussed in a properly conceived language of propriety.

There is a sense in which Hume can be said to have spent the rest of his intellectual career turning his account of the language of propriety into a vehicle for the reformation of manners. The *Essays Political and Moral* of 1741–7, and the *History of England*, for example, were exercises in showing how it could be used to encourage moderation in the use of political and historical language. But it was in the two *Enquiries*, the *Enquiry Concerning the Human Understanding* of 1748 and the *Enquiry Concerning the Principles of Morals* of 1751, and in the *Political Discourses* of 1752 that Hume addressed the problem of examining its relationship to the language of propriety and politeness that had developed in the early years of the century and showing how it could be used to reform the inadequate polite culture of an Addisonian world.

The most striking shift of linguistic emphasis Hume made in the second *Enquiry* was to introduce utility instead of interest into his

[41] *Treatise*, pp. 554–6.
[42] *Treatise*, pp. 566–7.

language of convention. In the *Treatise* he had admitted that his analysis had exposed facts of cognitive life which were often 'minute' and sometimes 'hideous' and had followed trains of thought which were often 'too subtle' for the vulgar to follow even although, as in the case of our reasoning about political obligation, ''tis certain that all men have an implicit notion of it.'[43] The appeal to utility rather than interest involved evading the emotive consequences of a dangerously Mandevillian vocabulary in favour of using the more familiar resources of the Ciceronian vocabulary from which the languages of propriety and politeness had been derived. So far as Hume's non-Christian account of the language of propriety was concerned, utility rather than natural theology now appeared as the principle on which an understanding of virtue depended and taste was to be valued as a means for refining our understanding of utility. The constraints of the language of propriety required Hume to show how the tensions between prudence, honesty and virtue could be eased. Here Hume subtly re-examined the principles of conversation. For Addison and Steele, the cultivation of politeness and natural theology ensured that conversation would lead to an understanding of virtue as well as prudence. For Hume, however, conversation would only teach virtue when fertilised with philosophy. As he had commented in 1742, modern philosophers should be 'ambassadors from the Dominions of Learning to those of Conversation' who had the task of supplying them with general questions about the principles of politics, morals, taste and even – so the *Dialogues Concerning Natural Religion* seem to hint – religion.[44] They would ensure that ordinary conversation became a vehicle for extending views of human interests from the confined and partial world of family and friends to society and, in the last resort, to that ultimate and universal source of morality, Hume's celebrated 'party of humanity'.[45]

In the second *Enquiry*, Hume's discussion of political authority was singularly terse. The discussion of political obligation was recast in a language of propriety which rested on a neo-Ciceronian

---

[43] *Treatise*, p. 550.
[44] 'Of Essay Writing', in David Hume, *Essays, Moral, Political and Literary*, ed. E.F. Miller (Indianapolis, 1985), p. 535. Henceforth cited as *Essays*. The point was refined in *Enquiries*, pp. 5–16 and again at the start of *Political Discourses* in 'Of Commerce'. *Essays*, pp. 253–5.
[45] *Enquiries*, p. 275.

appeal to utility, rather than interest. The problems of maintaining the rules of justice and morality in a commercial society were reserved for the *Political Discourses* of 1752. Here Hume's account of the problems of developing commerce in domestic and international politics were carefully interwoven with an elegant panegyric to its civilising powers which was cast in a language with which Defoe's readers were familiar and was also familiar to Scots who had debated the problem of generating economic growth in Scotland before the Union of 1707.[46] Here, as in the second *Enquiry*, Hume was careful to identify the importance of commerce in increasing sociability and making possible the conversation on which the spread of humanity and virtue depended.

The more these refined arts advance, the more sociable men become: nor is it possible, that when enriched with science, and possessed of a fund of conversation, they should be contented to remain in solitude, or live with their fellow-citizens in that distant manner, which is peculiar to ignorant and barbarous nations. They flock to cities; love to receive and communicate knowledge; to show their wit or their breeding; their taste in conversation or living, in clothes or furniture. Curiosity allures the wise; vanity the foolish; and pleasure both. Particular clubs and societies are everywhere formed: Both sexes meet in an easy and sociable manner: and the tempers of men, as well as their behaviour refine apace.[47]

It was no coincidence that the *Political Discourses* closed with essays on 'the Protestant Succession'; and 'the Idea of a Perfect Commonwealth'. These addressed the problem which lay at the heart of the political language of propriety, distinguishing the defence of the Revolution from the defence of Junto Whiggery. It was here that Hume explained how the Revolution and the Hanoverian Succession could be defended and how the constitution could be perfected. The first essay rehearsed, once again, the prudential reasons for adhering to the Hanoverian Succession and identified the cultural constraints on which an understanding of prudence and virtue depended.

But the settlement in the house of Hanover has actually taken place. The princes of that family, without intrigue, without cabal, without solicitation on their part, have been called to mount our throne, by the united voice of

---

[46] See my 'The Scottish Enlightenment', in *The Enlightenment in National Context*, ed. R. Porter and M. Teich (Cambridge, 1981), pp. 22–6.
[47] 'Of Refinement in the Arts', in *Essays*, p. 278. Cf. *Enquiries*, p.274.

the whole legislative body. They have, since their accession, displayed, in all their actions, the utmost mildness, equity, and regard to the laws and constitution. Our own ministers, our own parliaments, ourselves, have governed us; and if aught ill has befallen us, we can only blame fortune or ourselves. What a reproach must we become among nations, if, disgusted with a settlement so deliberately made, and whose conditions have been so religiously observed, we should throw everything again into confusion, and, by our levity and rebellious disposition, prove ourselves totally unfit for any state but that of absolute slavery and subjection?[48]

In 'The Idea of a Perfect Commonwealth', however, Hume broke new ground and in doing so, concluded his review of the Augustan language of propriety.[49] Like Grotius, Hume thought countries like England which possessed mixed constitutions in which there was no clear division of power between king and people were inherently unstable and prone to faction.[50] Nevertheless, he had already argued, in the *Essays Moral and Political*, that the recent growth in the influence of the crown and the wealth of the Commons had created a new balance between power and property which was favourable to the preservation of the constitution and could, if it was properly understood, even lead to its perfection. The essay on the 'Idea of a Perfect Commonwealth' was Hume's reply to Harrington, providing an imaginary model of a modern British polity in a post-Walpolian era to replace Harrington's image of a post-Cromwellian republic; a model which would beget a new, post-Harringtonian language of modern prudence to replace one that had been rendered redundant by the Revolution and the rise of commerce and empire. Here, Harringtonian notions of rotations and agrarian laws to redistribute power and property were abandoned. Here too, Hume demonstrated his fundamental distrust of Harrington's imperial designs for extending the military power of the republic to its peripheries. In Hume's model, constructed as his attention was turning from modern politics to the disastrous history

---

[48] 'Of the Protestant Succession', *Essays*, p. 511.

[49] 'Idea of a Perfect Commonwealth', *Essays*, pp. 512–29. For a contrasted view of Hume's perfect commonwealth as a model for a commercial society, see J. Robertson, 'The Scottish Enlightenment at the Limits of the Civic Tradition', in *Wealth and Virtue: the Shaping of Political Economy in the Scottish Enlightenment*, ed. I. Hont and M. Ignatieff (Cambridge, 1983), pp. 172–7.

[50] H. Grotius, *The Rights of War and Peace, in Three Books. Wherein are explained the Law of Nature and Nations, and the Principal Points Relating to Government . . . to Which are Added all the Large Notes of Mr. J. Barbyrac*. (1738), pp. 71–2.

of seventeenth-century Britain, creating trust between court and country was seen to be as integral to preserving the Revolution as creating trust between crown and parliament. That, however, was a matter of developing political institutions to regularise relations between court and country, a matter of placing parochial and county government on elective principles which were rooted in the claims of property rather than patronage and would serve as a foundation stone on which a new senate could be erected to engross the executive power of the realm. In this way – and Hume's modelling is highly intricate – court and country, power and property, the rule of the few and the many, would be held in balance within the framework of a system of limited monarchy which would mitigate the corruptions of party and the threat of those revolts of country against court which had destroyed the early Stuart constitution and could all too easily destroy that of the Hanoverians. It was a constitution which would not be immortal but would generate the culture required to limit the appeal of resistance. And in doing so it would vindicate a conception of revolution principles which referred to a Whiggish world which was far removed from that of the alternative forms of oligarchy proposed by the Junto and Bolingbroke. For what was on offer in Hume's language of propriety was a surprisingly radical defence of revolution principles whose future depended on the peaceful survival of the established order and on the expansion of commerce and culture.

CHAPTER 15

The rhapsody of public debt:
David Hume and voluntary state bankruptcy

Istvan Hont

I do not blame anyone if political evils make him begin to despair of the welfare and progress of mankind. But I have confidence in the heroic medicine to which Hume refers, for it ought to produce a speedy cure.

Immanuel Kant, 1798[1]

In his political discourse 'Of Public Credit', first published in 1752, David Hume delivered a judgement striking in its menace and severity: 'either the nation must destroy public credit, or public credit will destroy the nation'.[2] What did he mean?

In John Pocock's suggestive and elegant argument, his judgement was an expression of an inescapable ambivalence in Hume's vision of commercial modernity.[3] For Hume commerce was an essentially positive agency in world history, the handmaid of modern liberty and source of modern civilisation. Pocock suggests that in the Humean macrocosm commerce was to modern politics what, in Montesquieu's language, virtue was to republics: its 'principle'.[4] As it was the 'inner meaning of the republican thesis that virtue must sustain the conditions necessary to virtue', commerce, in order to carry the weight heaped on it by Hume's theory

I am grateful to Michael Sonenscher, Gregory Claeys, John Dunn, Quentin Skinner, Nicholas Phillipson and particularly to Fredric Paul Smoler for their generous help in refining this essay.

[1] Kant, *The Contest of the Faculties* (1798), Conclusion to Part 2: 'The Contest between the Philosophical and Law Faculties', in *Kant's Political Writings*, ed. Hans Reiss (Cambridge, 1970), p. 187.
[2] 'Of Public Credit' (henceforth PC), in David Hume, *Essays Moral, Political and Literary*, ed. E.F. Miller (Indianapolis, 1985), pp. 360–1.
[3] J.G.A. Pocock, 'Hume and the American Revolution: The Dying Thoughts of a North Briton', in his *Virtue, Commerce and History: Essays on Political Thought and History, Chiefly in the Eighteenth Century* (Cambridge, 1985), pp. 125–41
[4] *The Machiavellian Moment: Florentine Political Thought and the Atlantic Political Tradition* (Princeton, 1975), p.497.

ISTVAN HONT

of modernity, had to have the same self-preserving qualities. Tragically, as Hume himself realised (Pocock tells us), this was not the case, for commerce met its nemesis in the public debt. An agent of thoroughgoing corrosive power, public debt was created by the commerce it would eventually destroy.

Although on Pocock's account public credit and the expansion of trade are 'logically separable',[5] he reads Hume's essay as conjuring up 'a vivid image of a society destroying itself by heaping up the public indebtedness to the point where trade and agriculture were both brought to ruin'.[6] Hume was 'driven to adopt a jeremiad tone by the circumstance, now familiar to us, that commercial society did not contain any ultimate check on the forces making for its corruption.'[7] This explains, Pocock concludes, Hume's deep ambivalence and consequent censoriousness: 'if virtue and culture are ultimately unreconciled, and if the commerce the republic begets leads to a condition of public debt that destroys both liberty and prosperity, we are left with an account of the forces at work in history that is based upon a fundamental and acknowledged contradiction'.[8]

Pocock asserts that Hume's distress centres on the self-destructive tendency of commercial societies to generate debt. The thesis of this essay is that it is not commerce, but war (or the threat of war) that produces national debt, and that Hume's essay is in fact a meditation on the links between the fiscal necessities of national security and the social dislocations produced by debt finance. Hume's ambivalence is not the product of a vision of warring forces within commercial society. Rather, the scourge came from the conjuction of commercial society and international power politics.

The true antithesis to the danger of public debt was thus a durable peace, where public debt ceased to exist while commerce expanded. Hume had little hope for such a reordering of the world of warring states. In his 'Idea of a Perfect Commonwealth' he remarked that even the best of republics were as liable to be possessed by ambition as individuals, and ridiculed the idea of any

---

[5] 'Hume and the American Revolution', p. 130.
[6] Ibid. pp. 132–3.
[7] *Machiavellian Moment*, p. 497.
[8] 'Hume and the American Revolution', p. 133.

state forever escaping the dangers of the international regime.[9] The elimination of international conflict being impossible, Hume sought ways to minimise it while maintaining national security. The essay 'Of Public Credit' is a grisly demonstration of the consequences of a free commercial society failing to do so.

Hume's views about the origins of public debt are worth comparing with Montesquieu's. As Pocock has noticed, Montesquieu seemingly had two views of the national debt, one for the 'domain of external *virtù*', the other for domestic.[10] So far as the latter was concerned Montesquieu uncompromisingly claimed that the national debt had only drawbacks, and no advantages.[11] But when he considered the effects of the free constitution of England on its manners and national character, he believed that Britain's ability to use public debt effectively constituted the supreme guarantee of the republic's security from external foes. 'This nation would have secure credit because it would borrow from itself and would pay to itself' and supported by this 'immense fictional wealth', it could exceed its natural strength.[12]

Hume also believed that public credit would disturb commercial growth, but thought that Montesquieu had exaggerated the problem.[13] Hume could see advantages in interest-bearing government bonds, which allowed merchants and manufacturers to exploit interest income in competitive pricing strategies as well as providing them with opportunities for investments.[14] On the other hand, however, he refused to believe that the public debt could yield any positive benefit for the nation's security. The damage wrought by public debt to 'commerce and industry' was considerable, but 'trivial, in comparison of the prejudice that results to the state considered as a body politic, which must support itself in the society of nations, and have various transactions with other states in wars and negociations'.[15] And mirroring Montesquieu, Hume

---

[9] 'Idea of a Perfect Commonwealth', *Essays*, p. 529.
[10] *Machiavellian Moment*, p. 490.
[11] *The Spirit of the Laws*, trans. A. Cohler, B. Miller and H. Stone (Cambridge, 1989), p. 418.
[12] Ibid., p. 327.
[13] Hume to Montesquieu, 10 April 1749, *The Letters of David Hume*, ed. J.Y.T. Greig (2 vols., Oxford, 1932), vol. 1, pp. 137–8.
[14] *PC*, pp. 353–4. See these views reviewed in Sir John Sinclair, *The History of the Public Revenue of the British Empire*, 3rd edn. (4 vols., London, 1803), vol. 1, pp. 363, 354.
[15] *PC*, pp. 355–6, see also Duncan Forbes, *Hume's Philosophical Politics* (Cambridge, 1975), p. 174–5.

declared: 'The ill, there, is pure and unmixed, without any favourable circumstance to atone for it; and it is an ill too of a nature the highest and most important'.[16]

In light of this judgement we should concentrate our efforts on understanding this order of priorities, rather than on the economic and cultural parts of Hume's argument. His intricate essay was originally divided into two parts linked by a difficult bridge, and this interstitial material was greatly expanded in a 1764 revision. It is this expanded section that today seizes our attention, and seems to bear the bulk of the argument, and has distorted our readings. Understanding Hume's argument requires reading 'Of Public Credit' in reverse, against the order of Hume's own presentation, and initially ignoring the later insertion, thereby restoring Hume's sense of the political space available for analysis of the politics of public debt. I shall thus first reconstruct the arguments of 1752, and only then assess the 1764 revisions.

In 1752 Hume began with consideration of a favourite 'new paradox' of the Walpolean era, the thesis that modern-war finance had proved to be an engine of economic growth,[17] and attacked the notion of a voluntary state debt, incurred independently of the ultimate necessities of national security. Second, Hume tackled the vexed issue of the futurity of England's existing national debt. In what ways, if at all, was it possible to eliminate an established system of public credit? What might be the result of its continuing growth? It was in answering this latter question that Hume declared that 'either the nation must destroy public credit, or public credit will destroy the nation'.

Hume had for a decade argued that a perverse effect of free constitutions was that their very liberty produced a generic inability to use public credit with any moderation. In 'Of Civil Liberty' he had diagnosed this as a source of degeneracy which would eventually close the gap between free governments and the improving absolute monarchies of Europe.[18] Although both had acquired the habit of deficit finance and suffered terribly from it, absolute monarchies had an advantage in that their rulers could cancel the state's oppressive debt and even gain popularity by such action.

---

[16] *PC*, pp. 355–6.
[17] *PC*, p. 352. The direct reference to Walpole was dropped in 1770.
[18] 'Of Civil Liberty', *Essays*, pp. 94–6.

It was politically less easy for popular governments to attempt a managed bankruptcy (a 'cruel and barbarous' if occasionally necessary step), because their creditor-citizens were often the holders of the highest offices of state;[19] the difficulty of moving against their rights and interests was precisely the difference between a free and moderate regime and an absolutist one. The second part of 'Of Public Credit' extended this argument by looking more closely at this endemic difficulty under British conditions. Hume now argued that the only option open to popular governments was to imitate monarchies, and turn to the violent corrective device of voluntary bankruptcy (the 'natural death' of public credit). Otherwise they faced the ultimate catastrophe of a 'violent' death of both the nation and its debt, with the debt undermining the capability for defence. Since the call for a managed bankruptcy on patriotic grounds gained its credence from the long shadow of its apocalyptic alternative, our reverse reading of the essay might start with the calculatedly shocking option of Britain's 'violent death' by debt.

The 'violent death' that public credit threatened was the conquest of the nation by a foreign power. This usefully reminded Hume's readers that the origins and purpose of the national debt were not to be found in trade and commerce, nor in the sordid practices of stockjobbers, but in the defence problem. The loss of independence would obviate the need for further war finance with deadly finality. But how could the debt lead to such a monumental failure of practical judgement on the part of the British military and political leadership that they so grossly neglect Britain's defences?

Here Hume was taking a stand against an isolationist foreign policy.[20] Britain had a security problem in the shape of the expansionist ambitions of France. The Stuarts, by embroiling Britain in domestic upheavals for a great part of the Seventeenth

---

[19] 'Civil Liberty', p. 96.
[20] For a background on contemporary foreign policy debates see Jeremy Black, *A System of Ambition? British Foreign Policy 1660–1793* (London, 1991); J. Black, 'Mid-Eighteenth Century Conflict with Particular Reference to the Wars of the Polish and Austrian Successions', in J. Black (ed.), *The Origins of War in Early Modern Europe* (Edinburgh, 1987), pp. 210–41; J. Black, 'The Debate over Policy', in his *Natural and Necessary Enemies: Anglo-French Relations in the Eighteenth Century* (London, 1986), pp. 93–133; and H.M. Scott, '"The True Principles of the Revolution": The Duke of Newcastle and the Idea of the Old System', in J. Black (ed.), *Knights Errant and True Englishmen: British Foreign Policy, 1660–1800* (Edinburgh, 1989), pp. 55–91.

century, had let French power rise unopposed.[21] France, an immensely more agile and clever state than Spain had ever been,[22] had been kept from universal empire by a determined coalition of European states. It was in Britain's interest to participate in that coalition, since the 'balance of power of Europe, our grandfathers, our fathers, and we, have all deemed too unequal to be preserved without our attention and assistance'.[23] A universal monarchy would follow a collapse of the European balance of power precipitated by Britain's withdrawal from the anti-French coalition. Since Britain was an island nation, the temptation to avoid bloody and very expensive land wars on the continent was always present. If a future isolationist mood of apathy and false security were to be exploited by clever enemy propaganda, then, deprived of English financial and military help, France's European neighbours would fall one by one, eventually leaving Britain to face an unequal struggle against, and ultimately conquest by, an overwhelmingly strengthened European empire.[24]

Hume's scenario presupposed that Britain's attempts to increase an already high debt burden by further operations on the London credit market would fail, presenting the government with the choice of either substantially cutting defence or expropriating the funds earmarked for debt service. England's 'popular government'. Hume assumed, would be naturally reluctant 'to venture on so desperate an expedient, as that of voluntary bankruptcy' and suspend debt repayments.[25] More importantly, it would fail to get support from either house of parliament. Although landowners dominated the Lords and in large measure the Commons, their 'connections' to the 'proprietors' of stock would lead them to privileged public confidence in state finances over the long-term security problem. The financial establishment would press the ministers to prefer the short-term judgement of money markets to the national interest, to what 'prudence, policy, or even justice, strictly speaking requires'.[26] Put this way (and Hume did so) the dark shadow of 'conquest' seems less of a chimera than it might

---

[21] 'Of the Protestant Succession', *Essays*, p. 507.
[22] 'Of the Balance of Power', *Essays*, p. 338.
[23] *PC*, p. 364.
[24] *PC*, p. 365. See also 'Balance of Power', p. 340.
[25] *PC*, p. 365.
[26] *PC*, p. 364.

first appear. The violent (and thus total) death of the debt could occur if confidence in the financial system (in the security of mobile property) became a cornerstone of domestic policy,[27] if the apparent requirements of financial stability took priority over the nation's liberty in the international arena.

Hume's other option, engineering a 'natural death' of public debt, followed from this recognition. If the government faced a squeeze on its revenues at the same time that a major security scare erupted, it was important that it should not be paralysed diplomatically by considerations of debt finance. This would have been a legalistic fallacy characteristic of free governments. Instead of being caught up in the shadow world of fictitious wealth and paper commitments it could do better by remembering that its difficulties were not caused by real economic limits to its action, since the pre-existing debt system could function properly only if 'a large yearly revenue' from the 'funds, created and mortgaged' was 'lying in the exchequer, ready for discharge of the quarterly interest'.[28] Would it not then be a supreme political folly for statesmen who 'have the means of safety in their hands' to pretend that these sums were unavailable for the nation's use?

Hume returned to the keynote argument of the 'violent-death' scenario: governments and political classes had a duty to understand the true priorities of the political order they supervised. The preservation of 'public faith' was a question not only of political stability but of property and hence justice, but in his theory of political obligation Hume had been adamant that actual political leadership was impossible without a practical judgement concerning national priorities:

As the obligation of justice is founded entirely on the interests of society, which require mutual respect for property in order to preserve peace among mankind, it is evident that when the execution of justice would be attended with very pernicious consequences, virtue must be suspended, and give place to public utility. In such extraordinarily pressing emergencies the maxim *fiat Justitia & ruat Coelum*, let justice be performed, though the universe be destroyed, is false, and by sacrificing the end to the means, shews a preposterous idea of the subordination of duties. What governor

---

[27] See the often-cited passage from the anonymous *An Essay upon Publick Credit, in a Letter to a Friend Occasioned by the Fall of Stocks* (1748): 'The Debts of the *Public* are part of the *Constitution*, interwoven with all kinds of *Property*, and ... they cannot be separated, without *subverting the Constitution*' (p.5).

[28] *PC*, p. 363.

of a town makes any scruple of burning the suburbs, when they facilitate the approaches of the enemy?[29]

A state pays a debt only because it is in its advantage to do so, wisely anticipating a need for further credit; but a 'present necessity often forces states into measures', Hume added, 'which are, strictly speaking, against their interest.[30] *Salus populi suprema Lex*,[31] and in a real crisis the call for voluntary bankruptcy should be unanswerable: the 'right of self-preservation is unalienable in every individual, much more in every community'.[32] Since the 'violent death' of public credit might lead to the horrible political crime of sacrificing millions for the temporary safety of the creditors, Hume preferred the 'natural-death' scenario, and was quite ready to counsel sacrificing the property of thousands (he estimated that Britain had approximately 17,000 foreign and domestic creditors) on the altar of the nation's security interests. 'Necessity calls, fear urges, reason exhorts, compassion alone exclaims', as he described the hectic crisis leading to voluntary state bankruptcy, and 'the money will immediately be seized for the current service, under the most solemn protestations, perhaps, of being immediately replaced'.[33]

Did the creditors not know that at the end the 'public is a debtor, whom no man can oblige to pay'? How could these people, who speculated on the continuation of conflicts, believe that their precious paper property would be spared amidst the upheavals of general European wars in which sovereigns were willing to devastate the lives and the real property of so many of their subjects? It was in this context that Hume conjured up the famous image of the international order of eighteenth-century Europe which so pleased his reader in the Eastern provinces of Prussia, the Königsberg professor, Immanuel Kant. 'I must confess', Hume wrote in 1752, 'when I see princes and states fighting and quarrelling, amidst their

---

[29] 'Of Passive Obedience', *Essays*, p. 489.
[30] *PC*, p. 364. In 1752 the remark appeared in a footnote, but in 1770 Hume merged it into the main text.
[31] 'Passive Obedience', p. 489. See the debate about the applicability of this principle to Hume's views on the public debt and national bankruptcy between Giuseppe Giarizzo *David Hume Politico e Storico* (Turin, 1962), p. 32, and Duncan Forbes, 'Politics and History in David Hume: Review of *David Hume Politico e Storico by G. Giarizzo*', *Historical Journal*, 6 (1963), 287.
[32] *PC*, p. 362.
[33] *PC*, p. 363.

debts, funds, and public mortgages, it always brings to my mind a match of cudgel-playing fought in a China shop.'[34] Whatever was wrong with a system of state finance based on such fickle agencies as public confidence and credit from the viewpoint of domestic politics (and Hume thought that almost everything was wrong with it), the real danger lay in the intimate entanglement of public debt with the vagaries of international politics. The national debt was inextricably connected to the wars and imperial ambitions which would cause its destruction: 'the breach of national faith will be the necessary effect of wars, defeats, misfortunes, public calamities, or even perhaps of victories and conquests'.[35]

Hume's mention of 'victories and conquests' deserves our attention. It is sometimes supposed that Hume inserted his essay 'Of the Balance of Power' among his economic essays because of a presumed enchantment with the alluring symmetry between the titles of his essays 'Of the Balance of Trade' and 'Of the Balance of Power'. Perhaps so, but his readers may notice that the essay 'Of the Balance of Power' serves as a perfect introduction to 'Of Public Credit'. The essay, which could equally have merited the title 'Of Universal Empire', was a scathing indictment of all non-defensive warfare.

Unenchanted by the splendid retrospective view of Rome's mighty dominions entertained by many of his contemporaries, Hume categorically denounced the universal empire of the Romans along with the modern attempts of the Spanish and the French: 'enormous monarchies', he wrote, were 'probably, destructive to human nature; in their progress, in their continuance, and even in their downfal'.[36] He developed a distinction between 'wars of emulation' and wars of 'cautious politics', the latter being restricted to containing the ambition of the current contender for universal empire through the creation of a 'balance of power'.[37] Military and

---

[34] *PC*, p. 362. Kant cites this in a somewhat corrupt translation, *Political Writings*, p. 190.
[35] *PC*. pp. 361–2.
[36] 'Balance of Power', pp. 340–1.
[37] 'Balance of Power', pp. 334–5, 337. On the rise of the modern notion of the 'balance of power' see J. Black. 'The Theory of the Balance of Power in the First Half of the Eighteenth Century', *Review of International Studies*, 9 (1983), 55–61; M.S. Anderson, 'Eighteenth-Century Theories of the Balance of Power', in R. Hatton and M.S. Anderson (eds.), *Studies in Diplomatic History: Essays in Memory of D.B. Horn* (London, 1970), pp. 183–98; and E. Kaeber, *Die Idee des europäischen Gleichgewicht in der publizistischen Literatur von bis 16 bis zur Mitte des 18 Jahrhunderts* (Berlin, 1907). Hume, typically, claimed that Polybius already had a perfectly good understanding of the principle.

diplomatic activity which overstepped the boundaries of contain-
ment in pursuit of national glory was actuated by a zeal akin to the
'ancient Greek spirit of jealous emulation'[38] (the desire for pre-
eminence without territorial annexation) and was disastrous.

Hume sincerely believed that France's ambition had been the
primary cause of disturbance in the European state system since
the end of the seventeenth-century. France had been stopped only
by a broad coalition of states, among whom a vigilant and
courageous Britain had played a leading role as the 'guardian of the
general liberties of Europe, and patron of mankind'.[39] Britain's first
wars against France had 'begun with justice', even unavoidable
'necessity', but subsequent actions did not fall under the same
category. Britain had increasingly overstepped the boundaries of
'the prudent views of modern politics', and entered into unnecessary European commitments. The entirety of Britain's extraordinary need for continued war finance, 'all our public debts',[40] were
caused not only by France's ambition but by Britain's, Hume
concluded:

> To mortgage our revenues at so deep a rate, in wars, where we were only
> accessories, was surely the most fatal delusion, that a nation, which had
> any pretension to politics and prudence, has ever yet been guilty of. That
> remedy of funding, if it be a remedy, and not rather a poison, ought, in all
> reason, to be reserved to the last extremity; and no evil, but the greatest
> and most urgent, should ever induce us to embrace so dangerous an
> expedient.[41]

British posturing as the free nation guarding European peace, or
some other pathological manifestation of national *amour propre*,
Hume feared, would lead to unnecessary conflict. Even if this
'imprudent vehemence' could be dampened, he could not see a way
to wind down the debt-finance system under popular government.
This was in nobody's short-term interest. Landowners would not
tolerate 'unnecessary' high taxes and the creditors would not want
their money back merely to find for it, with great effort, some other

---

[38] 'Balance of Power', p. 339.
[39] Ibid., p. 635, cancelled in 1770.
[40] Ibid., p. 339.
[41] Ibid., p. 340. See the parallel passage in 'Public Credit', p.354. For examples of Walpole's
appeal to perceived necessity to justify his raids on the sinking fund, see his *Some
Considerations concerning the Publick Revenues, and the Annual Supplies, Granted by Parliament*
(1735), pp. 8, 39.

profitable investment.[42] More daring repayment schemes, mooted in England in the aftermath of the South Sea Bubble, were not only impracticable, but oppressive, socially insensitive and misconceived.[43]

Surveying all debt-reduction schemes, Hume's attention turned to French policy. Law's attempt at cancellation filled him with horror; it could lead only to national bankruptcy, with all its devastations but none of its political or economic benefits: public credit in this case would 'die of the doctor'.[44] The more mild experiment of revaluing the coinage more favourably impressed Hume,[45] and he admired the Dutch method of arbitrarily reducing the interest on the debt. But special factors in the politics of these countries made imitation very difficult. British political culture taught citizens to be 'good reasoners upon whatever regards their interest',[46] and accustomed them to the huge borrowing requirement if not to the likely consequences: in England 'a strange supineness, from long custom, creeped into all ranks of men, with regard to public debts'.[47]

'Of Public Credit' shows Hume reasserting his earlier thesis in 'Of Civil Liberty'. Public debt, particularly if coupled to the revival of 'ancient Greek jealousy', was under free and popular governments a degenerative force of the greatest magnitude, and Hume identifies a dangerous dialectic between ancient and modern political practices. In foreign policy and war strategy he appealed to modern prudence against ancient ambition. If that failed, Hume advocated a move back from modern practices to ancient financial prudence. Financing wars from accumulated savings and the

---

[42] *PC.* p. 638, dropped in 1770.
[43] *PC,* p. 361. Hume's target was Archibald Hutcheson's national-debt repayment plan in the wake of the South Sea Bubble, presented in his *A Collection of Treatises relating to the National Debts and Funds* (1721). In 1750 Andrew Hooke published a similar calculation in *An Essay on the National Debt and National Capital: Or, The Account Truly Stated, Debtor and Creditor. Wherein is Shewn, that the Former is but a Diminutive Part of the Latter* (1750).
[44] *PC,* p. 361.
[45] *PC,* p. 638, cancelled in 1770, see also 'Of Money', *Essays,* pp. 287–8. Hume's source of information on this was Dutot's *Political Reflections upon the Finances and Commerce of France* (1739), a polemical work written against French monetary experiments and particularly Melon's *Political Essay upon Commerce* and its advocacy of the policy of 'raising the coin'.
[46] *PC,* p. 638.
[47] *PC,* p. 360.

yearly revenue of the state could not stop adventurism altogether,[48] but did have clear, inflexible and tangible limits. Ancient prudence in finance, modern prudence in security policy was the winning formula, not the other way round.

How could one engineer a switch-over to sane principles? Peace was not a prospect, debt repayment was nearly impossible, financial quackery dangerous and neglecting national security suicidal. In comparison, the 'natural death' of debt had to be the favoured option. Cruel and barbarous, not quite an 'euthanasia', it was necessary. It did not even involve an inevitable decline to absolute monarchy, only an absolutist moment in the life of the popular state. The *coup d'état* against debt and creditors was the patriotic act of a desperate but ultimately responsible and virtuous leadership working within the confines of the mixed constitution.

In Hume's thoughts on war and public credit John Pocock hears the voice of Bolingbroke, as well as Swift's rhetoric under Marlborough and Pope's under Walpole.[49] He emphasises that there are important similarities here as well as dissimilarities, and this is certainly the case. Hume wasted remarkably little time on arguing about the fantastic qualities of credit and paper money and other issues of country moralising, and his essay goes far beyond the denunciation of frenzied stockjobbing and the South Sea Bubble which occupied the attention of 'Cato'.[50] The darling-country theme of wicked ministers using the public debt to engineer a monarchical *coup d'état* against the Revolution Settlement is entirely missing.[51]

A patriotic *coup d'état* against the regime of war finance is quite a

---

[48] PC, p. 351. Compare with 'Money', pp. 281–2. Hume perfectly well understood that modern warfare and national defence required tremendous spending power (p. 289), but he denied that the failure of Austria to pull its 'proportionable weight in the balance of Europe' would have been caused by their backward finances, by their 'scarcity of money'. Austria was not really a modern state, and the 'manners and customs' of the people were backward. 'We mistake, as is too usual, a collateral effect for a cause' (pp. 289–90); what Austria needed was commercial society and a modern tax system, not 'money' and public debt. Hume visited Austria in 1748, as a member of a British diplomatic mission, see his reports to his brother, *Letters*, vol. I, pp. 114–33.

[49] 'Hume and the American Revolution', p. 139.

[50] 'Of Publick Credit and Stocks', 15 December 1722, *Cato's Letters: or, Essays on Liberty, Civil and Religious, and Other Important Subjects*, 3rd edn. (London, 1723) vol. IV, pp. 12–23.

[51] This was the essence of Davenant's original 'rhapsody' of public debt, see his *An Essay upon the Probable Methods of Making a People Gainers in the Balance of Trade* [1699], in *The Political and Commercial Works of that Celebrated Writer Charles D'Avenant*, LL.D., ed. Sir Charles Whitworth (5 vols. London, 1771), vol. II, pp. 285–6.

different thing. Bolingbroke's own writings in the latter half of the 1740s, and particularly his 1749 'Some Reflections on the Present State of the Nation, Principally with Regard to her Taxes and her Debts, and on the Causes and Consequences of them', show that Hume's and Bolingbroke's thought ran along the same trajectory.[52] Bolingbroke similarly presented the conjoined problem of the public debt and Britain's security problem. An active defence policy was bound to cause yet a further increase of the cancerous debt, while a short-sightedly passive policy could lead to a sacrificing of Britain's rights, trade and dignity.[53] It was vital to reduce the debt burden, and the European power which first did away with its credit obligation, Bolingbroke asserted, 'will give the law to others, or be at least in a condition of not receiving it from one.'[54] He came to the conclusion that if ordinary persuasion and an appeal to patriotism could not make the creditors accept a retrenchment, then a patriotic bankruptcy had to be considered.[55]

If the creditors behaved 'in a state of civil society, much like Hobbes's men in his supposed state of nature', as 'individuals rather than fellow-citizens', then patriots, the landed men, had to explain to the men of money the fundamental law of all political societies: that 'the preservation of the commonwealth' is 'superior

---

[52] The essay, Bolingbroke's last work, was first published in *The Works of the Late Right Honourable Henry St. John, Lord Viscount Bolingbroke*, [ed. David Mallet] (4 vols., 1754), vol. III, pp. 143–79. Continental readers could easily make the association between Bolingbroke and Hume: the first French translation of Hume's 1752 economic essays appeared in vol. I, Bolingbroke's piece in vol. II of *Discours politiques* (Amsterdam, 1754, 1756), a miscellany of topical writing from Europe. The proximity of Bolingbroke's and Hume's position on national bankruptcy was rememberd up to the end of the century; see George Chalmers, *An Estimate of the Comparative Strength of Great Britain*, 2nd edn. (1794), p. 120 on Bolingbroke, and on Hume's 'cuckowes songe' of the bankruptcy of Great Britain in the 'Dedication to Dr. James Currie', pp. ix–xi.

[53] 'Some Reflections', p. 168.

[54] 'Some Reflections', p. 165, also p. 161. For a virtually identical assertion that if Britain would lag behind France in post-war debt reduction it will 'be necessitated to accept the Law from them; and be no longer able to oppose their Attempts for universal Monarchy' see *The Necessity of Lowering Interest and Continuing Taxes Demonstrated. In a Letter to G.B.* (1750), pp. 9–10. On the widespread use of this point for the better part of the eighteenth century see P.G.M. Dickson, *The Financial Revolution of England: A Study in the Development of Public Credit, 1688–1756* (London, 1967), pp. 22–3. Bolingbroke's preoccupation with power politics, the danger of universal monarchy and the balance of power is also very marked in his *Letters on the Study and Use of History* (first published in the *Works*, but written in the late 1730's in French exile), see Lord Bolingbroke, *Historical Writings*, ed. I. Kramnick (Chicago, 1972), p. 94 and at length in 'Letter 8', pp. 99–149.

[55] For Bolingbroke's consideration of the rise of the debt system to the status of a new 'reason of state' see 'Letter 2' of the *Letters on the Study and Use of History*, pp. 20–1.

to all other laws'.[56] The landed men, who were the 'true owners of our political vessel', would understand that the 'only effectual, and therefore necessary' way to liquidate the unbearable debt had to be a violent one. Patriots would also 'consider, and every man ought to consider, that if we cannot bear our distemper, and will not bear our cure, the political body must perish'.[57]

Hume's 'natural-death' scenario and Bolingbroke's patriotic bankruptcy are nearly identical. It was their considerations of the aftermath that differed. Bolingbroke, like Hume, preferred a post-debt policy of severe frugality but after bankruptcy he wanted a patriot king to lead the country out of its corruption.[58] As the ideal type of such leadership he turned to that emblematic figure of eighteenth-century European political imagination, Henry IV, and to the example of his virtuous minister Sully, who had successfully liquidated France's sixteenth-century debt.[59] In Hume's essay one finds none of this. The only comment Hume had on the post-bankruptcy situation announced the possible revival and continuation of the public debt even after such a nasty shock to 'public credit as a voluntary bankruptcy in England'. Hume pointed to the failings of human nature; men were governed by their imagination and their short-term interest, and if they wanted to believe in credit again they would find ways of accepting it and investing in it; in France public credit had eventually revived even after the tremendous mishap of the Mississippi Bubble. 'The fear of an everlasting destruction of credit, allowing it to be an evil', he concluded, 'is a needless bugbear.'[60]

Why did Hume, after strenuously arguing for the permanent elimination of the debt, assume its likely rebirth in the aftermath of a 'voluntary bankruptcy'? It was perhaps his way of dealing with at

[56] 'Some Reflections', pp. 174.
[57] Ibid., p. 168.
[58] 'The Idea of a Patriot King', *Works*, vol. III, p. 40. The call for a 'patriot king' was written in 1739, after Bolingbroke's return from France, with Frederick, Prince of Wales, as the next monarch in mind. The lessons Frederick had learnt about public credit are in his 'Instructions for my Son George, Drawn by Myself, for his Good, that of my Family, and for that of his People, According to the Ideas of my Grandfather, and Best Friend, George I', in G. Young, *Poor Fred: The People's Prince* (Oxford, 1937), pp. 172–5. On the future George III's own extensive education about the dangers of national debts see John L. Bullion, '"To Know This is the True Essential Business of a King": The Prince of Wales and the Study of Public Finance, 1755–1760', *Albion* 18 (1986), 429–54.
[59] 'Some Reflections', p. 159–61.
[60] *PC*, p. 363.

least some of the post-debt problems for which Bolingbroke needed a patriotic prince. Since Davenant's time it had been recognised that because credit instruments issued by the government served as a sort of paper money, a sudden stop in money flows following a bankruptcy could seriously damage the country's productive economy.[61] When Davenant, Bolingbroke and Hume called for frugality, they meant not a return to ancient simplicity but rather to a reliance on industry and trade. In Hume's case the prospect of a revival of public credit, and his insistence that the fear of a complete credit squeeze was unfounded, delivered much of his voluntary bankruptcy scenario from the accusation that engineering the 'natural death' of public credit would inevitably precipitate a disastrous commercial crisis and industrial recession.[62]

This analysis of Britain's public debt reflects Hume's position after the experience of the Austrian War of Succession. It expressed a widely shared and immediate worry about Britain's ability to carry its debt; the possible political conversion of Britain into a civilized European absolute monarchy in the long term is not brought into play. Bolingbroke was far more alarmist, emphasising that a voluntary bankruptcy, particularly one performed in the face of the danger of war, was purge 'by fire' which may 'beget universal confusion'. 'Out of confusion order may arise', but 'it may be the order of a wicked tyranny, instead of the order of a just monarchy. Either may happen: and such an alternative, at the disposition of fortune, is sufficient to make a Stoic tremble!'[63] In the light of this

---

[61] See a discussion of this in my 'Free Trade and the Economic Limits to National Politics: Neo-Machiavellian Political Economy Reconsidered', in John Dunn (ed.), *The Economic Limits to Modern Politics* (Cambridge, 1990), pp. 89–95. The point was frequently made throughout the century; see an example nearer to the date of Hume's composition of 'Public Credit' in the already cited *An Essay upon Publick Credit, in a Letter to a Friend Occasioned by the Fall of Stocks* (1748), p. 10.

[62] This possibility was the central point of Isaac de Pinto's famous criticism of Hume's voluntary bankruptcy plan: 'Mr Hume says, that, if a spunge were applied to the national debt, thousands would be sacrificed to the safety of millions. Without enquiring whether honor is, in any case, to be sacrificed to advantage, I affirm only, that the millions would for a long time feel the sacrifice of the thousands.' As a consequence of the general economic recession induced by the bankruptcy, the 'state, the government, would be without resources' for a considerable length of time and in this way Hume's worst-case scenario (the loss of independence through conquest by foreign powers), Pinto thought, might indeed come true. (*An Essay on Circulation and Credit*, ed. S. Baggs (1774), pp. 104–5).

[63] 'The Idea of a Patriot King', pp. 39–40.

scenario, Hume's 1752 essay was a calm, measured and even cautiously optimistic contemplation of the public debt.

Such stoic calmness did not survive the Seven Years War. Hume made substantial revisions to some of his essays at the time of the next edition. In the 1764 edition of his essays readers could find six new paragraphs in 'Of Public Credit'.[64] It is this insertion which is responsible for the reputation of Hume's essay as a jeremiad which can be read as the worst of eighteenth-century Country tracts.

Any assessment of Hume's ambivalence concerning commercial society must take account of his reaction to the effects of the Seven Years War on the public debt. His chief anxiety was not military failure or a credit squeeze making British support of the balance of powers impossible. The horrible truth was that Britain, against all odds, had won the war, and credit had expanded to finance the crazy consequences of Britain's quest for grandeur with an ease and speed which was historically unprecedented.[65] In the text newly inserted into the public-debt essay Hume acknowledged that in this war Britain had displayed prodigious military prowess, and had shown herself capable of exertions which 'much exceeded, not only our natural strength, but even the greatest empires'.[66] While the nation was apprehensive about what might happen if England's great-power status proved to be only momentary, Hume contemplated the even more sorry consequences if it did not. The 'abuse complained of' in his essay, Hume insisted, was this very 'extravagance'. Britain's quest for glory had to be denounced 'as the source of all dangers'.[67]

In 1752 Hume had expected Britain's voluntary bankruptcy to take place within 'half a century', although even then he clearly

[64] 1764 was the year the new version was published. The first indication of 'some pretty considerable Improvements' came from Hume in March 1763 (Hume to Andrew Millar, 10 March 1763, *Letters*, vol. I, p. 378) and he probably completed his revision in London, before his departure to France in the autumn of that year.

[65] For background see John Brewer, *The Sinews of Power: War, Money and the English State, 1688–1783* (London, 1989) and Richard Middleton, *The Bells of Victory: The Pitt–Newcastle Ministry and the Conduct of the Seven Years' War*, 1757–1762 (Cambridge, 1985). During the Seven Years War the British national debt almost doubled, between 1756 and 1763 it rose from £74 million to £133 million.

[66] *PC*, p. 358.

[67] *PC* (1764), p. 359. See also Hume's letter to Trudaine de Montigny, 25 May 1767: 'that horrible, destructive, ruinous War; more pernicious to the Victors than to the Vanquished', *New Letters of David Hume*, ed. R. Klibansky and E.C. Mossner (Oxford, 1954), p. 235.

recognised that the pessimistic predictions of an earlier generation of criticis were falsified by the 'duration' of Britain's credit 'beyond all reasonable expectation'.[68] Now it was not clear when to expect the drying-up of credit, although he thought the odds had shortened rather than lengthened. Indeed, it was precisely this which lent such urgency to Hume's rhetoric.[69] The extremities of the spectrum of choices remained the same, the most virtuous being frugality coupled with modern prudence, the worst being the loss of independence under the victorious sway of an universal monarch. Yet the meteoric rise in the volume of debt during the Seven Years War caused Hume to view the 'natural-death' scenario differently. Before he had argued that the debt had died while both the nation and its cherished free constitution had survived the crisis. In the 1764 insertion this last criterion is withdrawn.

A much larger debt implied a much larger bankruptcy and also a radical transformation in the balance of property and power within the nation even prior to that. The earlier 'natural-death' scenario had relied on the landed interest as the source of moderating opinion in the British political system. Under the conditions of the enlarged debt the property and hence the authority of landed men would be undermined to such a degree that the only way to put the debt to death would be to introduce domestic absolutism; the choice between honouring the debt obligations and resisting foreign domination implied that if independence was to be preserved the free constitution had to go.

While the scope of the debt was new, Hume's arguments were not. The scenario of 1764 had resonances of earlier 'Country' theories and elements of it were already present in Hume's 1741 essays, as well as in the first version of 'Of Public Credit'. The

---

[68] *PC*, pp. 364–5.

[69] Hume's response to the post-war economic recession ran opposite to his reaction to the increase of the war debt. As the Seven Years War drew to an end in 1762 Scotland's economy came under heavy financial pressure, leading to a liquidity crisis (see H. Hamilton, 'Scotland's Balance of Payment Problems in 1762', *Economic History Review*, 2nd ser., 5 (1953), 344–57) and at the height of the troubles the *Scots Magazine* (24(1962), pp. 33–9) provocatively reprinted Hume's 1752 essay 'Of Money' (which argued sharply against banks and paper money). In response to the debate which ensued Hume relaxed his well known anti-paper-money and anti-bank positions (see the 1764 amendments to 'Of the Balance of Trade', *Essays*, pp. 318–20). For further effects of this revision see also the related 1768 and 1770 corrections to 'Of Public Credit' (*PC*, pp. 636–7) and Hume's correspondence with Adam Smith concerning the 1772 bankruptcy of the patriotic land-bank at Ayr (*Letters*, vol. II, p. 264).

particular argument in the 1752 text which served as the platform for launching the 1764 insertion concerned the favourite theory of the advocates of modern finance that the national debt was a purely domestic phenomenon, because it was 'like transferring money from the right hand to the left'.[70] It was further argued that such transfer had its own natural limit: a certain proportion between productive and unproductive groups of the population had always to be maintained in any viable economy. Hence the nightmare of the patriots, a nation overtaxing itself in order to carry an ever-larger debt, was dismissed by the defenders of credit as a chimera. Hume begged to disagree.

Over-taxation was possible because of human imagination's boundless power of invention. If consumption taxes on luxuries were mortgaged to pay the national debt, the government would tax basic goods consumed by the poor; if this were exhausted it would raise the land tax. The national debt could not be accepted as a fairly innocent and self-checking economic device, it was bound to be ruinous and destructive to the political body. Hiking up the land tax would lead to an effective nationalisation of land, turning the landowning class into simple 'stewards to the public' who would function as oppressive tax farmers. The bloated debt would also engender a substantial rotation of property between the various economic classes: 'In 500 years', Hume ventured the opinion, 'the posterity of those now in the coaches, and of those upon the boxes, will probably have changed places, without affecting the public by these revolutions'.[71]

In 1764 Hume devised a thought experiment which examined the system at its theoretical upper limit, supposing the land tax 18 or 19 shillings in the pound (instead of the prevailing 4), and positing consumption taxes and customs increased to the limit still compatible with continued economic activity. The hypothesis left no scope for further domestic resource transfer from the productive to the credit economy. It had to be clear to the eye of even 'the most careless observer' that certain 'necessary consequences' had to follow from such developments.

---

[70] The source was probably Jean-François Melon, *A Political Essay upon Commerce*, ed. David Bindon (Dublin, 1739), p. 329. Melon's chapter 18, 'Of Public Credit', discussed the English public debt at some length.
[71] *PC*, p. 357.

Hume asked two questions. Could such a system be economically stable? And could it be managed politically? Even in peacetime such a system would keep tottering on a knife's edge: after running up a debt to the limits of a country's economic performance, 'any great blow given to trade, whether by injudicious taxes or by other accidents throws the whole system of government into confusion'. In Hume's measured judgement it was highly unlikely that parliament and government would not make 'both of wilful and involuntary error' in trying to run from the centre, through the tax system, the entire economy of an international trading nation.[72]

But even if one supposed 'great commerce and opulence' to continue, how could the government in a fully taxed economy raise the further sums required for its current expenditure, particularly for defence?[73] Hume now created a parallel scenario to the earlier crisis. Since in this 'unnatural state of society' the entire taxable revenue of the productive economy ended up as the income of the stock-holders, they were the only class which could shoulder the expenses of the community. There were two options, and the first was voluntary funding. In true republics citizens were willing to contribute to defence costs as a patriotic effort. Occasional extraordinary contributions, however, could 'never be the foundation of constant national defence'. What was needed was a regular contribution from the annuitants, a voluntary tax. Yet they were not at all the people from whom to expect such efforts. Hume refused to indulge in Montesquieu's fantasy of patriot creditors. In a vituperative attack he announced that these were 'men, who have no connections with the state, who can enjoy their revenue in any part of the globe in which they chuse to reside, who will naturally bury themselves in the capital or in great cities, and who will sink into the lethargy of a stupid and pampered luxury, without spirit, ambition, or enjoyment'.[74]

And what of the chances of involuntary contributions to the necessary expense of the political community? The crisis would come when the Lords and the Commons, now 'under the sway' of the creditors to the state, would refuse to remortgage the sinking fund. If their consent was not forthcoming, then the annuitants had

<hr>

[72] *PC*, (1764), p. 358.
[73] *PC*, (1764), p. 359. He supposed that defence requirements grew with the nation's wealth: 'these riches must be defended by proportional power'.
[74] *PC* (1764), pp. 357–8.

M

to be forced 'to contribute to their own defence, and to that of the nation'.[75] But who, by then, could force them? In 1752 it was the landowners who could preserve the constitution, who had less to fear from bankruptcy, because in comparison with the total dependency of the creditors on the state of financial confidence, 'the dignity and authority of the landed gentry and nobility is much better rooted'.[76] But the very large debt Hume now assumed could easily undermine their position.

The speed with which financial markets operated terrified Hume. 'The stocks can be transferred in an instant, and being in such a fluctuating state, will seldom be transmitted during three generations from father to son',[77] he wrote. Property in land would not remain stable enough to preserve the landed interest, and even if it were possible to build stable fortunes out of stocks and annuities, possession of such inherently mobile assets could 'convey no hereditary authority or credit to the possessor'. The quick rotation of mobile property would destroy the 'several ranks of men, which form a kind of independent magistracy in a state, instituted by the hand of nature'.[78] 'Adieu' then, Hume warned his readers, 'to all ideas of nobility, gentry and family'.

Ranks were not necessary simply to sustain a certain type of culture. The political outcome of the erosion of the system of ranks would be the collapse of the constitution: 'the middle power between king and people being totally removed, a grievous despotism must infallibly prevail'.[79] Insurrections could be resisted only by mercenary armies, and elections were bound to become corrupt. In the end the sole source of authority in the state would be the sovereign, and such a regime would necessarily be a political machine operated by place men.

The political stranglehold of the annuitant class over the Lords and Commons was an inevitable consequence of the debt. In the

[75] *PC* (1764), p. 359.
[76] *PC* (1764), p. 364.
[77] *PC* (1764), p. 358.
[78] *PC* (1764), p. 358. Rotation of property was an important theme in the work of Hume's friend, Patrick Murray, Lord Elibank, 'An Inquiry into the Original and Consequences of the Public Debt', in *[Three] Essays* (1755), p. 16, popularised by Malachy Postlethwayt, *Great Britain's True System* (1757), pp. 16–18. The view that the rotation engendered by modern financial markets was the modern equivalent of an agrarian law was developed by Sir James Steuart, *An Inquiry into the Principles of Political Oeconomy*, ed. A. Skinner (2 vols., Edinburgh, 1966), vol. I, pp. 316–8.
[79] *PC* (1764), p. 358.

1764 insertion Hume not only presupposed that the political judgement of the landed interest could be corrupted by its entanglement with monied men, as he had in 1752, but that the landed interest, as a political class, would virtually disappear. Hence only an absolute ruler could save the nation from the short-sighted and selfish policies of the creditors, and the necessary *coup d'état* had to be by the executive alone, against not only the monied interest but also the national councils of the state.

A post-debt absolute monarchy could be particularly dangerous. In a super-high debt regime the public was in effect 'the chief or sole proprietor of land' and in command of all the tax schemes 'which the fertile imagination of ministers and projectors have been able to invent'.[80] The absolute monarchy would inherit the hugely overgeared taxation system. The miscalculation of the monied men was in forgetting how easy it was in such circumstances to abolish their income. A post-debt absolutism, in which 'the whole income of every individual in the state must lie entirely at the mercy of the sovereign' would amount to a 'degree of despotism, which no oriental monarchy has ever yet attained'.[81]

Bidding adieu to the gentry and aristocracy meant not just waving goodbye to Britain's free government, but also renouncing any hope for its 'euthanasia'. The reason some European absolute monarchies were civilised governments of laws, not men, was because they gave security to the property and private economic and cultural activities of the subjects.[82] In civilised monarchies there were intermediary powers, and Hume distinguished the mild European monarchy from the 'maxims of eastern princes'. In a truly eastern monarchy the prince stretched 'his authority so far as to leave no distinction of rank among his subjects, but what proceeds immediately from himself; no advantages of birth; no hereditary honours and possessions; and, in a word, no credit among the people, except from his commission alone'.[83] It was to point out this difference that Hume insisted that a monarchical *coup d'état*, having inherited a homogenised social base, the effective public ownership of land and the entire revenue and excise, would create an absolute state more dangerous than any Europe had yet

---

[80] *PC* (1764), p. 360.
[81] *PC* (1764), p. 359.
[82] 'Civil Liberty', pp. 93–4.
[83] 'That Politics May Be Reduced to Science', *Essays*, p. 22.

envisaged. 'Such are the inconveniencies, which may be reasonably foreseen, of this situation', he warned his countrymen in 1764, 'to which Great Britain is visibly tending.'

Hume's lurid rhetoric of 1764 was widely noticed, but the methodological assumptions behind his extreme thought experiment confused many readers.[84] Sir James Steuart, with Adam Smith perhaps Hume's most attentive reader, knew what Hume meant, although he disagreed. In 1767, when he published *An Inquiry into the Principles of Political Oeconomy*, he dismissed voluntary bankruptcy on a purely indigenous state debt as neither 'lawful, honourable or expedient', and an act of desperate and ignorant madmen which was 'diametrically opposite to every principle of good government'.[85] Nonetheless, like Hume, he found it useful to construct scenarios based on strong assumptions and he re-ran Hume's thought experiment in two versions. In the first he came to the conclusion that the future of commercial society was indeed a perennial rotation, and his striking vision was of public credit as a kind of gyroscope, in which furious rotation co-existed with perfect stability.[86] His second scenario contemplated the character of the post-bankruptcy despotism and there he saw the possibility of a total state making the whole population and economy subservient to its invincible military machine, and destroying Europe's commercial society by forcing every other nation into a choice between following suit or falling under its domination.[87] It is clear from other of Steuart's detailed analyses that these models of socio-economic mechanisms provided a framework for his theories. Nonetheless, he tried to deflate the radicalism of such extreme visions by calling them no more than a lively and entertaining 'illustration of general principles', perhaps like 'a rhapsody',[88] or 'like a farce between the acts of serious opera'.[89]

---

[84] For an example see [Marquis de Chastellux], *An Essay on Public Happiness* (2 vols., London, 1774), vol. II, p. 335.

[85] *Political Oeconomy*, vol. II, pp. 648–53. He acknowledged 'the public good be alleged as an overruling principle, to which every other must give way', but only in cases of an escalating indebtedness to foreign creditors saw the need of invoking it as a justification for England's voluntary bankruptcy.

[86] *Political Oeconomy*, vol. I, pp. 180–2; vol. II, pp. 683, 647. Steuart's model, which was deeply influenced by Davenant's work, was a fully idiomatic implementation of the commerce-debt dialectic Pocock describes in 'Hume and the American Revolution'.

[87] *Political Oeconomy*, vol. I, pp. 226–7.

[88] Ibid., p. 182.

[89] Ibid., p. 227.

A 'rhapsody' it may have been; nonetheless the 1764 vision of a fully developed public credit was for Hume deadly serious, providing him with indices for marking the stages in Britain's march through war, empire and debt towards the destruction of its mixed consitution. He watched diligently for unnecessary wars and impending bankruptcy, and almost paranoically for the slightest signs of the weakening of authority and blurring in the distinction of ranks. The thrust towards popular patriotic government in the 1760s especially alarmed Hume; he felt the need for more governmental authority in order to stem the democratic republican tide, and recognised that public debt perhaps helped weak government in resisting it.[90] After the 1745 rebellion he had argued that domestic revolution could never bring down the debt system because too many people had an interest in avoiding bankruptcy.[91] In 1770, in the final addition to his essay. 'Of Public Credit',[92] he pressed the point again. It was not the debt that encouraged faction and fanaticism: if 'people factious, mutinous, seditious, and even perhaps rebellious' threaten a fragile free government 'which admits not of discretionary power' against its citizens, then the 'evil of national debts' was the only cure. 'All the stockholders', whose wealth depended on public faith and who dreaded any disorder, would immediately rally to the help of the government to calm the 'democratic frenzy'.[93] Hume had wished the population of London halved and the debt eliminated altogether;[94] now he was grateful for their existence. The desperation was clear in his private communications: the chimerical liberty of Britain, he wrote to his publisher, can scarcely be 'retrench'd without Danger of being entirely lost'.[95]

Once the immediate domestic radical threat had passed Hume returned to emphasising that the debt would prove the undoing of Britain. In his letters he repeated the warnings about the choice between the death of debt or nation,[96] and watched with agony the

[90] For accounts of Hume's views in this period see Pocock, 'Hume and the American Revolution', pp. 126–7, 137–9, Forbes, *Hume's Philosophical Politics*, pp. 187–91, and Donald W. Livingston, *Hume's Philosophy of Common Life* (Chicago, 1984), pp. 269–71.
[91] 'Protestant Succession', p. 511.
[92] For the 1770 edition Hume combed through all his essays for outdated notions and cancelled them.
[93] *PC* (1770), p. 355.
[94] Hume to Gilbert Elliot, Lord Minto, 22 July 1768, *Letters*, vol. II, p. 184.
[95] Hume to Strahan, October 1769, *Letters*, vol. II, p. 216.
[96] Hume to Strahan, 25 March 1771, *Letters*, vol. II, p. 237.

further manifestations of Britain's 'ancient Greek jealousy'. He thought the idea of expending a fortune fighting a war for the Falkland Islands the most stupid and dangerous folly ever attempted by his country. He thought, or perhaps hoped, that it would bankrupt first France and then Britain.[97] In 1771 he thought the British lacked prescience to a remarkable degree when taking pleasure in France's problems with her debt.[98] After his stay in France in the 1760s he had revised his view of the French danger, cancelling some of his wilder passages on universal monarchy and on Britain's role as the guardian of Europe's liberty.[99] But he kept all the paragraphs on the inevitability of international conflict and moderated none of his thoughts on the security dilemmas of the nation. He saw that the problems with America would exacerbate Britain's indebtedness; as John Pocock put it in his essay on 'Hume and the American Revolution', the 'reasons for calling the elder Pitt a wicked madman turns out to have been that the great war of empire that Pitt had waged had increased the national debt to near the point at which Hume thought it must prove ruinous to society'.[100]

In 1776 Hume returned to his 'rhapsody' of public debt, incorporating its lessons, as a parting shot, in the very last corrections to his great *History of England*, which were published only posthumously. To understand his message we need to recall Hume's conviction that the 'natural death' of public credit involved a deadly contest between justice and authority, with a double outcome: if the natural authority of the system of ranks aligned itself with prudent government the dialectics of authority and liberty could survive, if not, pure governmental authority without liberty would triumph over the debt. The problem of authority preoccupied Hume to such a degree that in 1776 he also sent to his publisher a new essay on the topic, entitled 'Of the Origins of

---

[97] Hume to Strahan, 21 January and 25 March 1771, *Letters*, vol. II, pp. 234–5, 236–7.

[98] Hume to Strahan, 25 March 1771, vol. II, p. 242.

[99] The final text of 'Of Public Credit', revised in 1770, mentioned just 'foreign enemies', while the original (1752) text was qualified by adding 'or rather enemy (for we have but one to dread)'. Remarks on French universal empire were dropped at the same time from 'Of the Balance of Power' and 'Of the Protestant Succession'.

[100] 'Hume and the American Revolution', p. 138. Hume did not live to see this, but during the American War the national debt almost doubled again, from £131 million in 1775 to £245 million in 1783.

Government'.[101] Natural authority and the order of ranks were 'essential to the existence of civil society', the traditional argument ran, and (unlike the intricacies of a free constitution) would always take care of themselves without constant vigilant attention. For Hume this trust in the robustness of traditional authority might turn out to be a disastrous underestimation of the fragility of the social and economic balance underpinning modern liberty. True, the modern political order rested increasingly on liberty rather than authority, but 'neither of them can ever absolutely prevail', and precisely because authority had functional and historical priority in supporting civil society 'in those contests, which so often take place between the one and other, the latter may, on that account, challenge the preference'.[102] Hume did not wish to shift opinion from the care for liberty to the care of ranks and authority in order to promote authoritarian regimes; rather, authority was sometimes necessary to preserve liberty. Putting a stop to public debt by a *coup d'autorité* was a case in point.

It seems, however, that by 1776 the odds for a benign voluntary bankruptcy had foreshortened to the point of extinction. First Hume echoed Montesquieu's famous dictum that after having removed 'all the intermediary powers that formed their monarchy' the English had better watch their liberty because 'if they were to lose it, they would be one of the most enslaved peoples on earth'.[103] Correcting errors of his youth Hume now described English government under Elizabeth I as a civilised European monarchy and re-drew the comparison between the ancient and modern constitution. England under Elizabeth 'though seemingly it approached nearer, was in reality more remote from a despotic and eastern monarchy than the present government of that kingdom, where the people, though guarded by multiplied laws, are totally naked, defenceless and disarmed; and besides, are not secured by

---

[101] The first mention of it is in a letter to William Strahan, 1 March 1774 (*Letters*, vol. II, p. 287); it was sent off for publication in the summer of 1776 (Hume to Strahan, 8 June 1776, p. 324) and appeared in the 1777 posthumous edition of Hume's essays.

[102] 'Of the Origin of Government', *Essays*, pp. 40–1. The convergence between Smith's and Hume's thoughts on authority is conspicuous, see *Lectures on Jurisprudence*, (A) IV. 1–38, V. 119–36; (B) 12–18; *Wealth of Nations*, V. i. b.4–13. and particularly the additions to the last (1790) edition of *The Theory of Moral Sentiments*, VI.ii.2. 8–18.

[103] *The Spirit of the Laws*, Pt. 1, ch. 4, pp. 18–19. Notice that in the next paragraph Montesquieu accuses John Law with destroying 'the intermediate ranks'.

any middle power, or independent powerful nobility, interposed between them and the monarch'.[104]

After asserting Britain's modern constitutional weakness, Hume (in a long footnote comparing Britain's war effort and war finances in the two periods) also presented its consequences.[105] With cutting sarcasm he depicted England's credit system as a folly worse than the delusions which had guided medieval crusaders: 'For I suppose', he wrote, 'there is no mathematical, still less an arithmetical demonstration, that the road to the Holy Land was not the road to Paradise, as there is, that the endless increase of national debts is the direct road to national ruin'.[106] What in 1764 had struck some readers as a delirious rhapsody was now to Hume actual reality.[107] The end had not come yet, but the moment for any virtuous 'natural death' of public debt had been passed:

It will be found in the present year, 1776, that all the revenues of this island north of Trent and west of Reading, are mortgaged or anticipated for ever. Could the small remainder be in a worse condition, were those provinces seized by Austria and Prussia? There is only this difference, that some event might happen in Europe which would oblige these great monarchs to disgorge their acquisitions. But no imagination can figure a situation which will induce our creditors to relinquish their claims, or the public to seize their revenues.

At this distance Hume's vision seems alternately rhapsodic, in the eighteenth-century sense, and eerily prophetic. Hume's apocalyptic scenario first came true not in the free state of Britain but in the civilised absolute monarchy of France, where anxieties about

---

[104] 'Appendix III', *The History of England from the Invasion of Julius Caesar to the Revolution in 1688* (8 vols., 1802), pp. 471–2.

[105] Duncan Forbes noticed a 'connexion' the reader might make between Hume's remark on the constitution and the footnote on public debt (positioned a page apart) but did not develop the argument, *Hume's Philosophical Politics*, p. 179. However, Forbes has convincingly shown the remarkable constancy of Hume's thought in the relevant respects and demolished Giarizzo's thesis of an increasingly conservative and Tory Hume.

[106] 'Appendix III', *History*, vol. v, pp. 475–6. Richard Price cited the addition to the *History* as 'a kind of dying warning from Mr Hume', *Two Tracts on Civil Liberty, the War with America and the Finances of the Kingdom*, 2nd edn. (1778), reprinted in B. Peach (ed.), *Richard Price and the Ethical Foundations of the American Revolution* (Durham, N.C., 1979), p. 132, and Thomas Paine echoed these views in his infamous 'The Decline and Fall of the English System Of Finance' (1796) in P.S. Foner (ed.), *The Complete Writings of Thomas Paine* (2 vols., New York, 1945), vol. ii, pp. 651–74.

[107] For Scottish assessments of the public debt in the same year see John Dalrymple, Earl of Stair, *The State of the National Debt, the National Income, and the National Expenditure. With Some Short Inferences and Reflections Applicable to the Present Dangerous Crisis* (1776) and, of course, the last chapter of Adam Smith's *Wealth of Nations*, 'Of Publick Debts'.

'public faith' in the instruments of debt finance made the monarchy fatally procrastinate when contemplating voluntary state bankruptcy.[108] From the ensuing disaster and revolution a regime more despotic than anything yet known arose. British use of public debt remained staggeringly effective for a century and a half. It allowed Britain and her allies to defeat the French military regime's attempt at universal empire. The danger of 'violent death' remained. When the time came Britain shouldered its Continental commitments as the patron of Europe's liberty and checked the attempt to absolute domination by 'Austria and Prussia'.[109] More recently, the nightmare of Russia's bid at universal empire has also passed: Hume's scepticism about the immense wisdom necessary to direct an entire national economy amidst the 'continual fluctuations of commerce' is again appreciated. *Sero sapiunt Phryges.*[110]

Pocock is thus certainly right when he argues that Hume's problems with the public debt were not a result of a 'blockage in his economic thinking'. He is also clearly correct when he asserts that by speculating about commercial society and the public debt Hume had 'built himself the scenario of an almost insuperable contradiction'.[111] It is perhaps useful to repeat that this stems from the tension between commercial society and international disorder, and ultimately the threat of war. Taking a hint from Pocock's essay on 'The Dying Thoughts of a North Briton', I can hardly believe that we have yet seen the end of this story. Today we are tempted to

[108] Hume's 'natural-death' scenario from 'Public Credit' was used as a warning against monarchical bankruptcy by Jacques-Pierre Brissot, *Pont de banqueroute ou Lettres à un créancier d'état sur l'impossibilité de la banqueroute nationale et sur les moyens de ramener le crédit et la paix* (3rd edn, 1787), pp. 136–7; he also used Hume's china-shop metaphor of international relations as his epigraph, p. 119. The clearest French call from voluntary bankruptcy came in Linguet's 'Réflexions sur la dette nationale en France: la Nation y est-elle obligée comme en Angleterre?' (*Annales politiques, civiles, et littéraires du dix-huitième siècle*, 15 (1788), 218–36, and republished in 1789); see Darlene Gay Levy, *Simon-Nicolas-Henri Linguet: A Study in Eighteenth-Century French Politics* (Urbana, Ill., 1980), pp. 239–45, 268, 281–96, 300–2. Kant saw in the king's failure to call for a bankruptcy, and his turn to the people – or the Estates General, for a solution instead (as Brissot demanded) – the immediate cause (and the primary legitimation) of the revolution (*Contest of the Faculties*, p. 164).

[109] Hume, travelling in Germany in 1748, wrote to his brother: 'Germany is undoubtedly a very fine Country, full of industrious honest People, & were it united it would be the greatest Power that ever was in the World' (*Letters*, vol. i, p. 126).

[110] 'The Phrygians learn wisdom to late': Kant's comment on Hume's metaphor about the international order and the china-shop (*Contest of the Faculties*, p. 190.)

[111] 'Hume and the American Revolution', p. 139–40.

indulge in the hope that Hume was indeed merely rhapsodising. The struggle between commerce and war, however, evokes the perennial conflict between liberty and authority: 'neither of them can ever absolutely prevail in the contest'.[112]

[112] 'Origin of Government', p. 40.

CHAPTER 16

Universal monarchy and the liberties of Europe: David Hume's critique of an English Whig doctrine

John Robertson

The Scottish Enlightenment presented English Whiggism with an unusual challenge. From a standpoint at once within and outwith the English political world, the Scots set themselves to rid English Whig politics and history of its parochial prejudices and ancient constitutional myths, and to interpret them afresh in a properly cosmopolitan perspective. Unsurprisingly, it was a challenge resented by most of its intended beneficiaries; and it is only recently that historians of English political thought have come to appreciate its significance. If the point is now generally taken, few have been as generous and imaginative in their pursuit of it as John Pocock.[1]

In pressing that challenge, no Scot was more tenacious or resourceful than David Hume. In Duncan Forbes's seminal phrase, Hume counterposed the cosmopolitan standards of 'sceptical Whiggism' to the parochial shibboleths of English 'vulgar Whiggism'.[2] But simply to insist upon Hume's scepticism, Pocock has argued, may be to underestimate the degree of ambivalence and even, in the end, of frustration expressed in Hume's political thinking. While it is almost certainly mistaken to interpret Hume's vigorous private hostility to Wilkes as evidence of a late conversion to Toryism, what Pocock characterised as 'the dying thoughts of a North Briton' seem to express an unease which goes beyond the sceptical.[3] In this essay, I wish to reinforce the impression of

---

[1] J.G.A. Pocock, 'The Varieties of Whiggism from Restoration to Reform', in *Virtue, Commerce and History* (Cambridge, 1985), esp. pp. 230–53; *The Ancient Constitution and the Feudal Law* (1957), *A Reissue with a Retrospect* (Cambridge, 1987), Part II, 'The Ancient Constitution Revisited', pp. 371–9.

[2] Duncan Forbes, *Hume's Philosophical Politics* (Cambridge, 1975).

[3] J.G.A. Pocock, 'Hume and the American Revolution: The Dying Thoughts of a North Briton', in *Virtue, Commerce and History*. The argument that Hume became a Tory was vigorously and ingeniously put by Guiseppe Giarrizzo, *David Hume politico e storico* (Turin, 1962).

serious Humean disenchantment with English Whiggism, by examining a hitherto almost unrecognised line of reflection within his political thought, that devoted to Britain's place in Europe.

It would be surprising had this dimension of British politics not been among Hume's concerns. In the space of seventy-five years after the Revolution of 1688, the British fought four major wars against the Bourbon Monarchy of France. The Nine Years War (1689–98) and the War of the Spanish Succession (1702–13) occupied virtually the entire period between the Revolution and the Hanoverian Succession. The Peace of Utrecht (1713) then secured thirty years of détente, until hostilities resumed in the War of the Austrian Succession (1743–8), followed by the still more extensive Seven Years War of 1756–63. At every stage the nature and extent of Britain's European involvement had been the subject of constant public discussion, and commentators were well aware of the link between these external commitments and the new agenda of domestic politics, above all in relation to the standing army and the public debt. If Hume was to fulfil his ambition to teach his contemporaries a lesson in political moderation, he must address both the foreign and the domestic dimensions of debate.

As we shall now see, Hume did reflect upon the purposes of Britain's involvement in Europe, as he did upon its domestic consequences. In doing so, moreover, Hume will be seen to have engaged with a central theme of Whig political thinking since the late seventeenth century, the threat presented to the liberties of Europe by the French aspiration to Universal Monarchy. It is Hume's treatment of this theme which my contribution seeks particularly to bring into focus. Although it could not escape Duncan Forbes's eye for Humean detail, it is not an aspect of Hume's thought which Forbes has chosen to develop.[4] The same may be said of Pocock, whose study of Hume's last years confined its attention to the problems of the debt and America.[5] Since that was written, however, the themes of universal monarchy and empire have come to the fore in another line of Pocockian inquiry, his interest in 'the politics of extent': what follows, therefore, is written rather in anticipation of a new debate than in revival of an

---

[4] For suggestive but brief remarks: Duncan Forbes, 'The European, or Cosmopolitan, Dimension in Hume's Science of Politics', *The British Journal for Eighteenth-Century Studies*, vol. I, no. 1 (1978), 57–60.

[5] Pocock, 'Hume and the American Revolution'.

old.[6] I shall first outline the course of Hume's reflection on the subject, as it was conveyed in successive collections of his *Essays*, and in the revisions he made to them. This will be followed by an interpretation of his arguments, in the context of the eighteenth-century debate over universal monarchy.

Sustained engagement with the issues raised by Britain's involvement with Europe only begins in the essays Hume published in 1752. His previous collection, *Essays Moral and Political* (1741–2), contained no more than a handful of remarks on the theme. In 'Of Liberty and Despotism' he had commented that the balance of power was a secret in politics only known fully to the present age, and was one indication of the general change for the better in modern government. In the same vein, he observed in 'Of the Rise and Progress of the Arts and Sciences' that modern Europe was a copy at large of what Greece was formerly in miniature, a cluster of distinct states enjoying 'the closest intercourse of commerce and learning'.[7] If these remarks had any contemporary implication, they would seem to have supported Walpole's last, unavailing efforts to maintain European peace.[8] Hume also passed a sharp comment on empires in the essay 'That Politics may be reduced to a Science', when he observed that free governments were much more oppressive than monarchies in their rule over dependent provinces. Thus Rome's provinces were less exploited under the monarchy than under the commonwealth; or – to take a modern example – the *Pais conquis* of France than Ireland, even though Ireland, 'being in a good measure, peopled from ENGLAND, possesses so many rights and privileges as should naturally make it challenge better treatment than that of a conquered province'.[9] Running through these early essays was the more general argument that modern 'civilized' monarchies, of which France was the outstanding example, were far from being 'despotisms': a civilised

---

[6] J.G.A. Pocock, 'States, Republics and Empires: The American Founding in Early Modern Perspective', *Social Science Quarterly*, 68, 4 (1987), 703–23.

[7] David Hume, 'Of Liberty and Despotism', retitled 'Of Civil Liberty' in 1758, 'Of the Rise and Progress of the Arts and Sciences', in *Essays Moral, Political and Literary*, edited by T.H. Green and T.H. Grose, 2 vols. 1898 (hereafter *Essays*), vol. I, pp. 160–1, 182–3.

[8] England had, however, already gone to war with Spain in 1739, and given the public clamour which had driven Walpole to this it is a little surprising that Hume did not comment further.

[9] Hume, 'That Politics may be reduced to a Science', *Essays*, I, pp. 101–3.

monarchy was no less, and in the case of dependent provinces rather more, committed to the rule of law than a so-called 'free government'.

By 1752, when the *Political Discourses* appeared, the issues seemed much more pressing. A general view of Britain's place in Europe was now set out in 'Of the Balance of Power'. Asking himself whether the idea of the balance of power, or only the phrase, was a recent invention, Hume argued that the idea was clearly known to the ancient Greeks: Demosthenes' oration for the Megalopolitans contained 'the utmost refinements on this principle, that ever entered into the head of a VENETIAN or ENGLISH speculatist'. Like ostracism, however, it was a principle which derived from the circumstances of the Greek cities rather than from reflection: it was the product of 'jealous emulation' when it ought to be a matter of 'cautious politics'. The antithesis of the principle was exemplified by Rome, whose war with Hannibal was 'a contest for universal empire', fatal alike to Carthage, the Greeks and the idea of the balance of power itself. The alternation of ideas had repeated itself after the fall of Rome. Based on vassalage and the feudal militia, the form of government established by Rome's northern conquerors had been inimical to further conquests. But once those institutions had been abolished, Europe had again been threatened by 'universal monarchy' through the union of so many kingdoms and principalities under the Emperor Charles V. Nor had the weaknesses of the House of Austria, from which its power collapsed within a century, removed the threat. In its place 'a new power succeeded, more formidable to the liberties of EUROPE, possessing all the advantages of the former, and labouring under none of its defects; except a share of that spirit of bigotry and persecution, with which the House of Austria was so long, and still is so much infatuated'. The Bourbons of France were the new aspirants to universal monarchy. While the latter idea was still a force in the modern world, however, Hume also found evidence of the countervailing influence of the balance of power. Despite being victorious in four of the last five general wars, France had failed to acquire a total ascendancy. If resistance was maintained, there was room to hope that the natural revolutions of human affairs would continue to preserve the world from so great an evil.

For the last three of those wars, Hume acknowledged, Britain had done most to maintain that resistance, standing as 'guardian of the general liberties of EUROPE, and patron of mankind.' But he cautioned against excessive ardour. The British appeared to have been motivated rather by 'the ancient GREEK spirit of jealous emulation' than by 'the prudent views of modern politics'. They were too ready to carry on wars in which they were only accessories, and to do so entirely at their own expense, mortgaging their revenues in the public debt, 'surely the most fatal delusion, that a nation, which had any pretension to politics and prudence, has ever yet been guilty of'. In the end, Hume feared, such excesses would lead opinion to swing in the opposite direction, rendering the British as careless of the fate of Europe, as the Greeks had been of that of Carthage.

The essay ended with the general reflection that 'enormous monarchies, such as EUROPE is at present threatened with', were likely to be destructive to human nature in their progress, continuance and even downfall. There was a recurrent pattern by which the military genius which aggrandised a monarchy left the court and the capital and moved to the frontier, whose defence then fell into the hands of mercenary and disloyal strangers. The Bourbons, whose nobility would not submit to languishing in garrisons in Hungary or Lithuania, would thus face the same fate as the Roman emperors, until the final dissolution of the monarchy.[10]

There was further reflection of Britain's involvement with Europe in two more of the *Political Discourses*. In 'Of Public Credit' Hume spelt out, in vigorous but sophisticated terms, the danger of allowing Britain's European commitments to be paid for by public credit. With but one foreign enemy to dread, the reluctance to accept the 'natural death' of public credit by voluntary bankruptcy was actually enhancing the danger of its 'violent death' by a conquest. Wearied by the struggle to maintain the balance of power while fettered by debt, the next generation of Britons were likely to sit by while their neighbours were overrun, 'till, at last, they themselves and their creditors lie at the mercy of the conqueror.'[11] The threat of universal monarchy owed less to the strength of

---

[10] Hume, 'Balance of Power', *Essays*, vol. 1, pp. 348–56. The reflection amplified a note in Hume's (probably early) Memoranda: 'Hume's Early Memoranda, 1729–40', ed. E.C. Mossner, *Journal of the History of Ideas*, 9, (1948), 517–18, note no. [258].

[11] Hume, 'Of Public Credit', *Essays*, vol. 1, pp. 373–4. See the contribution by Istvan Hont to this volume.

France than to the likelihood that British zeal for the liberties of
Europe would as suddenly collapse into passive indifference.

In a third essay, 'Of the Protestant Succession' (originally
written for publication in 1748), Hume contested the opinion that
the Hanoverian connection was damaging to British interests.
However much of a liability it might have seemed initially, it was
the Hanoverian Succession which had enabled Britain to win glory
across Europe, as the antagonist of the power which threatened
everyone with conquest. More practically, Hanover's place within
the Empire had served to connect Britain more closely with the
House of Austria, 'our natural ally'.[12]

Such arguments would seem to align Hume squarely with the
new direction in foreign policy adopted after 1748 by the Whig
Duke of Newcastle, and against those who believed that strict 'Blue
Water' principles of non-engagement with the continent should
continue to be followed. The latter believed that war with France
should be prosecuted overseas, in America rather than in Europe.
The Whigs, by contrast, held that Britain should revert to the 'Old
System' of William III, who had treated Bourbon France and
Spain as Britain's natural enemies, and the United Provinces and
Austria as her natural allies. If Britain now had to fight in North
America as well, the Whigs believed that it should not be by
sacrificing the 'liberties of Europe' and abandoning Britain's
commitment to the continental balance of power.[13] Hume had no
doubt become familiar with these assumptions during his period of
service in an embassy to the courts of Vienna (the supposedly
natural ally) and Turin in 1748. His essays of 1752 offered them
every support.

Following the Seven Years War, however, Hume's position
changed. He was still prepared to execute Whig diplomacy, serving
the embassy in Paris between 1763 and 1765, and as Under-
Secretary in the Northern department from 1767 until early 1768.
But while Whig statesmen continued to suppose that checking
French power was an essential condition of both European peace
and imperial security, Hume could no longer see a serious basis for

---

[12] Hume, 'Of the Protestant Succession', *Essays*, vol. I, pp. 474–8.
[13] H.M. Scott, '"The True Principles of the Revolution": The Duke of Newcastle and the
Idea of the Old System', in Jeremy Black (ed.), *Knights Errant and True Englishmen. British
Foreign Policy 1600–1800* (Edinburgh, 1989).

rivalry.[14] French apprehensions of Pitt, he assured a correspondent in 1766, were now without foundation.[15] Conversely, as he told Strahan, it was due to the peace-loving king of France that a war for the Falklands was averted in 1771.[16] More publicly, Hume also made a number of small but significant changes to the new editions of his *Essays* which appeared in 1768 and 1770.

The first such change, in 1768, was to delete from 'Of the Balance of Power' the suggestion that Europe was 'at present' threatened with enormous monarchies. A rather more substantial change to the same essay followed in 1770, when Hume removed the passage alleging that France had sought a universal monarchy for above a century, and celebrating Britain's role in defence of the liberties of Europe.[17] Similar alterations were made to the essays on 'Public Credit' and the 'Protestant Succession'. From the former went the parenthesis specifying that Britain had but one foreign enemy to dread; from the latter went the passage identifying Britain's glory with its having been the antagonist of the power threatening all Europe with conquest.[18] In deleting these passages, Hume now repudiated any suggestion that Bourbon France sought a universal monarchy. He did not, however, thereby dismiss the threat of universal monarchy altogether. As the essay on the 'Balance of Power' stood, the British people were still urged to maintain their vigilance on behalf of European liberty; and in that on 'Public Credit' he continued to warn against its violent death by conquest, although there was no longer an identifiable foreign enemy. The idea of universal, or at least 'enormous', monarchy remained valid, even when, in present circumstances, no serious aspirant could be identified.

This determination not to confuse the absence of an actual threat of universal monarchy with the end of the idea is indicative of more than political caution. It points to Hume's awareness of a larger,

---

[14] For the official view, H.M. Scott, *British Foreign Policy in the Age of the American Revolution* (Oxford 1990), pp. 341–3.

[15] Hume to the Marquise de Barbentane, 29 August 1766, in *The Letters of David Hume*, edited J.Y.T. Greig, 2 vols. (Oxford, 1969), vol. II, pp. 74–5, responding to a letter from Turgot, 23 July 1766, in E. Rotwein (ed.), *David Hume: Writings on Economics* (Edinburgh, 1955), p. 205.

[16] Hume to Strahan, 21 January, 11 March 1771, *Letters*, vol. II, pp. 234–7; it was not an informed view.

[17] Hume, 'Of the Balance of Power', *Essays*, vol. I, pp. 353, 355.

[18] Hume, *Essays*, vol. I, pp. 374 (Public Credit), 476 (Protestant Succession).

theoretical context for the discussion of universal monarchy, beyond the immediate concerns of British foreign policy. To turn from policy to theory, however, is not to suggest a radical divorce between the two. It was always a strength of English Whiggism (appreciated by Pocock as by few others) that its practice was closely supported by principles, whether theoretical or historical; and universal monarchy provides but one more case in point. Behind the commonplaces of Whig diplomatic doctrine can be traced a powerful line of English and anglophile argument upon both universal monarchy and Britain's proper contribution to its defeat. Only when Hume's arguments are seen in relation to this tradition does their full force become clear.

What I shall call the modern theory of universal monarchy, like the Whig 'Old System' which drew upon it, took shape in the first phase of Britain's continental commitment, between 1689 and 1712. To appreciate its modernity, however, we must first step still further back, and take a short view of the debate over universal monarchy in the previous two centuries.

The issue of universal monarchy in early modern Europe was tied to the rivalry between the Habsburg and Bourbon dynasties for supremacy in Europe. The pretension was first and most tellingly associated with Charles V; subsequently it was ascribed to the Spanish monarchy of Phillip II and his successors, and finally to Louis XIV of France. As an ideal it was capable of favourable construction, the most remarkable apologia being that written on behalf of the Spanish monarchy by the Neapolitan Campanella.[19] But generally universal monarchy was an accusation rather than an ideal, a term of condemnation, branding the alleged aspirant as an over-ambitious warmonger, bent on territorial aggrandisement by conquest.[20]

The history of English participation in this debate is only beginning to be written. It is unlikely that early modern Englishmen were as introverted in their political thinking as most modern historians have assumed; but we do not yet know what contribution they made before the middle of the century. For a brief period in

[19] Tommaso Campanella, *De Monarchia Hispanica* (Amsterdam 1640, previously published in German in Frankfurt in 1620).

[20] Franz Bosbach, *Monarchia Universalis. Ein politischer Leitbegriff der frühen Neuzeit* (Göttingen, 1988).

the 1650s the remarkable power of the military commonwealth made possible visions of a Roman imperial future, extending, in Harrington's Ciceronian formulation, to the 'patronage' if not to the empire of the world.[21] Although such visions faded with the Restoration, the English monarchy was now strong enough for intervention against would-be universal monarchs on the continent to be credible, and a vigorous debate over the source of the threat ensued. At first the danger was identified with the Dutch pretension to an 'empire of the sea', Dissenters alone insisting that the threat came from Louis XIV's France. After 1672, however, there was a consensus that the latter was the greater danger.[22] It was a major charge against James II that he had subordinated his kingdoms to French ambitions; and once William III had secured his new kingdoms, he could count on considerable support for his commitment to the struggle against Louis XIV. But the unprecedented scale of that commitment, its enormous military, financial and constitutional implications, also forced Englishmen and Scotsmen to reconsider the theory of universal monarchy for themselves, to assess more precisely its modern character, and to explore the alternatives to it.

In both England and Scotland the key thinkers were figures whose intellectual interest John Pocock was the first historian to recover: Charles Davenant and Andrew Fletcher.[23] As both Pocock and, more recently, Istvan Hont have demonstrated, Davenant's intellectual significance is not impaired by the notorious instability of his short-term political loyalties: he should be seen as having made a major contribution (matched only, among Englishmen, by that of Defoe) to the understanding of Britain's role in Europe and the world in the eighteenth century.[24] From the first Davenant

[21] James Harrington, *Oceana* (1656), reprinted in *The Political Works of James Harrington*, ed. J.G.A. Pocock (Cambridge, 1977), pp. 320–33.
[22] See Steven Pincus, 'Protestantism and Patriotism: Ideology and the Making of English Foreign Policy 1650–1665', Harvard University Ph.D., 1990, esp. Section III: 'Popery, Trade and Universal Monarchy'.
[23] J.G.A. Pocock, *The Machiavellian Moment, Florentine Political Thought and the Atlantic Republican Tradition* (Princeton, 1975), ch. 13.
[24] Istvan Hont, 'Free Trade and the Economic Limits to National Politics: Neo-Machiavellian Political Economy Reconsidered', in John Dunn (ed.), *The Economic Limits to Modern Politics* (Cambridge, 1990). Defoe's principal contribution to the discussion took the rather different form of a continuous commentary upon European affairs in his thrice-weekly review: *A Review of the Affairs of France: and of all Europe, as influenc'd by that Nation.* (1704–13).

assumed that the French king sought universal monarchy, and that Britain's liberties and the liberties of Europe alike depended on frustrating his designs.[25] Just what these designs entailed he spelt out in 1701, in the third of three *Essays upon I. The Ballance of Power, II. The Right of Making War, Peace and Alliances III. Universal Monarchy.*

The root of the ambition, Davenant argued, was the identification of fame with conquest. It was this imperial virtue whose passage through history explained the succession of empires. Although 'universal empire' had never actually been realised, the 'endless view of increasing' had led each aspirant in turn to conquer province after province in the hope of making itself perpetual.[26] Thus the mantle of empire had passed from the Assyrians through the Persians and the Macedonians to Rome; from Rome it was briefly assumed by Charlemagne, and then not claimed again until the emergence of the Spanish monarchy of Charles V. But this monarchy, Davenant thought, had been an accidental creation, too quickly acquired and too intolerant to last. The imperial virtue had since passed on to the French monarchy, whose strength had been built up more gradually, and which had the resources of manpower required to consolidate its acquisitions. If it too had made an error in expelling its Protestants, this was perhaps only to recommend itself to the bigoted Spaniards, to facilitate the annexation of their dominions. Should the French king achieve that, he would have 'for wealth, trade, number of inhabitants, and for power, a larger empire than the Turks possessed, or than that which Charlemagne erected.' There was no doubt, therefore, that the French were now 'the people most likely to invade the liberties of Europe'.[27]

Davenant next explained why universal monarchy was so dangerous, using the arguments of a Spanish historian of the time of Charles V, Pedro Mexia, as a foil.[28] There were three main reasons.

---

[25] Charles Davenant, *An Essay upon Ways and Means of Supplying the War* (1695), in *The Political and Commercial Works of Charles Davenant*, collected and revised by Sir Charles Whitworth MP, 5 vols. (1771), vol. I, p. 10 (hereafter Davenant, *Works.*)

[26] Davenant, *An Essay upon Universal Monarchy* (1701) *Works*, vol. IV, pp. 1–5, 23.

[27] Ibid., pp. 6–28, the final quoted passage on p. 28.

[28] Pedro Mexia, *The Imperiall Historie: Or the Lives of the Emperours, from Julius Caesar, the First Founder of the Roman Monarchy, unto this Present Yeere* (first published in Spanish in 1547, English translation, 1623). Davenant's reasons for using Mexia in this way are unknown.

First, it was not the case, as apologists like Mexia claimed, that a universal monarchy promoted peace. At every stage in their development, from infancy to dissolution, such monarchies were a source of wars, devastation and thraldom.[29] Second, a universal monarchy must engross the trade of the world:

> For, as we see in particular kingdoms, where there is one great city, it draws to it all the trade; so in a large dominion, composed of several provinces, be it a commonwealth, or a principality, whatever country is at the head of affairs, there will all the traffic center . . . Merchants will always resort to countries where they see a big Emporium, a luxurious people, and a pompous court.[30]

Finally, a universal monarchy will spread a uniform tyranny over all its provinces. Not only would these be taxed for the benefit of the court at the centre; they would enjoy no legal, cultural or religious independence. A universal monarch characteristically feels himself unsafe unless he has imposed uniformity in religion, preferably by Roman Catholicism.[31] In conclusion, Davenant observed that while it is not difficult to interrupt the rise of such a monarchy in its beginnings, once one has become established, other nations will crowd in under its yoke. Fear, interest and flattery will combine to induce submission, not a willingness to resist.[32]

But universal monarchy was only one form of empire: there were empires for preservation as well as for increase. One example of an empire for preservation was the German, divided into many principalities, and incapable of further conquest.[33] A second example, as Davenant explained elsewhere, was that of England. To the English, possessing a free government, foreign conquests were 'neither desirable, nor safe'.[34] Instead, England's empire was one of commerce. Still more than the French or the Dutch, the English had 'everything that can contribute to make us the foremost people of the whole commercial world', ports, situation, their own woollen manufacture and the products of their dominions in the West and East Indies.[35] Through trade, all this wealth

---

[29] Davenant, *Universal Monarchy, Works*, vol. IV, pp. 28–33.
[30] Ibid., pp. 33–4.
[31] Ibid., pp. 34–40.
[32] Ibid., pp. 40–1.
[33] Ibid., p. 23.
[34] Davenant, *Essays upon Peace at Home, and War Abroad* (1703), *Works*, vol. IV, pp. 284, 393.
[35] Davenant, *An Essay upon the Probable Methods of making a People gainers in the Balance of Trade* (1699), *Works*, vol. II, pp. 227–8.

should circulate about, enriching the chief seat of empire, and thence being dispersed through its parts. Such commerce, Davenant, argued, was most beneficial when least impeded: it was a mistake to protect weaker parts of the economy when others had greater potential. But this commitment to free trade was qualified in a crucial respect: it was reasonable for a superior kingdom to expect that its provinces, however they might enrich themselves, would not do so at the expense of the centre:

Where the seat of dominium is in a great emporium, . . . such a city will not only be the head of power but of Trade, governing all its branches, and giving the rules and price; so that all parts thereon depending, can deal but subordinately to it, til at last it is found that provinces work but to enrich the superior kingdom.[36]

In the case of England, this point had a quite specific application: Ireland must not be allowed to undermine English strength in woollen manufactures by its ability to sell its own more cheaply. Davenant justified this by arguing, contrary to Molyneux, that Ireland was a colony, which the mother country was required to protect, and over which it must therefore exercise supreme judgement for the benefit of the whole. Although this claim of empire could not be extended to Scotland, as a separate kingdom, Davenant urged the English to watch over all their neighbours, 'especially where they depend upon us'. In the last resort, he concluded, it was 'but a reasonable jealousy of state' to prevent Ireland undermining the principal foundation of England's trade.[37] If a free government, pursuing commerce not territory, was an empire for preservation rather than increase, this clearly did not mean that it should have no provinces, or that it could be expected to abdicate its sovereign authority over them.

As Hont has underlined, Davenant's reflections upon empire and commerce stand in a close and complex relation to those of Machiavelli and Harrington.[38] The distinction between empires for increase and for preservation was taken from them, but Davenant's preference for empires of preservation was the opposite of theirs.

---

[36] Ibid., pp. 237–8.

[37] Davenant, *Balance of Power, Works*, vol. II, pp. 236–59; as against William Molyneux, *The Case of Ireland's being bound by Acts of Parliament in England, Stated* (Dublin and London, 1698). For elucidation, see Hont, 'Free Trade and the Economic Limits to National Politics', pp. 78–89.

[38] Hont, 'Free Trade and the Economic Limits to National Politics', pp. 57–95.

Moreover, he did not adopt as his model empires for preservation those which Machiavelli and Harrington had criticised, Sparta and Venice.[39] Instead Davenant argued that an empire for preservation in the modern world could, and indeed should, aspire to be a commercial empire on a global scale. Only by becoming such an empire could England stand against a modern universal monarchy, with its own ambition to engross commerce as well as territory. To defy a universal monarchy, however, a commercial empire would need to be intensely Machiavellian in another respect: it would still have to match the universal monarchy in its 'virtue'. It would, in Davenant's revealing phrase, have to be prepared to show a ruthless 'jealousy of state', both towards its rivals and towards its own subordinate provinces.

Andrew Fletcher shared Davenant's conviction that the threat of universal monarchy had taken new forms, but came to differ sharply in his views both of the source of the threat and of the antidote. To Fletcher the pursuit of universal empire was as integral a feature of modern monarchy as the employment of standing armies. His initial treatment of the subject, in the *Discorso delle cose di Spagna* (1698), was an esoteric demonstration of the opportunity awaiting a King of Spain who could undertake a Machiavellian *renovatio imperii*. Fletcher anticipated Davenant in explaining that the mistake of previous Spanish rulers had been to grow too fast, and by their intolerance to depopulate the Monarchy. Nevertheless, he maintained, a successor who reversed this policy, encouraging toleration and the mechanical arts, and who allied himself with the English or the Dutch to gain mastery of the sea, could still expect to possess the empire of the world.[40] But if Fletcher's principal concern in 1698, like Davenant's in 1701, was the Spanish Succession, by the latter date he himself had identified a threat much closer to home. For it now seemed to Fletcher that William III was as ambitious as Louis XIV. In return for giving Louis Portugal as well as Spain, William hoped to be allowed to unite the three British kingdoms with all seventeen provinces of the Netherlands, thus obtaining for ever 'the empire of the sea, with an

---

[39] Davenant, *Balance of Trade, Works*, vol. II, pp. 275 (on Sparta), 379–80 (a less criticial remark on Venice, of which, however, Davenant made little).

[40] Andrew Fletcher, *Discorso delle cose di Spagna* ('Napoli', 1698), in *The Political Works of Andrew Fletcher* (1732), pp. 177–240.

entire monopoly of trade'.[41] Fletcher's final argument, in *An Account of a Conversation Concerning the Right Regulation of Governments for the Common Good of Mankind.* (1704) differed still further from Davenant's. The experience of Ireland as well as of the Scots' Darien venture showed that the English possessed exactly the same determination to uphold the superior interest of the centre as was characteristic of any empire. In logic the English might as well cut off all these outlying territories and have them sunk, the better to concentrate all wealth in London and the south-east.[4] As Fletcher now understood it, the problem of universal monarchy had ceased to be one of the personal ambitions of monarchs, and had become one of the insatiable demands of the metropolitan emporium: London was the new Rome.

While a maritime, commercial empire could thus be just as oppressive as a universal monarchy on land, Fletcher did not suppose that a modern nation could forego commerce, and the acquisition of colonial entrepots to facilitate its conduct overseas. (He himself was one of the most substantial investors in the Scottish Africa Company responsible for the Darien venture.) The problem was to identify the form of government which would make such commerce possible without reinforcing metropolitan predominance. The examples of Sparta and Venice were discounted, on the grounds that even in these aristocratical governments there were insufficent restraints on the desire of enlarging their dominions.[4] Instead Fletcher envisaged a remodelling of the entire pattern of government in Europe, to the end that it be divided into political communities roughly equal in size, which would be grouped into a smaller number of equal leagues or unions. Since these would be incapable of conquest (if not of war altogether), the common identification of the 'interest' of a nation with its 'advantage' over another would be broken. In its stead would come the recognition that the true interest and good of any nation were the same as that of any other, and that interest and justice were one.[44]

---

[41] Fletcher, *A Speech upon the State of the Nation: in April 1701* (1701), *Political Works*, pp. 261–3. A previous remark in another work of 1698, *A Discourse of Government with relation to Militia's*, that 'the sea is the only empire which can naturally belong to us. Conquest is not in our interest . . .', ibid., p. 66, had not had the same pejorative implication.

[42] Fletcher, *An Account of a Conversation concerning the Right Regulation of Governments for the common Good of Mankind* (1704), *Political Works*, pp. 403–16. I am grateful to David Armitage for discussions of Fletcher's theory of empire.

[43] Fletcher, *Account of a Conversation, Political Works*, pp. 437–8.

[44] Ibid., pp. 422–44.

Fletcher's reference to the Achaean League as the model for his plan suggests that it derived from the principles of confederation, exemplified in the modern United Provinces. Machiavelli too had admitted the possibility of equal leagues, and noted that they were inimical to conquest, an observation on which Harrington had elaborated.[45] But Fletcher had developed the idea in a direction quite antithetical to Machiavelli's and Harrington's preference for increase, while his denial that interest was to be equated with advantage was effectively a repudiation of the Machiavellian idea of competitive 'virtue'. In his analysis of empire, therefore, Fletcher can barely be described as a Machiavellian in any sense.[46] Accepting neither Davenant's distinction between an empire of commerce and universal monarchy nor his adherence to a Machiavellian 'jealousy of state', Fletcher's thinking constituted a direct, contemporary challenge to the English writer's attempt to redefine the terms of England's European and imperial commitments.

As Fletcher was almost certainly aware, however, such thinking was rapidly being rendered counterfactual. With the acceptance by his fellow-countrymen of parliamentary union with England in 1707 in return for free access to its trade, the attempt to construct an alternative, non-metropolitan theory of commercial empire appeared to lose its urgency. Subsequently the Peace of Utrecht could be taken to demonstrate that Europe's monarchies were now willing to abandon their territorial ambitions in favour of the balance of power, and the pursuit of purely commercial advantage. The moment for more radical thinking about European confederation appeared to have passed.

It was not only Fletcher's thinking which was overtaken by events. In England itself concern over the threat of universal monarchy was muted by the Peace, and the issue of empire lost some of its urgency. In his last writing, Davenant himself looked forward to the opening up of a peaceful, free commerce with France.[47] The radical Whig authors of *Cato's Letters*, John Trenchard and Thomas Gordon, continued to emphasise the evils of

---

[45] Machiavelli, *Discorsi*, II. iv; Harrington, *Oceana, Political Works*, pp. 323–4.
[46] See also John Robertson, 'Andrew Fletcher's Vision of Union', in R.A. Mason (ed.), *Scotland and England 1286–1815* (Edinburgh, 1987), pp. 216–18; and contrast with Hont, 'Free Trade and the Economic Limits to National Politics', pp. 117–19.
[47] Davenant, *Report to the Commissioners for the Publick Accounts of the Kingdom*, Part 1 (1712) *Works*, vol. v, pp. 378–97.

conquest, but with the qualifications that the modern absolute governments of Europe were not identical to the despotisms of Asia, and did not pose an immediate threat.[48] On the other hand, the conviction that the empire of the sea was the proper form of empire for a free state such as England was taken as confirmed; what was now flatly denied was any suggestion that this should involve Britain in continental European engagements. The navy, a militia and a few garrisons should be quite sufficient for the defence of British interests.[49] The moral of such reflection for Britain's place in Europe was drawn out, with a characteristic flourish, by one who regarded himself as the architect and embodiment of the Peace of Utrecht:

> By a continual attention to improve her natural, that is her maritime strength, by collecting all her forces within herself, and reserving them to be laid out on great occasions, such as regard her immediate interests and her honour, or such as are truly important to the general system of power in Europe, she may be the arbitrator of differences, the guardian of liberty, and the preserver of that balance, which has been so much talked of, and so little understood.[50]

This was Davenant's view of England's proper empire, but presented without Davenant's sense of the need to counter the threat of universal monarchy; the Machiavellian spark of acquisitive virtue was dimmed by Bolingbroke to a self-righteous glow.

Of far greater sophistication and significance were the reflections upon universal monarchy and empire of one who was not English, but who visited England between 1729 and 1731, and who knew and read Bolingbroke: Montesquieu. From his visit Montesquieu derived a highly favourable view of the English constitution, of which he proceeded to write a famous account; less well known, but equally favourable, was the opinion he formed of the English type of empire. But this opinion was not formed as quickly as the other: first Montesquieu had to settle his accounts with the long shadow of Louis XIV, and reconsider the question of universal monarchy.

---

[48] [John Trenchard and Thomas Gordon], *Cato's Letters*, 4 vols. (London, 1724), vol. III, pp. 303–11, vol. II, pp. 218–30; Thomas Gordon, *The Works of Tacitus, Volume I: The Annals. To which are Prefixed Political Discourses upon that Author* (1728) Discourse X, 'Of Armies and Conquest', pp. 116–24.

[49] *Cato's Letters*, vol. II, pp. 95–106, vol. IV, p. 144.

[50] Bolingbroke, *The Idea of a Patriot King* (1749), *The Works of the Late Right Honourable Henry St John, Lord Viscount Bolingbroke*, in 5 vols., published by David Mallett (1754), vol. III, pp. 107–8.

This he did immediately after his return from England, when he composed the *Réflexions sur la Monarchie Universelle en Europe* of 1734.

Montesquieu stated his conclusion at the outset of the work: a universal monarchy such as the Romans had possessed was, in the present state of Europe, 'moralement impossible' (a phrase later altered in manuscript to 'plus difficile qu'elle n'a jamais été'.) Montesquieu's explanations for this conclusion were various. Historically, he suggested, those rulers who, since the Roman empire, had been thought to aspire to universal monarchy had never seriously been in a position to achieve it. Charlemagne had no sooner acquired his territories than his family had forced him to divide them. The Spanish Monarchy had misunderstood and misused the wealth it had gained in the Americas. Most recently *un grand Prince qui a régné de nos jours* (Louis XIV), and who had been accused a thousand times of seeking universal monarchy, might have made himself the most powerful of Europe's kings, but could never have become the sole king of Europe. Indeed, Montesquieu noted, it was over 400 years since wars had caused great change in Europe; rather it was by marriages, inheritances and treaties that Europe had been and was being changed. To a considerable extent it was a matter of geography. Europe did not have the great enclosed plains found in Asia: it was naturally divided into states of smaller extent, inimical to the establishment of the autocratic despotisms required by great empires. Europe was *une grande République*, a nation composed of many nations, each of which possessed a spirit of liberty which defied conquest, and between which the speedy communication of new ideas ensured an equalisation of military force. In modern Europe, moreover, power was intimately related to commerce. But since success in commerce could never be permanent, no state could be assured of preeminence for long. This was because prosperity set bounds to itself: a state which grew rich in gold and silver would simply see its own prices rise, and other nations would be able to enter the market with cheaper goods.[51]

Although the *Réflexions sur la Monarchie Universelle* was no sooner published than withdrawn, the great majority of its arguments reappeared in the *Esprit des Lois* in 1748. A number were transposed

---

[51] Montesquieu, *Réflexions sur la Monarchie Universelle en Europe* (1734), in Montesqieu, *Oeuvres complètes*, 2 vols., ed. Roger Caillois, Bibliothèque de la Pléiade (Paris, 1951), vol. II, pp. 19–38.

verbatim, notably the analysis of the Spanish Monarchy's misuse of its silver, and the denial that Louis XIV ever came close to universal monarchy.[52] Others were elaborated to form one of the leading themes of the *Esprit des Lois*, the analysis of the politics of extent. Questions of scale, and of the form of government appropriate to different extents of territory, were central to Montesquieu's distinction of monarchy from despotism on the one hand, and from republics on the other. Despotisms were characteristically large empires, which could only be held together by arbitrary rule. But since the physical conditions for such large empires only existed in Asia, it was very much the implication of Montesquieu's analysis that the European monarchies were and could be expected to remain quite different in nature. The empire of Rome had been an exception, and there was no prospect of its being repeated. The monarchies of modern Europe ruled with moderation, and did not oppress their provinces as the Roman pro-consuls had done.[53]

At the same time, monarchies were naturally stronger than republics, whose form of government was suited only to small territories. Montesquieu did suggest, however, that republics might overcome the limitations of small extent by forming confederations, such as existed in Holland, Switzerland and Germany. These *républiques fédératives* would combine the internal advantages of republics with the external strength of a monarchy. But they would work well, Montesquieu warned, only when the participating republics were genuinely equal (which was not the case in either the Dutch or the German examples).[54] The idea of *républiques fédératives* was almost certainly of the same descent as Fletcher's plan for the reform of European government, but Montesquieu offered no opinion as to whether a *république fédérative* was in principle preferable to a monarchy. The implication of his discussion was rather that both forms of government had successfully demonstrated their capacity to accommodate to the historical and physical circumstances of Europe. With their respective strengths, they enabled Montesquieu to confirm the conclusion he had

---

[52] *Esprit de Lois*, Book xxi, chapter xxii, 'Des Richesses que l'Espagne tira de L'Amerique', was formerly Section xvi of *Monarchie Universelle*; likewise *Esprit des Lois*, Book ix, Chapter vii, 'Réflexions', incorporated the opening paragraph on Louis XIV from Section xvii of *Monarchie Universelle*.

[53] Montesquieu, *Esprit des Lois* (1748), in *Oeuvres Complètes*, Bibliothêque de la Pléiade, vol. ii: Book viii, Chapters xvii–xxi; ix, ix–x, xvi; xi, xix; xvii, iii–iv.

[54] *Esprit des Lois*, ix, i–iii.

reached in the *Réflexions*: it was ever more unlikely that a universal monarchy would be achieved in modern Europe.

This still left the island government of 'England' (as Montesquieu always referred to it), to be considered. Here Montesquieu's judgement was affected by what seems to have been a significant change of position. In the *Esprit des Lois* he no longer characterised commerce, as he had in the *Réflexions*, principally by the variability, the fickleness of its benefits. The suggestion that prosperity had natural limits was dropped, along with the confidence that poorer countries could catch up on richer by exploiting their price advantage. A country as poor as Poland, he now argued, should not trade with others, but should devote its grain surplus to the encouragement of its own, internal manufactures.[55] The nation to be admired was, rather, that which knew how to advance its commerce continuously, by ensuring that its merchants exploited its particular strengths, in woollens, coal and horses.[56] Such a nation was England. As Montesquieu explained in Book xix, chapter xxvii (which he explicitly presented as the sequel to Book xi, chapter vi, on the English constitution), the English had been uniquely successful in combining the spirit of liberty with the pursuit of commerce. As an island that nation had avoided conquests, and it set no great value on soldiering. But it did carefully regulate its commerce, to ensure that its trade with any particular nation was to its advantage. Where it established colonies, it had done so to extend its commerce, not its domination, and it had happily accorded them the form of its own government. It might be that it had reduced a neighbour nation (Ireland) to dependence, out of jealousy of its potential wealth. But England's empire was that of the sea, not of the land. Precisely because it did not aspire to territorial conquest, indeed, its friendship was the more sought by its neighbours. As an empire of the sea, it was in an excellent position to exert an impartial, moderating influence on the affairs of Europe.[57]

Crowning these blessings of England and Europe were the beneficial moral consequences of commerce. Commerce, Montesquieu proclaimed, was to be associated with *les moeurs douces*. By enabling the manners of all nations to be known and compared,

---

[55] *Esprit des Lois*, xx, xxiii.
[56] *Esprit des Lois*, xx, xii.
[57] *Esprit des Lois*, xix, xxvii; also xx, vii, xii.

commerce had freed the modern world of the aggressive values of the past. Between nations, if not between individuals, it promoted a regard for exact justice, and consequently peace.[58] These views did not entail a commitment to free trade. Montesquieu expected nations to trade to their advantage, and not to allow their merchants complete freedom, and he justified colonial monopolies as imposing order upon navigation, making it a matter for treaties. But he clearly regarded the adoption of such measures as quite compatible with *les moeurs douces*. By turning to commerce, he could claim, with an assurance Andrew Fletcher would have found incomprehensible, Europeans had at last begun to cure themselves of *machiavélisme*.[59]

With this the 'softening' of Davenant, begun in England after the Peace of Utrecht by *Cato* and Bolingbroke, was carried to a conclusion. The bogey of universal monarchy had been laid; in its place was the idea of a benign, beneficent English empire of commerce, which promoted peace in Europe, justice between nations, and the natural death of Machiavellianism. That France was once again Britain's enemy by the time the *Esprit des Lois* was published may have qualified the credibility of its argument dismissing the threat of universal monarchy; but Montesquieu's work still offered a remarkable apologia for England's pursuit of commercial empire as its contribution to the liberties of Europe.

Seductive as that argument might be, however, it was most unlikely to appeal to Hume. To the contrary, I wish finally to suggest, Montesquieu's arguments were just such as to provide Hume with the strongest of intellectual incentives to reconsider the prevailing English Whig doctrine of Britain's place in Europe. In the first place, Hume could not immediately or entirely accept that the threat of universal monarchy in Europe had disappeared. He was ready to agree with Montesquieu that the civilised monarchies of modern Europe were quite different from Asian despotisms. He would also acknowledge in 1752 that the French monarchy's repeated failure to capitalise on its victories afforded a strong presupposition against universal monarchy's ever being realised. But if to deny the French pretension to universal monarchy was, as

[58] *Esprit des Lois*, xx, i–ii.
[59] *Esprit des Lois*, xxi, xx–xxi.

Bolingbroke inferred, to remove all need for Britain to intervene directly in the affairs of the continent, then Hume was, in the 1750s, unwilling to go so far. Even when he became convinced, in the later 1760s, that the French had abandoned that ambition, he did not thence conclude that the days of conquest in Europe were over. The pattern of imperial ambition in the past, its close association with the dissolution of the feudal system and the onset of modernity, together with the vulnerability of modern systems of public credit, made it impossible to be certain that the threat of enormous, if not universal, monarchy would not recur. The arguments of Davenant and Fletcher that universal monarchy was a danger of the modern as well as the ancient world could not be discarded so lightly: the absence of an identifiable aspirant did not mean the end of the idea.

But it was Montesquieu's second line of argument, in praise of the English conception of commercial empire (the argument Montesquieu shared with Davenant), which Hume is likely to have found most dismaying. He spotted the difference between them immediately, in his complimentary but carefully written letter of 1749, when he commented on the chapter of the *Esprit des Lois* describing (and approving) the English approach to the balance of trade (chapter xii of Book xx). 'Il paroit', Hume wrote, 'que nous avons en Angelterre une trop grande jalousie de la balance de commerce.' The argument which Hume then summarised was a version of that which Montesquieu himself had originally used in 1734: the equalising effect of different prices in an international market.[60]

Fully to appreciate the importance of this point for Hume, however, requires reference to a range of Hume's essays not so far considered here. These are the essays with which he opened the *Political Discourses* in 1752, on 'Commerce', 'Money' and 'the Balance of Trade'. In them Hume offered his own account of economic development and its benefits, and of the futility of trading in order to increase a nation's stock of gold and silver. In pursuit of such an objective, he commented in 'Of the Balance of Trade', Britain had imposed innumerable barriers upon its commerce with France in particular, only to lose the French market for its woollen manufactures and to buy worse wine at a higher price from Spain and

---

[60] Hume to Montesquieu, 10 April 1749, *Hume Letters*, vol. 1, pp. 136–7. In the letter Hume refers to chapter xi; with the later addition of chapter vi, it became chapter xii.

Portugal.[61] To make the point quite clear, Hume added a further essay to the collection in 1758, on the subject 'Of the Jealousy of Trade', placing it between those on 'the Balance of Trade' and 'the Balance of Power'. In this new essay he dealt directly with the historic English obsession with woollen manufactures, arguing that if this 'staple' did not remain competitive against foreign manufactures, the spirit of industry ought easily to be diverted into production of other commodities. Emulation between nations and variety in the manufactures of each was the way to keep industry alive in all of them. Hume was thus happy to acknowledge that

not only as a man, but as a BRITISH subject, I pray for the flourishing commerce of GERMANY, SPAIN, ITALY, and even FRANCE itself. I am at least certain, that GREAT BRITAIN, and all those nations, would flourish more, did their sovereigns and ministers adopt such enlarged and benevolent sentiments towards each other.[62]

The immediate context of these arguments was provided by Hume's discussion with James Oswald and Josiah Tucker about the development prospects of poor countries in competition with rich ones – a problem originally debated by Fletcher and his contemporaries.[63] England's relation to Scotland and Ireland (the latter the subject of Hume's sharp comment in 1741, contrasting with Montesquieu's passing allusion) was clearly what Hume had most in mind, though his argument would have applied equally to Poland, Montesquieu's preferred example. As contemporary readers of the essay 'Of the Jealousy of Trade' realised, however, its argument was also, more generally, a wholesale critique of the prevailing English approach to commercial empire.[64] What Davenant insisted was the necessary, and Montesquieu had celebrated as the beneficent idea of commercial empire, Hume rejected as neither necessary nor beneficent. To promote such an idea was not to counteract or dispose of the danger of universal monarchy. It

---

[61] Hume, 'Of the Balance of Trade', *Essays*, vol. i, pp. 335–6.
[62] 'Of the Jealousy of Trade', ibid., pp. 345–8. The conflict between Hume's and Montesquieu's arguments revealed by this essay was noticed by Paul Chamley, though his discussion of it seems quixotic: 'The Conflict between Montesquieu and Hume. A Study of the Origins of Adam Smith's Universalism', in A.S. Skinner and T. Wilson (eds.) *Essays on Adam Smith* (Oxford, 1975), pp. 300–5.
[63] Istvan Hont, 'The "Rich Country – Poor Country" Debate in Scottish Classical Political Economy', in I. Hont and M. Ignatieff (eds.), *Wealth and Virtue. The Shaping of Political Economy in the Scottish Enlightenment* (Cambridge, 1983).
[64] Turgot to Hume, 23 July 1766, in *Hume: Writings on Economics*, p. 205.

was merely to set up another system of oppression and dependence, another obstruction to the progress of all nations. The conclusion was similar to Fletcher's, even if Hume used rather different economic arguments to reach it.

In the extended intellectual context provided by Davenant, Fletcher and Montesquieu, the significance of Hume's juxtaposition of his reflections on Britain's place in Europe with his arguments on commerce becomes obvious. It is clear that Hume's scepticism about the assumptions of the Whig doctrine of Britain's role in Europe reflects more than a growing conviction that France was incapable of achieving universal monarchy. Far more serious was the recognition that the Whig doctrine was used as a cover for the promotion of a dangerously misconceived idea of commercial empire. Not only did the British exaggerate the threat of France to the liberties of Europe; British commercial policy represented a threat still greater, and more immediate. The ultimate proof of this lay to hand in the American colonies, over which Britain was strenuously seeking to impose a trading monopoly. But such a monopoly, as Hume explained to the patient Strahan, could itself only be achieved by a war of conquest, followed by the annulling of all colonial charters and the investing of every governor with discretionary powers.[65] Colonial empire, in other words, must itself finally become territorial, and the free government of Britain would behave as oppressively as that of Republican Rome.

Hume's consequent prayer for the flourishing commerce of all the nations of Europe was probably the noblest expression of his cosmopolitanism. Yet the prospect of Hume at prayer should, perhaps, give pause. Was this a confession that he had little else to offer? It is notable that Hume had few ideas about the international political order which would best counteract jealousy in trade. Specifically, he did not take up the alternative of *républiques fédératives* canvassed on the basis of Europe's existing confederations by Montesquieu, and more speculatively by Fletcher. The closest Hume came to the idea was in the last of the *Political Discourses*, the 'Idea of a perfect Commonwealth'. At one point Hume defended the idea's practicality by claiming that it resembled the 'wise and renowned government' of the United Provinces; and it is just possible that the assurance that the model

---

[65] Hume to Strahan, 26 October, 13 November 1775, *Letters*, vol. II, pp. 300–1, 304–5.

was adapted to societies of large extent reflected an awareness of the potential for a new politics of extent offered by the North American continent, the scale of which was beginning to be appreciated.[66] But even if the essay can be seen as Hume's theoretical solution to the political problem in overcoming jealousy of trade, as to the more general problem of the relation between government and economic development,[67] the comparison with Montesquieu also suggests its limitations. As Hume admitted, the perfect commonwealth was an adaptation of the model of Harrington's *Oceana*, and it rested on the one-sided proposition, common to Harrington, and to Hume's early essay 'That Politics may be Reduced to a Science', that the character of a nation's politics depended simply on its form of government. Understandable as a reaction to Bolingbroke's moralism, this was exactly the type of political thinking that Montesquieu made to look archaic by the range and flexibility of his comparative analysis in the *Esprit des Lois*. It was Hume himself who reminded his nephew and namesake in 1775 of Montesquieu's observation, at the end of the chapter on the English constitution, that 'Harrington establishing his Oceana in opposition to the English constitution is like the blind men who built Chalcedon on the opposite [shore] to the seat of Byzantium.'[68]

Small wonder, then, that the dying thoughts of a North Briton tended to be ones of political frustration. The imminent prospect of a war to maintain Britain's commercial monopoly over its American colonies, and the likelihood that the threat of France would once again be invoked as a pretext, represented the triumph of errors which Hume's writings had sought in vain to expose. But if Hume's own arguments were to no avail (and he could not be aware of the inspiration which the framers of the American Constitution may have found in them), he had at least the

---

[66] Hume, 'Idea of a perfect Commonwealth', *Essays*, vol. I, pp. 490–3. Hume removed the qualification 'formerly' from the praise of the United Provinces in the 1770 edition.

[67] As I myself argued in 'The Scottish Enlightenment at the Limits of the Civic Tradition', in *Wealth and Virtue*, pp. 170–7.

[68] Hume to David Hume, 8 December 1775, *Hume Letters*, vol. II, p. 307. For a comparison of Hume and Montesquieu which illustrates the extent to which Montesquieu could make Hume's Harringtonian approach to politics seem archaic: David Wootton, 'Ulysses Bound?: Venice and the Idea of Liberty from Harrington to Hume', forthcoming in D. Wootton (ed.), *Republicanism and Commercial Society* (Stanford). Also, James Moore's early, scrupulous article: 'Hume's Political Science and the Classical Republican Tradition', *Canadian Journal of Political Science*, 10 (1977), 809–39.

intellectual consolation of living to welcome, early in 1776, two new works which would carry them on: one, Adam Smith's *Wealth of Nations*, a devastating critique of the whole edifice of British commercial empire; the other, Edward Gibbon's *Decline and Fall of the Roman Empire*, the supreme study of the power and corruption of universal monarchy.[69]

[69] Hume to Adam Smith, 1 April 1776; and to Edward Gibbon, 18 March 1776, *Hume Letters*, vol. II, pp. 309–12.

Part V

CHAPTER 17

A discourse of sovereignty:
observations on the work in progress

J.G.A. Pocock

I

The editors of this book have further honoured me with the opportunity of reviewing its contents. I shall attempt to comment on the series of essays which furnish in every sense the greater part of the book, indicating the problems to which they give answers and the further problems which they open up. This is much the same as indicating the contexts to which they belong and the nature of the enterprise in which we are all engaged. I take that enterprise to be the exploration of Anglo-British[1] history as presented in its political literature and the history of its political discourse. Within that scenario, the opening essay by J.H. Burns presents an initial challenge. The actors in his story were Scots whose intellectual and active careers were shaped and spent largely on the continent of Europe; yet the emphasis of the present book is overwhelmingly sub-insular and English – it presents a discourse formed in insular rather than continental Europe, and is focussed from near the beginning to near the end on the sovereignty of the English state and its problems. The Scottish theme launched by J.H. Burns does not recur until the concluding essay by John Robertson, when the question of Scotland within a British state and the character of that state itself are re-examined in ways that connect them with the current attempts at a re-consolidation of 'Europe'. Burns and Robertson might therefore be cast in the role of challengers to the complacent Anglocentricity of the rest of us, and a Eurocant might easily take shape, in which Anglo-British

---

[1] I borrow this useful term from Colin Kidd, 'Scottish Whig Historiography and the Creation of an Anglo-British Identity, 1689-c. 1800' (unpublished D. Phil. dissertation, University of Oxford, 1991). It denotes a British identity viewed from the standpoint of an English predominance, in this case historiographical.

J. G. A. POCOCK

history is first condemned as exceptional to the grand unifying themes of counter-reformation and baroque monarchy, French Revolution and the rise of the administrative state – privileged as constituting the true history of 'Europe' – and then deconstructed in order to assimilate it to what it has not been.

There is a certain amount of this sort of cant in circulation, but this book is entirely free of it. The reader would not know that 'British history' is in 'decline', nor can I find much reason for supposing that it is in anything but an exceptionally lively condition;[2] but what is to be learned from this and all recent work in the field is that Anglo-British historiography and history alike have been concerned with the maintenance of Tudor sovereignty over church and state, and that the question now before us is whether that sovereignty is to be continued, not whether it ever existed. That is the history which the British kingdoms bring with them into 'Europe', and the history of Europe will have to be written as modified by that history's presence if it is to make any sense at all. But precisely within this context, J.H. Burns reminds us of the careers which three Scotsmen pursued as inhabitants of a French and German continental setting, and as exponents of a Catholic monarchism already a good deal more Gallican than either papal or Caesarean; Blackwood's plain statement of the differences between an elected emperor and an anointed king is arresting, and later essays in this volume suggest that it was with Gallican monarchism rather than ultramontane papalism that Protestant England had to contend under the Stuart kings. Burns further reminds us, however, that if the Scottish-Catholic anti-monarchomachs were horrified by George Buchanan's theses concerning Christian kingship, they had no less reason to be concerned with his presentation of Scottish history. The rise of Buchananite historiography in the sixteenth century, and its sudden decline in the eighteenth,[3] form a principal thread in the pattern of discourse attending the matter of Scotland and the matter of Britain; and it may be added that as his opponents move from Scotland deeper

---

[2] David Cannadine's essay on 'British History: Past, Present and Future?' (*Past and Present*, 116 (August 1987)) is a lament for the present parlous state of universities and curricula, rather than for the intellectual condition of the discipline itself. I have stated a view of the significance of 'revisionism' in 'History and Sovereignty: The Historiographical Response to Europeanisation in Two British Cultures', *Journal of British Studies* (forthcoming, 1992).

[3] Kidd, 'Scottish Whig Historiography'.

into the Franco-German culture of adjacent western Eurasia,[4] Buchanan takes the road to the isles, his themes heading from a humanist and Protestant Latinity towards the kingdom of Dalriada, the myth of Fergus mac Erch and a Gaelic world at the limits of Anglo-Norman penetration.

J.H. Burns's essay is the only one of those before us to be set in the sixteenth century, reminding us that this volume presupposes some knowledge of both the Tudor origins of the problems dealt with by Klein, Mendle and Lamont, and the mid-Stuart origins, in the reigns of James V to Charles I, of the problems confronting Scotsmen in the War of the Three Kingdoms. These areas have been explored from time to time in seminars conducted by the Folger Institute Center for the History of British Political Thought, an enterprise[5] aimed less at surveying or summarising the history which supplies its title than at providing a series of maps to it; these maps differ in scale and relief. A seminar on Scottish political thought from the death of James V to the Union of the Crowns[6] has established something like a canon of major authors – John Mair, Hector Boece, John Knox, George Buchanan, James VI, Sir Thomas Craig – and has suggested a series of dialectics between kindred and royal law, baronial independence and Presbyterian discipline, Dalriadic and Norman historical perspectives, as unifying themes for a fuller history. The Union of the Crowns, however, raised the culminating problem of English monarchy and British state,[7] and brought Scottish history and political discourse into confrontation with English equivalents already formed and deeply rooted. The latter dominate the remainder of the present volume until Dr Robertson's concluding chapter.[8]

---

[4] I contend that the time has come to see Europe not as a continent but as a sub-continent, a peninsula of the Eurasian land-mass comparable with India.

[5] At the Folger Shakespeare Library in Washington, supervised since 1984 by Gordon Schochet, Lois Schwoerer and myself, with Lena C. Orlin, executive director of the Folger Institute for Renaissance and Eighteenth-Century Studies.

[6] Conducted in the fall semester of 1990 by R.A. Mason (University of St Andrews) under the title 'Scots and Britons: Scottish Political Thought and the Union of 1603'; publication forthcoming with Cambridge University Press, 1994. See also Arthur H. Williamson, *Scottish National Consciousness in the Age of James VI* (Edinburgh, 1979); Roger A. Mason (ed.), *Scotland and England, 1286–1815* (Edinburgh, 1987).

[7] Brian P. Levack, *The Formation of the British State* (Oxford, 1987).

[8] John Robertson conducted a Folger Center seminar in the spring semester of 1991, entitled 'Union, State and Empire: The Political Identities of Britain, 1688–1750', publication forthcoming with Cambridge University Press, 1994, as *A Union for Empire*.

Tudor political discourse, the necessary prelude to the contents of this book, has recently been re-evaluated by J.A. Guy.[9] There emerges, in the first place, an Erasmian humanism directed at the reform of clerical culture; second, a humanism of counsel having for its by-product the enigmatic masterpiece of Sir Thomas More, canonised as the first great text of post-medieval English political literature.[10] This Henrician humanism is distracted and partly destroyed by the terrifying politics of that king's reign,[11] but helps to produce a new vernacular consciousness of the realm itself, its topography, law and history, so that there are humanist foundations at the beginnings of English antiquarianism.[12] These in turn may be associated with the growth under Elizabeth of a courtly culture, interacting with the urban culture of London and Westminster and the London-based culture of the printing press to provide the setting for those formidable poetical and political statements put out by William Shakespeare, Sir Philip Sidney and Edmund Spenser. There is a Ciceronian and Senecan ethos of service and beneficence, favour and gratitude, which links the courtier of the Renaissance with the polite man of the Enlightenment; but the disillusionment and self-disgust to which courtiers are endemically prone – with or without a 'general crisis' to intensify it – gives rise to a cult of Tacitism which presents the evil counsellor or over-powerful favourite as converting divine kingship into tyranny,[13] and combines with the ancient baronial discontents of territorial magnates unwelcome at court to produce (or so we are assured) the austere and shadowy outlines of the first English republicanism.[14] Writings by Sir Walter Raleigh and Sir Francis Bacon[15] stand at the end of this line of development, drawing on

---

[9] J.A. Guy, *Tudor England* (Oxford, 1988).

[10] There is much recent literature on More and Utopia, most of it non-hagiographical. See J.A. Guy, *The Public Career of Sir Thomas More* (New Haven, 1980); Alistair Fox, *Thomas More: History and Providence* (New Haven, 1983); Richard Marius, *Thomas More* (New York, 1984).

[11] Alistair Fox and J.A. Guy, *Re-Assessing the Henrician Age: Humanism, Politics and Reform* (Oxford, 1986).

[12] Arthur B. Ferguson, *The Articulate Citizen and the English Renaissance* (Durham, N.C., 1965); Joseph M. Levine, *Humanism and History: Origins of Modern English Historiography* (Ithaca, N.Y., 1987).

[13] F.J. Levy, *Tudor Historical Thought* (San Marino, 1967).

[14] Blair Worden, 'Classical Republicanism and the Puritan Revolution', in Lloyd-James (ed.), *History and Imagination: Essays in Honour of Hugh Trevor-Roper* (Oxford, 1981); Jonathan Scott, *Algernon Sidney and the English Republic, 1623–1677* (Cambridge, 1988).

[15] Raleigh, *The Prerogative of Parliaments* (1615); Bacon, *History of the Reign of King Henry VII* (1621).

drawing on the new legal and antiquarian historiography to produce analyses of the decline in baronial military power.

Rich as all this is in providing an Elizabethan and Jacobean[16] political and cultural discourse, it is in the consequences of Henry VIII's Reformation that we find the enduring problematics of English political thought for the next three centuries. The Act in Restraint of Appeals (1533) formulates the English doctrine of sovereignty, laying it down that England is an 'empire', exercising a final and unappealable jurisdiction over itself in both church and state. This is the sovereignty to be defended and debated through civil wars, dissolutions and revolutions to the end of the English *ancien régime*. John Foxe's *Acts and Monuments* (1563) adds an apocalyptic dimension, presenting England as chosen by God to maintain religion's independence of Rome through exercise of the national sovereignty; [17] it is this union between Elect Nation and Ancient Constitution which William Lamont has shown motivating William Prynne, Richard Baxter and all the reluctant revolutionaries who laid claim to Godly Rule in the 1640s and 1650s.[18] But John Guy re-emphasised the fundamental ambiguity of the 'empire' from its beginnings[19]: was it ruled by an imperial crown whose authority over the church arose from the church itself, or by a crown-in-parliament which ruled the church according to the laws and customs of the realm? The proponents of the latter position could accuse the church of disrupting the national sovereignty and thereby selling itself to Antichrist; and opposed views of the church as a communion with Christ, opposed views in consequence of Christ's own body and nature, could arise from what was initially an argument over jurisdiction. The great discovery which we constantly make and remake as historians is that English political debate is recurrently subordinate to English political theology; and few of us know one-tenth of the theology available to competently trained divines and laymen among our predecessors.

---

[16] For the latter (chiefly a literature of court) see Linda Levy Peck, *Northampton: Patronage and Policy at the Court of James I* (London, 1982), *Court Patronage and Corruption in Early Stuart England* (Boston, 1990) and *The Mental World of the Jacobean Court* (Cambridge, 1991).

[17] William Haller, *Foxe's Book of Martyrs and the Elect Nation* (London, 1963) has not been displaced by the often-justified criticisms of Paul Christianson, *Reformers and Babylon: English Apocalyptic Visions from the Reformation to the Eve of the Civil War* (Toronto, 1978) and Katherine Firth, *The Apocalyptic Tradition in Reformation Britain, 1530–1645* (Oxford, 1979).

[18] William M. Lamont, *Marginal Prynne, 1600–69* (London, 1963); *Godly Rule: Politics and Religion, 1603–60* (London, 1969); *Richard Baxter and the Millennium* (London, 1980).

[19] *Tudor England*, pp. 132–4, 369–78.

II

By the end of Elizabeth I's reign there was enough tension in the English ecclesiastical structure to move the judicious Hooker to express his awareness that the state of things he set out to defend might pass away as in a dream.[20] Our dread of writing Whig history has grown to the point where any sense of crisis in the half-century preceding 1642 must be discounted with the reminder that there was no high road to civil war; yet Hooker's words do not read like a rhetorical convention and may therefore have meant something. He seems to have feared that Scriptural fundamentalism would lead to the dissolution of all authority, even Scripture's, and to have set out to display the full range of authority both sacred and natural, within which the authority of the preachers of the Word could only be one. He wrote in the grand medieval and scholastic tradition, and in the English tradition of monarchy according to law; and the *Laws of Ecclesiastical Polity* has achieved canonical status among the masterworks of English political thought (and even philosophy). Yet it is hard to define its exact place in the historical sequence which at present dominates our understanding of the Church of England's story; it is not easy, that is, to relate Hooker to the great cleavage between strict and Arminian Calvinism, and thereafter between Calvinism and theology not Calvinist at all, which opened up in Geneva-dominated Protestant Europe following the Synod of Dort or Dordrecht (1619). Hooker's environment was not one in which those who had reservations about the absolute decrees of grace would be instantly accused of going over to Rome, or (in England) of disrupting the sovereignty of imperial parliamentary monarchy which guarded the Elect Nation against the designs of Antichrist; an accusation promptly retorted against a Presbyterian clergy suspect of claiming a *jure divino* authority. Nor was it one in which those who dissented from either Rome or Dordrecht would be accused of subordinating grace to reason and following that road from Erasmus to Socinus in which the origins of Enlightenment have been detected.[21] But the next classic of Anglican apologetics, William Chillingworth's *The Religion of Protestants a Safe Way to Salvation* (1638), was written

[20] The opening words of the *Laws of Ecclesiastical Polity*, ed. A.S. McGrade (Cambridge, 1989).
[21] H.R. Trevor-Roper, *Religion, the Reformation and Social Change* (New York, 1967).

against a Jesuit opponent (Fisher or Knott) who insisted that if there
was not a single infallible church Socinianism must be the consequence, since Christ would lose the union of natures which had
permitted him to leave his mystical body behind him.[22] Chillingworth, after converting to Rome and back again, marshalled a
scrupulously probabilist argument in reply, but ended by proving
his opponent at least half right, in experiencing serious difficulty
before subscribing to the more Athanasian of the Thirty-Nine
Articles.[23] More than a century later, Edward Gibbon was to
rehearse his experience,[24] and discover anew that the real quarrel of
enlightened theology was with the doctrine of Incarnation.

The next group of essays in the order of review – those by
William Klein, Michael Mendle and William Lamont – take us
from before the Civil War, through its outbreak, to its retrospect in
the long career of Richard Baxter. Here the spectre of the high road
to civil war looms before us, and it may be worth reminding
ourselves that there do not necessarily cease to be roads when they
cease to constitute a four-lane highway; they may merely have been
tortuous, deceptively signposted, and turned back upon themselves. It is right to remember that 'the English Civil War' was an
aspect of 'the War of the Three Kingdoms'[25] and might never have
come about but for 'the fall of the British monarchies',[26] but the
English experience in the War of the Three Kingdoms was an
experience of civil war, and in that respect unlike the experience of
the other peoples. Civil wars are fought between citizens of the
same polity, who share a great many values and institutions but
have reached the point of violence in some radical disagreement
over how to maintain them; this is why contemporaries called the
English an 'unnatural' war,[27] and explains why civil wars may
issue in restorations and reactions, rather than revolutions. The

---

[22] *The Works of William Chillingworth* (10th edn, 1742), pp. 13–16 ('Preface to the Author of *Charity Maintained*').
[23] *Works*, introduction; Robert R. Orr, *Reason and Experience: The Thought of William Chillingworth* (London, 1968).
[24] Edward Gibbon, *Memoirs of My Life*, ed. Georges A. Bonnard (New York, 1966), pp. 58–63.
[25] I take this term from J.C. Beckett, *The Making of Modern Ireland, 1603–1923* (New York, 1966), where I first found it.
[26] Conrad Russell, *The Causes of the English Civil War* (Oxford, 1990); *The Fall of the British Monarchies* (Oxford, 1991).
[27] The term is used, and explained, in Thomas May's *History of the Parliament of England* (1647).

only campaign in which Scotsmen fought each other – that of 1644
to 1645 – was a Gordon rebellion under Montrose's dissenting
Covenanter leadership, combined with a Catholic incursion by
Clan Donald from Antrim and the isles;[28] while the prolonged and
atrocious wars of Ireland were (as always) the ethnic and religious
conflicts of an unsettled frontier, not a civil war at all. But the wars
in England were wars over the meaning and maintaining of the
Tudor sovereignty in church and state; wars of the empire with
itself, civil wars because they were interior to the polity and wars of
religion for the same reason. It does not matter if the internal
contradictions of the polity were insufficient to cause the war; once
there was war it came to be about those contradictions, and we may
argue forever about Harrington's chicken-and-egg problem – did
war cause dissolution of government, or dissolution of government
cause war?[29] It is an intellectually comforting consequence that we
may look for structural tensions in the polity without being guilty of
taking the high road.

William Klein's 'The ancient constitution revisited' takes us
back where (for this historian at least) it all began: with the first
discovery of an idiosyncratically English 'language' of political
discourse (though Butterfield, and in several ways Laslett,[30] were
previous discoverers). Idiosyncratic or indigenous? The language
certainly asserts that English law is indigenous, autochthonous and
that of a *tangata whenua*;[31] but whether the language arose auto-
chthonously, out of a 'common-law mind' built into the structures
of English thinking by the procedures of the courts, can be debated
for and against. I am glad I never wrote that the English knew no
law but their own, only that no other law obliged them to rethink
the history of the law that was theirs; this is why they liked citing
the tag *divisos ab orbe Britannos*; but this assertion of insularity is of
course an assertion, and it is permissible to ask why they made it as

[28] D.C. Stevenson, *Revolution and Counter-Revolution in Scotland, 1644–51* (London, 1977);
Alasdair MacColla and the Highland Problem in the Seventeenth Century (Edinburgh, 1980).
Alasdair's war might be considered an extension of the Irish conflict, and a history of
Clan Donald's role in this period might be worth having.
[29] *The Political Works of James Harrington*, ed. J.G.A. Pocock (Cambridge, 1977), p. 198.
[30] His edition of *Patriarcha and other Political Works of Sir Robert Filmer* (Oxford, 1949)
contained *The Freeholder's Grand Inquest*, which was published with Filmer's writings in
1679, and first drew attention to the complexities of the Filmerian controversy.
[31] This Maori term for an aboriginal or autochthonous people is further discussed below,
pp. 418–19.

well as why they believed it. There are several possible answers. It has been suggested that James VI and I's well-meant proclamation of a Kingdom of Great Britain[32] raised the fear that the king intended to dissolve the laws that were the ligaments of both his kingdoms, in order to reduce two mystical bodies to one and be no longer the husband of two wives; the affrighted English replied that even the British Solomon[33] could not reduce two wives to one substance. A quarter of a century later – and now under James's disastrous successor – we have the parliament of 1628 asserting the aboriginality and primacy of custom and statute in order to check the claim of the crown's lawyers that England was governed by several discrete laws and the king had discretion in choosing by which to proceed. A study of the 'ancient constitution' as produced by competition between the courts of common law and other kinds of jurisdiction, and by competition between Chief Justice Coke and other royal judges, was prefigured by Louis Knafla's study of Lord Chancellor Ellesmere[34] and may be brought to completion in a forthcoming work by Glenn Burgess.[35]

This is one of the few points at which I would now affirm that the ancient constitution was pleaded against the crown. We were all more Whiggish *circa* 1950 than we are now, and William Klein is right to point out that it is not Whig in Butterfield's progressivist sense to affirm the immemorial antiquity of English institutions as a whole. But I did not mean, even in those days, to establish a great divide between Coke on the one hand and Selden or Hale on the other. I think I knew that Coke too could see the process of adapting and interpreting custom as immemorial, separable there-fore – though it was not a separation he was much concerned to make – from the specific content of any custom. Whig history retained this dual perspective; while it was Whig to emphasise progress from a baronial towards a parliamentary order, the great Victorian Teutonists clung to the image of a pre-baronial and

---

[32] Jenny Wormald raised this possibility in a paper presented to R.A. Mason's seminar (n.6 above).

[33] Maurice P. Lee, *Great Britain's Solomon: James VI and I in his Three Kingdoms* (Urbana, 1990). To call James 'Solomon' complimented not only his wisdom but his union of two kingdoms, analogous to Judah and Israel. Jokes about 'Son of David' were an unfortunate by-product.

[34] Louis A. Knafla, *Law and Politics in Jacobean England: The Tracts of Lord Chancellor Ellesmere* (Cambridge, 1977).

[35] Glenn Burgess, *The Politics of the Ancient Constitution* (London, 1992).

pre-feudal liberty,[36] and the underlying question – first raised by
the philosophy of custom[37] – remained that of beginnings.[38]

The figure of Sir John Fortescue assumes greater importance as
scholars explore the implications of ancient-constitution argument,
and the king ruling both *regaliter* and *politice* is of course the king
who has two bodies; both in the sense that as ruling *politice* he is a
natural man acting as head of a mystical body, and in the sense
that as ruling *regaliter et politice* he can exercise absolute rule out of
parliament and the courts as well as in them – though, again, he is
more effectively absolute (he 'at no time stands so high in his estate
royal') in parliament than out of it. This is the king in whom
everyone desired to believe, ruling both absolutely and according to
law; it will seem longer to most contributors than it does to me
since R.W.K. Hinton suggested that this was the formula which
broke down on the way to civil war.[39] But to anatomise *rex
fortescuensis* is to re-assess the notion of conquest and find it much
more interesting than the repudiation of a Norman conquest by
itself suggested. The king ruling *regaliter* is the personification of
Nimrod, and does not lose this pedigree merely by converting
himself into a king ruling *politice*, in virtue of binding himself by
compact to leave his subjects their ancient laws and liberties;
George III did neither more nor less by the Quebec Act of 1774. It
was possible therefore to argue – and many did – that William I
had both been a conqueror and bound himself to be one no more;
which leaves unexplained the obsessive character of the counter-
argument that he had never had the option. There are two
hypotheses, which may be applied concurrently. One is to suppose
that the law of *meum et tuum*[40] had, by 1628, to be placed forever
beyond Nimrod's reach, with the consequence that the law of
tenure had to be made pre-Norman and immemorial. Without
meum et tuum there could be no law to which the king might bind
himself; no free man could have a property in his lands or goods, or

[36] J.W. Burrow, *A Liberal Descent: Victorian Historians and the English Past* (Cambridge, 1980).

[37] See William Klein, n. 26 on p. 32 above.

[38] It would be helpful to have some part at least of Sir Roger Owen's mammoth treatise in
print.

[39] R.W.K. Hinton, 'The Decline of Parliamentary Government under Elizabeth I and the
Early Stuarts', *Cambridge Historical Journal*, 13 (1957), 116–32; 'English Constitutional
Theories from Sir John Fortescue to Sir John Eliot', *English Historical Review*, 75 (1960),
410–25.

[40] Margaret A. Judson's *The Crisis of the Constitution* (New Brunswick, N.J., 1949) remains
the fullest study of the central role of this concept.

be any better than a villein. There is more of this rhetoric in the debates of 1628[41] than can be reduced to the mere superstructure of a court combination against the Duke of Buckingham; and it is essential to the strategy which the promoters of the Petition of Right attempted to adopt.

The second hypothesis supposes that the denial of conquest rendered immemorial the liberties of the Church of England, guaranteed in Magna Charta. Fortescue's dual monarch was since 1533 the church's supreme head and later governor, who might be exercising either his imperial monarchy or his monarchy in parliament, according to *lex terrae* and in short *politice*. Time had been, and would be again, when voices in parliament urged the king to use his imperial authority against the clergy themselves; but now there were those among the clergy who seemed to be urging him to disregard the authority which was his as head of the body mystical and political. It was part of Pym's case against Maynwaring that he had subverted the king's capacity to enter into counsel and compact with his subjects, and left him only the authority he had as conqueror.[42] This was not to enlarge royal authority, but to truncate it. To deny, therefore, that William I – emissary, as many supposed, of that most sinister of popes, Gregory VII – had ever had, let alone retained, the authority of a conqueror was a move in maintaining the indivisible sovereignty of England's king over the empire and its Christian freedom; one made less to deny that he possessed imperial authority over the church as Christ's vicar than to prevent the clergy filching it from him by destroying the necessary link with his authority at law and in parliament. We enter the world explored by William Lamont; the world in which ancient constitution and elect nation are at one, and the claim that the king is head of a church independent of the realm seems evidence of a Romish conspiracy against the independence of church and realm alike, and against the presence of God among His Englishmen. George III, as conqueror of Quebec, raised the darkest imaginable fears by legislating a compact which recognised the authority of the Church of Rome.[43]

---

[41] Robert C. Johnson, Mary Frear Keeler Maija, Jansson Cole and William B. Bidwell (eds.), *Commons Debates 1628* (New Haven, 4 vols., 1977–8), *passim*.
[42] Ibid., vol. IV, pp. 103–4. *Ancient Constitution* (1987), p. 300.
[43] Philip Lawson, *The Imperial Challenge: Quebec and Britain in the Age of the American Revolution* (Montreal, 1989).

This mental world furnishes the background to Michael Mendle's essay, focussed on the immediate (and English) preconditions to the outbreak of civil war in the English counties and the Welsh border in the fall of 1642. This war was a contest for control of the sword, drawn for British reasons to quell a rebellion in Ireland but revealing a climate in England of Hobbesian 'diffidence' so great that the parliamentary leaders dared not trust the king with it. There can be no better illustration of the theme that 'dissolution of the government caused the war' in England, although war elsewhere in Britain caused 'dissolution of the government', a term whose full meaning is apparent only in an English context. The Civil War was not fought to determine the location of English sovereignty, still less to transfer it from one locus to another; it was fought because the location of sovereignty had become disrupted, the king had left his parliament and proclaimed its leaders in rebellion, the parliament had employed the language of an army in mutiny when its members swore 'to live and die with the earl of Essex', and the war aim on both sides was to bring the king back to Westminster and the head back to its unity with the body (an objective satanically reversed on 30 January 1649). In this context those who fought the king insisted that they were fighting not him but his evil counsellors,[44] not his royal person but his 'seduced person', the perversion of his mystical body rather than his natural body (a claim Charles refuted by exposing himself in battle at Edgehill); and all resistance theory became a programme for restoring a king who must not be resisted. In the long view, Charles I was executed for not being a king, Louis XVI for being one; and this is the context in which we need to interpret the title of Michael Mendle's essay.

The sovereignty claimed for parliament in 1642 was not a legislative sovereignty, and in that sense not a Bodinian one. As Mendle shows, the two houses claimed to be 'the great council of the kingdom', and in that capacity to issue ordinances which had the force of law *although*, but were not statutes *because*, they lacked the royal assent and defied the king's refusal to give it. They were

---

[44] A medieval concept still alive in the era of Lord Bute, and perhaps not extinct today. I have been told of a conversation among officers of the Ulster Defence Regiment within living memory, in which it was asked what should be the response of Unionists should the Sovereign, at the advice of her ministers, put them out of her protection. After a short pause, the senior officer present said: 'Evil counsellors, of course.'

not statutes, that is, they did not claim to declare, still less to alter, any point in the common law; the issues of 1642 could not be settled by appeal to the ancient constitution in the strict sense, and the status of the law of *meum et tuum* was not among them. Consequently, parliamentary spokesmen insisted that their ordinances were not laws or exercises of the 'ordinary' power, either judicial or legislative; they were extraordinary actions, taken by the great council in times of extreme danger (namely, the seduction of the king by evil counsellors). In this light, both 'sovereignty' and 'absolutism' must be read as denoting extraordinary power, not a system of ordinary, normal or perpetual government. It is easy to see how Charles I could be suspected of a design to render the extraordinary ordinary, by exercising an authority to proclaim exceptional situations whenever he saw fit; the parliament had neither the capacity nor the intention to render its emergency powers perpetual, as its use of the term 'great council', and indeed the whole of its future in the 1640s and 1650s, makes sufficiently clear. If by 'absolute sovereignty' we mean Bodinian legislative sovereignty, this was a condition not a cause of the English Civil Wars; it existed already, everyone knew where it lay, and the catastrophe was simply that those who exercised it had grown unable to trust one another. They debated their roles in exercising it and accused one another of designs to subvert it; but this did not mean that they disagreed about its location or had any plans for locating it differently. The war was fought to restore its exercise; this is what made it a 'civil' and 'unnatural' war; and the objective of reuniting king and parliament, which seemed millennially out of reach in 1649, did not seem so in 1660.

The paradox is that legislative sovereignty had been established by the Tudors on foundations so largely medieval that the crisis of 1642 was confronted in largely medieval terms. The concept of parliament as the 'great council' of the kingdom, which could guard the crown against even the king himself, was a deeply baronial configuration, and went well with all those speculations about reviving the emergency authority of the marshal, the constable, or the steward, which recent scholarship has brought to light in both the 1590s and the 1640s and used in exploring a 'baronial' dimension to the civil war itself.[45] James Harrington,

[45] J.S. Adamson, 'The Baronial Context of the English Civil War', *Transactions of the Royal Historical Society*, 40 (1990), 93–120.

among the first to investigate this problem, might have agreed that
the great peers were still behaving like barons, but would have
asked if they retained the baronial power to do so; Saye and
Northumberland in their coaches may have accompanied Fairfax's
regiments entering London in 1647,[46] but that is not to say that
they commanded them as their clients or retainers. On the other
hand, the incoherences of 'medieval' behaviour in a 'modern'
setting do not necessarily mean the triumph of 'modernity' (Harrington thought that the 'modern', which was our 'medieval', was
dying and the 'ancient' about to return); and this is the essence of
anti-Whig historiography. There is much to be said for the view
that Fortescue and Thomas Cromwell between them held the field.
'The famed, flawed *Answer to the XIX Propositions*', as Mendle calls
it,[47] successfully reminded parliament that imperial sovereignty
bound those who exercised it so tightly together that the idea of a
'great council' must lead to disaster; the flaw, or 'poisonous
tenet',[48] was the unintended reduction of the king to an estate of his
own realm. Marchamont Nedham and Harrington after him were
to employ this to suggest that a better-balanced government might
be found without a king or House of Lords; but this very English
republicanism was to be part of the discourse of modern enlightenment but not of the modern state. Late in the eighteenth century it
passed out of the English mainstream altogether, and helped
constitute the American instead; and whether the federal republic
is a modern state in the European sense lies beyond the limits of
this volume. George III, the last great personal monarch in British
history, successfully defended (if it was ever attacked) the legislative sovereignty of king-in-parliament which is the most English
form of absolutism ever known. Only today is its future in real
doubt.

The central problem of 1642, it might seem, was that of
identifying the evil counsellors – the more so as they may not have

---

[46] J.S. Adamson, 'The English Nobility and the Projected Settlement of 1647', *Historical
Journal*, 30 (1987), 567–602. The controversy over J.S. Adamson's interpretation is not
relevant to my purpose here.

[47] Above, p. 116. See Corinne C. Weston, *English Constitutional Theory and the House of Lords*
(London, 1965); Corinne C. Weston and Janelle R. Greenberg, *Subjects and Sovereigns: The
Grand Controversy over Legal Sovereignty in Stuart England* (Cambridge, 1980); Michael
Mendle, *Dangerous Positions: Mixed Government, Estates, and the Answers to the XIX Propositions*
(Alabama, 1985).

[48] Weston and Greenberg, *Subjects and Sovereigns*, ch. 4.

existed; but we are provided with the most prevalent contemporary answer. William Lamont in the field of discourse, Caroline Hibbard in that of perception,[49] have told us who they were: the clerical enemies of monarchy feigning to be friends of absolutism, using the *jus divinum* of the throne to conceal the *jure divino* pretensions of the church, the 'Popish Plot' in which 'Arminians' inevitably became engaged once they claimed a jurisdiction sacred enough to exceed that of the crown. Against this threat those like William Prynne defended the union of ancient constitution with elect nation, the imperial sovereignty in state and church, unless and until they became persuaded that the clergy were, and always had been, betraying it from within; a role in which new presbyter might be but old priest writ large (the fear of 'priestcraft' is older than the word itself).[50] It is notoriously difficult to distinguish between those who were perceived as 'Arminians', those who perceived themselves as 'Arminians', and those who perceived themselves as something else and were or were not in sympathy with what they perceived 'Arminianism' to be; and in his essay in this volume, Lamont does not take us too deep into the tangled wood where Tyacke, Lake and White[51] debate how far there was a quasi-Calvinist consensus in the Church of England before Laud's advent and how far an 'Arminian' or some other assault upon it afterwards. Yet the problem is crucial in the history of English political theology and in Anglo-British–European historiography. In Dutch, French and Swiss Protestant history it is fairly easy to trace a sequence of developments – remonstrant in Amsterdam, universalist in Saumur – which seems to run directly from that tempering of the decrees of grace defeated at the Synod of Dort towards rational theology, Socinianism and Enlightenment; and H.R. Trevor-Roper has powerfully employed it in linking the world of Erasmus with that of Voltaire. But when he comes – as it is right that he should come – to assign the Church of England to its role in the history of Protestant Enlightenment,[52] recalcitrances appear. Not only are there Erasmian components in the writings of the

---

[49] Caroline Hibbard, *Charles I and the Popish Plot* (Chapel Hill, 1983).

[50] See Mark Goldie's essay in this book. Peter Harrison, *'Religion' and the Religions in the English Enlightenment* (Cambridge, 1990), has found a fully developed statement of the concept, minus the word, in Herbert of Cherbury.

[51] Lamont, n. 1, on p. 45 above.

[52] *Catholics, Anglicans and Puritans* (Chicago, 1988).

near-Socinian Chillingworth as in those of the sacramentalist Laud; nowhere but in England was 'Arminian' theology intimately linked with a doctrine of imperial and sacred monarchy and a desire to maintain community with the traditions and the liturgy of the universal catholic church. Trevor-Roper thus has difficulty reconciling the Erasmian and Arminian with what may be termed the baroque components in Laudian ritual and practice, and indeed the problem of the English baroque remains open.[53]

William Lamont tells his story through the writings of a great figure, Presbyterian without being altogether Calvinist: Richard Baxter, whose long life and acute intelligence enabled him to survey English history from the reign of Charles I into that of William III, and to tell us the Puritan story without imposing breaks in its continuity at the major watersheds. Baxter saw nothing much to dismay him in Arminian modification of the decrees of grace or leanings toward hypothetic universalism, and did not identify these tendencies with what he so deeply feared: the project of the Arminian Hugo Grotius to bring about a reunion of the churches through the calling of a general council. He seems in some way to have associated Grotian leanings in the English church and monarchy with the Irish rebellion of 1641 – they lulled Charles I into ignoring, if not complying with, what the fiends of Catholic Ireland were about to do in his name; yet Baxter did not think that Grotius's involvement in this sinister ecumenism was directly a product of his Arminianism. None the less, he saw Grotius's influence on English Protestantism exactly as Prynne had seen that of Laud, as a subversion of imperial monarchy in church and state. Reunion through a general council, he insisted, would be unacceptable because it would mean submission to a foreign jurisdiction. He therefore stands in the succession to Bale and Foxe and all the worthies of Godly Rule, to whom true religion and imperial sovereignty were one and the same; but though he joins with Andrew Marvell[54] in viewing most unsympathetically the history of general councils, he does not ground the supremacy of imperial monarchy in an Arminian-derived Socinianism and anti-clericalism (as Marvell very likely did).

---

[53] Linda Peck has in hand a project on 'England in the baroque age'.
[54] Andrew Marvell, *Historical Essay Concerning General Councils* (1676) in *Works* (ed. Grosart, 1875), vol. IV, pp. 91–161.

Baxter emerges, then, as a figure of the Elizabethan mainstream, who would have been at ease in the society of Abbot and Ussher and James I; yet towards the end of his life he has been caught by Lamont wondering whether James II does not stand for something new. In the age of Louis XIV there was such a thing as Gallicanism, and Baxter sought to distinguish between 'French' and 'Italian popery'. His prison notes of 1686 show him aware that powerful Catholic kings may repudiate the pope's right of deposition, and even summon councils to limit his authority. Under desperate conditions he came nearer to yielding to Grotius; and if we may think of James II's Catholicism as a kind of Anglo-Gallicanism, we may see the great nonconformist knowing himself tempted, like and yet unlike William Penn, to accept the king's offer of indulgence with eyes open to its risks. To this we shall have to return; for the present, it is crucial to note that imperial monarchy was a keystone of English thinking, and that the divine right of kings could be suspected of concealing a conspiracy against it.

III

The next group of essays I shall consider – those by Skinner, Tuck and Scott – take us into the mental world of the Interregnum, and oblige us to reflect on its character. It is not a world in revolution; Christopher Hill's 'world turned upside down' has come and gone, leaving the spectre of antinomian 'enthusiasm' to haunt the magisterial and clerical imagination for a century and a half. In these essays we are watching a world struggling to replace if it cannot retrieve its former equilibrium; the Interregnum as 'the quest for a settlement',[55] the debate over Engagement and *de facto* rule. The government is dissolved, and the people (in Harrington's phrase) 'a living thing in pain and misery';[56] it is the experience of an anomic condition which constituted the central trauma of English history, an open wound in the historical memory for a very long time to come. To understand the responses of printed discourse to this situation, we have to consider what government it was that authors perceived as having collapsed, and what they

---

[55] G.E. Aylmer (ed.), *The Interregnum: The Quest for a Settlement, 1646–60* (London, 1972).
[56] Harrington, *Political Works*, p. 838.

thought the conditions under which that collapse had occurred. In so far as we can find in seventeenth-century British thinking a concept of revolution in our sense of the term – a drastic change in historical conditions constituting a process – we may find it here; but it does not follow that the search for this concept should dominate our inquiry.

The government that had fallen, or been dissolved, was the English imperial monarchy. It was a loss of authority that the English had suffered – we may ask how far this was suffered by the governed as distinct from the governing classes – and the debate over *de facto* rule was a debate over the individual's responsibility, his obligation no less than his right, to reconstitute authority out of his own nature when left naked before heaven. Some saw this as a revolutionary opportunity, others as an intolerable burden, a few (like Harrington) as both. Because it was conducted in these terms, the Interregnum debate vastly reinforced the tendency to regard political discourse as a debate over *jus*, a term which could mean both right and authority; a tendency already so deeply entrenched in neo-Latin political thinking that political philosophy (where such a thing existed[57] was at bottom a philosophy of law. Political theorists at this day see the enterprise of political thinking as a juristic enterprise, coupled with a debate over its philosophical possibility; it was John Locke who laid down that political literature was concerned either with the origin and rights of government, or else with 'the government of men', about which he did not say very much.[58] Modern theorists are perturbed by a history of political discourse whenever it wanders from the high road of right and authority, and seek to bring it back under a juristic paradigm; but it is a cardinal rule of the historiography which defines itself as the recovery of languages that we must reconstitute the languages we find and follow the implications of their discourse wherever these may lead. This injunction seems to me conveyed in strong

---

[57] Oakeshott famously observed that *Leviathan* is not only the greatest, but perhaps the sole masterpiece of political philosophy in English. I would like to add that it is the first, and to inquire just what the historical meaning of 'political philosopher' is, and how to read the appearance of one at this moment in history. The point is taken up in 'Spinoza and Harrington: An Exercise in Comparison', *Bijdragen en Mededelingen Betreffende de Geschiedenis der Nederlanden*, 102 (1987), 435–49.

[58] 'Some Thoughts concerning Reading and Study for a Gentleman', in James L. Axtell (ed.), *The Educational Writings of John Locke* (Cambridge, 1968), p. 400.

terms by the essays of Skinner and Tuck on Hobbes, and in another way by that of Scott upon Harrington.

The government that had fallen was that of imperial monarchy, and the debate over the reconstitution of authority, strong in the years of civil war and stronger still after the catastrophe of regicide, has been intensively studied[59] in the works of Weston, Greenberg and Mendle on the *Answer to the XIX Propositions*,[60] in Quentin Skinner's essays on Hobbes and the Engagement controversy,[61] in John Wallace's work on the political setting of Andrew Marvell's poems,[62] and in Conal Condren's investigation of the writings of George Lawson.[63] Yet Marvell's *Horatian Ode* is among other things Machiavellian,[64] and a Machiavellian republicanism is to be detected in the works of both Nedham and Harrington.[65] In their hands republican theory became a response to the *de facto* predicament; it reminds us nevertheless that there was a humanist as well as a juristic and theological language of English politics, not incompatible with those it accompanied but at the same time very different from them. A civic or a civil humanism might be republican, but certainly need not be; and this leads the way towards the questions opened up by Quentin Skinner's examination of Hobbes's attitudes toward rhetoric.

The monarchy that had fallen was a monarchy of counsel; many thought of Charles I as a king who had not listened to counsel, had taken false counsel from his bishops, or had been misled and seduced by evil counsellors. In Fortescue the king ruling by law and the king ruling by counsel are one and the same, and those of

---

[59] Initially by Perez Zagorin, *A History of Political Thought in the English Revolution* (London, 1954).

[60] Above, n. 47.

[61] These have not been collected; cf. his 'History and Ideology in the English Revolution', *Historical Journal*, 8 (1965), 151–78; 'The Ideological Context of Hobbes's Political Thought', *Historical Journal*, 9 (1966), 286–317; 'The Context of Hobbes's Theory of Political Obligation', in Maurice Cranston and R.S. Peters (eds.), *Hobbes and Rousseau: A Collection of Critical Essays* (New York, 1972); 'Conquest and Consent: Thomas Hobbes and the Engagement Controversy', in Aylmer, *The Interregnum*.

[62] John M. Wallace, *Destiny His Choice: The Loyalism of Andrew Marvell* (Cambridge, 1968).

[63] Conal A. Condren, *George Lawson's Politica and the English Revolution* (Cambridge, 1990). To all these should be added Margaret A. Judson, *From Tradition to Political Reality: A Study of the Ideas set forth in Support of Commonwealth Government in England* (Hamden, Conn, 1980).

[64] A fact first noticed by J.A. Mazzeo, *Renaissance and Seventeenth-Century Studies* (New York, 1964), and developed by Wallace, *Destiny His Choice*: See Blair Worden, 'Andrew Marvell, Oliver Cromwell, and the Horatian Ode', in Kevin Sharpe and Steven M. Zwicker (eds.), *Politics of Discourse: The Literature and History of Seventeenth-Century England* (Berkeley, 1987).

[65] Harrington, *Political Works*, introduction, pp. 30–42.

his council are learned in the law; but in the two centuries since Fortescue's time had come the great revival of humanism, and the rhetoric studied by Professor Skinner is very much the rhetoric of counsel. Cicero, nevertheless, was a statesman in a republic, and his rhetoric is not used in advising a prince, but in the mouth of a legislator mobilises men to become citizens, or in that of an orator persuades citizens to adopt policies. Seneca and Quintilian lived under the principate, but even for them oratory is the instrument of counsel given in a highly public space, that (we might say) of a *res publica*. The profoundly monarchical English humanists had turned the oratory of the public space into a rhetoric of the council chamber;[66] but those whose *métier* or birthright was to advise the prince might both challenge the authority of professional rhetoricians who appeared among them – the problem is as old as More – and mistrust the latent republicanism of counsellors who spoke to one another, or to their Speaker, instead of addressing themselves to the ear of their king. It is no accident that the one pure *avis au prince* considered in this book was written by Hobbes's patron for Hobbes's pupil, and is couched not in the language of oratory but in the gruff allusiveness of the privy chamber, where 'sometimes, in a smoking-room, one learns why things were done'.[67] The status of rhetoric was unclear, never more so than after the catastrophe of both royal and parliamentary monarchy. Hobbes's dislike of oratory is, to the not-inconsiderable depth of its surface layers, a dislike of the eloquence of the republican citizen; the *vir dicendi peritus* who ceases to be *vir bonus* in proportion as his skill in speaking induces him to follow the imperatives of what he says instead of obeying the determinations of his sovereign, and the thunder of whose eloquence acts on other citizens with the same uncontrollable force as religious enthusiasm. Whether this mistrust extends to counsellors who bemuse the prince's ear with superfluous oratory Hobbes does not tell us. The 1650s were not the time for royalist *post mortems*, and *De cive* and *Leviathan* are in no sense discourses of the court.

The problem of Hobbes's humanism comes into view here, and I should like to suggest a renewal of emphasis on his translation of

---

[66] And much more than that: a physic for the spirit. See F.W. Conrad, 'A Preservative Against Tyranny: The Political Theology of Sir Thomas Elyot' (unpublished Ph.D. dissertation, The Johns Hopkins University, 1988).

[67] Rudyard Kipling, 'The Puzzler' (*Collected Works*, New York, 1941, vol. XXVII, p. 52).

Thucydides (mentioned here, I believe, only by Jonathan Scott).[68] Earlier in the history of humanism, the move towards Tacitus has been interpreted as a move away from the flowing oratory of the open republic towards the hard, knotted, gnomic sentences which teach us how to live under princes and observe their ways, teach princes the statecraft with which to rule us and observe our responses, and teach both them and us the darkness and complexity of our own behaviour and of the problems in which we are necessitated to make decisions. The maxim of state, itself arcane, is the exposition of some *arcanum imperii*;[69] and there is constantly the suggestion that only the prince is authorised, or otherwise empowered, to arrive at decisions about which there is always some darkness and mystery. The inscrutable judgements of providence, or the crooked counsels of the prince of this world? In Thucydides we find no prince, and consequently no Tiberius; but in his notoriously gnomic style, and his fascination by the perversion of political language. Hobbes could well have found the key to what was wrong with the thunderous eloquence of Pericles.

Yet there remains a problem. Is Leviathan operating in a world of *arcana* and mysteries of state? Is he dealing in rational or irrational integers? Much that we know about his author suggests that he is practising geometry, not algebra; that he is not an empiric, dealing by intuition (in which Hobbes did not believe) or experience (which 'concludeth nothing universal') with phenomena neither he nor his subjects fully understand. Richard Tuck suggests that Hobbes was in the end a utopian, and in utopia we are out of Plato's cave and there are no mysteries in the universal sunlight. On this showing, Leviathan requires of his subjects only the rational concurrence that there must be some final authority in determining where authority lies, and he can expect *ratio* to bring them to this decision without much need for *oratio* to assist them. But this would suggest that they need to be, and are, rationally

---

[68] See Gigliola Rossini, 'The Criticism of Rhetorical Historiography and the Ideal of Scientific Method: History, Nature and Science in the Political Language of Thomas Hobbes', in Anthony Pagden (ed.), *The Languages of Political Theory in Early Modern Europe* (Cambridge, 1987). I would agree with Professor Skinner that it is not precisely to 'science' that Hobbes was effecting a transition.

[69] Lionel A. McKenzie, 'The Guicciardinian Prince: Studies in the Meaning of Prudence from Bodin to Richelieu' (unpublished Ph.D. dissertation, The Johns Hopkins University, 1980). See also Peter S. Donaldson, *Machiavelli and Mystery of State* (Cambridge, 1988); Anthony Parel, *The Machiavellian Cosmos* (New Haven, 1992).

satisfied of the need for his authority, not of the rational content of his specific decisions; so that Hobbes would have withdrawn from *gubernaculum* into *jurisdictio*, from Locke's 'government of men' (the subject-matter of humanism) into the location of authority (that of jurisprudence and philosophy), from particulars into universals. In his much later *Dialogue of the Common Laws* he was notoriously unsuccessful at showing how the content of the sovereign's decisions could be justified by the same reason as that which demonstrated the need for sovereign authority; yet it seems certain that *circa* 1650 the dissolution of government seemed to present the universal problem of authority, rather than any particular problem in prudence or statecraft.

Quentin Skinner isolates one problem more. In *Leviathan*, it seems, Hobbes's sternness towards eloquence abates, and he allows a legitimate role for *oratio* in persuading men to follow certain courses as just and prudent. Another essay would be needed to explore the grounds of this shift in attitude,[70] and certainly it is hard to imagine Leviathan either making speeches to his subjects in the manner of Olphaus Megaletor the legislator, or receiving counsel from them which he weighs in his own deliberations. What is more, Leviathan's relation to his subjects is that of the theatre, not the forum. He represents, which is to say that he impersonates them; he is both a great body in which every citizen finds himself incorporated, and a great mask (this does not appear in the frontispiece) in which every citizen sees his own face. He persuades them not of the wisdom of what he says or does, but of the necessity that they own his actions as taken by them; and for the actor to expound and explicate his actions in their name would be to take the audience behind the scenes and encounter the dilemma faced by Henry V in his dialogue with the soldiers on the night before Agincourt.

Perhaps it is not Leviathan who has need of eloquence, so much as his Frankenstein. I have sensed a duality of theme in Quentin Skinner's essay: there is Hobbes's *doctrine* of rhetoric, considered as a force in morals and politics, and there is Hobbes's *use* of rhetoric in his own authorial performances. Certainly the rhetoric of *Leviathan* is a rhetoric of a very special kind. It is tempting, though

---

[70] Thus Skinner, above, p. 93. I will not pursue here the question how far his British Academy lecture, and the other works he cites on Hobbes and rhetoric, go towards a temporary filling of this lacuna.

it is probably facile, to resolve Skinner's problem by putting the two together, and suggest that Hobbes softened *towards* rhetoric in *Leviathan* because he saw, by the time he wrote the Review and Conclusion, that he had great need *of* rhetoric if he was to persuade his readers to two very radical decisions. One was to abandon the monarchy and submit to the sovereignty (whatever it was) being exercised in England in 1651. The second was to abandon episcopacy, and regard both it and presbytery as knots to be untied in succession to that of papacy, as steps toward the independence of congregations under a strong civil government. This was the most drastic, and nearly the most disastrous, step taken by Hobbes in the whole of his career as a publicist; it carried him irrevocably into the company of militant anti-clericals; and we hear far more from those whom the rhetoric of *Leviathan* repelled from following this step than from those who were attracted towards it.

It is Hobbes's breach with the Church of England, in exile and after restoration, which dominates Richard Tuck's remarkable essay, developing an interpretation of this part of *Leviathan* which he generously associates with my writings more than twenty years ago.[71] What I certainly did not appreciate then was the context of Hobbes's move in the politics of the exiled Stuart court. Tuck reveals that the first to notice, and react against, what Hobbes was up to were his old associates of the Great Tew circle, Clarendon and Hammond, the former bearing up for the Church of England in the unfriendly atmosphere of France, the latter labouring to ensure its continuity by underground activity in England; and he further notes that they had good cause to be outraged, since Hobbes had expressly upheld the authority of an apostolic church in *De cive* (which they might know about) and his reply to Thomas White (which they might not). I am tempted to add that Great Tew, while it might have made them suppose that Hobbes was of their ecclesiastical persuasion, might also have alerted them to the dangers which he now presented; since doubts about the immortality of the soul and the meeting of two natures in Christ cannot have been unheard of in the circle of Chillingworth and Falkland.

[71] I am startled to learn that I credited myself with expounding this reading in a paper of 1968, which I no longer have, since I vividly remember working it out at Churchill College during a snowstorm in 1969. I also doubt if I deserve the praise implicit in Richard Tuck's remark that Hobbes scholars engrossed in 'the Taylor–Warrender debate' have taken twenty years to catch up with what I wrote then. This congratulates me too much for neglecting the Taylor-Warrender debate altogether, as I fear I did.

It was 'the looser sons of the Church, and the king's party' whom Hammond feared would be seduced by the 'farrago of Christian atheism'[72] to be found in *Leviathan*, and the compound, though recognisable, is not a simple one. Churchmen, including those as orthodox and sophisticated as those of Great Tew, were always tempted to regard points even of doctrine as not necessary to salvation, incapable of determination by human wit, and therefore meet to be enjoined by authority of the magistrate, until they must recoil from the point where all spiritual substance was emptied from the church and only the magistrate remained; and *Leviathan* was moving in that direction with planetary mass and speed. 'The looser sons of the Church' might here reveal themselves as of 'the king's party' and nothing more; both Hammond and Clarendon saw Hobbes's apostasy with eyes bent on the doctrine that the king's party must also be the church's. Some of the writing, the publication and the initial reception of *Leviathan*[73] coincide in time with Charles II's expedition to Scotland, his taking of the Covenant, and the campaigns of Dunbar and Worcester. Clarendon was persuaded that Henrietta Maria had incited her son to take the Covenant in the expectation of undermining the Church of England and the national sovereignty established by the Tudors, and preparing the way for an eventual Catholic restoration.[74] It is the kind of strategy always easy to suspect in French policy, and we can see how Hobbes's calculated breach with Church of England doctrine, his advocacy of a monarchy which could move at will among the confessions, would appear among his fellow-exiles. If he understood his own timing, one must ask what he intended.

At this point great interest must attach to Richard Tuck's exploration of the possible links between Hobbes's philosophical scepticism – that is, his scepticism regarding philosophy – his anti-ecclesiastical materialism, and the arguments of Thomas White (alias Blacklo) and the latter's patron Sir Kenelm Digby. These English Catholics, at variance with Rome but by no means out of its communion, had followed the Jesuit Petau in arguing that the ante-Nicene fathers had held no consistent doctrine of the Trinity, and that it was only the influx of Greek philosophy which

---

[72] Above, p. 122.
[73] For a closer study of this chronology, see Glenn Burgess, 'Contexts for the Writing and Publication of Hobbes's *Leviathan*', *History of Political Thought*, II (1990), 675–702.
[74] *History of the Rebellion and Civil Wars in England* (Oxford, 1731), vol. v, p. 344.

had raised questions for emperor and council reluctantly to answer. Petau was anticipating Richard Simon's contention that the authority of Scripture, thus challenged by philosophy, was subordinate to the authority of the church; but White and Hobbes further perceived how easily that authority might be re-invested in the civil sovereign. By questioning the immortality of the soul – Hobbes did this more drastically than White – both challenged the church's claim to be part of the everlasting communion of the saints with God and to have a role in the distribution of eternal rewards and punishments. Digby and White were active in promoting some revision of the relations between Rome and the civil powers, and we find ourselves at a point where English Protestant fears of conspiracy begin to look less fantastic. If Clarendon or Hammond – William Lamont would have us add Baxter – had been confronted with evidence that Hobbes derived some part of his 'farrago' from debate with a camarilla of libertine papists, they would have nodded grimly and said it was just as they feared. It is the spectre of the Grotian conspiracy again; Hobbes and White remained intimate if argumentative[75] after both returned to England in the 1650s, and both were threatened with parliamentary banishment in 1666.[76] The hunt for the Beast was still up in the year of its Number.

Hobbes therefore belongs in the context of a controversy antedating the regicide, as to how far the restoration of the monarchy was to be a restoration of the church (as bearing apostolic authority and as by law established); and something soon after 1649 moved him decisively in a libertine-monarchist direction. In inquiring what this was, Richard Tuck is led to inquire into Hobbes's larger historical vision, and he credits me with having 'noticed' that 'he was a kind of Utopian'.[77] I am unable to find any text in which I expressed this perception, but I am happy to endorse it now. I find that I said he followed the common strategy of removing from political time into political space,[78] and this certainly sounds utopian; but I am not sure it makes the point we are pursuing. I had in mind his construction of the state in nature rather than history, but what Tuck and I now consider 'utopian' in Hobbes is a

[75] Anthony Wood, *Athenae Oxonienses* (Oxford, 1848), vol. III, p. 1247.
[76] Above, p. 137.
[77] Above, p. 137.
[78] *Politics, Language and Time* (1971), p. 157.

matter of history. Tuck's Hobbes is Epicurean – he had Epicurean friends in Paris – in his desire to liberate humans from unnecessary fear of the gods; but where Lucretius saw philosophy as a liberation from mythology, Hobbes wants to liberate them from the fear of eternal punishment, which is founded on the false doctrine of immortality invented by philosophers and gives the church the means of defying the civil ruler. He therefore looks to an imminent future in which philosophy will have ceased to dictate to theology, and the latter will be safe in the hands of the magistrate. This involves the assumption that humans will fear annihilation at death less than they fear damnation after it, which is not as certain as philosophers suppose. It also makes the assumption that the means now exist of dispelling forever the false lights of Greek philosophy, with its real essences, immortal souls, and the rest of the kingdom of the fairies. A time is at hand when 'men can live without false beliefs'; this Richard Tuck characterises as 'the greatest of the English revolutionary utopias'.[79] I would want to add only that it is not a utopia of place, but an eschaton or anti-eschaton situated in imminent futurity; we are not in space but in history. The history of philosophy, for Petau, for Hobbes, and very soon for Cudworth, is taking its place alongside the history of the church and even sacred history.

The problem of utopia recurs in the case of James Harrington, the subject of Jonathan Scott's essay. *Oceana* is an ideal commonwealth, and in this loose sense a utopia; but it is not an imaginary *topos* or place, and in this sense not a *eutopia* or *outopia*. It is not reached by voyaging in imaginary space, but by developing a theoretical conception or model (a word much used by Harrington) of history. It is situated in the imminent future of a lightly fictionalised England, and of a Europe whose history is not presented in fictionalised form. The problem is what utopia is doing in a context of history, and of a scheme of historical thought more sophisticated than any other of its time. This is a problem which I think Jonathan Scott is trying to dismiss rather than to recognise.

As the author of two remarkable studies of Algernon Sidney,[80] he is giving an account of English republican thinking alternative to

---

[79] Above, p. 138.
[80] *Algernon Sidney and the English Republic, 1623–1677* (Cambridge, 1988); *Algernon Sidney and the Restoration Crisis, 1677–1683* (Cambridge, 1991).

that constructed around the figure of Harrington. There emerges an austere, aristocratic, somewhat baronial republicanism, Platonic in the double sense that it can be traced back both to Algernon's ancestor Sir Philip's *Arcadia*[81] and to images of Venice founded in Plato's *Laws*. So stated, it is not Machiavellian; it did not follow Machiavelli's deliberate rejection of Venetian serenity and eternity in favour of Roman dynamism and glory rather than length of days, and did not echo his acceptance of a democratic component in the republic, with the tensions and violence that reinforced Roman dynamism. Jonathan Scott, however, traces in Sidney's career and writings an indestructible identification with the 'good old cause', which brought him in the end to the scaffold, but first to a realistic acknowledgement that England faced a 'Machiavellian moment', occurring in real time and to be solved only at the cost of real violence. Harrington's construction of a Venetian if democratic[82] utopia, on the contrary, Scott sees as an exit from history and even from the republic; an attempt to stop the *vicissitudo rerum*. His Harrington abandons Machiavelli for Venice; his Sidney moves in the opposite direction.

The question is that of how utopia is related to history. It might be pointed out that even Machiavelli had left the choice between Venice and Rome open, and that his follower Donato Giannotti had attempted to sketch a Venetian-style republic for Florence on Machiavellian principles.[83] It must be emphasised that Harrington took Machiavelli's idea of necessary tensions between nobles and people and turned it into a motor of historical change: the monarchy destroys the feudal tenures which are the basis of nobility in 'modern prudence' (alias the 'Gothic balance') and liberates a people who in their turn destroy what is left of Gothic monarchy and nobility together. But – as Jonathan Scott rightly discerns – the destruction of modern prudence is both a return to ancient prudence, and an exit from history (the 'goods of fortune') into utopia (the 'goods of the mind').[84] The 'Machiavellian

---

[81] See also Blair Worden, 'Classical Republicanism'.

[82] Harrington continuously stresses this component.

[83] *The Machiavellian Moment*, pp. 286–320; Giovanni Silvano (ed.), *Donato Giannotti: Republica Fiorentina* (Bologna, 1990); Giuseppe Biscaccia, *La 'Repubblica Fiorentina' di Donato Giannotti* (Florence, 1978). Giannotti sought to combine Venetian stability with popular participation; Harrington Venetian immortality with Machiavellian expansiveness. To the extent that Oceana is an empire, it is not in utopia at all.

[84] I develop this thesis in an edition of Harrington's *Oceana* and *A System of Politics*, Cambridge Texts in Political Thought, (1992).

moment' is transformed into a quasi-millennial *occasione* or *kairos*. In *The Machiavellian Moment* I was trying to argue that this was always a possibility within the 'republican synthesis'; Jonathan Scott, to the contrary, sees the move as an abandonment of the republic altogether. However Algernon Sidney may have perceived matters, Harrington shared with Milton and Vane the perception that England must either embrace or reject an opportunity of completely transforming its nature, but profoundly disagreed with their conviction that this must be achieved through a rule of the saints.[85] To the extent that utopia is more pagan and less Christian than the millenium, Harrington was more utopian than Milton and Vane; but his utopia is situated on the millennial side of the 'Machiavellian moment'.

This is the point at which I am not persuaded by Scott's contention that Harrington's utopia ceases altogether to be a republic and becomes a Hobbesian experiment in the control and mechanisation of human speech and action. It rests on his reading of the elaborately fantasised 'orders' of Oceana (printed in black letter in the original text), which are to make men good whether they are so or not, and therefore (says Scott) are to replace free action by the human personality with the regularised conduct of automata. Hobbes and Harrington (he says) both reduced the social and natural world to one of billiard balls in motion and impact; where Hobbes set up a mortal god to command the balls' movements, Harrington devised a grid which could be imposed on the whole table. He rendered the republic a creature that moves in predestinate grooves, not even a game but a plan. There are two crucial steps that bring him to the point thus interpreted by Jonathan Scott: one is the institution of the dance-like marching and counter-marching of the Venetian ballot, the other – implicit in it but explicit in his text – the rigorous separation of the legislative process into deliberation, conducted only in the speech-making but non-balloting senate, and decision, conducted in silence by the balloting assembly. As he did in the analogy of the two girls sharing a cake, Harrington has reduced the free exercise of personality to two intellectual faculties, those of reflection and action, and has institutionalised and mechanised them both to a point where the human person simply disappears from politics. There are resem-

[85] Harrington, *Political Works*, introduction, pp. 108–10, 111–13, 118.

blances between his utopia and Hobbes's, in which knowledge
proceeds without disputation and decision is taken without apparent recourse to rhetoric.

There are several points to be made here. One is that Harrington
knew what he was doing, and made a joke about it. He set up the
comic character Epimonus de Garrula – note the name – to object
that this was mere 'playing at billiards with the commonwealth of
Venice', and that 'in the parliament of Oceana you had no balls or
dancing, but sober conversation; a man might know and be known,
show his parts and improve them'.[86] Here is the free exercise of
personality which utopias habitually eliminate, and Harrington is
showing himself aware of the case for it. It might of course be
objected that by 1656 the 'sober conversation' of the House of
Commons was as thoroughly discredited as most other components
of the traditional politics. A few years later it was to be noted of Sir
Arthur Haslerig in Richard Cromwell's parliament that 'he was full
of jests and in great heart today',[87] not long before the Quaker cried
out on him that his beast would carry him no further and he must
down. Epimonus is a jester, a lord of misrule; and he is so because
he (and the parliament of Oceana) are still living in the decay of
'modern prudence', where men are merely what they are and their
free personalities merely the exercise of their passions uncontrolled
by reason. He is doomed, therefore, to play on a cloth untrue, with
a twisted cue and elliptical billiard balls. It is of no small interest
that the billiards metaphor appears to recur in Newcastle's advice
to Charles II, where it is said of utopians that 'if they govern
themselves by those Rules what men should be not what they are
they will miss ye Cushion very much'.[88] It is the function of utopia
to depict men as other than they are, but it is the aim of revolution
to make them so. Harrington and Milton were to share the entirely
correct conviction that if the political habits of Englishmen could
not be transformed, they would choose them a captain back to the
Egypt of the ancient constitution;[89] and this is why Harrington's
utopia is to be read as an attempt to change history and not to stop

---

[86] Harrington, *Political Works*, pp. 242–3. Epimonus has trouble in refraining from addressing the Lord Archon as 'Mr Speaker'.
[87] J.T. Rutt (ed.), *Diary of Thomas Burton* (London, 1828), vol. IV, p. 106.
[88] Above, p. 168
[89] Harrington, *Political Works*, pp. 112–3, 114–15, 762–3, 797–8; Milton, *Prose Works*, vol. VII
(New Haven, 1980), p. 463.

it. In contemplating Englishmen in their history, he knew very well what he was up against. This is also why 'neo-Harringtonians', adapting Harrington to the history of a restored ancient constitution, were resolved to go on with English history as it had been, not as it might be.[90] Montesquieu said of Harrington that he had built Chalcedon with Byzantium before his eyes;[91] but Byzantium was precisely what he and Milton did not want. It was part of the history of reason of state, 'the true theatre of expedient-mongers and state-empirics, the deep waters wherein that Leviathan the minister of state takes his pastime.'[92] The allusion is probably to Jean de Silhon rather than Hobbes, but is aimed at a Leviathan not utopian or revolutionary enough. The mortal god is more than a merely empirical minister of state, or should be.

It also needs emphasising that the utopia of the ballot is a Platonic republic. Scott (and J.C. Davis before him)[93] seem to me mistaken in insisting that Harrington was trying to manipulate humans as non-rational actors into a rational system. Human beings are not kittens[94] or Cartesian automata; they are not to be made inert cogs in a rational machine, but debaters and deciders in a community of reason higher than their individual natures. Hence the utopian, and if you will anti-human enterprise of making some only debaters and others only deciders; it is the kind of enterprise attempted by Plato (though Harrington distinguishes them on the basis not of caste but of function) and leads to the Platonic vision: 'The contemplation of form is astonishing to man, and has a kind of trouble or impulse accompanying it, that exalts his soul to God. As the form of a man is the image of God, so the form of a government is the image of man.'[95] This contemplation is not for chained kittens, but for philosophers escaped from the cave. Platonism on this scale is a long way from Machiavelli, and what we have to realise is that Harrington's grasp of history, his 'Machiavellian meditation on feudalism', prepares the way for an exit into a Platonic utopia, from 'the goods of fortune' making men what they are to 'the goods of the mind' which will make them what they

[90] *Contra*, Scott, p. 141.
[91] *Esprit des Lois*, XI, 6.
[92] *Political Works*, p. 853.
[93] Scott, pp. 150–1 and 153 above.
[94] *Political Works*, p. 744; Scott, p. 159 above.
[95] *Political Works*, p. 837.

should be. Taken in isolation, the parts of *Oceana* printed in black letter are the dead lunar landscape which Jonathan Scott takes them to be. He has doggedly read them through, and so have I; but there is not much reason to suppose that many others have. Harrington's readers in the history of English discourse paid attention to the context in roman type, and there found him in two personae. One was the historian of government in relation to property, the pioneer of social-change explanations of the causes of the civil wars and of a manner of historical interpretation which permanently changed the character of English historical thinking, and will outlive the decline of Marxism and include it.[96] The other was the Platonist, one of a group whom Coleridge saw ploughed under by Bacon at the Restoration and Locke at the Revolution, and left to be rediscovered by his own generation.[97] We know now the sources of Coleridge's perception. Harrington, Milton, Sidney and Ludlow, formed into a republican canon by John Toland, were idealised by later historians of the Commonwealth – Catharine Macaulay[98] and William Godwin[99] – as a group of lost philosopher-rulers who might have transformed the corrupt nature of the English had not Cromwell, Charles II and William III sold them back to Egyptian darkness. The belief of several of them in a God of reason, incarnate more in the human mind than in Christ's person, was transformed into a philosophical idealism and made part of a Platonic rebellion against both orthodox and enlightened religion. Both aspects of Harrington – the Machiavellian and the Platonic, the history and the utopia – lived on into the nineteenth century. To explain their co-existence in a single mind is part of the problem of the 1650s.

IV

In Newcastle's advice to his prince, Conal Condren lets us hear the voice of the baron as counsellor, speaking at a disconsolate time

---

[96] Cf. Scott, p. 154.

[97] John Morrow, *Coleridge's Political Thought: Property, Morality and the Limits of Traditional Discourse* (New York, 1990).

[98] Rolando Minuti, 'Il Problema Storico della Libertà Inglese nella Cultura Radicale dell'Età di Giorgio III. Catharine Macaulay e la Rivoluzione Puritana', *Rivista Storica Italiana*, 98 (1986), 793–860.

[99] John Morrow, 'Republicanism and Public Virtue: William Godwin's *History of the Commonwealth of England*', *Historical Journal*, 34 (1991), 645–64.

when the Ciceronian, even the Senecan rhetoric of counsel had not much to offer. A prince in exile, even one about to return to his kingdom, was an uneasy hybrid of *principe nuovo* and *principe naturale*, and Newcastle's advice may recall that given by Stephen Gardiner (or one of his household) to Philip II, a *principe naturale* if ever there was one, on how to acquire England by marriage and rule there as a *principe nuovo*.[100] Is this, however, advice on the violent restoration of a normal politics violently disturbed – the joyous entry of May 1660 – or the hard voice of the *arcana imperii*, the habitual discourse of the inner sanctum? Celebrants of 'high politics' might plump for the latter, and Newcastle was such a celebrant himself. Is it – to frame a somewhat different question – advice on the restoration of the Tudor sovereignty after an interlude of rebellion, as in the more golden visions said to have been entertained by Clarendon; or is there a sense of 'new things for a new world', such as the baroque absolutism replacing civil and religious war, just then taking shape in France? If the latter, we might look for something superseding Machiavelli, since Robert Bireley's study of 'the Counter-Reformation prince' has shown that the great anti-Machiavellians, from Botero and Lipsius to Ribadeneira and Fajardo, were persuaded that Machiavelli had not known how a monarchical state was constructed and had therefore misunderstood the nature of its morality.[101] But the Tudor empire in church and state, it might be answered, was never such a monarchy, never baroque and never bureaucratic, and we get no nearer such great pioneers of *Politik* and *Staatswissenschaft* than – Sir William Petty?[102] Certainly, Newcastle does not seem to get much beyond the *arcana imperii*: how the prince is to maintain his state in his court and maintain his guards in his realm. Matthew Wren, Harrington's adversary – admired by Jonathan Scott as a true Machiavellian[103] – came nearer 'modernity' in advocating a commercial society in which the sovereign ruled the fluctuating interests of men, and their taxable wealth made possible the maintenance of a standing army.[104] Harrington

---

[100] Peter S. Donaldson (ed.), *A Machiavellian Treatise by Stephen Gardiner* (Cambridge, 1976).

[101] Robert Bireley, *The Counter Reformation Prince: Anti-Machiavellism or Catholic Statecraft in Early Modern Europe*, (Chapel Hill, 1990).

[102] E. Strauss, *Sir William Petty: Portrait of a Genius* (London, 1954). A treatment in the light of recent thinking seems desirable.

[103] Above, pp. 153–4. I see him as an authentic member of that rare species, the Macphersonian possessive individualist.

[104] For Wren, see Harrington, *Political Works*, (introduction), pp. 83–9.

had attacked Wren's politics as those of a 'mathematician'; he seems to have meant less the political geometry of Hobbes than the calculus of probabilities and experimental weighing of forces, developed by the Oxford connection to which Wren belonged and attacked by Hobbes in the controversy about the squaring of the circle. Wilkins and Boyle, not Hobbes, were to furnish the new philosophy of the restored monarchy.[105]

Conal Condren's Newcastle is therefore a man for the new prince, but not for the new monarchy. He is closest to Hobbes (whom both he and his sovereign knew personally) in his anti-intellectualism; books are to be mistrusted, lawyers (like corporations) are caterpillars of the commonwealth, and both the 'Bible-mad' enthusiasts and priests of every persuasion claiming an authority of the spirit are guilty of the Hobbesian offence of supposing ideas learned from books or speech to assert values independent of those of the sovereign. Therefore learning is to be discouraged, not (as the enthusiasts supposed) because words resist the authority of the spirit, but because they encourage the illusion of its presence. Ceremony is to be preferred, because it may become habit, forming the mind through custom which is stronger than discipline. Condren, seeing how this anticipates Hume,[106] is aware how the 'ceremonies' of the court might become the 'manners' of polite and commercial society, so much celebrated in the discourse of the next century as furnishing the cement of civilisation. But for the present discourse is to be discouraged; too much learning, too much speech, make men disobedient, finding authority in themselves. Hobbes had distrusted rhetoric and preferred decision, the *ultima ratio regum*; if this had changed as Hobbes moved away from the church, the clerics of the Restoration were sometimes prepared to impose silence. Gordon Schochet's formidable protagonist Samuel Parker was unafraid of saying that the church should observe a short way with dissenters, putting them to silence wherever possible and maintaining as much silence as possible in

---

[105] Steven Shapin and Simon Schaffer, *Leviathan and the Airpump: Hobbes, Boyle and the Experiemental Life* (Princeton, 1985). Hobbes, *Six Lessons to the Professors of the Mathematics.* (1656).

[106] Above, p. 175.

its own dealings with them.[107] There should be no disputing with those to whom dispute itself was the occasion of disobedience.

'To put the case fully', says Mark Goldie, 'would require an institutional and intellectual history of the Restoration church'.[108] Such a history would indeed be a boon to historians engaged in the enterprise to which the present volume contributes. It might begin with Gilbert Sheldon and Henry Hammond, intimates of the captive Charles I – whose first request to Cornet Joyce was that he might be allowed their company – and examine their work in keeping an episcopal connection alive, before and after the regicide. We need as precise an account as possible of what elements of a 'Laudian' or 'Arminian' programme they kept alive as they and their associates emerged to seek control of ecclesiastical life after the Restoration,[109] but there is more to be done on the character of clerical resistance and collaboration under the Cromwellian regime. From the standpoint of the present volume, we can note of Hammond that he singled out for attack in Hobbes's 'farrago' its insistence that the ordinations carried out by the apostles were civil rather than spiritual acts, implicitly subject to the authority of a sovereign; and that it was Harrington who came to Hobbes's aid against Hammond,[110] insisting that these were acts of *chirotonia* rather than *chirothesia*, not performed by a priesthood but by a self-sustaining civil republic. Hobbes and Harrington further agreed that Israel from Moses to Samuel had been a theocracy directly under God and *therefore* a civil society in immediate control of its own religion; whether it had been a monarchy under the high priests or a republic mattered less, at least to Harrington, than that the priests had claimed no authority independent of the elect nation's civil structure. Both further believed that the mission of

---

[107] 'The way then to prevent Controversies, and to avoid Schisms, is not to define, but silence groundless and dividing Opinions. The Church should in such cases imitate *Socrates's Daemon*, that never gave any positive Answer, but as oft as it was consulted answered either *No*, or *Nothing*; because they are usually started about matters uncertain, and consequently undeterminable.' Parker, *A Free and Impartial Censure of the Platonick Philosophie* (Oxford, 1666), p. 90.

[108] Above, p. 212. See now John Spurr, *The Restoration Church of England, 1646–1689* (New Haven, 1991), which did not reach me in time to be utilised in this essay.

[109] J.W. Packer, *The Transformation of Anglicanism: With Special Reference to Henry Hammond* (Manchester, 1969); C.N. Lettinga, 'Covenant Theology and the Transformation of Anglicanism' (unpublished Ph.D. Dissertation, The Johns Hopkins University, 1987).

[110] Hobbes, *Leviathan*, ch. 42; Hammond, *A Letter of Resolution of Six Quaeres, of Present Use in the Church of England* (1653); Harrington, *The Prerogative of Popular Government* (1658), Book II.

the Son had been to restore and universalise the theocracy exercised by the Father; if this was to Judaise or Socinianise Christ, diminishing his divinity and the doctrine of the Trinity, they (like Milton) were prepared to accept the consequence. That Hobbes was an Epicurean materialist (as well as a monarchist), Harrington a Platonic idealist (and republican), did not yet have primary importance; what mattered was the discomfiting of the church's spiritual substance. We can now see what Hammond was about in this and other controversies: the defence of the priesthood, of the apostolic church and of the Nicene and Catholic christology; the defence of Christian monarchy was part of this programme.

Hobbes and Harrington also had their collisions with the group around John Wilkins and John Wallis at Oxford, clerics who could accept ordination and benefices under a non-episcopal regime yet conform to the church restored by Sheldon and his associates, who nevertheless regarded them with reservations. This is one source of the later categories of 'Cambridge Platonists' and (non-identically) 'latitudinarians', and the history Mark Goldie envisages will have to investigate both the prosopography and the theology of the Restoration Church. Its intellectual politics will distinguish between the Baconism of Oxford men setting up the Royal Society in London and the Platonism set up by other ex-Presbyterians in Cambridge. Both saw themselves as antidotes to prophetic enthusiasm; yet the first publication by Samuel Parker, an ex-Presbyterian who had attached himself to Sheldon, was a savage assault on the Platonic doctrine of essences as conducive to both Roman priestcraft and sectarian enthusiasm. Anglican clerics could denounce transubstantiation as priestcraft while retaining belief in the apostolic succession; the rhetoric of 'priestcraft' studied by Mark Goldie – which extended the Hobbesian epigram into the blanket assumption that all priests were unpleasing – they saw as begotten in an unnatural but intelligible marriage between enthusiasm and atheism. Christopher Hill's 'world turned upside down' is there to tell us that their diagnosis was not always wrong.

The Restoration church's insistence on the supremacy of the civil power was strong enough to bring down the accusation of 'Hobbism'[111] and to remind us that they had had no quarrel with

[111] John W. Marshall, 'The Ecclesiology of the Latitude-Men, 1660–89; Stillingfleet, Tillotson and Hobbes', *Journal of Ecclesiastical History*, 36 (1985), 407–27.

Hobbes before he broke with episcopacy in *Leviathan*. Yet I have suggested that Parker saw Hobbes' materialism as not far removed from enthusiasm,[112] and Professor Schochet more centrally reminds us that (like Ralph Cudworth) Parker saw the ego-centred conduct depicted in Hobbes's state of nature as opposed to any doctrine of natural law and morality, with which the church could not dispense. If the apostolic succession, and its accompanying doctrine of Christ's nature, provided one vocabulary in which Hobbes was altogether rejected, another – which need not, but sometimes did, point in Arian or Socinian directions – arose from the emphasis on religion as the practice of morality in obedience to authority, on natural law reinforced by assurance of rewards and punishments in an afterlife. Hobbes's mortalism, as well as his egoism, undercut this doctrine, and where mortalists were not sceptics or atheists they were often enthusiasts and millenarians. Platonic arguments for the soul's immortality were much taken up by churchmen, and Cudworth was only one who sought to Christianise as much as possible of the Platonic cosmology, finding in the Demiurge the prototype of a benevolent creator who directed the fall of atoms by rational law.[113] He aimed to conduct Plato in the direction soon to be taken by Newton, but the fear of enthusiasm led others to follow Parker in rejecting Plato and arriving at a reasonable religion, the rational benevolence of whose God (and man) might leave little need for an Incarnation or a Trinity. The enemies of priestcraft studied by Mark Goldie might end as deists, whose God had no need of dogmas or mediators; but within the conforming clergy and the laity who upheld the church, there was room for orthodoxy to move away from its own traditions, for latitudinarians to take the Arian side in the debate over the Council of Nicea, finding themselves uncomfortably close to those who thought the whole debate ridiculous and a display of the sinister powers of priestcraft. To see the Church of England as radically divided into Trinitarians and Socinians would be a serious exaggeration; for the next hundred years, nevertheless, there is evidence of a recurrent minority holding opinions of the latter kind,[114] and to explain its presence we may look back to

---

[112] 'Thomas Hobbes: Atheist or Enthusiast? His Place in a Restoration Debate', *History of Political Thought*, II (1990), 737–49.

[113] Cudworth, *The True Intellectual System of the Universe* (1678).

[114] J.C.D. Clark, *English Society, 1660–1832* (Cambridge, 1986); John Gascoigne, *Cambridge in the Age of the Enlightenment* (Cambridge, 1990).

Chillingworth, explore the alternative strategies before the church of the Restoration, and spend much time focussing our attention on the ecclesiology and theology of Locke.[115]

Goldie and Schochet do not explore in this book – as both have elsewhere[116] – the multiple complexities of tension between church, crown and parliament, between persecution, comprehension and toleration, which arose in the gap between Acts of Uniformity and Declarations of Indulgence, between the shaken but determined Tudor church-state and the monarchy which was its unreliable head; but both writers leave us in no doubt that this is the key to Restoration politics. Schochet follows Parker into the last months of his life in early 1688, when as bishop of Oxford he supported (while attempting to moderate) James II's intrusion of Catholics into the fellowship of Magdalen College, and went so far as to write in favour of the abrogation of the Tests. Since we have learned from J.C.D. Clark to regard the Test Act as a pillar of the English church-state, falling with it only in 1829 to 1832, it is (as he would agree) valuable to be reminded that Parker could see it not as an assertion of Cavalier principle, but as a Shaftesburean and Whig subversion, part of an attempt to invoke the imperial monarchy against the church itself. Church and king had done without it, and need not welcome it. Yet Parker was going further than Sancroft and his brethren would find it possible to go a few months after his own death, and we must ask whether Parker and Cartwright were mere timeservers, and in any case what they envisaged. Did they see dependence on the royal power of dispensation as a sure means of reducing English Catholics to harmlessness, or would they in the last extremity have accepted a Church loosely linked with Rome but preserved by the Act of Supremacy in a more than Gallican independence? They must have considered the question, and the exact nature of James's (or Dryden's) Catholicism needs further investigation. Richard Baxter in prison is there to remind Lamont and us that the Grotian spectre still walked, and it is a pity that none of the tercentennial studies of 1688 (as far as I know) has

---

[115] John W. Marshall, 'John Locke in Context: Religion, Ethics and Philosophy' (unpublished Ph.D. dissertation, The Johns Hopkins University, 1990). See further his 'John Locke's Religious, Educational and Moral Thought', *Historical Journal*, 33 (1990), 993–1002.

[116] Tim Harris, Paul Seaward and Mark Goldie (eds.), *The Politics of Religion in Restoration England* (Oxford, 1990); Gordon J. Schochet (ed.), *Restoration, Ideology and Revolution: Proceedings of the Folger Institute Center for the History of British Political Thought*, vol. IV (Folger Shakespeare Library, 1990).

enquired into that year's transactions from the point of view of the Vatican. What is clear is that James II fell, like his father before him, because he was perceived as subverting his own sovereignty over a church still given to persecution; what is less clear is how the church was brought to that partial abandonment of persecution which Mark Goldie presents as a turning point in history. The politics of toleration are not a principal theme of this book, but appear to have been linked with an increasingly active Socinianism, since a Christ about whom one could agree to differ was not a Christ present in his mystical body the church.[117]

In an essay published elsewhere,[118] Mark Goldie has reminded us of the powerfully effective act of passive resistance practised by the Seven Bishops in the summer of 1688, and more diffusedly by numbers of Anglican justices of the peace behind them. Nonobedience stopping short of resistance was normally thought of as a moral stance, expressing the limit to which the subject might justifiably go under the unjust orders of a divinely legitimised ruler. Here, however, it proved to be a political act, performed in *verità effettuale*; a ruler who could find nobody to execute his commands was being effectively stopped in the exercise of his authority, and moreover found his leading supporters publicly declaring them illegitimate. So decisively had the clergy brought James's policies to a halt that Mark Goldie depicts them as the more astonished and outraged by his subsequent removal from the throne; they thought they had done all that was needful. Passive resistance therefore supplies one setting in which it is valuable to read Lois Schwoerer's study of resistance theories more decisively Whig. Much resistance theory, active as well as passive, implies the ultimate legitimacy of the government being resisted *in exercitio*, and does not reach the point where it is declared *absque titulo* and is dissolved. John Locke, however, raised as all know the possibility of a situation in which a people discover and declare that their government is making war upon them, and by issuing an appeal to heaven bring it to be dissolved.

---

[117] J.G.A. Pocock, 'Within the Margins: The Definition of Orthodoxy', presented to the Eleventh Le Moyne Forum on Religion and Literature, 'The Margins of Orthodoxy: Heterodox Writing and Cultural Response' (Le Moyne College, Syracuse, New York); publication expected.
[118] 'The Political Thought of the Anglican Revolution', in Robert A. Beddard (ed.), *The Revolutions of 1688: The Andrew Browning Lectures, 1988* (Oxford, 1991).

We do not consider in this volume the fascinating problem of the historical moment at which Locke wrote his chapter on dissolution, or ask whether the appeal to heaven he envisaged could have been other than an appeal to civil war.[119] If the Second Treatise is an Exclusion tract, it has little to say about exclusion; yet part of its setting must be the circumstances that though James as a Catholic could easily be presumed at war with his Protestant people, he nevertheless won (before he lost) universal acceptance as still the divinely sanctioned imperial ruler of the Tudor monarchy in church and state. The memory of that government's dissolution was less than thirty years old, an appalling trauma which nobody desired to repeat or claimed the right to precipitate. This is a good setting in which to read Lois Schwoerer's demonstration that much but not all established resistance theory presupposed a situation in which a dissolution of government had already occurred, and concerned itself with the people's right to act in that situation. It thus joined hands with the debate over *de facto* authority after 1649, so much of whose literature was reprinted in 1689 and after. There existed the logical consequence that it must be decided whether a people possessed the right, or the authority, to determine and proclaim that a dissolution of government had occurred, to determine what acts on a ruler's part constituted a making of war on his people; but it remains extraordinary that Locke should have chosen to raise that issue in the murky political circumstances existing in 1683 or earlier, when he must have been envisaging some form of civil war and writing words that incited the people to precipitate it by an appeal to heaven. It is even more extraordinary that James II should have come by December 1688 to a point where it seemed that he was attempting to dissolve the government and the people were acting by means of constituted authority to prevent his doing so. These were the circumstances in which Locke's *Treatises of Government* were published, with the result that it takes a major effort of the historical imagination to read them as they must have been written. So extraordinary were these circumstances, however, that we must accept Lois Schwoerer's reminder that those there were who both had and wished to take a view of the events of the winter of 1688 to 1689 implicitly and explicitly the same as Locke's;

[119] J.G.A. Pocock, 'The Fourth English Civil War: Dissolution, Desertion and Alternative Histories in the Glorious Revolution', *Government and Opposition*, 23 (1988), 151–66.

who declared that a dissolution of government had indeed occurred, that the people were authorised to proclaim such a dissolution,
and that they were now acting to continue the government or
entrust it to new hands, 'as they list'. In her study of the
Declaration of Rights,[120] she has argued that those of this persuasion succeeded in writing some of their claims into statute law, with
some permanent effects.

Twenty years later, at the time of the Sacheverell trial, someone
remarked that it was necessary to decide 'whether we lie under a
national guilt or not'.[121] The words make, in strong because
theocentric language, the point weakly because deistically made by
the Declaration of Independence's 'decent respect for the opinions
of mankind': that a people which has acted to change its government must answer for its having done so. The two speech-acts differ
on the point of whether a government has been dissolved or not; in
1710 this is not certain, in 1776 it is. They differ in the answers they
give to questions they implicitly agree must be asked: what it is that
has just been done, by what authority it has been done, and to what
authority those who have done it are required to answer. It is a long
way from the judgement of heaven, to which one appeals, to the
opinion of mankind, to which one owes respect; a long way too –
one might add – from the opinion of mankind to the judgement of
the market, to which the in many ways Lockean revolutionaries of
1989 and 1991 are obliged to appeal by the want of any other
standard. But the difference between 1689 and 1776 is in large
measure a difference in religion, made in one perspective by the
eighteenth-century liberalisation of Christian doctrine – a God
concerning whom one has opinions is no longer a God who makes
known his judgements – and in another by the divergence between
Anglo-British and American history. The dissolution of government and the reversion of power to the people are a dreaded
aberration in the British historical memory,[122] but a corner-stone
and foundation in the American (where the God who gives
judgement in battle shows his face only in 1861–5). The Lockean,

[120] Lois G. Schwoerer, *The Declaration of Rights, 1689* (Baltimore, 1981).
[121] The authoritative account is that of Geoffrey Holmes, *The Trial of Doctor Sacheverell* (London, 1973). I should be obliged to any reader who can supply the source of the words quoted.
[122] Though one would not have known this from the official celebrations of the 1988 tercentennial, when a radically Tory regime adopted the most conventional of Whig readings.

still more the 'commonwealth' or republican reading of the Revolution of 1688 was the opinion of a significant dissenting minority in England and Scotland in the eighteenth century; to understand Anglo-British history we have to treat it as such. Those who emphasise its persistence – Lois Schwoerer and other successors to Caroline Robbins, in a rather different way Richard Ashcraft – do so because they are Americans, historically justified in being Whig historians. The foundations of the American polity lie in the secession from Anglican imperial monarchy of certain English colonies culturally dominated by dissenting and 'old Whig' alienation from the form that monarchy took after 1688 to 1714. Without the religious and political mentality of these dissentients the United States could not have existed in the form we recognise, and American historians are thus obliged to write the history of old-Whig and old Dissent persistence and to require us to look at British history from the standpoint and in the light it provides. Without American, as without Scottish, Irish and Dissenting history, it is not possible for English history to become British.

James Tully, on the other hand, writes history as a Canadian, who understands the persistence of imperial sovereignty without its reversion to the people. He therefore understands democracy in its British rather than its American sense – that is, there is a binding convention that the sovereign acts by the counsel and consent of the people, given in electoral decisions – and he further understands his own polity as a partnership between 'layers' of sovereignty. The latter, however, is far from being the form of the Anglo-British polity, and its reality calls for explanation. James Tully's essay is concerned with Locke, and I must find especially satisfying his perception of what I was trying to say about that figure in various writings[123] – something which American historians have now and then had difficulty in comprehending. Because Tully and I see Locke as a powerful but not a central figure, we can agree that his very great importance can be assessed only when we understand, first, in what ways his doctrines were contested, and second, in what ways they interacted with discourse arising out of concerns other than those addressed by him. Americans rightly see Locke as a central figure – their history does begin with dissolution, appeal

[123] Most recently, 'Negative and Positive Aspects of Locke's Place in Eighteenth-Century Discourse', in Martyn P. Thompson (ed.), *John Locke and Immanuel Kant: Historical Reception and Contemporary Relevance* (title also in German: Berlin, 1991), pp. 45–61.

and reversion[124] – and some of them are tempted to regard this debate among historians as a zero-sum game, in which points in favour of Locke's importance are weighed and counted against points which seem to diminish that importance, and a numerical decision is given one way rather than another. This rather primitive procedure has extended into a series of great (and very American) debates about the relative importance, in foundational and enduring American values, of elements called 'republican' and elements called 'liberal'[125] – the latter derived from eighteenth-century commercial individualism and identified rightly or wrongly with Locke's writings. There are real questions within this unmanageable mass of argument, but Tully does not go into them; nor do I wish to open them up here.[126] What is important to notice is that we are at a point where Anglo-British political discourse is extended to North America, of which part secedes and transforms it and part does not secede.

James Tully's second major perception – as I find myself reading his essay – has to do with Locke's relevance to the politics of those whom Canadians call 'first nations', Australians call 'aboriginals', and New Zealanders refer to by the Maori term *tangata whenua*.[127] These peoples inhabit the lands in which Lockean settlers establish themselves, but because they do not cultivate them by arable techniques of 'commercial agriculture' (Tully's term for it) are regarded by the settlers as not mixing their labour with it, appropriating it or thus constituting themselves as a 'people'. They are thus silently excluded from what the Declaration of Independence has to say about the equal rights of all 'peoples'; American

---

[124] The Anglo-American distinction is emphasised by Clark, *Revolution and Rebellion*, pp. 168–9.

[125] There is a bibliography of the historiographical literature, complete to dates of publication, in Robert S. Shalhope, 'Toward a Republican Synthesis: The Emergence of an Understanding of Republicanism in American Historiography', *William and Mary Quarterly*, 3rd series, 29 (1972), 49–80, and 'Republicanism and Early American Historiography', *William and Mary Quarterly*, 39 (1982), pp. 334–56; and Peter S. Onuf, 'Reflections on the Founding: Constitutional Historiography in Bicentennial Perspective', *William and Mary Quarterly*, 46 (1989), 341–75.

[126] Perhaps I may cite 'Between Gog and Magog: Republicanism and *Ideologia Americana*', *Journal of the History of Ideas*, 48 (1987), 325–46, and 'States, Republics and Empires: The American Founding in Early Modern Perspective', in Terence Ball and J.G.A. Pocock (eds.), *Conceptual Change and the Constitution* (Lawrence, Kans. 1988).

[127] Americans for their part call them 'Native Americans', a term containing some interesting tensions. Here, as elsewhere, the problem is that of incorporating as 'Americans' those who did not arrive by the way of voluntary immigration.

discourse and practice seem to have been in fact ambivalent as to whether 'Indians' constituted 'peoples' and 'nations' or not. When the 'agriculturist' premise operates to exclude hunter-gatherer cultures from the category 'civil society', the Lockean state of nature is redefined as the 'state of savagery' and moves towards becoming the Hobbesian *bellum omnium contra omnes*; the lands over which hunter-gatherers move may be appropriated by agriculturists without their consent, and the wars that ensue may become ethnocidal or genocidal because they are fought outside the domain of *jus gentium* if not natural law. This issue is implicit in the schemes of stadial or 'four-stage' history propounded by French and Scottish jurists and social theorists in the eighteenth century, all of which tended to identify the hunter-gatherer, if not also the shepherd nomad, with the 'savage'.[128] Tully emphasises Locke's role as an instigator of such schemes; I myself have some doubts how far they arose in response to his writings, which are certainly consonant with them. Locke's Indian has property in the fruit he picks or the deer he kills, but not in the land over which he moves to do so; only the act of tillage mixes labour with the land and binds it to the person. What we have historically refused to recognise is that societies of this kind have in fact an immensely strong sense of bonding with the land, as expressed in the word *whenua* which means both 'land' and 'placenta'.

Tully's central point is that the crown, being imperial, operates differently from the Lockean people, who are settlers in a wilderness originating themselves. It seeks fellow sovereigns with whom it can negotiate *imperium*, or whom it may conquer; it is therefore capable of acknowledging a species of sovereignty in a newly discovered people, without seeking the origins of sovereignty in that people's social structure, and claims for itself only a prior and exclusive right, founded in discovery or first contact, of negotiating what transfers of property or sovereignty may subsequently occur. Lockean peoples, on the other hand, engaged in the appropriation of land and the constitution or reconstitution of themselves as peoples, can recognise in strict logic neither the sovereignty of the crown over themselves, nor the prior sovereignty of a 'first nation' over itself, if neither the crown nor the native-born

---

[128] See 'Tangata Whenua and Enlightenment Anthropology', *New Zealand Journal of History*, 26 (1992), 28–53.

appear to be engaged in the acquisitive individualism of agricultural appropriation. In consequence, Americans employing Lockean theory, like Jefferson, very easily moved to seeing themselves as
self-justified by the act of appropriation, and as exercising rights of
conquest in exclusion of those who had occupied the land as
wilderness without appropriating it as property. Chief Justice
Marshall was able to recognise Indian tribes as 'nations' only by
supposing – to Jefferson's deep displeasure – that the United States
government had acquired the imperial authority formerly exercised
by the British Crown.

James Tully proceeds to a post-Lockean image of his own
Canada, now renegotiating its character as a confederation, as a
blending of distinct but 'layered' modes of crown sovereignty,
exercised by right of discovery followed by treaty in respect of
Indian 'first nations', by right of conquest followed by compact and
concession in respect of Quebec, and by right of direct dominion in
respect of provinces settled by itself. These sovereignties (that of
the crown having been 'repatriated') must now negotiate immediately with one another. It is a vision of history profoundly
un-American, both more imperial and (one is tempted to add) less
imperialist. To it I am in a position to adjoin the case of New
Zealand, a unitary state now redefining its sovereignty in the light
of the Treaty of Waitangi, drawn up in 1840 between the crown, at
the point of proclaiming British sovereignty, and the several Maori
tribes or 'nations' (the word is *iwi*).[129] Precisely because the New
Zealand Company, an organisation of settlers, was not party to this
treaty, it took the form of a quasi-Lockean compact in which
something resembling *dominium* (in Maori *rangatiratanga*) was
reserved to the Maori signatories, and something resembling
imperium (the word is *kawanatanga*) established in the crown.
Precisely because the terms of this compact have not been observed, claims to compensation are now made under it, and there
ensues (*inter alia*) the question of how the crown's sovereignty has
been vested in a democracy which has never claimed a Lockean
capacity to originate itself.[130] Tully and I both find ourselves in

[129] I.H. Kawharu (ed.), *Waitangi: Maori and Pakeha Perspectives on the Treaty of Waitangi*
(Auckland, 1989); Andrew Sharp, *Justice and the Maori: Maori Claims in New Zealand
Political Argument in the 1980s* (Auckland, 1990).
[130] J.G.A. Pocock, 'Law Sovereignty and History in a Divided Culture: The Case of New
Zealand and the Treaty of Waitangi', the Iredell Lecture, Lancaster University, 1991
(publication expected).

post-modern historical situations to which the issues of what happened in 1688 and 1776, as well as in 1840 and 1867, remain directly relevant, and the issue of aboriginal sovereignty raises the question of pre-agricultural human ecology.

v

The concluding group of essays – those by Lawrence Klein, Nicholas Phillipson, Istvan Hont and John Robertson – bear witness to a major qualitative change that came over Anglo-British political discourse in the last decade of the seventeenth and the first of the eighteenth century. The long-standing issues of right and authority, ecclesiastical as well as political, were in no way diminished – dynastic and ecclesiastical instability, before and after 1714, saw to that – but were joined by a new discourse, cultural, imperial and historical, with which political theorists, trained at the points where law and philosophy meet, are still finding it hard to deal. In the decade of the Nine Years War, England became a powerful military and financial state,[131] and standing army and public credit were seen as introducing new sets of historical conditions, neither ancient nor Gothic. In the decade of Anne's reign, this process continued, and England became the centre of an 'enormous', meaning a multi-national, British monarchy, obliging Scots to surrender their political autonomy and with it their national historiography.[132] Political discourse became British, in the sense that it was concerned with the archipelagic order and the place of England and Scotland within it; European, in the sense that it sought to locate Britain in the struggle between universal monarchy and a system of states; and historicist, to the extent to which it was involved in the transition to a 'commercial' order, based on new forms of property, new modes of social interaction, and new perceptions and fashionings of the self.

In addition to all this and interacting with it, the processes termed 'enlightenment' continued. To the left of Anglican latitudi-nariansim and English if not Scottish Presbyerianism, Arian and Socinian theology took their toll of the divinity of Christ – despite

---

[131] John Brewer, *The Sinews of Power: War, Money and the English State, 1688–1763* (New York, 1990).

[132] This was the theme of John Robertson's seminar, described in n. 8 above, as well as of Colin Kidd's dissertation, 'Scottish Whig Historiography'.

the denial of the benefits of the Act of Toleration to non-Trinitarians[133] – and both reinforced and weakened (by rendering scandalous) the powerful and widespread impulse to reduce religion to a mode of social behaviour, reasonable and good-humoured, in which neither superstition nor enthusiasm would disturb the authority of the social order. Sociability took the place of the sword and crozier of Leviathan, and a cult of 'manners' and 'politeness' offered itself as the remedy for civil and religious war. Politeness, while deeply rooted in a courtly and more remotely in a Ciceronian past, was part of a cult of modernity; it associated itself with the rise of *le doux commerce*,[134] and proposed to replace the rough virtue of the ancient citizen or Gothic freeman, the metaphysics and disputatiousness of the patristic or scholastic philosopher-theologian, and the superstition and enthusiasm of Catholics and Protestants alike, with nothing more or less than the behaviour codes of an interactive society. Lawrence Klein's central figure, the third earl of Shaftesbury, followed his tutor, John Locke (as did Joseph Addison) in the enterprise of taking philosophy out of the scholar's study and locating it in the conversation of the gentleman's drawing-room. Politeness was a cult of conversation (itself a codeword for the interactiveness of an increasingly commercial age), a rebellion of the gentility against the clerisy – against divines, scholars, jurists, antiquarians[135] and scientists – of the amateur against the professional, the consumer of culture against its producers and expert mediators. It was more aristocratic than bourgeois, being full of Aristotle's *megalopsychia*, Cicero's *otium cum dignitate* and Castiglione's *sprezzatura*; it owed much to Versailles and the *honnête homme*; yet if not bourgeois it was urbane, situated at the points where the city interacted with the court.[136] Shaftesbury has much of the Country Whig about him, but Addison and Steele set about the civilising of rustic foxhunters and monied cits alike, in the club where Sir Roger conversed with Sir Andrew. Defoe promoted the same process, looking westward from Temple Bar;

[133] Clark, *English Society*, and John Gascoigne, *Cambridge in the Age of the Enlightenment*.
[134] Albert O. Hirschman, *The Passions and the Interests: Political Arguments for Capitalism before its Triumph* (Princeton, 1977).
[135] Joseph M. Levine, *The Battle of the Books: History and Literature in the Augustan Age* (Ithaca, N.Y. 1991).
[136] J.G.A. Pocock, 'Clergy and Commerce: The Conservative Enlightenment in England', in R. Ajello (ed.), *L'Età dei Lumi: Studi Storici nel Settecento Europeo in onore di Franco Venturi* (Naples, 1985).

but the Spectator Club was only a few blocks from Grub Street and Hogarth's crowds grimaced and grabbed outside its windows, bringing Mandevillean reminders of politeness's murky under-pinnings.[137] It was a fragile enterprise in an unpoliced age, but acquisitiveness and even corruption were less to be dreaded than fanaticism; it was Lord George Gordon, not Jonathan Wild or even Jack Wilkes, who broke the windows in the last act. Shaftesbury moved away from Locke towards a refined Platonism and even enthusiasm, but is at his most characteristic in the truly extraordi-nary reflection that Christianity is 'in the main, a witty and good-humoured religion'.[138] In the juvenescence of the year came Christ the tiger, and there are times when the tiger is more to be respected than the pussy-cat; but we may hear the voice of Gibbon murmuring that after the Reformation 'the nature of the tiger was the same, but he was gradually deprived of his teeth and fangs',[139] to be answered only by William Blake growling, 'If he'd been Antichrist, Creeping Jesus, he'd have done anything to please us.'[140] There was something quixotic about the enterprise of politeness, and Edmund Burke was to see the Revolution as the rebellion of mental energy against the history of manners and the discipline of property.[141]

Politeness attempted hegemony in a singularly impolite age; Samuel Parker was hardly qualified to argue that Christianity should be a sociable religion, and that only dissenters stood outside politeness. When Shaftesbury says one should not dominate the conversation or strive to terminate it, the figure of Samuel Johnson looms at the head of the table; churchmen knew there were some issues that could not be smoothed away. At a considerable distance, we anticipate Burke contending that Harrington and Shaftesbury had been wrong to believe that society could do without a landed clergy, or that all human ills could be traced to its origins in Egypt; we look beyond Burke to Coleridge's perception that clerical culture must be re-structured (and re-endowed) as a

---

[137] Ronald Paulson, *Hogarth: His Life, Art and Times*, 2 vols. (New Haven, 1971); *Hogarth: The Modern Moral Subject*, 1697–1732 (New Brunswick, 1991).
[138] Above, p. 284.
[139] Edward Gibbon, *History of the Decline and Fall of the Roman Empire*, ch. 54 (ed. Bury, London, 1912), p. 133.
[140] William Blake, *The Everlasting Gospel (Complete Poems*, Harmondsworth, 1986), pp. 857–9.
[141] *Virtue, Commerce and History*, pp. 198–9, 205–9.

third party in the dialectic of land and commerce.[142] Under the first
two Hanoverians, however, the social order was endangered by all
the forces implicit in its historical situation, by fanaticism, faction
and corruption; and could not come to a reckoning with them short
of re-assessing its place in the history of England, Britain and
Europe. Our last three essays deal with how this re-assessment was
attempted by David Hume, whose greatness as a philosopher
should never have obscured the comprehensiveness of his capacities as a commentator on his age. Of the three, Nicholas Phillipson's stands closest to Lawrence Klein's, sharing his concern with
politeness. Phillipson continues his demonstration that the *History
of England* is a great expansion of the field of polite discourse,[143]
carrying the latter far beyond the foundations laid by Shaftesbury,
Defoe and Addison, and contending both that English history must
be understood through a narrative of the forces making for and
against a polite society, and that politeness itself must be situated
in the context of the history thus narrated. In this way the *History of
England* becomes a philosophical history, as the age understood the
term 'philosophy' and was henceforth to apply it to the term
'history'. But Phillipson further contends that as Hume's understanding of English history, and of his own time as situated in it,
grew deeper, tougher and more complex, he came to see that
politeness itself required deeper foundations, and must be transformed first into the 'prudence' (a Ciceronian virtue) of Phillipson's
title, and second into the 'propriety' there mentioned – a language
of judgement as to what language it was proper to use. Language
must not only be free, forbearing, witty and polite; these virtues
were valuable but superficial. It must be carefully weighed – since
it could so easily disturb the balance – and must call things by their
proper names, which implied neither realism nor nominalism so
much as a judgement of its own propriety. But 'propriety' could not
be separated from 'property'; it was not long since the two words
had been interchangeable; and Hume saw language as acquiring
the capacity for prudence in proportion as commerce rendered

---

[142] The theme developed in *On the Constitution of the Church and State according to the Idea of Each*
(1830). Morrow, 'Republicanism and Public Virtue', pp. 142–8. The alliance between
state and culture endured until its brutal disruption in the 1980s, when a state claiming
to limit its own powers moved to destroy the independence of universities, motivated by
contempt for their nature and function.

[143] Initiated in his *Hume* (London, 1989).

property more interchangeable, human relations more open to sociability, conversation more accessible to women and thus more effective in the moderation of the passions and the deflection of fanaticism. This was doubly the language of the philosopher in history.

Phillipson, however, leaves Hume at the point where he concluded his *History* with the defence of the Revolution of 1688, and allowed it to be carried on to his own time by the far more restless and subversive pens of Tobias Smollett and Catharine Macaulay.[144] They took a jeremiad and proto-revolutionary view of the history and prospects of the Hanoverian regime, and so – though as their adversary – did Hume; Phillipson shows that he always regarded it as a precarious enterprise, and Hont and Robertson explore the origins of the dark pessimism of Hume's last years, when he felt himself to be dying in the failure of the history he had done so much to write. In an essay of this length, it is difficult to treat the discourse of the eighteenth century as fully as that of the seventeenth; a whole new mental as well as historical world needs to be reconstructed. But it can be stated that Hume's fears arose less from the interior structure of the monarchy imperial in the Tudor sense, than from its place at the centre of an imperial power exercised in a space British, European and finally American. The years 1688, 1707 and 1714 were making themselves felt as he died in 1776. Istvan Hont studies the inwardness of Hume's fear of the effects of public debt; I do not disagree with him that Hume saw war rather than commerce as debt's principal cause, but there are certain connections between the two, and even a utopia of free trade, in which states engage in commerce and study war no more, does not seem to eliminate the international fluidity of indebtedness. Hume was asking what would happen to a state the whole of whose capital was mortgaged to creditors beyond its borders; this might annihilate its civility while leaving its commerce intact, and civility (or politeness) was the only protection known against fanaticism. It was a recrudescence of fanaticism that Hume feared as he died, and less than twenty years later Burke would be

---

[144] Smollett, *A History of England from the Revolution to the Death of George III. Designed as a Continuation of Mr Hume* (1763–5); Macaulay, *The History of England from the Accession of James I to that of the Brunswick Line* (1763–71, 1781–3); *The History of England from the Revolution to the Present Time, in a Series of Letters to a Friend* (1778).

diagnosing the general indebtedness of Europe as occasioning the
birth of a species of enthusiasm entirely new because it was
atheistic.[145] The sole hope lay where Montesquieu had placed it, in
the capacity of Great Britain to contain the national debt within the
national economy; a proposition of many resonances as the collapse
of the Soviet Union furnishes the bicentennial of the collapse of the
ancien régime.

Hume in 1776 had lost faith in that capacity because he was
dismayed by the vast expansion of the national debt under Pitt's
ministry in the Seven Years War. It was a question how that war
was to be characterised and so conducted. John Robertson situates
the debate, and Hume's judgement on it, in the context of the
discussion over universal monarchy.[146] Since the Nine Years War,
or as early as 1672, it had been a commonplace that France
threatened to revive the world empire of Charles V or the Roman
Caesars, and that if Europe was to move out of an antiquity of
conquest into a modernity of commerce, universal monarchy must
be replaced by a *république des républiques*, a plurality of trading
states. Histories as massive as Robertson's *Charles V* and Gibbon's
Decline and Fall had been constructed around this theme, and Hume
himself had seen the balance of power as necessary to enlightenment and sociability. But the struggle against France had turned
Britain into an imperial state, and Andrew Fletcher had feared that
an Anglo-Dutch monarchy might seek that universal empire of the
seas of which the Netherlands had long been accused in the role of a
new Carthage. Hume warned the British against slipping into the
pursuit of universal hegemony in the struggle against it, but as a
good Hanoverian did not fall into the Tory opposite of advocating

---

[145] For a study of Burke's counter-revolutionary thought with this and allied themes at its
centre, see 'The Political Economy of Burke's Analysis of the French Revolution', in
Virtue, Commerce and History; 'Introduction' to J.G.A. Pocock (ed.) *Edmund Burke: Reflections
on the Revolution in France* (Indianapolis, 1987); 'Edmund Burke' in Bruno Bongiovanni
and Luciano Guerci (eds.), *L'Albero della Rivoluzione: le interpretazioni della rivoluzione
francese* (Turin, 1989); 'Edmund Burke and the Redefinition of Enthusiasm; The Context
as Counter-Revolution', in François Furet and Mona Ozouf (eds.), *The French Revolution
and the Creation of Modern Political Culture: Vol. III, The Transformation of Political Culture,
1789–1848* (Oxford, 1989).
[146] It was a remarkable achievement of his seminar (n. 8 above) to show in how many ways
the creation of the United Kingdom of 1707 was situated in perceptions of this concept
and its problems.

an empire on blue water.[147] What he beheld with horror was Pitt's expansion of debt and war in Europe, ending in the pursuit of continental empire in the Americas and the oceans of the world. He followed Swift and Bolingbroke in urging a renunciation of empire and peace with France in a partnership of self-moderating power in Europe, and he did so in the belief that a debt-ridden politics would destroy what balance there was in the constitution and unleash the powers of fanaticism yet again. He was not remote from Josiah Tucker's fear that anti-Trinitarian dissenters in England and the American colonies might join to subvert the church in the empire, if the latter were not liquidated in time;[148] a fear not remote, in its turn, from Burke's linkage of debt and revolution.

The very complex moment of 1776 passed, and much was to follow it; but 'I cannot conclude a circle, and such is this commonwealth, without turning the end into the beginning'.[149] John Robertson's essay ends the book where J.H. Burns's began, with a cosmopolitan Scottish vision of Europe, into which has to be integrated the Tudor sovereignty in church and state that has been the unifying theme of all these contributions, and around which so many languages of discourse have taken shape. That sovereignty, however, has now become the image of an enlightened and in many respects a post-religious society, while at the same time becoming the centre of a multi-national and multi-ecclesiastical British imperial state. There are tensions between what is English and what is British about it, while furthermore it has assumed a permanent role in the history of both western Europe and North America. Global and historical issues have therefore to be discussed in the language of what is still an Anglocentric discourse about a culture maintaining itself through sovereignty in church and state. Because it ends with three essays on David Hume, this book looks somewhat ahead to 1776 and does not address the intellectual politics of the first half of George III's reign, in which period much of my own work has recently been centred. Themes

---

[147] Guido Abbatista, *Commercio, Colonie ed Impero alla Vigilia della Rivoluzione Americana: John Campbell pubblicista e storico nell'Inghilterra del sec. XVIII* (Florence, 1990) contains a detailed examination of blue-water policy arguments. See the forthcoming dissertation by Eliga H. Gould (The Johns Hopkins University) and his 'To Strengthen the King's Hands: Dynastic Legitimacy, Militia Reform and Ideas of National Unity in England, 1745–1760', *Historical Journal*, 34 (1990), 329–48.

[148] *Virtue, Commerce and History*, ch.9.

[149] Harrington, *Political Works*, p. 339.

428   J. G. A. POCOCK

emerging there include: the flowering of Scottish historical sociology in the wake of Hume and Robertson;[150] the imperial crisis
and the formation by secession of an American political culture; the
beginnings of Canadian, modern Irish and Anglo-Indian political
discourse; the consolidation of monarchy after 1783; Burke and the
response to the French Revolution; and in the second half of the
reign, and more generally in the half-century from 1780 to 1830, the
emergence of intellectual and material forces hard to fit into the
world which took shape from William III and looks back to Henry
VIII. We should enter the stormy seas of the Victorian mind under
the banner of the Noble Science of Politics,[151] though a less
Scottocentric approach to the age is said to be in the making.[152]
The story would remain, however, that of a discourse of sovereignty, which now challenges the future as much as it is challenged
by it.

[150] I see my present study of Edward Gibbon as fitting partly into this context; see 'Edward
Gibbon in History: Aspects of the Text of the *Decline and Fall*', in Grethe B. Peterson
(ed.), *Tanner Lectures in Human Values*, vol. xi (Salt Lake City, 1989), 289–364.
[151] Stefan Collini, Donald Winch and John Burrow, *That Noble Science of Politics: A Study in
Nineteenth-Century Intellectual History* (Cambridge, 1983).
[152] Meditated by Mark Francis (University of Canterbury) and John Morrow (Victoria
University of Wellington). Additionally, much may be learned about the period after
1790 from the books and articles of Gregory Claeys. See M. Francis, 'A Prolegomenon for
the History of British Political Thought during the Nineteenth Century', *Political Science*,
38 (1986), 70–85, and 'After the Ancient Constitution: Political Theory and English
Constitutional Writings 1765–1812', *History of Political Thought*, 9 (1988), 283–302.

J.G.A. Pocock: Publications

1951 'Robert Brady, 1627–1700: A Cambridge Historian of the Restoration', *Cambridge Historical Journal*, 10, 2
1957 *The Ancient Constitution and the Feudal Law: A Study of English Historical
Thought in the 17th Century* (Cambridge: Cambridge University Press)
1960 'Burke and the Ancient Constitution: A problem in the History of
Ideas', *The Historical Journal*, 3, 2
1962 'The History of Political Thought: A Methodological Enquiry', in
Peter Laslett and W.G. Runciman (eds.), *Philosophy, Politics and
Society: Second Series* (Oxford: Basil Blackwell)
1962 'The Origins of Study of the Past: A Comparative Approach',
Comparative Studies in Society and History, 4, 2
1964 Ed. and introd., *The Maori and New Zealand Politics* (Hamilton:
Blackwood Paul)
1964 'Ritual, Language, Power: An Essay on the Apparent Political
Meanings of Ancient Chinese Political Philosophy', *Political Science*,
16, 1
1965 'Machiavelli, Harrington and English Political Ideologies in the
Eighteenth Century', *The William and Mary Quarterly*, 3rd series, 22, 4
1966 'The Only Politician: Machiavelli, Harrington and Felix Raab',
Historical Studies: Australia and New Zealand, 12, 4
1967 Paperback reprint, *The Ancient Constitution and the Feudal Law* (New
York: W.W. Norton)
1968 'Civic Humanism and its Role in Anglo-American Thought', *Il
Pensiero Politico*, 1, 2
1968 'Time, Institutions and Action: An Essay on Traditions and their
Understanding', in Preston King and B.C. Parekh (eds.), *Politics and
Experience: Essays presented to Michael Oakeshott* (Cambridge University
Press)
1970 'James Harrington and the Good Old Cause: A Study of the
Ideological Context of his Writings', *Journal of British Studies*, 10, 1
1970 'Time, History and Eschatology in the Thought of Thomas Hobbes',
in J.H. Elliott and H. Koenigsberger (eds.), *The Diversity of History:
Essays in Honour of Sir Herbert Butterfield* (London: Routledge and
Kegan Paul)

1971 'Custom and Grace, Form and Matter: An Approach to Machiavelli's Concept of Innovation', in Martin Fleisher (ed.), *Machiavelli and the Nature of Political Thought* (New York: Atheneum)

1971 *Politics, Language and Time: Essays in Political Thought and History* (New York: Atheneum)

1971 'Working on Ideas in Time', in L.P. Curtis, Jr. (ed.), *The Historian's Workshop* (New York: Knopf)

1972 British edn. *Politics, Language and Time* (London: Methuen)

1972 'Virtue and Commerce in the Eighteenth Century', *Journal of Interdisciplinary History*, 3, 1

1973 'The History and Historiography of New Zealand Universities', *New Zealand Journal of Educational Research*, 8, 2

1973 *Obligation and Authority in Two English Revolutions* (Wellington: Victoria University of Wellington)

1973 'Political Thought in the Cromwellian Interregnum', in P.S. O'Connor and G.A. Wood (eds.), *W.P. Morrell: A Tribute: Essays in Early Modern History* (Dunedin: University of Otago)

1973 'Verbalising a Political Act: Towards a Politics of Language', *Political Theory*, 1, 1

1974 Reprint, *The Ancient Constitution and the Feudal Law* (Bath: Cedrick Chivers Ltd)

1974 'British History: A Plea for a New Subject', *New Zealand Historical Journal*, 8, 1

1975 'British History: A Plea for a New Subject (with Comment and Reply)', *Journal of Modern History*, 47, 4

1975 'Early Modern Capitalism: The Augustan Perception', in Eugene F. Kamenka and R.S. Neale (eds.), *Feudalism, Capitalism and Beyond* (Canberra: Australian National University Press)

1975 *The Machiavellian Moment: Florentine Political Thought and the Atlantic Republican Tradition* (Princeton: Princeton University Press)

1975 Paperback edition, *The Machiavellian Moment*

1975 'Modes of Action and their Pasts in Tudor and Stuart England', in Orest Ranum (ed.), *National Consciousness, History and Political Culture in Early Modern Europe* (Baltimore: The Johns Hopkins University Press)

1975 'The Prophet and the Inquisition: Or, a Church Built upon Bayonets Cannot Stand', *Political Theory*, 3, 4

1976 'Between Machiavelli and Hume: Gibbon as Civic Humanist and Philosophical Historian', *Daedalus*, 105, 3

1976 'The Classical Theory of Deference', *American Historical Review*, 81, 3

1976 'Modes of Political and Historical Time in Early Eighteenth-Century England', in Ronald C. Rosbottom (ed.), *Studies in Eighteenth-Century Culture*, vol. 5 (Madison University of Wisconsin Press)

1977 'Comment', in John W. Eadie (ed.), *Classical Traditions in Early*

America (Ann Arbor: Center for the co-ordination of Ancient and Modern Studies)

1977 'Between Machiavelli and Hume . . .' (1976), reprinted in *Edward Gibbon and the Decline and Fall of the Roman Empire*, ed. G. W. Bowersock and J. Clive (Hardback edition, Cambridge Mass.: Harvard University Press)

1977 'Gibbon's *Decline and Fall* and the World View of the Late Enlightenment', *Eighteenth-Century Studies*, 10, 3

1977 *The Political Works of James Harrington*: edited with an introduction (Cambridge: Cambridge University Press)

1978 'Contexts for the Study of James Harrington', *Il Pensiero Politico*, 11, 1

1978 'Machiavelli and Guicciardini: Ancients and Moderns', *Canadian Journal of Political and Social Theory*, 2, 3

1979 'To Market, to Market: Economic Thought in Early Modern England', *Journal of Interdisciplinary History*, 10, 2

1979 'The Mobility of Property and the Rise of Eighteenth-Century Sociology', in Anthony Parel and Thomas Flanagan (eds.), *Theories of Property: Aristotle to the Present* (Waterloo, Ontario: Wilfrid Laurier University Press, for University of Calgary Institute for the Humanities)

1979 'Reconstructing the Traditions: Quentin Skinner's Historians' History of Political Thought', *Canadian Journal of Political and Social Theory*, 3, 3

1979 'Saeculum Saeculare', *Eighteenth-Century Studies*, 12, 2

1980 'Authority and Property: The Question of Liberal Origins', in Barbara C. Malament (ed.), *After the Reformation: Essays in Honor of J.H. Hexter* (Philadelphia: University of Pennsylvania Press)

1980 'Civil Wars, Revolutions and Political Parties', in Patricia U. Bonomi (ed.), *Party and Political Opposition in Revolutionary America* (Tarrytown, N.Y.: Sleepy Hollow Press)

1980 'Hume and the American Revolution: The Dying Thoughts of a North Briton', in David Fate Norton, Nicholas Capaldi and Wade L. Rolison (eds.), *McGill Hume Studies* (San Diego: Austin Hill Press)

1980 '*Mito di Venezia* and *Ideologia Americana*: A Correction', *Il Pensiero Politico*, 12, 3

1980 *Il Momento Machiavelliano: il pensiero politico fiorentino e la tradizione repubblicana anglosassone*. Vol. I: *Il pensiero politico fiorentino*. Vol. II: *La 'repubblica' nel pensiero politico anglosassone*. (Bologna: Il Mulino) (Italian translation of *The Machiavellian Moment: Florentine Political Thought and the Atlantic Republican Tradition*, with an introduction written for the Italian edition)

1980 'The Myth of John Locke and the Obsession with Liberalism', in J.G.A. Pocock and Richard Ashcraft, *John Locke* (Los Angeles: William Andrews Clark Memorial Library)

1980 'The Origins of Study of the Past: A Comparative Approach' (1962), reprinted in P.B.M. Blaas (ed.), *Geschiedenis als Wetenschap* (The Hague: Martinus Nijhoff)

1980 'Political Ideas as Historical Events: Political Philosophers as Historical Actors', in Melvin Richter (ed.), *Political Theory and Political Education* (Princeton: Princeton University Press)

1980 'Post-Puritan England and the Problem of the Enlightenment', in Perez Zagorin (ed.), *Culture and Politics: From Puritanism to the Enlightenment* (Berkeley and Los Angeles: University of California Press)

1980 'Providenza, Fortuna e Virtu' (chapter 1 of *Il Momento Machiavelliano*), *Il Mulino*, 29, 442–66

1980 Review of *Political Theory: Tradition and Interpretation*, by John G. Gunnell. *Political Theory*, 8, 4, 563–7

1980 Editor and contributor ('Introduction', '1776: The Revolution Against Parliament'), *Three British Revolutions: 1641, 1688, 1776* (Princeton: Princeton University Press: Folger Institute Essays, for Folger Shakespeare Library)

1980 'Tra Machiavelli e Hume: Gibbon umanista civile e filosofo della storia' (translation of article published in 1976 and 1977), in Franca Rovigatti (ed.), *Gibbon: Niebuhr: Ferrabino* (Rome: Instituto della Enciclopedia Italiana)

1981 'An Appeal from the New to the Old Whigs? A Note on Joyce Appleby's "Ideology and the History of Political Thought"', *Intellectual History Group Newsletter* (no date or number), 47–51

1981 'Gibbon and the Shepherds: The Stages of Society in the *Decline and Fall*', *History of European Ideas*, 2, 3, 193–202

1981 '*The Machiavellian Moment* Revisited: A Study in History and Ideology', *Journal of Modern History*, 53, 1 49–72

1981 'Political Theory, History and Myth: A Salute to John Gunnell', and 'Intentions, Traditions and Methods: Some Sounds on a Fog-Horn', *Annals of Scholarship*, 1, 4, 3–25 and 57–62

1981 'A Reconsideration Impartially Considered', *History of Political Thought*, 1, 3, 541–5

1981 Review of *Country and Court: England, 1658–1714*, by J.R. Jones, and *Stability and Strife: England, 1714–1760*, by W.A. Speck, *Eighteenth-Century Studies*, 15, 1, 95–7

1981 Review of K.C. Hsiao, *A History of Chinese Political Thought*, vol. I, *International Studies in Philosphy*, 13, 2, 95–100

1981 Review of *Studi su Machiavelli pensatore*, by Stelio Zeppi, in *Journal of the History of Philosphy*, 18, 3, 349–51

1981 Review of *Utopian Thought in the Western World*, by Frank E. Manuel and Fritzie P. Manuel, in *Renaissance Quarterly*, 34, 1, 86–9

1981 'Virtues, Rights and Manners: A Model for Historians of Political Thought', *Political Theory*, 9, 3, 353–68

1982 Review of Lester H. Cohen, *The Revolutionary Histories: Contemporary*

Accounts of the American Revolution, *Journal of American History* (March 1982), 920–1

1982 'The Limits and Divisions of British History: In Search of the Unknown Subject', *American Historical Review*, 87, 2, 311–36

1982 'The Political Economy of Burke's Analysis of the French Revolution', *The Historical Journal*, 25, 2, 331–50

1982 'The Reconstruction of Discourse: Towards the Historiography of Political Thought', *Modern Language Notes*, 96, 959–80

1982 'Superstition and Enthusiasm in Gibbon's History of Religion', *Eighteenth-Century Life*, 8, 1, 83–94

1983 'Cambridge Paradigms and Scotch Philosophers: A Study of the Relations between the Civic Humanist and the Civil Jurisprudential Interpretation of Eighteenth-Century Social Thought', in Istvan Hont and Michael Ignatieff (eds.), *Wealth and Virtue: The Shaping of Political Economy in the Scottish Enlightenment* (Cambridge: Cambridge University Press)

1983 'English Historical Thought in the Age of Harrington and Locke', *Topoi*, 2 (1983), 149–62

1983 'Josiah Tucker on Burke, Locke and Price: A Study in the Varieties of Eighteenth-Century Conservatism', in Marie Peters, ed., *Essays Presented to Professor N.C. Phillips*, (Privately printed, the University of Canterbury), pp. 5–48

1983 'Radical Criticisms of the Whig Order in the Age Between Revolutions', in Margaret Jacob and James Jacob (eds.), *The Origins of Anglo-American Radicalism* (London: Allen and Unwin)

1983 Review article: 'Outgrowing the Hucksters: *A History of the University of Auckland, 1883–1893*, by Keith Sinclair', *New Zealand Journal of History*, 17, 2, 185–91

1983 Review of George Shelton, *Dean Tucker and Eighteenth-Century Economic and Political Thought*, *Journal of Modern History*, 55, 1, 116–18

1983 Review of Lionel Gossman, *The Empire Unpossess'd: An Essay on Gibbon's Decline and Fall*, *History of European Ideas*, 4, 2, 223–5

1983 Review of Michael Oakeshott, *On History and Other Essays, Times Literary Supplement*, 4,203, October 21, p.1,255

1984 'The European and English Inheritance', in Jack P. Greene (ed.), *Encyclopedia of American Politics*, (New York: Scribner and Sons), vol. II, pp. 513–34

1984 'Recent Scholarship on John Locke and the Political Thought of the Late Seventeenth Century: A Review Article', *Theoretische Geschiedenis*, 11, 3, 251–61

1984 Review of Christopher Hill, *The Experience of Defeat: Milton and Some Contemporaries*, in *Times Literary Supplement*, 4,265, 29 December p. 1,494

1984 Review of J.A.W. Gunn, *Beyond Liberty and Property: The Process of Self-Recognition in Eighteenth-Century Political Thought*, in *Eighteenth-Century Studies*, 18, 1 (Fall), 112–15

1984 'Verbalising a Political Act: Towards a Politics of Speech' (1973), reprinted in Michael Shapiro (ed.), *Language and Politics* (New York University Press), pp.25–43

1985 'Behind the Crisis: New Zealand and the United States', *Baltimore Sun*, February 12

1985 Review of Christopher Hill (ed.), *Winstanley: The Law of Freedom and other Writings*, in *Political Theory*, 13, 3, (August), 461–5

1985 'Clergy and Commerce: The Conservative Enlightenment in England', in Raffaele Ajello, Luigi Firpo, Luciano Guerci and Giovanni Ricuperati (eds.), *L'Eta dei Lumi: Studi Storici sul Settecento Europea in onore di Franco Venturi* (Naples: Jovene Editore), vol. I, pp. 523–622

1985 'Commentary' (on a paper by Ann Gorman Condon), in Prosser Gifford (ed.), *The Treaty of Paris (1783) in a Changing States System* (Washington: University Press of America), pp. 203–6

1985 'The History of British Political Thought: The Creation of a Center', *Journal of British Studies*, 24, 3, pp. 283–310

1985 'Machiavelli in the Liberal Cosmos', *Political Theory*, 13, 4, 559–74

1985 'The Sense of History in Renaissance England', in John F. Andrews (ed.), *William Shakespeare: His World, his Work, his Influence*, 3 vols. (New York: Charles Scribner's Sons), vol. I, pp. 143–58

1985 'Trading Traditions: A Report from the High Barbary', *Annals of Scholarship*, 3, 3, 103–12

1985 *Virtue, Commerce and History: Essays on Political Thought and History, Chiefly in the Eighteenth Century* (Cambridge: Cambridge University Press)

1985 'What Is Intellectual History?' (contribution to a symposium), *History Today*, 25, 52–3

1986 'English Historical Thought in the Age of Harrington and Locke', reprinted in F. Fagiani and G. Valera (eds.), *Categorie del Reale e Storiografia: Aspetti di Continuita e Trasformazione nell' Europa Moderna* (Milan: Franco Angeli Libri), 1986, pp. 371–401

1986 'The Influence of British Political Thought on the American Constitution: Magna Carta in Context', in Robert S. Peck and Ralph S. Pollock (eds.), *The Blessings of Liberty: Bicentennial Lectures at the National Archives* (Chicago: ABA Press, 1986), pp. 11–20

1986 'A New Bark Up An Old Tree', *Intellectual History Newsletter*, 8 (April), 3–9

1986 'Political Theory, History and Myth: A Salute to John Gunnell.' Reprinted in John S. Nelson (ed.), *Tradition, Interpretation and Science: Political Theory in the American Academy* (Albany: State University of New York Press), pp. 21–42

1986 Review of John Dunn, *Rethinking Modern Political Theory: Essays, 1979–83*, in *History of European Ideas*, 7, 701-2

1986 Review of Philip Corrigan and Derek Sayer, *The Great Arch: English*

State Formation as Cultural Revolution, in *Albion*, 18, 2 (1986), 294–6

1986 'Tra Gog e Magog: I Pericoli della Storiografia Repubblicana.' (Translated by Roberto Vivarelli. *Rivista Storica Italiana*, 98, 1, 149–94

1987 *The Ancient Constitution and the Feudal Law: A Reissue with a Retrospect* (Cambridge: Cambridge University Press)

1987 'Between Gog and Magog: The Republican Thesis and *Ideologia Americana*', *Journal of the History of Ideas*, 48, 2, 325–46

1987 *Edmund Burke: Reflections on the Revolution in France*, edited with introduction and notes by J.G.A. Pocock (Indianapolis/Cambridge: Hackett Publishing Company)

1987 'Enlightenment and Revolution: The Case of North America', in *Seventh International Congress on the Enlightenment: introductory papers* (Oxford: The Voltaire Foundation), pp. 45–58

1987 'Modernity and Anti-Modernity in the Anglophone Political Tradition', in S. N. Eisenstadt (ed.), *Patterns of Modernity: Volume I: The West* (London: Francis Pinter Publishers), pp. 44–59

1987 Review of John Robertson, *The Scottish Enlightenment and the Militia Issue*, in *Parliamentary History*, vol. VI, pt. 2, pp. 343–4

1987 '1660 and All That: Whig-Hunting, Ideology and Historiography in the Work of Jonathan Clark', *Cambridge Review*, 108, no. 2,298, October, 125–28

1987 'Spinoza and Harrington: An Exercise in Comparison', in *Bijdragen en Mededelingen Betreffende de Geschiedenis der Nederlanden*, 102, 3, (1987), 435–49

1987 'States, Republics and Empires: The American Founding in Early Modern Perspective', *Social Science Quarterly*, 68, 4, 703–23

1987 'Texts as Events: Reflections on the History of Political Thought', in Kevin Sharpe and Steven N. Zwicker (eds.), *Politics of Discourse: The Literature and History of Seventeenth-Century England* (University of California Press), pp. 21–34

1988 Contribution (pp. 114–16) to Juliet Gardiner (ed.), *What is History Today?* (London: Macmillan)

1988 'The Fourth English Civil War: Dissolution, Desertion and Alternative Histories in the Glorious Revolution', *Government and Opposition*, 23, 2, 151–66

1988 'Political Science at Canterbury: A View from the Top', *University of Canterbury Chronicle*, 83, 2 (June)

1988 *The Politics of Extent and the Problems of Freedom: The William Jovanovich Lecture* (Colorado Springs: Colorado College Studies, 25)

1988 'Religious Freedom and the Desacralization of Politics: From the English Civil War to the Virginia Statute', in Merrill D. Peterson and Robert C. Vaughan (eds.), *The Virginia Statute for Religious Freedom: its Evolution and Consequences in American History* (Cambridge: Cambridge University Press), pp. 43–73

1988 Review of R.J. Smith, *The Gothic Bequest: Medieval Institutions in British Thought, 1688–1863, Albion*, 20, 1, 105–7

1988 Terence Ball and J.G.A. Pocock (eds.), *Conceptual Change and the Constitution* (University Press of Kansas). Incl. reprint of 'States, Republics and Empires' above (pp. 55–77)

1988 'Transformations in British Political Thought', in *Political Science* (Victoria University of Wellington, vol. 40, no. 1, July), pp. 160–78 (special issue, 'Theory in History: English Political Thought, 1640–1832', guest editor Mark Francis)

1989 'The Book Most Misunderstood Since the Bible: John Adams and the Confusion about Aristocracy', in Anna Maria Martellone and Elizabetta Vezzosi (eds.), *Fra Toscana e Stati Uniti: il Discorso Politico nell' Età della Costituzione Americana* (Florence: Olschki), pp. 181–201

1989 'Conservative Enlightenment and Democratic Revolutions: The *Government and Opposition*/Leonard Schapiro Lecture, 1988', in *Government and Opposition*, 24, 1, pp. 81–105

1989 'Edmund Burke and the Redefinition of Enthusiasm: The Context as Counter-Revolution' and 'Comment, or Pièce Retrospective', in Francois Furet and Mona Ozouf (eds.), *The French Revolution and the Creation of Modern Political Culture, vol. 3: The Transformation of Political Culture, 1789–1848* (Oxford: Pergamon Press), pp. 19–36, 36–43

1989 'Edmund Burke', translated into Italian by Marco Pustianaz, in Bruno Bongiovanni and Luciano Guerci (eds.), *L' Albero della Rivoluzione: le interpretazioni della rivoluzione francese* (Turin: Einaudi), pp. 89–96

1989 'Political and Historical Existence in Eastern and Western Philosophy', translated into Japanese by Masao Kikuchi, *Matsusaka University Journal*, 6

1989 *Politics, Language and Time: Essays on Political Thought and History.* Republished by the University Press of Chicago

1989 Reprint of 'Burke and the Ancient Constitution: A Problem in the History of Ideas', in Jack Lively and Andrew Reeve (eds.), *Modern Political Theory from Hobbes to Marx: Key Texts* (London: Routledge), pp. 159–82

1990 'Edward Gibbon in History: Aspects of the Text in *The History of the Decline and Fall of the Roman Empire*', in Grethe B. Peterson (ed.), *The Tanner Lectures on Human Values*, II (Salt Lake City, University of Utah Press), pp. 289–364

1990 'Gibbon and the Idol Fo: Chinese and Christian History in the Enlightenment', in David S. Katz and Jonathan I. Israel (eds.), *Sceptics, Millenarians and Jews* (Leiden: E.J. Brill), pp. 15–34

1990 *Politica, Linguaggio e Storia*, trans. Guiseppe Gadda Conti, ed. Ettore A. Albertoni (Turin: Comunità)

1990 'The Political Limits to Pre-Modern Economics', in John Dunn (ed.), *The Economic Limits to Modern Politics* (Cambridge: Cambridge University Press), pp. 121–41

1990 Review of David Womersley, *The Transformation of the Decline and Fall of the Roman Empire*, in *Eighteenth-Century Studies*, 23, 4, 318–21

1990 'Samuel Butler e L.G. Pocock: le scoperte delle isole', translated by Nat Scammacca, *Trapani Nuova*, July 16; 'Realtà e allegoria, storia e mito', September 14

1990 'Thomas Hobbes: Atheist or Enthusiast? His Place in a Restoration Debate', *History of Political Thought*, 11, 4, 737–49

1991 'City and Empire: Rome and its Fall in Eighteenth-Century Thought', in E. Brix, T. Fröschl and J. Leidenfrost (eds.), *Geschichte zwischen Freiheit und Ordnung: Gerald Stourzh zum 60 geburtstag* (Graz/Vienna/Cologne: Verlag Styria), pp. 339–48

1991 'Deconstructing Europe', in *London Review of Books*, 19 December, pp. 6–10

1991 'Negative and Positive Aspects of Locke's Place in Eighteenth-Century Discourse', in Martyn P. Thompson (ed.), *John Locke and Immanuel Kant: Historical Reception and Contemporary Relevance* (Berlin: Duncker and Humblot), pp. 45–61

1991 Review of Anthony Pagden, *Spanish Imperialism and the Political Imagination: Studies in European and Spanish-American Social and Political Theory, 1513–1830*, in *American Historical Review*, 96, 5, 1,505–6

1991 Review of John Brewer, *The Sinews of Power: War, Money and the English State, 1688–1763*, in *Eighteenth-Century Studies*, 24, 2, 270–2

1991 Review of Paul Monod, *Jacobitism and the English People, 1688–1788*, in *History of European Ideas*, 13, 5, pp. 644–6

1991 'Sicilian Origins of Homer's Odyssey. Samuel Butler and L.G. Pocock: The Discovery of Islands', in *The Press* (Christchurch N.Z.), July 20

1991 'The Significance of 1688: Some Reflections on Whig History', in Robert Beddard (ed.), *The Revolutions of 1688: the Andrew Browning Lectures, 1988* (Oxford: The Clarendon Press), pp. 271–92

1991–2 Review of Isaac Kramnick, *Republicanism and Bourgeois Radicalism: Political Ideology in Late Eighteenth Century England and America* in *Eighteenth Century Studies*, 25, 2, 219–27

1992 'The Ideal of Citizenship since Classical Times', in *Queen's Quarterly*, 99, 1, 33–55

1992 'The Language of Political Discourse and the British Rejection of the French Revolution', in Eluggero Pii (ed.), *I Linguaggi Politici delle Rivoluzione in Europa, XVII–XIX secolo* (Florence, L.S. Olschki: Il Pensiero Politico, Biblioteca 16), pp. 19–30

1992 'Tangata Whenua and Enlightenment Anthropology', in *The New Zealand Journal of History*, 26, 1, 28–53

Index

Ideas in Context

Edited by Quentin Skinner (general editor), Lorraine Daston, Wolf Lepenies, Richard Rorty and J.B. Schneewind

Forthcoming titles include works by Martin Dzelzainis, Mark Goldie, Noel Malcolm, Roger Mason, James Moore, Nicolai Rubinstein, Quentin Skinner, Martin Warnke and Robert Wokler

Titles marked with an asterisk are also available in paperback.